From the Ghetto to the Melting Pot

Portrait of Israel Zangwill, 1904. Postcard. Issued by the Rotary Photographic Series (U.K.). Edna Nahshon's personal collection.

From the Ghetto to the Melting Pot

Israel Zangwill's Jewish Plays

Three Playscripts
by Israel Zangwill

Edited, with Introductions
and Commentary, by
EDNA NAHSHON

W

Wayne State University Press   Detroit

14 13 12 11 10   5 4 3 2

Library of Congress Cataloging-in-Publication Data

Zangwill, Israel, 1864–1926.
From the ghetto to the melting pot : Israel Zangwill's Jewish plays : three playscripts /
by Israel Zangwill ; edited, with introductions and commentary, by Edna Nahshon.
p. cm.
Includes bibliographical references and index.
ISBN 0-8143-2955-1 (pbk. : alk. paper)
1. Jews—Drama. I. Nahshon, Edna. II. Children of the ghetto. III. Melting pot.
IV. King of Schnorrers. V. Title.
PR5921.N37 2006
822'.8—dc22
2005015539

ISBN-13: 978-0-8143-2955-9
ISBN-10: 0-8143-2955-1

For Ken,
with boundless love

Contents

List of Illustrations   ix
Acknowledgments   xi
Preface   xv

Prologue   1
Introduction
   Israel Zangwill: Child of the Ghetto   5

Children of the Ghetto
   Introductory Essay   61
   Playscript   111

The Melting Pot
   Introductory Essay   211
   Playscript   265
   Appendixes   365

The King of Schnorrers
   Introductory Essay   389
   Playscript   401

Epilogue   513

Notes   519
Index   547

Illustrations

Portrait of Israel Zangwill (1904)   frontispiece

The market scene in the New York production of *Children of the Ghetto* (1899)   71

Blanche Bates as Hannah in the New York production of *Children of the Ghetto* (1899)   73

Wilton Lackaye as Reb Shemuel in *Children of the Ghetto* (1899)   75

The confrontation scene in *Children of the Ghetto* (1899)   85

Reb Shemuel blesses his daughter, Hannah, in the New York production of *Children of the Ghetto* (1899)   90

Bessie Tomashefsky as Hannah in the New York Yiddish production of *Children of the Ghetto* (1904)   108

Postcard image of America emerging from the melting pot (1914)   212

Caricature of America as a teacup from *Puck* (1889)   216

David expounds the melting pot vision in the London production of *The Melting Pot* (1914)   220

Vera Revendal and David Quixano in the London production of *The Melting Pot* (1914)   229

Kathleen O'Reilly in the nose scene in the London production of *The Melting Pot* (1914)   231

David and Vera reunite in the final scene of the London production of *The Melting Pot* (1914)   239

America as melting pot from the cover of a promotional brochure for a touring production of the play (1916)   253

Poster of the film version of *The Melting Pot,* cover of *Kinematograph and Lantern Weekly* (U.K., 1919)   255

Newspaper collage of the cast of the London production of *The King of Schnorrers* (1930)   397

Acknowledgments

It is a delightful task to record my gratitude to those who have assisted me in this project. I thank my home institution, the Jewish Theological Seminary of America, for awarding me the Sol Stroock Fellowship, and the Lucius N. Littauer Foundation for providing a grant that covered many of my research expenses. I am especially indebted to Oxford University's Centre for Hebrew and Jewish Studies for granting me a Skirball Fellowship that enabled me to spend half a year in what may be termed a scholar's paradise.

It gives me particular satisfaction to thank friends and colleagues for their interest and support. Their names are arranged in chronological and geographical order. In the United States: Professor Ismar Schorsch, Chancellor of the Jewish Theological Seminary of America, who believed in this work since its inception; Professor Arthur Goren of Columbia University, whose command of American Jewish history helped define my research in its earliest stages; Professor Barbara Kirshenblatt-Gimblett of New York University, a constant beacon of wisdom and kindness; and Professor Dov-Ber Kerler of Indiana University, formerly of Oxford University, a friend and colleague par excellence. I also wish to thank David Lincoln, senior rabbi of New York's Park Avenue Synagogue; Ed Cramer, theatrical attorney and Zangwill enthusiast; Professor Jeffrey D. Feldman of the Department of Museum Studies, New York University; and Edward Portnoy, a specialist on Jewish cartoons.

In the U.K. my thanks go to my friends at Oxford University's Centre for Hebrew and Jewish Studies. First and foremost among them are José and Professor David Patterson, president emeritus of the Centre, who welcomed me to their home and taught me more than they will ever realize. I also thank Mr. Peter Oppenheimer, president of the Centre, and professors Glenda Abramson and Martin Goodman for their attentive kindness. Special kudos go to the dedicated staff at Yarnton Manor, most particularly Mrs. Joan Sinclair, who created a home away from home. Additionally, I thank Carol

Seigel, formerly of London's Jewish Museum, and Marion Baraister, publisher and playwright, and author of *The Crystal Den,* a play about Eleanor Marx and Israel Zangwill. It was a treat to get to know Professor Nick Zangwill, who teaches philosophy at Oxford University. Nick is the grandson of Mark Zangwill, Israel's brother.

I wish to express my great appreciation for the generous support extended to me by librarians and archivists, most particularly the remarkable Dr. Kathryn Johnson, archivist of the Lord Chamberlain's Collection at the British Library. I am grateful to Joshua Lunn and the entire staff of the British Library Manuscript Reading Room, whose friendliness made every visit such a pleasant experience. I am most thankful to the librarians and staff of the Bodleian Library—especially Nigel James and Stuart Ackland; the British Film Institute; the Theatre Museum in London; and the Leopold Muller Memorial library at the Oxford Centre for Hebrew and Jewish Studies, where I benefited from the expertise of its chief librarian, Brad Sabin-Hill, currently Dean of the Library of the YIVO Institute in New York.

In the United States I wish to thank my friends at the Library of the Jewish Theological Seminary of America, especially Lissa Weinberger and Yisrael Dubitsky, who are not only knowledgeable but are always ready to lend a helping hand; Dr. Peggy Pearlstein of the Library of Congress; the staff at the New York Public Library, especially at the Manuscript and Archive Division at the Humanities and Social Sciences Library, and Library for the Performing Arts; the staff at the YIVO Institute for Jewish research; and Raymond Wemmlinger, librarian of the Hamden-Booth Theater Library at the Players Club.

In Israel I am beholden to the staff of the Central Zionist Archives in Jerusalem and the Jabotinsky Archive in Tel Aviv, especially Amira Stern and Irit Sivan, the latter a dear friend since our adolescent years.

I appreciate the goodwill of the libraries and archives that extended reproduction permission of the images used in this book: the Central Zionist Archives; the Museum of the City of New York; the Harry Ransom Center at the University of Texas–Austin; the Michigan State University Museum; the Special Collections Department, University of Iowa Libraries; and the library of the Jewish Theological Seminary.

This book owes much to Tim Oliver, my incomparable editor and pal. I will always be in his debt.

I also extend my thanks to my Wayne State University Press editors, Kathryn Wildfong and Kristin Harpster Lawrence.

Finally, I thank my husband, Gad, and my son, Ken, for listening, assisting, and making my work worthwhile. Ken's spontaneous peal of laughter when he first read *The King of Schnorrers* was music to my ears. This book is dedicated to him.

Preface

This volume presents three plays written by Israel Zangwill, two of which, *The King of Schnorrers* and *Children of the Ghetto,* have never been published before. Their discovery began with a cursory interest in the 1899 American theater production of *Children of the Ghetto.* I soon learned that the whereabouts of the playscript were unknown. The Library of Congress confirmed that *Children of the Ghetto* had been copyrighted in 1899 but that it was not in possession of the text. The Central Zionist Archives in Jerusalem, the repository of Zangwill's papers, had but a preliminary draft of the play's first act. However, when I found that the play had been briefly performed in London I recalled that until 1968 plays intended for theatrical production had to be submitted for license to the Lord Chamberlain's Office, with its Examiner of Plays acting as the government censor. And there, among a legion of scripts that make up the Lord Chamberlain's Collection, housed in the British Library, I found the unpublished playscripts of *Children of the Ghetto* and *The King of Schnorrers* and the original version of *The Melting Pot.* Ironically, Zangwill's texts had been preserved by the very institution he had opposed, one that in 1912 banned production of his play *The Next Religion.* This topsy-turvy finale would have undoubtedly produced a sparkling witticism from Zangwill, a wry humorist. At the same time, he would have been well pleased by the publication of these Jewish works, particularly *Children of the Ghetto,* his first full-length play, which was most dear to his heart.

The three plays included in this volume were not written as a trilogy and are united here by virtue of their shared Jewish subject matter. They appear in the order in which they were written and produced. At the same time, I wish to suggest that they can also be read in the order of their historical settings, beginning with *The King of Schnorrers.* Such sequence takes us on a two-hundred-year journey that begins in eighteenth-century London, with its intra-Jewish tensions farcically depicted in *The King of Schnorrers,* to a drama of its nineteenth-century immigrant ghetto, at a crossroads between tradition and modernity, portrayed in *Children of the Ghetto,* and finally to the shores of twentieth-century America, where the survivor of a Russian pogrom delivers a messianic gospel of tolerance and racial fusion in *The Melting Pot.* Bound together, these plays dialogue with one another while highlighting complementary themes and motifs.

Although individual essays precede each playscript in this text, even readers who are interested in only one of the playscripts may benefit from reading all the introductory essays in sequence to get a better sense of Zangwill's life as well as the context and interconnectedness of the plays.

Great care has been taken to reproduce the playscripts as close to their original texts as possible. However, some minor technical corrections, notably, punctuation and capitalization, have been inserted in accord with current publishing style.

Prologue

Shortly before sailing to America for the premiere of *The Melting Pot,* Israel Zangwill (1864–1926), England's preeminent Jewish writer, presided over a festive dinner at London's Great Central Hotel.[1] This elegant affair, organized by the Maccabeans, a prestigious Jewish cultural society, was held to honor the dramatists, actors, and critics of the London stage. Zangwill, then president of the society, chaired the event. He was flanked by two illustrious figures: Herbert Beerbohm Tree (1853–1917), the supreme actor-manager of his time, and Henry Arthur Jones (1851–1929), a leading dramatist who was instrumental in promotion of serious drama on the English stage. Other notable guests included Brandon Thomas (1856–1914), author of the immensely successful comedy *Charlie's Aunt;* Arthur R. Ropes (1859–1933), who as "Adrian Ross" wrote the lyrics for many popular comic operas; Edward Morton (1858–1922), author of the hit musical comedy *San Toy;* Anthony Hope (1863–1933), author of *The Prisoner of Zenda;* William Poel (1852–1934), founder of the Elizabethan Stage Society, which had a tremendous impact on modern staging of Shakespearean plays; Alfred Sutro (1863–1933), prominent playwright and fellow Maccabean; and Laurence Housman (1865–1959), illustrator and writer, a committed socialist and pacifist who, like Zangwill, was a member of the Men's League for Women's Suffrage.

Zangwill said in his welcome that while some of the guests were not Jewish, the Maccabeans were "akin to them all in spirit," for both guests and hosts cared greatly for the dramatic arts. He teased Tree over a caricature made by his half-brother, Max Beerbohm (1872–1956), that ridiculed Zangwill's Jewish political activism by showing him riding on a donkey, leading the way to Zion. He wisecracked that in the picture the only creature to accompany him was the donkey and suggested a companion cartoon in which he should be shown successful, with the theaters of Europe "closed for repairs" as a result of the Jewish exodus. He quipped that it was generally thought that the first to feel the effect of the absence of Jews would be the stock exchange, but that it would not be hit half as hard as the stage. He then paid tribute to Jewish men and women of the theater, noting there were far too many to name. Playfully mocking hackneyed stereotypes while evoking biblical references to Jewish bravery, he remarked with pride and humor that "the Jewish race . . . has run to art even more than to money, as becomes the descendants of a people who were always fighting the Philistines." As he concluded, he reminded his audience that "the greatest Jew of modern times, Dr. [Theodor] Herzl," was a dramatist and mused, "if Moses lived in our day he would have written, not pentateuchs, but plays."

This event, largely a paean to Zangwill, demonstrates the high esteem in which he was held in both Jewish and non-Jewish circles and the pivotal position from which he could link the two. We catch glimpses of some of his personal traits: erudition, a penchant for clever maxims, a splendid sense of humor, sarcastic candor, and a thinly veiled intolerance for criticism. Also evident are an enthusiasm for the theater combined with a belief in its power to transform human affairs. These, and a commitment to women's suffrage and universal justice, were fused with a devotion to the promotion of Jewish interests and a tacit demand to be publicly recognized as both an Englishman and a Jew. Zangwill's extolment of Herzl, the founder of political Zionism, is telling, as is the parallel he draws between Herzl and Moses and, by extension, with himself, as playwright and architect of Jewish destiny.

The dinner, with its bright repartee and celebration of the camaraderie of Jewish and Gentile genius, calls to attention a nexus of social and cultural issues that inform the present book: spaces of ethnic identity and intercultural communication between Jews and their host society, particularly in the sphere of the performing arts; the growing visibility of Jews in mainstream theatrical life as artists, managers, spectators, and benefactors; the stereotypical construction of Jewish characters on the stage; and the emergence of Jewish self-representation on the mainstream stage. These constituted important topics in the cultural landscape of the late nineteenth and early twentieth centuries, an era when theater fulfilled the role now associated with the popular mass media of cinema and television.

Israel Zangwill, man of letters, Jewish nationalist, and man of ideas in the world of affairs, was a towering figure in modern Anglo-Jewish life. His literary oeuvre includes novels, plays, short stories, humorous pieces, essays, and poems, on a wide array of topics, but it was his Jewish writings that gained him international acclaim and celebrity. His voice was heard worldwide, with particular resonance in his native England, where he was perceived as Judaism's primary cultural interpreter and advocate. After his death, one author explained Zangwill's unique position as follows:

> When a Jewish question was taken up by the press, or a Jewish question was discussed in Parliament, or anything Jewish appeared on the surface, the English world would not listen to [Lord] Rothschild, the head of the Jewish community, nor to the Board of Deputies, nor to the Chief Rabbi, but to Israel Zangwill because he was considered the authoritative Jewish spokesman and the ambassador of the Jewish people at the Court of St. James.[2]

Zangwill's role as an interpreter of Jewish life extended to English and American theater, where he revolutionized the portrayal of Jews and, by extension, of subsequent immigrant groups, on the mainstream stage.[3] He was keen on quoting Shylock: "If you deny me, fie upon your law! There is no force in the decrees of Venice." The justice he demanded for Jews was always part of a larger humanistic outlook. In the address he delivered at the 1911 Race Congress in London, he explained, "Civilization is not called upon to save the Jews, but it is called upon to save itself. If there is no justice in Venice for Shylock, then alas for Venice."[4] This justice he demanded in politics, in literature, and on the stage.

Introduction
Israel Zangwill: Child of the Ghetto

THE EARLY YEARS

Israel Zangwill was born on January 21, 1864, at 10 Ebenezer Square, in London's East End, within earshot of Bow Bells, traditionally the mark of a true Londoner. He often referred to himself as a "Cockney Jew," an identity composed of the polarized amalgamation of indigenousness and outsiderness. His parents, Ellen Hannah and Moses Zangwill, were immigrants from czarist Russia. Moses, a native of Zemiatchy, a small town in Latvia, escaped the life of a Cantonist (a boy soldier seized and conscripted into the Russian army), arriving in London in 1848 at the age of twelve, destitute and alone.[1] Moses is described as a meek and pious man who meandered sheepishly amid the hustle and bustle of Anglo-Jewish immigrant life. Israel would immortalize his father in his novel *Children of the Ghetto* (1892), modeling the character of Moses Ansell after him. Like his literary simulacrum, Moses Zangwill tried hard to provide for his growing family, often shifting occupations, succeeding in none. Moses Ansell's job history is listed as "glazier, synagogue beadle, picture-frame manufacturer, cantor, peddler, shoemaker in all branches, coat-seller, official executioner of fowls and cattle, Hebrew teacher, fruiterer, circumciser, professional corpse-watcher, and out-of-work tailor," the versatility wryly attributed to the fact that "there was nothing he could not do badly."[2] Zangwill's deadpan remarks should not obscure a profound empathy with his father's misery, as the jocular description develops into a tender account of the loneliness and abuse Moses had experienced as an alien and Jew as he went peddling about the English countryside:

> To Moses, "travelling" meant . . . carrying the red rag of an obnoxious personality through a land of bulls. It meant passing months away from wife and children, only occasionally alleviated by a Sabbath spent in a synagogue town. It meant putting up in low public houses

and common lodging houses, where rowdy disciples of the Prince of
Peace often sent him bleeding to bed, or shamelessly despoiled him
of his merchandise, or bullied and blustered him out of his fair price,
knowing he dared not resent.[3]

The memories of his father's humiliation never vanished. Years later, on his
last visit to New York to give a major policy speech, titled "Watchman, What
of the Night?" the fifty-nine-year-old Zangwill invoked again the days when
his mendicant father was subjected to "endless sneers and persecutions because he was a Jew."[4]

Although Moses Zangwill was looked down upon as a shlemiel in practical matters, he was respected in his community for his religiosity and Talmudic erudition. As the eldest son, Israel received special attention from his
father, who took him to synagogue early every morning. The boy would retain a lifelong love of Jewish liturgy, which he also translated into English.[5]
Late in life he also translated the Hebrew religious poetry of Solomon Ibn
Gabirol (ca. 1020–ca. 1070), the great Spanish Jewish poet and philosopher.[6]
Like many of his contemporaries, the adolescent Israel abandoned the devout
lifestyle of his father. This was a source of great sorrow to Moses. Joseph
Leftwich, Zangwill's biographer, recounts an incident when Dayan Susman
Cohen, a rabbinic scholar and friend of Moses Zangwill, introduced the latter
as the father of the famous author. Moses reproached his friend privately, saying he did not wish to be known as the father of a "renegade" and used a fierce
epithet: "yimakh shmo" (may his name be obliterated).[7] In his later years, the
father left London to live in Jerusalem, where, supported by his successful
son, he lived the humble pious life he had so craved.[8] They met for the last
time there in 1897. It was an emotional reconciliation that culminated in a
joyful celebration of the Passover seder at the father's humble apartment and
inspired the heartrending "To Die in Jerusalem," a story in which the errant
son finally wins his father's absolution.[9] Moses died in Jerusalem in August of
1908, shortly before the premiere of *The Melting Pot*.

Israel's mother, Ellen, born Hannah Marks in 1840, in Ravinisek, a village near Brest-Litovsk on the road to Warsaw, possessed different mettle.
According to a brief biographical sketch of the family prepared by Mrs. Mielziner, a family friend, Hannah was about twelve when she was brought to
England with a group of children rescued from a Polish pogrom.[10] It was at
the home of her London relatives that she met Moses Zangwill. They married
in 1861 and moved to Plymouth, and later to Bristol, finally settling in London's immigrant community. Hannah, who could barely read or write, was a

feisty and vocal woman whose determination kept the family afloat. Despite poverty, her children were kept in school rather than sent out to work. The price of securing a future through education was perhaps steep for Israel, who later in life blamed his constant bad health on poor nutrition during his early years. It is not surprising, then, that both *Children of the Ghetto* and *The King of Schnorrers* are laced with references to food—its sale, purchase, and preparation.

It was mainly the family's two oldest children—Leah (b. 1863) and her younger brother Israel—who most vividly remembered the times of brutal poverty. Years later, Leah would recount the family's hardships, how they would wait weeks for a postal order to come from the "traveller" father while landlords threatened eviction and how mother's hands "were worn to the bone saving for her little ones."[11] Mrs. Zangwill is portrayed in Joseph H. Udelson's biography of her son as lax in her commitment to traditional Jewish practices, including the keeping of a kosher household.[12] But this was not so. With so many mouths to feed—by then including her elderly mother-in-law, three boys, and two girls—she probably expressed her frustration much like the impoverished Mrs. Ansell in *Children of the Ghetto,* who wondered about "the value to God, man or beast," of learned rabbis who spend all their time studying when "they would be better occupied in supporting their families."[13] While more Anglicized and not as religiously pedantic as her husband, she was remembered by Eleanor Cowen, her old-time friend, as "very pious and very meticulous in keeping all religious laws" (see note 10). The aforementioned biographical sketch of the family clarifies further that "even in her old age her [Mrs. Zangwill's] stubbornness often made her escape her family, at that time prosperous enough to send her to the Synagogue by carriage on Sabbath and Holy Days, and go by herself afoot as was piously correct, straight across London from their home in Hampstead to the West End Synagogue."[14] When her husband left for Jerusalem, Mrs. Zangwill stayed in London, where her grown children were greatly attached to her, and always remembered the want she had known.

Israel was eight years old when his family settled permanently in London. England was at its apex as a world power. London, the seat of empire, was prosperous, rich in the arts and sciences, but also had large pockets of dire poverty. Growing rapidly, its population doubled to 6 million between 1851 and 1901. Its Jewish community was growing as well, mostly due to the mass immigration from the czarist empire during the last quarter of the nineteenth century. In 1800 there were about 8,000 Jews in the whole of England; by 1850 there were 20,000 in London, and by 1887 that figure had reached

50,000, 80 percent of them living in the immigrant quarter, the East End. In 1894 this number climbed to 60,000, and then to 160,000 in 1900. Historian Lloyd Gartner noted that in 1914 London stood third, after New York and Chicago, in the number of East European immigrants.[15]

Israel Zangwill experienced these changes firsthand. He was a child in the 1870s, when immigration changed from primarily Dutch and German to predominantly East European, first due to the 1869–1870 expulsion of Jews from the border regions of northeastern Russia and pressure on Romanian Jews to emigrate, and later in 1875–1876, when Jews fled to avoid service in the czarist army during the Russo-Turkish War.[16] He was a teenager when in the late 1870s the immigrant quarter began to develop a cultural pulse with the arrival of such intellectuals as Yiddish writer Morris Winchevsky, and he was a young man in 1881–1882 when the massive Jewish exodus from the czarist empire was gaining momentum in the aftermath of widespread pogroms in southern Russia.

The growing community of East European immigrants found a home in the East End, a sprawling mass of thoroughfares, narrow streets, courts, and alleys, riddled with dark and squalid slums. In 1894 the *American Hebrew,* a New York–based weekly associated with the city's affluent uptown community, offered a London correspondent's view of the scene:

> We are in the centre of Spitafield in the heart of the Jewish quarter. All about is Jewish! Men with beards, others clean-shaven of face. Women with *shitels* [wigs] or *lint* [kerchiefs], girls gaudily dressed, boys in the corduroy suits of the Jews' Free School—all Jewish. Posters in Yiddish, some religious, some socialistic, bills in crude colors, notices of rooms to let in the same tongue. Patois in the ear and in the eye, the tone, the habit, the idea is foreign.[17]

The imperiously detached tenor of this description is not surprising. Native English Jews assisted their kindred with paternalistic generosity but at the same time were disconcerted by the huge influx of immigrants. They regarded their penury and foreignness as distasteful and detrimental to their own recently won position in British society. The offense felt by the immigrant poor, their culture condescendingly rebuffed, would linger. In 1927 Louis Zangwill (1869–1938), Israel's younger brother and a novelist himself, sarcastically delineated the sharp demarcation of "locality and purse" that divided the "London Judea" of the 1880s, noting that "there were the Uncivilized and there were the Civilized!" The "Uncivilized" comprised the foreign

Jews of the East End, while the "Civilized" were the "Somebodies" who were the "Magnates or Nobs," men with "assured positions in the Heathen universe"—Lord Rothschild, Samuel Montagu, and Sir Julian Goldsmid—who had "the weight of authority, a suggestion of awe, even frightfulness." These autocrats, he wrote, were followed by an army of sycophants, who represented the "Nobodies" who comprised the mass of established Anglo Jewry, whom he found "sterile and repellent," absorbed in "assimilating in the British Philistinism of the day."[18]

Once in London, Israel was sent to the Jews' Free School, which offered its students, mostly the children of poor immigrants, a rigorous curriculum of secular and Jewish studies. There was no tuition, and such basic needs as clothing, food, and medical care were often provided. It was a formidable institution. In 1876 its staff of a hundred—teachers, assistant teachers, and pupil-teachers—was educating 1,350 boys and 1,000 girls, a total that by century's end would top 4,000. Their charges were all strictly disciplined by headmaster Moses Angel, who presided over the school magisterially for five decades, until his death in 1898.[19] Dubbed "the Bismarck of Bell Lane" by students, Angel had little respect for their background and deemed their parents "the refuse population of the worst parts of Europe."[20] Supported by Jewish philanthropists, especially the Rothschild family, the school prided itself on its perpetuation of "Englishness," which it equated with morality, the headmaster declaring that before the children had been "anglicized or humanized" it was difficult to tell the state of their "moral condition."[21] The school's emphasis on teaching English language skills to children born in so-called imperfectly civilized countries stemmed to a large measure from the desire to erase markers of ethnicity in the hope that linguistic invisibility would discourage anti-Jewish prejudice.[22] Angel's successor, Louis Abrahams, stressed that the teachers' mission was "to wipe away all evidence of foreign birth and foreign proclivities" so that the children would be identified with "everything that is English, in thought and in deed, that no shadow of anti-Semitism might exist."[23]

This drive to Anglicize proved a mixed blessing. On the one hand, it enabled a child like Israel Zangwill to attain a dazzling command of the language and claim a stake in England's intellectual and artistic heritage; on the other, it created anxiety when first- and second-generation youngsters had to negotiate between the establishment's pressure to acculturate, its disdainful view of their background, and their natural affection for the culture of family and community. Perhaps because of his stellar academic performance, Israel may have found it easier to reconcile the two cultures. Writing in his school notebook with characteristic verve, he vividly reported his fascination with the rich lore transmitted by his grandmother, who was a treasure trove of proverbs and phrases that he learned by heart and repeated to her on all possible occasions.[24]

Israel distinguished himself in his studies, winning the prestigious Commemoration Prize for academic excellence twice (1877–1878).[25] In his teens he was a pupil-teacher, eventually becoming a full member of the faculty. While teaching he completed all the required examinations and in 1884 graduated from London University, receiving his BA with triple honors. Some years earlier he had come to the attention of Lord Rothschild, the school's main benefactor, who offered to send the precocious youth to Eton and Oxford. Israel declined, because, as he later explained, he did not wish to feel indebted and thus be prevented from criticizing his would-be patron in the future, as indeed he eventually did, referring to him on more than one occasion as "The Lord I do not worship."

Becoming a Writer

Zangwill's literary career began at age seventeen with the publication of his short story "Professor Grimmer." At eighteen he joined forces with Meyer Breslar, a fellow pupil-teacher, and wrote "Motso Kleis" (Matza Balls), a vivid depiction of the shopping pandemonium of Petticoat Lane on the eve of Passover, in which the authentic lingo of a market—a hodgepodge of Yiddish and mispronounced English—was faithfully reproduced. Twenty thousand copies of the novella were printed as a pamphlet by the enterprising duo and hawked on the street. The author's name was given as the inane "Shloumi Yoshki ben Shlemeal." The revelation of the identities behind this nom de plume led to an uproar of sorts. Breslar was summarily expelled, and Zangwill was reprimanded and summoned to appear before school authorities. Some fifteen years later, he would recall:

> One dread afternoon, when all Nature seemed to hold its breath, I was called down to interview a member of the committee. In his hand were copies of the obnoxious publications. . . . In the course of a bad quarter of an hour, he told me that . . . the prose novelette was disgusting. "It is such stuff," said he, "as little boys scribble on walls. . . . Confess you are ashamed of yourself," he reiterated, "and we will overlook it." "I am not," I persisted, though I foresaw only too clearly that my summer's vacation was doomed if I told the truth. "What is the use of saying I am?"[26]

He was given the option of dismissal or promising to publish only after approval from a school committee. He chose not to publish until departing from the school. It was the first recorded incident in a lifelong struggle against censorship.

Zangwill's schoolmasters were enraged by his realistic portrayal of market life, which they believed would turn Jews into objects of Gentile ridicule, always a sensitive issue. They were particularly scandalized by the use of Yiddish expressions, as they regarded this language of immigrants as a debased jargon that represented all that was undesirable in Jewish life. Although at the time Zangwill shared the widespread view of Yiddish as a lowly dialect—evidenced in his novel *Children of the Ghetto* by its jocular description as "the most hopelessly corrupt and hybrid jargon ever evolved"—it would be incorrect for us to now judge this comment as an expression of personal ethnic unease. Yiddish in the early 1890s was generally referred to as "jargon," and modern Yiddish literature, a major source for the language's later respectability, was in its infancy.[27] Moreover, for Zangwill, who was reared at home with a mixture of Yiddish and English, the notion of linguistic hybridity did not carry negative overtones. As a realist, he introduced Jewish terminology and colloquialisms into his writings as a natural expression of community. He argued against those who opposed its inclusion, saying it was as if "English-speaking Scotsmen and Irishmen should object to 'dialect' novels reproducing the idiom of their 'uncultured' countrymen."[28] For this reason Zangwill had originally refused to furnish *Children of the Ghetto* with a glossary of the Jewish words and phrases that peppered its pages. But though the first British edition published by Heinemann did not include one, the American edition that appeared several weeks later did, anonymously provided by Cyrus Adler (1863–1940), a noted scholar, the first American PhD in Semitics, who in the following year founded the American Jewish Historical Society. In the preface to the third edition (1893), which did contain a glossary, Zangwill wrote that he had reluctantly consented to its inclusion and that it was "based on one supplied to the American edition by another hand."[29] Zangwill's earlier insistence on this point has its subversive aspect. The inclusion of a Jewish vocabulary not only enabled the marginalized voice of the immigrant Jew to be heard within the dominant culture but also suggested a decentering of its hegemonic discourse. And he was not alone in this. Critic Holbrook Jackson mentioned Zangwill in his 1913 book *The Eighteen Nineties* with reference to the popularity of the use of dialect in fiction.[30] Jackson notes that this trend was inaugurated by James M. Barrie in 1888 in his sketches of Scottish life, *Auld Licht Idylls,* and was advanced in 1892 by Jane Barlow in her depictions of Irish peasants in *Irish Idylls* and *Bog-land Studies.* He links these writers with an interest in "local colour" and the revival of the Cockney dialect in both serious and comedic fiction.[31]

Zangwill dealt with issues of linguistic "purity" and hybridity in his essay "Language and Jewish Life," written in 1903.[32] He discussed the roles of Jewish languages—Yiddish, classical and modern Hebrew, and Ladino—and concluded that at present it was Yiddish that fit the definition of a living language. He regarded it as the principal medium of communication among the Jewish masses, noting that it "vibrates with their history, follows the mould of their life and thought, and colours itself with their moods."[33] He praised the ability of Yiddish to absorb and transform foreign words, considering linguistic appropriation as proof of the dynamism of a living language. Moreover, he repudiated the willful eradication of Jewish words from the language of Americanized and Anglicized Jews, a practice he equated with the weakness of Jewish life outside the ghetto. He pointed to the untranslatability of key cultural concepts and suggested that for Jews to become genuine members of the human community their unique terminology must be added to the global thesaurus.

Zangwill's affection for and indebtedness to Yiddish as the language of authentic Jewish life can be gleaned from an excerpt from the new introduction he wrote for the Yiddish translation of *Children of the Ghetto:*

> In being translated into Yiddish this book undergoes an exceptional fate. For while most books when translated are altered into a foreign tongue, this book is really translated into its own tongue, for in the spiritual sense of the words, Yiddish is the language in which it was really conceived, and I had great difficulty in translating Yiddish ideas and expressions into phrases which Englishmen could understand.

Then, directly addressing his Yiddish readers:

> You will understand the pictures which I have tried to draw and the purpose which I had in mind in drawing them. You will not think that this book is an attack upon the Jews, as some of the English-speaking Jews did who were frightened at the thought that the world would now discover that they were not exactly like English Christians; as if the world did not know it the whole time. You are not ashamed of being what you are, and you are familiar with stories and plays written about your own lives.[34]

Zangwill was familiar with the rapidly growing Yiddish literature of the period and assisted its practitioners when they came to London. In 1900, for example, he sponsored a public reading by poet Morris Rosenfeld. Zangwill's sponsorship created a bit of a journalistic fracas when he was criticized by the *Jewish World* of London for having "forgotten how to speak Yiddish" because he introduced the poet in English. In a letter to the editor the upset Zangwill retorted that as a born Londoner, he never mastered Yiddish well enough to address an audience in it, adding, "anything more electric than the effect of Mr. Rosenfeld on his audience I have never witnessed."[35] Eight years later he wrote the part of the old grandmother in *The Melting Pot* entirely in Yiddish. Not a single critic commented on its incomprehensibility. The press conference organized in New York shortly after the opening of the play marked the first time both English- and Yiddish-language journalists were invited as members of the city press corps, signaling the incorporation of Jewish immigrant culture into the city's cultural mainstream. Zangwill maintained a connection to Yiddish throughout his life. In his 1923 visit to New York he gave a speech at Maurice Schwartz's Yiddish Art Theatre in which he commended the Yiddish stage as superior to the commercial English-language fare in artistry and literary seriousness.

For the young Zangwill, his teaching position was a source of increasing dissatisfaction. E. Jaffe, a fellow teacher, recalled his colleague's frustration: "His mind revolted against the dull dreary monotony of the whole business, the constant repetition *ad nauseam* of the names of capes, rivers, heights of mountains, &c., and in the soul-killing, sing-song style that could be heard by any passer-by at any Board School in those days."[36] The pen would be Zangwill's way out.

In 1888 a new pseudonymous work written by Zangwill in collaboration with Louis Cowen, another school colleague, appeared. As in his previous co-venture, Zangwill did nearly all the writing. Titled *The Premier and the Painter; a Fantastic Romance,* it recounts the adventures of a "world-weary" Tory premier and an ultra-radical atheist housepainter who switch places and identities, the latter directing a conservative administration with much success. The authors' names were hidden behind the pseudonym "J. Freeman Bell," according to Zangwill an abbreviation of "Jews' Free School, Bell Lane," though one can also interpret it as a declaration of independence from the tyranny of the school administration, servility, and intellectual drudgery. With the resumption of his literary activity, Zangwill's teaching career ended. His and Cowen's resignation from the school led to a confrontation with Lord

Rothschild, who let it be known publicly that the two had been dismissed. Cowen and Zangwill responded with an open letter to the *Jewish Chronicle* in which they claimed that Rothschild's insinuation was libelous and demanded that he publicly apologize for damaging their reputations, an apology that never came.[37] Thirty-five years later, while recounting this story in New York, Zangwill stated, "I after all was only the son of a Russian peddlar."[38]

The Premier and the Painter gained little attention and did not further its author's career.[39] The twenty-two-year-old Zangwill began to work as a journalist at the very bottom. It was the beginning of an exuberant four years during which he would hone his pen in a dazzling array of literary genres and befriend some of the most creative persons in the worlds of Jewish and English letters. In 1888 he was hired by the *Jewish Standard*, a weekly devoted to promotion of the interests of Orthodox Judaism, recently founded by Dutch Jews unhappy with the *Jewish Chronicle*, which they regarded as insufficiently traditional. There he served first as subeditor and later as editor, contributing stories, poems, and translations. As "Marshalik" (jester, in Yiddish) he wrote a satirical column, "Morour and Chorouseth," named for the bitterest and sweetest dishes of the Passover seder. He commented on any topic that struck his fancy: he bemoaned the disappearance of Jewish intimacy, particularly in regard to hospitality and charitable giving, which in the past had been conducted in the home and were now in the hands of bureaucrats, limited to the office hours of the United Hebrew Charities; he lamented the disappearance of the picturesque character of the *schnorrer*, whom he would later immortalize in his novella and play; and he ridiculed the social pretensions of well-to-do Jews, especially as they masked their identity behind high-sounding English names. This distaste for Jews who try to pass and deny their humble origins is a recurring motif in Zangwill's work.

In his *Children of the Ghetto* Zangwill depicted in great detail the idiosyncratic ambience of the *Jewish Standard*, thinly masked as "The Flag of Judah." He delighted in the eccentricities of its contributors, particularly Naphtali Herz Imber (1856–1909), an extravagant poet whose "Hatikvah" (The Hope) would become the anthem of the Zionist movement and the State of Israel. Zangwill was taken by the brassy fancifulness of the vagabond Imber, encouraged him to write in English, translated his poem "The Watch on the Jordan," and published his articles, which included fantastic claims that the Talmud contained references to modern technological and scientific phenomena, including the recently constructed Eiffel Tower. This magnificently madcap character found his way into the novel and the play under the long-winded moniker Melchitsedek Pinchas.[40] Imber, who left London for

America in 1891, did not forget Zangwill's kindness. In 1892 he devoted a long article to him and called him "a poet by the grace of God," comparing him to Mark Twain, Heinrich Heine, and Benjamin Disraeli.[41] The article refers to Zangwill's current work on *Children of the Ghetto* and sheds light on his humble circumstances, as "the most ill paid of literary men," who, according to Imber, worked "only for the purpose of supporting his parents."[42]

In addition to the time-consuming and poorly paying job at the *Jewish Standard*, Zangwill continued his literary work. Again using the name J. Freeman Bell, he published "Under Sentence of Marriage," a story about a young rabbi in a small provincial congregation whose employment hinges on the synagogue's stipulation that he marry within a year of being hired. A year later, as the "Baroness von S.," he published "Satan Mekatrig" (Satan the Accuser), a story full of supernatural elements, in which the forces of evil are embodied in a hunchback dwarf. The next year, finally under his own name, he published "Diary of a Meshumad" (Diary of an Apostate), a chilling tale of a Russian Jew who converts to Christianity and is slaughtered during a pogrom fueled by the anti-Semitic tirades of his son.

At that time Zangwill became associated with an informal circle of Jewish scholars who met at one another's homes for intellectual discussions on Jewish topics. The group, calling itself the Wanderers, since they did not adhere to any prescribed subject but meandered freely from one topic to another, consisted of people whose work would have an enormous impact on the modern study and interpretation of Judaism. In addition to Zangwill, it included Asher Myers (1848–1902), later editor of the *Jewish Chronicle;* Joseph Jacobs (1854–1916), scholar of history, anthropology, and folklore; Solomon Schechter (1847–1915), appointed Reader of Rabbinics at Cambridge in 1891, who in 1901 would leave for New York to lead the Jewish Theological Seminary; Israel Abrahams (1858–1925), author of the seminal study of Jewish life in the Middle Ages and Schechter's successor at Cambridge; Lucien Wolf (1857–1930), journalist, scholar, and Jewish diplomat, who would later participate in the 1918 Paris Peace Conference; Herbert Bentwich (1856–1932), lawyer, first president of the English Zionist Federation, and one of the founders of the Hebrew University in Jerusalem; Solomon J. Solomon (1860–1927), respected painter, who in 1918 became president of the Royal Society of British Artists; and Arthur Davis (1846–1906), engineer and accomplished Hebrew scholar. The group inspired the formation of the Maccabeans, a club that sought to bring together Jewish "gentlemen" engaged in literature, science, and the arts and declined admittance to people engaged in business and finance. The two associations found their way into the *Children of the Ghetto,* portrayed as the Asmonean Society, where "brilliant free-lancers, each thinking himself a solitary exception to a race of bigots, met one another in mutual astonishment."[43] Impelled by his scholarly milieu, Zangwill contributed to the *Jewish Quarterly Review,* an academic journal founded in 1888, edited by Claude Montefiore and Israel Abrahams. His essay "English Judaism; a Criticism and Classification," which appeared in the July 1889 issue, offered a lengthy response to two articles concerning the nature of Judaism, one by Solomon Schechter, the other by eminent historian Heinrich Graetz.[44]

While closely involved in Jewish circles, Zangwill made forays into the world of English letters. He associated with a loosely knit group of comic writers, among them Barry Pain (1864–1928) and Jerome K. Jerome (1859–1927), whose set included Eden Phillpotts, J. M. Barrie, Rider Haggard, H. G. Wells, Arthur Conan Doyle, W. W. Jacobs, Hall Caine, Thomas Hardy, and Rudyard Kipling. In 1890 Zangwill became editor of a short-lived humorous magazine, *Ariel, or the London Puck,* which modeled itself on *Punch,* where he serialized stories that in 1891 he put into book form as *The Bachelors' Club,* joined a year later by a companion volume, *The Old Maids' Club* (1892). The two, which were well received by the public, were later published in one volume as *The Celibates' Club.*[45] After Jerome's monthly *The Idler* was founded in 1892, Zangwill became a frequent contributor and serialized *The King of Schnorrers* in the magazine, thus bringing specifically Jewish humor into the mainstream. Jerome's "New Humour" would later fall out of critical favor, and Zangwill, now devoted to more serious fare, was commended for giving up fluff. Yet a humorist even in the face of adversity, Zangwill completely rejected a contemptuous view of comic literature. In his preface to the sixth edition of *The Celibates' Club,* he charged the critics with an antihumor prejudice and criticized fellow authors who were eager to cover up their "humorous" pasts in the belief that it would diminish their stature, remarking, "it is . . . your university prigs who never descend to a jest, not your Shakespeares and Heines."[46]

Trying his hand at a variety of literary formats, Zangwill also experimented with the burgeoning genre of the detective novel, writing *The Big Bow Mystery* (1892), originally serialized in 1891 in the *Star.* This work is recognized as the first literary story based on the concept of "the locked room," a crime committed where all the exits are locked from the inside and no one else is there.[47] *The Big Bow Mystery* remains popular to this day, and several films based on it have been produced.

His love for the theater led Zangwill to join the Playgoers Club, of which he became president in 1904. He befriended Herbert Beerbohm Tree, who, though always denying rumors of his partial Jewish ancestry, was clearly interested in Jewish dramatic characters and would in later years play Svengali, Fagin, and Shylock to great acclaim. Tree was close enough to Zangwill to have been a guest at the November 13, 1892, dinner celebration of the publication of *Children of the Ghetto,* where he disclosed that he was preparing to play the Jewish character in his production of Kingley's *Hypatia* and announced that he had just asked Zangwill to write a play about Uriel Acosta for him.[48] This plan never came to fruition, though Zangwill's prose portrayal of Acosta was incorporated into his book *Dreamers of the Ghetto.* Zangwill had always hoped that Tree would play the title role of *The King of Schnorrers,* but this project also never materialized. In 1911 they finally collaborated when Tree produced and starred in Zangwill's ambitious antiwar blank-verse drama, *The War God.*

Zangwill also befriended J. T. (Jacob Thomas) Grein (1862–1935), a major force in the nonprofit stage, who in 1891 founded the Independent Theatre, an innovative venture whose goal was the presentation of new drama of artistic merit without commercial considerations. Grein was a Dutch Jew who settled in England in 1885, and it was through Zangwill's recommendation that he got his first job as theater critic for the London weekly *Life* in 1890.[49] He made theater history when he produced the English premiere of Henrik Ibsen's *Ghosts* (1891) and inaugurated George Bernard Shaw's theatrical career in 1892. Grein produced Zangwill's play *The Revolted Daughter* in 1901, and in the twenties their paths crossed again within the framework of the Jewish Drama League, of which Zangwill was the honorary president.

In January 1890 Zangwill entered another facet of London life when he obtained a reader's ticket to the library of the British Museum.[50] There he may have met Beatrice Potter, who was investigating the Jewish East End as a researcher for Charles Booth's monumental inquiry published under the title *Life and Labour of the People of London.*[51] At the library, described by Potter as home to "decrepit men, despised foreigners, forlorn widows and soured maids, all knit together by a feeling of fellowship with the great immortals," Zangwill befriended Eleanor Marx [Aveling] (1855–1898), Karl Marx's youngest daughter, a brilliant writer and orator, regarded by her father as his political and intellectual heir.[52] An active socialist, she had joined William Morris in 1884 to form the Socialist League and in 1885 played an pivotal role in organizing the International Socialist Congress in Paris. She was active in the campaign for women's equality and worked closely with the Women's Trade Union League.[53] Through Marx, Zangwill probably met her social circle of emigré revolutionaries, socialists, feminists, and literati, among them Vera Zasulich, George Bernard Shaw, Havelock Ellis, and Olive Schreiner.

Their friendship, which led to joint authorship of the playlet *A Doll's House Repaired* (1891), was propelled by a shared interest in two subjects: Jews and the theater. Eleanor was the only one of Marx's family to take an interest in her Jewish roots. In 1889 she had translated Amy Levy's *Reuben Sachs*, a bitter exposé of the Anglo-Jewish bourgeoisie, into German, the only book Eleanor translated from her native English.[54] In 1890 she was moved to activism. In her response to an invitation to speak at a mass Jewish socialist meeting held in the East End to protest Jewish persecutions in Russia, she wrote, "I shall be very glad to speak at the meeting on Novm. 1st, the more glad that my father was a Jew."[55] And there is additional evidence of her growing interest. A Russian visitor meeting with Eleanor at the time quoted her as saying, "My latest linguistic acquisition is Yiddish." Eleanor explained that she was politically involved with Jewish workingwomen in Whitechapel and used her knowledge of German to deliver lectures in Yiddish. She added, "the Jewish language is akin to my blood . . . in our family it is thought that I am like my paternal grandmother, who was the wife of a learned Rabbi."[56] Though it is difficult to assess Zangwill's role in Eleanor's growing Jewish consciousness, there is little doubt that Jewish issues did come up in their meetings. Possibly, their friendship led him to a partial reconsideration of the controversial *Reuben Sachs,* which he had parodied in the *Jewish Standard* yet depicted more favorably in *Children of the Ghetto.*

Eleanor loved the theater, and in her youth had seriously contemplated an acting career. She was now a proponent of Henrik Ibsen (1828–1906), two of whose plays, *The Lady of the Sea* and *An Enemy of Society,* she had translated in the mid-1880s. She was particularly interested in Ibsen's *A Doll's House;* she and her common-law husband, Edward Aveling, performed the lead roles of Nora and Torvald Helmer in a private reading in December 1886, with G. B. Shaw in the role of the extortionist Krogstad and William Morris's daughter May as Mrs. Linde. This event heralded the emergence of "Ibsenism," a political and cultural constellation of Marxists, socialists, Fabians, and feminists who regarded the playwright as social philosopher and spokesman for their respective causes.[57] Ibsen's plays attracted great attention, aroused bitter controversy, and became the touchstone for the New Drama.[58]

Ibsen came to represent the dividing line between two opposing camps: Ancients and Moderns. Chief spokesman for the New Drama was William

Archer (1856–1924), an Ibsen translator and critic, who disapproved of plays written as vehicles for acting and emphasized the intellectual aspect of drama. The standard-bearer for the old school was Clement Scott (1841–1904), London's dominant theater critic until the late 1890s. Scott, who wrote for the *Daily Telegraph* beginning in 1872, was an ardent devotee of actor Henry Irving and is remembered for his notorious dismissal of Ibsen's *Ghosts* as "an open drain; a loathsome sore unbandaged."

A Doll's House, professionally produced in 1889, marked the first Ibsen play given a public performance in England. It had the effect of a thunderbolt, stunning audiences with its manner and content, and according to Harley Granville-Barker was "the most dramatic event of the decade."[59] The play's conclusion, culminating in Nora's departure, magnified by the sound of a slamming door, created an uproar. The notion that a wife and mother would walk away from her family in quest of selfhood was deemed immoral and unnatural to most Victorians. Marx and Zangwill mocked this haughty condemnation in their dramatic spoof *A Doll's House Repaired,* where Nora repentantly begs for her husband's forgiveness and meekly remains at home.[60] Their rewrite of the final scene playfully twists elements of the original, ending in a parodic reversal as Helmer enters his bedroom, slamming that door from the inside. The piece was written for people familiar with the play and the expletives of its critics. It is not known if this sketch was given a public reading. The sixteen-page text appeared twice in printed form, first in the London monthly *Time,* and later in a small pamphlet.[61] This essentially minor composition points to Zangwill's familiarity and sympathy for the women's movement early in his literary career. While his biographers hinge his involvement in the women's suffrage movement to his marriage to Edith Ayrton in 1903, the prior connection through Eleanor Marx suggests the presence of a conscious feminist aspect in his work in the early 1890s and invites a consonant reading of his work of this period.

CHILDREN OF THE GHETTO THE NOVEL

Israel Zangwill's great break, though he may not have realized it at the time, came in 1890, when Judge Mayer Sulzberger (1843–1923), chair of the publications committee of the recently founded Jewish Publication Society of America, was visiting London, looking to commission a Jewish novel.[62] Following Lucien Wolf's recommendation, and personally impressed with Zangwill's work, Sulzberger offered the twenty-six-year-old author a contract. It is quite astounding from today's perspective that there was no American contender for the task. At home, Sulzberger came under some fire for offering the job to a "foreigner," yet no alternate candidate was even proposed. Zangwill hesitated. For although he assured Sulzberger that he had "a Jewish novel" inside him, he was uncertain whether he wanted to present himself so early in his career as a parochial writer. In addition, he feared that by taking the commission he could be subject to pressure that might compromise his artistic freedom, and this concern was not altogether imaginary. Zangwill's correspondence with Sulzberger reveals that the Americans were pressing for validation of their ideals and sensibilities. They were eager to have the novel's heroine emigrate to America, and upon receipt of the manuscript, Sulzberger suggested that Zangwill change the unhappy ending of the Hannah Jacobs–David Brandon romance so as to not frustrate the American penchant for "fair play."[63] Though Sulzberger gave Zangwill a free hand and backed his focus on the life of the East European immigrant Jewish community, his comment that "fine flowers doubtless grow on the muck-heap" bespeaks the instinctive distaste with which the ghetto was regarded even by the most open-minded of upper-class Jews.

The title Zangwill chose was brilliant in its simplicity. It echoes the biblical designation of the Jews as children of Israel, while presenting the current immigrant Jewish community not only as a product of common ancestry but of a tangible geographical environment, thus implying the question of their identity once they leave the ghetto. Zangwill layered the medieval meaning of "ghetto" as a compulsory area of residence with the added modern signification of a homogenous urban enclave with its own subculture.[64] He drew his reader's attention to the new meaning with which he had imbued the centuries-old term. The proem to the novel opened with an explanation of the difference between the modern ghetto of London and the medieval ghetto of Rome: "Not here in our London Ghetto the gates and gaberdines of the olden Ghetto of the Eternal City. . . . It is no longer the stage for the high-buskined tragedy of massacre and martyrdom; only for the obscurer, deeper tragedy that evolves from the pressure of its own inward forces, and the long-drawn-out tragi-comedy of sordid and shifty poverty."[65] Some opposed the change in meaning. The correspondent of the *American Hebrew* scolded, "despite the picturesqueness of the term, let us not give so free license to the pen that it may term the East End quarter a ghetto. Ghetto indeed! Elysium is this to refugee and oppressed."[66] In its revised designation the term may have been academically inaccurate, but the allure of its sweeping brevity guaranteed absorption into the cultural vocabulary. It was subsequently used with great frequency. Within a decade of its publication, Zangwill's novel had inspired such titles as Abraham Cahan's *Yekl: A Tale of the New York Ghetto* (1896); Herman Heijermans's play *The Ghetto* (1899); the English translation of Morris Rosenfeld's Yiddish poems under the title *Songs of the Ghetto* (1899); Hutchins Hapgood's *The Spirit of the Ghetto* (1902); and actor David Warfield's *Ghetto Silhouettes* (1902). When Louis Wirth wrote in the late 1920s his classic study *The Ghetto,* it was natural for his discussion of "Modern Ghettos" to begin with substantial quotations from the work of Israel Zangwill.[67] As early as 1903, Jack London further elasticized and appropriated the Jewish term by calling the entire area of East London "a ghetto" to which the dominant economic class had confined its undesirable yet necessary workers.[68]

   Children of the Ghetto is comprised of two parts: "Children of the Ghetto" and "Grandchildren of the Ghetto." It offers a panoramic view of the London ghetto in its first part, and in the second a portrayal of the identity quandary and spiritual malaise of the Jewish bourgeoisie. It is constructed of a series of loosely connected sketches, some linked only tenuously to a central story line, thereby endowing it with a cinematic quality of shifting gaze, focus, tone, and mood. It was a work of "astounding vitality," wrote William Archer in a private note to the author, with "not a 'dead' page in it."[69] The book took the reader on a literary-ethnographic tour, navigated with confidence, erudition, and humor by the ever-present author in the role of storyteller, interpreter, guide, critic, and advocate. In offering a sweeping pageant of Jewish life in the ghetto, Zangwill drew upon a vast treasury of personal experiences collected at home, in the street, and at school, synagogue, and workplace. He tapped into the tales and epigrams of his grandmother, the Talmudic deliberations of his father, the complaints of his mother, the pomposity of the philanthropists, and the flamboyance of a poet. With the confidence of a native son, he immerses his readers in a lush mélange of the smells, sounds, and colors of the ghetto's congested terrain, introducing a colorful gallery of characters who form its human landscape. When *Children of the Ghetto* appeared, the *Jewish Chronicle* equated the scope of its dramatis personae with the large canvas of London life drawn by Charles Dickens:

> Noble figures and despicable; grotesque figures and commonplace; humorous . . . and pathetic . . . ; figures at which we laugh, figures at which we weep, figures which we fain would have been absent from the picture, figures that we know, figures that we wish we knew; spiritual figures and "men of the earth"; poets and peddlars; beggars and millionaires; Rabbis and unbelievers; gentle women and fishwives; artists and artizans; Jews of every school of creed, of every shade of

culture, of every phase of defiant vacillation in belief and every shade of naive uncertainty. It is a generic image, or rather, a kaleidoscope, to which the Jews of all the ages lend a feature or ray of colour.[70]

In an interview, Zangwill explained that the goal of his book was "to give a conspectus, or a coup d'oeil" of the whole life of the Jews of London. He explained it was because Jews had been so poorly treated in English literature, both in an artistic and moral sense, that he had chosen for his book a broad format with a large number of characters, with the intention of exhibiting that Jews, like Englishmen, could not be "summed up in any single, or indeed in any score, of types."[71] The charge that English letters failed to recognize the diversity of the country's Jews was not new. Ten years earlier, Charles Kensington Salaman (1814–1901), a prominent Anglo-Jewish musician, protested in his book *Jews as They Are* the reduction of all Jews to a uniform matrix, regardless of the fact that they differ in character and condition.[72]

The critical consensus was that *Children of the Ghetto* was highly original and unlike any other book authored by a Jewish writer. Rabbi Stephen Wise observed in hindsight that it "was not a book; it was an event," the first "conscious act of self-disclosure" to occur after a long history of Jewish self-effacement.[73] Lucien Wolf praised the book, for in it "the real heart and soul of Jewry were uncompromisingly laid bare." It was a project, he noted, that had thus far remained unfulfilled even when tackled by the sympathetic George Eliot, author of *Daniel Deronda,* who, despite her "intuition," had remained the brilliant outsider, or by Jewish writers like Amy Levy and Mrs. Sidgwick, who had produced near-caricatures.[74] Having three years earlier contributed an ethnographic account of Jewish life in the East End to the London periodical *The Graphic,* Wolf was especially attuned to the revolutionary nature of Zangwill's ethnic self-presentation.[75] In 1887 Wolf and Joseph Jacobs stood at the helm of the Anglo-Jewish Historical Exhibition, presented in London's Royal Albert Hall, whose aim was to create interest in Jewish history and legitimate the Anglo-Jewish community.[76] Wolf recognized the enormous leap from the presentation of carefully manipulated objects that conveyed a universal message of commitment to home and faith, to the vibrant pen sketches of individual characters, who, albeit tender, were mostly poor and uncouth.

Zangwill's depiction of Russian immigrant Jews as harbingers of the spirit of Judaism was received with trepidation by an English Jewry that was nervous about its public image, a reaction anticipated by the author. Raphael Leon, one of the novel's main characters, explains to the fictionalized Amy Levy: "In no work of art can the spectator be left out of the account. . . .

In a world full of prejudices a scrap of paper may start the bonfire. English society can afford to laugh where Jewish society must weep. That is why our papers are always so effusively grateful for Christian compliments."[77] Indeed, it was only when Gentile cultural arbiters declared *Children of the Ghetto* a "great book" that Jewish public opinion joined, loud and clear, in the chorus of praise. It soon became evident that the book was one of historical consequence, compared in retrospect to *Uncle Tom's Cabin* for its immense impact on public attitudes. Zangwill's literary portraits became the lens through which sympathetic Gentiles now saw the real-life immigrant Jew. M. C. Birchenough, a Gentile writer who was asked to review the book for the *Jewish Quarterly Review* as one who had no connection to the ghetto, recommended a tour to the "far country" of the East End, where, she noted: "The 'Children of the Ghetto,' who cross your path in the flesh, recall over and over again, the types in the book."[78]

Children of the Ghetto was widely translated—into German, Russian, French, Yiddish, and Hebrew—and would remain on the publishers' "active list" for nearly two decades after its author's death. The book and Zangwill's subsequent writings on the ghetto influenced greatly the way Jews of the day looked at themselves. Writing in America in 1914, Louis Lipsky explained, "Above all, the *Children of the Ghetto* for the first time revealed to us, the first or second generation of the Russian immigration, an adequate picture of how we, our parents and grandparents, appeared in the sight of the world" and "gave us an inkling of our own position in the world about us."[79] With time, as Gentile culture learned more about the Jews, and as a whole genre of Jewish immigrant literature developed, the historic role of the book became blurred. Its readership eventually consisted mostly of the great-grandchildren of the urban ghettos of a century past, who had found in its dense tapestry a fountain that energized their sense of ethnoreligious identity.

The composition of a Jewish work of this magnitude forced the young Zangwill to confront his own identity as a Jewish writer. Cyrus Adler recalled their 1892 meeting in London, when he was trying to determine the status of the yet-undelivered manuscript on behalf of the Jewish Publication Society.[80] Zangwill reported that he had finished the book but didn't think the JPS would want it, explaining, "I have been very frank and truth-telling, having given my own picture of Jewish people as I saw them, and I do not think that an official Society would wish to give its imprint to such a book." Adler asked, "How do you look upon the Jewish people in this book?" "As artistic material," was the reply. Adler inquired further, "Have you no other interest in the Jewish people except as artistic material?" "No." Adler responded, "If that is the case, we do not want your book." A couple of days passed. As Adler was about to sail back to America, a package was left for him. It contained Zangwill's story "Diary of a Meshumad" with a note: "I am leaving for you one of my stories. . . . You will probably judge from it that I have more than an artistic interest in the Jewish people." The manuscript of *Children of the Ghetto* followed soon afterward.[81]

With the ghetto, Zangwill had found his own original voice, and to many it seemed the source of his best literary work. In 1893 he published two major volumes: *The King of Schnorrers,* where he combined his talent for humorous writing with his interest in Jewish life, and *Ghetto Tragedies,* a collection of stories that would be republished in 1899 with additional material as *They That Walk in Darkness.* In 1898 came *Dreamers of the Ghetto,* regarded by some as his magnum opus, and in 1907 *Ghetto Comedies.* Meanwhile, he continued to publish on non-Jewish subjects. Some of his frequent contributions to major periodicals of the period were collected in *Without Prejudice* (1896). His novella *Merely Mary Ann* (1893), later to be included in the collection *The Grey Wig* (1903), and *The Master* (1895) drew much praise and were followed by two other non-Jewish novels, *The Mantle of Elijah* (1900) and *Jinny the Carrier* (1919), and his travelogue, *Italian Fantasies* (1910). Near the end of his life he was working on a Jewish novel, *The Baron of Offenbach,* which he did not complete. Zangwill also produced important essays on an array of political and cultural topics, some of which appeared in book form, a book of poetry, and translations of the Hebrew liturgy and the religious poems of Solomon Ibn Gabirol. He was also a prolific dramatist, his body of work including nearly twenty plays, most of which were published and produced.

THE THEATER

The year 1892 marked Zangwill's modest debut as a produced playwright. *The Great Demonstration,* a one-act farce written with school chum Louis Cowen, was produced as a curtain-raiser, a short piece preceding a full-length drama, at London's Royalty Theatre. It had probably been written a few years earlier and merited production on the coattails of the successful *The Bachelors' Club* and *The Old Maids' Club,* as can be gleaned from the introductory remarks of a review in *Theatre* that referred to Zangwill as the author of the two books, "which scintillate with diamond-like wit, hard and clear and brilliant."[82] Like *The Premier and the Painter,* the plot of *The Great Demonstration* revolves around a willful change of identities across class lines. The lighthearted playlet was highly praised for its wit and cleverness by the theatrical press.[83]

Zangwill's next play, *Six Persons,* a one-act duologue, opened on December 22, 1893, at the Haymarket and received considerably more critical attention. It was produced by Herbert Beerbohm Tree as a curtain-raiser for his successful star vehicle *Captain Swift.* In *Six Persons* Zangwill presents three phases in the relationship of a young couple who become engaged during the course of an evening, regret it in the morning, each thinking they could do better, each hoping the other will break it off, without exposing their own rancor, but finally falling for each other, the young man's sentiments aided by a revelation that the woman has a generous yearly income. The idea for the piece, as well as its title, derives from Oliver Wendell Holmes's (1809–1894) *The Autocrat of the Breakfast Table,* popular on both sides of the Atlantic. In it the eminent American physician, poet, and humorist developed a theory of interpersonal communication wherein there are at least six distinct personalities present in every dialogue: each party as only God knows them, each as they think of themselves, and each as conceived by the other.

Though the playlet was applauded as very clever and entertaining, a "sparkling and spirited piece of writing," the critics were disappointed that it did not reflect its "weighty" title.[84] The *Era* complained, "We have been led to expect so much in the way of psychological analysis and exposition—that the audience sat [and waited for the] illustration which was to come of one of Holmes's ingenious theories." For the reviewer, this attitude of "puzzled expectation" diminished the enjoyment derived from the piece.[85] The play was published by Samuel French in 1898 and was quite popular with amateur players. When it was revived in 1912 for a special charity concert at the Royal Court Theatre, it was reported to have caused "much amusement," even though by then its humor was considered "somewhat old-fashioned."[86] In 1895 another Zangwill farcical skit, *Threepenny Bits,* was staged as a special matinee at the Garrick Theatre, but garnered little attention.

Clearly, these short pieces were not commensurate with Zangwill's lionized position in the London literary world. All in all, until the 1899 production of his first full-length play, *Children of the Ghetto,* Zangwill was positioned at the doorstep of the professional London stage, immersing himself in the rapidly changing theatrical scene of the 1890s in anticipation of a major career as a dramatist.

Zangwill had been drawn to the theater at a young age, and the stage features frequently in his novels and short stories. His biographer, Joseph Leftwich, wrote that in his youth Zangwill found his way to the Britannia Theatre in neighboring "Gentile Shoreditch" and to the Pavilion Theatre in Whitechapel.[87] A visit to the Britannia, situated outside the tightly defined Jewish territory, was a thrill for the East End boy, who likened his daring explorations outside the ghetto to the expeditions of Haroun Al Raschid, the ancient Caliph of Baghdad. Little did the young offender know that going to the local English theater had been popular with the Jews of the area in the earlier years of the nineteenth century, before they had moved out to wealthier parts of town. Indeed, this is how some Jewish youngsters, including Arthur Wing Pinero—eldest son of a Portuguese Jewish family, later a leading dramatist—found their way to the then-demimonde of the theater. Henry Mayhew, author of *London Labour and London Poor* (1861–1862) among other sources, offers evidence of Jewish patronage of the East End stage and its popularity among the younger generation. In his evidence to the Select Committee on Public Houses, given in 1854, J. Balfour described the phenomenon as follows: "the Jews on our Saturday night, after the Sabbath, were great frequenters of theatres; the theatres in their quarters are crammed. If you were to go to the theatres near the Jews' quarter, you would find the gallery and pit filled with Jews and Jewesses."[88]

In his comprehensive and richly illustrated article "The Jews in London," Lucien Wolf noted the Jews' fondness for the stage and offered a list of English-language plays produced in East End playhouses with an eye toward a Jewish clientele.[89] In 1899, in conjunction with the forthcoming opening of *Children of the Ghetto,* the *Jewish Chronicle* stated in a matter-of-fact way that it was well known in the metropolis that Jews were "quite the best patrons of the drama."[90] Ten years later the *Jewish World* commented on the popularity of the English stage with East End immigrants and joked that the gallery at Covent Garden was referred to as "the meeting place of Chazonim [cantors]."[91] The article gave a rather spirited account of this infatuation:

> Jewish playgoers are among the most inveterate confraternity of theatrical worshipers. On "first nights" and other special occasions they muster in great force. It is a veritable new Exodus from the homes of Israel that makes its Holy Land the theatre district nightly, and the sons and daughters of the community who lay their homage at the feet of the footlight favourites revel in the mystic freemasonry which had its birth in the hours of waiting outside pit and gallery door—periods of weariness rendered cheerful, fascinating even, by a comradeship the like of which no other hero-worship has yet known.[92]

There are no statistics regarding the Jewish attendance of that time, but it is clear that though the numbers were not extremely large in themselves, they were far larger than the proportion of Jews in the general population.

Zangwill's childhood dream palaces, the Britannia and the Pavilion, were enormous houses, with respective seating capacities of 3,700 and 4,700. The Brit, as it was commonly dubbed, was a popular institution that maintained its own stock company and stock repertory, specializing in pantomimes and magnificent spectacles for the locals. The Pavilion, known as the "Drury Lane of the East," which also presented pantomimes and melodramas, was since 1870 in the possession of Morris Abrahams and managed by Isaac Cohen. Its location in the very heart of the Jewish neighborhood made it the central entertainment venue for the immigrant community. Responding to the new clientele, it began to offer Yiddish shows in the 1890s and from 1906 to 1934 was primarily devoted to Yiddish productions.

Sporadic theatrical activity in Yiddish had already begun in the East End in 1880 at the Garrick Theatre on Leman Street, but it was in the hands of amateurs and remained limited in scope. The situation changed with the mass influx of immigrants from Russia and particularly in the aftermath of the 1883 czarist ban on Yiddish performances that brought many actors to London, though most of them would eventually sail to America. Most prominent among the arrivals was the yet unknown Jacob P. Adler (1855–1926), who would later become the most revered actor of the Yiddish stage. In January 1894 his Russian Jewish Operatic Company began producing musicals by Abraham Goldfaden, melodramas, and Judaized adaptations of popular European plays. They played in local workers' clubs converted into theatrical venues, where they could avoid rigorous safety regulations required by the authorities for regular theater houses, and were doing well enough to have a local kosher butcher invest in the construction of a performance space on Princes Street. Disaster struck on January 18, 1887, during a performance of *Gypsy Girl,* a popular operetta. With the theater packed, someone screamed out "FIRE" when there was none. The audience panicked, and seventeen were killed in the stampede, the worst disaster in the history of the Jewish stage. The horrified East End was grief-stricken. The theater closed, and Adler left for America. This tragic episode as well as other Yiddish theatrical tidbits were incorporated into the novel *Children of the Ghetto.*

Zangwill's zest for the theater was undoubtedly fueled by the boom in theatrical activity during his youth. Theater historian Michael Booth notes that by the end of the nineteenth century the theater and music hall business in London had developed into a full-blown mass entertainment industry. In 1892 London had 550 places of amusement, 50 of them theater houses, all of which catered to a potential clientele of half a million nightly.[93] This proliferation of theatrical activity was brought about by the great social changes of the

Victorian era, in particular a process of rapid urbanization that doubled the population of London in the second half of the century and a rise in income and wages that allowed increased spending on leisure activities. Booth cites additional influential factors such as the development of a railway network that made it possible for middle-class suburbanites to come to the metropolis for an evening's entertainment, the shortening of work hours, improved street lighting, which resulted in a decline in crime, and the development of international tourism. Reminiscing in 1932, Pinero (1855–1934), whose *The Second Mrs. Tanqueray* (1893) was a major signpost in the evolution of the New Drama, explains to readers, now flocking to the movies, that in the 1880s play-going "was the chief evening amusement."[94] The only rival to the theater was the music hall, he goes on to note, but it was not considered proper for upper- and middle-class women, and such leisure activities as dancing and dining in public had not yet taken root.

While in the early 1880s audiences were primarily drawn to the theater to see star performers, by the end of the decade the drama drew increased attention, marking the dawn of the age of the playwright. This development was closely linked to the phenomenon of the "long run," a result of the great increase in the number of theatergoers. A run of a hundred consecutive performances was now considered a mark of success for a serious drama, while a hit show like *Charlie's Aunt* (1892) surpassed that fifteen times over. The long run led to a significant improvement in the economic condition of playwrights, who could now receive royalty payments in lieu of selling their scripts and whose work was now protected from transatlantic piracy under the American copyright law of 1891. All this reduced the practice of "churning out" plays, many of them adaptations from the French, and encouraged writers of distinction to contribute to the stage. Copyright-protected plays began to be published in book form, often with prefaces and extensive stage directions, intended for the reader as much as for the stage manager, as exemplified by Zangwill's *The Melting Pot.* With the advent of Pinero and Henry Arthur Jones, and especially George Bernard Shaw, and following the monumental impact of Ibsen, the theater had become a major participant in the discourse of the age. "No other branch of art," noted Pinero, "can be credited with such strides" during this period.[95]

FROM ZIONIST TO TERRITORIALIST

During the 1890s Zangwill became a political man, a process that began on November 21, 1895, when Theodor Herzl (1860–1904), a Viennese writer and dramatist with no name recognition in the English-language world, called on Zangwill in his London home. Herzl, the founder of political Zionism, his historic *Judestaat* (A Jews' State) (1896) not yet published, had just arrived from Paris, with the hope of enlisting support for his revolutionary Zionist vision. Though he had decided that the focus of the nascent Zionist campaign ought to be relocated to the British capital, London was an unfamiliar territory, devoid of personal contacts. The suggestion that he approach Zangwill, whose work he had not read, had been made two days earlier in Paris by Max Nordau (1849–1923), an early ally of Herzl. Nordau, who had attracted considerable attention with his recently published *Degeneration,* was an eminent author and physician. He had just met Zangwill at the home of the English publisher they shared, William Heinemann.[96]

Israel Zangwill's brother Louis was also present at the meeting. The brothers received the aristocratic-looking stranger in the somewhat shabby study they shared in the family home in Kilburn.[97] Herzl, who was not conversant in English, spoke French at his hosts' request, and his words were a total surprise. He spoke of the despondency of European Jews, explained his idea for a Jewish state, and laid out with great precision a practical plan for the acquisition and organization of a new national Jewish terrain. The Zangwill brothers were awed by his vision. The last thing they expected in staid London, Louis wrote later, was "the abrupt appearance of a new St. Paul, preaching to Jew and Gentile alike, and compassing sea and land to make even one proselyte for his scheme of a new and modern Jewish nation."[98] Herzl explained he had come to England to present his plan and gain the support of English Jews and requested that his host direct him to leading members of the community. Though not an instant convert to Zionism, Israel immediately put his knowledge and connections at his visitor's disposal. Three days later Herzl outlined his Zionist program at a dinner organized by the Maccabeans. Clearly, Zangwill recognized the dramatic component in Herzl, acknowledging that "perhaps it is the playwright's habit of moulding events in the dream-world that leads to these attempts to manipulate the tougher material of the real."[99] In years to come he would on more than one occasion refer to the underlying similarity of dramatists and political leaders. "Playwriting," he declared in his presidential speech at the Playgoers Club, "is a Branch of Politics."[100]

Recording the meeting at the house in Kilburn in his diary, Herzl writes that Zangwill was in full agreement on the need for Jewish territorial independence, but that they differed in their respective definitions of Jewish identity. Zangwill's view, writes Herzl, was that Jews were a "race," then a standard view rooted in biology, that stressed "blood relations" and common ancestry.[101]

Herzl rejected this interpretation, explaining, "We are an historical unit, a nation with anthropological diversities. . . . No nation has uniformity of race."[102] The importance of Herzl's rejection of a racial component in his construction of Jewish identity and his fascination with Jewish racial variety—he had been thrilled to learn about the existence of nonwhite Kurdish, Persian, Indian, and Ethiopian Jews—is quite outstanding, notes political scientist Shlomo Avineri, when seen against the racial theories of nationalism then prevalent in Central and Eastern Europe.[103] Zangwill was to espouse Herzl's view of the Jewish people. In a 1903 interview with the *Daily Mail,* he explained with romantic flamboyance his vision of gathering and molding into a nation the Jews, whom he termed a chameleon-like, universal race. He offered an exotic list of candidates that emphasized Jewish racial and ethnic diversity: "the beni Israel, who are the flower of your Indian Army, strange yellow Talmudists from China, Dellvalles and Toledanos from Curacao and Colon, Cohens and Levis from Whitechapel and New York, bandoliered brigands from the Caucasus, ringletted horse dealers from Galicia."[104] In "The Jewish Race," a speech delivered in 1911 at the Race Congress in London, he explained that "every people is a hotch-potch of races" and emphasized that though Jews were mainly a white people, they had a black, brown, and yellow "fringe."[105] This embrace of Jewish heterogeneity would inspire his vision of America in *The Melting Pot.*

Herzl's reception in England during this and subsequent visits ranged from cautious to enthusiastic, the latter exemplified by the one he was accorded by the Jewish Working Men's Club in Whitechapel, where he spoke to East European immigrants on July 13, 1896. Yet he failed to enlist a massive commitment from English Jewry, who were entrenched in a secure existence and relative comfort. His small circle of supporters, according to historian Todd M. Endelman, consisted mostly of the veteran immigrants of the *Chovevei Zion* (Lovers of Zion) Association, a proto-Zionist organization, and middle-class, mostly native-born professionals and businessmen of Zangwill's background and generation, who, suggests Endelman, also intended to use the new movement as a force in opposition to the oligarchic rule of the Anglo-Jewish elite.[106] The stirring of the new movement was strongly felt among members of the Maccabeans club, who in 1897 organized a springtime "pilgrimage" tour of Palestine, which was Zangwill's only visit to the country where his father had settled in old age. It was both exhilarating and disenchanting. His heart sank at the sight of Jerusalem's filthy alleys, its stony desolation, and its mostly unemployed Jewish community. After the lush greenness of England, Palestine struck him as "a waterless, treeless waste," infested with malaria and Ottoman corruption.[107]

In August 1897, Zangwill attended the First Zionist Congress in Basle, Switzerland, as an observer. He imparted his impressions in the poetic chapter "Dreamers in Congress" that appeared in his acclaimed *Dreamers of the Ghetto* (1898). His pen captured with excitement the physical diversity of the participants, who came from many lands. The "strange phantasmagoria of faces," he noted, belied the claim to the existence of a "Jewish type."[108] He caught the rapture of the event, as well as the charisma of Herzl, but he also felt the ironic doubt of a bystander who found in Herzl both the glory of the Assyrian king Tiglath-Pileser and the pauper's grandeur of his own King of Schnorrers.[109]

The writer Reuben Brainin recalled that at the time of the First Zionist Congress, Zangwill impressed him as a "citizen of the republic of letters," with nothing in him of the politician or the partisan.[110] Although sympathetic to the movement, Zangwill was still ambivalent, as can be gleaned from his 1899 essay "Zionism."[111] In it, he offers several courses for the so-called Jewish problem, one passive and three active: national regeneration, religious regeneration, disappearance, and nonaction. He presented the arguments of those opposed to political Zionism as unnecessary and impractical, spoke of Palestine's physical desolation and corrupt Ottoman administration, yet went on to express his belief in the feasibility of the Zionist enterprise. His conclusion was un-ideological. "Even a Jewish state," he professed, "would not remove all the *Judenschmerz,* and only a quack could offer a single simple remedy for such a complex problem."[112] Thus, he declared, of the four options, he was inclined to accept all. In its editorial the *Jewish Chronicle* called the essay a "brilliant and puzzling performance" that came from a man "of hesitating judgement," whose words would leave both Zionists and dispassionate readers hungry for definiteness.[113] Zangwill, it said, was torn between his reason and his heart, the first telling him the Basle Plan was implausible, the second hankering for the Zionist idea.

By December 1901 Zangwill abandoned his observer's position and joined the Zionist Federation, serving as an official representative in the Fifth Zionist Congress. From that point on, his energy, his pen, and his connections were placed with magnanimity and flamboyance at the service of Jewish national renaissance, so much so that he declared he had ceased to be a novelist and had become a Zionist. He published a major essay, "The Return to Palestine," wherein he made the famous statement, "Palestine is a country without a people; the Jews are a people without a country. The regeneration of the soil would bring there generation of the people."[114] He contended that with the crumbling of the ghetto walls, the Jew had reached a crucial "parting of the way," where he had to decide to either exist as "merely a member of an international religious community welcoming the world to Abraham's bosom," or "obey the trumpet call of Isaiah" and actively pave the way for a resumption of a national existence with its own culture.[115]

In April 1903 the Jewish world was traumatized by the horrific pogrom that took place in the Russian city of Kishinev, the capital of Bessarabia. (See the 1914 appendix to the playscript of *The Melting Pot* herein.) The official statistics of the devastation—49 Jews dead, 500 wounded, 700 houses and 600 shops and businesses looted and destroyed, and 2,000 families left homeless—merely itemize the appalling acts of vandalism that took place. The Kishinev pogrom acted as a thunderbolt. Although the popular and official nature of Russian anti-Semitism had been well known beforehand, the world was shaken by the hideous butchery carried out, in broad daylight, by a gleeful mob, with curious onlookers and considerable police and military forces not taking action, reflecting the tacit support of the czarist authorities. New means of communications that enabled the dispatch and publication of photographs of the atrocities brought home the existence of savagery close to the heart of Europe, leading newspapers like the *Pall Mall Gazette* to question whether Russia could be counted among the civilized nations. For Zionists, Kishinev was a morality tale that demonstrated the hopelessness of Jewish diasporic existence. In a 1903 address, Zangwill stated, "The poor people of Kishinef [*sic*] tried to save themselves by putting in their windows sacred Russian images. It is our history in a nut-shell. In moments of danger we put up the flag of the enemy. And it avails nothing in the long run—the image-imitators at Kishinef were the people particularly chosen for crucifixion."[116] To those who criticized Zionism as contradicting the universalist principles of the Jewish prophets, he replied that the prophets saw that "internationalism must be rooted in nationalism," that there cannot be "a brotherhood of peoples" without "peoples to be brothers," and that before one can have a brother "there must be a 'me' to have a brother." He concluded with a typical Zangwillian witticism: "It takes two to make one brother."[117]

The deteriorating situation of Romanian and Russian Jews highlighted the need for a Jewish place of refuge. At the Sixth Zionist Congress, which took place in Basle during August 1903, Herzl discussed the collapse of the project to establish a Jewish colony in the Sinai Peninsula and brought to the floor a proposal made by the British government that offered a large tract of territory in East Africa for colonization by Jews, who would have an autonomous government under British suzerainty. This offer represented an enormous breakthrough for Herzl's diplomacy, for this marked the first time, explains historian Stuart A. Cohen, that "the government of one country proposed to enter into a formal and territorial relationship with Jews representing Jews of several others, without apparent regard for either immediate financial profit or short-term civic return."[118] Herzl called upon the congress to give serious attention to the offer, which was strongly supported by Nordau and Zangwill. Commonly termed the "Uganda Scheme," the proposal aroused immense opposition that nearly tore the young movement apart. Russian Zionists were enraged by the suggestion of the establishment of a national settlement outside Zion and somewhat derogatorily termed as "Territorialists" those inclined to consider any non-Palestinian location. Finally, by a vote of 295 to 178, with 98 abstentions, it was agreed to organize an expedition to examine the possibility of a Jewish settlement in the proposed territory. Zangwill showed his Territorialist leanings in an article written in October 1903 when he suggested that the road to Zion might include a stopover in a land "less beset with political and religious pitfalls," where Jews could acquire skills in cooperation and self-government, could strike a balance between old customs and modernity, and then await the most opportune moment to colonize Palestine.[119]

Herzl's premature death in the summer of 1904 left the "Uganda Scheme" unresolved. In the Seventh Zionist Congress, held the following year, the debate concerning the question of settlement outside Palestine was renewed. The British offer was rejected; the original Basle Platform, which called for the creation of a Jewish homeland in Palestine, was reconfirmed; and there was a majority vote against the formation of a national home anywhere outside Palestine or its immediate vicinity. Eager for a quick answer for the rapidly deteriorating conditions of East European Jewry, beleaguered by dire economic circumstances and a battery of devastating pogroms, Zangwill was enraged by this rejection of an autonomous territory that could serve as a place of refuge.[120] He walked out of the congress in protest, broke with the Zionist movement, and together with other discontented members founded the Jewish Territorial Organization, of which he became president. As the situation in Russia continued to worsen, and in view of the fact that Zionism was making few gains at best, the ITO (the Yiddish acronym for the organization) gained momentum and enlisted the support of prominent figures, many of whom the Zionists had been unable to attract.[121] Zangwill tried to resurrect the British East Africa offer on behalf of the ITO, but it had been withdrawn. What then followed was a series of globe-trotting ITO searches for a suitable territory for colonization, for a so-called Itoland. Canada and Australia were briefly considered, and geographical commissions were sent to Mesopotamia, Cyrenaica, and Angola. These extensive searches did excite the popular imagination and gave the ITO an activist and dynamic image, yet in the end they failed to bear any fruit. Although Zangwill rejoined the Zionist movement in 1917 in the aftermath of the Balfour Declaration, he remained wary of what he considered the indecisiveness and naïveté of the Zionist leadership and its hopeful wish that the Arab population would accept the Jewish colonizers. In 1920 he wrote, "The only chance of reconstructing a nationality without the sword is to colonise, as the Jewish Territorial Organisation projected, an unpopulated territory. It was because I foresaw that the Palestine problem could yield only to force that my own energies have been diverted for so many years to the quest for a comparatively unoccupied region, sufficiently large, healthy and fertile to contain the potentiality of a Jewish State."[122]

In the summer of 1906, Zangwill was approached by Jacob H. Schiff (1847–1920), an American Jewish philanthropist, with an offer to join forces to implement an innovative plan to organize a methodical and supervised stream of Jewish immigration from Eastern Europe to the western United States. Schiff had no interest in Zangwill's agenda for political autonomy. Concerned about the severe hardship of Russian Jews, he was afraid that open immigration to America would soon be terminated and concerned that anti-immigration sentiments were inflamed by the rapid growth of overcrowded urban Jewish quarters in the Northeast, particularly in New York City. He thus sought to divert Jewish immigrants to the country's hinterland, hoping that the first settlers, carefully selected and assisted in their relocation, would encourage a future flow of newcomers. In his correspondence with Zangwill, Schiff laid out the project, noting that if they were able to transport and settle twenty-five thousand people over a ten-year period, he would consider it a success.[123] ITO's task would be to recruit suitable immigrants in Russia, preferably skilled workers below the age of forty, and to see to their needs until they reached the German port of Bremen, where the *Hilfsverein der Deutschen Juden* (Society for the Aid of German Jews) would care for them until they sailed to America.

Zangwill hesitated at first to collaborate with Schiff, as the proposed project was far removed from ITO's grandiose plans. Moreover, he had a dislike for dictated top-down immigration policies, believing that a stream of immigration had to be formed spontaneously, by pressure of its own forces.[124] He finally decided to join Schiff, possibly because he thought the project would contribute to ITO's activist prestige and would afford practical experience in immigration practices that could prove useful when Itoland was established. The project came to be known as the Galveston Plan, named for the Texas city that would serve as the port of entry where immigrants would be processed and sent on to their respective destinations. Members of the first group, eighty-seven in all, arrived on July 1, 1907, and were dispersed to Missouri, Minnesota, Iowa, Colorado, Nebraska, Illinois, Wisconsin, Oklahoma, and Texas, unconventional destinations for East European immigrants.[125] Some ten thousand Jews passed through Galveston by the end of the project in 1914. Beset by numerous social, cultural, and governmental problems in both Russia and America, the project was regarded as only partially successful. Naomi Cohen, Schiff's biographer, faults the philanthropist for treating the immigrants as pawns rather than partners. Schiff "may have praised the ideals and cultural baggage that the newcomers brought with them," she writes, "but his approach bespoke less a desire to comprehend the needs of the Russians than to refashion them in an American mold."[126]

The Melting Pot was by its author's own account a direct product of his involvement in the ITO and the Galveston movements. In an interview with the *New York Times*, he said that the play developed out of three years of observation and involvement in Jewish immigration and settlement issues in which he had been immersed. He had encountered sights and situations, he said, that had left their imprint on his "soul and heart." "The average business man could go through the experience that I have gone through, settle the problems insofar as he could, and go to his way and think no more of the matter," he tells us, "but with a literary man it is different. With him such things are bound to produce a lasting effect which sooner or later must manifest itself in his writings."[127]

AMERICA, 1898

Zangwill visited America for the first time in 1898, yet the American horizon was already present in his earlier work. America as the penultimate goal of East European Jewish immigration was an ingrained facet of the London Ghetto, the city serving as both a final destination and a major venue for transmigration.[128] Although the majority of the hundreds of thousands of Jews proceeding through British ports used them as points of transit in their transatlantic voyage, others lingered for months and years, seeking to earn enough money for passage, biding time before joining their families overseas, or trying their luck in London before resuming their journey. Though London was then regarded as the "capital of the world," it was New York City that was quickly becoming the primary urban Jewish center in the West, its Jewish population rising from 80,000 in 1880 to 225,000 in 1890, and climbing to

580,000 in 1900, almost 17 percent of the city's total population of nearly 3.5 million.

Zangwill's interest in America was piqued after the Jewish Publication Society in Philadelphia commissioned his work in 1890, and it was intensified by his personal friendship with Judge Mayer Sulzberger and Cyrus Adler, who both stood at the heart of the communal and cultural life of American Jewry. Although *Children of the Ghetto* was initially greeted with discomfort by many American Jews, for largely the same reasons it had caused anxiety among Anglo Jewry, the book's roaring success allayed nervousness about loss of face in Gentile society and allowed acculturated Jews to savor its colorful characters and take pride in Zangwill's acclaim.[129]

From 1892 on, Zangwill's name featured prominently on the American literary map, as his writings were serialized in magazines and published in book form in tandem with British publication. The young Willa Cather (1873–1947) wrote in 1898 that she was drawn to Zangwill's first lecture in New York due to her admiration for his novel *The Master,* a non-Jewish story of the moral quandaries of a Nova Scotia artist, which was serialized in *Harper's Weekly* in 1894 and published in New York by Harper and Brothers in 1895.[130] In 1898 the New York *Bookman,* an important literary journal, published a profile of Zangwill that included an interview conducted in London in anticipation of his soon-to-be-released *Dreamers of the Ghetto.*[131] The article foreshadows Zangwill's first American visit and his career as a dramatist. In the interview Zangwill speaks about his future plans, which, he says, include the composition of a play, though he offers no specifics regarding its subject matter and title. He mentions that numerous London theater managers asked him to write for the stage and that actor Richard Mansfield offered him carte blanche to write four plays and was interested in producing and starring in *The King of Schnorrers.* Mansfield (1854–1907), known for his bravura performance style, was regarded by many as America's leading actor-manager. He excelled in such roles as Dr. Jekyll/Mr. Hyde, Ivan the Terrible, Beau Brummel, and Don Juan, and he could have been a spectacular Manasseh. The proposition, however, never came to fruition, and Mansfield went on to star in and achieve great success in Edmund Rostand's *Cyrano de Bergerac.*

In the interview Zangwill positions himself as a "literary" dramatist and dismisses the commercial stage as a place where "a manager looks upon a playwright as a tailor who must cut to measure." He declares that his play would be written "as a piece of literature" and that he might publish it in book form before offering it to a theater manager. He also says he is opposed to the "distortion" of one's books into playscripts, especially the custom of altering the original ending to a happy one for purposes of the stage. Five years later Zangwill would be faulted of doing just that in his highly popular dramatization of his novella *Merely Mary Ann*. He announces that if he did dramatize one of his books, he would strictly adhere to the spirit of the original work, a pronouncement that would be put to the test within a year. Zangwill also speaks of the possibility of coming to America on a personal visit, possibly combined with a lecture tour.

At that time, the Unites States offered a lucrative cultural market, as evidenced by many tours of English theatrical companies, notably Henry Irving's troupe, which crossed the Atlantic eight times between 1882 and 1903.[132] A lecture circuit of visiting English "oratorial performers"—writers, explorers, and public figures—had also developed, feeding the great demand of popular American adult education programs affiliated with the Lyceum movement. Lecture tours were organized by professional bureaus, and the star impresario in the field was Major J. B. (James Burton) Pond (1838–1903), owner of the Redpath Lyceum Bureau, who in 1895 had organized Mark Twain's world tour. Pond had been an agent for many star speakers: Henry Ward Beecher, Ralph Waldo Emerson, and journalist/explorer Henry M. Stanley, whom he paid the then-gargantuan sum of $50,000 for a series of fifty lectures. A master of public relations, Pond was known to have extended a standing offer of $100,000 to William E. Gladstone, four-time British prime minister, to come to America and lecture. In his memoirs, *Eccentricities of Genius,* Pond writes that he first called on Zangwill in 1897, after receiving many inquiries about him from all over America, especially from Jewish societies.[133] This commercial interest reflects the emergence of a Jewish cultural market and attests to Zangwill's celebrity status in America.

The original London meeting between impresario and writer was friendly but inconclusive, with Pond remarking that it seemed almost impossible to come to "any kind of an understanding" with Zangwill, who was convinced there was a great public waiting for him in America but "couldn't understand" why Pond should get a third of the profits. Pond quoted a steep five-hundred-dollar fee for a Zangwill lecture, a sum that the two wealthy Jewish clubs in New York, the Harmonie and the Freundschaft, could pay, though there was some balking by smaller Jewish organizations that were frustrated by an inability to afford it.[134] Zangwill, who was most generous with people and causes dear to his heart, was at the same time alert to the economic value of his work, often protesting against publishers and middlemen who profiteered from an author's labors. As a professional writer financially dependent on his own pen, he was not romantic in his acceptance of the commodification of his writing. In his own work he maintained a firm separation between the creative process, where "the laws of art alone" governed, and the final product, which he believed the artist had the right to sell "in the best market."[135] His lifelong correspondence with Macmillan, his American publishers, attests to a close vigilance over sales and royalties.

Zangwill sailed to New York aboard the *Lucania* in August of 1898, accompanied by Judge Mayer Sulzberger, who had set up the trip and would be Zangwill's host in Philadelphia, and Louis Loeb (1866–1909), an American Jewish artist and illustrator, a close friend whom he had met in Paris. They arrived on August 27 and were greeted by three prominent Jewish leaders—philanthropist Daniel Guggenheim, Zangwill's host in New York; David Blaustein, superintendent of the Educational Alliance; and Philip Cowen, editor of the *American Hebrew*. Still unable to secure a contract, Pond organized an impromptu press conference, where Zangwill cleverly fielded a rapid barrage of questions. Press coverage the next day was enthusiastic, and, according to Pond, "the interest in the great Jewish novelist was manifest everywhere."[136] Lecture committees called and letters of inquiry poured in, but Zangwill hesitated to obligate himself, as a result of which some excellent invitations were lost. By the time an agreement was drawn up, nearly all the lyceum offerings around the country had been finalized, and Pond had to invest in renting halls, left to depend on individual ticket sales. If that was not enough, Zangwill himself was not a malleable performer. He insisted on speaking without notes and opposed reading aloud from his work, as was the custom of lecturing authors, contending that writers should not offer such recitals unless endowed with the dramatic flair of Charles Dickens.[137] He was not entirely correct in this contention. Audiences to this day enjoy author readings not for actorly skills but for the intimacy offered by the reunion of author and text. By the end of the tour Zangwill softened his position, and when he gave his most favorably received lecture, "The Ghetto," he concluded the presentation with a recitation of one of his poems, "The Hebrew's Friday Night."[138]

Zangwill's first lecture in America, on "The Drama as a Fine Art," took place on Tuesday afternoon, October 11, 1898, at the beautiful seven-hundred-seat Lyceum Theatre in New York.[139] It is debatable whether this was the best way to introduce Zangwill to the general American public, as his reputation rested foremost on his ghetto writings, and his authority in Jewish customs and mores was universally accepted. Though he had lectured on the ghetto in Jerusalem, and later in Ireland and the Netherlands in 1897, his experience as a public speaker was limited. Had he opened his lecture series with his talk on the ghetto, he would have had the advantage of working with a familiar presentation and could have possibly avoided the nervousness he displayed. It thus stands to reason that the decision to have Zangwill's inaugural lecture be on a non-Jewish topic stemmed from a strategy intended to avoid ethnic labeling. Nevertheless, his Jewish identity featured prominently in reports of his lectures, and the frequent references to his "race" reveal an ambivalence toward a cultural icon with a public Jewish persona. By his very corporeality, he unwittingly became a site of Jewishness, impelling his audience to negotiate its perception of Jews. This is evidenced by a remark in the *New York Dramatic Mirror* in late November, near the end of the lecture tour, that the people at first "went to see Zangwill," while later on "they went to hear him."[140]

Werner's Magazine, devoted to speech and drama, offered the most comprehensive coverage of the "Drama" lecture. Its report opens not with a biographical sketch or a list of the speaker's credentials in drama, but with a discourse on his name and a telling anecdote aimed at revealing that his first initial stands for "Israel." In the same vein, it refers to the considerable Jewish presence in the audience, stating that "blood is thicker than water," and neglects to mention the fact that, in Pond's words, the crowd was "as intelligent and fashionable an audience as New York could turn out."[141] Having confirmed Zangwill's Jewish identity, *Werner's,* which did not contain illustrations, offers a detailed description of his physical appearance that was anchored in the period's stereotype of "The Jew." Thus, Zangwill's body became a representation in itself, as the magazine informs its readers that he "looks his race," itemizing the anatomical signs that fit the stereotype: pale skin, undersized bony figure, and curly and very dark hair. To this it adds that his "upper incisors" are "so prominent as to make it a trifle of a muscular effort to mask them with his upper lip," an observation that was probably not merely a comment on the speaker's orthodontics, but was a reflection of the racialist belief in the "bestial" qualities of Jews and their Negroid characteristics, then a mark of racial inferiority.[142] It continues, "the man is Jew from bone to skin and back again," with "the combination of nose, eyes, lips and hair that marks the transplanted Oriental."[143] One can hardly miss the similarity between the magazine's portrayal of Zangwill and the depiction of Svengali, the villainous Jewish mesmerist in George du Maurier's immensely popular novel *Trilby,* an equally successful dramatized version of which had opened in New York in 1895: Svengali has "thick, heavy, languid, lustreless black hair," with "bold, brilliant black eyes, with long heavy lids," and a "thick, sallow face." *Werner's* coverage offered scant mention of Zangwill's Englishness, and then only in connection with the externals of his accent and his clothes, stating that "being an Englishman, it is but natural that his clothes do not fit him except in violent wrinkles."[144]

Even Willa Cather, greatly impressed by Zangwill's literary work, was watching him through a racialist prism, assuring her readers that though the gentleman was not handsome, neither was he a "freak." "His physiognomy," she writes, "is typically Semitic, the bold nose, the pale, olive skin, the full lips, the heavy dark eyes, the shaggy black hair, suggest not only the Jew, but Oriental Jew."[145] At the same time, she invokes a philo-Semitic paradigm of the Jew as philosopher and prophet, describing his face to be "full of the idealism of his race," with a wit "as sharp and fantastic as Heine."[146] She explains, "besides its pawnbrokers, its sweatshop toilers, its itinerant pedlars, its Shylocks and money-hagglers, its money barons and pillagers, the ghetto has always had its dreamers, and their dreams have changed the course of history and founded empires."[147] An allusion to Heinrich Heine and an indirect reference to Benjamin Disraeli, both regarded as pinnacles of Jewish intelligence, were often applied to Zangwill, reflecting a racialist belief in Jewish intellectual genius, a quality whose downside was believed to be a high rate of insanity and mental disorders.[148]

In the lecture Zangwill discussed the development of drama out of religious rites, its eventual separation from the Church, and its rejection and condemnation by the Puritans. He extolled Ibsen as the greatest living master of the drama and rejected the naturalism of Emil Zola, explaining that dramatic verisimilitude does not require photographic literalness, but rather the faithful expression of humanity's grand passions. No lovers ever spoke like Romeo and Juliet, he said, yet their words expressed the feelings of all lovers. He praised the plays of his contemporaries Arthur Pinero and Henry Arthur Jones and pronounced most of the old plays dead, declaring that the only English comedies since Shakespeare to have life in them were *The School for Scandal* and *She Stoops to Conquer.* He then embarked on a sharp-tongued critique of the commercial stage, praised the French theater for preserving its literary traditions, and denounced the English for appropriating, twisting, and emasculating French drama. He dismissed the theatrical manager as shopkeeper, the actor as egotistical and stupid, and the critic as ineffectual, and concluded with a call for the drama to rid itself of banality and reflect the grandness and heroism of the age, which he likened to the Elizabethan period, when England produced its greatest dramas.

Major Pond writes that Zangwill offered "a shower of epigrams interspersed with sparkles of wit" that carried his audience with him from the beginning to the very last word and that he was recalled and cheered vociferously at the end of the lecture.[149] However, Zangwill's severe censure of theater critics, many of whom were in attendance, was the ultimate faux pas and resulted in an avalanche of bad press. Zangwill was damned for things he said and for much he did not say, for having the wrong accent and wearing the wrong clothes, and was accused of suffering from an attack of "swelled head" brought about by indiscriminate flattery. The levelheaded *New York Dramatic Mirror,* the city's major theatrical paper, tried to explain to its readers that the controversy was caused not by the speaker's idealistic albeit extremist arguments, but rather by his lack of discrimination and his proclivity to form "sentences that bite into his subjects" and to "hit one or two nails on the head very hard."[150] The tumult was such that on October 23 the *New York Times* declared, "It's time to stop talking about Mr. Zangwill's lecture, what he said, and what he didn't say, or what any one else thinks he ought to have said."[151] The *American Hebrew* implied that anti-Semitic motives lay behind the press attacks. A short item in the *Dramatic Mirror* indirectly suggests that the ruckus might also be attributed to cultural misreadings between England and America.[152] It turns out that three other British authors engaged that year as lecturers by Pond—Anthony Hope, Richard Le Gallienne, and Hall Caine—were faulted by the New York press for inappropriately "having fun" at the expense of the American public, though there is no reason to suspect that was their intention.

Zangwill was received with great enthusiasm by New York's Jewish community and was applauded by its upper echelon, who regarded him as their ambassador to the world of letters, one who conferred prestige on his people by his universal literary acclaim and public Jewish stance. A special banquet was arranged in his honor on October 24 by the Judaeans, a society that was analogous to the London Maccabeans. Many, though not all, of the seventy-eight who attended were affiliated with the American Reform movement and were members of the largely German-Jewish financial and intellectual elite. Held at the Tuxedo Club, the dinner was kosher, with grace delivered by the Reverend Dr. H. Pereira Mendes, English-born rabbi of the orthodox Congregation Shearith Israel. The event's special guests were Judge Sulzberger, Louis Loeb, and Abraham Cahan, who was then writing for the *Commercial Advertiser* and had attracted literary attention with his stories of the New York ghetto. Zangwill was introduced by the association's president, Dr. Henry M. Leipziger, a native of Manchester, England, and noted New York educator, who spoke of current developments, including the Dreyfus Affair, and hailed the guest for having "enhanced the good name of the Jew."[153] Additional speakers included Judge Sulzberger, Chicago University law professor Julian W. Mack, Columbia professor of political economy Edwin R. Seligman, and Abraham Cahan. Their recurrent theme was Zangwill's historic contribution to Jewish self-esteem by virtue of his "legitimization" of the ghetto and of past Jewish life. Mack emphasized the role of the ghetto as the "protoplasm of Judaism" and rejected the parvenu who in their upscale status turned up their noses at the ghetto, likening them to the butterfly that disdains the worm that preceded it and to which it owes its existence. Sulzberger praised Zangwill for reconnecting emancipated Jews to the ghetto, thus enabling them to liberate themselves from the psychological shackles of self-effacement. Cahan took a more poetic approach, embedded in the culture of his Lithuanian youth, and described Zangwill as a *charef* (someone with a very sharp intellect) and a *gaon* (a genius), and likened him to the mythological *Sambatyon,* a turbulent river with fantastic rapids that was said to separate the lost ten tribes from the rest of Israel.

Meant as a compliment, the *Sambatyon* metaphor also pointed to some of the turbulence that Zangwill's elegant address had propelled. Hidden behind the beautifully crafted language was a critique of Reform Judaism for having lost the sense of wonder and poetry of authentic Judaism and for becoming literal and rigid in its own way. Zangwill was grieved by the Reform prayer book, particularly its abandonment and excision of the traditional Hebrew liturgy, and asked rhetorically, "With a sacred language far easier to acquire than Greek, why write new prayers in nineteenth-century journalese?"[154] He criticized the excessive decorum he encountered in Reform synagogues, where the minister and choir were performing onstage with minimal congregational participation. He reminded his audience that "Judaism is not Christianity minus Christ" and called upon American Judaism to evolve into one that would combine a modern standpoint with medieval poetry. He quoted the Old Duke from *As You Like It:* "The toad, ugly and venomous, wears yet a precious jewel in its head," predicting a Jewish Renaissance, a time when Israel would again "take the centre of the world-stage." The latter quote was a typical tactic reflecting his fusion of cultures. To Jews he quoted Shakespeare and Dr. Johnson and Richard Lovelace, whose famous lines—"Stone walls do not a prison make / Nor iron bar a cage"—he used in his lecture on the ghetto. To Gentiles he quoted Talmudic stories, not thinking twice of concluding a survey of the London theater season with a clever tale about Rabbi Hillel in a Jerusalem marketplace.

The response to Zangwill's critique was swift and written to appear in the same issue of the *American Hebrew* in which the lecture was published. A comparatively mild letter came from Rabbi Maurice H. Harris of Temple

Israel of Harlem, and a fiercer one from Dr. Kaufman Kohler (1843–1926), a pillar of American Reform Judaism and rabbi of the prestigious Temple Beth-El in New York. Referring to Zangwill as "the gentleman from England," Kohler accused him first of generalizing despite his unfamiliarity with the American scene, and second, of personal hypocrisy. Alluding to Zangwill's nonobservant lifestyle, he wrote, "No one will venture in this country to extol the Shulchan Aruch, while at the same time indulging in Trefa [unkosher] meals. No one will dare expatiate on the poetry of religious symbols in the Jewish home and at the same time think of taking into his own household a non-Jewish wife."[155] Kohler was correct in some of his criticism. Zangwill's understanding of the position of American Jews was bound to be superficial. For example, Zangwill commented that American Jews made too much of upper-class social anti-Semitism and of the refusal of fancy hotels and resorts to accommodate a Jewish clientele.[156] He mentioned that Rudyard Kipling had once told him that Americans were sensitive because they were "new," to which Zangwill added that the Jews were "old" and could afford to smile.[157] He went on to inform his audience that the irony of the situation was that the criticisms directed toward American Jews by their countrymen were those that Europeans so often levied against Americans. Clearly, compared with virulent European anti-Semitism and czarist persecutions, closed doors at exclusive clubs and hotels seemed insignificant. From an American Jewish perspective, though, this was a painful reminder of the prejudice from which even the prosperous elite were not immune.

Leaving behind New York controversies, Zangwill set out on a successful lecture tour that included Boston, Philadelphia, Buffalo, Cincinnati, Cleveland, Chicago, St. Louis, Memphis, Birmingham, and Atlanta. The scene had quieted down by the time he returned to New York in November, and he delivered three well-received lectures at the Waldorf Astoria. He again offered his "Drama" lecture, then spoke on "Fiction, the Highest Form of Truth." The third, "The Ghetto," drew a particularly large crowd and was very well received. At the end of this American tour, Zangwill told Pond that he would never be a professional lecturer, a promise he kept. Though undoubtedly exhausting, his visit had served him well. He saw much of the nation with his own eyes, came into close contact with American Jews, and forged friendships with notable Americans, among them Governor-elect Theodore Roosevelt. Pond wrote that, at the time, Zangwill was "the best-advertised man in the country" and that many offers and dazzling propositions were sent his way.[158] One was an invitation to dramatize *Children of the Ghetto* for a major production on the American stage.

THE SPECTACULAR GHETTO

In its depiction of an entirely traditional Jewish milieu, the drama *Children of the Ghetto* marks a watershed in the representation of Jews on the mainstream English-language stage. The play was produced by George C. Tyler (1867–1946), a maverick newcomer to Broadway, who in 1898 founded Liebler and Company, a production organization named for Theodore Liebler Jr., a partner and original investor. Formerly an advance man for actor James O'Neill, Tyler was moderately successful before "hitting the jackpot" in 1898 with Hall Caine's *The Christian,* a play previously rejected by London and New York producers.[159]

A non-Jew, born and raised in Chillicothe, Ohio, Tyler was a seasoned public relations man, with a well-honed instinct for popular sentiments and taste. Quite a flamboyant character, he became an ardent admirer of Zangwill's, hailing him as a genius and "the noblest and most earnest Jew alive."[160] His admiration was genuine, but that does not fully explain why he decided to invest heavily in the yet-to-be-written stage adaptation of *Children of the Ghetto.* With its multiple plots and episodic structure, the novel did not easily lend itself to dramatization, especially within the conventional dramatic format of linear plot development. Several of Zangwill's short stories would have been more amenable to stage adaptation, particularly the inherently theatrical novella *The King of Schnorrers.*[161] Perhaps the reason was, as Tyler explains in his memoirs, that Zangwill and his novel *Children of the Ghetto* were then "right in the middle of the public eye," though one could argue that Zangwill's literary star was then at its brightest, and anything he wrote for the stage would have drawn attention, even if not directly linked to his first novel.[162]

Tyler's decision to develop this project clearly hinged on the fame of the novel and its theme. He believed that there was popular interest in Jews, especially East European immigrants, and that the public would be willing to pay to see the ghetto's habitat and lifestyle re-created on stage. The newspapers and books of the day attest to the general public's curiosity about Jews, primarily triggered by the massive influx of Jewish immigrants who were changing the human topography of major American cities, especially New York. Additional factors that converged to make the Jews the subject of popular attention include the hair-raising reports of Russian blood-libels and pogroms; the increasing presence of acculturated Jews in politics, the professions, commerce, and the arts; and the prominence of the Rothschilds and other banking families. The shockwaves of the ongoing saga of the Dreyfus Affair, by century's end universally regarded in England and America as a monstrous travesty of justice, also piqued curiosity and heightened certain philo-Semitic sentiments. This interest is manifested, for example, in the 1900 publication of *Jewish Laws and Customs: Some of the Laws and Usages of the Children of the Ghetto* by the Reverend A. Kingsley Glover. The book was dedicated to "Israel Zangwill, the Interpreter of Jewish Life" and was presented as a companion piece to the popular novel.[163] In his introduction, Glover explained the timeliness of his enterprise:

> The Jewish people throughout the world present to-day, from a variety of causes, an unusually attractive subject for Gentile study. The world-famous Dreyfus case, the poetry of Emma Lazarus, the philanthropy of Moses Montefiore, of the Hirsch family and the Rothschilds, the persecution of the Russian Jews, the vigorous life of both orthodox and reformed Judaism in Europe and America, the Zionist movement and its enthusiastic following, as exhibited at the Jewish congresses at Basle, all invite the Gentile to pay his respects to the Jewish people by a careful study of both their racial and religious characteristics.[164]

Some of the interest in Jews was religiously motivated, as Protestant scholars and clergy who acknowledged the Jewish origins of Christianity were intrigued by Jewish rituals, which they romanticized as authentic vestiges of biblical times. In the 1890s it was not unusual to encounter reports in the Christian religious press on synagogue life and on the celebration of Jewish holidays, as well as praise for Jewish religious devotion.[165] These often offered an ahistorical and exoticizing gaze that mythologized the Orthodox Jew as a patriarch directly linked with primal spiritual resources. The old unacculturated immigrant Jew was now marked as the harbinger of authentic Judaism, the ultimate performer of ancient Jewish rituals. William Dean Howells (1837–1920), acclaimed as the dean of late-nineteenth-century American letters, observed the market of the Jewish Lower East Side in the 1890s as follows: "Everywhere I saw splendid types of that old Hebrew world which had the sense if not the knowledge of God when all the rest of us lay sunk in heathen darkness. There were women with oval faces and olive tints, and clear, dark eyes, relucent as evening pools, and men with long beards of jetty black or silvery white, and the noble profiles of their race," and the aristocratic Bostonian found himself thinking, "it was among such throngs that Christ walked, it is from such people that he chose his Disciples and his friends."[166]

This biblical mystique captured the imagination of other touring aesthetes, who found in the grim urban humanscape great spiritual beauty. "How impressive the old men look," exclaimed art critic Sadakichi Hartmann, "whole chapters of the Bible seem to be personified in them."[167]

The interest that Jews were attracting was also motivated by a growing preoccupation with an expanding slum population, especially in New York, where 43 percent of the city was foreign-born by 1890, many living in abject poverty. Throughout the 1890s the city slums were in the public eye, and its residents were both feared as a potentially dangerous underclass and paraded as thrilling subjects by reporters, novelists, photographers, writers, muckrakers, and social reformers. Well-to-do bohemian thrill-seekers embarked on "slumming" tours, the city's hot new tourist attraction. The less adventurous enjoyed the surrogate experience of these "hidden spaces" offered by journalists, who as intra-urban explorers and connoisseurs provided vibrant depictions of the city's "rough" districts. In his study *The Incorporation of America*, Alan Trachtenberg explains how the nature of life in the modern metropolis, combined with new technologies of communication, gave birth to a spectatorial culture in which city-dwellers became consumers of images and sensations produced by the press in its ceaseless search for the melodramatic and the gory.[168] The slum, explains Walter Fuller Taylor, became the new literary frontier, as unknown and exciting to readers of the 1890s as "the solitary forests and great lakes of interior America had been to the reader of Fenimore Cooper's time."[169] The key text of this trend was *How the Other Half Lives: Studies among the Tenements of New York* (1890), written by reformer and photojournalist Jacob A. Riis (1849–1914).[170] Based on a story that appeared in an 1889 issue of *Scribner's Magazine,* it was the first American book on the subject of the urban slums to contain photographs, many of them taken with a new lighting technology that enabled Riis to enter homes and depict the intimate texture of poverty. His attitude toward his subjects was ambivalent. His section on "Jewtown" demonstrates a distanced attitude, one that pulsates with empathy, stereotyped images, and caricature.

The Jewish Lower East Side, a congested habitat and the nerve center of most of the city's Yiddish-speaking immigrants, was later delineated by more sympathetic reporters, for whom Abraham Cahan served as native savant. Most prominent among them was Hutchins Hapgood (1867–1944), a colleague of Cahan at the *Commercial Advertiser* and a well-to-do Harvard-educated midwesterner, whose *The Spirit of the Ghetto* (1899) portrays the intellectual and artistic life of Jewish immigrants. Critic Irving Howe, who wrote the introduction for its 1966 reprint, praised Hapgood as "marvelously open in his curiosity, free of prejudice or sentimentalism."[171] In the spirit of the 1960s, Howe compares Hapgood's journey and collaboration with the young ghetto artist Jacob Epstein, who provided more than fifty illustrations to the work, to the journey of poet James Agee and photographer Walker Evans through the Deep South during the Great Depression. It is noteworthy that Hapgood devoted considerable space to descriptions of the Yiddish theater of Lower Manhattan and is fascinated by its popularity, intimacy, emotional appeal, and artistic aspirations. The Yiddish theater became a magnet for visiting uptown theater people, and so, while offering its immigrant patrons theatrical spectaculars, it also provided a spectatorial site for visiting outsiders. It is in this context that one must regard the curious 1903 production of the *Merchant of Venice* in which Jacob P. Adler, the foremost dramatic actor on the ghetto stage, performed the role of Shylock in an English production entirely in Yiddish.

Hapgood was not alone in finding kindred souls in the tenements and coffee shops of Lower Manhattan. Lincoln Steffens (1866–1936), son of a wealthy California family who would become one of America's most celebrated journalists and the author of the muckraking *Shame of the Cities* (1904), also became emotionally invested in the ghetto during the 1890s. In his memoirs, written more than thirty years later, he devoted a full chapter to "The Ghetto," reminiscing that at the time he was "almost a Jew": "I had become as infatuated with the Ghetto as eastern boys were with the wild west, and nailed a mazzuza [*sic*] on my office door; I went to the synagogue on all the great Jewish holy days; on Yom Kippur I spent the whole twenty-four hours fasting and going from one synagogue to another. The music moved me most, but I knew and could follow with the awful feeling of a Jew the beautiful old ceremonies of the ancient orthodox services."[172] Steffens empathized with the hardships of ghetto life so much that he did not neglect to scornfully recall in his memoirs a socially prominent Jewish matron who once wrote to his editor complaining that "so much space was given to the ridiculous performances of the ignorant, foreign, East Side Jews and none to the uptown Hebrews."[173] Little did she understand that in a culture of the touristic gaze, the upwardly mobile acculturated Jew who aspires to genteel respectability was seen by people like Steffens and Hapgood as a dull and inauthentic copy of the bland American bourgeoisie, against which they were in rebellion within their personal lives.

The uptown/downtown clash over legitimate Jewish representation mostly transpired behind the scenes. It came out into the open early in 1900 on the heels of production of *Children of the Ghetto*. In January the editor of *The Bookman* denounced the antagonistic attitude of Americanized Jews toward ghetto literature and revealed threats to boycott publications that gave platform to such portrayals. His comments created quite a stir, and in the February issue the periodical counterposed two articles under the umbrella title "The Ghetto in Literature." The first, by Annie Nathan Meyer (1867–1951), an American-born Jewish writer and philanthropist, vented the frustration of the acculturated uptown milieu. She paid lip service to the "genius of Mr. Zangwill" and the "cleverness of Mr. Cahan," but did not mince words in expressing the modern Jews' distress over the excessive interest of her "Gentile brethren" in "the foreign-looking, strange-speaking Hebrew of the Ghetto, with Talmudic lore at the end of his tongue, and a frayed *talith* [prayer shawl] at the end of his shoulder."[174] She added wryly that, clearly, the ghetto type provided infinitely better "copy" than the modern Jew and hinted at the shallowness of Gentile interest, suggesting it existed only "within the covers of a book." She argued that the "Americanized Hebrew" was denied any literature that described him seriously, and that, like his "Gentile brother," he desired to "hold up his resemblances rather than his differences," suggesting that an emphasis on otherness may encourage anti-Jewish sentiment. Finally, she likened Jewish irritation with Gentile exoticizing to the objection of Americans to the trite English stereotype of the American as cowboy with six-shooter.

Martin B. Ellis, a Gentile writer, offered the counter-piece, in which he demonstrated a dislike for Meyer's world.[175] He offered a tale resembling Steffens's. A few days after writing an admiring portrayal of the ghetto's Yom Kippur observance, Ellis was summoned by his editor, who handed him a letter from "a well-known uptown Jewish woman, active in reform and charities," who complained that the story had ridiculed the Jews. When they met, she stated that his writing about downtown Jews was an act of mockery. Incensed by her haughty manner and identifying with the humble subjects of his story, he disparaged her narrow-mindedness thus: "that there was beauty [in the East Side] and an unstudied life full of interest, was beyond her comprehension. That the ancient religion of Israel was a moving and living force was unthinkable."[176] When this outraged matron challenged Ellis as to why he would not come uptown and describe the services at one of "our synagogues," he responded, "because there is nothing characteristic or beautiful in them. They are conventional concerts, like a Christian service, and with no great hold upon the congregation." Ellis concludes his tale with an angry condemnation of the "kind of Jews" who frowned on Zangwill and tried to have Cahan's stories boycotted because they were ashamed of their Jewish identity. They were "rich, Philistine, semi-Christianized Jews of the uptown Golden

Ghetto" who were "snobs and social climber[s], arrogant and material and commonplace."[177]

Zangwill's name featured prominently in the Gentile discourse on Jewishness. Glover suggested that his *Jewish Laws and Customs* would help "lovers of Zangwill" understand the laws and social ideas that molded the lives of his admired writer's "picturesque personages."[178] Steffens offered as testimony to his familiarity with Jewish life the fact that when Zangwill came to New York he asked him to be his guide during his tour of the East Side.[179] Hapgood took Zangwill's presence for granted to such an extent that he referred to him by last name only, and Hartmann conceded that the Gentile saw the ghetto through the lens provided by George Eliot and Israel Zangwill.

THE STAGE JEW

The announcement of the forthcoming American production of *Children of the Ghetto* created quite a buzz in the theater world. The *Dramatic Magazine* spoke for many in the profession when they asked if it were possible to succeed with the yet untried dramatic characterization of the Jew, "presented from a standpoint of serious purpose."[180] Their mention of "serious purpose" as a novelty alludes to the traditional portrayal of the stock type known as the "stage Jew" and to the prominence of the Hebrew comic on the popular English-speaking stage. The Hebrew comic came into vogue during the 1870s and would become a durable fixture in American vaudeville and British music halls and pantomimes. Famously delineated in the 1880s by American comedian Frank Bush and other garden-variety imitators, the type was an unsavory caricature of a mean-spirited foreigner, a sleazy coward in perpetual pursuit of financial gain, whose shenanigans, intended to trick Gentiles, are finally exposed and deflated. Typically named Solomon, Levy, or Moses, he was a pawnbroker, a dealer in old clothes, or some other petty merchant, his Jewishness instantly recognizable by his mannerisms and appearance. An unmanly sort, he was dark and shabby, his accoutrements including a worn black coat, a long beard, an exaggerated Semitic nose, and a comical German or Yiddish accent and dialect woven into silly and mispronounced English. A typical Frank Bush song went as follows:

Oh, my name is Solomon Moses I'm a bully Sheeny man,
I always treat my customers the very best what I can.
I keep a clothing store 'way down on Baxter Street,
Where you can get your clothing now I sell so awful cheap.

Chorus: Solomon, Solomon Moses,
Hast du gesehen der clotheses?
Hast du gesehen der kleiner kinder,
Und der sox iss in der vinder?
I sell to you for viertel dollar,
You will say was cheap,
Oskaploka overcoats
For fimpf sehn dollar and half.

My name is Isaac Levy Solomon Moses hast du gesacht?[181]

The equally popular British variant of the type was similar in appearance, language, and miserliness. Its lineage dates back to at least 1777, when a performer named Wewitzer appearing at Foote's Little Theatre in the Haymarket was described as "the best representative of comic Jews and foreigners that perhaps ever was or ever will be."[182] The characteristics of the type's more modern incarnation were described by author Hall Caine in his lecture on "The Jew in Literature" at an 1892 London dinner of the recently formed Maccabeans:

We all know the worthy gentleman in his little shabby hat and his long sack coat, with his nasal snuffle and his mincing walk. The silly old buffoon is never so high in histrionic rank as the low comedian, for that is a jester whom the public is expected to laugh with, whereas the Jew is the living gargoyle that they are expected to laugh at. His characteristics are cunning and cowardice, usually tinctured with the greenest stupidity. Every fool scores off him, and his latter end is usually one of battered hats and eclipsed eyeballs.[183]

Caine, a philo-Semite with close ties to London's Jewish community, did not regard the character as a manifestation of willful anti-Jewish sentiment but rather as a reflection of Jewish powerlessness that made it possible to turn Jews into the convenient butt of humor. He explained, "I will not say that this foolish person is invented solely in order that the public may indulge itself with laughter at the Jews, but that some butt of ridicule being necessary, it is safer in England to make him a Jew than a Quaker, or a Plymouth Brother, or even a Mormon."[184]

Although Caine equates Jews with other religious groups, the stage Hebrew belonged essentially to a gallery of so-called racial comics, which included the Scot, the Welsh, and the Irish in England, and the German, the Irish, and the Negro in the United States, at times portrayed by entertainers of the same ethnicity who used the stereotype to catapult their careers. Many Jews were greatly chagrined by the popularity of Hebrew comics and felt they positioned the Jew as a target for mockery, while other racial comics, such as the Irish, though also portrayed in an objectionable manner, at times succeeded in creating a good-natured rapport that helped win over audiences.[185] A lively exchange on this subject took place in the letters-to-the-editor section of the London *Jewish Chronicle* during the winter of 1911, its sensitive nature highlighted by the fact that many of the writers posted their comments anonymously. Some suggested that the Jews were perhaps too thin-skinned: as they were enjoying with the rest of the audience the performance of Scot and Irish comics, so they should reciprocate in goodwill and allow others to enjoy jokes made at their own expense and "take a broader view of life generally."[186] Others considered the Jewish comic a stimulant for anti-Semitism, arguing that equation with Scot and Welsh comics was misdirected, since the Jews were an isolated and persecuted people.[187] A Jewish campaign against racial impersonators, begun in America and extended to England, resulted in their gradual elimination.[188] Their memory lingered, though. In 1942 Lord Halifax, then British ambassador to the United States, noted in his diary, after a visit by Rabbi Stephen Wise and a colleague, that the latter's manner of speech was "exactly like that of a stage Jew." Halifax also noted that he could hardly keep a straight face when the man chimed in. The subject of their conversation was Nazi deportation of French Jews.[189]

America of the 1880s witnessed somewhat of a positive transformation of the Stage Jew into what Harley Erdman calls a "jolly good fellow," incorporated in the comic melodrama *Sam'l of Posen; or, The Commercial Drummer* (1881), starring M. B. Curtis, a Detroit-born son of Jewish immigrants.[190] Curtis portrayed a manly, good-natured, and fast-talking character without the standard external markers of the Stage Jew. Though the performance was dismissed by some critics as lightweight and vulgar, it was immensely successful, inspiring numerous imitations. Erdman regards Sam'l as a forerunner of theatrical "crypto-Jews" like Groucho Marx—comedians whose Jewishness manifests itself in an abrasive wisecracking performance.[191]

The Jew also inhabited English and American melodrama, usually appearing as a villainous character, who, albeit sinister, was mostly treated comically. Originally English, when exported to America the type gradually acquired local color. Dion Boucicault (1820–1890), one of the most prolific and successful playwrights of the Victorian stage, whose life and work were divided between England and America, introduced several such unsavory Jewish characters. His *Flying Scud* (1867) presented "Mo" Davis, a farcically treacherous and spineless member of a gang. A year later, his *After Dark* (1868) featured the criminal Dicey Morris, a gambling-house proprietor, whose appearance is described in a penny-novel version of the play as follows: "His curly black hair was lustrous with oil; and so were his whiskers, which almost came round to his nose—a nose that revealed the Israelites a mile off, though Mr. Dicey Morris has the impudence to deny he was born one of 'the Peoplesh.'"[192] Although the Stage Jew transformed to reflect sociological changes, dramatists were reluctant to abandon its stereotypical core. Thus, for example, the rise of a wealthy strata of American Jews late in the nineteenth century led to elasticization of the stock type to include the vulgar nouveau riche. One such unsavory character from the 1890s, recorded in Louis Harap's extensive survey *The Image of the Jew in American Literature,* is the Jewish crook in Charles Townsend's *Jail Bird* (1893). According to the playwright, Solomon Isaacs represented "a vulgar, brutal Jew" and was accordingly bedecked in "loud and vulgar dress; checked trousers, short velvet coat, flashy tie, profusion of diamonds."[193] Rich or poor, of the ghetto or the mansion, the stage Jew of the late nineteenth century continued to be distinguished in most cases by his silly or grotesque physical and linguistic otherness.

Even when the public image of Jews was improving, the basic schemata of the character was retained, much like the stock types of the *Commedia dell'arte.* Abraham Dreyfus (1847–1926) touched upon this in a lecture titled "Le Juif au théâtre" (The Jew in the Theater) delivered to the *Société des Études Juives* in Paris. When the stage caricature is protested, he said, the dramatist responds, "but what are we to do? . . . You don't want any more types of Jew-usurers, Jew-thieves, Jew-Murderers, Jew-apostles! . . . And if we represent on the stage any Jewish types which are not different from the Christians,—why, the Jews won't seem to be Jews at all! Then why should we call them Jews?"[194] The pejorative traits of the theatrical type were so well entrenched that many playwrights and producers of Jewish ancestry deliberately avoided inclusion of Jewish characters in their plays. In his talk, Dreyfus also quoted Adolph d'Ennery (1811–1899), one of France's most successful nineteenth-century playwrights and the author and coauthor of some two hundred dramatic texts. In explaining the absence of Jewish characters from his work, d'Ennery argued that a dramatist could not use the stage to fight against popular sentiment. Thus, if he introduced Jewish characters into his plays, they would need to be "usurers, swindlers, or traitors—in short, villains." Being a Jew himself, this would be disagreeable. "What was I to do then?" he asked, and then responded, "I have suppressed the Jew entirely in my plays."[195]

The most hideously criminal Jew of Victorian theater was Fagin, who made his stage debut in 1838. This was followed by a slew of dramatic adaptations of Dickens's *Oliver Twist*, a beloved story that guaranteed yearly revivals and periodic mountings that often did turn-away business. M. J. (Myer Jack) Landa, author of the encyclopedic *The Jew in Drama*, argued that the appearance of Fagin had seriously adverse implications for the portrayal of Jews on the mainstream stage because the character "codified anew" the portrayal of the Stage Jew, now "relegated to the lower and repulsive order of beings."[196] The quintessential predatory Jew, Fagin is an embodiment of every parent's nightmare, a kidnapper and corrupter of innocent Christian children, whom he sets on a hellish life of criminality and destruction. Dickens endowed him with the standard characteristics of the devilish medieval Jew: red matted hair, a hooked nose, and clawlike hands. A creature of the night, his shuffling gait is likened to a slithering reptile. Dickens's vivid description of Fagin's last night out reads like ready-made stage directions: "It seemed just the night when it befitted such a thing as the Jew to be abroad. As he glided along stealthily, creeping beneath the shelter of walls and doorways, the hideous old man seemed like some loathsome reptile; engendered in the slime and darkness through which he moved: crawling forth, by night, in search of some rich offal for a meal."[197] Though Dickens would later amend the text of *Oliver Twist*, reducing the number of references to Fagin as "the Jew," there was no misunderstanding as to his identity. Discussing the reductive uniformity of stereotyped Jews, Zangwill once commented wryly that while Fagin was seen by Gentiles as the epitome of the Jew, no Jew would suppose that the criminal Bill Sikes stood for the Englishman.[198]

The most infamous demon-Jew of the 1890s was the musician-mesmerist Svengali, who stands at the fulcrum of du Maurier's *Trilby* (1894), a sensational best-selling novel with a dense sexual and racial subtext. An itinerant musician of East European origin, Svengali hypnotizes Trilby, a young English artist's model living in Paris. Though she has no musical abilities, he transforms her into a zombielike diva who enchants audiences throughout Europe with her glorious singing voice. Paul M. Potter's dramatized version of *Trilby* was the hit of the 1895 New York theater season and was subsequently taken throughout the country by numerous touring companies. Wilton Lackaye (1862–1932), who originated the role, became a major star. He often returned to the part and would always be associated with it in America.

Ironically, four years later he was to originate the role of Reb Shemuel in *Children of the Ghetto*. Herbert Beerbohm Tree realized the enormous potential of *Trilby* as a vehicle and hastened to buy the English rights. In his immensely successful London production, he played Svengali and further emphasized the Jewish aspect of the character, concluding a near-death scene with the crescendo of the Hebrew prayer "Shema Yisroel Adonai Eloheno Adonai Echod!"[199]

The young Jewish female, the so-called *belle Juive,* at times generically referred to as "Rebecca" after the beautiful heroine of Walter Scott's *Ivanhoe* (1819), fared better on the mainstream stage, though her fortune was universally tragic. Passionate and mysterious, she was the object of Gentile male desire, yet doomed to loss of identity through conversion, or to unrealized love due to internal and external barriers to a Jewish–Christian union. The character was best represented in *Leah, the Forsaken* (1863), an adaptation of *Deborah,* by Salomon Herman von Mosenthal (1821–1877), an Austrian Jewish dramatist and poet. It tells the pathetic story of Leah's betrayal by her Gentile lover, her hateful vow of revenge, and her ultimate conversion to self-sacrificing forgiveness. A child of the forest, clad in flesh-revealing tatters, passionate and distraught, she offered a grand vehicle for some of the most distinguished actresses of the nineteenth century, including Fanny Janauscheck and Sarah Bernhardt, the latter's Jewish identity playing an important role in her highly exoticized public persona.

While *Leah, the Forsaken* achieved enormous popularity, the two foremost classical German plays with noble Jewish male characters that served as pleas for religious toleration—Gotthold Ephraim Lessing's *Nathan the Wise* (1779) and Karl Guzkow's *Uriel Acosta* (1847)—were not seen on the English stage until the twentieth century.[200] Still, there were sporadic efforts to counterbalance the predominance of Jewish villains and petty knaves. The first philo-Semitic advocacy on the English stage was *The Jew* by Richard Cumberland (1732–1811), produced at Drury Lane in May 1794. Its protagonist, Sheva the Jew, is a usurer and a fanatical miser willing to subsist on potato peels and water so as to bestow his wealth upon a young Christian aristocrat. Albeit a farfetched character, Sheva serves as a mouthpiece for the author's honorable agenda when he explains the pathetic lot of Jews: "We have no abiding place on earth—no country, no home. Everybody rails at us, everybody points us out for their may-game and their mockery. If your playwriters want a butt, or a buffoon, or a knave to make sport of, out comes a Jew to be baited and buffeted through five long acts, for the amusement of all good Christians."[201] The author's sentiments were noble, but the play was considered poor fare, mainly remembered by Jews who were thankful for its spirit of tolerance. Another idealized Jew hit the London stage a century later. *An Old Jew*, by Sidney Grundy (1848–1914), a popular Victorian playwright, opened on January 6, 1894, at the Garrick Theatre, and starred John Hare. Its Jewish protagonist leaves his adulterous Christian wife and two children, though not without providing handsomely for their needs, and returns twenty years later under a masked identity, now as rich as Croesus, willing to use his boundless resources to solve all the problems of his spoiled children. Like Cumberland's Sheva, he is essentially a pale reversal of the villainous stage Jew, defined by the prescribed contours of the character as alien and fantastically wealthy. Both Cumberland's and Grundy's quixotic do-gooders were lifeless embodiments of Christian ideals and virtues and performed their extravagant charity as lone outsiders in an entirely non-Jewish context.

The Stage Jew was ultimately challenged and elevated from theatrical tawdriness not by the pen of a playwright but by the brilliant originality of Henry Irving, the reigning actor-manager of his time. He first tackled the Jewish issue, albeit indirectly, in his production of *The Bells* (1871), an adaptation prepared by Leopold Lewis (1828–1890), a London Jewish writer, of Emile Erckman and Pierre Alexandre Chatrian's *Le Juif Polonais* (The Polish Jew). This sensational production propelled Irving to the top rank of English-language tragedians, and he kept it in his repertory and performed it throughout England and America until his death thirty-four years later. The psychological melodrama tells of an Alsatian burgomaster who is tormented by his memory of a traveling Polish Jew he had murdered for his gold on Christmas Eve exactly fifteen years earlier. The juxtaposition of Christmas and the robbery, and the murder of an alien Jew by a Christian, identified the offstage Jewish character not merely as victim but associated him with the crucified Christ.

The Jew as an alien biblical patrician who is victimized and made degenerate by barbaric Christians made his most striking appearance in Irving's revolutionary production of Shakespeare's *The Merchant of Venice* (1879). His powerful interpretation, which enlisted audience sympathy on the side of Shylock, was recognized as a milestone in the representation of the Jew. Shylock was a seminal figure, whose name had entered the language as a commonly employed anti-Semitic slur. The character had a long and rich theatrical history, evolving from the Elizabethan red-haired, elephantine-nosed buffoon to Charles Macklin's portrayal as a malicious and vindictive usurer (1741), an interpretation that was basically preserved by actors Edmund Kean and William Charles Macready in England, and Edwin Forrest and Edwin Booth in America. The character of Shylock was instrumental in the formation of the popular image of the Jew. Charles Kensington Salaman, in his passionate defense of English Jewry, *Jews as They Are,* devoted considerable attention to Shylock, whose "purely imaginary" inhuman desires, he said, "have balefully recoiled upon the whole Jewish race, with an injury to the character of modern Jews which may be regarded as irremediable."[202] Irving's sympathetic interpretation portrayed Shylock as a tragic figure, a representative of a maltreated and abused people, majestically striving to assert his right to full humanity. When Irving died in 1905, Malcolm C. Salaman wrote that by his impersonation of Shylock, Irving "made himself the creditor of every self-respecting Jew."[203] While Irving's Shylock was construed as an orientalized character, Tree further Judaized and contemporized *The Merchant of Venice.* He situated Shylock within the milieu of the ghetto, his house faced by the synagogue, which had streams of worshipers coming and going. *Kol Nidrei* was played by the orchestra, with Hebrew chants performed during the "ghetto scenes."[204]

Zangwill was fascinated with Shylock and embellished this mythical character in his imagination. He envisioned Shylock as a deeply intellectual Jew of Spanish origin, attached to his daughter and a dead wife. When Shylock first appears on the stage, he wrote, he should be pondering over "some old Talmudic folio," or engaged in a "picturesque ceremony," with a wine cup and spice box, his daughter Jessica holding a candle in her hand.[205] With the insight of an emancipated Jew, he understood Shylock's desire for the love and respect of the "lordly Christians," for, he added knowingly, "when has a Jew not coveted that?"[206] He also saw the connection between Shylock's relaxation of religious dictum by accepting the Christians' invitation to dine with them and the catastrophe that befalls him in his daughter's betrayal. Zangwill's fanciful reconstruction of Shylock deemphasizes authorial intent: "it is not important what Shakespeare meant, as what he might mean to us."[207] He acknowledged that practically every age rewrites the old masterpieces, as part of an ongoing reinterpretation. His play *Children of the Ghetto* is in many ways his Jewish version of the myth of the old Jewish usurer and his beautiful young daughter.

In the twilight of his life, when he became honorary president of the Jewish Drama League (1925), Zangwill spoke about *Children of the Ghetto* in terms of the role he had envisioned for it as the basis for a Jewish dramatic repertoire, what he called "a school of Jewish drama."[208] Whether such a school exists is a matter for debate, but there is no doubt that *Children of the Ghetto* kicked wide the door of the English-language stage to ethnic Jewish drama. Once open, a long line of Jewish dramatists would follow.

Children of the Ghetto

Introductory Essay

THE PLAY

The dramatization of the dense canvas of *Children of the Ghetto* was a complex task. Though only that part of the novel devoted to ghetto life would be used in the play, this still represented a considerable volume of text, which had to be compressed into the dialogic conventions and time strictures of the theatrical medium. The interrelation between the text of the novel and that of the play came up when Macmillan, Zangwill's American publisher, became concerned that a proposed publication of the play by Small, Maynard, and Company, a new Boston house, might jeopardize Macmillan's copyright on the novel. In his response, Zangwill explained that those speeches in the play that roughly coincided with the book constituted scarcely two or three pages out of four hundred. He noted that he stood to gain little financially if the play were to be published and that he had consented to its publication "in the interest of art" and with the hope of promoting in America the idea of literary drama, namely "drama that could face print without blushing."[1] Several months later, without explanation, Zangwill informed Macmillan that upon "reconsideration" he had advised Small, Maynard not to proceed.[2] Consequently, the play was not to be published until now, herein.

Since the novel includes several tenuously linked narratives, its dramatic adaptation was not merely a matter of condensation, but required selection of a central story line. Zangwill focused on the side story of the Hannah Jacobs-David Brandon romance, doomed by the prohibition of Jewish law against marriage of a male Cohen (descendant of the priestly tribe) to a divorced woman, in effect even when the divorce was a mere technicality used to resolve a legal entanglement. Although Zangwill retained many of the novel's colorful characters, the foregrounding of the Hannah Jacobs episode required the elimination, alteration, and consolidation of several of the novel's incidents and led to hierarchical repositioning of its dramatis personae. In addition to Hannah, Reb Shemuel, and David Brandon now occupying center stage, Melchitsedek Pinchas was promoted and assigned functions previously relegated to others—now it was he, rather than the original Old Hyman, who declares the mock wedding ceremony as valid—while others, notably Esther Ansell, the novel's most central character, were now consigned to the subset of minor figures. All in all, though the drama shares its title and one story line with the novel, the cuts, rearrangements, and additions of source material resulted in a new work that, despite its similarities, is different in details, theme, and message.

A formal consequence of the recasting of the story in the dramatic genre was its division into acts. Zangwill followed Ibsen's four-act model.[3] The four acts together present a symmetrical structure, and their titles—"The Letter of the Law," "The Spirit of Love," "The Letter and the Spirit," and "Love and Law"—posit the play's central theme: the conflict between adherence to Jewish law and the yearnings of the heart. They are organized chronologically, each grounded in a Jewish festival or holy day—Chanukah, Purim, Friday night, and Passover—used as temporal markers that could also be understood by a Gentile audience, Chanukah being associated at the beginning of act 1 with Christmas, and Passover with Easter. The use of these holidays offered dramatic justification for the enactment of Jewish rituals and offered a symbolic interpretation, particularly in the last scene, where the celebration of the Children of Israel's liberation from Egyptian bondage commented ironically on Hannah's psychological surrender to the yoke of tradition.

Various artistic and cultural factors led Zangwill to concentrate on Hannah's story and to focus on Reb Shemuel as the drama's tragic protagonist. One possible reason was the popularity of religious topics in both melodramas and "problem plays" during the late 1880s and 1890s. Henry Arthur Jones devoted two plays—*Judah* (1890) and *Michael and His Lost Angel* (1896)—to the predicaments of clergymen, and the dramatization of Hall Caine's *The Christian,* whose protagonist is a tortured London minister, was enormously successful in America. Such serious fare was also connected, albeit inadvertently, to another immensely popular class of religious drama known as toga plays—namely, melodramatic extravaganzas that typically revolved around the romance between a masculine Roman patrician and a plebeian beauty belonging to a forbidden Christian sect. Set in the world of early Christian martyrdom, the melodramas were based on the conflict between powerful and hedonistic paganism and the moral force of Christianity.[4] The genre's most triumphant specimens were *The Sign of the Cross* (1896) in England and *Ben-Hur* (1899) in America, productions that reached mass audiences, many of whom had never been to the theater. A London periodical, *The Sketch,* commented in November 1899 on the abundance of "some very startling, not to say daring, 'religious,' or religiously named 'dramas'" and listed the titles staged during the previous year: *The Sign of the Cross; No Cross, No Crown; Forgive Us Our Trespasses; Defender of the Faith; The Power and the Glory; The Christian Cross;* and *The Christian.*[5] In later years, Zangwill would tackle non-Jewish religious issues in two plays: *The Next Religion* (1912), banned by the British censor, and *Plaster Saints* (1914), whose subject is a puritanical minister with a skeleton in his closet, based on the Henry Ward Beecher scandal.

One of Zangwill's most important amendments to the novel in dramatizing *Children of the Ghetto* was eliminating the character of Levi, Hannah's brother. By refashioning Hannah as an only child, and by greatly diminishing the role of her mother, Zangwill emphasized the father-daughter relationship, a popular theme of Victorian drama and, more importantly, one that evoked Shakespeare's Shylock–Jessica pair. This intertextuality is suggested not merely by Zangwill's great interest in Shylock but also by the immense popularity of *The Merchant of Venice* in the discourse of the period, so much so it was deemed a late-Victorian obsession.[6] The play's characters, particularly Shylock and Portia, were often invoked in the press in debates on Jewish and feminist issues. This popularity was also evident in America, where Jewish organizations would later lead a long campaign for removal of the play from school curricula. Zangwill alluded to the impact of this widespread familiarity with *Merchant* when he quoted an English lady who declared, "Shylock is the only Jew most of us know personally."[7]

Shylock's iconic status in Western culture elicited a broad spectrum of Jewish artistic and scholarly responses. For Jews, among the most troubling aspects of the play was Jessica's betrayal of her father. She deserts him, steals his money, finds a home among the Christian elite, the very ones who tormented him, and converts to their faith. Heinrich Heine's poetic ear detected the moan "Jessica, my child!" of the old Jew, defrauded of child and descendants, at the closing of the Yom Kippur service.[8] Subsequent writers and artists have created a body of Jewish texts that prune, revise, and rewrite the play and imagined sequels where Jessica is poetically penalized by the scorn of her husband and Christian society or, consumed by remorse, yearns to return to her ancestral home. Zangwill, too, discredited Jessica, whom he regarded as "the most detestable and least Jewish character in all fiction," and suggested that the part "ought to be rewritten."[9] Though he did not rewrite Shakespeare, he did in effect write a play that acted as a countertext by indirectly inverting and reflecting on the original that inspired it. Like *The Merchant of*

Venice, Children of the Ghetto is monopolized by a legalistic theme, contrasts native and outsider, mixes tragedy and comedy, and even uses a ring as a dramatic device. Hannah's tragedy begins when the mischievous Sam Levine puts a ring on her finger and unwittingly becomes her husband. Shakespeare features three rings, two of which are given by Portia and Nerissa to their suitors as oaths of love. The third, given to Shylock by his beloved wife, Leah, now dead, is traded in Genoa by Jessica, their daughter, for a pet monkey.

In his rendition of Reb Shemuel and his daughter, Hannah, Zangwill offers a Jewish reading of the deep-rooted literary tradition of the old detestable Jew and his beautiful daughter, institutionalized in English letters by Shakespeare's Shylock and Jessica, Christopher Marlowe's Barabas and Abigail (*The Jew of Malta*), and Walter Scott's Isaac of York and Rebecca (*Ivanhoe*). Zangwill reverses things: his old Jew is not a nasty usurer but a friendly ghetto rabbi, generous and kind to a fault, acceptant of people's failings and idiosyncrasies, as long they do not impinge on the absolute sovereignty of Jewish law. He is the antithesis of the avaricious stereotype of the Stage Jew. He shares his clothes and household money with the poor, is sensitive to his daughter's romantic needs, and welcomes her suitor, even though he is a lax Jew. Yet this affable rabbi assumes prophetic and tragic dimensions when he adheres to a strict interpretation of Jewish law, to which his submission is absolute. Even when it is about to devastate his daughter's life, he devoutly fulfills the divine dictate, much like Abraham in following God's command to sacrifice his beloved Isaac. The price of his unquestioning faith is steep. Not only does he deny his daughter personal happiness, but he also denies himself future descendants. It is fitting that at the high point of his daughter's dilemma, which takes place during the night of the seder, Reb Shemuel dons his *kitl,* the white garment worn by the Orthodox Jewish male when he marries and when he is buried. Like a tall tree that cannot bend with the wind, the house of this patriarch is doomed to disappear, while the coarse members of the community adjust, compromise, and attain a modicum of financial and personal success.

Hannah, like Jessica, is unhappy with her father's restrictive universe and yearns for poetry and romantic love. However, though in a moment of amorous rebelliousness she agrees to flee with David to America, when the time to leave arrives she is incapable of cutting herself off and stays, overcome by filial tenderness and deep attachment to the traditional world that had nurtured her. Unlike Jessica's lover, David Brandon, Hannah's beloved is a Jew, but in the world of orthodoxy in which she lives he is as forbidden to Hannah as a Christian would be. Indeed, on several occasions he is indirectly associated with the Christian world that surrounds the ghetto. In act 3, when Hannah prepares her father for the revelation of her love to the non-devout David, she jokingly teases him with the speculation, "Suppose . . . I wanted to marry a Christian." In act 4, when he urges Hannah to elope to America, David suggests that she share a cabin aboard a ship with a female "Christian friend" of his. The introduction of the female friend is supposed to reassure an audience of David's honorable intentions, when they might otherwise frown at the idea of an unmarried woman crossing the Atlantic without a chaperone. At the same time, though, it singles out David as the only character in the play with close personal ties to the Christian world. If Hannah were to go along with David's plan, she would not only give up the security of home and community; she would also begin the voyage to her new life by sharing her personal space with a Gentile. The significance of David's suggestion is underscored by the fact that it is an addition to the typed playscript, written in Zangwill's own hand over the original, in which David describes the prospective companion as a "sister of my dead chum."[10] Furthermore, toward the end of the play, when David rattles the door at Hannah's house in his desperate attempt to will her to join him, Mrs. Jacobs explains away the noise as caused by a "Christian rough." A moment later, when Hannah bolts the door and David throws a stone at the window, Mrs. Jacobs repeats, "There! I told you it was a Christian rough," to which Reb Shemuel retorts, "It is worse—it is some Jewish rough."

Practically all the problems in the play are created by men arriving in the ghetto from the outside world: Sam Levine, who foolishly puts the ring on Hannah's finger, has returned from months spent pursuing his livelihood in the English countryside; David Brandon has just come home from years in South Africa, where he made his fortune; and Melchitsedek Pinchas appears at the London Ghetto after he had journeyed all over Europe and Palestine. In this manner the play suggests that departure from the ghetto marks the beginning of the Jew's journey into assimilation. At the same time, the way back to authentic Jewish life represented by the ghetto is equally impossible, as David's final cry of "I am shut out!" demonstrates. A man of the world, David suggests to Hannah that America is the answer. There, he tells Hannah, any rabbi would marry them, presumably referring to the practice of Reform Judaism. Hannah, though a nonbeliever, rejects this option, or any suggestion of a more progressive understanding of Jewish law. As she sees it, her options are either full adherence to orthodoxy or complete rejection of Judaism. In this respect she serves as a mouthpiece for Zangwill, who could not embrace Reform Judaism as a viable alternative to the traditional Judaism he loved but did not practice. Like Hannah Jacobs, Zangwill was a rebel and a modern, who was umbilically attached to traditional Judaism, to its rich literature, to the music of the synagogue, to the familial ceremonies of the Sabbath and Passover. One did not leave such richness, he suggests, for Reform Judaism, which he regarded as a watered-down replacement that smacked of Christianity. The monumental tragedy of modern Jewish life, Zangwill seems to be saying, is that the alternative to the authentic Jewishness of the ghetto is total abandonment of tradition and full submersion in a secular though essentially Gentile world.

His views are expressed in the prologue to the play, which was not read from the stage but handed out in printed form to the audience:

PROLOGUE

Behold, O friends, who stern in judgment sit,
A hidden world the footlights ne'er have lit:
A world whose day and night, whose sun and shade,
By spinning round the ancient Law are made;
Whose springs and winters take—whate'er the clime—
From Old Jerusalem their changeless time.
Still in God's love the chosen people basks,
But ah! What tragic price Jehovah asks.
How strange a miracle this deathless life,
Aye with itself and all the world at strife,
This life that links us to the purple past
Of Babylon and Egypt, all the vast
Enchantment of the ancient Orient,
And yet with London and New York is blent;
The life that lives, though Greece and Rome are dust,
And Spain's inquisitorial racks are rust;
And, though so faded from the ancient glory,
When kings and prophets shone in Israel's story,
Is brightening once again, yet who shall say
With light of Eastern or of Western day?
Our drama shows a phase transitional,
Young love at war with ancient ritual—
How dead laws living, loving hearts may fetter,
The contest of the Spirit and the Letter.
Yet noble, too, that kissing of the rod,

That stern obedience to the word of God,
In godless days when sweated Hebrews scout
The faith their sunless lives are dark without.
But do not deem the Ghetto is all gloom!
The comic spirit mocks the ages' doom,
And weaves athwart the woof of tragic drama
The humours of the human panorama.
The poet vaunts, the hypocrite goes supple,
The marriage-broker mates the bashful couple,
The peddler cries his wares, the player aces,
Saint jostles sinner, fun with wisdom paces,
The beggars prosper and the babes increase,
And over all the Sabbath whispers, "Peace!"
* * *

We draw the curtain from this world *in petto,*
Entreating grace for "Children of the Ghetto."

I. Zangwill

Preparing the Production

On April 11, 1899, George Tyler, producer of *Children of the Ghetto,* wrote from New York to Zangwill in London:

> I enclose you a letter from Mr. James A. Herne written in answer to a proposition I made to him to work with you in staging the play. Mr. Herne occupies the highest position of any American producer. What is more, he is a man of wealth and one who rarely devotes his services to any other than his own plays. Insomuch as I have heard you speak of him I take it for granted that you are somewhat familiar with his style of work. However his letter will give you a pretty good insight into the serious character of the man. From a literary stand-point his work always commands the greatest respect in America. He has devoted his entire life fathering beautiful and original ideas. The association of a man of this character will prove of great value both from an artistic and financial standpoint. The American press will be induced to give us added attention, being the first time that two men occupying such exalted positions in their respective fields have associated themselves. I hope you will thoroughly appreciate

the importance of the step and realize that you will have a congenial spirit to assist in producing what promises to be the novelty of the century.[11]

James A. Herne (1839–1901), the director, merits special attention. His involvement in the production was of particular importance in light of his status as a distinguished elder dramatist, a director, and an actor who had a pioneering role in the introduction of realism on the American stage.[12] His own *Shore Acres* (1893) was regarded by Henry Irving as the best American play he had ever seen, one that marked the beginning of a genuine school of American drama. Writer Hamlin Garland (1860–1940) spoke for many when he wrote in his diary that Herne was "the most original of our dramatists."[13] A master of stagecraft, Herne began his career at the bottom of the theatrical ladder as a "utility man," toured America with various companies, and later collaborated with David Belasco in San Francisco, eventually co-writing *Hearts of Oak* (1890), in which Herne and his wife, Katharine, played the leads.[14] During the early 1880s he settled in Boston, where he developed a friendship with Hamlin Garland, who introduced him to the local literati, notably William Dean Howells, considered by many the foremost writer of the day. As he became associated with Boston's intellectual elite, Herne was greatly influenced by the evolutionary theories of Charles Darwin and Herbert Spencer and by the economic and taxation reforms proposed by Henry George. An agnostic himself, he became an ardent supporter of William Jennings Bryan.

Herne familiarized himself with Europe's new polemical drama, particularly with the work of its herald Henrik Ibsen, whose plays, rarely produced in America in the late nineteenth century, were denounced by the country's leading theater critics, including William Winter, as the gospel of "disordered mentality, distrust, despondency, bitterness, and gloom."[15] Herne developed a taste for realism and its emphasis on the nexus of human psychology and social reality. In his own plays, which he always directed and acted in, he strove to create an illusory world that had the "look" of reality, free from such overt theatrical traditions as asides and soliloquies. His productions appeared simple and were infused with local color, creating a sense of the social and physical milieu within which men and women actually lived and revealed themselves. The characters were ordinary Americans who expressed themselves naturally, using a spoken, often colloquial, language. Herne articulated his dramatic convictions in an essay titled "Art for Truth's Sake in the Drama" that appeared in *The Arena,* a radical political/cultural magazine edited by the maverick Benjamin Orange Fowler. In it Herne contrasted "art for art's sake," which he defined as art that is inoffensive and aesthetically pleasing, with "art for truth's sake," whose goal is to express "a *larger* truth"—truth being not always beautiful but always indispensable. He declared, "I stand for art for truth's sake because it perpetuates the everyday life of its time, because it develops the latent beauty of the so-called common places of life, because it dignifies labor and reveals the divinity of the common man."[16]

In 1891 Herne produced his *Margaret Fleming,* starring himself, with Katharine in the title role. The play was considered so radical that producers declined to invest in it or even book it in a commercial theater. It was finally presented in Boston's Chickering Hall, a recital space that he turned into a theater, which set a precedent for using nonconventional venues for dramatic productions. Fowler and Garland worked vigorously to promote this production and billed it as "An American Play without a Soliloquy." The play, which examines society's double sexual standard, is regarded by historians as marking the birth of modern American drama and garnered Herne the sobriquet "the American Ibsen."[17] The critical reception outside Boston was similar to that for Ibsen's plays. The *New York Times* called the play "the quintessence of the commonplace," explaining, "its language is the colloquial English of the shops and the streets and the kitchen fire-place. Its personages are the everyday nonentities that some folks like to forget when they go to the theatre. It is constructed in defiance of the laws of Aristotle and Horatius Flaccus and Corneille and Hazlitt. . . . The life it portrays is sordid and mean, and its effect upon a sensitive mind is depressing."[18] This trailblazing production, now a landmark in the history of the American stage, barely lasted three weeks in New York City.

Zangwill first met Herne during the last Boston run of *Shore Acres* in the winter of 1898, and according to Herne's daughter, Julie, the two hit it off immediately. Zangwill later attended a New York performance of Herne's production of his *Griffith Davenport,* accompanied by Hamlin Garland and Mr. and Mrs. Daniel Guggenheim.[19] He then told Tyler he wanted Herne to direct *Children of the Ghetto.* In April of 1898 Herne received a letter from Tyler inviting him to direct the play, to be produced with an all-star cast. According to Julie, her father was not interested in the project, as he did not expect it to be successful and wished to devote his time to another play of his, *Sag Harbor.* Herne resisted Tyler's request twice. He had suffered a severe financial setback with *Griffith Davenport,* though, and finally capitulated after the offer of an exceedingly large salary, signing an agreement on May 17, 1899.[20] By the time Herne was hired, a New York theater was secured, an opening date was announced on Liebler and Company stationery, and most of the leading parts were cast, all accomplished in the spirit of Tyler's contract with Zangwill, in which the producer promised first-class treatment in terms of the house, manner of production, and cast.[21] Their letters show that Tyler and Zangwill collaborated on various production aspects, including casting the leads, with Tyler affirming Zangwill's emphasis on "avoiding the grotesque and offensive" and refraining from caricature.[22] Since a major objective of the production was to present an accurate rendering of the ghetto, much of the management of the production's Jewish details was entrusted to Zangwill. Tyler wrote, "I leave the matter absolutely to you, and you will pay whatever price you think is proper."[23]

In London, Zangwill contacted Frederic Hyman Cowen (1852–1935), an eminent musician and fellow Jew, but the plans for him to compose the score did not materialize, one possible reason, though probably not the determining one, being a disagreement with the producer over the size of the orchestra.[24] The job was eventually entrusted to William Furst (1852–1917), an established Broadway composer, who wrote a prelude that included such "Hebrew melodies" as "Maoz Tsur," as well as themes from cantorial pieces, and selected and arranged works by other composers.[25] Zangwill felt that music played an important role in the production and offered as an example the synagogue music in act 4.[26] When Hannah hears the prayers she grew up with, she is thrown into emotional turmoil and abandons her aspirations for a new life, unable to discard her home and community for the man who is the love of her life.

The pursuit of authenticity also applied to the visual aspects of the production. The ground plan and sketches for the costumes and the exterior and interior sets were prepared by Zangwill's artist brother, Mark. In a letter to Tyler, Zangwill reports plans to spend Passover Eve at the London Jewish market accompanied by Mark with a Kodak camera in order to collect visual material. Mark also made watercolor sketches of the main characters from the novel that were used by the costume designer and widely reproduced for the publicity campaign. In an interview with the *Jewish Chronicle*, Zangwill explained that his intention was not to reproduce a particular part of the London Ghetto, but to achieve scenically what the play did in literature, namely, represent "the essence of the spirit of locale."[27]

Zangwill and Tyler were also in consultation with each other about casting decisions. Much of the discussion evolved around the eagerness of the two men to hire David Warfield for the role of Melchitsedek Pinchas, which confirms the centrality of this character in their vision of the play. Warfield

The market scene. New York production of *Children of the Ghetto,* act 4 (1899). Photo by Byron. Museum of the City of New York, Byron Collection.

(1866–1951) was a major star who popularized the turn-of-the-century Hebrew comic type with such characters as Solomon Yankle in *Hurly Burly* (1898), Isidore Nosenstein in *Helter Skelter* (1899), and Shadrach Leschinski in *Fiddle-Dee-Dee* (1900).[28] On February 3, 1899, Zangwill wrote Tyler, "I hope you will secure Warfield, even if he is high. It would probably be difficult to replace him"; a few days later Tyler responded, "I don't think I will have any trouble securing Warfield." However, Warfield hesitated to leave a lucrative vaudeville engagement with Weber and Fields, where he was offered a princely $350 a week to stay another year. On June 24, 1899, Tyler informed Zangwill that he had hired William Norris for the part. Norris was a versatile actor who had performed alongside Richard Mansfield, had replaced David Warfield in "The Belle of New York" (1897), and was currently performing in the hit production of *His Excellency the Governor.*[29]

The other parts for *Children* proved easier to cast. On February 19, 1899, Tyler wrote that he had arranged with Blanche Bates (1873–1941) to play Hannah and that he had offered the part of Reb Shemuel to Wilton Lackaye (1862–1932), who had gained theatrical fame when he originated the role of Svengali. Both were then appearing in the hit Liebler production of *The Musketeers* starring James O'Neill. In a letter sent on March 28, 1899, Tyler noted Bates's talent and prospects for stardom and praised Lackaye as a favorite New York actor and one of the best in the country. Three months later, on June 24, Tyler notified Zangwill of additional casting, stating: "I have spared no expense whatever and everything is very promising." He wrote that the salary list of the principals alone would be in the neighborhood of $2,300 per week, which meant a total running expense of about $3,500 a week, adding that Mr. Herne was to receive $500 a week for his work as stage director.[30] According to Julie Herne, her father was dispirited when he realized he had practically no say in selection of the cast and that he found Tyler unnecessarily wasteful, paying exorbitant salaries to top actors for bit parts. He felt he could have cast the play, with its more than thirty speaking parts, much better for half the money. Moreover, he disliked all-star casts, as he felt the actors were less interested in ensemble acting and more eager for audience attention.[31]

Rehearsals were to begin on August 21, 1899. Zangwill arrived three weeks earlier and received a celebrity's welcome, finding himself surrounded by the press. According to Julie, he was as "delighted as a child" with the attention. Herne met Zangwill upon his arrival and brought him out to Herne Oaks, his Long Island estate, where they could work in peace far from the sweltering city. Zangwill's easy ways and vivacious personality endeared him to the family, and a genuine friendship developed. He frolicked with the children and was particularly fond of the young Chrystal Herne, who nine years later would originate the role of Vera in *The Melting Pot*. According to Julie, Zangwill knew little about the practical aspects of the theater, which he was happy to leave to Herne, though he was protective of every word in the script. Whenever Herne suggested a cut, Zangwill would exclaim, "Is it for the good of the play?" When convinced this was the case, he would relent, though sighing, "Very well. Then you may cut the line. I will consent to any change that is for the good of the play." He insisted that he would not agree to any cut whose purpose was simply to get the curtain down by eleven, as was then customary.[32]

As rehearsals began, problems soon arose among the all-star cast, who were constantly trying to upstage each other, and the director, whose theatri-

Blanche Bates as Hannah in the New York production of *Children of the Ghetto* (1899). Photo by Byron. Museum of the City of New York, Byron Collection.

cal vision called for toned-down, realistic ensemble acting. Things were particularly tense with Wilton Lackaye, in the lead role of Reb Shemuel. According to Julie Herne, he had not learned his lines and was still ad-libbing when rehearsals were moved to Washington, D.C., just days before the play was to open. It finally came to open confrontation. Having futilely addressed him several times before, Herne admonished, "It is [the author's] right to have his words delivered exactly as he wrote them, for he is held responsible for them by the critics and the public. A generation ago, when we used to change the bill every night, it was permissible to 'fake' and paraphrase, since no memory could hold all the lines exactly; but nowadays, when plays are classed as literature, and we devote months of study and rehearsal to them, there is no excuse."[33] Herne then gathered the cast and in his quiet drawl reaffirmed his authority. Bruised egos were calmed and work continued in earnest.

Ten years later, Lackaye discussed his acting method and shed light on his work on the part of Reb Shemuel. Lackaye regarded actors as a sort of highly observant collectors who noticed the littlest peculiarities and eccentricities of the persons around them, archived the data, then reassembled various details for their stage characterizations, which were essentially composites of the people they had met. It was most unusual, he said, to base a part on one specific person, unless for the purpose of burlesque or imitation. However, his experience with Reb Shemuel had been unique and defied his usual approach to character building. He explained that as he was studying the part, he went to the ghetto on the Lower East Side of New York and for weeks mingled among the local Jews. Several times he sat unrecognized in the Essex Market Police Court and studied the various people who came there. One day a rabbi entered the courtroom, having been summoned to conduct a wedding in a seduction case. "That's 'Reb' Shemuel," he thought. Lackaye followed the rabbi to Grand Street, then to Pitt and Clinton, and through other ghetto byways. He was so taken with the man, he took pains to copy every detail of his dress and mannerisms. Lackaye recalled that after opening night, Zangwill asked him how he had formed his idea for the part, noting, "Your Shem[uel] is an exact reproduction of the original as I first found him in London." The actor recounted how he had found his Shemuel, and the author said he wanted to see him for himself. One afternoon they went to Grand and Pitt, and before long Zangwill cried out, "There, there—there is my 'Shem'! The last time I saw him was in 'Houndsditch'—he was coming through Petticoat Lane."[34] In his reminiscence of his acting career, Lackaye notes that the only characters he had originated that were essentially imitative and not artistic composites were Reb Shemuel and Svengali. Remarkably, both were Jewish

Wilton Lackaye as Reb Shemuel in *Children of the Ghetto* (1899). Harry Ransom Humanities Research Center, University of Texas at Austin.

parts and the ones that largely defined his career. Lackaye was not the only actor to find inspiration in the ghetto. Cyrus Adler, Zangwill's friend and host in Washington, remembered that many actors went to the East Side of New York and other Jewish neighborhoods in order to acquaint themselves with the "downtown Jews" whose lives they were going to portray.[35] Eventually, the mostly non-Jewish cast came to identify so strongly with the spirit of the play that they refused to hold a rehearsal on the Yom Kippur a few days before the opening.

Jewish nervousness about the production mounted as the Washington premiere drew near, especially as the aggressive promotional campaign was not fully attuned to the sensibilities of American Jewry. With anti-Semitism still a common aspect of American life, advertisements in the press that *Children of the Ghetto* would "show the Jew as he really is" created strong anxiety, especially when they were adjacent to such pronouncements as this one that appeared in August 1899 in *Leslie's Weekly:*

> Mr. Zangwill deals with a phase of life not understood by the people of New York, for between the Hebrew of this city and the Hebrew of London there is as much affinity and sympathy as between a Zulu and a Choctaw Indian. In the Hebrew of Whitechapel the sentiment of pride in race, of exclusion from association of all those who are not of his blood and faith, of hatred and contempt for the "Goyim," of adherence to the ancient forms and ceremonies of his faith, burns brightly through all the broadening changes and influences of a later civilization.[36]

Mindful of the unsettling effect of such notices on the Jewish community, Tyler issued a soothing press release in early September.[37] It began by acknowledging that "fear has been expressed" that Zangwill would offensively contrast types of Jewish life and that this would present Jews in an undesirable light. It went on to pledge that the playwright's "picturesque personalities" were drawn in the most considerate manner and that they had no affinity with the vulgar caricatures of the Stage Jew, noting that only two or three characters spoke in "dialect," all others reading their lines in "pure English." At the same time, the producer tried to disassociate the production from an overly ethnic matrix, explaining that the play was not written as a "special appeal" to Jews. With some bravado it stated that Mr. Zangwill never depended on Jewish influence for success and that his aim was to write a play whose dramatic merit would "please all classes of people without distinction as to nationality or creed."

FACING AUDIENCES AND THE CRITICS

Children of the Ghetto opened at the National Theatre in Washington, D.C., on September 18, 1899. Jews in America and England regarded it as an event of great importance and monitored it anxiously, acutely aware that the embodied nature of theatrical presentation opened a new frontier in image formation. Given the significance conferred on the production as a historic first, detailed reports written by figures with intellectual stature were dispatched to the Jewish press in America and England. Richard Gottheil (1862–1936), professor of Semitics at Columbia University and president of the American Federation of Zionists, who had just returned from two months in Europe, informed his English readers that nothing newsworthy was currently transpiring for American Jewry aside from the "Zangwill month." The newspapers, he said, "have been full of Zangwill, of the Ghetto, and of its children; but chiefly of Zangwill."[38] Gottheil, who readily acknowledged his unfamiliarity with the theater, wrote that the play did not interest him half as much as the response it elicited from Jewish and Christian spectators of the "theater-going fraternity," an ephemeral entity he must have regarded as representative of the American public. He expressed the Jewish quandary when he mused, "But the Ghetto put upon the stage and brought upon the lurid glare of the footlights, carried from East Broadway to Fifth Avenue (or from Whitechapel to the Strand) and framed in gilt—what impression would it make upon the outside world, what impression would it make upon the Ghetto itself?"[39]

Cyrus Adler prepared a special report on the production for the London *Jewish Chronicle* that began by situating the opening in the public life of the American capital and highlighted its appeal and impact on non-Jews.[40] He emphasized the massive interest in the premiere and amplified its significance by explaining that the social season had not yet begun in Washington, since official and diplomatic activity did not resume until December. In addition to underscoring the event's social importance, this statement endowed the opening with an aura of national significance, though, in truth, for theater professionals, Washington was a site for out-of-town previews, referred to in show business parlance as a "dog." In addition, Adler de-ethnicized the event by reminding his readers that the number of Jews in the city was tiny, less than one percent of the population, and did not take note of Jews in the audience, though a non-Jewish reporter with a decidedly positive approach toward the production mentioned that the audience "naturally was largely composed of men and women of Mr. Zangwill's religious faith."[41] The Adler narrative makes it clear that he, like Gottheil and many others, was primarily concerned with the impact of this first bona fide Jewish presentation of self on the Gentile world. The overriding social nature of his interest is made even clearer in the concluding lines of his coverage of opening night: "I believe that . . . the effect upon the outside world will be salutary and that the Jew will be an ennobled creature in the eyes of all who have gazed upon Mr. Zangwill's drama. Who can tell—it may even bring about a Jewish revival. His is the most inspired of Jewish pens that now commands the attention of English-speaking people, and all Jews may rest secure that his high artistic instincts are saturated with a noble sympathy which will place the Jew aright before the world."[42]

Numerous newspaper reports and reviews confirm the success of the Washington production. The house was filled to capacity, breaking a record set the year before at the opening of *The Christian,* Tyler's great hit. The audience is described as attentive, responsive, and greatly stirred by the last scene of act 3. The *New York Times* reported that audience enthusiasm "broke forth at every possible point, and sometimes interrupted sentences,"[43] and the *New York World* noted that there were eleven curtain calls.[44] Though the evening ran quite a bit longer than was customary, the performance lasting between three and a half and four hours, Herne and Zangwill were cheered vigorously and called on to speak after the final curtain. The consensus was that *Children of the Ghetto* had proved a success and that the opening "unmistakably augured a long run."[45]

Audience response to the thematic novelty of the play was also monitored by theater producers, many of them Jews, who had maintained there was not sufficient general interest in the Jew as a serious stage character and that Jewish audiences would not support a dramatic venture whose main interest was Jewish life and customs.[46] The production also attracted the attention of younger intellectually minded critics, young Turks who were serious about realism and literary drama. One of them, John Corbin, fresh out of Harvard and Oxford and in 1899 the drama critic for *Harper's Weekly,* devoted more attention than others to Herne's direction, noting favorably that his imprint was immediately recognizable in the realism of details and individualization of extras. Somewhat tactlessly, Corbin went on to compare *Children of the Ghetto* with Herne's own *Shore Acres* and *The Reverend Griffith Davenport* and deemed Zangwill's play superior, faulting Herne as a dramatist for his incompatible mix of a homely milieu evoked through pedantic realism, with plots grounded in dated melodrama. Zangwill's play, he said, had none of the latter, his scenes progressing with a simplicity and inevitability that was "worthy of comparison with the best of Ibsen."[47]

After Washington the production proceeded to play for a week in Baltimore and then moved for a two-week engagement at the Walnut Street Theatre in Philadelphia. Zangwill had spent some time there during his 1898 lecture tour and was a close friend of Judge Mayer Sulzberger, whom he saluted on opening night as the "Grandfather of the Ghetto," reminding the audience that it was Sulzberger who had commissioned *Children of the Ghetto* for the Philadelphia-based Jewish Publication Society. As in Washington, the play was glowingly received by both Jews and Gentiles. The local press described the audience as spellbound, with the *Evening News* remarking on the respectfulness of the galleries, which were largely occupied by "the youth[s] who easily yield to ribaldry."[48] The play was hailed for its skillful writing. The prominent *Evening Item* announced that with the single exception of *Cyrano de Bergerac,* no play made known in America in recent years had shown such mastery of the "artistic and aesthetic value of subtle culmination of interest." The *Evening Telegraph* proclaimed, "Mr. Zangwill has given to the stage a very notable play and one that will endure for more than a season," and the *North American* predicted that the play was destined to become a classic, not only to Jews but also to the "literature of peoples." The *Philadelphia Press* particularly emphasized the ethnic theme, declaring Zangwill a pioneer of racial drama. It explained that "sectional studies" were an important part of American literature in fiction and drama, stressing that a work of such extensive scope as Zangwill's, one that attempted the representation of a whole people, with their distinctive traits and their religion in its "human manifestations," all integrated into a consistent and coherent dramatic story, was a project that had not yet been accomplished. The actors, most notably Wilton Lackaye as Reb Shemuel, were applauded, as was the richly detailed milieu created by Herne, particularly in act 4, where more than a hundred extras were on stage.[49]

The play was praised first and foremost for its stirring presentation of Jewish life. The *North American* alluded to the recent reconviction of Alfred Dreyfus in Rennes and exclaimed, "that France might see and feel a play like this!" They also assigned to the theatrical production social and political consequence: "if anything further was needed to [set] the Hebrew free from the bondage of prejudice and disdain to which he has been subjected, this play will accomplish it to all who can see, think and feel."[50] A rather thoughtful review appeared in the *Public Ledger.* It spoke of the play as provoking discussion, raising three subjects for debate: first, the future capitalization of the "newly-opened-up field of Judaism"; second, the issue of religion as a subject for the stage and the extent to which the stage could go without offending the public; and third, the debate concerning adaptation of books for the stage. These issues would become topics of intense contention when the production arrived in New York.

Jewish Philadelphia adored the production. Henrietta Szold (1860–1943), a Zionist, social reformer, author, and future founder of Hadassah, analyzed and praised the play in a talk given at a meeting of the Council for Jewish Women.[51] The *Jewish Exponent,* the city's chief Jewish paper, was permeated with a sense of restored ethnic and religious pride. Rabbi Charles I. Hoffman, writing as "Publius," described the transforming effect of the play.[52] In a confessional mode, he admitted that, like others, he was at first ill at ease with the public display of Jewish orthodoxy and its strict adherence to Jewish law in front of Christian spectators and initially felt superiority vis-à-vis the story's characters, thinking that modern Jews were "clear of such absurdities" as the matrimonial entanglement presented in the play. Such things only happened to "benighted Russian Jews," and people like himself, he thought, "cannot and ought not to be represented as responsible for such conditions."[53] However, as he became immersed in the play, he felt transformed by the serenity and sanctity of the religious sentiment enacted on stage and by the presentation of the great forces of "God-fearingness, obedience and loyalty" that offered a true portrait of Judaism, its "harsh and repellant external appearances" notwithstanding. This, he said, reinforced his identity and made him prouder than ever of being a Jew. Speaking directly to his Jewish readers, he assured them that although the outer world may not understand or appreciate the nature of Judaism so fully captured by the play, "you and I may well repeat the benediction contained in the daily ritual: 'Blessed art thou, O Lord, our God, King of the World, who hath made me an Israelite.'" Like Adler, he concluded that his fear that the production might have an injurious effect was unfounded and that the play "fully substantiates and confirms Zangwill's title to the possession of genius."[54]

En route to Broadway the production underwent some revision, including a new title: *The Zangwill Play,* with *Children of the Ghetto* as a subtitle.[55] This barely raised an eyebrow in Philadelphia, but once in New York it prompted derisive remarks about Zangwill's insatiable hunger for self-promotion. Harrison Grey Fiske, editor of the *New York Dramatic Mirror,* gibed that "the play, the programme, the electric signs and what not else connected in the production was so much and laboriously labelled all over with the name of Zangwill that one had to lift the bushel to find the light."[56] Zangwill defended the change in title as intended to avoid confusion with *The Ghetto,* an adaptation of Herman Heijermans's play that had opened at New York's Broadway Theatre on September 15.[57] One of the Netherlands' major playwrights, Heijermans (1864–1924) was an assimilated Dutch Jew who was severely critical of religious orthodoxy and bourgeois values.[58] His play, which had already drawn Jewish protest in Amsterdam, was successful in the Netherlands and France, while its English adaptation drew negative reviews in both London and New York, where it was rejected both as old-fashioned and declamatory and as anti-Jewish in its unappetizing portrayal of the ghetto as intolerant and avaricious. Zangwill regarded the producers of *The Ghetto* as interlopers and claimed that Liebler and Company had suffered in terms of publicity, since the "best" part of their title—the catchword "ghetto," toward which he felt proprietary rights—had been snatched by a competing group that tried to capitalize on the advance publicity of Zangwill's play. He claimed that this led to confusion, so that people who had purchased tickets for the Heijermans play thought they were going to see *Children of the Ghetto.* He did not criticize Heijermans directly, though he let it be known that the novel *Children of the Ghetto* had long been available in Dutch, that *Dreamers of the Ghetto* had been translated into Dutch in 1898, and that he had lectured two years earlier on "The Ghetto" in the main cities of the Netherlands.[59]

Zangwill soon became a favorite target, particularly for the sensational press. The New York *Sun* went as far as to suggest that Zangwill was actually pretending to be the play's author and credited James Herne with the dramatic adaptation of the novel, stating, "The materials were supplied by Zangwill, their modeling into dramatic shape was probably done by our own playwright."[60] Zangwill was so infuriated by this accusation that he instituted a $25,000 libel action against the *Sun,* which was later dismissed.[61] In fact, the first rumors that Zangwill was not the real author of the play had been circulating well before his arrival in America, in the wake of the hiring of Herne, a playwright himself, as stage director. In a letter dated June 24, 1899, George Tyler wrote to Zangwill, then still in England: "There is an individual by the name of Richardson who writes a column on a 'Tenderloin' paper called the Morning Telegraph, who is not at all friendly with this firm. His reason for unfriendliness was brought about by our refusal to consider any blackmailing proposition. It was this person who originated and published the story to the effect that Mr. Herne was engaged 'to remedy the defects of your stage craft.'"[62] Tyler went on to belittle the significance of the story and said that the best policy was to ignore the *Morning Telegram,* which he deemed a newspaper of "no consequence" that had printed many stories of the same sort about Liebler's other enterprises. Nevertheless, the defamation of Zangwill as quasi-plagiarist persisted enough so as to move Herne to assert its falsehood in his curtain speech at both the Washington and New York openings.

Stories about blackmail and bribery in the theater world were not uncommon at the time. With the exception of a handful of leading critics, the theater critics for daily papers were not held in high journalistic esteem and were poorly compensated. At the same time, they could significantly influence the economic viability of a producer's investment. This inevitably led to occasional intellectual and financial dishonesty. J. B. Pond recalled a story of a successful theatrical manager who, aware of his friendship with William Winter, the top New York drama critic of his time, asked Pond to facilitate an offer of $2,500 in exchange for a positive review. When told that the critic was not bribable, the frustrated manager told Pond that he had already secured the next best drama critic for half that amount.[63] Such shenanigans were not unknown in England either. The widow of London theater critic Clement Scott included in her memoirs, *Old Days in Bohemian London,* a chapter titled "Bribery and Temptation," in which she recounts incidents, albeit without identifying details, of playwrights and actors in London and New York who tried to bribe her husband, mostly by offering jewelry to her. She admits to being tempted yet insists her husband was a straight arrow.[64]

In his book on the American theater of the period, *The Stage in America,* Norman Hapgood, theater critic for the *Commercial Advertiser,* spoke openly of links between producers and newspapers and their common practice of "puffing." He wrote that the *Sun's* dramatic criticism was colored by its close association with the Theatrical Syndicate, a powerful organization of managers and theater owners whose monopoly dominated the theatrical life of the country.[65] Hapgood wrote that if *Children of the Ghetto,* which he considered an unusually strong play, had been produced by Charles Frohman, the Syndicate mainstay in New York, the producer would have been praised for his "high ideals," whereas had Liebler and Company produced some of Frohman's hits, they would have been met with a "storm of condemnation."

The *Sun's* libelous accusation as well as personal attacks by other papers were not innocently motivated. Among others, George Tyler and the *Jewish Chronicle* interpreted this anti-Zangwill campaign as payback for Zangwill's attack on critics in his infamous lecture a year earlier.[66] This was confirmed by Zangwill, who wrote with typical panache, "Ever since I lectured on the 'Drama as a Fine Art' I have been told that all the world of insect life, squirming in the sun when the old moss-grown stone was rolled over, was waiting for my blood."[67] Hapgood, who admired Zangwill's work, credited the assault to Zangwill's prickly persona. He wrote that when in public Zangwill "treated everyone badly" and that in his indiscriminate critique of managers, playwrights, actors, public, and critics, "making no explicit exception beyond himself," he understandably aroused their antipathy.[68] Zangwill exacerbated the antagonism of the theatrical press on opening night when he reiterated his argument that high-caliber literary men did not write for the stage in England and America and wisecracked that the acting and management of *Children of the Ghetto* were so perfect that if any critic could find fault with the play, the fault would lie with Zangwill or with the critic.

Anti-Zangwill sentiment among New York critics became so intense that in 1900, when his one-act *The Moment of Death* was produced by Tyler as part of a double bill, Zangwill's name was deliberately underpublicized, and the production was advertised by the title of the first lengthy piece, Harriet Ford and Beatrice de Mille's *The Greatest Thing in the World.* When Tyler commissioned the one-act play, he explained to Zangwill, "My chief object will be to force down the throats of the New York critics a Zangwill production, and secure from them, without their knowledge, a genuinely enthusiastic endorsement of his achievement. To this end I shall let no living soul know who the author of the piece is, and I write you now in regard to it, without telling my business partner. I shall not exploit the piece much in advance, and depend upon its merits alone to do the work; then, if it proves a triumph, I shall afterward let the public [know] the name of the author."[69]

The New York premiere of *Children of the Ghetto* took place on October 16, 1899, at the Herald Square Theatre. It was a glamorous affair. In his memoirs, George Tyler recalled that the audience was composed of the cream of the social register, with Sir Thomas Lipton and Lady Cunard of tea and shipping fame, respectively, in attendance.[70] The "plush and ermine audience went wild over the play," according to Tyler, a description confirmed by various journalistic sources, which reported on the packed house, the attendance of the "literary set," and the audience's enthusiastic response. Having done so well out of town, and emboldened by the initial New York response, the *Children of the Ghetto* team left the theater that night "walking on air," dead sure they had a hit on their hands.

The next day they were surprised to wake up to less than a chorus of critical praise. Most of the reviews in the daily press were mixed, though the *New York Times* declared that the play "was found to justify the expectations of its worth."[71] The acting was generally praised, especially in the confrontation scene in act 3. Blanche Bates and Frank Worthing as the young lovers were said to have rendered aboveboard portrayals, and the supporting cast, especially Adolph Lestina as Moses Ansell, Ada Dwyer as Malka, and Mabel Taliaferro as Esther, were applauded for their finely tuned portrayals. William Norris as Pinchas received mixed reviews, the feeling being that there was too much of him and that his conspicuousness ought to be moderated. Wilton Lackaye won unanimous accolade for his Reb Shemuel. His performance was hailed for its rare emotional power, humor, and tenderness, with the *New York Times* comparing him to Coquelin, the legendary French actor. His must have been a memorable performance, for six years later, when the play was produced in Yiddish, Abraham Cahan noted that the "Christian" Lackaye had offered a richer and far more genuine portrayal of the rabbi than did the Yiddish star-actor Sigmund Feinman.[72]

The positive view of the actors was not extended to the playwright, however. A savage tone prevailed in the critical din, leading Tyler to describe it as a "lynching party."[73] One of the most vitriolic notices appeared in the *Sun,* which stated that "the Zangwill Play" was not a play, but a series of incidents in ghetto life combined with a number of studies of Hebrew characters, that its central theme was tenuous and constantly interfered with by interpolations of little or no moment, that its argument was founded on a Talmudic law that was obsolete among modern Jews, and that the story, after brave pretense at something, ended in nothing.[74] That was so, it said, because the play defied "the laws of romance, the spirit of the hour, the impulses of the human heart"—presumably referring to its unhappy ending, a major point of contention ever since the infamous door slam at the end of Ibsen's *A Doll's House.*[75] The critique of the play as unsatisfactory for its lack of a strong unifying dramatic plotline depended largely on where one stood in the cultural conflict between Romantics and Realists. These opposite approaches were suggested by the *New York Times* prediction that the play would appeal more to erudite "students of the drama" than to spectators who went to the theater for occasional diversion. A voice for the former was Norman Hapgood of the *Commercial Advertiser,* who thought highly of the play. He wrote that despite the slightness of plot, the individual scenes were so greatly effective in and of themselves, and were so well staged and acted, that the dramatic interest was sustained. Moreover, the plot, though slender, was interesting, the dialogue exquisite, the production intelligent, and the stage picturesque. He regarded the characters, notably Pinchas, the crooked poet; Moses Ansell, the learned pauper; and Esther, the child grown old by responsibility, as strikingly original.[76]

Abraham Cahan, himself a realist writer who was familiar with the new Continental drama, contributed a lengthy article on the production to *The*

"It is the Law!" The confrontation scene, *Children of the Ghetto,* act 3, with Blanche Bates as Hannah, Wilton Lackaye as Reb Shemuel, and Frank Worthing as David Brandon. Photo by Byron (1899). Museum of the City of New York, Byron Collection.

Forum and proclaimed *Children of the Ghetto* "a piece of art."[77] He situated the production within what he termed the "literary anarchy" of the departing nineteenth century, where, he said, aesthetic emotion was often confounded with interest in plot and incident.[78] Cahan rejected those who judged a novel or a drama by the amount of plot it contained, as if the disentanglement of a complex set of events stood at the heart of artistic enjoyment, and compared them to the little girl who skips all the descriptive passages in the novel in order to quickly find out if at the end the hero marries the heroine. *Children of the Ghetto,* he said, did not belong to the "blood-and-thunder" school of drama and instead offered a canvas of artistically crafted details and characters that blended harmoniously into a rich tapestry of human life, with all its fun and sadness, against which the basic event evolved in the most "natural" way. He regarded the play as an artistic totality of "singular power and beauty" and assigned it to the same class as *The Weavers* by Gerhart Hauptmann (1862–1946), an innovative German dramatist who would be awarded the Nobel Prize in 1912. *The Weavers* (1892), considered Hauptmann's greatest master-piece, is a social drama focused on the 1844 revolt of Silesean weavers. Written in the spirit of naturalism, it subordinates action to circumstances and is known as a play without a hero, since it depicts an entire community, with individual characters rising and fading as the action develops. Hauptmann's work was not very well received in turn-of-the-century New York. His *Hannele*, which opened at the Fifth Avenue Theatre in 1894, was criticized as formless and blasphemous and ran for less than two weeks. *The Weavers* was produced in German in 1896 at the Irving Place Theatre and was granted a moderately successful English-language production only in 1915. It was only in the 1960s that the play found new relevance and prominence in America.

Tyler recounts that the "lynching party" was headed by Clement Scott (1841–1904), recently arrived in New York as guest critic at the *New York Herald,* a newspaper with ties to London's *Daily Telegraph,* where he had served as drama critic since 1872.[79] In addition to his ferocious *Herald* review, Scott also sent a fire-and-brimstone piece to the *Sketch* in London.[80] The latter was so acrimonious that the editor, undoubtedly taken aback, clarified in his foreword that the publication did not endorse "in any way" Scott's "philippic" and, in an obvious attempt at counterbalance, mentioned that Zangwill's *Children of the Ghetto* was "emphatically a novel to read" and that the play based on it was an important piece to see.[81] Previously London's most influential drama critic, Scott had recently been forced to resign from the *Telegraph* as a result of a major scandal created by his tirade about the immanent promiscuity of stage actresses. Though now in his dotage, and regarded by the young as an "old fogey" out of touch with the changing fabric of society and the new trends in the theater, he was still highly respected by his mostly conservative New York colleagues. C. Lewis Hind made the case that Scott wielded enormous power in the theater world precisely because he did not write for the intellectual elite, and that his readership consisted of "the great middle class of England, sane, sentimental, and entirely inartistic."[82] Scott belonged to a time and tradition where great actors ruled the stage, and plays, which served primarily as vehicles for performance, were not regarded as a branch of literature or sociology. He worshiped Henry Irving, abhorred Ibsen, and poured his wrath out on the New Drama, which he termed the "drama of the dustbin." Hind remarked wryly that if Clemmy (Scott's nickname) had his way, one would have been "debarred" from enjoying Ibsen, Chekhov, Brieux, Gorki, Shaw, Galsworthy, and others, and would be condemned "to sit out the intolerable inanities of *The Sign of the Cross,*" deprived of the self-questioning aroused by *The Second Mrs. Tanqueray* and *Mrs. Warren's Profession.*[83]

Scott opened his *Herald* review with the imperial bellicosity with which he targeted dramatic revolutionaries and Ibsenite drama. He began with explicit use of the first person: "As I write after an evening of boredom and astonishment, the Zangwill play seems to me one fine dramatic moment [i.e., the confrontation scene in act 3] sandwiched between a somewhat silly farce and an occasionally blasphemous pantomime."[84] Most of his ire was directed at the Jewish material, finding its "episodic matter" excessive. He conceded patronizingly that it might be interesting to a "Hebrew audience," but deemed it wholly uninteresting to Christians. He dismissed act 4 and its depiction of Passover Eve in the ghetto as a tedious parade of people going in and coming out of a nearby synagogue and haughtily remarked: "[The scene is] most attractive to the inhabitants of the Ghetto, I am prepared to admit, but a little tedious to those who have not a camera at hand to take snapshots at this scene of pantomime detail." Scott was especially incensed by the character of Melchitsedek Pinchas, the Hebrew poet, whom he regarded as "a very offensive Jew," one who "out-Herods Herod," and declared him "the worst stage Hebrew ever known in farce or melodrama."[85] Christians, he complained, had been admonished for ridiculing the Jews with the tawdry stage Hebrew, but Pinchas, he said, in vulgarity and noise outdid even Svengali and the crude Jewish characters created by Harry Jackson at Drury Lane. He practically accused Zangwill of dramatic anti-Semitism, saying, "here we have a Hebrew author showing the seamy side of Judaism on the stage in a manner that has never been done before, and with all accuracy of realistic detail," and went on to ask rhetorically whether Israel Zangwill was laughing up his sleeve at his own people.[86] He evoked Irving, his hero, and thundered indignantly, "At a time when a Henry Irving has shown us a pathetic and poetic Shylock, it has been reserved for a Zangwill to create a Pinchas, and to put in his mouth words which made at least one Christian shocked at the profanity that no sense of realistic art can justify."[87]

It would be facile and not altogether wrong to deride Scott as old-fashioned, ethnocentric, and patronizing, a voice of empire deigning to allow an alien Jew to exist within the hegemonic face of an Irving. At the same time, the extremism of his comments notwithstanding, his anger points to some genuine issues that arise when an ethnic or minority culture is presented on the mainstream stage to an auditorium made up of two audiences with different cultural codes and expectations. Jewish religious legalism, synagogue prayers, and the frantic preparations for the Passover holiday carry emotional weight for Jewish spectators, but could fatigue an audience unfamiliar with the "hum and buzz of implication." Even John Corbin, who applauded the production when he saw it in Washington, interjected into his accolades a comment that the meaning of some "details of stage realism" were not presented clearly "to the Gentile mind," even though the more "recondite features" were explained in the program.[88]

Some reviewers took the matter beyond the question of comprehensibility. Edwin S. Bettelheim, while praising the "splendid collection of Hebrew sketches," raised the issue of Gentile interest, questioning the appeal of the production, "considering we have almost a Ghetto on our own East Side."[89] Though his implied contrast of "we" as opposed to an unspecified "them," presumably the immigrant Jews of the Lower East Side, is annoying, his query regarding the interest of a mainstream audience in an ethnographic-driven depiction of traditional Jewish life is not insignificant from a theatrical point of view. While in Zangwill's novel Jewish customs and mores were translated and explained by the omnipotent voice of the author, on stage they existed independently, expected to transmit meaning and aesthetic pleasure despite their relative opaqueness. Indeed, Gottheil, who was interested in and familiar with the ghetto, argued that in and of itself the ghetto was neither interesting nor outwardly beautiful, that it was Zangwill who, with his sparkling wit and artistic presentations, had made it engaging and beautiful, that is, had romanticized its drab reality.[90] Once presented on a realistic stage, with its accent on verisimilitude, the play lost the "Zangwill atmosphere" and was, he said, probably of interest to Jews only.[91]

Problems in intercultural communication extended beyond ceremonies and objects. Scott, for one, felt lost and frustrated when faced with the self-deprecating nature of Jewish humor, which, as in his denunciation of Melchitsedek Pinchas, he also failed to see contextually. He wrote with astonishment about the many Jews in the audience who did not flinch when "allusions to the 'Messiah' are coarsely tossed out of the lips of the comic and profane Jew, when this same individual on the night of the Passover sneers at the 'Paschal Lamb' and calls it the 'Paschal Pig.'"[92] Scandalized and repelled by realist depiction of lower-class life, he warned that if the use of coarse language could be justified as authentic, the stage would soon be deluged with "the verbal filth and vocabulary offal of the Seven Dials," a London area notorious for its poverty, crime, and prostitution.[93] Again, Gottheil addresses this issue almost as if in response to the feeling of cultural disorientation that emerges from the reviews of Scott and others. In Gottheil's opinion, such responses demonstrated how impossible it was for a Gentile to genuinely understand the Jewish character "of the Ghetto type." He explained, "the inclination to make sport of himself, to speak in a humorous way of things which are very sacred to him is a characteristic which must necessarily jar upon the ears of the outsider. He cannot understand the difference between this humour and rank blasphemy; he cannot understand how an audience, composed largely of Jews, can applaud such humour and listen to it with complacence."[94]

Another major issue of critical contention, again presented most vociferously by Clement Scott, was the performance of religious rituals, especially prayers, on stage. In his repudiation Scott reflected England's rigid policy of protecting the dignity of religion on the stage. A firmly established protocol that was pedantically maintained by the Examiner of Plays at the Lord Chancellor's Office included a ban on presentation of biblical subjects and the ridicule of clergy, as well as on the frequent use of God's name and the enunciation of oaths and scriptural verse. Scott explained his credo as follows: "I hold that religion, or a realistic reproduction of religious ritual dear to anyone in the audience, be it in favour of Jew or Gentile, Catholic or Protestant, has no more right to be discussed or represented on the stage than any religious topic [has] a right to be brought up in mixed society at the dinner-table or in the drawing room. Good taste forbids them in society; good taste should forbid them on the stage."[95] Such opinions were indeed the norm until 1880, but by century's end they had fallen behind public opinion, where those objecting to religious drama were but a conservative minority.[96] It was in this spirit that Zangwill's play *The Next Religion* was refused a license in January 1912, with the censor objecting to incidental phrases such as "The real Good Friday would be that which brought the cure to cancer."[97]

To Scott's mind, the "crowning act of daring" in *Children of the Ghetto* happens in act 4, when Reb Shemuel, dressed in his "shroud," blesses his daughter on stage with a direct allusion to the "Almighty God." This demonstrates yet again the cultural misunderstandings that surrounded the production. Unlike Jewish spectators, Scott was unaware of the fact that the "shroud" was a *kitl,* a white robe that is not limited to serving for burials but is also the traditional garment donned by the leader of the Passover seder. Nevertheless, Scott tried to hinge his objection on a statement by Dr. Herman Adler, the chief rabbi of London, who, according to Scott, had condemned as offensive the use of Hebrew prayers and hymns in the London production of Heijermans's *The Ghetto* (1899).[98] Adler's protest, though, was undoubtedly connected to the perceived anti-Jewish sentiment of Heijermans's play. Moreover, it must have been influenced by English, not Jewish norms, as demonstrated

Reb Shemuel (Wilton Lackaye), dressed in a *kitl,* blesses his daughter, Hannah (Blanche Bates). New York production of *Children of the Ghetto,* act 4. Photo by Byron (1899). Museum of the City of New York, Byron Collection.

by the fact that one of the most beloved and emotionally satisfying features of the Yiddish stage, clearly a genuine expression of Jewish theatrical tradition, was the performance of religious ceremonies and the singing of cantorial music. Given the thorniness of the sacrilege accusation, Abraham Cahan took it to two orthodox rabbis of the New York Ghetto. The first, Rabbi Chaim Yaakov Widerwitz, a much-respected Talmudic scholar, confirmed the validity of the play's legal entanglement and offered an opinion regarding the question of sacrilege: "If they don't utter the Name, and the whole play is not calculated to make fun of our religion or our people, there can be no objection."[99] He explained further that as the explicit name of God did not appear in the Kaddish prayer, and if the cantor did not pronounce the Name in *Yigdal* and *Borchu*—the prayers over which Scott was fuming—there was no offense in performing them on the stage.[100] Rabbi Samuel Wine took a similarly lenient approach, dismissing the question with "there are much graver sins in the world than to sing *Kaddish* in a theatre."[101] Unlike Scott, who decontextual-ized the subject of sacrilege, the rabbi concluded that it all depended on the spirit in which the religious material was taken; if the play told the truth, and no scorn was intended, then there was no sin.

Furious over Scott's damaging transatlantic offensive, Zangwill wrote a stinging response that appeared in London's *Jewish World* and was reproduced in Philadelphia's *Jewish Exponent.* He mocked Scott's "shock" over the play's use of terms such as "Messiah" and "Paschal Lamb," saying that he ought to know that in a Jewish context they had none of the invested Christian asso-ciations. In Jewish thought, he said, the Messiah was merely a man and the Paschal Lamb merely a shadowy survivor of the ritual offering in Jerusalem. In this Zangwill implicitly demanded that Scott, here a representative of the majority's Christian culture, adopt a bicultural lens that would allow him to appreciate concepts that hold a specific meaning for him through the eyes of the Jewish minority. Additionally, he ridiculed Scott, whom he labeled the "austere preacher of morality on the London stage," by contrasting his agita-tion over the performance of religious rituals and prayers with his enthusiastic endorsement of *Zaza,* a sexually provocative hit show. Addressing Scott in the second person, he said, "Your being shocked at these is really comic, for as you are not a pious Jew yourself, your only shock could have been that the Jews present were not shocked."[102] Why should they be shocked any more than Christians were by the hymns and organ anthems used in dramas from *Faust* to *The Christian?* he asked. The stage, Zangwill asserted, is as holy as a pulpit in a cathedral or a synagogue, for "where ever an honest man stands, there is holy ground."[103]

Not only was the press hostile, but New York Jews did not offer a warm communal embrace either. Again, Richard Gottheil foresaw much of what would happen when he wrote immediately after the New York opening:

> I have not yet seen what the Jewish press has to say about it. But from my talk with a number of people who were present I should qualify my own statement [that the play would be of interest only to Jews] and say, only to Jews who have still retained connection with the Ghetto and understand its life. The "Up-towners" are largely weak-kneed, and do not like to think that a Ghetto still exists or that they have any reason to be identified with it. They are faint-hearted and fear the impression of themselves, as if in some way Children of the Ghetto as well will work them ill in their social aspirations. They are to be pitied.[104]

On October 18, two days after the New York premiere, the *New York Times* took the unusual step of publishing an editorial about the production. Written from an unmistakably uptown Jewish perspective, it made no mention of the play's artistic attributes nor of the paper's own theatrical review, but was ghosted by its proprietor's ethos. The *Times* had been owned since 1896 by Adolphe S. Ochs (1858–1935), the son of German Jewish immigrants, who had transformed it from a near-defunct publication into a powerhouse in the life of the city. Ochs was married to the daughter of Rabbi Isaac Mayer Wise (1819–1900), the greatly admired leader of the Reform movement in America, and was soon to become a devoted trustee of Temple Emanu-El. He was also very sensitive about being Jewish, that being, according to author David Halberstam, "a dominating characteristic about him."[105] The *Times* editorial reads as follows:

> It will seem to many, we think, that in making *The Children of the Ghetto* what it is, Mr. Israel Zangwill has utilized his knowledge of a race and a religion in a way to tempt criticism at once just and severe,—has as it were, betrayed confidences made to him, not as a novelist or a playwright, but as a man born and bred in a certain faith. Mr. Zangwill has always emphasized the fact that he is a Jew. Thereby he voluntarily assumed, both toward his own people and toward others, an especially heavy responsibility. His co-religionists can fairly demand from him a loyalty beyond question or suspicion, and to the followers of other faiths he owes absolute accuracy when he undertakes to explain the peculiarities of his own to them. *The Children of the Ghetto* meets neither of these demands. Its author presents the most sacred of Jewish rites, not in their highest, but in their lowest phases, not as a plea for respect, but as an excuse for laughter. This is disloyalty. He repeatedly ignores both the probabilities and the possibilities of Jewish life, and this is to misinform and mislead such of his auditors as he does not grieve or offend. Of course, no hard and fast line can ever be drawn between the facts of personal knowledge and experience which the artist may use with propriety and those which he should hold sacred from any artistic exploitation. But that a distinction of this sort does nevertheless exist, real though constantly changing with motive and circumstance, would hardly be denied, even by those who claim for the artist the widest liberty in the choice of his material. If, in the effort to display his talent or his genius, and to win the rewards, monetary and other, of such display, he passes the

wavering limits of taste and decency, his offense is a most grave one. Of this offense all sensitive playgoers, whatever their creed, will be sure to convict the author of *The Children of the Ghetto.*[106]

Such stern editorial condemnation undoubtedly intensified the anxiety and confusion experienced by uptown Jews that had been brewing since the announcement of the forthcoming production. The *American Hebrew,* the city's leading English-language Jewish weekly, had been full of stories on Zangwill and the ghetto since September. The paper's ample preopening coverage encouraged interest. At the same time, it conveyed a disquieting double message, promising that Zangwill's play would be a powerful tool for creating a truer appreciation of "what the Jew is and what he stood for" in America, while reassuring readers they need not fear that the play would cause them to be confused for ghetto Jews, a statement that awakened the very fear it wished to allay.[107] Given the production's perceived importance, substantial coverage of it and related topics continued well after the New York opening. The *American Hebrew* was inundated with letters to the editor, reports of sermons pertaining to the play, and scholarly essays on its central legal issue, whereby rabbis and communal leaders seized an opportunity to further their respective causes. Other material focused on topics tangential to the production: there was an essay on religion in dramatic art, a report from Denver on the recent trials and tribulations of the poet Naphtali Herz Imber, the model for Melchitsedek Pinchas, and proposed theories on the origins of the name "Zangwill."

The focus of much of the scholarly debate concerned the legal validity of the mock marriage between Hannah Jacobs and Sam Levine and the question of whether it required a divorce, and whether a divorce in such a special case would indeed constitute an impediment to marriage of a divorced woman with a Cohen. In an admiring review of the play, Rabbi Maurice H. Harris, a London native serving as rabbi of Temple Israel in Harlem, maintained that Zangwill presented Jewish law accurately, labeling it "a triumph of Jewish law," a pronouncement subsequently used as an advertising blurb and posted in New York streetcars, undoubtedly to the chagrin of many uptown Jews. Writing from Louisville, Kentucky, Lewis N. Dembitz, a prominent lawyer and legal scholar, offered differing Mishnaic and Talmudic texts to demonstrate the legal indeterminacy of the case. Although he accepted Zangwill's rendition of the law, he argued that if indeed Judaism suffered from this "ugly defect" that would thwart the marriage of Hannah and David, it would be better "to cover the naked spot" than to bring it into the public gaze and charged that Zangwill had done so merely to gain wealth and fame.[108] Rabbis Morris Mandel, from the nation's capital, and Dr. Frederick de Sola Mendes of the West End Synagogue of New York, separately wrote that the mock marriage was nonbinding, since Jewish law required the consent of the bride to a marriage.[109] Distraught over the play, De Sola Mendes roared, "Hannah does not consent to a real marriage. Nor can a betrothal hold with one who is already betrothed, as Levene [*sic*] is. Therefore, there is no marriage; therefore, there is no divorce; therefore, Hannah may legally marry Brandon; therefore, the 'play' falls to pieces (as it deserves)." Laymen, he warned, should not meddle with the law, and the play, if a triumph of anything, was the "triumph of ignorance of Jewish Law."[110] Not so, argued Rabbi Dr. Gotthard Deutsch with great authority. A professor of Jewish history and philosophy of religion at the Hebrew Union College of Cincinnati, he cited two pertinent cases mentioned in Rabbinic literature, one in the Responsa of Samuel Aboab, rabbi of Venice (1702), the other in the Responsa of Z'bi Ashkenazi, rabbi of Sarajewa, Altona, Amsterdam, and Lemberg (1712).[111] He explained that legally a mock marriage is considered "dubious matrimony," that it does necessitate a divorce, and that after the divorce the woman could not marry a Cohen, so that Zangwill's presentation was entirely accurate.

Some rabbis appropriated the play as a sermon topic to promote their own agendas. Samuel Schulman, a young rabbi, gave a Sunday sermon at Temple Beth-El in which he denounced Zangwill, stating that he had "done his people an injury." He complained that the "badness" of the play resulted from its incomplete depiction of the full scope of Jewish life and suggested that the author should have made the character of David Brandon the representative of modern Reform Judaism. He went on to argue that if Reb Shemuel did not object to David Brandon's violation of Leviticus by shaving his face, why would he force him to abide by the law regarding the marriage ban on the union of a Cohen and a divorcée and thus bring tragedy to his beloved daughter?[112] This feeble argument was appropriated for mockery by those opposed to Sunday Jewish services, then a contentious issue in Reform Judaism, and a vociferous dispute ensued.[113]

Rabbinic muscle-flexing notwithstanding, the crux of the debate among Jews was the presentation of Jewishness to Christian America. Reflecting this anxiety of its readership, the *American Hebrew* solicited the opinion of the Honorable Thomas L. James (1831–1916), postmaster general under President James A. Garfield. In a brief introductory note, the editors explained that James's opinion had been invited to offer an idea of how the play had affected "persons not of our faith and unfamiliar with the forms and ceremonies delineated upon the stage."[114] James's statement was simple and direct. He considered the play "strong, sinewy and powerful." Greatly different from anything he had ever before seen, it revealed "phases of human life" entirely new to him.[115] He was not at all put off by its religious nature and found its portrayal of Jewish orthodoxy vivid and realistic, revealing Jewish tradition in all its sternness and ruggedness. He found it "not at all unlike the Puritan belief of 'thus saith the Lord' of a century ago," a statement undoubtedly relished by many of the paper's readers most keen to assert their American identity.[116]

The Jewish laity response to the New York production of *Children of the Ghetto* was unanimous. Jacob H. Hollander, author and professor of political economy at Johns Hopkins University, praised the construction of the play as marking a new development in American drama, hailed its sympathetic portrayal of Jewish life, which he said would foster Gentile comprehension of a "misunderstood people," and predicted that it would have an energizing effect on the modernization of Judaism.[117] Max Ellinger, on the other hand, considered Zangwill's Jews to be a travesty, a caricature of a degenerated ghetto. "To bring the distorted figures of the East End Ghetto," he wrote, "which teems with superstition and ignorance upon the stage and make the world believe that these figures are the types of true orthodox Jew, these Jews that present no redeeming feature to our modern eye, is a wrong, which should not only meet with the protest of every Israelite who thinks something of the fair game of his people, but most decidedly of every orthodox Jew."[118]

The *American Hebrew* also published two letters written by women, each representing an opposing view of the theatrical production. The first, by a Miss Malka Pinchas, was a paean to the play, preceded by an admission of initial reservations. The second, by Gertrude Veld, disapproved of the production for practical, not artistic reasons, explaining that "our religion is sufficiently made a farce of as it is, without having it *staged,* to be ridiculed, perhaps."[119] Ms. Veld, not a very fluent writer, but a self-described "aspirant for histrionic honors," drew attention to the tangible aspect of the theatrical performance and to intra-audience communication. She recalled her visit to the Herald Square Theatre. About 75 percent of the audience were Christian. "Do you think they come out of respect to the Jew?" she asked, "No! Merely as I heard some, who were seated in the row behind me, to make sneering remarks, and look upon the entire play as a farce to amuse them." Veld's close attentiveness to the reactions of Gentile spectators is typical of the interaction that transpires in an auditorium with two distinct audiences, be the dividing line religion, ethnicity, race, or gender. The auditorium reverberates with the tension of mutual looked-at-ness, with the spectators who identify with the hegemonic group often taking their cues from the minority members. Those, in turn, like Veld, secretly monitor the mainstream response to the material presented on stage. Veld's simplistic conclusion was that Zangwill's "beautiful pictures" ought not have been paraded in the flesh, but rather should have "remained in the book from which they originated."[120]

One voice conspicuously absent from this medley of opinions was that of the ghetto. It did not occur to anyone at the *American Hebrew* to go downtown and ask the people whose lives were depicted onstage what they thought and felt. It was a year later when Hutchins Hapgood, whose sympathies lay with the ghetto, described the dichotomy in the uptown/downtown responses to the production: "the organs of the swell up-town German-Jew protested that it was a pity to represent faithfully in art the sordidness as well as the beauty of the poor Russian Ghetto Jew." The uptown Jews, he explained, were ashamed to have their proletarian brethren as subject of literature and drama. The downtown Jews received the play with pleasure and found it to express "truthfully their life and character, of which they are not ashamed."[121]

The heated controversy surrounding the play had an adverse effect on the box office. This had been predicted by the *New York Times* critic, who wrote that an "excess of notoriety" would hurt rather than help the play, citing as example *The Sign of the Cross,* a production that had enjoyed phenomenal success in England but failed in America due to public controversy.[122] Tyler, who at first hoped for a repetition of the phenomenon surrounding *The Christian,* a play that was ill-received by the critics but a great hit with the theatergoing public, remained to the end completely devoted to Zangwill's play, which he regarded as grand. He fought tooth and nail to keep the production up, blaming the critics for discouraging both Christians and Jews from attending, and even produced a two-page broadsheet in which he accused "a certain coterie of the so-called dramatic critics of New York" of maliciously plotting to destroy the production. (See the entire text of the pamphlet at the end of this section.) In an interview with the *Jewish Chronicle* Zangwill alleged yet another source of conspiracy to destroy his play: "Almost the whole of it was the work of pseudonymous Jewish journalists, men who are without a scrap of religion, with their tongues in their cheek and their bribes in their pockets."[123] Whether there was in fact such conspiracy is impossible to ascertain. However, the strikingly different receptions in Washington, Baltimore, Philadelphia, and New York leave open the possibility that strings had indeed been pulled behind the scenes.

As is usually the case, fighting the press proved a lost cause. Tyler, who had originally made vague plans for a parallel London production, decided to ship the entire American cast to the West End, and on November 25, bruised and battered, the New York engagement of *Children of the Ghetto* was terminated.

New York Criticism

The management of the Zangwill Play, "Children of the Ghetto," have a word to say to the theatre-going public of New York, and it takes this method of saying it for the simple reason that its members are not the owners of a newspaper and are hence voiceless, so far as press opportunities go, in its own defence.

They respectfully assert that "Children of the Ghetto" was presented in three cities before its merits and demerits were offered for analysis by the theatre-going public of New York. In those cities it had large audiences, ordinarily much larger than were obtained by rival attractions, and the consensus of opinion was so pronouncedly in its favor that the management does not hesitate to say that never before in the history of the American stage were such enthusiastic notices published of an attraction, never before was such a unanimity of sentiment shown, never before has there such a disregard for space been evident, as in the treatment extended the Zangwill Play by the press in Washington, Baltimore and Philadelphia, in which cities it had alone appeared before entering New York. There was scarcely a voice raised save in praise, and this was given without persuasion and without stint. To an intelligent mind it is simply the height of absurdity to credit this to the work of "the press agent." There is neither common-sense nor sense of fairness in the pretense that the dramatic critics of the newspapers in those cities are all numbskulls, or all venal.

It is the knowledge of the facts embodied in the above paragraphs, and not with an egotistical confidence in their own judgement alone, that the management herewith respectfully files its protest against the eagerness and banditti-like concert of action with which a certain coterie of the so-called dramatic critics of New York seek to destroy, either for pecuniary compensation or with a malevolence that would charm the soul of an Australian bushman, all theatrical attractions which do not emanate from their own peculiar source of supply, or which, perchance, in their cafe councils, for other reasons, "deserve to be knocked." These men have made their profession a byword and a subject of contempt in nearly every household in New York. So unfair has been the treatment accorded, that it has become a recognized, palpable fact to every intelligent reader in the city. Thank God there are honorable exceptions to this rule, and when this management speaks of a "coterie" it wants it distinctly understood that it recognizes the fact that there are newspaper critics in New York whose reviews, whether favorable or reverse, always command respect, as the honest opinions of honest men.

The management of "Children of the Ghetto" do not speak for themselves alone, who have had to suffer much, and without recourse, at the hands of these banditti, and it speaks for every theatrical management in New York engaged in honest endeavor, who should have a right to present such productions as they may deem becoming and worthy, and submit them to an intelligent public, for its approval or condemnation, without being subjected to an attempt at assassination by a mercenary and malevolent clique organized for that purpose, and to whom an inscrutable Providence has, for some singular reason, given temporary power and opportunity. It speaks for the theatre-going public as well, who, as these gentlemen will eventually find out, are crying as loudly for protection as the managers themselves.

In their strictures upon the Zangwill Play there was as much to be observed that would excite amusement as contempt. For instance, the writer has collated a parallel column of extracts from the so-called criticisms of the first night production, in which the play was extolled, in

its entirety and in its detail, while in the adjoining collated column it is violently condemned. That is to say,
one critic finds fault with this and praises that, while another does his knocking at another portion and praises
that which the other condemns. It is an interesting parallel column, and shows not only how much little sincerity
there is in the criticisms but also how much value should
be placed upon such lucubrations.

There is much, however, that was deserving of the se-
verest censure, and was well calculated to try the temper
of even a modest and peace loving man. Language was
put into mouths of men that had never been used, facts
were misrepresented, a gentleman, whose life has been
blameless, and whose intellectual standing is such that
he has ever been the recipient, wherever he might go,
of naught but kindly distinction and deserved consideration, is treated like a pick pocket and a tramp, the whole
purport and purpose of his play distorted, and with a
venom born either of ignorance or malicious intent, an
effort is made, through the vilest misrepresentation, to
prejudice against his play his own people—a people for
whose up-building and in a demand for justice for whom
he has perhaps devoted more energy and zeal than any
other living man.

Among intelligent communities everywhere the very
name Zangwill stands for the pleas for justice for the Jew.
What has he done to bring down upon his head this malevolent and vicious diatribe? Some months ago he delivered a lecture in the Lyceum Theatre on "Drama as a
Fine Art," which did not tickle the fancy of these hydro-
cephalic arbiters of fate. This was the sum and substance
of his offending, no more.

The management asks for nothing but fair and honest
criticism, and will not complain if that criticism be unfavorable. It respectfully protests, however, against virulent and mendacious abuse, indulged in for the basest of
purpose; and owing no newspaper it proposes to say so, if

it has to say it in handbills pasted on the bill-boards and deadwalls. It is with the public The Zangwill Play has to deal, and to its fairness the management is not afraid to submit its destiny, standing ready to abide the issue, no matter what that verdict may be.

We believe "Children of the Ghetto" is a great play, one of the greatest if not the greatest of the season. In this view, almost without exception, all fair-minded and un-biased newspaper men who have seen it have coincided. If the theatre-going public of New York do not think so let it die the death, so far as New York success is con-cerned, but we must respectfully protest against its death at the hand of the hired assassin.

LIEBLER & CO.

THE AFTERMATH

Tyler admitted in his memoirs that when he sent the American production of *Children of the Ghetto* to London, the English stage was for him a totally un-tried field. "All I knew about it when I started," he wrote, "was that I'd had to pay twelve thousand dollars cash down to get a London theatre to play in."[124] He risked the money, he said, because he was "sore" about the New York debacle and was hoping for a big "British victory," one that would vindicate his efforts and secure the future of the production, in which he staunchly believed.[125] Yet while the American production had been carefully prepared and heavily advertised, its transportation to the West End was fraught with difficulty and characterized by unfamiliarity and a paucity of time and local contacts. This was manifest in, among other things, the dearth of a well-thought-out publicity campaign aimed at the English market. Stung by bitter experience, Tyler had specifically asked that the play not be advertised as a "Jewish play," a label he believed to be at the heart of their misfortune in New York.[126] The production was thus trumpeted as a great American success, a claim ridiculed by the London *Times,* which noted, "If *Children of the Ghetto* was really as successful in New York as we have been told, it is difficult to understand how America can have spared it to London so soon."[127]

Though the production was transferred basically intact, including such offstage staff as Tyler's property man, electrician, and stage carpenter, some cast changes proved inevitable. Blanche Bates and Frank Worthing, who had originated the roles of Hannah Jacobs and David Brandon, jumped ship in favor of *Naughty Anthony,* a new David Belasco production scheduled to open at the Herald Square Theatre, just vacated by *Children of the Ghetto.* Bates was replaced by Rosabel Morrison, her understudy, who took over the part during the play's last week in New York. Morrison was a Jewish actress whose only shortcoming, according to Tyler, was that she was not as beautiful as her predecessor.[128] Robert Edeson, the new David Brandon, was a well-respected professional who had costarred two years earlier with Maude Adams in James M. Barrie's hit *The Little Minister,* a play whose denouement hinged on the old Scottish law—also mentioned in *Children of the Ghetto*—that determined that if a couple declared themselves man and wife before witnesses, they were considered married. In addition, English actors were engaged locally for some of the smaller parts.

In his haste to transport the production and keep the ball rolling, Tyler overlooked some important factors. He brushed aside the possible impact of the Boer War (1899–1902), which had begun in October, and disregarded the fact that the Adelphi Theatre, where the play was to open, had traditionally catered to devotees of melodrama, a genre with which it was popularly associated. Additionally, he opted to open shortly before Christmas, less than ideal timing for a realist portrayal of Jewish ghetto life, and did not consider the negative residual effect of the recent failure of Heijermans's *Ghetto,* a production that had received much more attention in London than in New York. Moreover, Tyler was abroad, arriving in London only days before the opening. The effect of his absence became all too obvious when upon arrival he saw the locally hired extras, who should have been rehearsed letter-perfect. He recalls in his memoirs: "And, lord, what a mess I ran into! The bright young man I'd sent over to arrange matters had hired a bunch of rank cockneys and made them up to look like Jews—which they didn't at all—they looked like Weber and Fields with a dash of Fagan [*sic*]. I blew up completely at that point—went diving in among them and started pulling putty noses right and left."[129] Two days before the opening, with Zangwill at his side, Tyler hastened to London's Petticoat Lane, where the playwright, a celebrity beloved of the ghetto, was hauled onto a platform and required to make a speech. When Tyler offered two shillings a night for extras, double the going rate, there was a great clamor to be chosen, and seventy-five people were hired. With a rich selection of authentic extras, the crepe beards and fake noses were discarded, and the appearance of verisimilitude, crucial for the Passover Eve scene, was restored. Much maligned in New York, this scene went on to win praise in

London for its "subtly wrought interaction" of music and color, which one reviewer termed "a revelation."[130] Interestingly, the actors' American accents, though commented on, did not particularly jar English ears.

When *Children of the Ghetto* opened on December 11, 1899, at the Adelphi, English theatergoers had not been prepared for the production and, as some reviewers suggested, were mostly uninterested in the performance of Jewish lore. Unlike some sections of Protestant America, Londoners did not identify with Reb Shemuel's religious fundamentalism. The literary success of Zangwill's depictions of Jewish life notwithstanding, English society was insular, unaccustomed to the diversity introduced by mass immigration; nor was it free from anti-Semitic sentiment, recently augmented by rumors that London Jewish financiers had conspired with coreligionist mine owners in South Africa to push Britain into a war that would serve their personal economic interests. Even acculturated Jews were generally regarded as an alien element; all the more so ghetto Jews, who some intellectuals and artists found quaint, but many more viewed as repellent. For example, the *Queen*, a genteel self-described "Lady's Newspaper," did not beat around the bush when it pronounced, "To be quite plain, the fact of the matter is that the ordinary English play-goer does not find illustrations of Jewish life and customs in the least entertaining."[131] In the same vein, the *Athenaeum* remarked, "that the Yiddish language in which Mr. Zangwill is an adept should win its way further across the footlights is scarcely to be desired. It is not now spoken in average Jewish circles, but is confined to the inhabitants of what Mr. Zangwill calls, rather arbitrarily, 'The Ghetto.'"[132]

The *Outlook*, which admired the production, described the Jewish life presented in the play, though located in the heart of the capital, as more exotic and remote from Gentile London than any sights David Brandon could have encountered in his wanderings "between the Table Mountain and the Zambesi."[133] Though it admitted that the real children of the ghetto "talk English no better and no worse than the rest of their fellow citizens in Shoreditch" and do not differ from other English subjects in superficial aspects such as the clothing and entertainments they favor, it said their essential alienness was seen when one looked at their faces and gained entry to their thoughts. Though the *Outlook* was captivated by the ghetto characters, citing the wonderful multifacetedness represented in Guedalyah, a lowly greengrocer who while selling cabbages all day is preoccupied with plans for effecting a Jewish return to Zion, it confirmed Guedalyah's and the other characters' fundamental un-Englishness. In a similar vein, the respectable *Athenaeum* declared authoritatively that the play demonstrated that "the Jew remains always a Jew."[134]

Even though Jews had resided in London for generations, their religious customs were neither comprehensible nor particularly intriguing to most critics. The reviewer for the *Era,* the city's foremost theatrical paper, exclaimed, "It is all very odd and curious," suggesting with a mix of cluelessness and xenophobia that perhaps in lieu of the playwright's rhymed prologue, the audience should have received an explanatory dictionary. "Let us understand," he wrote, "why the characters in *Children of the Ghetto,* as they enter a house, rub their hands upon a kind of match-striker nailed to the wall, and afterwards suck them. Let us be informed why the Jews in the East-end of London a generation ago draped their brick stoves with velvet table covers bearing an 'Abracadabra.'"[135] Mocking the play's topic and realistic style, he suggested that the author deliver a lecture on "Hebrew home life a hundred years ago" in the intervals between acts, so that his stage pictures might serve "the same purpose as the magic lantern views which are often employed to illustrate instructive discourses."[136]

Still, the influential London *Times* gave the production an excellent review, though not of the sort that would suggest mass appeal. It paid attention not only to the unconventional subject matter but also to the play's construction, linking it to Continental realism. It suggested that Zangwill's aim was not to create a tight, compact drama, but to construct a picture, much like Hauptmann's *The Weavers.* The author, it said, had characters coming and going without direct reference to the central story, but, it noted, they contributed to the overall effect, which, on the whole, the *Times* found most interesting. It reported that the first two acts dragged somewhat and commented that the weakness of the story stemmed from the fact that its motive held little appeal for the ordinary playgoer. At the same time, it was greatly impressed with the presentation of the conflict between the old world and the new, between faith and passion. Like most, it commended the high quality of the acting, most particularly the portrayals of Reb Shemuel and Melchitsedek Pinchas.[137] J. T. Grein, who served as a clarion of the New Drama and was an admirer of the Paris naturalist Théâtre Libre of André Antoine, praised Zangwill in his *Sunday Special* review for breaking new ground and directing his gaze at a part of London life of which the West End was "strangely ignorant." He found the story "engrossing" and its treatment "artistic," and the production, he said, was "palpitating with life."[138] He conceded that the play would find fewer adherents in England than in other countries, where, he said, the public had been more theatrically sophisticated, with an appreciation for the playwright as "the miniature painter of life no less than the skillful inventor of fascinating intrigues."[139] He reiterated his high opinion in his year-end theater survey, where he listed the play as one of the three most important productions on the London stage, the other two being *The Only Way,* by the Rev. Freeman Wills, and George Bernard Shaw's *The Devil's Disciple.*[140]

Like their American counterparts, English Jews had been concerned about the impact of the production on their status and public image, but the early dispatches from America must have had a calming effect. Already in September, London's *Jewish World* proclaimed after the Washington opening, "The nervous can be re-assured. The fears of many may be allayed. Mr. Zangwill has done the right thing. He has avoided caricature; scoffing is alien to the characters he has drawn."[141] Unlike New York, London held local pride in Zangwill, the community's successful son. Accordingly, as soon as it received news of the London production, the *Jewish Chronicle,* in addition to its usual ongoing reports on Zangwill's activities, began to drum up interest by including related material in every issue—a "soft" interview with Zangwill about the play, a "chat" with the American manager, a serious essay by Israel Abrahams on "Reb Shmuel as a Lawyer," as well as various short items of questionable newsworthiness. The subject of Jews and the drama was also given prominence, as if the approaching "absolutely Jewish play" would allow the community to claim distinction as producers and consumers in another popular field of British life.[142]

According to the *Jewish World,* the opening-night audience was almost entirely Jewish. The ceremonial aspect of the opening was not lost on Sir Samuel Montagu, MP (Member of Parliament) for the East End, who choreographed his entry to earn cheers from his constituents in the gallery, stepping in while the orchestra was playing the "Maoz Tsur" part of the musical prelude. The audience was a microcosm of London Jewry, assembled to see and immerse itself in the representation of some aspects of its life and heritage. Every detail was observed through the filter of personal knowledge and memory. While Gentile critics found the religious details incomprehensible, the *Jewish World* remarked on minute stage inaccuracies—a six-branched candlestick instead of the eight-branched Chanukah menorah, a calendar error for the Hebrew date of Chanukah, a mezuzah misplaced indoors, and the wrong tune for Passover prayers—and flinched at Pinchas's crude violation of the Sabbath at Reb Shemuel's house and at the latter's onstage recitation of the priestly blessing. It also noted historical anachronisms—for example, the tailors' strike and Brandon's return from the Cape (South Africa) would have taken place in 1890, and not at mid-century—and pointed out, not unreasonably, that a woman with Hannah's upbringing would not permit the matrimonial jest that stood at the core of the play, that her mother would have drummed into her to never permit a man to put a ring on her finger. Unlike most, it found Lackaye's portrayal "hardly Jewish enough."[143]

The *Jewish World* also offered a socioeconomic survey of the auditorium, in which it correlated ticket price, personal appearance, degree of Anglicization, and presumed geographic identity. The audience response, it said, reflected their position in English society, ranging from the interest mixed with disappointment and doubt of upper-class Jews, to the sheer enjoyment of the ghetto-dwellers, who recognized themselves on the stage. It reported that there were some interruptions originating in the gallery from Adelphi regulars, who expected the thrills of melodrama and were upset with the unhappy ending. Grein suggested that these "brutes" were "palm-greased hirelings, no doubt, of Whitechapel orthodoxy," who set out to disrupt the evening.[144] Whether or not that was the case, Grein's certitude underscores the Jewish apprehension that accompanied the production.

The two Jewish papers differed in their assessment of the play. The *Jewish World*'s review was mixed and, like quite a few others, noted that the play lacked dramatic intensity, yet praised its brilliant points and striking incidents.[145] The *Jewish Chronicle,* a Zangwill bastion, was entirely congratulatory, praising the combination of theme and innovative form. It exclaimed that the playwright attempted "what no contemporary dramatist has so far ventured," namely, a realistic play that consisted of a series of "living pictures," and concluded with an endorsement: "Mr. Zangwill has the right to expect that his earnest and original effort shall be seen and admired by very many. For our part, we heartily hope that he will receive the reward due to his genius and his high ideals."[146]

External events conspired against the production, however. December 11 was the Monday of Black Week, when British forces in South Africa seemed to be facing disastrous defeat. M. J. Landa offered a parallel day-to-day calendar: "Two days before the production . . . General Gatacre had met with check at Stromberg; while the people were waiting outside the Adelphi to enter the theatre for the first performance, Lord Methuen was sustaining defeat at Magersfontein; and before the week was over news came of General Buller's reverse on the Tugela on his way to the relief of Ladysmith."[147] With this grim news, Tyler writes, the London theater district "went out like a light," along with the added misery of a two-day dense fog that discouraged the bravest playgoer. His coffers emptying rapidly, Tyler decided to close the show and headed back home after the final Saturday night performance. *Children of the Ghetto* played London for six nights and one matinee—gone by week's end. With the exception of the London *Times,* nearly all the newspaper reviews appeared on the day the show closed, or later, so that, unlike New York, where the press took an active role in "killing" the production, the effect of the London reviews was inconsequential. Were it not for his New York experience, and had he not been in a foreign country, Tyler would probably have held on longer. Whether the play stood a chance for popular success is pure conjecture.

The London theater world was startled by the abrupt removal of *Children of the Ghetto*. An irate Israel Abrahams, who had just written the glorious review for the *Jewish Chronicle*, vented his anger in a feisty piece riddled with legal terminology, in which he spoke of Zangwill being denied a hearing, of justice and revenge.[148] He implicitly put the blame at the doorstep of London's Jews, who in their hesitancy had shied away from the theater during its opening week. Referring to the surprise and disappointment expressed by many at its sudden disappearance, he remonstrated, "the public and the critics who now lament the withdrawal have only themselves to thank." His mention of the "unstinted praise" that appeared in the English press was probably intended also to needle his readers for their fence-sitting, for waiting to see how Gentile England would respond, perhaps as had been the case when Zangwill's novel was published in 1892. Sounding like a raging schoolmaster wagging his finger, he snapped, "People are all regretting that they did not see the play; they have real cause to regret."[149] Abrahams prophesied that *Children of the Ghetto* was not dead, and envisioned that, with some minor revisions, it would one day be a complete success. The "corpse," he said, was destined for a speedy resurrection.

A fortnight after the play closed, on December 31, Tyler sent a telegram to Zangwill in London: "Will experiment further with Zangwill play provided you wave royalties in case financial failure. If any profit contract stands."[150] With this stipulation in tow, Tyler decided to keep the show going, more certain than ever of the intrinsic merits of *Children of the Ghetto*. Despite its reputation, which even he said made managers shy away from it as if it were "smallpox," he put together an American tour. His personal friendship with the manager of the Grand Opera House in Chicago helped him land a week's engagement. Again, the press was all over them. Before the company arrived, Lyman B. Clover, the critic for the Chicago *Herald*, wrote a column whose main tagline was "the awful thing is coming!"[151] When Tyler protested in person to him about maligning a play he had never seen, Clover responded that this was payback, as he considered Zangwill's assault on the theatrical critics a personal affront. Surprisingly, after attending opening night, Glover reversed himself, joined local reviewers' enthusiasm, and admitted in print that he had been wrong. Chicago marked a reversal in the production's fortunes. Tyler felt it could have run indefinitely, but the theater had been prebooked, and the company had to move on. He did manage to keep it going the entire season, taking it on the western, southern, and New England circuits, where it was favorably received. And although he lost $75,000 on the production, Tyler never lost faith in Zangwill. In his memoirs, written thirty-five years later, Tyler writes that it made his blood boil to see "the savage way" the papers slandered Zangwill for writing "one of the best plays of that generation."

On December 23, 1904, a Yiddish production of *Children of the Ghetto* opened at New York City's People's Theatre in the Bowery. The text had been translated by playwright Leon Kobrin—who shortly afterward wrote his own Yiddish Ghetto play, *Di East-Side Ghetto*—and starred Sigmund Feinman as Reb Shemuel, and Boris and Bessie Tomashefsky as David Brandon and Hannah Jacobs. Within the safe boundaries of Jewish ethnicity, the story was received without much discussion. No longer a vehicle for Jewish self-presentation, it did not raise issues of identity and evoked none of the controversy that had choked the original to death. It was now enjoyed with laughter and tears as a colorful tragicomic tale of traditional Jewish life, with a complication that everyone understood, and its unhappy ending, typical of much of Yiddish drama, taken as a matter of fact. Abraham Cahan, by then the influential editor of the *Forward,* the most popular New York Yiddish daily, informed his readers that the play had originally been written for a non-Jewish audience and poetically likened its presence on the English stage to a crimson mark on a white background. He could appreciate the difference in productions, but to his immigrant readers the comment was a piece of theater history of marginal value. Transported into its original idiom, the play's greatest merit, according to Cahan, was the playwright's skill at intertwining a brilliant sense of humor with moments of great sadness. In an ironic twist, he faulted Feinman, a star of the Yiddish stage, for failing to create a genuine Lithuanian or Polish rabbi and investing the role with the tone of a Shakespearean hero.[152]

In 1915, as the ghetto proved to be one of the more popular themes of American cinema, the William Fox Film Corporation produced a silent black-and-white film version of *Children of the Ghetto.*[153] Directed by Frank Powell, with a script written by Edward José, it was based on both the novel and the play, though Zangwill was not involved in any capacity in the production. The film opened with a paean to the novel, with Wilton Lackaye as himself reading from the book, as the character of Reb Shemuel, also played by Lackaye, appears at the other side of the table. This sentimentalized screen version introduced the kinds of changes that could have transformed the original stage play into a popular melodrama. The story was now moved to New York and reintroduced Levi, Reb's Shemuel's brazen son. He is seen arriving

Bessie Tomashefsky as Hannah in the Yiddish production of *Children of the Ghetto* at the People's Theatre in New York (1904). Harry Ransom Humanities Research Center, University of Texas at Austin.

drunk at the Passover seder, insulting his father and blaspheming God. After being gravely injured in a cabaret brawl and about to die, Levi begs for and receives his father's forgiveness. Hannah and David are not separated, but are married in a civil ceremony, after which she becomes estranged from her father, who is handed an additional blow when his wife dies. Several years pass. Reb Shemuel is shown conducting a lonely seder, at a table surrounded by empty chairs. Now widowed, Hannah appears with her two children, and her father accepts them all with open arms. The film was rich in ceremony, including a wedding and three Passover seders—at the first seder rabbi, wife, son, and daughter are together; all but the son are present in the second; and Reb Shemuel is alone at the third. Sixteen years after he had originated the role, Lackaye's exquisitely honed portrayal was again praised, credited by *Variety* for making the film far better than the usual fare.[154]

While the novel *Children of the Ghetto* maintained its popularity, the play completely disappeared from the public eye. However, in 1924, two years before Zangwill's death, two interesting though unrelated occurrences took place. *Hannah,* a play by Jolanda Cividalli based on the novel, was presented at the first Jewish studies conference in Italy in 1924. With no awareness of its original dramatic precursor, it was praised as a pioneering attempt to create a modern Jewish theater in Italy, with critics finding Zangwill's story an analogue for the vacillation of Italian Jews between traditional Judaism and assimilation into the bourgeoisie.[155] In the same year, precisely a quarter century after the original production, the *New York Times* drama critic paid homage to *Children of the Ghetto.* In a review of *We Moderns,* a recently opened Zangwill play, the memory of *Children* was tenderly evoked as a profound and universal tragedy of the ghetto, the life of which the playwright had observed with humor and integrity. It had failed, the reviewer suggested, because it was too groundbreaking and advanced for the "golden nineties," when Broadway had not yet learned to "look back on the Bowery with true reverence." To remedy this wrong, the *Times* called on the prestigious Theatre Guild, which was committed to the idea of a national repertory, to revive this "masterpiece of . . . our national drama." The call went unanswered.

Although *Children of the Ghetto* never became the hit Zangwill and Tyler hoped it would, the play should not be judged by the conventional standards of theatrical success and failure. The first Jewish play presented on the Anglo-American English-language stage, it was a milestone that called attention to the relationship between hegemonic culture and minority voices and demonstrated the difference in comfort levels between the embodied theatrical performance and the literary text. The differing responses to the production point to the great variance in regional reception and to the distinct meanings a cultural product assumes in different places, with their respective set of issues. It was in New York, with its large Jewish population, that the production fully problematized the complex issue of Jewish self-representation on the mainstream stage. Self-representation would become an increasingly contentious issue as works on Jewish identity entered the public artistic sphere, their creators usually disturbing the status quo, their work raising nervous internal arguments summed up by the questions "What will the goyim say?" and "Is it good or bad for the Jews?" Zangwill addressed this question when he said to one interviewer, "Are you aware . . . that still more people think that Jewish life should not be represented on the stage of the world! So long as a community does exist, its tragedy and comedy must be expressed by writers. That is one of the ways in which a community learns to understand itself, and to think out its future. If Jewish writers do not deal with Jewish topics, others will. The question is, which is preferable?!"[156]

Visibility, self-editing, and self-effacement have long been a major vein that runs through Jewish artistic productions in England and America. In 1946, writing in the immediate aftermath of the Holocaust, author Ben Hecht (1893–1964) pointed an accusing finger at his mostly Jewish Broadway audience with the words of the young hero of his *A Flag Is Born:* "You with your Jewish hearts hidden in your American boots! You with your Jewish hearts hidden behind English accents—you let the six million die—rather than making the faux-pas of seeming a Jew."[157] In 1996 the Jewish Museum in New York created a controversy reminiscent of the one that engulfed *Children of the Ghetto* with its provocative exhibition of *Too Jewish?: Challenging Traditional Identities.* Such sensitivity surrounding issues of self-presentation is by no means uniquely Jewish. Quandaries regarding image formation have beleaguered most ethnic and minority groups who participate in the mainstream discourse. Accordingly, the debates concerning *Zoot Suit, Capeman,* and *M. Butterfly,* to name a few, constitute an important chapter in the history of the American stage.

CHILDREN OF THE GHETTO

A Play in Four Acts
by Israel Zangwill

[Founded on the Writer's
Novel of the Same Name]

[Editor's Note: *Children of the Ghetto* opened in New York City on October 16, 1899, at the Herald Square Theatre. The cast list reproduced herein follows the order of the Herald Square Theatre program with one emendation (see * below). This list includes the explanations for characters who appear in the program's list but are not included in the playscript's "Persons of the Play."]

Cast of Characters

'Reb' Shemuel	Wilton Lackaye
David Brandon	Frank Worthing
Melchitsedek Pinchas	William Norris
Moses Ansell	Adolphe Lestina
*Simon Wolf	John D. Garrick
Guedaliah	Gus Frankel
Michael Birnbaum	Emil Hoch
Ephraim Phillips	Frank Cornell
Sam Levine	Fred Lotto
Sugarman	Charles Stanley
Shosshi Shmendrik	Richard Carle
Father Sol	
(oldest inhabitant of the Ghetto)	Phineas Leach
Barney Aurato	
(a millionaire from Australia)	E.J. Raymond
Fishmonger	A. Ghaistly
Purse-Trickster	John D. Garrick
Clothes-Dealer	O'Frederick Hoffman
Showman	Gus V. Devere
Schnorrer (Beggar)	William Singerman
Boy Salesman	Master Buckley
The Pious Partisan	Frank Bailey
Cake-Seller	H.F. Dolan
The Butcher	C.E. Odlin
The Chazan (Cantor)	L. Greenberg
B. Rotman (Chorister)	S. Swartz

B. Schultz (Chorister)	N. Trucks
Mrs. Belcovitch	Madame Cottrelly
Becky	Ada Curry
Mrs. Jacobs	Louise Muldener
Malka	Ada Dwyer
Milly Phillips	Laura Almosnino
Leah	Rosabel Morrison
Widow Finklestein	Sadie Stringham
Esther Ansell	Mabel Taliaferro
The Sabbath Fire-Woman	Isabel Preston

An Irish woman, who tends the Ghetto fires and candles on Friday nights and Saturdays, it being unlawful for a Jew to touch fire on the Jewish Sabbath)

Mrs. Montmorency	
(a grandchild of the Ghetto)	Jennie Buckley
Her Friend	
(a fashionable visitor to the Ghetto)	Zelle Davenport
Beggarwoman	Mary Stoner
Hannah Jacobs	Blanche Bates

* In the Herald Square Theatre program the roles of both Simon Wolf and Guedaliah are listed as played by Gus Frankel. However, newspaper reviews list John D. Garrick as playing Simon Wolf. I have amended the cast list accordingly.

PERSONS OF THE PLAY

Reb Shemuel	(The Ghetto Rabbi)
Melchitsedek Pinchas	(Hebrew Poet)
Moses Ansell	(A Pauper Alien)
Simon Wolf	(Freethinker and Labour-Leader)
Guedalyah the Greengrocer	(A Zionist)
Michael Birnbaum	(President of a Synagogue and married to Malka)
Ephraim Phillips	(A Business Man, married to Malka's daughter, Milly)
Sam Levine	(A Commercial Traveller, engaged to Malka's daughter, Leah)
Sugarman the Shadchan	(A Marriage-Agent)
Shosshi Shmendrik	(A shy Carpenter)
David Brandon	(A young man from the Cape)
Hannah Jacobs	(Reb Shemuel's daughter)
Mrs. Jacobs	(Her Mother)
Malka	(Business woman and head of her clan)
Milly Phillips & Leah	(Malka's Daughters)
Mrs. Belcovitch	(An imaginary invalid)
Becky	(Her buxom daughter)
Widow Finkelstein	(Owner of a grocery)
Esther Ansell	(A girl of twelve)

Fire-Woman, Lamp-Lighter, Policeman, Beggars, Congregation, Dancers, Pedlars, Pedestrians, &c. &c.

The action takes place in the Jewish settlement in East London, a quarter of a century ago, and covers a period of a hundred days.

ACT I
THE LETTER OF THE LAW.
At Milly's in Zachariah Square.
(*On the Feast of Chanukah.*)

ACT II
THE SPIRIT OF LOVE.
At the Ball in the People's Club.
(*ON THE FEAST OF PURIM. SEVENTY-TWO DAYS LATER.*)

ACT III
THE LETTER AND THE SPIRIT.
At REB SHEMUEL'S.
Friday evening. On the great Sabbath.
(*Twenty-five days later.*)

ACT IV
LOVE AND LAW.
In the Ghetto Market-Place.
On the Eve of Passover.
(*Three days later.*)

ACT I

The Letter of the Law

(*The Scene represents the Living-Room in* MILLY PHILLIPS' *house, giving on Zachariah Square by Door RIGHT, and on kitchen by door LEFT. On mantelpiece, which is covered with fringed green cloth, stands, amid cheap china dogs and lustres and quill pen in ink-bottle, a seven-branched candlestick with six candles in it. On top of a chest of drawers are decanters of liquor and a clothes-brush. A high guard is in front of the fire.* MICHAEL BIRNBAUM *and* EPHRAIM PHILLIPS *in negligée attire and carpet slippers are discovered playing cards and smoking cigars.* MICHAEL BIRNBAUM *is a fresh-coloured young man of thirty, rather good-looking with side-whiskers and a keen eager glance.* EPHRAIM PHILLIPS *is a sallow-looking, close-cropped Pole.*)

Michael	Trump it! Yes, Ephraim, the old woman is in one of her tantrums to-day.
Ephraim	Five of spades! Well, she always gets flustered on Fridays with her marketing. But it's rather rough on us to have our Christmas holiday spoiled like this.
Michael	My game! (*Empties saucer of money.*) Perhaps she thinks as we are Jews we oughtn't to enjoy Christmas, eh?
Ephraim	Ha! Ha! But you forget, Michael, it's Chanukah, too. And we have a right to enjoy our own festival.
Michael	Well, the old woman thinks it enough enjoyment for us to light up all those candles up there and to sing *Mooz-tsur ye-shuosi.* (*Sings.*)
Ephraim	Ha! Ha! If she only spoilt Christmas. But do you remember last Passover?

Michael	Do I remember last Passover? (*Hands cards.*) Shuffle! I felt I wanted to go back to Egypt!
Ephraim	Ho! Ho! Ho! Whatever made you marry her?
Michael	What made you marry her daughter?
Ephraim	True. (MICHAEL *deals cards in silence. Pauses. Throws card.*) Diamonds! But Milly is a good soul. Michaelis Malka—as good as gold. (*Winks.*)
Ephraim	I don't suppose there is a girl in the lane who fries fish better than my Milly. (*A knock.*)
Michael	My trick!
Ephraim	Come in!
	(*ENTER SAM LEVINE, a muscular young Jew with a pink-and-white complexion, a tawny moustache and an overflow of animal spirits.*)
Ephraim & Michael	(*Jumping up.*) Hullo, Sam, got back for Christmas?
Sam	Hullo Ephe, and Mike! (*All shake hands.*)
Michael	Had a good season?
Sam	Not bad. Though up in Scotland those new firms are cutting down prices fearfully. But where's Leah?
Michael	Out marketing with the old woman. Have a cigar!
Sam	Thanks. (*Taking it.*) Then I shall come across her in the lane. (*Going.*)
Ephraim	Don't be do devilishly romantic. Leah'll keep.
Michael	Sit down and take a hand. Why, in a fortnight's time you'll have Leah all day long.
Ephraim	And longer. He! He!
Michael	Ha! Ha! Come—we'll have a game of Solo Whist. Milly!
Milly	(*From kitchen.*) Ye-es!

Michael	Come and make up a game of Solo Whist.
Milly	I can't—I'm making the noodles.
Ephraim	Oh, come along, old girl. (*Rushes into kitchen and drags* MILLY *out. Her arms are bare with morsels of dough clinging on.*)
Milly	Oh, you wretch. Whatever will mother say! Hullo, Sam.
Ephraim	That's what mother'll say. You're looking blooming, Milly. How's the kid?
Milly	Little Zeky's fine! Not to beshrew him. If only his grandmother didn't worry over him so—she considers him hers more than mine or Ephraim's!
Ephraim	Yes, we give you fair warning, Sam. Malka is the head of the family.
Michael	Yes, and when you marry Leah, my wife will stay with you and quarrel with you and carry off your clothes-brush forgetfully, so as to have a handle for coming back and staying with you again.
Milly	Don't you choke Sam off. I want another household for mother to stay at. (*All laugh.*)
Michael	Tired of *me*, eh? (*Laughter.*)
Milly	You don't count. You just go with mother. (*Laughter.*)
Sam	Well, as the old lady is presenting our house and furniture it's only fair she should look in now and then.
Ephraim	Now and then! She'll live with you always as she does with us.
Sam	But she has her own house across the square, haven't you, Michael?
Michael	Yes, but we only remove over there when she quarrels with Ephraim or Milly—or the baby. (*Laughter.*)
Sam	Well, she'll soon quarrel with me. (*Laughter.*)
Ephraim	Ah, but she'll come back. With the clothes-brush! (*All laugh*

except SAM.)

Sam	With the clothes-brush!
Milly	Whenever she quarrels with us and goes home, mother slyly carries away that clothes-brush there. (*Points.*)
Sam	And what's the use of that?
Milly	Why, it gives her a handle for coming back.
Ephraim	When she's sulked herself out, she comes across the square on pretext of returning it.
Sam	Ha! Ha! Ha! Well, in my house there won't be any clothes-brush. (*Laughter.*)
Michael	Oh, won't there. Isn't she presenting the furniture in your house? There'll be a clothes-brush, depend upon it.
Sam	I don't care. I shall be away such a lot, travelling.
Milly	That's right, Sam. Don't be frightened off.
Michael	(*Shuffling the cards.*) Well, don't let us waste our one quiet hour. Come, you be *my* partner, Milly.
Milly	But mother wanted me to make the noodles—
Ephraim	Bah! when the cat's away—
Sam	The mice play cards, ha! ha! ha! Come, Milly, you shall be <u>my</u> partner.
Milly	But Michael asked me first.
Sam	All right. But you'll do better to be my partner. Look! (*Holds up sparkling diamond-ring.*)
All	Oh!
Michael	Leah's in luck.
Milly	Oh, what lovely diamonds! Yes, I *will* be your partner. (*Laughter.*) Let me look!
Sam	(*Slipping it on her finger.*) By this ring behold thou art con-

secrated unto me according to the Law of Moses and Israel. There! you must be my partner now. I have married you. (*Laughter.*)

Ephraim   Hear, O Israel, you *have* studied-up your marriage ceremony in good time.

Michael   Ha! Ha! How Sam's head is running—

Ephraim   Into the noose.

Michael   Well, then I suppose I must content myself with Ephraim. Shillings, I suppose. (*Business. Deals cards. Play commences. A knock at door.*)

Sam   (*Jumping up.*) There's Leah.

Milly   Nonsense, she wouldn't knock. Here, take back her ring though. (*Returns it.*) It is a beauty. Come in!

Sam   Well, I flatter myself I know a good stone.

(*The door is opened and the head of MELCHITSEDEK PINCHAS is stuck in with cigarette in mouth. He is a shabbily picturesque, slim, dark, little man with long matted black hair and a hatchet-shaped Aztec face with brilliant eyes. He carries under arm a heap of small paper-covered books.*)

Pinchas   I vish Mr. Michael Birnbaum. I have been to his house—she is empty.

Michael   I am Mr. Birnbaum.

Pinchas   (*Rushing in ecstatically and kissing the hem of his garment.*) You, the highly celebrated President of the great Vitechapel synagogue, the Gates of Mercy!

Michael   (*Playing.*) Don't—go away—I am busy.

Pinchas   I am busy, too. But I find time to pay my respects to the lion of learning, the eagle of visdom.

Michael   And who the devil are you?

Pinchas   Melchitsedek Pinchas.

Michael	Who?
Pinchas	Yes, Pinchas himself. You are surprised. You think I live always in Galicia, that only my poems—my divine songs—fly through the vorld. But England, she cries out to look on my face, and I come, I fly over with my new poems, I kiss the dust of the feet of the patrons of learning and the Muses. (*Whisks out book.*) Five shillings!
Michael	But it is Hebrew—who's going to understand this?
Pinchas	Ah, you be right. England—she stinks with ignorance. You and me are the only two men in England who write Hebrew grammatical.
Michael	You have been misinformed. Here, Ephraim, this is more in your line. You understand your Hebrew prayers. I only say them.
Ephraim	(*Taking book.*) Metatoron's Flames.
Pinchas	Ah, he understands. (*Rushes to kiss his hand.*) In this heathen country, to meet a scholar, it is like seeing the sun. Metatoron's Flames. Is she not a beautiful title? Ven Enoch was taken up to heaven while yet alive, he vas changed into flames of fire and became Metatoron, the great spirit of the Cabalah. Even so—I—Melchitsedek Pinchas—am caught up into the heaven of poesie and I become all fire and flame and light. (*Noticing cigarette has gone out.*) You have a match?
Sam	Here's a match. (*PINCHAS strikes a light.*)
Ephraim	(*Throws book on chest of drawers and money on table.*) And here's five shillings and get out.
Pinchas	(*Lighting cigarette.*) Five shillings! (*Puffs.*) How can the heavenly flame live on five shillings?
Milly	You said five shillings.
Pinchas	Five shillings for a Man-of-the-Earth. But for a scholar like your husband, he must have a book with a dedication in my own handwriting. And she costs seven and sixpence . . . Ah, there is pen and ink! (*Rushes to mantel and takes down pen and ink.*)

Ephraim	I won't have a dedication. (*Deals cards.*) Get out!
	(*PINCHAS sadly counts money, adjusts books and EXIT.*)
Sam	I didn't know people wrote Hebrew now-a-days. Five of spades. I thought Hebrew was a dead language; only used for religion.
Ephraim	Seven of spades. Oh no, Poland is full of uncombed chaps with long ear-locks who talk Hebrew just like you and me talk English.
Michael	Aren't you forgetting our own Reb Shemuel, Sam? Trumps.
Milly	Reb Shemuel! I thought he talked Yiddish to all those *greeners*.
Ephraim	Yiddish, too. King of hearts. But he *can* talk Hebrew—like a Patriarch.
Milly	He looks like one. By the way, I expect Reb Shemuel's daughter this morning.
Michael	Hannah!
Sam	That pretty girl! Good idea—I'll ask her for a waltz for the Purim ball.
Ephraim	Take care—Leah'll be jealous.
Milly	The Purim ball now! Why, you'll be married before then.
Sam	True, but one must look ahead. (*Laughter.*)
Michael	I suppose Hannah comes about Charity, as usual.
Milly	Yes, she wanted us to help in establishing a new one—a Home for Incurables. I wrote her she'd better come and talk it over. We have so many *old* charities a-begging.
Michael	Hannah is quite the Queen of *Schnorrers.*
	(*The door opens, and PINCHAS's head re-appears, finger to nose and a cajoling smile. All turn.*)
Pinchas	You von't have dedication?
Ephraim	(*Roars.*) No! (*Door closes.*) My game!

Michael   Well, that's the *King* of *Schnorrers*.

Sam   He ought to marry Hannah, then.

Michael   What a ghastly idea. You've got marriage on the brain.

(*The door opens and* PINCHAS's *head re-appears.*)

Pinchas   You shall have her for two shillings.

Milly   Don't have a fit, Ephe. *I'll* present you with a dedication. Perhaps it'll bring little Zeky luck and blessing. Here's half-a-crown. (*Throws.* PINCHAS *catches it, then seizes her hand and kisses it.*)

Pinchas   Ah, my Miriam, my Deborah, I vill write you a poem too. (*To* EPHRAIM) Vat name?

Milly   Ephraim Phillips.

(PINCHAS *writes in book while the game proceeds.*)

Pinchas   (*To* MILLY) You vill not honour the illustrious President with a Dedication also?

Michael   No, no.

Pinchas   Ah, I see you have the Chanukah candles. But Chanukah— she means Dedication. (*Smiling cajolingly.*) Make a feast of dedication, hey?

Michael   (*Half-laughing, half-angry.*) Why, the fellow is a regular *Schnorrer.*

Pinchas   (*Drawing himself up proudly.*) *Schnorrer?* Beggar? Me? In Russia, in Turkey, in Germany, in Romania, in Greece, in Morocco, in Palestine—every vere the greatest Rabbis have leapt like harts on the mountains vid joy of my coming. They have fed and clothed me like a prince. I have preached at the synagogues—from miles and miles around the people have come to be blessed by me. But in England—in England alone, vat is my velcome? Do they say, velcome, Melchitsedek Pinchas, velcome as the bridegroom to the bride ven the long day is done and the feast is over, velcome to you vid the torch of your genius, vid the mountain of your learning. Here, we have no great and vise men. Our chief Rabbi is an idiot. Come thou and be our Chief Rabbi. Do they say this? No, they call me a *schnorrer*. (*Indignant EXIT, door slams.*)

Milly	You've insulted the man.
Michael	Well, how could I know he was so devilish important? His collar was dirty enough. King of Clubs. (*Play continues. Door re-opens.* PINCHAS's *head re-appears, finger to nose.*)
Pinchas	Such a sweet savour of incense from your kitchen vindow rises to heaven!
Milly	Are you hungry?
Pinchas	Like on the Day of Atonement.
Milly	Come into the kitchen, I'll find you something. (*EXEUNT.*)
Michael	That Milly of yours is too soft-hearted.
Ephraim	But she plays a good hand at solo! (*Draws at cigar.*)
Sam	Here, throw that away—have one of mine. (*Offers cigar-case.*)
	(*Door bursts open. ENTER* LEAH, *beautifully-dressed, and parcel-laden.*)
Leah	(*Breathless.*) Listen—quick—mother's fish—
Sam	(*Spilling cigars.*) Leah!
Leah	Sam! (*Drops parcels. He embraces her, but after the first kiss she repulses him.*) Don't stop me—I've just dodged mother—to run in and tell you—how much she paid—for her fish.
Michael & Ephraim	(*Breathlessly.*) How much?
Leah	Thirty shillings. (*Is rushing out.*)
Sam	(*Seizing her.*) But what's all this about?
Michael	Why the old woman is in a frightful temper to-day and if we guess double—

Ephraim	So that she thinks it's a bargain.
Leah	We'll have a peaceful holiday.
Sam	I see. Ha! Ha! Ha!
Omnes	(*Loudly.*) Ha! Ha! Ha!
Milly	(*Looking in wonderingly.*) What's—
Ephraim	(*Breathlessly.*) Milly, the fish cost thirty shillings.
Milly	Leah, you're a duck!
Leah	But she'll catch me if I'm not sharp. (*Rushes out—returns.*) Oh my parcels! (*Collects them, rushes out.*) Here's mother coming. I'll go the back way. (*Rushes though kitchen. Shrieks. Returns.*) Who's that?
Pinchas	(*Following her into room with fork.*) Angel of Beauty, be not alarmed.
Milly	It's all right. He's only a Poet. (*Breathlessly pushes them both back and closes the kitchen door, as through the street-door comes* MALKA, *timidly followed by* ESTHER ANSELL, *a clean but poverty-stricken child of 12.* MALKA *has a tanned gipsy-like face, and a tall, imperious figure.*) Hullo, mother, where's Leah?
Malka	I don't know. I lost her in the crowd. I have to squeeze and sweat while you squat yourselves down here to play cards.
Sam	(*Coming forward.*) It's my fault, mother.
Malka	Sam!
Sam	Yes, back again, like a bad penny. And you're looking as bright as a new one.
Malka	It's because we elders keep our bones active; the new generation wants to keep Sabbath all the week and expects the ceiling to pour puddings.
Michael	Well, it doesn't pour such puddings as you make, mother.
Malka	And why isn't Milly making the noodles?
Milly	I just came out to see the fish—oh, what beauties! Put them

	down, Esther.
Esther	Yes, miss.
Milly	Why do you call me miss?
Esther	I beg you pardon, ma'am. I am so used to talk to teacher.
Michael	Why, those plaice look alive!
Ephraim	What a turbot! Did you ever?
Sam	(*Admiring.*) Tut! Tut! When I'm married, my mother-in-law shall buy *my* Sabbath fish.
Malka	Yes, Black Jonathan can't fool me. I saw Mrs. Sugarman buying some gurnards, stuffed with brown paper. Ha! Ha!
All	(*Glad to vent their laughter.*) Ha! Ha! Ha!
Malka	And what do you think I gave for these?
Michael	I'm afraid you've been too extravagant, mother.
Milly	These fish—nobody would let them go under three golden guineas.
Malka	Sixty-three shillings! Nonsense!
Ephraim	You want things too cheap, Milly. They'd be a bargain at seventy.
Malka	Lucky I don't let *you* do my marketing.
Sam	Yes, he'd be a nice, fishy customer.
Malka	Esther—here's your shilling.
Esther	Thank you, miss—I mean, ma'am.
Sam	May I guess? You're all on the wrong tack. *We* couldn't get them under seventy, but I wager mother got them for fifty. Eh, come now.
Malka	(*Very pleased.*) No-o-o!
Michael	Not *less* than that?

Malka	Ye-e-s.
All	Is it possible? Tut, tut, tut!
Milly	Forty-five.
	(*MALKA shakes head.*)
Michael	Forty?
	(*MALKA shakes head.*)
Ephraim	Thirty-seven and sixpence.
	(*MALKA shakes head.*)
Michael	Well, it's no use going lower than that. Give it up.
Malka	Twenty-five!
All	(*With mixture of genuine and feigned astonishment.*) Twenty-five!
Malka	So sure as I stand here. (*MILLY, still admiring takes fish to kitchen, the others resume game. MALKA turns and perceives ESTHER is shocked and is angry at being overheard in a lie.*) Well. What are you waiting about for? <u>Nu</u>, there's a peppermint.
Esther	Thank you. But I thought you might want me for something else. And I—I—
Malka	Well, speak up, I won't bite you.
Esther	I—I—nothing. (*Opens door.*)
Malka	Here, turn your face round, child. Don't be so sulky. You poor mother was like that—peace be on her soul. She'd want to bite my hand off, if I hinted that your father was not the man for her. Thank God, we have no tempers like that in this house. I couldn't live for a day with such people. Come, tell me what ails you, or your dead mother will be cross with you.
Esther	I thought you might lend me the three and sevenpence halfpenny—
Malka	The three—?

Esther	Four and sevenpence halfpenny were stolen from me in the lane—how can I make Sabbath for father and the children?
Malka	Lend—why, how can you ever repay it?
Esther	Oh yes, I have lots of money in the bank.
Malka	Eh? What? In the bank?
Esther	Yes. I won a five pound prize at school, and next year I shall be allowed to draw out the money.
Malka	Five pounds? Your father never told me that! Ah, he is a true *schnorrer*, is Moses.
Esther	(*Hotly.*) My father hasn't seen you since. If you had come round when my poor brother Benjamin died—
Malka	Impudence-face! Do you forget who you're talking to?
Esther	No! You are my father's cousin, that is why you ought to have come when father was sitting the seven days.
Malka	I am not your father's cousin, God forbid. I was only your mother's cousin and I don't wonder you drove her into the grave among the lot of you? From this day I wash my hands of the whole ungrateful pack. Sell matches. Not another thing will I do for you.
Esther	Ungrateful! Why, what have you ever done for us? You made my mother work like an Irish Fire-woman.
Malka	Impudence-face! What have I ever done for you? Why— why—I—I—shameless hussy! And this is what Judaism is coming to in England? This is the manners and religion they teach you at your school, eh? What have I—impudence-face! And at this very moment you hold one of my shillings in your hands.
Esther	Take it! (*Throws it away, it rolls and rolls on floor in a terrible silence.*)
Michael	(*Rising from card-table.*) Eh? Eh? What's this, my little girl? What makes you so naughty?

(*ESTHER bursts into hysterical sobs.*)

Sam	Don't cry like that, don't.
Milly	(*Coming out of kitchen and leaving the door open.*) What's the matter with the girl, mother?
Malka	She's mad, raving mad. I found her in the lane gushing with the eyes over a lost purse—a *schlemihl* like her father—and I've given her a shilling and a peppermint. And you see how she turns on me, you see.
Sam	Poor little thing. Here, come here my child. (*ESTHER does not budge.*) Come here. See, I will make up the loss to you. Take the pool. I've just won it, so I shan't miss it. (*ESTHER sobs louder. SAM rises and empties the saucer into her pocket. MICHAEL and EPHRAIM both add silver and so does MILLY. SAM opens the door and puts ESTHER outside.*) There! Run away, my little dear and be more careful of pick-pockets.
Malka	(*Darting after her and hauling her back.*) Give me that money. (*She rifles her pocket—and counts out the coins.*) Seventeen shillings and sixpence. How dare you take all this money from strangers and perfect strangers? Do my children think to shame me before my own relations? (*Throws money back into saucer, produces her own purse, extracts a gold piece and presses it into ESTHER's hand.*) There! Hold that tight! A Golden guinea—twenty-one shillings. And if ever I find you taking money from any one in this house but your mother's own cousin, I'll wash my hands of you for ever! (*ESTHER moves dazedly towards door.*) Stop! Where is your father now?
Esther	Standing in the lane with lemons!
Malka	A fat lot he sells—stands dreaming of Bible and Talmud, I warrant, instead of minding his business. There's a never-do-well! A nice match for my poor cousin, peace be upon her. Send him to me. He needs some advice on the bringing-up of children. Do you hear?
Esther	Yes, ma'am. (*EXIT ESTHER.*)
Malka	And nicely my own children reward me for the way I've brought *them* up. (*Glares. Dread silence. She sidles to chest of drawers and surreptitiously seizes the clothes-brush. Then stalks*

majestically towards door. It bursts open and LEAH *rushes in, with her parcels.*)

Leah	Why, mother! Home already!
Malka	I can't stand about gossiping all day.
Leah	Goodness, is that Sam back?
Sam	My darling! (*Flies to her.*)
Milly	(*At window.*) Why, here is Hannah Jacobs coming to see you, mother, about that Home for Incurables.
Malka	Oh of course! I'm made of gold.
Michael	No—but your heart is, mother. (*Kisses her.*)
Malka	(*Softening.*) I know I'm too good.
Michael	Well, mother, it all gets written down in heaven.
Ephraim	And printed on earth.
Malka	All the same that Hannah Jacobs is a nuisance always coming pestering. I shall give her a piece of my mind. (*A knock.*) Come in! (*ENTER HANNAH JACOBS with a collecting card.*) Ah, Hannah! (*Sweetly.*) Beautiful weather, isn't it?
Hannah	Lovely. How are you? (*As HANNAH extends her hand MALKA becomes aware of the clothes-brush in her own. She stoops down and pretends to brush her skirt.*)
Malka	So muddy out! What a stranger you are to be sure, Hannah!
Michael	Yes, quite angel's visits.
Ephraim	An angel of mercy, though, judging by the looks of that card.
Hannah	That kind of angel's visits people like to be few and far between.
Malka	Only stingy people. Here, Hannah. Here is something towards the new Home. (*Giving her pool from saucer.*) Seventeen and six, I think.

Michael	Oh I say, mother, some of that is Sam's.
Malka	And why shouldn't Sam go to heaven?
Sam	(*Who is kissing* LEAH.) I'm there!
Malka	Such goings-on! I do declare. When I was first married in Poland I never even saw my husband till the day after.
Sam	And Leah hasn't seen me for three months. . . . Oh, what a donkey I am! (*Producing ring.*) Look, Leah!
Leah	O-o-o-h!
Sam	(*Teasing.*) No, no snatching. You are not the only pretty girl in the room. (*Holds it up.*) Here is a ring and a very pretty ring, and which pretty girl will be the owner of this pretty ring? Ha, I see Miss Jacobs *would* like it.
Hannah	(*Smiling.*) Certainly—towards the Home for Incurables.
Sam	Then hold out the second finger of your right hand. (*HANNAH obeys smilingly,* SAM *slips it on her finger.*) "By this ring behold thou art consecrated unto me according to the law of Moses and Israel."
Michael	Ha! Ha! Ha! Now he's married Hannah!
Malka	Ha! Ha! Ha! The droll rascal will have his little joke.
Pinchas	(*Who has come unobserved to kitchen-door, smoking cigarette.*) Little joke! But this is no joke, good people!
All	(*Turning.*) Eh?
Malka	Who's this?
Milly	A poet, mother. I gave him some dinner.
Malka	Ah, these *schnorrers*. They'll eat me out of house and home.
Pinchas	I am no *schnorrer*. I am a man learned in the Law, and I tell you this young man has really married this beautiful maiden. (*Sensation.*)
Hannah	(*Horror-struck.*) Married! (*Pulls off ring and throws it on floor. It rolls unregarded.*)

Leah	What's that?
Sam	Oh nonsense, nonsense. What are you talking about?
Pinchas	You not vant her! A wife beautiful as the Queen of Sheba!
Sam	Damn the Queen of Sheba! Do you mean to say we are married?
Pinchas	Such is the law of Moses. If before two vitnesses a man takes a voman—
Leah	(*Hysterically.*) Sam. What have you done?
Michael	Ephraim, do you remember any such nonsense?
Ephraim	I am beginning to. In Poland when—
Malka	I told you what would come of your godless jokes! I told you so.
Sam	But it can't be true.
Hannah	(*In quiet despair.*) Anything may be true in our religion.
Milly	But at that rate Sam married me, too.
Ephraim	No, you were married already.
Sam	And I was engaged already.
Pinchas	That's nothing.
Sam	But it can't be legal. Who ever hear of such a marriage-law?
Pinchas	Who ever heard? Vy, it's just like the Scotch marriage-law!
Sam	My God! So it is. I heard of a case this very trip.
Malka	You rogue! You planned all this. You thought—
Leah	Oh, mother!
Sam	(*Savagely.*) But surely there must be some way out of this, some dodge or other. I know you Talmudical rascals can split hairs. Can't you make one of your clever distinctions, even when there's more than a hair in the balance?

Pinchas	(*Pondering.*) A vay out? A vay out? (*They hang breathlessly on his words.*) Of course there's a vay out!
Hannah	Thank heaven!
Malka	I told you so! I told you so!
Sam	What is it? What is it?
Pinchas	(*Craftily puts finger to nose.*) You shall see. I go away—vay out! I come back. In ten minutes (*going*) the beautiful maiden will be free. (*Conscious dramatic EXIT.*)
Sam	Well, I'm jiggered!
Malka	This comes of making mock of holy things. (*Door re-opens. PINCHAS's head re-appears, finger to nose.*)
Pinchas	But vat I get for my services?
Sam	Anything—everything. I'll buy all your books.
Ephraim	With dedications.
Pinchas	No, I am a poet, not a tradesman! I rescue the beautiful Princess from the dragon.
Sam	Eh?
Pinchas	And I must marry the Princess.
Hannah	What?
Sam	All right. You shall marry your Princess! Hurry up now. (*Door closes.*) Don't take him so seriously, Miss Jacobs.
Hannah	There are some things that have to be taken seriously, Mr. Levine.
Sam	That's right. Pitch into me all round. I deserve it. (*Approaches LEAH.*) And so it was frightened, my poor little girl.
Leah	Don't come near me.
Michael	It'll all be all right, Leah. He's gone to look up some old book or the other.

(*Door re-opens.* PINCHAS's *head re-appears, finger to nose.*)

Pinchas	You von't forget—I must marry the Princess!
Sam	Yes, yes—fly! (*Pushes him out.*)
Michael	Don't look so serious, Miss Jacobs.
Hannah	I am not so sure as all of you. We are strangled by strange old laws—they are coiled about us like serpents.
Malka	What did I say? What did I say? Ah, God forgive you, Sam. (ALL *relapse into gloom. A timid knock at door.*)
Sam	If that fellow's back again, I'll kick him out of the Square. (*Rushes to door and throws it open, discovering* ESTHER ANSELL, *with* MOSES ANSELL, *a frowsy pedlar with ear-locks, and a bent, broken attitude. A* CARPENTER's *bag of lemons is slung from his neck.*)
Esther	Please ma'am, here's father!
Malka	(*Exultant.*) Ah Moses! Here is my cousin Moses! Now we shall know the Law. Come in, Moses, come in! (MOSES *shuffles in.*)
Moses	(*Humbly.*) Sie haben für mir geschickt, Malka?
Esther	(*Pulling his coat half whispers.*) Don't speak Yiddish, father. You promised me always to speak English.
Moses	(*Humbly.*) I can't remember, Esther. Ah, you haf send for me, Malka?
Malka	Yes—to ask you a question about the Law.
Moses	(*Raising head like a war-horse.*) About the Law!
Malka	Yes, suppose a man puts a ring on a girl's finger and says the marriage-words. Are they married?
Moses	(*Chanting with legal unction.*) Ven a man puts a ring on a girl's finger and says the marriage-vords. Are they married? *No.*
All	No?
Moses	Dere must be two witnesses.

All	Ah!
Malka	Then that makes them married?
Moses	Yes. The Talmud speaks not about the ring. The ring only stands for money. The man he buys the bride with it. But the Geonim of Babylon—
Sam	Bother Babylon. Suppose it's only a joke, Mr. Ansell.
Moses	(*Drawing himself up rebukingly.*) A joke—ve must not make jokes about holy tings.
	(*A silence.*)
Hannah	But surely, Mr. Ansell, there is some way of undoing such a marriage!
Moses	*Nu gewiss.* I mean certainly.
All	(*Eagerly.*) Yes?
Moses	The man must give the voman *Get.*
All	*Get!*
Esther	Father means divorce.
Sam	Yes, we know. Oh what fools we were! Of course! Divorce! Good old Jewish Law. Hannah, I divorce thee. Ha! Ha! Ha!
Malka	I told you so, Leah, I told you so. My cousin Moses—he knows the Law.
Michael	Ha! Ha! Ha! You can get out as quick as you get in.
Hannah	(*Quietly.*) I am not so sure about that.
Sam	Nonsense—you trust Moses. The Law of Moses, ha! ha! ha! Here, Moses, those lemons for sale?
Moses	(*Relapsing into humility.*) Yes, they are. Two a penny each.
Sam	I buy the lot. (*Tosses them up. Sings.*) Oranges and lemons— the bells of St. Clements. Orange—blossoms for marriages; lemon—for divorces. Come, old girl, (*to LEAH*) gi's a kiss.
Leah	You silly old Sam! (*Kisses him.*)

Hannah	(*Smiling.*) I am afraid you still belong to me, Mr. Levine. I am quite sure my father goes through much more elaborate forms when he divorces couples.
Malka	My cousin Moses will tell us.
Moses	(*Legal chant again.*) The *Shulchan Aruch*—
Malka	(*Impressively.*) A-a-a-h! The *Shulchan Aruch*—that's the book.
Moses	The *Shulchan Aruch* in the chapter *Eben Haezer* gives exactly one hundred and one rules for *Get*.
Sam	One hundred and one rules!

(*Door opens.* PINCHAS's *head appears, finger to nose.*)

Pinchas	Remember, I must marry the Princess!
Malka	Go away. We have no need of strangers—my cousin Moses knows as much Law and Talmud and Gomorrah as the angels in heaven. (MOSES *stands humbly.*)
Hannah	And my father, sir, is Reb Shemuel. He will arrange the divorce.
Pinchas	Reb Shemuel, your father! Vy I just vent to fetch him to give you *Get*. Ah, he loves poets. He vill see I get my rights. Here he comes. (*Looks out.*)
Esther	Why, here is a ring on the floor. (*Picks it up.*)
Leah	It's mine. (*Slips it on.*) Thank you, Esther.

(PINCHAS *throws door wide, and obsequiously makes way for* REB SHEMUEL, *a patriarchal white-bearded figure in a long coat. He holds a roll of parchment, longer than broad.*)

Reb Shemuel	(*After kissing the door-amulet.*) Peace to you all.
All	(*Murmuring.*) Peace!
Hannah	Oh father! Don't be angry.
Reb Shemuel	You here, Hannah! What is it?
Hannah	I am the girl.

Reb Shemuel	The girl?
Hannah	The wife. The wife of the joke.
Reb Shemuel	The wife I have to give divorce to!
Hannah	Yes.
Reb Shemuel	And who is your husband?
Sam	I am, sir.
Reb Shemuel	I am sorry to meet my son-in-law with rebuke.
Sam	I deserve it all, sir. I never will jest with holy things again. And I'll study up on religion too, lest—
Reb Shemuel	Than this, too, may be for good. But we shall need a scribe.
Pinchas	I write the Hebrew beautiful—
Malka	No, my cousin Moses—
Reb Shemuel	Ah, Reb Moses! The very man!
Moses	God is good to me to-day.
Reb Shemuel	A pen and ink!
Pinchas	(*Darting to mantel, flourishes quill.*) Ah, ve pierce the dragon.
Reb Shemuel	No, not a quill. Some authorities say the *Get* should not be written with a quill pen. We had best be on the safe side.
Esther	I have a pen! (*Produces from pocket.*)
Reb Shemuel	(*To PINCHAS.*) Will you, Mr.—I forget your name—
Pinchas	Melchitsedek Pinchas!
Reb Shemuel	Yes—will you ask some of the neighbours to step in? We have not ten men for a congregation.
Pinchas	Yes—anything—for the Princess! (*Kisses his hand to* HANNAH, *and EXITS.* MOSES *arranges himself clumsily at table,* ESTHER *helps him.*)
Reb Shemuel	You understand how the law directs it to be written?

Moses	Yes—clear, not crooked, each letter and each line separated, no— vat you call them, Esther?—no blots, no scratch-out, no altering—
Reb Shemuel	Well, there's only the particulars to fill in, but be very careful. If ink drops on one letter, a new *Get* must be written.
Moses	I know.
Reb Shemuel	Now, Mr. Levine, you must buy the parchment and pen and ink from Reb Moses: so the *Get* becomes altogether your property.
Sam	All right. How much, Moses?
Moses	(*Abstractedly.*) Two a penny each.
Esther	Father! (*Shaking him.*) Well, say sixpence.
Sam	Oh no, it's worth its weight in gold. Say a sovereign.
Esther	Oh, that's too much.
Sam	Well, I haven't paid for the lemons yet. Reckon it square, Moses.
Moses	Tank you, sare. Hare you are. (*Gives materials to Sam, who holds them.*)
	(*RE-ENTER* PINCHAS, *importantly marshalling in five or six neighbours, including* GUEDALYAH THE GREENGROCER.)
Pinchas	I've explained to them.
Reb Shemuel	Ah, thank you, good friends. Keep your hats on. And yours, too. (SAM *and the others put hats on.*) But I shall want two special witnesses to sign the *Get*.
Pinchas	Me! I vill kill the dragon.
Reb Shemuel	(*Peering.*) Ah, is that my neighbour, Guedalyah the Greengrocer? You be the other witness. You are neither of you relations of Mr. Levine?
Pinchas & Guedalyah	No, no.

Reb Shemuel	Well, you're not of Hannah. Good. Now, Mr. Levine, we begin. Do you give this *Get* of your own free will, without any compulsion, or vow or oath?
Sam	Yes.
Reb Shemuel	Give Reb Moses the materials and order him to write you a bill of divorce for your wife Hannah, the daughter of Reb Shemuel.
Sam	(*Obeying.*) Reb Moses, write for me a bill of divorce for my wife, Hannah, the daughter of Reb Shemuel.
Reb Shemuel	Now appoint the witnesses.
Sam	And you, Mr. Pinchas, and you Mr.——er——
Guedalyah	Guedalyah.
Sam	Guedalyah, be witnesses.
Reb Shemuel	(*To SAM.*) And attest this *Get* for my wife, Hannah, the daughter of Reb Shemuel.
Sam	And attest this *Get* for my wife, Hannah, the daughter of Reb Shemuel.
Moses	Your father's name, Mr. Levine?
Sam	Joseph.
Moses	(*To witnesses.*) See, I write this *Get* in the name of Samuel, the son of Joseph, for the purpose of divorcing his wife, Hannah, the daughter of Shemuel. (*Writes. PINCHAS bends over. Breathless silence.*)
Pinchas	Now I sign.
Reb Shemuel	Not yet—not yet, the ink must be dry.
Pinchas	Ah, the black blood of the dragon!
Reb Shemuel	Guedalyah, you sign first. See, just here, on the right, next to margin.
Guedalyah	(*Taking pen.*) I sign this *Get* on behalf of Samuel the son of Joseph, for the purpose of divorcing his wife, Hannah, the

daughter of Shemuel. (*Signs.*)

Pinchas (*Snatching pen.*) I sign this *Get* on behalf of Samuel, the son of Joseph, for the purpose of divorcing his wife, Hannah, the daughter of Shemuel . . . and marrying her to me. (*Signs.*)

Reb Shemuel (*Takes parchment and reads aloud.*) Listen all! This is the sense, translated into English: "On the sixth day of the week and the twenty-first day of the month of Kislev in the year 5634 since the creation of the world, I, Samuel the son of Joseph of the town of London, thus determine, being of sound mind and under no constraint; and I do release and send away and put aside thee, Hannah, daughter of Shemuel, of the town of London, who hast been my wife from time past, hitherto; and hereby I do release thee and send thee away and put thee aside that thou mayest have permission to be married to any man whom thou desirest, and no man shall hinder thee from this day for ever. And these presents shall be unto thee from me a bill of dismissal, a document of release and a letter of freedom according to the Law of Moses and Israel." (*To* MOSES.) Is this the *Get* which you have written at the request of the husband for the purpose of divorcing his wife, Hannah, the daughter of Shemuel?

Moses Yes.

Reb Shemuel (*To* PINCHAS *and* GUEDALYAH.) Did you hear the husband give the order to write it?

Pinchas
& Guedalyah Yes.

Reb Shemuel Did you sign it at the husband's request and for the purpose of divorcing his wife, Hannah, the daughter of Shemuel?

Pinchas
& Guedalyah Yes.

Reb Shemuel Do you recognise your signatures?

Pinchas
& Guedalyah Yes.

Reb Shemuel (*Handing the* Get *to* SAM LEVINE.) Do you give this bill of divorce of your own free will?

Sam	(*Holding* Get.) Yes.
Reb Shemuel	You will not hereafter protest, or otherwise annul.
Sam	No.
Reb Shemuel	(*Solemnly.*) If any man present knows ought to invalidate the *Get,* or why it should not be delivered to Hannah, let him speak before it is delivered. For after it is delivered I shall pronounce the ban of Excommunication upon any one who shall attempt to invalidate the *Get.* Hannah!
Hannah	Yes, father.
Reb Shemuel	Remove all rings from your fingers.
Hannah	I have only one. (*Obeys.*)
Reb Shemuel	Stretch forth your hand to receive the *Get.*
Hannah	There, father! (*Holds out her hand.*)
Reb Shemuel	(SAM—*holding forth* Get—PINCHAS *moves to pass it on.*) No, no, no one must assist her. Lay it on her palm. (SAM *obeys.*) Don't close your hand on it yet, Hannah—not till the words "any man!" repeat after me, Mr. Levine—"This is thy *Get.*"
Sam	This is thy *Get.*
Reb Shemuel	And thou art divorced by it from me.
Sam	And thou art divorced by it from me.
Reb Shemuel	And art permitted to be married to any man.
Sam	And art permitted to be married to any man.
	(HANNAH's *hand closes feverishly on parchment.*)
Reb Shemuel	(*Taking parchment, and solemnly tearing it cross-wise.*) For ninety days it is forbidden thee to be betrothed again.
Hannah	Oh, father! (*Falls on his breast, exhausted.*)
	(LEAH *rushes into* SAM's *arms.*)
	CURTAIN.

ACT II

The Spirit of Love

(*The scene represents the general lounging-room of the People's Club, giving on the Ballroom [CENTER], the buffet [LEFT], and the EXIT [RIGHT]. It is the end of the supper interval at the Purim Ball. Seated round the table, or standing, or moving to and fro, a motley crowd of all ages, half in stylish evening dress, half anyhow; chatting, laughing, eating, drinking. On a central plush lounge are MALKA, MILLY and LEAH, the younger women fashionably attired, LEAH in red. EPHRAIM PHILLIPS, likewise stylish, approaches them with a plate of sandwiches.*)

Ephraim	Any more sandwiches for anybody?
Milly	Thank you, dear. I've had enough supper.
Ephraim	Won't you try a beef sandwich, mother?
Malka	A beef? Ma? How do I know it's kosher?
Leah	Oh, mother (*eating*)—a Jewish Club!
Malka	Jewish! (*The music plays a provincial bar.*) Such Judaism would have made my grandmother turn in her grave.

(*ENTER SAM LEVINE, as Steward and M.C.*)

Sam	Take your partners for the waltz. (*A lively waltz commences.*)
Leah	(*Half dancing.*) Such Judaism would make anybody turn in their grave. (*EPHRAIM takes back plate. General movement to ball-room.*)
Malka	Well, say what you will, children, I call it disgraceful to dance with other women's husbands.

Leah	Well, if we had enough husbands of our own to fill up our programmes with—! You can't dance all the time with the same man.
Malka	While you were engaged, you danced all the time with the same man.
Leah	Ah, it's not the same man now. Besides Sam is busy as steward and M.C.
Malka	But Milly has no such excuse.
Milly	Why mother, *I* haven't been dancing with other women's husbands.
Malka	I'll smack your face if you tell me such lies.
Milly	Lies! My partners were all bachelors.
Malka	Still worse. Ah, I don't like these modern ways of keeping Purim. I prefer the old way—
Leah	What old way?
Malka	Oh, more religious—the men dressing up as Queen Esther and all that.
Leah	You call that religious—for a man to dress as a woman! I call it indecent.
Malka	(*Looking scathingly at her low dress.*) I call it more indecent for a woman to dress as a woman.
Milly	If we went by your ideas of religion we should all wear wigs.
	(*Ephraim returns.*)
Leah	Oho, fancy Ephraim as Queen Esther.
Ephraim	What's that?
Malka	I say it's time you danced with my Milly.
Ephraim	So it is. This is our waltz, I believe, Milly.
Milly	(*Looks at programme.*) Yes.
	(*They go in.* LEAH *laughs.*)

Malka	What are you laughing at?
Leah	Nothing.
Malka	You call your mother nothing! Of course now she's found you a husband and given you a house and furniture, she's nothing. (*The waltz strikes up.*)
Michael	(*Coming from buffet.*) There's a clothes-brush look in her eye. (*Aside.*) Why, what's the matter, mother?
Malka	The matter! You must go and smoke, while my children insult me. (*A young man hurries up to* LEAH, *she takes his arm and goes into ball-room.*) There! I've a good mind to do as everybody else, and dance with other women's husbands. It would be only what you deserve.
Michael	I should bear my punishment like a man.
Malka	Eh?
Michael	(*Kissing her.*) All right, mother: but you won't dance even with *me*.
Malka	My, lamb, let us go somewhere, where there are not so many people. (*They go towards the buffet. The stage is now almost clear. ENTER DAVID BRANDON door RIGHT. He looks round, then opens door of dancing-hall, the music swells merrily. He stands looking in.*)
Sam	(*Coming up.*) Can I introduce you, sir, to any of the ladies?
David	(*Laughing.*) How can you introduce me, Sam, when you don't know me?
Sam	What David! David Brandon! Back from the Cape.
David	Yes, I knew you at once. (*Vigorous hand-shake.*)
Sam	Well, I suppose you've made your pile, like all the other boys.
David	(*Laughing.*) I haven't come to grief like *some* of the other boys. But it's been a rough time: life reduced to the bare rock. By Jove, it's good to come back to old England and hear somebody talk of something outside money-getting.

| Sam | Wife-getting, eh? Ha! Ha! That's the next step, isn't it, with the Cape boys. |

Sam   Wife-getting, eh? Ha! Ha! That's the next step, isn't it, with the Cape boys.

David   Don't call me a Cape boy. That's the name we give the Kaffirs out there.

Sam   Oh is it? Well, let me introduce you to some of the Club-girls.

David   (*Laughing.*) No thanks—I'm *not* hunting for a wife.

Sam   Then they'll hunt you.

David   They'll catch a Tartar. No, no, leave me my dream of romance. I hate the idea of marrying just because you can afford to keep a wife.

Sam   Well, but when else are you to marry?

(*The waltz-tune is now soft and dreamy.*)

David   When I meet the girl I dreamed of in those lonely African nights under the great throbbing stars.

Sam   My stars! (*Perceives SUGARMAN emerging from the buffet.*) And what is to become of Sugarman?

David   Sugarman?

Sam   Sugarman the Shadchan—there he is, marriage-broker and lottery agent.

David   (*Laughing.*) What a strange combination of businesses!

Sam   Not at all. Isn't marriage a lottery? Supplies German lottery tickets and English wives—all prizes and no blanks, he says. Sugarman!

Sugarman   (*Eagerly.*) Yes, Mr. Levine!

Sam   Here is a young man back from the Cape, simply wallowing in gold and diamonds, and yet lacking the one real treasure—a wife.

Sugarman   Ah Sir! Let me get you one. A man of your age! Why, you ought to have a wife and three children.

David	Thanks! I don't want a wife and three children.
Sugarman	No, of course not, sir—not in a lump. I mean a maiden. If I get you a maiden with a dowry of a thousand pounds—a thousand golden sovereigns paid on the wedding morning—what commission will you give me?
David	The maiden!
Sam	Ha! Ha! Ha!
Sugarman	Do not make fun of holy things. How stands it written in the Talmud? Eve was taken from Adam's rib, and every man's Eve is his lost rib, without which he is not complete.
David	And so you go about fitting the lost ribs into the right owners, eh?
Sam	Ha! Ha! Well, come and look for your own rib, David. I've just found mine without assistance. (*Dragging him in.*)
David	What! You married!
Sam	To the dearest girl in the world. (*EXEUNT.*)
Sugarman	The cheapest, you mean! Not a penny on her to anybody! Ah no good, no good, all these modern young men—no religion left in them. Romance they call it—I call it just sinful passion. The next step will be to marry Christian girls altogether. Bah! (*ENTER* SHOSSHI SHMENDRIK *excitedly from ball-room. He is an awkward, ungainly young man in ill-fitting morning-dress.*) Hello! Shosshi Shmendrik, you at a ball!
Shosshi	Yes, and I want my money back.
Sugarman	What, isn't the ball good enough for you?
Shosshi	Don't twist my words—you know what I mean. Give me back that commission money.
Sugarman	What! Haven't I found you the most buxom bride in all Whitechapel? Becky Belcovitch!
Shosshi	You found me Becky's mother.
Sugarman	Well, that is half the battle, and you only advanced me half

the commission.

Shosshi	But Becky herself will never say one word to me.
Sugarman	Many a man would like a wife like that.
Shosshi	Yes, if she'd only say she'd *be* my wife.
Sugarman	She is so modest—a virtuous woman is a crown to her husband.
Shosshi	But she isn't so modest with the other fellows. I'm the only one she won't dance with! I have to dance attendance on her mother instead—I've only just escaped her.
Sugarman	Well, better have her mother's company before marriage than after.
Shosshi	There won't be any after—Not a single dance, look. (*Shows programme.*)
Sugarman	Then dance with the other girls.
Shosshi	They're just as bad as Becky. Why there she is. (*ENTER BECKY BELCOVITCH in beautiful evening dress on the arm of a fine young man. SHOSSHI approaches her. She freezes him with a glance, then sweeps by, giggling unrestrainedly, into the refreshment room.*) What did I tell you? I must have my money back.
Sugarman	Business is business. (*Mops brow with bandanna.*) But I tell you what I will do.
Shosshi	(*Eagerly.*) Yes?
Sugarman	If you were to buy this ticket for the Hamburgh lottery, you would probably win that money back—and more, too.
Shosshi	I want my money back.
Sugarman	Here is your mother back. (*ENTER MRS. BELCOVITCH—a little, dried-up, imaginary invalid. Escapes.*)
Mrs. B.	Oh, there you are, Shosshi. What became of you?
Shosshi	(*Savagely.*) I was looking for Becky—I want her to dance with me.

Mrs. B.　She is shy of you. It is only natural. Give her time. You are a carpenter earning good money, she cannot hold out for ever and I would dance with you myself—only I have such ill-matched legs. One is a thick one and the other a thin one. And so one crawls around. It must be time to take my medicine. (*Produces bottle.*) Shosshi, could you get me a glass and a spoon? (*SHOSSHI goes towards Buffet, meets BECKY and her YOUNG MAN coming out. Again she stares haughtily and passes by, giggling unrestrainedly.*) Becky!

Becky　(*Turning at door.*) I'm in a hurry, mother.

Mrs. B.　Can't you stay a little with me and Shosshi? I feel so ill.

Becky　Shosshi will look after you. (*Preparing to waltz; to YOUNG MAN, aside.*) It's all nonsense, her illness. She pays our doctor a penny a week in sickness or health, so she doesn't like to lose by being well. I've given up going for the medecine—I just put water in her bottle. (*Waltzes in.*)

Shosshi　You see, Mrs. Belcovitch, you see. (*EXIT—lurches against PIN-CHAS, emerging from Buffet with a cigarette. The cigarette falls to the ground.*)

Pinchas　Schlemihl! (*Picks it up and walks, a shade drunkenly, to door of ball-room and looks in.*) Ah, youth, beauty, music, vine—it is a glorious vorld. Only they vill not let me smoke in there—the fool-men. Ah, (*takes cigarette out of mouth*) if I could find my Princess! I save her from the Dragon—and she give me not one leedle smile. Ah, these English maidens—I cannot understand them. All over Europe—in Bucharest, in Berlin, in Budapest, the virgins make eyes at me. Be I not a tall handsome cavalier, vid the poet's fire. (*Puts cigarette in mouth.*) Ah, she go out. I go in. (*EXIT to ball-room.*)

(*Re-ENTER SHOSSHI with glass and spoon.*)

Mrs. B.　Ah, quick, quick, I feel so bad. (*SHOSSHI hastens. Drops spoon. Business.*) Schlemihl! (*Drinking.*) Ugh! But I feel better. It's good stuff. Will you drink with me?

Shosshi　Thank you—I— (*She looks offended.*) There's no glass.

Mrs. B.　And isn't my glass clean enough for you?

Shosshi	Yes, yes, I shall be glad. (*Business. Drinks.*) Why, it tastes like water!
Mrs. B.	(*Angrily.*) Water! My enemies shall drink such water.
Shosshi	I—I—mean—it isn't as nasty as my mother's cod-liver oil.
Mrs. B.	Your mother—it's all fancy with her! She coddles herself too much. May my children's children never be any worse. If your mother had my health, she would be lying in bed with it. But I go about in a sick condition. I can hardly crawl around. Look at my legs—has your mother got such legs? One a thick one and one a thin one! (*ENTER* PINCHAS *and* SIMON WOLF *arm-in-arm from ball-room. The music becomes very gay.* MRS. BELCOVITCH *begins to hop.*) Ah let us go and look on. (*Seizes* SHOSSHI.) Come! (*Dances him in.*)
Simon	Yes, they come dancing here, instead of combining against the sweaters who make their lives a misery. Ah, I have no patience with them. The coming Passover would be more appropriately celebrated by a strike for freedom than by feeding on unleavened bread. Unleavened bread. Pooh! Unleavened idiots! I've a good mind to propose at next Sunday's meeting that all Jewish socialists in London should organise a monster mock Passover service—a parody of the Seder with loaves and beer instead of *motsos* and raisin-wine.
Pinchas	(*Lighting his cigarette.*) Ah, you be a great man, Simon Volf, a heaven-born leader of the poor and the oppressed. But you be a fool-man. You frighten them away with your irreligious talk. They tremble for the heavenly lighting. Ah, you have no statesmanship. There is one vise man to a million fool-men, and he sits on their heads. Let *me* address your meeting next Sunday—then you vill see. I vill speak to them vid their own tongue—my vords vill rush like the mountain-torrents, sweeping away the sweaters. You know Simon, I and you are the only two people in the East-End who speak the English grammatical.
Simon	But these speeches must be in Yiddish.
Pinchas	Gewiss. But who speak her like you and me? You must give

	me one leedle speech.
Simon	I cannot. So many of the old leaders want to speak.
Pinchas	Old leaders! Bah! What have they done? Me and you, ve vill be the Moses and Aaron to lead the people out of the land of bondage. Ve vill get a great following, ve vill put up for Vitechapel at the elections, ve vill both become members of Parliament, me and you, eh?
Simon	(*Smiling.*) I'm afraid there's not much chance of that.
Pinchas	Vy not? There are two seats. Vy should you not have the other?
Simon	Ain't you forgetting about Election expenses?
Pinchas	*Nein!* I forget nothing. Ve vill start a fund.
Simon	We can't start a fund for ourselves.
Pinchas	Vy not? You for me. Me for you.
Simon	You won't get much.
Pinchas	Think not? P'raps not. But *you* vill for *me*. See, my name, Melchitsedek Pinchas, she already makes M.P., Member of Parliament.
Simon	I'd advise you, Pinchas, not to let the tailors and shoemakers get wind of your ambitions. My own motives are absolutely unselfish, I swear to God. Yet you saw that malicious pamphlet that was circulated against me in Yiddish—silly illiterate scribble.
Pinchas	(*Angrily.*) Scribble! She vas vair beautiful. Sharp as the sting of the hornet. Ah, you vill see how I speak Yiddish.
Simon	(*Threateningly.*) Pinchas! *You* wrote that pamphlet.
Pinchas	(*Running away.*) Me? Me? I love you like a brother—almost like a voman. (*At door of the Buffet, turning.*) Von leedle speech.
Simon	It is impossible! I should stir up a wasp's nest.
Pinchas	Just this vonce—I vill be grateful to you all my life.

Simon	Get out. (*Threatening.*)
Pinchas	I vill never give you my ideas again. (*Angry. EXIT to Buffet.*)
Simon	Dance on! Sweaters and sweated in one merry union. But the day will come when *my* union—
Pinchas	(*His head re-appearing at door, cajoling finger to nose.*) Von leedle speech.
Simon	Go to the devil. (*Threatening. EXIT Pinchas.*)
	(*ENTER* EPHRAIM *with* HANNAH JACOBS. *She wears violets at her bosom.*)
Hannah	Ah, what a relief to get a breath of fresh air!
	(*They sit down.*)
Simon	Reb Shemuel's daughter! Ah, if it weren't for her father—he preaches contentment, damn him!—pious resignation to the will of heaven. Pious resignation! Pah! Pinchas is all wrong—I *will* get up that Passover parody, and when they see you *can* eat bread without bringing down thunder and lightning, . . . why, they'll be crying for butter, too. (*EXIT from club.*)
Hannah	Oh, how foolish of me! I left my fan somewhere. (*Half rising.*)
Ephraim	Let me get it for you. It was a feathery thing, wasn't it? (*EXIT.*)
Hannah	Yes, thank you. (*Sits down.*) Oh, how stupid life is! (*Falls into reverie.*)
Pinchas	(*Popping in head again, finger to nose.*) Simon, just von leedle—ah, my Princess! (*Stands, staring.*)
David	(*Relinquishing a* LADY *at ball-room door. Yawns.*) Oh, what a bore civilization is after all. (*Suddenly perceives* HANNAH.) Now if Sam had introduced me to *her!* (*Stands staring.*)
Pinchas	(*Aside.*) Beautiful as the Queen of Sheba.
David	(*Aside.*) There's the first girl with poetry in her.
Pinchas	(*Advancing.*) Ah, my royal maiden, that I saved from the

	Dragon.
Hannah	(*Smiling.*) You here, Mr. Pinchas?
Pinchas	Yes, vy shall I not follow you here? Ven I come to your father's house, I cannot get von leedle vord vid you. You have received my poem?
Hannah	Yes, but I could not understand it.
Pinchas	Not understand! She vas as clear as the blue lake and as beautiful.
Hannah	(*Smiling.*) But she was in Hebrew.
Pinchas	Ah! You—Reb Shemuel's daughter—you understand not Hebrew.
Hannah	Very little—I am only a woman.
Pinchas	Ah, a voman is vorth all the Rabbis in the vorld. Vat is learning, Talmud,—musty nonsense. Life, life, she is varm, beautiful. Ah, I love you! (*Comes nearer.*) You belong to me—I saved you from the Dragon.
Hannah	Go away! You are drunk.
Pinchas	(*Advancing on her.*) Your eyes make me drunk—your lips— (*HANNAH springs up in alarm—PINCHAS tries to embrace her. DAVID springs forward, catches him by coat-collar and throws him aside.*) British bull-dog! I saved her from the Dragon!
David	Save yourself from the flagon! Aren't you ashamed of yourself, sir?
Pinchas	(*Shaking fist.*) Your name, British bull-dog. Oblige me vid your name.
David	(*Smiling.*) Oh, you want to fight a duel, do you? Well, my name's David Brandon—at your service.
Pinchas	David Brandon. Ah, I vill write an acrostic at you. (*Counts on fingers.*) D-a-v-i-d B-r-a-n-d-o-n.—Ah, she vill be terrible. (*Goes towards Buffet.*)
David	Oh she will, will she. (*Stopping PINCHAS.*) No, no more drinking. That's the way out. Go quietly or I'll call the steward.

(*EXIT PINCHAS.*)

Pinchas	(*Popping in head.*) D-A-V-I-D—ah, I vill wrap her round a bullet and shoot you vid it. (*EXIT*).
Hannah	Don't take him seriously, Mr. Brandon. Accept my sincere thanks.
David	I can't take your thanks seriously, either. I only wish he had been a little more dangerous.
Hannah	(*Smiling.*) That *is* kind.
David	No, of course, I don't mean that. But—but—er—do you know who the fellow is?
Hannah	Only a half-mad rogue of a genius who is sponging on my father. But then everybody does that.

(*ENTER EPHRAIM with fan, laughing.*)

Ephraim	Ha! Ha! What do you think? I hunted everywhere till I suddenly caught sight of old Mrs. Belcovitch flirting behind it with—ha! ha! With Shosshi Shmendrik, the carpenter.
Hannah	Mr. Phillips, let me introduce Mr. David Brandon.
Ephraim	Pleased to know you, Mr. Brandon. Jolly dance, isn't it?
David	Delightful. How the old place has developed since I knew it. There weren't so many dress-coats in those days.
Hannah	You have been out of England?
David	Out of all civilization.
Hannah	Ah, I thought you brought a refreshing breath of something new.
David	Thank you.
Ephraim	Ha! Ha! You came out here to get a breath of fresh air—and you seem to have got it.
Hannah	But I have to leave it. (*Rises.*) My next partner will be looking for me.

David	May not I have the pleasure of a dance?
Hannah	I am sorry. My programme's full. (*Holds it up.*)
Ephraim	Perhaps there's one of mine you can give him. (*Looks at it.*)
David	You are very kind.
Ephraim	Why, your next partner is Michael, Mr. Birnbaum and he's in a dark corner, ha! ha! With Mother Malka, trying to smoothe away his other dances with the girls. He'll be delighted to be let off the engagement.
Hannah	(*Hesitating.*) Well, if you'll explain—
David	Of course he'll explain—
Ephraim	There's the Lancers. Excuse me!
David	Certainly. (*EXIT EPHRAIM.*) What a charming young fellow!
Hannah	Yes. Shall we join a set?
David	Didn't I hear that you preferred the fresh air?
Hannah	Well—yes—if you like.
David	I'd just as soon talk. (*Sits down.*) Besides, it's such a jam inside. (*Moves nearer.*)
Hannah	(*Moving back.*) And you are used to great spaces.
David	Ye-es.
Hannah	Tell me something about your adventures.
David	Oh, they no more deserve to be called adventures than to-night's.
Hannah	You don't call this an adventure!
David	Well—er—I mean, not the *fighting* part.
Hannah	Oh, I see. Well—
David	Well—the worst was when I was alone!
Hannah	Is that an adventure—to be alone!

David	Well, if you keep interrupting—
Hannah	Well, tell your story your own way.
David	There isn't any story. I just worked.
Hannah	How unromantic!
David	Do you like romance?
Hannah	We all like what doesn't grow in our garden.
David	But it must grow in *your* garden.
Hannah	You are mistaken—nothing grows in my garden but cabbages. To tell the truth, there isn't even a garden and I get the cabbages from Guedalyah the Greengrocer. But even Guedalyah dreams of Zion, and the return of the Jews, while I—I—
David	You dream of something, too.
Hannah	No, (*very sadly*) nothing. I have no outlook, none.
David	It is impossible. We all dream.
Hannah	What do you dream of?
David	I—I—of violets!
Hannah	How happy you must be! Everybody is wearing them to-night.
David	I did not notice it.
Hannah	No? You dream with your eyes shut, then.
David	What dreamer would wish his eyes opened?
Hannah	You say pretty things. Roughing it has not roughened you.
David	Then I deserve some of those dainty violets.
Hannah	(*Shaking her head.*) This is not a world in which virtue meets its deserts.
David	Oh please! Let us forget the real world.
Hannah	Then I give you one little violet—in the dream-world. (*She gives it to him—he places it on his button-hole.*)

David	Thank you—I wish I had dreamed you gave me more than one dance.
Hannah	That is all you asked for.
David	May I have a bunch?
Hannah	No, of course not. A moment ago, my programme was full. Do you think miracles happen?
David	Yes, yes, I think—miracles happen.
Hannah	(*Lightly.*) My father would be delighted with you.
David	Your father?
Hannah	He believes in miracles too—swallows all the Bible ones as unquestioningly as the food mother puts on his plate.
David	You are laughing at me?
Hannah	I? (*Looks at programme.*) Sam! I think it's time I found him. (*Rising.*)
David	Who's Sam?
Hannah	Sam? Sam's—(*with a twinkle of fun*) the man I was married to.
David	What?
Hannah	What's the matter?
David	Did you say you were married?
Hannah	I did have that misfortune.
David	To Sam Levine! My old schoolfellow! I *guess* it! You are the—
Hannah	Yes—the very Sam! (*Pause. Joyous music heard.*)
David	You said—misfortune?
Hannah	Yes.
David	Sam must be a regular brute. He ought to have his head punched. (*Looks into ball-room.*)
Hannah	No, no—no more melodrama to-night.

David	(*Gloomily.*) Don't be alarmed—I only wanted to see if—yes, he is still carrying on with that fat thing in red.
Hannah	Don't run Leah down. She's a friend of mine.
David	They always are.
Hannah	I suppose he thinks he owes her some compensation—he was engaged to her before he married me.
David	Then he is doubly a brute. And now he goes back to her!
Hannah	Naturally.
David	How came you to marry him?
Hannah	Accident.
David	Accident!
Hannah	The purest.
David	You *are* making fun of me! Show me your hand.
Hannah	(*Snatching it away.*) No, I'm not so simple as to show my hand.
David	I don't believe you're married at all!
Hannah	I didn't say I am. I said I was. There, I've shown you my hand. Still puzzled?
David	But Sam's alive.
Hannah	It's very simple.
David	I give it up.
Hannah	He gave me up. I was divorced.
David	You?
Hannah	I. (*Laughing.*)
David	And he has gone back to that fat thing! (*Looks in again.*) You are playing with me!
Hannah	No. True as the law of Moses, as father would say. In fact, the law of Moses is to blame for the whole thing.

David   Won't you explain?

Hannah   Well, only our little circle knows it. We asked the witnesses
            not to speak of it and even mother does not know. If you will
            keep it a secret—

David   I will keep it as sacred as this violet.

Hannah   Well, your old schoolfellow got joking one day with a dia-
            mond ring he had bought for Leah and he slipped it on my
            finger, saying "By this ring I consecrate thee unto me accord-
            ing to the Law of Moses and Israel." This was before wit-
            nesses, so that constituted a marriage.

David   The devil! I beg your pardon.

Hannah   No, thank you for saying it. That was what I wanted to say at
            the time.

David   But that's not the law of England.

Hannah   It's the law of Scotland, and it's the Jewish law. And of course
            my father puts Jewish law before everything else—even com-
            mon sense.

David   Who is your father?

Hannah   Reb Shemuel!

David   Reb Shemuel! That dear old chap! He often used to bless me
            when I was a boy. And he always gave me a penny afterwards.
            Lots of us boys went to be thus blessed. And so, I suppose, he
            made you go though a formal divorce . . . I am so glad.

Hannah   Glad?

David   I mean . . . amused. It's so queer. Fancy such things in our
            century.

Hannah   You are not very respectful of the Law of Moses.

David   Oh well, I don't see how we can keep *all* of it nowadays. It's
            absurd to expect a man to go without meat, when he's travel-
            ling up country, just because it hasn't been killed by a licensed
            slaughterer. But I oughtn't to be saying such things to Reb
            Shemuel's daughter.

Hannah	What nonsense! Haven't you discovered I am not so pious as my father?
David	Oh, I knew you couldn't be quite so pious. A woman is not expected to be. Let me see—didn't I use to say a prayer thanking God for not having made me a woman?
Hannah	(*Smiling.*) It seems to have been a long time ago.
David	It was. When I was a boy. When I was a *boy*—ha! ha!
Hannah	Ah, don't laugh. You ought to thank God still. A woman has no voice in her destinies.
David	Oh, I don't see that.
Hannah	Do you not? My marriage with Sam is only a violent sample. Any marriage I might make would be just as forced, really.
David	How so?
Hannah	Well, I should have to marry a pious man, for the sake of father's position.
David	And you don't like pious men?
Hannah	This eternal concern with pots and pans, with prayers and phylacteries—ugh!
David	But your father would not forbid you to marry a man you—you cared for . . . just because he wasn't pious.
Hannah	I am sure he would.
David	But that would be cruel.
Hannah	*He* wouldn't think so, he'd think he was saving my soul. And remember he can't imagine anyone not seeing the beauty of the Yoke of the Law.
David	He seemed to me the kindest creature in the world.
Hannah	Oh so he is, so he is. But when religion's concerned, the best-hearted of mankind are liable to become hard as stone.
	(*The music ceases. SUGARMAN ENTERS from Buffet and looks at them.*)

David	Well—couldn't—couldn't he pretend to be pious?
Hannah	Who?
David	Your—your lover?
Hannah	Such a lover, Mr. Brandon, I shouldn't love. If I took on a new life, it must be a life of Truth and Freedom. But it will never be—I shall never marry.
David	Don't prophesy. You may marry tomorrow—as suddenly as the first time.
Hannah	(*Laughing.*) Impossible. Why I can't even be betrothed till ninety days after the *Get*.
David	And when is the time up?
	(*ENTER SAM.*)
Hannah	(*Still speaking.*) Our time is up. For here is Mr. Levine, coming for his waltz. Ha! Ha! How serious we got! And you never told me your adventures after all.
David	I'll tell you next time of my—adventure.
Hannah	Do. Yes, Mr. Levine. This is ours. (*To David, laughing.*) Won't you ask Leah to dance?
David	I shall not dance any more to-night.
Hannah	What a shame! What will you do?
David	I shall dream.
Hannah	Of violets?
David	Of one violet.
Hannah	Well, it will be with your eyes open. (*Takes SAM's arm, looks back over shoulder at DAVID, nods. DAVID makes a step towards her. EXEUNT SAM and HANNAH. DAVID stands looking after her.*)
Sugarman	Another commission gone!
	CURTAIN.

ACT III

The Letter and the Spirit

(*Interior of Reb Shemuel's book-lined parlour. The Sabbath ta-ble with snow-white cloth, two candles burning, twisted loaves, fried fish, wine-cup vase of violets &c. The* REB *in black skull-cap at head of table,* HANNAH *and* MRS. JACOBS *on either side. The meal is finished and the* REB *is just joyously concluding the Grace. As the curtain rises all join in chanting the Hebrew, ending in a silent muttering.*)

Reb Shemuel (*Stretching himself.*) So you see, my dear, in spite of all your worrying, we *did* have fish for Sabbath.

Mrs. Jacobs You mean *because* of my worrying. If I relied on you, we shouldn't even have bread.

Reb Shemuel (*Smiling.*) Of course not. You must rely on the Almighty.

Mrs. Jacobs But what's the use of His sending you money, when you waste it on dirty beggars.

Reb Shemuel If I could find clean beggars, I would willingly give them the preference. Don't you see that that is just God's greatest gift to us—the power of helping others!

Mrs. Jacobs Others! Others! And I can't even have a servant-girl to help me!

Hannah Oh mother! You know you always discharge them.

Mrs. Jacobs Discharge them! I'd like to discharge them from a cannon. Unless you stand over them like the Egyptian taskmasters over our forefathers, do they ever do a stroke of work—except breaking the crockery? And the dust they leave on every-thing!

Reb Shemuel	Except on my papers. They *will* mix them up.
Mrs. Jacobs	You shouldn't leave them about—how are the poor girls to know?
Reb Shemuel	Yes, the fault is mine. Let us not disturb the Sabbath peace.
Mrs. Jacobs	But I must disturb it—there's no servant to clear the table. (*Begins to clatter with the dishes.*) If it wasn't against the religion I should have to make up the fire!
Hannah	(*Rising.*) Let me clear, mother.
Mrs. Jacobs	No, no: I must not lean on you, or else when you're married—Ah, if you had been a proper father, Shemuel, you would have saved up your money for Hannah's dowry.
Hannah	Don't begin with that again, mother.
Mrs. Jacobs	I've never left off.
Reb Shemuel	That's true.
Mrs. Jacobs	It makes me a laughing-stock to have an unmarried daughter of Hannah's age. You find husbands easily enough for other men's daughters.
Reb Shemuel	I found a husband for your father's daughter.
Mrs. Jacobs	You didn't even do that. My father found you. He told me you were so learned.
Reb Shemuel	And he told me you were so good-tempered. (*Kisses her.*) I know what it is, my Simcha—you have another of your headaches.
Mrs. Jacobs	(*Sweetly.*) Yes, Shemuel, I think I'll go to bed early.
Reb Shemuel	Do, my dear.
Mrs. Jacobs	As soon as I have cleared.
Hannah	Oh, mother, I *shall* help you.
Mrs. Jacobs	No, no. (*Carrying a dish and the vase into the kitchen.*)
Hannah	Don't take away the violets, mother.

Mrs. Jacobs	Yes, yes, they'll fade in this heat. Tomorrow is also a day. Give your father his Song of Solomon. (*EXIT.*)
Reb Shemuel	Poor Solomon—with his thousand wives.
	(*HANNAH takes a book from shelves.*)
Hannah	I always preferred David. And David was a man after God's own heart. There, father. (*Hands book.*)
Reb Shemuel	Thank you Hannah. (*Commences to chant it. HANNAH takes up photograph of DAVID and kisses it surreptitiously. Then gets herself a book, sits and reads. There is a little tap, followed immediately by the entrance of the Sabbath FIRE-WOMAN, an old Irishwoman who without saying a word snuffs the candles, pokes the fire and EXIT. Neither the REB nor HANNAH looks up or pays the least attention to her. A pause.*) What are you reading, Hannah?
Hannah	The Bible, father.
Reb Shemuel	Ah, that is right.
Hannah	I also want to read the Song of Solomon—only in English.
Reb Shemuel	You!
Hannah	Yes—why have you to read it on Friday nights?
Reb Shemuel	Because like the Sabbath it is an expression of God's love for Israel.
Hannah	God's love for Israel? (*Reads.*) "I charge you, O ye daughters of Jerusalem, by the roes and by the hinds of the field, that ye stir not up, nor awake my love, till he please." What has that to do with God or Israel?
Reb Shemuel	It is metaphorical, dear. The Midrash explains that it means that we must not stir up Israel to return to Palestine till God pleases.
Hannah	It seems to me just a simple song of human love. Listen. (*Reads ecstatically.*) "I am my beloved's and his desire is towards me. Come, my beloved, let us go forth into the field: let us lodge in the villages. Let us get up early to the vineyards, let us see if the vine flourish, whether the tender grapes appear and the

pomegranates bud forth." I wish it had mentioned violets. (*A stone strikes window.*)

Mrs. Jacobs   (*Rushing in.*) What was that?

Reb Shemuel   Must have been a stone.

(*Derisive voice at keyhole:* "Jew! Jew!")

Mrs. Jacobs   Those Christian roughs again.

Reb Shemuel   Alas, we are still in Exile.

Hannah   (*Aside, bitterly.*) God's love for Israel.

Mrs. Jacobs   You always will keep the shutters open, so they can look in.

Reb Shemuel   Why should we not display our holy Sabbath peace, our harmless lives?

Mrs. Jacobs   That's what aggravates them. Close the shutters, Hannah.

(*As HANNAH opens window to close shutters MRS. BELCOVITCH and SHOSSHI SHMENDRIK appear outside.*)

Mrs. B.   Good Sabbath, all. We are just coming in with a question. May we?

Reb Shemuel   Certainly, Mrs. Belcovitch.

Mrs. B.   Go on, Shosshi.

(*SHOSSHI ENTERS sheepishly. He puts finger to amulet of door-post and kisses it.*)

Reb Shemuel   Sit down. (*MRS. JACOBS offers seats. HANNAH closes shutters. Business.*)

Mrs. B.   We wish you to decide between us.

(*SHOSSHI nods with sickly smile.*)

Reb Shemuel   With pleasure, if I can.

Mrs. B.   Shosshi was engaged to my daughter, Becky. The contracts were written out.

Shosshi   But Becky—

Mrs. B.	Let me speak. Whoever broke off the match had to pay ten pounds damages. Now what happens? Shosshi breaks off with Becky—
Shosshi	But Becky—
Mrs. B.	Let me speak! Shosshi breaks off with Becky and wants *me* to pay the ten pounds.
Shosshi	But Becky—
Mrs. B.	Will you never let me speak? Do you want the judge to hear only one side? You say Becky broke with you, I know. But didn't you purposely shock her by showing her—
Shosshi	But Becky—
Mrs. Jacobs	Hush! Hush, dear people. You make my head split.
Reb Shemuel	Well, well, Mr. Shmendrik. What do you want to say?
Shosshi	Becky laughed whenever—whenever she saw me. And when I brought her some of my work to see she told me to get out.
Mrs. B.	Some of your work! Get out!
Shosshi	I brought her specimens of my carpentry—some cradle-rockers!
Reb Shemuel	Cradle-rockers!
Mrs. B.	Cradle-rockers. And such things one shows to a maiden!
Shosshi	They were my best carving—one was a thin one and the other was a thick one.
Mrs. B.	Shameless droll! Do you make fun of my legs, too?
Mrs. Jacobs	Ach, what bad tempers some people have!
Shosshi	I won't pay a penny more. I've lost enough over Sugarman the Shadchan.
Reb Shemuel	Do you withdraw from the contract, Mrs. Belcovitch?
Mrs. B.	No! I do not.
Reb Shemuel	Then do you, Mr. Shmendrik?

Shosshi	But Becky—
Mrs. B.	Answer the question!
Shosshi	But Becky laughs when she sees me.
Reb Shemuel	Would you have her cry? Come, this is not a question for the Sabbath. The prohibition against touching money refers even to our thoughts. Come to me on Sunday with Becky.
Mrs. B.	Come to you again—with *my* legs! I can hardly crawl around. I am in a sick condition.
Reb Shemuel	Sosshi will give you his arm. Good Sabbath.
Shosshi	But Becky—
Mrs. B.	Hold your peace and obey the Reb. (*Takes his arm.*)
Shosshi	But Becky—
Mrs. B.	On Sunday. (*Drags him out.*) Good Sabbath. (*EXEUNT.*)
Reb S. & Hannah	Good Sabbath.
Mrs. Jacobs	Half my headaches come from these people who come bothering you. Why don't they leave you alone on Sabbath at least?
Reb Shemuel	It is better that they come to me than drag their affairs before the English courts.
Hannah	Well, I think Becky's perfectly right to refuse to be contracted away. She laughs—ha! ha! ha!—laughs away the customs of the ages. Delicious. Ha! Ha! Ha!
Mrs. Jacobs	The impudence-face! I'd smack it if I were her mother!
Reb Shemuel	Well, my dear, you can't say Shosshi is the ideal of a maiden's day-dream.
Mrs. Jacobs	Everybody can't have a fancy goods man.
Reb Shemuel	That's true, but Shosshi is very plain goods.
Hannah	I am glad our people weren't always so unromantic. Listen,

	mother, to the Song of Solomon. "Set me as a seal upon thine heart, as a seal upon thine arm: for love is strong as death!"
Mrs. Jacobs	But Mr. Shmendrik earns a good living—
Hannah	(*Reading.*) "Many waters cannot quench love, neither can the floods drown it: if a man would give all the substance of his house for love, it would utterly be condemned!"
Pinchas	(*Outside.*) Yes, yes, Guedalyah, you shall come in and ask him for yourself.
Hannah	Why, there's that Pinchas again!
Reb Shemuel	(*Rubbing his hands.*) Ah, now we shall talk poetry and holy lore.
Mrs. Jacobs	Not in my hearing. That noisy little *schnorrer* will make my head beat like a hammer. I'll go to bed at once.
Reb Shemuel	Won't you wait for the Fire-woman to light you to your room? (*Pinchas knocks.*)
Mrs. Jacobs	No, no, I can feel my way.
Hannah	I'll help you, mother. (*They mount the stairs.*)
Reb Shemuel	Come in!
	(*ENTER* PINCHAS *and shyly behind him,* GUEDALYAH *the Greengrocer, a tall loosely-built man with a pasty complexion and shining, enthusiastic eyes.* PINCHAS *ostentatiously kisses the door amulet.*)
Pinchas	Ah, peace to you all. (*Catching sight of* HANNAH *up the stairs.*) Good Sabbath, Princess? Vy you fly from me?
Hannah	Come, mother! (*They disappear.*)
Reb Shemuel	Good Sabbath! (*Peering.*) Is not this Guedalyah the Greengrocer?
Pinchas	Yes, I saw him at his door as I was coming to you, and we talked of Zion.
Reb Shemuel	(*Piously.*) Whose glory may God restore!

Guedalyah	Amen.
Pinchas	He vished me to ask of you a favour—but I persuaded him to ask of you himself.
Reb Shemuel	Ah. Take a chair, Guedalyah.
Pinchas	That is vat he vishes to ask *you*. He! He! He! (*PINCHAS wanders to book-shelves and opens books.*)
Guedalyah	Yes, Reb Shemuel, since Pinchas has come to the point at once. I want to ask you to honour us by taking the chair at the opening meeting of the Holy Land League; which a few of us are founding to promote the return of the Jews to Palestine.
Reb Shemuel	(*Shaking head.*) I fear the days of the Messiah are not yet.
Guedalyah	(*Flaring up.*) And when then?
Reb Shemuel	We know not. We are in exile. It is God's will. We must submit.
Pinchas	(*Turning round.*) No, I agree with Guedalyah. Vy ve submit? Ve can be our own Messiah.
Reb Shemuel	But how?
Guedalyah	We will collect a fund—slowly but surely. It is the poor, the oppressed, the persecuted, whose souls pant after the land of Israel, as the hart after the water-brooks. With the first-fruits of our collection we will send out a little party of persecuted Jews to Palestine, then another and another. The movement will grow like a sliding snow-ball that becomes an avalanche.
Pinchas	(*Getting excited.*) Yes, I vill come. I vill make a mighty speech, for my lips, like Isaiah's, have been touched with the burning coal. I vill write our *Marseillaise*. Singly, ve are the sand-grains, united ve are the simoom. I shall be the trumpet to gather the dispersed from the four corners of the earth . . . yea, I shall be the Messiah himself. (*Takes out cigarette and puts it to candle.*)
Reb Shemuel	(*In excited reminder.*) Ah! The Sabbath!
Pinchas	(*Drops the cigarette.*) I forgot. I fancied the Messiah was al-

ready come, and the Yoke of the Law abolished.

Guedalyah   Let us be practical. We are not yet ready for *Marseillaises* or Messiahs. The first step is to get funds enough to send one family to Palestine.

Pinchas   Yes, yes, but ve must look ahead! See, my name Melchitsedek Pinchas—she already makes M.P., Messiah, Palestine. But I will not go rashly—one family at a time. Eh, how does that strike you, Guedalyah?

Guedalyah   Yes, yes, that is my idea.

Pinchas   Aha! You see I am not a Napoleon only in great ideas. I understand detail-prose as well as poetry. Ah, I see Zion laughing on her mountains, and her fig-trees skipping for joy. I vill be the treasurer of the fund.

Guedalyah   (*Dryly.*) No, I prefer you to write the *Marseillaise*. Well, what do you say, Reb Shemuel?

Reb Shemuel   I will think. If it is only sending a few families . . . But when God wishes us to go back, He will stretch out His right hand, and lead us by pillars of cloud and pillars of fire.

Guedalyah   I believe in columns of subscriptions.

Reb Shemuel   Except the Lord build the house, it shall not stand. Till that great day our Zion is here. Wherever three men are gathered together to discuss the law, there is the Divine Presence.

(*Another stone crashes at window-shutters, and another derisive cry is heard.*)

Guedalyah   There is the Devil's Presence.

Reb Shemuel   We are in Exile. We must suffer.

Guedalyah   We deserve to suffer . . . Good-night. (*Turning back.*) The day will come when you will see I was right.

Reb Shemuel   You are no more right than Simon Wolf. He rebels against God's decree, wickedly. You, piously. But you are both rebels.

Guedalyah   Are you coming, Pinchas?

Pinchas   No, I have important things to say to Reb Shemuel. Go, go, leave me to convince him. (*Aside.*)

Guedalyah   Good Sabbath. (*EXIT.*)

Pinchas   Ah, Guedalyah has only greengrocer's ideas—small potatoes. I and you vill light this great signal-fire.

Reb Shemuel Not to-day, Pinchas. It is the Sabbath. Leave all that to our Fire-woman. What else do you wish to say?

Pinchas   To ask you to give your daughter this poem. She says she understand not Hebrew, so I write English—my first English poem—for her!

Reb Shemuel Ah! (*Taking it.*)

Pinchas   You see I made it acrostic—Hannah—like the Hebrew. Oh, very clever—H-A-N-N-A-H.
Hebrew Hebe
All-fair Maid,
Next to Heaven
Nightly laid,
Ah, I love thee
Half afraid.

Reb Shemuel Very pretty.

Pinchas   It is beautiful—Ah (*finger to nose*) but I vant you to tell her that vat I write her is not a millionth part of vat I feel, that she is my sun by day and my moon and stars by night, that I must marry her at once or die, that I think of nothing in the vorld but her, that I can do, write, plan, nothing vithout her, that once she smiles on me, I vill write her great love-poems—greater than Byron, greater than Heine, greater than Solomon, the real Song of Songs, which is Pinchas's—that I vill make her immortal as Dante made Beatrice, as Petrarch made Laura, that I valk about wretched, bedewing the pavements vith my tears, that I sleep not by night, nor eat by day—you vill tell her this!

Reb Shemuel I will tell her. You are a son-in-law to gladden the heart of any scholar. But I fear the maiden looks coldly on wooers. Besides, you are fourteen years older than she.

Pinchas	Then I love her twice as much as Jacob loved Rachel. For it is written, "Seven years were but a day in his love for her." To me fourteen years are as a day in my love for Hannah.
Reb Shemuel	Ha! Ha! But have you the wherewithal to support her?
Pinchas	Not in this ignorant country, may be. But ve vill go abroad— to your birth-place, Reb Shemuel, the cradle of great scholars.
Hannah	(*At top of stairs.*) Father!
Reb Shemuel	Yes, my dear.
Hannah	Can you come up to mother?
Reb Shemuel	Excuse me—my wife is unwell.
Pinchas	Ah, tell Hannah now, tell Hannah now.
Reb Shemuel	Yes, yes, good Sabbath.
Pinchas	Good Sabbath. (*Ostentatiously kisses door-amulet and EXIT. REB SHEMUEL mounts stairs, the house-door opens. PINCHAS re-appears, finger to nose.*) You vill tell her?
Reb Shemuel	Yes, I will tell her.
	(*House-door closes. REB SHEMUEL disappears round top of stairs; house-door re-opens, PINCHAS's head re-appears. Seeing coast is clear, he comes in, picks up his cigarette from the floor, lights it at candle, and canters out in a cloud of smoke.*)
Reb Shemuel	(*Re-appearing at top of stairs.*) Ah, you naughty creature. So it was only a trick to be rid of Pinchas.
Hannah	Well, mother will never fall asleep if I stay, she *will* talk. And I couldn't come down while *he* was there.
	(*They descend.*)
Reb Shemuel	What a shame! And he was telling me how much (*sniffs smoke*) he loved you! (*Sniffs.*)
Hannah	(*Sniffing.*) Yes, I know all about that. But (*sniffs*) I hate your snuffy scholars and poets.

Reb Shemuel   That is wrong, my daughter. Wisdom and learning and piety must be respected even if they appear in rags. Abraham entertained God's messengers though they came as weary travellers. See, here is a poem Pinchas addressed to you. (*He sits down to his Hebrew Bible at the table, and murmurs. She sits opposite reading the poem. A silence. She studies his face.*)

Hannah   Father!

Reb Shemuel   Yes, my child.

Hannah   You don't seriously entertain the idea of—of my marrying Pinchas.

Reb Shemuel   (*Smiling.*) *He* does.

Hannah   Ah, I knew you didn't. You know I could never marry a man like that.

Reb Shemuel   Your mother could.

Hannah   Dear old goose! (*Pulling his beard.*) You are not a bit like that. You know a thousand times more. (*He holds up hands of comic deprecation.*) Yes, you do. Only you let him talk so much. You let everybody talk and bamboozle you.

Reb Shemuel   (*Feeling her hands with a puzzled look.*) The hands are the hands of Hannah, but the voice is the voice of her mother.

Hannah   All right, dear. I won't scold you any more. I'm so glad it didn't really enter your great, stupid, clever old head that I was likely to care for Pinchas. And you wouldn't really want me to marry any one I didn't like?

Reb Shemuel   God forbid! My little Hannah shall marry whomever she pleases.

Hannah   You don't mean that, father.

Reb Shemuel   True as the Law of Moses. Why not?

Hannah   Suppose . . . I wanted (*smiling*) to marry a Christian.

Reb Shemuel   Ha! Ha! Ha! My Hannah would have made a good Talmudist. Of course we know that would never occur.

Hannah	(*Lightly.*) Yes, but if I was to marry a very, very, very lax Jew, you'd think it almost as bad.
Reb Shemuel	No! No! That's a different thing altogether. The worst of Jews cannot put off his Judaism. His unborn soul undertook the yoke of the law at Sinai.
Hannah	Then you really wouldn't mind if I married a lax Jew.
Reb Shemuel	(*More gravely, with dawning suspicion.*) I should mind. But if you loved him, he would become a good Jew.
Hannah	But if he wouldn't.
Reb Shemuel	I should pray. While there is life there is hope for the sinner in Israel.
Hannah	And you would really not mind whom I married?
Reb Shemuel	Follow your heart, my little one. It is a good heart and it will not lead you wrong. (*HANNAH turns away to hide her emotion. He resumes his reading. After a silence she places her wet cheek to him.*)
Hannah	Father, forgive me. I am so sorry. I thought that—that I—that you—oh! Father! Father! I feel as if I had never known you before to-night.
Reb Shemuel	What is it, my daughter? What have you done?
Hannah	I have betrothed myself. I have betrothed myself without telling you—or mother.
Reb Shemuel	To whom?
Hannah	To a Jew.
Reb Shemuel	(*Relieved.*) Ah!
Hannah	But he is neither a scholar, nor pious. He is newly returned from the Cape.
Reb Shemuel	Ah, they are a lax lot. Where did you meet him?
Hannah	At the Club Ball.
Reb Shemuel	Your mother would have you go. What is his name?

Hannah   David Brandon. He is a noble soul.

Reb Shemuel   You were not betrothed at the first meeting.

Hannah   Oh no, father. Besides the ninety days were not up.

Reb Shemuel   (*Softened.*) You remembered that?

Hannah   Yes, father. And I saw him several times before.

Reb Shemuel   At the Club?

Hannah   At the club. (*The* REB *strokes her hair.*) I would not have said "Yes" so quick, father, but David had to go to Germany and would not leave England till I had promised. (REB *stands with bent head, pondering.*) He is so masterful and sudden, father; a man of action, not a woman of dreams, like poor me. Perhaps that is what fascinates me. You are not angry with me, father?

Reb Shemuel   No, Hannah. But you should have told me from the first.

Hannah   I always meant to, father. But I feared to grieve you.

Reb Shemuel   Wherefore? The man is a Jew. And you love him, do you not?

Hannah   As my life, father. (*Quoting.*) "I am my beloved's and his desire is towards me."

Reb Shemuel   It is enough, my Hannah. With you to love him, he will become pious. When a man has a good Jewish wife like my beloved daughter, who will keep a good Jewish house, he cannot be long among the sinners. The light of a true Jewish home will lead his footsteps back to God. (*A silence. He puts his hands on her head.*) May God make thee as Sarah, Leah, Rachel and Rebecca.

Hannah   Dear Father! (*Embraces him.*)

Reb Shemuel   And now I had better see if your poor mother has managed to doze off.

Hannah   You will not tell her yet?

Reb Shemuel   Tell her! Why she'd be awake all night! (*Mounts the stairs, smiling.*)

Hannah	(*Looking after him.*) A true Jewish home! He almost persuades me that I shall keep one after all. I am glad I have never told him of my doubts. Dear David! How happy he will be! (*Takes out his picture. There is a timid knock.* HANNAH *puts picture in her pocket.*) Come in!
	(*ENTER ESTHER ANSELL.*)
Esther	Good Sabbath, miss.
Hannah	Good Sabbath, Esther. What brings you out at this hour?
Esther	Well, I wanted to come some other day, but what with school and the children Sabbath is my only free time. And then only Friday night after I have put the little ones to bed.
Hannah	(*Kissing.*) Poor Esther! You are a hardworked little mother.
Esther	Oh, I wouldn't mind the work, bless you, if—if—
Hannah	If what—
Esther	Oh nothing.
Hannah	Tell me, dear.
Esther	Well, if there were enough to manage on. But I mustn't complain. Next year we shall be quite rich.
Hannah	How is that?
Esther	I shall be allowed to draw out the five pounds I won at school.
Hannah	Five pounds! That is indeed wealth. Why what will you do with it all?
Esther	Trust me to know what to do with it all.
Hannah	But tell me.
Esther	I can't. (*Hangs head.*)
Hannah	Yes do. I want to know.
Esther	Well, father must have a new coat, that is the first thing, and

a box of paper collars. Oh, but I didn't come to talk about father, only about my little brother.

Hannah	Well, what about your little brother?
Esther	I am thinking of putting him up as a candidate for the Orphan Asylum at the next election, and I wonder if your father would use his influence—
Hannah	Certainly, certainly.
Esther	You see father being alive, my brother is not a perfect orphan, and that damages his chance. And the injustice is, that father doesn't earn much more than if he *were* dead.
Hannah	But I thought he sold lemons.
Esther	Oh no, he doesn't sell lemons. That's the trouble. He only stands with lemons.
Hannah	Well, you tell him to send me fifty lemons, will you?
Esther	No, miss, I can't.
Hannah	Why not?
Esther	It is the Sabbath. I mustn't accept a business order on the Sabbath.
Hannah	I beg your pardon. You funny little thing. Well, I'll try and remember—on Sunday.
Esther	And please, miss, would you make a knot in your handkerchief about the orphan asylum?
Hannah	Certainly—I (*takes out handkerchief and portrait.*) No. I'll do better. I have an orphan of my own (*looks at photograph*)—that'll keep me in mind of it.
Esther	(*Alarmed.*) A rival candidate?
Hannah	No, dear. Look.
Esther	(*Looks.*) Oh a grown-up! I don't consider a grown-up an orphan.
Hannah	Well. He hasn't got any one in the world to look after him all

the same.

Esther	Well, that's his own fault. He is old enough to have little orphans of his own—like father.
Hannah	(*Laughing.*) What a horrible idea! Do you like his face?
Esther	Oh yes—but not so much as Lord Byron's.
Hannah	(*Laughing.*) Oh dear, Esther, you are so funny. Well, you had better run home now, I think!
Esther	Yes, miss.

(*HANNAH accompanies her to door, and opens it.*)

Hannah	Aren't you afraid of being out so late?
Esther	Me, miss! I should be afraid if father was. The roughs call after him so. Good Sabbath, miss. (*EXIT.*)
Hannah	Good Sabbath, *missus.* (*Stands at door, looking after her, then looks fondly at portrait and presses it to her lips. DAVID suddenly embraces her. She screams slightly and lets photograph fall.*) David!
David	My darling Hannah.
Hannah	(*Disengaging herself.*) But—
David	But you have let my picture fall. (*Picks it up.*) What a bad omen!
Hannah	(*Taking it.*) It's your own fault for startling me so. Why do you come here?
David	Because my ship has just brought me—because I couldn't bear to be in London without seeing you. Because I was resolved to speak to your father this very night and brave all.
Hannah	What sudden madness.
David	Sudden, I admit. You said that when I asked for the violet. You said that when I asked for you. But mad? We shall see.
Hannah	You were not mad, dear. Come in. (*He follows her, wondering. She closes the door.*) Father has consented.

David   Eh?

Hannah   I told father—and he has consented.

David   (*Passionately.*) Hannah! (*Solemnly.*) My wife!

Hannah   My husband! (*They embrace.*) "Set me as a seal upon thine heart, as a seal upon thine arm: for love is strong as death." (*There is a tap on the door. The lovers hurriedly stand apart. The old* FIRE-WOMAN *ENTERS, silently, walks between them, pokes the fire, snuffs the candles and walks out without a word.*) That's a reminder, David, you can't stay long. At nine the old Fire-woman puts out all lights.

David   (*Laughing.*) And you all visitors, eh?

Hannah   Yes—father will be shocked enough at your coming at all. Hadn't you better wait till the morning?

David   Morning! Why this *is* morning. Here *is* the sun-rise, the bar of burning gold across the blue, the sweet clean air. Don't you hear the birds? Oh, Hannah, Hannah, it is morning at last.

                 (*REB SHEMUEL heard at head of stairs, humming a synagogue-tune. The lovers look up.*)

Reb Shemuel   She is sound asleep.

Hannah   Father! (*REB stands still at head of stairs.*) This is Mr. David Brandon. He has just got back from Germany and—and—

Reb Shemuel   (*Smiling.*) Ah, love is worse than the river Sambatyon. Even that rests on the Sabbath.

David   I hope, sir, my love for your dear daughter will never have a holiday.

Reb Shemuel   Ah, ah, we begin on that height but— (*descending slowly and shaking his head*) Well, well, (*offering his hand*) may the Most High bless you! May you make my Hannah as good a husband as she will make you a wife.

David   Trust me, Reb Shemuel.

Reb Shemuel   (*Lightly.*) Hannah says that you are a sinner in Israel. But I suppose you will keep a Jewish kitchen.

David	If it is only to have the pleasure of entertaining you, sir—
Reb Shemuel	(*Laying hand on shoulder.*) Ah, you will soon become a good Jew. My Hannah will teach you. God bless her. I was a bit lax myself before I married.
David	No, not you, Reb Shemuel. I warrant you never skipped a precept, even as a bachelor.
Reb Shemuel	Oh yes, I did. For when I was a bachelor, I hadn't fulfilled the precept to marry, ha! ha! ha!
Hannah	Is marriage reckoned a good deed then?
Reb Shemuel	In our holy religion everything one ought to do is reckoned a good deed, even if it is pleasant.
David	(*Laughing.*) Then even I must have laid up some good deeds. Really, it isn't such a bad religion after all.
Reb Shemuel	Bad religion! Wait till you've tried it. You've never had a proper training, that's clear. Are your parents alive?
David	No, sir. They both died when I was a child.
Reb Shemuel	I thought as much. Fortunately my Hannah's didn't. (*He smiles. HANNAH presses his hand.*) She will teach you. (*She lets his hand drop.*) Ah, it will be all right. God is good. You have a sound Jewish heart at bottom, David, my son. Hannah, bring back the wine. We will drink a glass together. (*EXIT HANNAH to kitchen-door.*) Sit down, sit down, my son. We have let you stand . . . (*DAVID sits.*) I suppose Hannah told you of her . . . her prior matrimonial misadventure.
David	Yes. Do you mean this is the second? Ha! Ha!
Reb Shemuel	Ha! Ha!
David	Sam Levine was one of my schoolmates, too. Well, I'm glad he's married now, so there's no more danger of mix-ups. And the sooner I'm married, too, the better.
Reb Shemuel	Then I suppose you have the means?
David	Oh yes, I can show you my—

Reb Shemuel	I don't want to see anything. My girl must be supported decently—that is all I ask—that and the Jewish home—
David	Ah, you mustn't think me quite a lost soul, Reb Shemuel. You often blessed me in the synagogue at the corner—when I was a boy.
Reb Shemuel	Did I really?
David	Ah, but not with the blessing you give me to-night, sir.
Reb Shemuel	Ahem! (*Coughs with emotion.*) Perhaps you'll like a seat for the coming Passover at the old synagogue, then.
David	I should be delighted . . . oh, I forgot—I am so sorry.
Reb Shemuel	About what?
David	I had already promised Mr. Birnbaum to attend *his* synagogue—near the Halfpenny Exchange. For, talking of blessings (*smiling*) my own services are wanted.
Reb Shemuel	Your services . . .
David	Yes, as—as—I forgot the Hebrew name. As Priest.
Reb Shemuel	Oh, as *Cohen*.
David	Yes, as *Cohen*. Mr. Birnbaum's congregation suffers from a scarcity of the tribe of Aaron. So they want me to help in—what's the Hebrew word again?—in blessing the congregation.
Reb Shemuel	(*With a change of face*). What! Are you a *Cohen*?
David	(*Smiling.*) Of course I am. Why they got me to bless them in the Transvaal last Atonement Day. (*REB rises.*) So you see I'm *not* altogether a sinner in Israel . . . What is the matter? You are ill. (*Rises.*)
Reb Shemuel	(*Shaking his head and striking his brow with his fist.*) Ach Gott? Why did I not think of finding out before? But, thank God, I know it in time.
David	Finding out what?

Reb Shemuel	My daughter cannot marry you.
David	(*Blankly.*) Eh? What?
Reb Shemuel	It is impossible.
David	What are you talking about, Reb Shemuel?
Reb Shemuel	You are a *Cohen.* Hannah cannot marry a Priest.
David	Not marry a Priest! . . . Why I thought they were Israel's aristocracy.
Reb Shemuel	That is why. A Priest cannot marry a divorced woman.
David	(*In dazed whisper.*) Do you mean to say that I can't marry Hannah?
Reb Shemuel	Such is the law. A woman who has had a *Get* may not marry a *Cohen.*
David	But you surely wouldn't call Hannah a divorced woman?
Reb Shemuel	What else? A married woman?
David	Great God! Then Sam has ruined our lives . . . (*Dazed pause, hoarsely.*) This is some of your cursed Rabbinical laws, it is not Judaism, it is not true Judaism. God never made any such law.
Reb Shemuel	Hush, blasphemer! (*Taking up HANNAH's English Bible.*) Listen to the voice of God Himself. Leviticus, Chapter XXI, verse 7: "Neither shall the Priest take a woman put away from her husband: for he is holy unto God. Thou shalt sanctify him therefore, for he offereth the bread of thy God; he shall be holy unto thee: for I the Lord, which sanctify thee, am holy."
David	But God never meant it to apply to a case like this.
Reb Shemuel	We must obey God's law.
David	Then it is the Devil's law.

(*They face each other scowling. Pause. ENTER HANNAH with a large bunch of violets, taken from the vase, in her breast, and carrying a tray with glasses and biscuits.*)

Hannah	There you are, father . . . (*The tray clatters with her sudden alarm.*) What has happened?
David	Take away the wine—we shall drink nobody's health to-night.
Hannah	My God! (*Throws down tray, runs to the REB.*) What is it? Oh what is it, father? You haven't had a quarrel? (*Silence. She looks appealingly—from one to the other.*)
David	No, it's worse than that. You remember your marriage in fun to Sam Levine?
Hannah	Yes . . . merciful heavens! I guess it. The *Get* wasn't valid, after all.
David	No, not that. But this blessed religion of ours reckons you a divorced woman, and so you can't marry me because I'm a *Cohen*, Priest!
Hannah	Can't marry you because you're a *Cohen?*
Reb Shemuel	We must obey God's law. It is your friend Levine who has erred. Not the law.
David	The Law cannot visit a mere bit of fun so cruelly and on the innocent, too.
Reb Shemuel	When King David numbered the people, the plague fell upon *them.* God's ways are not our ways, His thoughts are not our thoughts.
Hannah	Father! Can nothing be done? (*He shakes his head. She totters into a chair.*)
David	(*Thunderously.*) Something must be done, something shall be done. I will appeal to the Chief Rabbi.
Reb Shemuel	And what can he do? Can he go behind the Law?
David	He will see our case is an exception.
Reb Shemuel	The Law knows no exceptions. The Law of God is perfect, enlightening to the eyes. Be patient, my dear children, in your affliction. The Lord giveth and the Lord taketh away—bless ye the name of the Lord.

David	Not I! But look to your daughter. She has fainted.
Hannah	(*Moans.*) Oh, I wish I had. (*Plucks mechanically at petals of the violets: some fall to the floor.*)
Reb Shemuel	(*Laying hand on her head.*) Be a good girl, dear, and bear your trouble like a good Jewish maiden. Come now—rouse yourself. Tell David you will always be a friend, and that your father will love him as though he were indeed his son.
Hannah	I can't, father, I can't. Don't ask me.
Reb Shemuel	Do you love him so much, Hannah? (*She leans her head on the Bible and sobs.*) But you love your religion more, my child. That will bring you peace.
Hannah	(*Raises head.*) Many waters cannot quench love. Neither can the floods drown it. (*Lowers head again.*)
David	(*Exultantly.*) Do you hear, Reb Shemuel. Do you hear?
Reb Shemuel	Oh God! God! What sin have I committed that Thou shouldst punish my child thus?
David	Don't blame God! It's your own foolish bigotry. Is it not enough your daughter doesn't ask to marry a Christian? Be thankful, old man, and put away all this antiquated superstition. We're living in the nineteenth century.
Reb Shemuel	And God lives in all centuries. His Law is eternal, unchangeable, for the good of all, not of one. Is it to be obeyed only when it is easy? Come, thank God, for you cannot have all the desire of your heart or the inclination of your eyes.
David	The desire of my heart! Do you imagine I am only thinking of *my* sufferings? Look at your daughter, think of what you are doing to *her,* and beware before it is too late.
Reb Shemuel	Is it in my hand to do or to forbear?
David	Yes. Who need ever know that Hannah—
Hannah	No, David, no concealment. I appeal from the letter to the Spirit.
David	Yes, only be sensible! Just think! What am I better than an-

	other Jew—than you yourself for example—that I shouldn't marry a divorced woman?
Reb Shemuel	It is the Law. You are a Priest.
David	A Priest ha! ha! ha! In the nineteenth century! When the Temple has been destroyed these two thousand years.
Reb Shemuel	(*Raising hand mystically.*) It will be rebuilt. We must be ready.
David	Oh yes, I'll be ready. Ha! Ha! Ha! a Priest, Holy unto the Lord. A Priest up-to-date, too holy to marry your daughter. *I!* Ha! Ha! Ha! And so the first sacrifice the Priest is called upon to make is the sacrifice of your own daughter. But I won't, Reb Shemuel, mark my words. Not till she offers her own throat to the knife. If she and I are parted, on you and you alone the guilt must rest. You will have to perform the sacrifice.
Reb Shemuel	What God wishes me to do, I will do. What is it to that which our ancestors suffered for the glory of God's name.
David	Yes, but it seems you suffer by proxy.
Reb Shemuel	My God! Do you think I would not die to make Hannah happy? But God has laid the burden on her—and I can only help her to bear it. And now, sir, I must beg you to go. You do but distress my child.
David	What say you, Hannah? Do you wish me to go?
Hannah	Yes—what is the use? Now?
Reb Shemuel	My child. (*Straining her to his breast.*)
David	Very well. I see you are your father's daughter. (*Turns to go.*)
Hannah	David! (*He does not turn.*) David! You will not leave me.
David	(*Turning, exultant.*) Ah, you will come with me. You will be my wife.
Hannah	No—no—not now, not now. I cannot answer you now. Let me think—good-bye, dearest, good-bye. (*DAVID takes her in his arms, kisses her passionately, and EXITS quietly.*) Oh, it is

cruel, your religion, cruel. (*Sits staring hopelessly at* REB SHEM-UEL, *who falls into a chair and buries head in his book.*)

(*There is a little tap. The* FIRE-WOMAN *ENTERS, pokes out fire to ashes, puffs at one candle, then at the other. All dark. She goes out silently and closes the door with a little slam.*)

SLOW CURTAIN.

ACT IV

Love and Law

(*The Ghetto Market-place in front of* REB SHEMUEL's *house, half-an-hour before sunset on Passover Eve (Eve of Yontov). Next door separated by a picturesque Arch is the* WIDOW FINKELSTEIN's *grocery. Other shops on both sides, including a public-house with a white sheet, marked "Kosher Rum," and then giving on a little alley the door of the Synagogue up a flight of railed steps near the left wing, with some of its upper windows showing. In the road in front of the old-fashioned houses and down Arch and alley stretches a double line of barrows and stalls on either side of which a crowd, going both ways at once, jostles. Some go in and out of shops. There are people of all styles and dresses, from the very rich to the very poor. There is a cake-seller, a fishmonger, a butcher, a greengrocer, a second-hand clothes-dealer, a showman, a trickster, a beggar-woman, dealers in holy foods, but the centre of the scene is occupied by* MOSES ANSELL *standing in front of* REB SHEMUEL's *with his bag of lemons,* SHOSSHI SHMENDRIK *with his woodwork stall on one side and a fishmonger on the other. On the walls are Hebrew bills and theatrical posters.*)

Vendors	(*In different keys.*) Yontovdik! Yontovdik!
Cake-seller	Here's you caikes! Passover caikes! Motsos, only fourpence a pound. Almond-caikes, worsted balls Palavas . . .
Guedalyah	(*The green-grocer.*) Cowcumbers, Cowcumbers! Bitter herbs, horse-radish, Charoises ready-made! Cowcumber!
Butcher	Buy! Buy! Finest fowls—sausages—saveloys—
All	(*Together.*) Yontovdik! Yontovdik! &c.
Passer-by	(*Stylishly dressed. To a shabby.*) Hullo Sol! Don't you remember

me—Jake who went to Australia? Ah. Of course you do. It does one good to see your phiz again. Come and have a glass of rum and shrub. (*Drags him towards white-sheeted public-house.*)

Showman   (*Beating drum.*) This wye for the real live tattoed Hindian from the Hafrican Harchpelago. Walk up! Walk up!

Clothes-dealer Trousers, gentlemen. Dirt-cheap. As good as new and better fitting. Braices thrown in!

Fishmonger   All live O! Turbots, Soles, live Soles!

Butcher   Buy! Buy!

Guedalyah   (*Outside his shop.*) Bitter herbs! Bitter herbs in memory of Zion and sweet mixture in hopes of recovering it.

All   (*Together.*) Yontovdik! Yontovdik! &c.

Trickster   (*On a stand.*) Three shillings for one—one, two, three. S'elp me Gawd, gentlemen. (*Holds up purse.*)

Beggar-
Woman   (*To* SAM *and* LEAH.) A penny, beautiful couple, the Lord send you a hundred gran'children.

Sam   This would please your mother, better than us, eh, Leah.

               (*She laughs. They pass on.*)

Beggar-
Woman   May a thousand wagons shoot black curses over you.

Cake-seller   Motsos, the finest motsos!

Esther   (*Struggling through crowd.*) Father! (MOSES ANSELL *broods, without answering. She pulls at his coat and calls louder.*) Father!

Moses   (*Startled.*) Fine lemons, two a penny each! Two a penny each!

Esther   Don't say each, father. How often must I tell you?

Moses   (*Hanging his head.*) I can't remember.

Vendors	Yontovdik! Yontovdik! &c.
Esther	Haven't you taken sixpence, yet?
Moses	No, Esther.
Esther	And in half-an-hour it will be Passover! Oh dear, dear, and the children did think we should have fish this Passover.
Moses	But we have potatoes.
Esther	Potatoes! The Soup Kitchen gave us that! And the children get so tired of having nothing but potatoes with their mot-sos.
Moses	But God has sent us wine!
Esther	Yes, I've just finished making that.
Shosshi	Hullo, little Esther! Wouldn't you like something from my stall, a Passover present?
Esther	Thank you, but the children can't eat cradle-rockers or paper-cutters.
Shosshi	But these paper-cutters are olive-wood from Jerusalem.
Moses	From Jerusalem! Oh Esther, take one, take one. The Almighty bless you, Mr. Shmendrik. Now we shall have a blessed Passover.
Showman	Walk up! Walk up!
Fishmonger	Live soles! May I die if they ain't. Hi, what's your hurry, all of you?
Voices	(*Mingled.*) Yontovdik &c.
Fashionable W.	(*To* LADY FRIEND.) Picturesque. Is it not, Winifred? Like an Italian market-place.
Old Ike	(*A shabby* OLD MAN. *To fashionable* WOMAN.) Hullo, can that be you Betsy?
Fashionable W.	(*Confused and cold.*) I beg your pardon.

Old Man	Why, you remember old Ike! Lord, lord, what a fine woman you've growed! And to think that you're little Betsy who used to bring her father's corfy in a brown jug when he sold slippers at this very spot! Little Betsy!
Fashionable W.	I'm in a hurry. Good evening. (*To her friend.*) No use talking to a drunken man.
Friend	Certainly not, Isabel. (*They pass on.*)
Old Ike	Isabel! If you're Isabel, Then I *am* drunk. But I haven't tasted anything stronger than your father's corfy, little Betsy! Isabel. Ho! Ho!
Butcher	I can't cut it any leaner, mum. The bones go with it.
Mingled Voices	Yontovdik &c. (*A POLICEMAN elbows his way through throng.*)
Trickster	(*Waving purse.*) Hi, where's your pluck! Never see such a pack of cowards in my life. I offer you three shillings for one, and there ain't one of you with the heart of a mouse. Where's your pluck? Where's— (*Perceives POLICEMAN, jumps down himself and disappears down Arch in crowd.*)
Voices	Yontovdik &c. (*POLICEMAN passes on.*)
Moses	Fine lemons, two a penny! Fine lemons, two a penny!
Esther	Ah, that's right, father.
Moses	But they don't sell any better.
Esther	Right is right, whether we gain by it or not.
Moses	(*Eagerly.*) Yes, as it stands written in the Sentences of the Fathers. (*Shaking his head in pious reflection.*)
Malka	(*Appearing suddenly.*) Well, good-for-nothing dreamer, why aren't you crying your wares?
Moses	(*Startled.*) Two a penny each, two a penny each.
Malka	Ho, and there's Esther, too, lazying about, when she might be carrying people's bags. What's she got there—a paper-cutter?

	Only thinking of her books—always reading books. I never read a book in my life except a prayer-book, and yet I've got three businesses and two grandchildren.
Moses	But it is from Jerusalem. Show her, Esther,
Malka	Ah, from Jerusalem. (*Kisses it.*) May we all be there next year!
Esther	And what would you do with your three businesses?
Malka	Impudence-face! Mind your own business. And I was just going to buy some fish and let you carry it home.
Moses	God shall bless you.
Malka	For the merits of your father, who is a great saint, not for your own, you shall carry my fish. Do you know, Moses, my Milly thought she could do the marketing better than her old mother, and the fish she brought home this morning—well it was like having the drains up. I'll show her what fish is. (*She picks out some at the stall.*)
Vendors	Yontovdik. Yontovdik &c.
Guedalyah	Bitter herbs, bitter herbs in memory of Zion.
Malka	(*To* FISHMONGER.) There! How much for that lot?
Fishmonger	Well, you're an old customer and fish is cheap to-day. Take 'em away for twenty-five!
Malka	Twenty-five! Why, I got better this morning for eighteen.
Fishmonger	Eighteen! Why, I'll have to end up in the Almhouses.
Malka	You shall have my vote and interest then. We pay two subscriptions a year.
Fishmonger	Sold for eighteen! (*Cleaning them.*) Live soles! Where's your hurry ladies? They're live but they won't bite.
Malka	You see, Esther, the old woman knows how to get bargains. Take 'em to my Milly and say mother sends them with her love and she's to boil 'em immediately.
Esther	Yes, miss—ma'am.

Malka	(*Turns back.*) You'll smell Milly's fish as soon as you get in—just wrinkle up your nose and say "Pooh! What's the matter?" Do you hear? (*Going LEFT.*)
Esther	Yes, miss.
Malka	And oh, Esther! (*Taking brush from pocket.*) Just slip this clothes-brush on Milly's table. It's a—it's a present I bought her.
Esther	It looks second-hand.
Malka	Mind your own business. (*Going LEFT.*)
Esther	(*Tugging at her dress.*) But you haven't given me anything.
Malka	Impudence-face!
Esther	You told me to mind my own business.
Malka	I'll give it your father. I won't have you waste it on cakes—and paper-cutters. Get along now. (*ESTHER goes.*) Here is a shilling, Moses.
Moses	May the Highest One bless you and send you a happy Yontov.
Malka	He *has* blessed me, Moses. I shall be a grandmother again before the New Moon, and I shall call the boy Reuben, after my father, peace be to him.
Moses	But suppose it's a girl.
Malka	A girl! No, no, Moses, I have faith in the Almighty. (*EXIT LEFT.*)
Vendors	Yontovdik &c. (*Drum beat, &c.*)
Esther	(*Running back, breathlessly.*) Father, how much?
Moses	A shilling.
Esther	Then we may have fish after all! Give it to me, quick. (*He gives it to her.*) Please, sir, let me have the best shillingsworth you can. It's all I've got.
Fishmonger	Certainly, my little dear. There—and there—and there!

Esther	Oh, but that's too much for a shilling.
Fishmonger	Not at this late hour, my child. I'd rather they went to you than to— ha! ha! ha!—to the dogs.
Esther	Thank you, sir. Oh, how glad the children will be!
Fishmonger	Live soles! Only sixpence the pair. Now's your chance, hurry up!
Esther	(*Dropping the fish in* MOSES's *lemon-basket.*) Run home at once, and put them in salt before you go to Synagogue—I'll fly back in time to cook 'em with your own lemons before Yontov.
Moses	(*Flustered.*) Yes, Esther—fine lemons,—ah, thank the Highest we shall have a happy Passover. (*Going—turns back.*) You see the blessing in the Jerusalem paper-cutter.
Esther	Yes, yes—but mind you wash yourself before you go to Synagogue.
Moses	I always wash myself for Passover.

(*EXIT LEFT,* ESTHER *EXIT RIGHT.*)

Fishmonger	All alive O!
Vendors	Yontovdik! Walk up! Passover cakes! &c., &c.

(REB SHEMUEL *comes out of his house and speaks to the* STALL-KEEPERS *in front of it.*)

Reb Shemuel	Good people—it is time for synagogue.
Fishmonger	Time for you, Reb Shemuel, bless you. Too early for us.
Reb Shemuel	The sun will soon set.
Old Beggar-woman	(*Rushing up.*) Reb Shemuel! Reb Shemuel! Take pity! I haven't had a crumb of bread all day.
Reb Shemuel	And you won't have any for eight days more, unless you're a bad Jewess. Here (*giving her money*) and beg better.

Beggar-woman	A thousand years may you live! (*Other* BEGGARS *rush up.*)
Beggars	For Yontov! Reb Shemuel! (*He scatters largesse.*)
	(*A* BEGGAR *limps up, in tatters, shivering.*)
Reb Shemuel	My poor fellow. God help you! (*Turns out his pockets to show he has no more.*)
Beggar	Haven't you got an old coat?
Reb Shemuel	Do you object to a new one? Here— (*Gives him his coat.*)
Beggar	Oh the Almighty— (*Falls to kissing his hand.*)
Reb Shemuel	Put it on, you fool. (*Sneezes.*) Atschew! (*Runs back to house.*)
	(*Noises of market-babble of* BEGGARS. *Stalls begin to pack and move.* FISHMONGER's *stall moves away.* REB SHEMUEL *appears at his house-door, with his wife wringing her hands.*)
Mrs. Jacobs	Ah, you'll ruin me, Shemuel! You'd give away the shirt off your skin.
Reb Shemuel	If the other man had only his skin! Why not? Atschew! Perhaps my coat may have the honour to cover Elijah the prophet in disguise. (*Moves away.*)
Mrs. Jacobs	Great heavens.
Reb Shemuel	What is it?
Mrs. Jacobs	All your money was in that coat.
Reb Shemuel	(*Startled.*) Was it? (*Remembering.*) No, no, it wasn't. I took it all out first.
Mrs. Jacobs	God be thanked! Let me take care of it.
Reb Shemuel	I—I gave it away.
Mrs. Jacobs	Gave it away!
Reb Shemuel	Yes—I couldn't carry money into the synagogue.
Mrs. Jacobs	Then this is the last time you carry money out of my house. (*Shuts door with a bang.*)

Reb Shemuel	Come, come, brethren, see the sun sets. Go home to your wives and keep the Passover.
Shosshi	(*Dolefully.*) I've got no wife.
Reb Shemuel	(*Smiling.*) Then you have especially to thank the Lord for delivering you from the House of Bondage.
	(*Passes on up the steps to the Synagogue, which begins to be lighted up. SHOSSHI begins to pack up. ENTER MRS. BELCOVITCH, laden with parcels.*)
Mrs. B.	Ah, Shosshi, a happy Yontov to you!
Shosshi	I should have been happier if I had never met your Becky! Now I shall never—(*Takes up a cradle-rocker and surveys it wistfully with a great sigh.*)
Mrs. B.	Don't rake up old dust-bins. Yontov is the time for making up quarrels and I looked for you on purpose, though I can hardly crawl around. I am in a sick condition.
Shosshi	I am sorry. How are your legs?
Mrs. B.	They do not change.
Shosshi	And Becky!
Mrs. B.	(*Sighing.*) She always changes. She has two new young men with her now. (*Calling.*) Becky, what has become of you?
	(*BECKY, magnificently clad, appears between two oddly matched YOUNG MEN, each parcel-laden. She sniggers as usual, as she passes SHOSSHI and EXIT with her mother.*)
Shosshi	(*Glaring after the YOUNG MEN.*) One is a thin one and one a thick one. (*He sighs, and begins to wheel off his barrows. The CROWD and the stalls are fast melting away.*)
Widow F.	(*Darting from her shop.*) Hi! Where's my sixpence?
Shosshi	What sixpence, Widow Finkelstein?
Widow F.	For the stand in front of my shop.
Shosshi	But I haven't taken a penny. (*Wheels off again.*)

Widow F.	(*Clinging to barrow.*) My sixpence!
Shosshi	Let go!
Widow F.	Not without my rights. (*He see-saws her up in air.*)
Shosshi	Let go—or I'll run away with you.
Widow F.	I shouldn't mind being run away with by a nice young man.
Shosshi	(*Drops handles, startled, she see-saws down.*) I'm not a nice young man.
Widow F.	If I had as nice a young man to help me with the shop I could make ten pounds a week.
Shosshi	Ten pounds a week! (*See-saws her up in his excitement.*) But how do you know I'm not married?
Widow F.	Sugarman told me all about you.
Shosshi	Sugarman! No, no—no Sugarman for me!
Widow F.	No, nor me. I believe in falling in love.
Shosshi	You do. (*He lets her fall down. They gaze at each other in silence.*) Ah . . . this will be a happy Passover.
Widow F.	Won't you come and read the *Seder* service for me to-night?
Shosshi	I will go home at once and clean myself.
Widow F.	And I will shut up at once. (*Seizes a shutter.*)
Shosshi	Can't I help you? (*Business ad lib: they kiss behind the shutters. SHOSSHI again commences to wheel off his barrow but stops.*) Here is your sixpence!
Widow F.	(*Breaking it.*) Here is your half!
Shosshi	(*Wheeling off.*) He! He! He! I always knew I should fall in love . . . Well, I'm even with Becky now. He! He! (*EXIT.*)
	(*The market-place is now almost empty. The lamp-lighter goes on his rounds. The houses are lighted up. The synagogue windows are especially brilliant. People mount to it. Dusk falls deeper and deeper as the Scene proceeds. The first sounds of prayer are heard from the synagogue. ENTER* MRS. JACOBS *from the house.*)

Mrs. Jacobs	They are beginning—I am late. (*Runs back.*) Hannah!
Hannah	(*At threshold, very subdued in manner.*) Yes, mother!
Mrs. Jacobs	I do believe I forgot the bitter herbs.
Hannah	(*Looking within.*) I see the sweet mixture and the shankbone and the parsley and the roasted egg—no, not—
Mrs. Jacobs	It's your father's goings-on that drive things out of my head—
Hannah	Don't come back—I will attend to it.
Mrs. Jacobs	Perhaps it's a good omen for the coming year that I only remembered the sweet mixture.
Hannah	I hope so.
Mrs. Jacobs	Perhaps—perhaps it means you will find a bridegroom in it.
Hannah	You will be late for synagogue.
Mrs. Jacobs	There you are! Always jumping down my throat! I dare not mention a young man to you. If you would only find one for yourself. But you have never in all your life given a young man a finger-tip of encouragement.
Hannah	Have I not?
Mrs. Jacobs	Never! A mother's eye—that sees everything.
Hannah	Or nothing.
Mrs. Jacobs	Nothing, indeed! It sees you are getting on in years, my girl. Well, well (*kisses her*), don't forget the bitter herbs.
Hannah	(*Wearily.*) I won't forget the bitter herbs. (*EXIT MRS. JACOBS to synagogue.*) If she only knew! But no! She sees me and father all day long and never sees the skeleton secret that stands between us, yet unites us. Oh God. (*Looks up.*) And you too, you stars that seem to look down on us with love. You are only blind worlds that see nothing—great blind worlds as black as our own.
	(*A burst of prayer from synagogue: she goes slowly in doors. Nothing is heard but prayers. Through the lightly curtained window,*

HANNAH is seen giving mechanical touches to the picturesque Passover table, which with its candles, strange dishes and white table-cloth gives the impression of holiness and peace. ENTER DAVID BRANDON cautiously. He peeps in through the window.)

David	(*He taps: raises the window cautiously and calls.*) Hannah!
Hannah	(*Startled, drops dish.*) David!
David	Yes—are you alone?
Hannah	But father—
David	Safe at synagogue. I have watched. (*Goes to door.*) Let me come in.
Hannah	No, no, he might return. (*Runs to door and bolts it.*)
David	He can't yet. (*Turns handle.*) You have bolted the door against *me!*
Hannah	Have I, dear? I didn't mean to. There— (*shows herself at aperture.*) No, no, no, don't come in.
David	Then come out.
Hannah	I am afraid.
David	Afraid! Afraid of me.
Hannah	Of myself—and father will be coming back. It is such a short service to-night. (*Shuts door.*) Stay where you were. We can talk. (*Reappears at window.*) Why have you come?
David	I could not feed on your letters, nor breathe courage into you with mine. (*He throws up window higher.*) You must hear my resolution from my own lips.
Hannah	(*Moving back.*) What have you resolved?
David	Never to give you up while I live. Oh my darling—(*takes her hands*), do not shrink back. Feel that it is I, your own David who will slay all these Philistines. (*He draws her to him.*)
Hannah	(*Surrendering herself.*) My own dear David.

David	Then you will come with me?
Hannah	(*Startled.*) Come with you? Where?
David	To America.
Hannah	America!
David	Yes—here there will be endless heart-worries and discussions and shrinkings-back. The ocean will wash it all clean. Let the old world bury its dead—a new life in a new world.
Hannah	But when?
David	Now—to-night—at once.
Hannah	Oh no, it is too sudden.
David	Death is sudden sometimes, why not life? Listen, darling, Providence has arranged it all. A Christian friend of mine—Mrs. Dannheim—sails from Southampton in the morning. You can share her cabin. The boat is half empty this time of year.
Hannah	You take my breath away.
David	You will have time to get it back—on the Atlantic. It is the only way. Come—your hat and cloak.
Hannah	But my other clothes!
David	Half-an-hour at the stores.
Hannah	No; no, I cannot—I cannot leave the house unprotected. Not—not yet.
David	By the next steamer your courage will ooze out again. Come with me—no one shall part us—for ever and ever. Think what it means, sweetest, together, you and I, for ever and ever.
Hannah	But father—I must have a last look at him—a last kiss—remember I am going across the ocean—
David	Ah! You *are* going!
Hannah	Yes.

David	My dearest. Oh thank God, thank God! Heaven open before me.
Hannah	And before me.
David	Sweetest! In America we shall have none of these difficulties. No one will know that I am a priest or you a . . . (*contemptuously*) a divorced woman. Any Rabbi will marry us.
Hannah	Why should we be married by a Rabbi?
David	Why?
Hannah	Yes, why?
David	Because we are Jews.
Hannah	You would use Jewish forms to outwit Jewish laws!
David	Oh, those laws were only meant for the days when we had a Temple in Palestine, but these old fools—I beg pardon, these fanatical Rabbis—
Hannah	No, David, no more deceit. What need have we to seek the sanction of any Rabbi? The State will marry us. If Jewish law cannot do so without our hiding something, let us have done with Jewish law. This must be a break, a complete break, don't you see, dear? All this ceremony—it has always coiled stiflingly round my soul—we must break away from it all. Must we not eat bread on board instead of Passover cakes? Yes, we have kept our last Passover. This is our Exodus—we go out towards the great free new life.
David	Yes, darling, towards the great free new life.
	(*The Marseillaise sounds in the distance down the Archway.*)
Hannah	What is that? I never heard that here.
David	An omen, Hannah, the music of our march to freedom.
Hannah	It is coming this way—we must not be seen together. (*Shuts window. DAVID moves aside. She comes to the door and looks out.*)
	(*ENTER through Archway a grotesque procession of Jewish Freethinkers, led by SIMON WOLF, and MELCHITZEDEK PINCHAS, and*

followed by a rabble. PEOPLE, *including* WIDOW FINKELSTEIN
*at her toilette, look out of doors and windows. The band plays
the Marseillaise, the flags bear inscriptions: "The Paschal Pig,"
"Down with the Rabbis," "Try our Passover Bread." Some carry
loaves of bread stuck on poles and broom-handles.*)

Simon	Halt! (*The procession pauses.*) Silence!
	(*The band leaves off. Prayers are heard from the synagogue.*)
Hannah	Jews with bread!
Simon	Fellow-sufferers in Israel. Here at the synagogue-door I announce to all that we shall hold *our* Seder at the Freethinkers' Club in Hamburg Street, where the staple dish will be bread, where the bitter herbs will be replaced by bitter beer. I invite one and all to eat with us the bread of freedom.
Man	(*In crowd.*) Free beer too?
	(*Laughter.*)
Simon	No, but the spirit of freedom. (*Laughter.*) Instead of the Pascal Lamb we shall sacrifice the Paschal pig.
Pious Man	(*In crowd.* Shut up, you *Meshumad.*
Pinchas	Ve vill not shut up. Ve keep open.
Pious Partisans	Yah! Hoo! *Meshumad!*
Pinchas	Slaves in Egyptian darkness! Stupid men of the earth! Don't you know it's all lies about the miracles in Egypt? (*A stone smashes his hat.*) May the Ten Plagues of Pharaoh rot you! (*Snatches a loaf of bread and aims it at crowd.*)
The Crowd	Yah! Booh! Down with the bread-eaters!
Simon	To hell with the Rabbis and their miserable dupes.
	(*A free fight commences with much shouting.* REB SHEMUEL *appears at door of Synagogue on top of steps.*)
Reb Shemuel	(*In thunderous rebuke.*) Brethren. (*All turn and look up. The fight ceases slowly.*)

Hannah	(*To DAVID, who has crept near her.*) My father! Go! Go!
David	He won't see me in the crowd.
Hannah	No, no. Hide. (*He slips down Archway.*)
Reb Shemuel	Brethren. What means this brawling on the Passover?
Simon	It means that we are redeeming Israel from the house of bondage, from the slavery of superstition.
Pinchas	Yes, ve keep the Passover truly. This is the true Exodus!
Reb Shemuel	(*In horror.*) You, Pinchas, you, the scholar, the sweet singer in Israel!
Pinchas	Yes, me, who else shall be the Moses? She laughed at me—your Hannah—but she vill see, ven I am King of the Jews. Down with the Pharaohs who sweat de people to build them treasure-houses. Let them drown in a Red Sea of Blood. *Allons, enfants de la patrie.* (*Sings and swaggers about.*)
Reb Shemuel	Silence!
Pinchas	I vill not silence. Too long ve have listened to Rabbis vith big beards and big stomachs, who drowse us vid prayers. Ve must fight for freedom.
Wolf's Followers	Bravo! Hooray!
Reb Shemuel	Peace, fools! Freedom? Freedom to go astray after the desires of your hearts and the lust of your eyes. Three thousand years the law of Moses hath preserved us—shall we not preserve *it?*
Pinchas	Three thousand years—time for a second Moses.
Reb Shemuel	Nay, remember what the first Moses said. Deuteronomy, Chapter IV. "Ye shall not add unto the word which I command you, neither shall ye diminish ought from it, that ye may keep the commandments of the Lord your God, which I command you. Take heed unto yourselves, lest ye forget the covenant of the Lord your God, which he made with you—lest ye forget."

Simon   But the Lord has forgotten us. (*His* FOLLOWERS *laugh.*)

Reb Shemuel   The Guardian of Israel neither slumbereth nor sleepeth. Though we are in exile for our sins, we are still His chosen people. His blessing is still over us, and under us are the everlasting arms. I know your lives are hard—hard sometimes as the Egyptian bondage—but in your shibboleths—in your socialisms and atheisms—there is no healing. With good humour, with cheerfulness, with love we may ease each other's burdens; with faith and hope in God we may bear our own. Think—think, (*sweeping his arms solemnly over the Ghetto*) over how many poverty-stricken homes this Passover night the Angel of Peace will hover, shedding celestial light upon the humbly festive tables, think how many a toil-worn brother, sitting with wife and children, will chant to them the hymns of deliverance from Egypt, as he lolls joyously upon his Passover pillows. All your strikes and Sabbath-breakings will bring him—what? Sixpence a day more? And for sixpence a day he is to sell his faith, his joy, his dream, the dream of centuries, the brotherhood of Israel, the Messianic hope, his share in the World-To-Come.

Simon   D——n the world-to-come. We want this world. Play up. (*The band commences.*)

Reb Shemuel   Peace! Peace I say! (*Band stops, overawed.*) Disturb not the Passover or the Lord will *not* forget you. The Lord shall smite you with madness and blindness and astonishment of heart. You shall grope at noonday as the blind gropeth in darkness. The heaven that is over your head shall be brass, and the earth that is under you shall be iron. Go home, go home to your family-table and serve the Lord with joyfulness at the immemorial *Seder*. (*The procession marches off sullenly.* REB *raises his hands in blessing.*) May He who maketh Peace in the high heavens, make peace upon us and all Israel, and say ye Amen.

The Crowd   Amen. (*They disperse,* REB SHEMUEL *re-*ENTERS *the Synagogue.* HANNAH *stands with her head buried in her hands.* DAVID *timidly approaches her.*)

David   Hannah!

Hannah	Did you hear? Did you hear?
David	Yes, I heard—the old, old cant.
Hannah	No, it is not cant.
David	Hannah! You are faltering.
Hannah	Father is—oh you see how he quiets these rebels.
David	My darling! Be strong. For Heaven's sake don't draw back now.
Hannah	Is it for Heaven's sake?
David	(*Fiercely.*) For Hell's sake then. You cannot break your promise. (*Marseillaise breaks out again.*) There! You hear! He quiets them—but only for a moment. (*Music louder.*) You are coming with me. Do you understand?
Hannah	Yes. (*With a gesture of resolution.*) It was but a spasm.
David	Thank God! My own dear Hannah again.
Hannah	Yes, what does he offer them but words . . . words? No, they shan't take you away from me. I won't let you go.
David	That's my brave girl! Come, get your things.
Hannah	Yes, yes. (*Running in.*) See I hang my hat and jacket behind the door. In a moment I can slip out.
David	But I meant come at once.
Hannah	This minute?
David	Yes, you did get a farewell sight of your father's face—Providence again.
Hannah	Yes—it is true—I will put on—no, no, not yet, I promised— I promised mother not to forget the bitter herbs. There are things to do—things to get together—things with childish memories—your letters. Hark! They are singing *Yigdal*—the last hymn. Father will be back. Go! Go!
David	Why should I go? The Southampton train leaves at eight. I will remain near by till you are ready.

Hannah	(*Rapt.*) Hush. Listen.
	(CANTOR *and* CONGREGATION *continue the Hymn.*)
David	The train goes at eight.
Hannah	The train . . . yes, yes. The same old melody I have heard from childhood. I see myself a little girl before I had learned to think and doubt—oh how sweet and enchanted life was then! Listen—it winds itself about my soul.
David	But we shan't catch the boat, darling. It is a quarter to seven. Do you hear?
Hannah	Yes, yes, I hear. To-night was the night I used to fancy the Angel would come out.
David	The angel?
Hannah	Yes, father told me when I was a little girl that on Passover night an angel sometimes came out of the doors of the ark from among the scrolls of the Law. Year after year my eyes were fixed on the purple curtain, waiting, waiting.
David	(*Impatiently.*) But there was no angel.
Hannah	But there was no angel. And yet (*pointing to the window, through which the Passover table is visible*) when I look at the peaceful Passover table with its quaint dishes, I almost see him hovering over it. Ah, if you could have sat with us to-night! I should have felt a Jewess again, lapped in faith and trust. Oh God, oh God! (*Breaks down.*)
David	Compose yourself, dearest. Let us take what remains. There was no angel.
Hannah	No, there was no angel or he would have some to save me to-night.
David	Then it is I must save you, Hannah. It shall be mine to make you happy. Trust yourself to me. The train leaves at eight.
Hannah	At eight! I—I—Give me till seven.
David	It is but ten minutes—I will wait.
Hannah	Not here.

David	I will get our cab and wait in that—round the corner. You'll slip out with your things—at seven!
Hannah	Yes, at seven; go, go; the service is closing. (*Stands in a daze, listening to the hymn.*) Ah, why is religion so cruel? Why is this terrible alternative forced upon me—to stab my parents or David.

(*The* BEADLE *throws open the door of the Synagogue, the last verse thus sounds louder and the* CANTOR *sings it with great passion. The* PEOPLE *begin to troop down.* HANNAH *remains, as if hypnotized.* PASSERS-BY *cry* "Good Yontov," *but she does not respond. Others pass her by without knowing her and bid each other* "Good Yontov!" *as they part.* SHOSSHI *knocks at* WIDOW FINKELSTEIN'*s shop and is welcomed in. The air is full of peace and joy.*)

Ephraim	Good *Yontov,* Hannah.
Michael	Good *Yontov.*
Mrs. Jacobs	What are you standing in the cold for? Have you attended to the bitter herbs?
Hannah	The bitter herbs!
Mrs. Jacobs	Moon-struck again! I suppose I'll have to see to them myself. It's all bitter herbs for me, not even a servant to help me, and all our money wasted on dirty *schnorrers.* (*She goes in.*)

(*Other* PEOPLE *pass. Then* MOSES ANSELL, *wearing a white collar for the first time and shabbily spruced up, comes from the Synagogue, arguing with* REB SHEMUEL.)

Moses	But it stands so in the Talmud, Tractate Passover.
Reb Shemuel	Yes, yes, you are right, Reb Moses. I had forgotten the passage. Well, I hope God has sent you a good Passover.
Moses	A king could fare no better. The Almighty has even sent us fish.
Reb Shemuel	I am so glad. Good *Yontov.*
Moses	Good *Yontov.*

(*EXIT, carolling a holy melody.*)

Reb Shemuel   Hannah, you will catch cold.

Hannah   I—I cannot breathe indoors.

Reb Shemuel   You have a headache.

Hannah   Yes—and a heartache too.

Reb Shemuel   My poor child! I have so prayed to the Almighty. It will pass, it will pass.

Hannah   Never—whatever happens.

Reb Shemuel   You are a sacrifice to the Law, but think, dear, how many the Law redeems. Come in to the *Seder* service.

Hannah   You are not beginning *Seder* yet.

Reb Shemuel   Yes, as soon as you have helped me on with my shroud. Come!

Hannah   With your shroud!

Reb Shemuel   Have you forgotten I always wear it on *Seder* night? Come!

Hannah   (*Shuddering.*) No! No! It is too ominous.

Reb Shemuel   Nonsense, dear. Only solemn.

Hannah   Help you on with your shroud!

Reb Shemuel   Not if it suggests sad thoughts to you, my child. But if you *must* stay a little in the air for your headache, you must put on your hat and jacket. I'll fetch them—oh here they are! Hanging on the door. (*He wishes to put them on her.*)

Hannah   No, don't help me! Let me put them on myself. (*He goes in.*) Oh God, what irony is this! He bringing me my hat and jacket (*putting them on*), I—helping him to his shroud.

Reb Shemuel   (*Re-appears at door, his white shroud over his garments, looking very solemn and spiritual.*) At least you don't want to go without my Festival blessing.

Hannah   (*Startled.*) Go? I—No, father. I will not go without your blessing.

Reb Shemuel	(*Places hands on her head, the moonlight shines on them.*) God make thee as Sarah, Leah, Rachel and Rebecca. "The Lord bless and keep thee, the Lord make his face to shine upon thee and be gracious unto thee: the Lord turn his face unto thee and give thee Peace." (*A pause—his hands resting on her head. A clock chimes slowly seven.*)
Hannah	(*Looks round desperately. The* REB *turns to go in; he is shutting the door.*) Father, father, don't shut the door. I am coming in.
	(*She goes to door—gives a last terrified look round, and goes in. As door shuts,* DAVID *ENTERS cautiously.*)
David	She is late. (*He steals towards window.*) She has her hat and cloak on, thank Heaven. (*Goes towards door. Another clock strikes seven with different chime.*) Ah, the clocks disagree. She will come now, my darling. (*Agonized pause. Paces to and fro. Returns to window.*) She is taking off her hat and jacket. My God, will she fail me after all? She is drawing to the *Seder* table . . . (*The* REB's *prayer is heard.*) She holds the wine-cup. Perhaps they suspect her—she is biding her opportunity. Her head is bowed. She seems in reverie. Has she forgotten? Has she forgotten? I shall go mad. Ah! They are drinking the wine. Will she slip out now? Yes she moves. No, she is holding the ewer as he washes his hands. . . . She sits down again. O, my God, she celebrates her ancestors' exodus, not ours, not ours! (*He rattles the door.*)
Reb Shemuel	What is that?
David	My God, she celebrates her ancestors' exodus, not ours, not ours.
Mrs. Jacobs	Some Christian rough.
Hannah	No, only the wind, mother.
Mrs. Jacobs	Bolt the door then, Hannah, it won't rattle so. Well, why don't you go?
Hannah	I am going.
David	She will slip out now. (*The bolts are shot with a harsh sound.*) I am shut out! (*A pause.* REB *praying within.* DAVID *takes up a stone and throws it at the window.*)

Mrs. Jacobs	There! I told you it was a Christian rough.
	(*Marseillaise heard again faintly in distance.*)
Reb Shemuel	(*Within.*) No—do you hear that music? It is worse—it is some Jewish rough. (*Marseillaise grows a little louder.*)
Mrs. Jacobs	I always tell you to have the shutters closed.
Reb Shemuel	Close them, Hannah dear.
	(*HANNAH goes to window and opens it to get hold of shutters. DAVID seizes her hands.*)
David	(*In a hoarse whisper.*) Are you coming? (*Marseillaise louder.*)
Hannah	I am sucked back; I am sucked back. Go alone, dear: in a new country you will forget me more easily. (*Marseillaise triumphant as if procession is passing near by.*)
David	And you?
Hannah	It would break their hearts.
David	You break mine. (*Drops her hands.*)
Hannah	And my own. (*Closes shutters with harsh clang, leaving the stage much darker. The Marseillaise dies away.*)
David	(*Falling on knees, his head on the window-sill.*) I am shut out, I am shut out.
Reb Shemuel	(*Loudly, within.*) Pour out Thy wrath on the heathen who acknowledge Thee not and on the Kingdoms which invoke not Thy name; for they have devoured Jacob and laid waste his Temple. Pour out Thy indignation upon them and cause Thy fierce anger to overtake them. Pursue them in wrath and destroy them from under the heavens of the Lord.

(*SLOW CURTAIN.*)

The Melting Pot

Introductory Essay

The Play

In response to the findings of the 2000 U.S. Census that there had been major shifts in the country's racial and ethnic composition and a significant increase in the number of people of multiracial parentage, syndicated columnist Ben Wattenberg wrote a piece titled "The New American," which opened with the salute "Welcome back, Israel Zangwill" and identified his play *The Melting Pot* as "the biggest Broadway hit—ever."[1] Like much that has been said about the mythologized melting pot metaphor and its putative author, this statement blends fact with fiction. Though the play enjoyed a respectable New York run of 136 performances—a bit below the 148 of Zangwill's most successful Broadway production, *Merely Mary Ann* (1903)—it pales in comparison with such mega-hits of the decade as Charles Klein's *The Music Master* (1904), a David Belasco production that enjoyed a Broadway run of 951 performances. The impulse to aggrandize the stage production of *The Melting Pot* is understandable, as nearly a century later the figurative term is an intrinsic element of American discourse and functions as a key image in the country's self-definition, one that is repeatedly revisited and reformulated in tandem with changing realities and attitudes toward immigration and racial and ethnic interaction. The symbol's prestige has fluctuated, yet its appeal has never vanished, and even though the term "melting pot" was originally associated with America, it has gained global currency and is now used in discussions of various multiethnic societies and nation-states that struggle with issues of immigration and diversity. An essay titled "*Le Melting-Pot:* Made in America, Produced in France" (1999), whose author surveys France's internal debate on immigration, acculturation, and assimilation, opens with the declaration, "Israel Zangwill is fast becoming one of the hottest references on the French academic scene," noting that his has become the name to know

American postcard (dated July 2, 1914, postmarked Lincoln, Nebraska). The image exemplifies the quick incorporation of the melting pot metaphor into American popular culture. Edna Nahshon's personal collection.

for those interested in "melting pots," multiculturalism, universalism, and multiple identities.[2]

The metaphor's potency is highlighted by the fact that even its critics counter it with imageries grounded in it.[3] Yet unlike its major competitors—salad bowl, stew, mosaic, and symphony—the melting pot image focuses on process, not on outcome, and presents a prophetic vision that is entirely futuristic. Its allure is multifaceted. It conveys great dynamism—it is described in the play as roaring, bubbling, stirring, seething, melting, and fusing—and is suffused with medieval echoes of alchemy and the occult, as well as with the hominess of the kitchen, invoking associations of both gold and nourishment, with their respective olfactory, tactile, visual, and symbolic properties.

Zangwill's rhetoric of immigration is embedded in the Exodus saga, with God as the dynamo that propels a grand human fusion. He thus bestows upon America and its people the glory of being providentially guided, party to a divine covenant. This religio-mystical tenor of the play was disturbing to some, especially outside the United States. The British left-wing periodical *The New Age,* for example, blasted Zangwill's prophesy that in America the races of the world would "unite to build the Republic of Man and the Kingdom of God" and his vision that "one day there will be neither Jew nor Greek."[4] The latter, it said, taken from St. Paul's proclamation that there "is neither Jew nor Greek, there is neither bond nor free, there is neither male nor female; for ye are all one in Christ Jesus," suggested that Zangwill practically regarded America as the mystical body of Christ.[5] This is not altogether surprising. Like some other Jewish artists of the period, Zangwill was fascinated by Jesus, whom he reappropriated as a Jewish prophet, whose message, he said, was later corrupted by Christianity's introduction of pagan elements. In this vein, he opened his book *Dreamers of the Ghetto* with a poem titled "Moses and Jesus," in which he imagined a meeting of the two prophets where their eyes interlock "In one strange, silent piteous gaze, and dim; / With bitter tears of agonized despair."[6]

For nearly a century, the powerful symbol of the melting pot has been assailed by racialists, antiassimilationists, and cultural pluralists, the latter disregarding Zangwill's explanation in his 1914 "Afterword" (reproduced in the appendixes to *The Melting Pot,* p. 377) that "the process of American amalgamation is not assimilation or simple surrender to the dominant type, as is popularly supposed, but an all-round give-and-take by which the final type may be enriched or impoverished."[7] In 1923 Zangwill repeated his aversion to the reductive message of uniformity that was being read into his title. He warned against an America that "itches" to turn into a "China," populated by "monotonous millions of hundred-percenters" and misunderstands "the richness produced by the diversity of its peoples."[8]

The impact of the play's title and central metaphor invites an outline of its development both for antiquarian reasons and for a more thorough understanding of authorial intent. The two main sources for examining this development are the author's personal correspondence and the script located in the Lord Chamberlain's Collection, which predates the final published version. These two sources reveal the transformation of the play's title. Zangwill first named it "The Mills of God," which bespeaks the author's theological interpretation of history and, like the "melting pot," offers as its central image a mechanical apparatus used for dissolving, distilling, mixing, and processing the ingredients of food.[9] When alerted by his producer George Tyler that this title was similar to that of the unsuccessful 1907 Broadway production of *Mills of the Gods,* a play by George Broadhurst, Zangwill changed the title to

"The Crucible," which, he said, was "better . . . in some ways though not in others."[10] President Theodore Roosevelt had some part in the use of this new metaphor, which is acknowledged by the author in a letter to the president in which he wrote that the play "dramatises your own idea of America as a crucible in which the races are fusing into the future America."[11] That Zangwill became attached to this new title is evidenced by his July 21 letter to George Tyler in which he assures the producer that the word "crucible" was not uncommon, suggesting previous criticism, and cites as proof a recently arrived clipping of the *American Hebrew* in which America is referred to as such.[12] He writes that he considers the image "very necessary" to his idea of the play and adds that he had already written to his American artist friend Louis Loeb, requesting that he make a design of an "Alchemist stirring a Crucible." He even notes with childlike enthusiasm that he had come to realize that the map of the United States bears a rough resemblance to the shape of a crucible and indicates that this visual affinity could be "worked in."[13] At the same time, he raises the issue of the existence of an American book of the same name—most certainly referring to Mark Lee Luther's *The Crucible,* serialized in *Cosmopolitan* in 1907 and due to be published in 1909 by Macmillan, Zangwill's American publishers. Of uncertain mind, he notes further that in England the use of an identical title in a play and a book does not constitute a problem, yet at the same time he offers an alternative title, "The God of Our Children," a phrase he is "anxious to put upon the market" while being wary of possible objections to it on religious grounds.[14] By summer's end Zangwill calls his script *The Melting Pot,* and the front page of the typed manuscript submitted to the Lord Chamberlain's Office shows the title "The Crucible" crossed out by hand and replaced with its final title, *The Melting Pot.*[15]

The timing of the play was propitious, and its title quickly became familiar to millions who never read it or saw it performed. The massive waves of immigration of the period, predominantly from southern and eastern Europe, and the heavy concentration of immigrants in urban enclaves drew tremendous attention and raised great uncertainties and troubling questions concerning the changing fabric of America. Historian Philip Gleason grounds the great popularity of the melting pot symbology in the historical moment and contends that it prospered because it provided a concreteness to a cluster of ideas and attitudes that developed independent of Zangwill.[16] With immigration high on the national agenda, he writes, there was a felt desire for a compact and generally accepted image, remarking that "more favorable circumstances for launching the new symbol could hardly be imagined."[17]

The genealogy of the melting pot imagery dates back to *Letters from an*

American Farmer (1782) by Frenchman J. Hector St. John de Crèvecoeur (1735–1813), whose answer to the question "What Is an American?" drew attention when reprinted in a 1907 issue of *The Chautauquan.* Crèvecoeur offered as an example a family whose grandfather was an Englishman, his wife Dutch, their son married to a Frenchwoman, with the couple's four sons married to wives of different nations, and explained, "Here individuals of all nations are melted into a new race of man, whose labours and posterity will one day cause great changes in the world."[18] Other early antecedents include a statement by De Witt Clinton, who believed that the English language was "melting us down into one people," and Ralph Waldo Emerson's prophetic 1845 pronouncement:

> [A]s in the old burning of the Temple at Corinth, by the melting and intermixture of silver and gold and other metals a new compound more precious . . . was formed; so in this continent,—asylum of all nations,—the energy of Irish, Germans, Swedes, Poles, and Cossacks, and all the European tribes,—of the Africans, and of the Polynesians,—will construct a new race, a new religion, a new state, a new literature, which will be as vigorous as the new Europe which came out of the smelting-pot of the Dark Ages.[19]

While these passages emphasize the idea of "melting," a striking visual representation of America as receptacle appears in an 1889 caricature in the popular humor magazine *Puck,* in which America is portrayed as an about-to-be-stirred full-to-the-rim teacup, the reference to the "one element that won't mix" alluding to Irish immigrants. A lesser-known evocation of the "melting pot," and possibly one noticed by Zangwill, was made by Rabbi Samuel Schulman in his sermon "Should American Judaism Surrender Its Ideals?" delivered at New York's Temple Beth-El on Passover, March 30, 1907. In it the rabbi described America as "the melting pot of nationalities, which has most hospitably received a variety of races and creeds," yet emphasized that while becoming Americans, Jews must remain faithful to their religion.[20] It must be called to attention, though, that such precursors had limited impact. It was unquestionably Zangwill's play that endowed the metaphor of the melting pot with gravity and made it into a household word.

Perhaps because the melting pot is intrinsically associated with America, students of the symbol's lineage hardly ever direct their gaze to English letters, in whose climate it originated. In a postscript article written fifteen years after his original piece, Gleason admits this shortcoming and contends that had

THE MORTAR OF ASSIMILATION—AND THE ONE ELEMENT THAT WON'T MIX.

An early precursor of the image of America as a melting pot. The caricature by C. J. Taylor appeared on June 26, 1889, in *Puck*, a popular American humor magazine. The "one element that won't mix" refers to the Irish. Courtesy of Michigan State University.

Zangwill been an American it is unlikely he would have used the melting pot metaphor. The reason he offers is that English writers use it differently, as "a generic metaphor for any process involving basic change."[21] This observation may be correct, but Gleason's lexical approach, whose aim is to demonstrate dissimilarity, neglects the fact that the symbol of the melting pot was used in England in the very same sense as Zangwill's by at least one other author—Ford Madox Hueffner [Ford], in his nearly forgotten *The Spirit of the People: An Analysis of the English Mind,* published in London in 1907.[22] The book, the third in a trilogy of an "impressionistic" history of England that delineates the character and spirit of the English, includes a chapter titled "The Melting Pot," in which the author praises the strength England gained from the arrival of foreigners who were "the bad eggs, the adventurous, the restless, the energetic of their several nations."[23] Moreover, Hueffner [Ford] offers the observation that "England is not a nation, not the home of a race, but a small epitome of the whole world, attracted to a fertile island by the hope of great gain, or by the faith that there a man may find freedom."[24] This definition was commented on by Paul Peppis, who notes the modernity of its outlook and explains, "a racially mongrel population becomes 'English' because it inhabits the British isles and internalizes English culture, acquiring the proper national spirit."[25] Hueffner's view, more American than European insofar as it regards national identity as predicated by place rather than bloodline, may have been influenced to some extent by the fact that his father was a naturalized German immigrant. Zangwill, likewise the son of immigrants, offers an index of English identity in his 1914 "Afterword" to *The Melting Pot.* He opens with a quote from Tennyson's lines in welcome of Princess Alexandra—"Normans and Saxons and Danes are we"—which he extends with a list of other groups who have immigrated to Britain: "Huguenots and Flemings and Gascons and Angevins and Jews and many other things."[26] In 1924 he stated clearly that "England, like every other country, has been a melting pot."[27]

As in *The Melting Pot,* Hueffner [Ford] concluded his chapter with a picture of immigrants at the harbor. He describes the scene with nearly as much pathos as Zangwill:

> The other day I was down at the docks, watching the incoming of a ship that brought many Jews from Odessa. As man after man crossed the gangway he knelt down and kissed the muddy coping of the wharf. That was because still, as for the Anabaptists and the Huguenots, England appears to the bad eggs of the nations to be the land of freedom. And it is not impossible that one of the children of one

of these adventurers may be, like another Disraeli, the man who will help England to muddle through.[28]

There is no indication that Zangwill knew of Ford's use of the term when composing his play.[29] The significance of the similarity lies in the fact of two voices expressing almost simultaneously a concept that completely diverged from the racialist conception of English nationality and the notion of "Anglo-Saxon" supremacy, offering a new and positive perspective on immigrants as valuable contributors to society.

Zangwill's theorizing of nationalism, most eloquently expressed in his *The Principle of Nationalities,* developed within a culture preoccupied with the study of race and genetics.[30] He abhorred racial ranking and grading and in his speech to the 1911 Race Congress in London mocked current doctrines of racial hierarchy.[31] On numerous occasions he asserted that all races are "really akin" to one another and pronounced that "the primitive notion of the abysmal separateness of races can scarcely survive under Darwinism" and that the notion of racial purity is but dangerous nonsense.[32]

Writing in 1998 and citing Zangwill's "Afterword," historian David Biale raised the issue of Zangwill's ambiguity with regard to the position and meltability of blacks in America.[33] One does indeed detect a certain fuzziness in Zangwill regarding this issue. Undoubtedly, Zangwill was essentially Eurocentric and did not engage in original deliberation regarding race relations in America. Aside from an instinctive moral center, he largely accepted the opinions of those he considered qualified in such matters, including President Roosevelt. His primary devotion was reserved to alleviation of the plight of persecuted Jews and their resettlement. Indeed, he used a suggestion of their "whiteness" to facilitate a potential settlement in the South, though he was later aghast at the deadly 1906 race riots in Atlanta, which he called a "black pogrom," and wrote that he was fearful of "trusting the Russian Jews among the Southern savages."[34] Yet, as Zangwill became more familiar with American racism, and especially in light of the militancy of the Americanism movement of the day, his vision crystallized. In 1924 he wrote, "At the congress of races in London just before the war, it was urged by an eminent anthropologist and unanimously accepted that all races contain the raw materials of development—in other words, can rise. If this is so, the negro can rise, and if he can rise he ultimately can attain the Anglo-Saxon level. It is only a question of opportunity and time."[35] In its review of *The Melting Pot,* the *Washington Post* was quick to recognize the interracial implications of the play's message. It made it clear that fusion might work well and might even be advantageous for

Aryans and Semites but would be "most dangerous" when applied to Aryans and another race. Such a doctrine, it predicted, would never be popular in America.[36]

Zangwill believed that human history is an ongoing process of fusion. Even the Jews, he said, a group less inclined to intermingle than most others, were a racial mix, who, though mainly white, included nonwhite members in India, China, Jamaica, and Africa. He propounded that since the Jew has entered all the diverse incarnations of the human race and has managed to be at home in completely different environments, he was in fact the "common measure of humanity," a live evidence of the supremacy of geography and spiritual heritage, and a proof that color "is not an unbridgeable and elemental distinction."[37] He saw the Jew not merely as a link to all living humanity, but also to the extinct people of antiquity—the Babylonians and Assyrians—and thus concluded, with unabashed romanticism, "one touch of Jewry makes the whole world kin."[38]

Given that every nation is a melting pot, the uniqueness of the American process, said Zangwill, lies not merely in human fusion, but in the unprecedented large scale and simultaneity of immigration. Its fusion process is normal, he asserted, but is magnified and diversified beyond all historic experience, thus turning America into the ultimate melting pot. Though he idealized America in his play, he did not shrink from criticizing it. Quincy Davenport, the only "real American" in *The Melting Pot,* is obnoxious, shallow, and infantile. He is an ostentatious and unproductive multimillionaire who apes the flippant mores of Europe's corrupt aristocracy, is devoid of both intelligence and moral weight, and professes a complete disregard of matrimonial vows. Even his anti-Semitism is disingenuous, a thoughtless copy intended to ingratiate himself to Baron Revendal, whose daughter, Vera, he wishes to marry. Everything that is positive about America—seriousness of purpose, idealism, creativity, and talent—is represented in the immigrant characters. In 1914, in response to a letter with valid complaints about America's social ills, Zangwill wrote, "That America is not yet fit to be a 'melting pot' I quite agree. But the object of my play is to shame it into greater fitness. . . . I have recalled America to the noble conception of its constitution. It is up to America to do the rest."[39]

America captivated Zangwill as an embodiment of an ideal. Its ecology, its rivers and mountains, its smells and colors, did not feed his imagination like the ghetto or even rural England did. His contact with the nation was largely through its Jews, and thus for him America and Judaism were inextricably linked. He declared that American ideals were not Christian but Jewish,

David expounds the melting pot vision to Vera. *From left:* Frau Quixano (Inez Ben-susan), Mendel Quixano (Hugh Tabberer), Vera Revendal (Grace Lane), and David Quixano (Walker Whiteside). *The Melting Pot*, act 1. London production (1914). Central Zionist Archives, Jerusalem.

for the Puritans founders were "Old Testament men."[40] This argument is posited by David Quixano, who proudly tells the sneering Quincy, "Yes—Jew-immigrant! But a Jew who knows that your Pilgrim Fathers came straight out of his Old Testament." David is the quintessential immigrant not only because, as Zangwill wrote in his "Afterword," he has no other homeland, but because the country he is immigrating to is based on his heritage. The final effect of the play, according to Biale, is that it turns all Americans into crypto-Jews.[41] This observation can be corroborated by the fact that with all the talk of melting and fusing, the Jews in the play, regardless of their religious devotion, never attempt to imitate the Gentiles with whom they interact face-to-face. Rather, it is the Gentiles who are influenced by the Jews, as manifest in the character of Kathleen O'Reilly, the Irish servant, who by play's end is babbling in Yiddish and seems to have grown into a quasi-expert on Jewish holidays and religious customs. This merger of Judaism and Americanism is apotheosized in the play's grand finale, with its patriotic amalgam of the

Jewish Sabbath and the Fourth of July, and the Statue of Liberty, bearing the words of Emma Lazarus, a Jewish poet, beckoning and shining her light upon the vessels filled with immigrants from all corners of the earth arriving in this New Jerusalem.

In addition to giving voice to Zangwill's engagement in problems of immigration and issues of nationality, *The Melting Pot* was deeply grounded in his personal life. On November 26, 1903, he married Edith Ayrton (1875–1945), an aspiring writer, and a non-Jew. She grew up in a family of distinguished scientists, the only child of Professor William E. Ayrton, a physicist and electrical engineer, and Matilda Chaplin, a physician. When Edith was eight, her mother died, and two years later her father married one of his students, Sarah (Hertha) Marks, a brilliant scientist who as Hertha Ayrton was the first female member elected to the Institution of Electrical Engineers in 1899. Hertha, whose name was often mentioned in the same breath as that of her colleague Marie Curie, was an ardent feminist. She was the third of eight children born to impoverished Jewish immigrants who had fled Poland for England, and though an agnostic who had broken away from her orthodox upbringing, she was always proud of her heritage, making it clear that she had never "exchanged" the faith into which she was born.[42] Israel and Edith were married in a civil ceremony. The London *Times* reported on the wedding and listed the names of the guests at the reception held at the bride's parents' home.[43] The roster included some impressive names, among them the groom's old friends, authors Hall Caine and Jerome K. Jerome, but not a single member of the Zangwill family, nor any of Israel's Jewish friends. Evidently, his mother, his pious old father then living in Jerusalem, and other relatives and Jewish associates would not sanction his union with a Gentile and boycotted the wedding.

Though philosophically receptive to intermarriage well before he met Edith, maintaining that it was the natural result of the modern social exchange between Jew and Gentile, there are indications that Zangwill struggled with the issue at the personal level. His October engagement and November wedding occurred in the immediate aftermath of the cataclysmic Kishinev massacre, which marked the beginning of a series of devastating pogroms in Russia. The linkage of Kishinev and intermarriage and the emotional turmoil involved in marrying outside of Judaism right after such a heinous event constitute the major conflict of *The Melting Pot,* where David Quixano is tormented not by religious differences but by the personal and collective trauma of persecution and bloodshed. An oblique indication to Zangwill's hesitancy to marry can be gathered in a letter from Edith Zangwill to actress Annie Russell some years later, in which she confessed, "And once in my life when things were very unhappy & I did not feel that I would marry Israel & at the same time I did not feel that I could ever marry anyone else, this possibility [of not having children] cut out of my life seemed a great sorrow."[44] Zangwill's fiery commitment to Jewish nationalism, which he regarded as "the only channel left for the young and faithless," eased his passage across the Rubicon.[45] During the ceremony, which took place at a London registry office, the groom startled the presiding registrar when he stretched out his arm in the middle of the proceedings and exclaimed loudly the Zionist oath—"If I forget thee O Jerusalem, may my right hand forget its cunning"—and remarked to those present, "that makes our marriage Jewish!"[46]

The repercussions of Zangwill's marriage within the Jewish community are difficult to gauge. According to Joseph Leftwich, his first biographer, there was a storm of protest, while Joseph H. Udelson, his most recent biographer, notes that it evoked no public comment and considers the silence "deafening."[47] Zangwill responded to criticism with his typical mix of bravado, erudition, defiance, and vulnerability. His wife, he said, had "the same Jewish ideals as those with which you credit me," chiding his detractors for having forgotten the spiritual message of Moses, thus indirectly reminding them that Israel's first prophet and lawgiver had married Zipporah, a Midianite.[48] He offered as palliative the fact that Edith's parents were nonbelieving Christians and topped it off with a dash of braggadocio, flaunting Hertha Ayrton, Edith's stepmother, as a "brilliant Jewish scientist," who was believed to have been the original for Mirah, the heroine of George Eliot's *Daniel Deronda*.[49] Zangwill's allusion to Moses' wife and his use in *The Melting Pot* of Ruth the Moabite's well-known words, repeated by Vera Revendal, the Gentile heroine—who tells David, her Jewish beloved, "I come to you, and I say in the words of Ruth, thy people shall be my people and thy God my God!"—relate to biblical women who cast their lot with the Jews and "intermarried" into the community of the children of Israel.[50] In the original manuscript, Vera tells David before their final reconciliation, "It is more than love now, I am telling you. It is love purged in the river of blood—it is a passionate yearning over the martyred boy—it is a craving to give myself to your service, body and soul, anything, everything, that might wipe out a bit of my debt."[51] Thus Zangwill's version of intermarriage reverses the traditional paradigm: it is the Jew who accepts the Christian, pardoning historical wrongs, showing the mercy associated with Christian doctrine.

Like Zipporah and Ruth, Edith fully integrated herself into Jewish life. Leftwich mentions a Zionist meeting where Edith spoke of the Hebrew she was studying and made so-called kosher puns, speaking of a Jewish state where "the orthodox Jew could follow his own religion without let or hindrance."[52] Edith's active participation intensified after her husband established the Jewish Territorial Organization (ITO). In a letter to Annie Russell written on January 21, 1909, she mentions a recent speech before an audience of four thousand. In another letter, she refers to delivering speeches at large ITO meetings in Whitechapel and Leeds: "They are all so extraordinarily nice to me," she writes, "they reduced me to tears at Leeds." She adds that she did "so little," that it was Israel who did all the real work, yet sneaks in a modest boast that sometimes she got even bigger ovations than her husband.[53] It should come as no surprise, therefore, that in 1909, when asked whether once a Jewish territory was secured he would settle there permanently, Zangwill answered that he was ready to leave England and move there with his wife and children right away.[54] In 1923 he reiterated his and Edith's personal commitment, saying, "Believe me, when I had hopes of the establishment of a Jewish State, whether in Palestine or elsewhere, it never even occurred to me that I should not settle there. For years my wife and I lived on an uncertain footing, never knowing when the call might come, and if and when it did come I had hesitated to answer it, I am sure she would have gone off first."[55] Leftwich, who kept in touch with Edith after Zangwill's death, notes with some bitterness that even though Edith always maintained her interest and commitment to Jewish affairs, the 1946 *Jewish Year Book* failed to mention her death. When Leftwich protested, he was told that Mrs. Zangwill "never was in any sense a Jewess, and the inclusion of her name in a list of Jewish obituaries would therefore be inappropriate."[56]

Zangwill was not the only member of the original Zionist leadership to intermarry. Max Nordau had married a Gentile before he became a devotee of Zionism, though he would later consider it a flaw in his political work, as implied by a letter Herzl wrote to him shortly before the First Zionist Congress, in which he assured Nordau that his marriage would not hamper his service to the cause. In the Jewish state, Herzl assured him, intermarriage would be accepted and the offspring of such unions would be fully recognized as Jews.[57] Likewise, Herzl was friendly to Edith and wholeheartedly congratulated her on her marriage. Russian Zionists, however, were considerably more censorious, as demonstrated by a letter from Chaim Weizmann to Menachem Usishkin, written in December 1903. In it Weizmann acknowledges that the couple was received with applause when they appeared at a London Zionist meeting, but accuses the marriage of being a contributing factor to the decline in prestige of Zionism in England.[58]

By all accounts, the Zangwills' was a happy union, with Israel lending his prestige and active support to the fight for women's suffrage, his wife's and mother-in-law's great cause. Writer Herman Bernstein, who in 1915 spent a weekend with the family, which by then included three children, described a home where "an atmosphere of happiness and refinement prevailed."[59] Issues of identity nevertheless did present themselves with the birth of the couple's three children—Ayrton Israel (b. 1905), Margaret Ayrton (b. 1910), and Oliver Louis (b. 1913). In a somewhat rambling piece titled "My Religion," written a year before his passing, Zangwill states that by "marrying out" he tried to make it clear that to him Judaism was not racial yet admits he had failed to "get the idea over."[60] He reveals that he did not make firstborn Ayrton "a son of the covenant," because his vision and knowledge of history prevented him from carrying on what he calls the Jewish tradition of trying to "sit between two stools," which he had deplored long before his marriage. In 1900, speaking about the next generation, he urged, "let not their brains be muddled and tampered with, as mine was, by two contradictory teachings, nor their natural absorption of English idea, ideals, and traditions checked and confused by tales of what happened two thousand miles away two thousand years before they were born."[61] Oliver, the youngest, he informs his readers, was circumcised only because the doctor advised it.

Ayrton, the father of Zangwill's only grandchildren, eventually became neither Englishman nor Jew. He left England in 1930 to work in Mexico as an engineer, where he met and married Sara Terrazas Olivares in 1934, and though he never converted, his children were raised as Catholics. In 1955 Rabbi Floyd S. Fierman met Ayrton in El Paso, Texas, by then his home. Ten years later, writing about their meeting for the *Jewish Spectator*, Fierman exclaimed, "Israel Zangwill's grandchildren and great-grandchildren are Catholics!"[62] Some years after Israel's death, his daughter, Margaret, suffered a mental breakdown and spent the remainder of her life in a Swiss sanatorium. Oliver Zangwill, thirteen when his father died, became his mother's mainstay when she grew older and gained renown as a professor of experimental psychology at Cambridge University. Living in England with a famous name, he could not avoid questions of identity. After Oliver was appointed to his professorship, the *Jewish Chronicle* called Joseph Leftwich to find out if Oliver considered himself a Jew and thus whether his appointment should be reported in their paper. Without asking Oliver, Leftwich told them that it should. When he mentioned the matter, Oliver responded, "I don't really know whether I consider myself a Jew or not, but certainly I am flattered if other people see fit to consider me one."[63] It was he who decided to donate his father's papers to the Central Zionist Archives in Jerusalem after the establishment of the State of Israel.

The Melting Pot touches on other issues related to the elements of Zangwill's life aside from intermarriage. Like David Quixano, Zangwill believed that he was "of Spanish blood" on his father's side.[64] A Sephardic pedigree was considered a stamp of Jewish aristocracy, especially in England, as *The King of Schnorrers* demonstrates so humorously. Such ancestry resonated with romance, invoking a direct connection to the Golden Age of Spain, when Jews reached the pinnacle of scholarly and artistic creativity. It evoked pride in the heroism of those who suffered torture rather than convert to Christianity and created a mystical link between the expulsion of Jews from Spain in 1492 and the discovery of America, where they would prosper again. David, who serves as the playwright's voice, is portrayed in his author's image as an inspired artist with a grand message for humanity. Like Zangwill, he is associated with Moses, whom Zangwill considered the noblest figure in all of history. The play's final scene, where David stands on the roof of the settlement house gazing at the ocean with Vera beside him, blessing the arriving immigrants, pulsates with the semblance of Moses on Mount Sinai, where God delivered the Ten Commandments and entered into a covenant with the people of Israel through him. It also suggests the final moments of his life, when, after blessing the Israelites, he climbs to the peak of Mount Nebo, gazes upon the Promised Land he would never enter, and dies. The association between Zangwill and Moses was poetically portrayed by scholar and benefactor George Alexander Kohut (1874–1933) after Zangwill's last visit to America (1923), during which he blasted American Jewry for its halfhearted support of Zionism.

> Zangwill—the Clarion
> What clamor fills the tents of Shem
> From Gotham to Jerusalem?
> A second Moses, come to view
> The idols of the misled Jew.
>
> Commuting long, he's fresh from God,
> The faithless mob is overawed;
> He bears the sacred tablets twain
> And shatters them in grief and pain.
>
> The motley multitude is still

In presence of his conqu'ring will
He makes it drink the molten brew
In penance for the truth it slew.

And yet contrition has not cleansed
The race his wrath has recompensed
And all the petty tyrants cry
Anathema against the sky.

O men of little faith refrain
From hindering this man of main
Grim, great and dauntless, in his hands
He holds inviolate commands.

He speaks with thunder in his voice
The very hills of God rejoice
No watchman of the darkling night
Sees clearlier the dawning light.

Ye carping critics, ponder this:
Our lion-hearted leader is
The noblest statesman of them all—
His challenge is a clarion-call!

While he wrote himself into David, Zangwill's Old Frau Quixano was probably inspired by his mother, to whom he was deeply attached. Various anecdotes attest to their bond. Louis Golding recounted that for quite a while after his marriage—he was thirty-nine at the time—Zangwill could not bring himself to move his books from his mother's house to his new home for fear of hurting her feelings.[65] This attachment to his mother and his memories of her days of privation gave him insight into the deep loneliness and desolation underlying Frau Quixano's muttering complaints and endow the character, one who could easily become a living prop or caricature of an old hag, with emotional gravity. Her world might be doomed, but it still commands respect and affectionate tenderness. Speaking only in Yiddish, she is spared the comic effect produced by Kathleen's Irish brogue, Pappelmeister's German accent, and the Baroness's frenchified English. Her life story is similar to Hannah Zangwill's. Her husband, David Quixano tells Kathleen, who is distraught by the ill temper of her mistress, was a pious scholar, who was able to immerse himself in the study of the "holy books" because she did all the chores for him and the children; and though his death left her penniless and alone, she devoted herself to visiting the sick and watching over the dead of her congregation. The original manuscript of the play offers additional details that accent her hardship: David tells Kathleen that Frau Quixano's husband took sick and "lay bedridden many years and then he was more useful for he taught students. But she was the real school-manager, yes, and the mother to all those students too."[66] Although Frau Quixano is irrelevant to David's futuristic vision, he craves her approbation and love. Accordingly, in the last scene of the play the union of Vera and David is preceded by a touching reconciliation with the religiously observant Frau Quixano, who in order to not desecrate the Sabbath has walked all the way from her house and, shunning the elevator, climbs to the roof to share in David's moment of glory. It is not difficult to read into this Zangwill's yearning for maternal acceptance of his marriage to Edith.

The characters of the anti-Semitic Baron Revendal and his daughter, Vera, were inspired by historical figures as well. Revendal was probably named for Levendall, the chief of police in Kishinev, who mingled with the rioters and encouraged the murder and mayhem. Vera was possibly fashioned after Vera Zasulich (1849–1919), a Russian radical who had inspired Oscar Wilde's first play, *Vera,* and whom Zangwill probably met through his friend Eleanor Marx. The revolutionary Zasulich was first arrested in 1869 and served two years in jail and four in exile. In 1876 she joined the Land and Liberty group in St. Petersburg, and when one of her comrades was arrested and illegally flogged, she shot the city's chief of police in revenge. Charged with attempted murder, she was granted a jury trial, where antigovernment sentiment combined with disclosure of police abuses and her own genteel behavior won an acquittal, with the crowds in the street cheering her and protecting her from a rearrest order. She fled to Europe and joined forces with Pavel Plekhanov and Pavel Axelrod. She arrived in London in 1894 and stayed for three years, during which time she immersed herself in the library of the British Museum and befriended Eleanor Marx and Edward Aveling, who introduced her to their circle of friends. Zasulich staunchly opposed the anti-Semitism of the Russian Left. In the 1880s she signed a manifesto composed, but never completed, by Pavel Axelrod, that censured the Left's accommodation of peasant anti-Semitism. Later, as a member of the editorial board of *Iskra,* she insisted that the publication be totally free of anti-Semitic overtones and in the spring of 1903 published a harrowing account of the Kishinev pogrom.[67] Unlike Vera Revendal, Zasulich never came to America. She returned to Russia during the 1905 revolution, but in the aftermath of its disastrous failure she gave up on political activity.

The play's groundedness in the here and now reveals itself in several other details. The simultaneity of the Sabbath and the Fourth of July that occurs in act 4 reflected the actual calendar of 1908, when the holiday fell on a Saturday, a symbolism expounded upon in sermons delivered in American synagogues. Davenport's silly suggestion that his orchestra become *Judenrein* [free of Jews] may have been inspired by a story that appeared in the *American Hebrew* about such an attempt in Russia. The use of Yiddish in the play was enhanced by preparations for the forthcoming Czernowitch Conference, where Yiddish would be declared a national Jewish language. Even the theme of America as the healer of old hatreds and the scene of the marriage of a Russian Jewish refugee with the daughter of his Russian persecutor had already appeared in Ezra S. Brudno's novel *The Fugitive* (1904), the story of a Russian Jew whose life is devastated when his father is framed and executed for the ritual murder of a Christian child, and who years later in America marries the daughter of the architect of the libel.

In *The Melting Pot* Zangwill furthered his mission to dispel and reconfigure the stereotypical image of the Stage Jew. His strategy begins with the protagonist's name—names being a major marker of a character's ethnic and social identity. Zangwill chose for his protagonist one with a blurred ethnic code. Quixano—a genuine Sephardic name—is put to dramatic use in the first scene when Vera comes to the family home, not suspecting that David is Jewish. When told, she exclaims, "Oh, but it is impossible!" and nearly runs out. She is won over by Mendel Quixano's civility and by the cultural icons that surround her—classical music scores and volumes of poetry by Shelley and Tennyson. Doubtless, had David's last name been more typically Jewish, Vera would not have initiated a visit to his house. Once she overcomes her initial shock, she reflects on his first name, pronouncing, "A Jew! . . . But then so was David the shepherd youth with his harp and his psalms, the sweet singer of Israel!" By constructing an association with a biblical king revered by both Jews and Christians, who is believed by Jews to be a descendent of Ruth the Moabite and by Christians the progenitor of the line that culminated in Jesus, the poor Russian immigrant is romanticized as the offspring of kings and poets.

The connection to King David also emphasizes the musical genius of David. Jews and music were a much-discussed issue at the time, especially in the aftermath of Richard Wagner's vitriolic contention that Jews were racially incapable of creating great music. Wagner (1813–1883) began this campaign

Vera Revendal (Grace Lane) meets David Quixano (Walker Whiteside) as he arrives at his home. *The Melting Pot,* act 1. London production (1914). Central Zionist Archives, Jerusalem.

in 1850, when he pseudonymously published "Judaism in Music," which he expanded and published under his own name in 1869.[68] He considered the Jew a demonic presence in German art, one who by his innate alienness can at best parrot the externals of the native yet lacks the inner authenticity that is the wellspring of true art. Rootless, unable to access the folk spirit that is the fountain of life, the art he creates is like a mirror—shallow, cold, trivial, ornamental, and ultimately ruinous. Wagner's anti-Semitic gospel was perpetuated by Houston Stewart Chamberlain (1855–1927), his devoted, Germanized, English-born son-in-law, and found currency outside Germany, especially in France. In a similar vein, composer Vincent d'Indy, a member of the anti-Semitic party L'Action Française, accused Judaism of corrupting French music with inferior works for the sake of silver. The theme of the Jews' manipulation of Europe's musical scene was reflected in George Du Maurier's *Trilby*, in which Svengali, a Jewish musician, cannot find success in his own right and needs to voice himself through the body of a young Christian woman whom he manipulates professionally and personally. David Quixano is the ultimate riposte to musical anti-Semitism. His talent is of the highest order. He is an originator, a genius whose talent is so perfect that no human teacher can improve it. The greatness of his composition does not derive from or depend on others. It is a godsend, a transmission of beauty to the new Promised Land. David's portrayal as a violinist was most probably influenced by the appearance of a succession of young Russian-born Jewish violin virtuosos of extraordinary talent. The most glittering was Mischa Elman (1891–1967), the wunderkind son of impoverished shtetl Jews who at eleven was admitted to the St. Petersburg Conservatory and at thirteen created a sensation in Berlin. The next year Elman performed at Buckingham Palace for King Edward VII and King Alfonso of Spain and on December 10, 1908, made his historic Carnegie Hall debut. The transforming effect of his music was described by Carl Sandburg, who wrote in his poem "Bath" of a despairing man who went to hear Elman play and emerged revitalized, with "a singing fire and a climb of roses everlastingly over the world he looked on."[69]

David Quixano is also portrayed by Zangwill so as to dispel the money-hungry image of the stage Jew. Completely engrossed in Olympian spiritual and artistic spheres, he is oblivious to financial need, so much so that the aristocratic Vera mildly chastises him for it. His personal modesty and indifference to monetary gain are highlighted by the counterposition of Quincy Davenport's selfish and squandering behavior. David, though inattentive to his own needs, is acutely attuned to the pain and misery of New York's dispossessed. Though his career may depend on Quincy's generosity, David rebukes him for his reckless spending while women and children are dying of hunger.

It is no wonder that *The Melting Pot*, in which racial stereotypes are deconstructed, employs the holiday of Purim, which celebrates the deliverance of the Jews from a plot to exterminate them, with masquerading an important part of the celebration. The creative tension between the mask and the identity behind it is used in the scene where the myth of the Jew's historically fetishized nose, a central ingredient of anti-Semitic iconography, is ridiculed in a hilarious scene. Kathleen dons a fake nose as part of the merriment and then loses it amid the excitement. What follows is a farcical romp in which

Kathleen O'Reilly (E. Nolan O'Connor) in search of the fake nose, with Vera Revendal (Grace Lane), Herr Pappelmeister (Clifton Alderson), and Quincy Davenport Jr. (P. Perceval Clark) in the Quixano living room. *The Melting Pot,* act 1. London production (1914). Central Zionist Archives, Jerusalem.

she crawls under the furniture in an effort to retrieve the nose, thus exposing it for what it is—a fake theatrical prop that fits everyone's face and belongs to none.

Zangwill intended *The Melting Pot* to arouse sympathy for the plight of Russian Jews by anchoring it in the Kishinev pogrom. However, David Quixano's graphic account of the atrocities, which appears in act 3, was a late addition to the original manuscript. Walker Whiteside, who originated the role of David, wrote in a 1910 essay about his experience with the play and its production, including a discussion of David's monologue that presents a chillingly detailed description of the pogrom. The actor's account is fully confirmed by Zangwill's correspondence with Tyler.[70] When he first read the play, Whiteside writes, he felt there was an element missing from the third act. He shared this sentiment with Tyler, explaining that while the pogrom in which David's entire family was slaughtered was mentioned in the text, it called for detailing the sort of horror that had the power to impel David to reject Vera upon the discovery that her father was in charge of the butchery. Tyler put the actor on a steamer to England the next day. Zangwill's first response to Whiteside's idea was that such a description would be too revolting, but on further consideration he created one, and it came to be regarded by many as the most intense moment of the play.[71]

The inclusion of the speech changed the tenor of the confrontation between Baron Revendal and David. While in the final version David "stonily" faces the baron, who threatens him with a pistol and speaks "mystically" of the blood of his brothers crying out from the ground, in the original version he appears more earthy and is consumed, albeit briefly, with a desire for revenge. His violinist's hands at first do not recoil from the metal of the gun. The original version goes as follows:

Baron	(*Whipping out his pistol*) Back, dog! (*David's bow descends instantly on the Baron's knuckles—he drops the pistol, which David swiftly picks up and covers him with, letting fall his bow.*)
Baron	Help! Help!
Vera	David! Give me that pistol! (*Runs toward him*)
David	Stand back! This man's life is mine.
Vera	No! No! he didn't mean to shoot you.
David	(*Ignoring her*) For crimes beyond human penalty—for obscenities beyond human utterance—for nails driven through bold men's eyes—for—
Vera	You are raving.
David	Would to God I were. (*Takes better aim*)
Baron	(*Frantically*) Vera!
Vera	But this is my father!
David	Your father! . . . God! (*Staggers back, relaxes pistol into Vera's hand*)
Baron	You have saved me. Oh my darling! (*Tries to embrace her*)

Vera	(*Frenziedly, shrinking back*) Don't touch me!
Baron	(*Starting back in amazement*) Vera!
Vera	(*Hoarsely*) Say it's not true.
Baron	What is not true?
Vera	What David said. It was the mob that massacred—*you* had no hand in it.
Baron	(*Silently*) I was there with my soldiers. (*Takes his pistol half-mechanically from her drooping hand*)
David	(*Leaning, pales, against a chair, hisses*) And you looked on with that cold face of hate—while my mother—[72]

The segment replaced by David's recital of the horrors of the pogrom originally went as follows:

David	Easy words to you. You never saw that red flood bearing the mangled breasts of women and the spattered brains of babes and sucklings. Oh! (*Covers eyes with hands*) You Christians can only see that rosy splendour on the horizon of happiness. And the Jew didn't see rosily enough for you—ha! ha! ha! the Jew who gropes in one great crimson mist.[73]

At the end of the scene, when the Baron hands him the pistol, saying, "You were right! Shoot me!" David's original lines were:

David	Shoot you? (*Looks quietly at pistol. Vera looks up dazed. Ceasing to sob*) Why should you be luckier than I? (*Drops pistol. Turns back towards door, then with a sudden recollection, turns again and shuffles towards his violin on the floor, picks it up, surveys it caressingly, murmurs*) I must get a new string! (*Picks up bow, puts violin in case and case carefully under arm, resumes his dragging march towards the*

> *door, with bent head, never looking at Vera. Repeats*
> *maunderingly*) I must get a new string!
>
> (*Exit R. Quick Curtain*)[74]

While the pogrom narrative was an addition to the original script, the other changes, with the exception of slight rewordings of stage directions and occasional changes of "crucible" to "melting pot," are deletions. Some of the excised material reveals where the playwright was most emotionally invested. Act 1 has the fewest deletions, and the only one of substance is the previously mentioned lines related to Frau Quixano's past hardships. The text removed from act 2 belongs to the David Quixano–Quincy Davenport exchange and was originally intended to highlight Quincy's imitative frivolity and David's passionate advocacy of Jewish immigrants. In his account of the Venice-inspired bacchanalia, Quincy offers Vera these additional details: "We got real gondoliers from Venice in liveries of green, blue or yellow, and had the most wonderful silks trailing at the sterns of the gondolas—in exact imitation of the Venetian nobility in the great water fetes. It was a fairy scene of twinkling lights and delicious darkness."[75] The next excision is from David's response to Quincy's dismissive "You, Jew-immigrant!" Following the line where David accuses Quincy and his sort of "turning the last and noblest hope of humanity into a caricature," David says in the original version, "Look around at your Jew-immigrants—how they have climbed from the pack of the pushcart to equality with you idle inheritors of easy gold; how they stand before America—white [here meaning free from evil intent] men of Wall Street, incorruptible Judges, honest politicians, scrupulous traders, princely philanthropists, scholars, thinkers, artists—an ever-growing army of grateful patriots, anxious to repay America's hospitality by making her still greater among the nations."[76] A few lines later he accuses Quincy of "bringing all the follies and fetishes of yesterday trying to bring back Europe," referring to its most corrupt aspects. The love scene with Vera a little later in act 2 is made more romantic. When Vera says, "Your genius lifts you to the stars," in the original version David responds, "No, no; it is you who lift me—I float now with you in the great starry spaces," to which she responds, "Yes, we float together, Oh, David."

The major change in act 4 is the excision of Vera's mea culpa cited earlier, which ends with her admission, "But I am bankrupt. That is why I say good-bye," to which the "dazed" David replies, "You love me and you leave me?" eliciting her despairing response: "What else can I do?"[77] Its elimination smoothes out the later reconciliation between the lovers and changes the emotional balance, reducing Vera's despondency, presenting her more as partner than penitent. It is probably for this reason that Vera's previous line—"It is my love for myself that is dead"—was taken out as well. In the original, Vera also offered a professional-like analysis of the effect of David's symphony: "If they were somewhat tickled by the pizzicato passages depicting the bubbling and seething of the crucible, and rather dazed by that staccato fortissimo episode of the forging and hammering of the American, the rest left them rapt, softened, illumined."[78]

Zangwill, who was said to play the piano with the ecstasy of a Hasidic rabbi, must have heard the music in his mind's ear. Interestingly, aside from the patriotic "My Country 'Tis of Thee," the only musical piece he specifies in his stage directions is the cathedral music from *Faust,* which surges as David and Vera reconcile. Taken from Charles Gounod's opera, this music must have been chosen for its soul-stirring intensity. In this scene Margueritte cries out, frightened and agitated, with the choir singing of the dreadful Day of Judgment, Mephistopheles pronounces her doom, and she collapses. Did Zangwill choose the piece only for its rousing music? Or did it vent a deeply buried fear that in forsaking his heritage for a glorious futuristic vision David Quixano might be selling his soul?

Zangwill was always ambivalent about full assimilation into Gentile culture. In his poem *The Goyim,* written in the aftermath of the barbarism of World War I during which East European Jews were dispossessed and murdered en masse, he expresses great disillusionment with Christian civilization.[79] He describes a boy much like himself, yearning to experience life outside the ghetto, who grows up and discards the customs of his ancestors and comes to worship Plato, Virgil, Shakespeare, Shelley, Bach, Beethoven, and Michelangelo. "But behold him today," the poet cries out:

> Little Jacob once more,
> Bowed small by the years and calamities,
> With his tragical eyes,
> The Jew's haunted eyes,
> That have seen for themselves,
> Seen history made
> On the old Gentile formula,
> Seen the slums written large
> In the red fields of Europe,
> And the *Goyim* blood-drunken,

Reeling and cursing
As on Saturday night.

Back, back, he cries, brethren,
Back to the Ghetto,
To our God of Compassion,
To our dream of Messiah,
And our old Sabbath candles!
For the others are *Goyim,*
Who despite all their Platos,
Their Shakespeares and Shelleys,
Their Bachs and Beethovens,
Drink human blood.
Not only ours but their kinsmen's.

THE PRODUCTION

Writing to George Tyler some two months before the Washington premiere of *The Melting Pot,* Zangwill voiced uncertainty about whether he would be able to be there.[80] He surmised that the trip to America would take five weeks from door to door and could conflict with a trip he might have had to take to Cyrenaica in North Africa, where an ITO scientific expedition, two years in the making, was conducting a thorough investigation of the land's potential for Jewish colonization.[81] Cyrenaica was found to be unsuitable, and Zangwill did sail to America. This envisioned conflict demonstrates how imminent the prospects for the establishment of an autonomous Jewish land were for him and points to the connection between his territorial endeavors and his vision of America and American Jewry. Indeed, when asked, "Why are you going to America?" in an impromptu interview conducted in London two days before he embarked on the *Teutonic,* Zangwill responded, unequivocally, "I am going entirely in connection with the Jewish problem."[82] He went on to speak mostly about the ITO, Galveston, the prospects for Zionism, and his planned meetings with Oscar Strauss, the secretary of commerce and labor and America's first Jewish cabinet member, and other policy-makers regarding immigration. As to his play, he said that it dealt with both the Jewish question and general American issues and treated the former as part of the latter.

This nexus would confound the many American critics who puzzled over the fact that the firebrand advocate of Jewish nationalism was proposing to thrust Jews into the American cauldron, where they were bound to lose their separateness. In a brief editorial written in the aftermath of the premiere of *The Melting Pot,* the perplexed *American Hebrew* concluded that Zangwill constituted "a brilliant paradox" and wondered whether his progression from Zionism to Territorialism to Assimilation was his in fact his ultimate "answer to the Jewish question."[83] Gentile writers also expressed surprise, noting, "it seems hard to reconcile this Jew and his Zionistic propaganda with the play."[84] It would be facile to explain away this incongruity, as some have, with the condescending statement that these ideological zigzags demonstrate that Zangwill was consistently inconsistent. The key lies in his interpretation of Jewish history and his contention that Jews had come to a fork in the road. He articulated this view on numerous occasions, including in an interview with the *American Hebrew* conducted upon his arrival in New York. He said, "Jews cannot go on as they are, a separate nationality among the nations [and a] distinct but inactive religion among the creeds. Either the nationality must find a state to express itself in or the religion must be revived and appeal to all, or Jews and Judaism will be absorbed into the other nations and creeds. There is no other alternative."[85] Zangwill enunciated the idea that the emancipated Jew had reached a moment of decision in his "Zion, Whence Cometh My Help" speech, delivered in London in 1903:

> Zionism forces upon the Jew a question the Jew hates to face. Without a rallying centre, geographical or spiritual; without a Synhedrion; without any principles of unity or of political action; without any common standpoint about the old Book; without the old cement of dietary laws and traditional ceremonies; without even ghetto-walls built by his friend the enemy; it is impossible for Israel to persist further, except by a miracle—of stupidity.
>
> It is a wretched thing for a people to be saved only by its persecutors or its fools. As a religion, Judaism has still magnificent possibilities, but the time has come when it must be de-nationalized or re-nationalized.[86]

The demand for a decision between a national and a religious life was put forward in *The Melting Pot* in a line that is missing from both the original Lord Chamberlain's version and from the published text but is referred to by Zangwill in a July 23, 1909, letter to Tyler, at which point the play had been on the road for an entire season and was being readied for its New York opening. In it Zangwill directed that David tell his uncle Mendel, "America or Zion, it is up to *us* to choose."[87] Dr. Judah Magnes (1877–1948), then assistant rabbi of Temple Emanu-El, one of the few who fully understood the ideology behind these lines, was the only one to notice the absence of these words from the printed text. An ardent Zionist, Magnes considered *The Melting Pot* pernicious from the point of view of Jewish survival and considered its message a "backward" form of Zionism. He forcefully rejected Zangwill's polarized view, asserting that Zion was the complement to America, not its alternative.[88]

Such an either/or approach typified Zangwill's vision of Jewish affairs. In its coverage of the premiere of *The Melting Pot,* the *Jewish Comment* of Baltimore suggested that such extremism was essentially non-American and evidenced the English origins of the play. The subdivision of Jewry into rigid orthodoxy and accelerated assimilation, it said, was alien to American reality, where there were "a hundred halting places" between the strict Sabbath-keeping Jew and the one who contributes to the human race by willfully marrying a Christian.[89] The innate non-Americanness of *The Melting Pot,* later heralded as The Great American Play, was also raised in a hostile piece that appeared in the *New York Press* and was reprinted in the *Jewish Comment.* Half of it a personal and nativist assault on Zangwill, the article refers to him as "this man, who is novelist one day and dramatist the next," who has "pitched his tent on American soil," accused him of audacity in the selection of his play's title, and jibed, "what does this Englishman know about [the melting pot]?" With ill-disguised cynicism, it added, "of course, there is a possibility that Zangwill may know us better than we know ourselves, yet it is hard to believe that the wisest, most discerning of men, can search our hearts at a distance of 3,000 miles."[90]

Zangwill's involvement in the preparatory work of staging *The Melting Pot* was considerably less than for *Children of the Ghetto.* In addition to being occupied by ITO business, he was now an experienced playwright who was comfortable with the production process and had several productions under his belt: *The Moment of Death* (1900, U.S.), *The Revolted Daughter* (1901, U.K.), *Merely Mary Ann* (1903, U.S.; 1904, U.K., revival 1907, U.S.), *The Serio-Comic Governess* (1904, U.S.), *Jinny the Carrier* (1905, U.S.), and *Nurse Marjorie* (1906, U.S.). With a cast of only nine, *The Melting Pot* did not necessitate the careful logistics required by *Children of the Ghetto,* with its enormous cast and ambitious replication of milieu. The play was directed by Hugh Ford (1868–1952), not a theatrical innovator like James A. Herne, but rather an accomplished professional, one who would go on to direct several successful Broadway productions and have a career in silent films.[91] The play,

David (Walker Whiteside) and Vera (Grace Lane) reunite on the rooftop of the settlement house in the final scene of *The Melting Pot.* London production (1914). Zionist Archive, Jerusalem.

whose first three acts take place indoors, required little more than realistic and functional sets, props, and costumes. Only act 4, where David and Vera unite on the rooftop of a settlement house, invited scenic ingenuity, richly provided by Ford, complete with a background vista of New York's skyline and harbor. A stereopticon, a powerful multiple-lens magic lantern, projected the image of an illuminated Statue of Liberty, one of the first visual links between Lady Liberty and mass immigration.

The statue was included in the text as well. At the end of David's speech in act 1, he tells Vera, "when I look at our Statue of Liberty, I just seem to hear the voice of America crying: 'Come unto me all ye that labour and are heavy laden and I will give you rest—rest—.'" Interestingly, the summons he hears comes from Matthew 11:28–30, where Jesus' disciples are urged to commit to Christ for salvation. This is quite different from Emma Lazarus's famous lines: "Give me your tired, your poor, / Your huddled masses yearning to breathe free, / The wretched refuse of your teeming shore. / Send these, the homeless, tempest-tost to me, / I lift my lamp beside the golden door!"

Overall, Zangwill's correspondence with Tyler demonstrates a limited interest in the practical aspects of the production, so much so that he even suggests, possibly with an eye to frugality, that Tyler reuse the set of *Nurse Marjorie*, which was now ending its run on the road, with the revision that the wall decorations and props should include Jewish books and a piano.[92] This was so because Zangwill regarded *The Melting Pot* as a literary play of ideas, a *Tendenz-Schauspiel*, wherein the task of enunciating the script would fall mostly to the actors. Consequently, the sporadic comments he makes to Tyler regarding production primarily concern casting. Zangwill questioned casting Walker Whiteside (1862–1942), of whom he'd never heard, for the lead, and Tyler assured him that he was a first-rate actor who had not yet achieved stardom because of his slender physique. Once Whiteside visited him in England, Zangwill quickly came to appreciate his talent. A native of Indiana, Whiteside had begun his career as a Shakespearean actor and was gifted with a sonorous voice that was ideally suited to the character's oratory. Said to be in pursuit of the mantle of Edwin Booth (1833–1893), the greatest American tragedian of the nineteenth century, a goal he would never achieve, Whiteside did garner enormous critical praise for his portrayal of David Quixano.

After the opening, Zangwill possibly came to regret his scant presence. His letters to Tyler are now inundated with complaints about unauthorized changes, some of the sort that would normally be worked out during rehearsals. One month after the premiere, he complains about the "American idea" that a director should be allowed to make changes regardless of the original intent of the dramatist. He cites Ford's decision to bring down the first curtain at a point when the beautiful celebration of the Sabbath reaches its peak, thus giving the opposite impression of what he had intended, namely the disruption of the Sabbath caused by the pressures of economic survival.[93] Some years later he would further clarify his intention in a letter to London's *Jewish Chronicle*.[94] He explained that for Frau Quixano lighting the candles was the only bit of ritual left in the "melting pot" of New York, that the traditional bread and salt were absent from the table because no ceremonial meal could be eaten by the men who were rushing off to work on the Sabbath. He explained to those who wished that the first act would end harmoniously with the peace of Sabbath blessings that he aimed "not to depict the Sabbath peace but its profanation."[95] He did not do so lightly. The Sabbath celebration at home is a cherished concept for Zangwill. It is featured in all of his Jewish plays and appears as a recurring theme in other literary work. His "The

Hebrew's Friday Night," an ode to its sanctity, concludes as follows: "The simple love of home and child and wife, / The sweet humanities which make our higher life."[96] The muddled Sabbath at the Quixano home and the generational discord over adherence to its observance communicated a sense of great loss. This sadness is portrayed in Zangwill's postwar political play, *The Forcing House,* where Baron Gripstein, a powerful financier who had converted to Christianity to further his career, yearns for the serenity of the Sabbath of his poverty-stricken childhood. When asked why he had not returned to that "happiness," he replies, "On the road of life there is no returning."[97]

Zangwill wrote to President Theodore Roosevelt on August 25, 1908, inviting him and the members of his family to the opening of *The Melting Pot.*[98] In the same letter, he reminds him of their earlier exchange about the future of America and muses briefly of his strange adventures in the search for a Jewish territory. Within a week and a half, a letter from the White House confirmed that the president and Mrs. Roosevelt would be "very glad" to accept the invitation.[99] When the play opened on Monday evening, October 5, at the Columbia Theatre in Washington, the audience included President and Mrs. Roosevelt; William Loeb, the president's advisor; Secretary of State Elihu Root; Secretary of Commerce and Labor Oscar Strauss; and Jewish leaders Simon Wolf, a prominent jurist and philanthropist, and Isaac Solomon, a wealthy Baltimorean. The *Jewish Exponent,* taking tremendous pleasure in the public fraternity of the nation's power elite and Jewish philanthropists, exclaimed, "Even Washington might be pardoned for dividing its attention between a new play and such auditors."[100] Roosevelt is reported to have watched the play intently. His enthusiastic response was such that a local paper opened its coverage with the remark, "When President Roosevelt likes a play, he likes it!"[101] After David's first grand speech about America, Roosevelt was the first to burst into applause, and he applauded throughout. When Zangwill took a curtain call, the president stood in his box, was reported by some to bow, and cried out, "It is a great play, Zangwill!"

Roosevelt had but one friendly criticism of the play, which he shared with the author the next day during lunch at the White House. In act 3, shocked to hear of Vera's love for David, the baron cries out, "God in heaven—are you married already?" On opening night Vera responded, "In the sight of that God we are: not being true-born Americans, we hold even our troth eternal." Roosevelt objected, feeling that Vera's line demeaned Americans. Zangwill, standing corrected, changed the line to, "No, but not being unemployed millionaires like your Davenport members of the 400, we hold our troth eternal," undoubtedly suggested by Roosevelt, "the 400" being those considered by the

Astors to be the cream of New York society, the sort of people whom the president held in contempt.[102] The story about the changed text was widely reported and took the form of a juicy anecdote that helped publicize the production. It was also incorporated into a national debate on the declining state of the family, triggered by a government survey that reported that one in twelve married couples in America were ultimately divorced, data denounced by many moralists as "a great black spot upon American civilization."[103]

Roosevelt's admiration for the play was long-lasting. Three years later, in 1911, he wrote:

> That particular play I shall always count among the very strong and real influences upon my thought and my life. It has been in my mind continually, and on my lips very often, during the last three years. It not merely dealt with the "melting pot," with the fusing of all foreign nationalities into an American nationality, but it also dealt with the great ideals which it is just as essential for the native born as for the foreign born to realize and uphold if the new nationality is to represent a real addition to the sum total of human achievement.[104]

Six years later, in a wartime appeal titled "The Children of the Crucible" (September 1917), Roosevelt invoked the play when he wrote, "We Americans are the children of the crucible. It has been our boast that out of the crucible, the melting pot of life in this free land, all the men and women of all nations who come hither emerge as Americans and as nothing else."[105]

Zangwill had first met the president in 1898, when he was governor-elect of New York. Roosevelt mentioned their conversation in a May 15, 1901, letter to George Briggs Aiton, editor in chief at the National Encyclopedia Company in Chicago, in which he expressed his views on American Jews:

> As I told Zangwill when he was over here, I made up my mind it would be a particularly good thing for men of the Jewish race to develop that side of them which I might call the Maccabee or fighting Jewish type. I was confident that nothing could do more to put a stop to the unreasoning prejudice against them than to have it understood that not only were they successful and thrifty businessmen and high-minded philanthropists, but also able to do their part in the rough, manly work which is no less necessary.[106]

Roosevelt went on to praise the gallantry of the Jews who enlisted in the

Rough Riders, prided himself on bringing Jews into the force when he was New York City police commissioner and seeing to it that they would serve on an equal footing, and clearly enjoyed regaling Aiton with the anecdote of how he dealt with one Rector Alward, an anti-Semitic evangelist who had come to preach in the city. Roosevelt assigned forty Jewish policemen as Alward's bodyguards. He also assisted American Jewish leaders in their campaign against official Russian anti-Semitism. He publicly voiced the sympathy of his administration and the American people for the victims of the Kishinev pogrom and ordered the State Department to deliver a letter of protest to the Russian government, which refused to accept it. At a 1905 London banquet Zangwill, who a year earlier had met with the president in the White House, declared, "in the whole history of the world the Jews never had a better friend than President Roosevelt."[107]

Zangwill recalled his 1904 visit with Roosevelt in his famous speech to the American Jewish Congress, Watchman, What of the Night? (1923): "In 1904 I myself discussed with President Roosevelt at the White House the whole subject of the relation of American Jews to a Jewish autonomous colony. Roosevelt thought that any official opinion on the subject had better come personally through Secretary Hay, the Minister for Foreign Affairs, who, accordingly, after a most sympathetic conversation, empowered me to publish his opinion that it was open to all American Jews, without the faintest imputation on their patriotism, to take part in the foundation of such a colony."[108] Zangwill maintained a lifelong admiration for Theodore Roosevelt and dedicated the published version of the play to him.

CHICAGO—NEW YORK—LONDON

The Washington premiere of *The Melting Pot* was hailed as a striking success. It was expected to move to New York within a short time, though no explicit date or venue was named. Remarkably, Tyler decided to take the production directly to Chicago, where it opened on October 18 at the Grand Opera House. In an article titled "Zangwill's *The Melting Pot* Plays Chicago," Guy Szuberla writes, "Just why the Leibler [*sic*] & Co. Syndicate sent Zangwill's play to Chicago—rather than New York or some other theatrical venue—is hard to say with anything like certainty and directness."[109] The answer is to be found in Tyler's correspondence with Zangwill. Although nine years had passed since the New York debacle with *Children of the Ghetto*, its memory was still fresh in the producer's mind. In a letter to Jacob Schiff soliciting an endorsement for *The Melting Pot,* Tyler wrote, "Warned by the fate of our production of Mr. Zangwill's 'Children of the Ghetto,' which was really one of the strongest and most meritorious plays that ever found a place on the American stage, and the only fault of which was in its presentation of the education of the public, and the prejudice that was excited by maliciously inclined critics, I naturally seek to avoid similar results in this dilemma and this must be my excuse for my present missive to you."[110] Tyler's fear of again aggravating Jewish New York is clearly stated in a letter to Zangwill wherein he responds to the writer, putting the play in the same class with *Children of the Ghetto,* and his advising that "Jews must never be touted for directly": "I know this fact already," he writes, as "bitter experience had taught it to me."[111] The problem, he posits, is to know at just what point to leave off soliciting Jewish patronage, especially when working with press agents and managers who might be overzealous or not sensitive enough to ethnic concerns. Although the Chicago run lasted nearly the entire season and was immensely successful, just days before the New York premiere Tyler again expressed anxiety to Zangwill: "We are up to the opening for 'THE MELTING POT,' and frankly, I am very nervous—more nervous than I would be over any other play, but I must confess my nervousness is based on the old "Children of the Ghetto" results. You know a burnt child dreads the fire, and I cannot get the fear out of my system."[112]

The Melting Pot opened in Chicago on October 18, 1908, for a three-week run. Success was immediate. The production garnered a religio-patriotic aura expressed in newspaper reviews that made frequent use of such terms as "burning flames," "prophecy," and "genius" to describe Zangwill's sermonizing. The play's long-winded speeches, generally anathema to theatergoers, were received with enthusiasm. Burns Mantle, the critic of the *Daily Tribune,* praised the "wonderful amount of preaching," which captured the audience's attention with its authoritative tone and eloquent expressiveness. There was "nothing spiritually finer," he wrote, nothing "dramatically more tremendous" on the Chicago stage than this "voicing of the prophet's message."[113] The *Unity* declared that "the United States never received on the stage a more worthy or glorious characterization than in this play," and Constance Skinner, writing for the *Evening American,* felt that the grandiosity of the play elevated it to a sphere where dramatic criticism is rendered irrelevant.[114] She acknowledged that it had some flaws in terms of construction, but compared them to spots on the sun that become insignificant when its "splendor . . . is bursting over the world." For her, the play burned with "the spirit-white [i.e., pure] fire of genius," and its author, though a foreigner, had achieved what American dramatists had thus far failed to do, that is, compose The Great

American Play, one that showed "the white soul of America and interpreted to all lands her message." *The Melting Pot,* she assured her readers, "is a play you will remember all your life."[115]

Audiences were captivated by the grandiose theme and intense emotionalism of *The Melting Pot.* Writing for the *Evening Post,* Percy Hammond noted that they "listened raptly, with that precious silence so infrequent in the theater" and at the dramatic climax in the third act burst into applause that continued long after the curtain fell.[116] Whiteside's Kishinev soliloquy left many breathless and sobbing.[117] The cathartic effect of the finale was enhanced by audience participation. Zangwill's papers include a sheet with the lyrics of "America" (the actual title of "My Country 'Tis of Thee"), handed out to the audience, inviting them to sing along, which suggests that in some performances, possibly those on the Chatauqua circuit, ended with the audience and cast singing this national hymn in collective patriotic affirmation.[118]

Approval was not unanimous, however. Two of the city's seven dailies posted negative notices that crackled with nativism and anti-Semitism, mixed in with aesthetic comment. Amy Leslie of the *Daily News* rejected Zangwill's "avalanche of brilliant arguments" as steeped in "red, white and blue, with a kind of mongrel spread-eagle screaming liberty."[119] She accused him of rhetorical excess and "Yiddish hysteria" and of having written a "long Niagara of the woes and faults of Judea" instead of a truly American drama. Zangwill's melting pot idea was for her but a "crucible of elimination." And the Jews, she suggested, did not wish to be "melted up," nor were Americans eager to melt with them—or with the Irish, the Dutch, or the "Hottentots"—any more than other nations would. In a similar vein, Charles W. Collins of the *Inter Ocean* regarded the play as "Semitism run rampant," a Jew's cry for deliverance that merely used Americanism for "incidental dithyrambs" and "majestic background."[120] Collins posited the existence of two disparate audiences, each with its own sociocultural baggage. The first, with which he identified, consisted of the old-stock native-born, whose heritage afforded them the emotional detachment he considered imperative for dispassionate artistic appreciation. The second was comprised of "immigrants and sons of immigrants, particularly of Jewish blood," who approached the play in a "subjective" and personal manner. Clearly, for Collins, only the former could be true arbiters of taste. He dismissed Zangwill as a trickster with little artistic sincerity, who beguiled the audience's "primitive" sense of "artistic illusion," much like George M. Cohan's exploitation of simplistic patriotism and theatrical razzle-dazzle.

Perhaps out of a desire to balance their dismissal of such a popular play, both Leslie and Collins showered glowing compliments on Walker Whiteside in the lead role. Collins opened by hailing Whiteside as an artist in whom "burns the flame of genius, strong and unmistakable" and extolled him as a towering actor with a magnetic temperament and an exceptional emotional range. This praise, though hyperbolized, was not disingenuous. The actor's interpretation was applauded by all critics for its introspection, thoughtfulness, and sensitive detail. Notices that compared him favorably with David Warfield, one of the country's greatest actors, guaranteed stardom, a status reflected in newspaper ads with Whiteside's name featured above the play's title. The remainder of the cast were also highly commended, including Chrystal Herne, James A. Herne's daughter, who played Vera Revendal.

The impact of the negative reviews was not significant, in no small way thanks to an aggressive advertising and public relations campaign conducted by Tyler, which in addition to broad-spectrum and strategic advertising, courted civic and religious leaders. He organized a special matinee and invited clergymen from all denominations. More than 150 attended, many with their spouses. They became a cadre of emissaries who publicized and legitimized the production among their respective congregations.[121] He then solicited written endorsements from them and other prominent Chicagoans, which he included in a 5½- x -3½- inch booklet. One hundred thousand copies were distributed. They included exuberant blurbs by many of the religious leaders and other high-caliber figures, among them Jane Addams (1860–1935), pioneer social worker and leader in the women's suffrage and pacifist movements, who was to be a 1931 Nobel laureate, and Clarence Darrow (1857–1938), America's eminent labor lawyer, who would appear in some of the country's most celebrated cases, from the Scopes "Monkey" trial to Leopold and Loeb. The booklet was prefaced by photos and endorsements from Theodore Roosevelt, Jacob Schiff, and Oscar Strauss. Newspaper ads displayed snippets from these endorsements, boasting that the play had "created more discussion than many international subjects" and exclaiming, "No Play Ever Presented in Chicago Has Received Such Encomiums As These." The production became a "must-see" not only for the regular theatergoing public but also for those who wished to be informed and to partake in the discourse of the day.

Business was excellent, with the third week bringing in ten thousand dollars.[122] When the Grand Opera House was to be given over to the next booking, Tyler, convinced that local potential had not been exhausted, decided against moving to New York. Waiting for the theater to again become available, he kept the show going in one-night stands in the area, and on December 6 it reopened at the Grand Opera House, with the option for an indefinite run. Zangwill was not entirely happy with this arrangement. Chicago did provide handsome revenues, but he was eager to have the play open in New York, one reason being that his contract with Macmillan stipulated that publication would only follow a New York opening. Tyler, however, continued to send reports about the magnificent business *The Melting Pot* was doing in Chicago and argued that if the production were moved to New York in mid-season they would get only a four-month run before the summer, when the city's theaters would close, with no guarantee of resumption in the fall. After the Christmas season ended, and with the onset of a severe Midwestern winter, the box office began to decline, and in March 1909 the production left Chicago for a tour that would include St. Louis, Cincinnati, and Minneapolis.

The Melting Pot's approbation of mixed marriage raised quite a controversy within the American Jewish community but did not prompt much heated exchange in Chicago. America's second largest city, with a population of around two million, Chicago had a relatively small numbers of Jews—less than one hundred thousand—over 65 percent of them of East European descent, many of them immigrants not able to understand an English-language production nor afford the ticket price. The city's prominent Jews were mostly of German descent, much of their elite belonging to the city's largest and most prestigious temple, the Sinai Congregation. Its rabbi, Emil G. Hirsch (1851–1923), was an eminent figure in Reform Judaism and a leading Chicagoan, who had worked closely with progressive reformers like Jane Addams. A religious radical, he was opposed to "physiological Judaism," was a staunch believer in a universalized American Judaism, and took an unusually liberal approach to intermarriage. Already in 1904 he wrote that he had officiated at "so called 'mixed-marriages,'" though with the stipulations that the parents of both parties gave their consent and that the non-Jewish spouse was not a confessing Christian, and with the understanding that the children would be raised as Jews.[123] Revisiting the issue in a sermon triggered by the production, he spoke favorably of Zangwill's thesis that intermarriage, as Hirsch put it, could be "the most potent agency in extending the boundaries of Israel's religious fellowship."[124] He argued that intermarriages were common in biblical times and that until the triumph of Christianity proselytes were accepted by Judaism, at times in great numbers, and that unions with Gentiles ended only after the church began to ostracize and persecute Jews. These views must have had some influence on the local Yiddish press. In a piece titled "Zangwill's

Great Success," Leon Zolotkoff, editor of a local Yiddish newspaper, sang the praises of Zangwill and defended the play's thesis, arguing that its critics refused to see the amalgamation that was already in effect whether they liked it or not.[125] However, Hirsch's approval did create a backlash among Reform clergy outside of Chicago. One rabbi called it "crooked, maniacal and anti-Jewish," another accused Hirsch of being unpatriotic, and the *Jewish Tribune* dismissed him as "owner of a Sinai of his own"—referring to his life appointment at his synagogue—and a pursuer of tawdry sensationalism.[126]

Aside from Chicago, the play's intermarriage theme had aroused intense opposition from the beginning. In its otherwise enthusiastic coverage of the Washington premiere, the *Jewish Exponent* noted that the one element of the drama that struck "a false and illogical note" was the introduction of the marriage between Jew and Gentile as "a factor in the process of amalgamation."[127] The Jewish people, it said, had a vital interest not to engage in the "race suicide that would follow absorption." The issue was mainstreamed by the *New York Herald,* whose Sunday magazine section featured a heavily advertised "conversation" between Israel Zangwill, "the English Author," and Daniel Guggenheim, "the Colorado Millionaire," titled "Should Jews Marry Christians?"[128] Zangwill, who did most of the talking, spoke as a nationalist rather than a proponent of assimilation. He voiced the need for a Jewish territory; glorified notable Jewish figures in the arts, finance, and philanthropy; and also mentioned the "thousand forms" in which anti-Semitism manifested itself in America. Presenting himself as an observer rather than a propagandist, he explained, "My view [what he saw] and my views are not the same. What I observe and what I desire are different." His ideals, he said, were of "a pure Jewish religion and a solid Jewish nation." What he saw was "the broken fragments of a homeless race struggling to maintain its religion and race in the face of almost hopeless obstacles and prejudices." "I see Jews," he lamented, "with little pride of race and with no remnants of the old faith, changing their names, denying their parentage and losing themselves in the new conditions." As for intermarriage, he pointed to the fact that overall it was on the rise and had become commonplace in Australia, and especially in Denmark, where such unions were "obliterating the whole [Jewish] race." As a Jew he might lament this, but as an artist he could only "record the truth." Guggenheim's response was straightforward in its opposition to intermarriage, stating, "no man can respect himself or win respect who sacrifices his God for gain of any sort." He patriotically attested that in America there was no need for Jewish self-negation and evoked George Washington's famous letter to the Jewish congregation in Newport, in which he wrote, "For, happily, the Government of the United States, which gives to bigotry no sanction, to persecution no assistance, requires only that they who live under its protection, should demean themselves as good citizens."[129]

Hirsch's pronouncements and the *Herald* piece created much media hoopla. The *Jewish Tribune* hastened to "survey" the opinions of "prominent New Yorkers," a group that included Daniel Guggenheim; Leon Kamalky, editor of the *Jewish Daily News;* and rabbis Joseph Silverman and Judah L. Magnes of Temple Emanu-El, Stephen S. Wise of the Free Synagogue, Samuel Schulman of Temple Beth-El, Aaron Eiseman of Temple Beth Israel Bikur Cholim, and Dr. Pereira Mendes of Shearith Israel, who unanimously opposed intermarriage and agreed that it was a recipe for the extinction of Judaism.[130] Broadway followed the pulpit and the press with "intermarriage plays," notably Thomas Addison's *Meyer and Son* and J. Hartley Manners's *The House Next Door.* The intermarriage uproar was largely a case of art highlighting an issue in advance of life, the *American Hebrew* noting that there had been no marked increase in the very small number of mixed marriages between Christians and Jews in the United States and that the subject had come to the fore because of Zangwill's play.[131] While this controversy was raging, *The Melting Pot,* the match that had ignited it, remained safely tucked away in Chicago, its message debated in New York by those who had not seen nor read the yet unpublished play.

The Melting Pot opened in New York on Monday, September 6, 1909, at the newly built Comedy Theatre, a small 650-seat Broadway house built by the Shuberts, who were now replacing the Theatrical Syndicate as the major power of the American stage. The premiere attracted great attention, given the play's nationwide fame, with interest bolstered by Tyler, who was again conducting an extensive publicity blitz that included press releases, newspapers ads, and billboards brandishing superlative snippets by Roosevelt, Strauss, Schiff, and others. Opening night was an important event on the social calendar, and the audience's response, as described by the *Morning Sun,* was a producer's dream. The *Sun* reported that the spectators "not only clapped their hands with a remarkable enthusiasm, but they cheered in a way not usually heard in a New York theatre," their enthusiasm such that "there was difficulty in keeping count of the curtain calls."[132] This portrayal is supported by several other accounts, though an alternative description is presented in an antagonistic account given by the *New York Press.* After commenting on the significant number in the house who were "of Zangwill's blood," it described the audience as not knowing what to make of the play as it progressed, with an audience that at first was "in ready spirit to applaud" but later responded in "doleful silence."[133]

The next day, September 7, Tyler telegraphed Zangwill in England, "Audience's reception magnificent. Press divided. Success safe."[134] This opaque summation of press reaction was diplomatic. True, the *Herald* hailed *The Melting Pot* as "a big play," but many other reviews ranged from mixed to dreadful, with the *Evening World* labeling the production "the greatest disappointment of the season."[135] The *New York Times* reviewer did not mince words. He deemed *The Melting Pot* a "very bad play," ranking it as "hardly second rate," and branded its characters as mere sawdust and words. Though acknowledging the greatness of the subject matter, the *Times* dismissed Zangwill's handling of it as "cheap and tawdry" and appraised the play as "awkward in structure, clumsy in workmanship and deficient as literature."[136] The speeches, which had drawn much excitement in Chicago, were rejected in New York as long and dreary Fourth of July oratory, at best fit for the lecture hall. Alan Dale—the pen name of Alfred J. Cohen—drama critic of the *American,* regarded it as a "heavy, gloomy, mournful and unenjoyable thing" in dire need of an editor's blue pen.[137]

Zangwill's melting pot theory was given scant attention by the critics, some of whom regarded his motive for writing a play full of "claptrap patriotism" as purely commercial. Adolph Klauber, drama critic of the *Times,* suggested that Zangwill had a tendency "to keep his ear to the ground for the murmur of popular approval."[138] In a critical yet positive review, the *World's* Louis V. De Foe was equally cynical, commenting that the play's "high-sounding laudations of our ideals of freedom and citizenship, intermingled with long-winded panegyrics to our flag, our Constitution and even to our borrowed national hymn, do not drown the sound of metal at the box office."[139] David Quixano's idealism was regarded with skepticism, with some deeming him a bore, a "neurotic with a violin."[140] Annoyed with his verbosity and "patronizing air," the *Evening Sun* dismissed the character, saying, "a worse mannered and more insufferable prig than this David Quixano has never trod a stage."[141] Walker Whiteside's interpretation of David was not received with kudos either. Many critics paid tribute to his beautiful voice and fine elocution but regarded his acting style as declamatory, monotonous, "roady," and artificial.

While Chicago regarded *The Melting Pot* first and foremost as a play about America, New York saw it primarily as a Jewish play. Its use of Jewish materials drew diverse reactions, reminiscent of those evoked by *Children of the Ghetto.* Arthur B. Walkley, reviewing the American production for the London *Times,* thought little of the play but was greatly taken with its "delicately sympathetic" portrayal of traditional orthodox Jewish life.[142]

He credited Zangwill for making "an exquisite thing" of Jewish tradition and was especially impressed with his portrayal of the home ritual of the Sabbath. He was so moved by it that he suggested that Zangwill's tender picture undermined the assimilatory message of the play. It was a "grievous pity," he suggested, to have the authentic Jews represented by Mendel and Frau Quixano melted in the great American pot and reminted as "crude, shiny, brand-new Americans." Seeing Mendel through a romantic and exoticizing lens, he wrote of Mendel's "oriental dignity" and Isaiah-like "solemn simplicity." Cast into the "melting pot," he predicted, Mendel would come out "chewing gum and drinking cocktails, holding on by one hand to a subway strap and reading one of Mr. Hearst's papers in the other, saying, 'It's up to you' and 'This is a sinch [*sic*]!'"[143]

Alan Dale of the *American* took an opposite view. He recalled *Children of the Ghetto* and made the case that, as then, Jewish customs neither spoke to nor appealed to non-Jews and that Jews did not appreciate seeing them footlighted. Moreover, Klauber of the *New York Times* found Zangwill's representation of Jewish life disrespectful and inauthentic. He probably drew on personal knowledge when he complained that the characters spoke German not Yiddish, and he accused Zangwill of deliberately using Frau Quixano for cheap comic effect. The scene that he and other critics regarded as particularly objectionable was the Purim frolic at the end of act 2, when Frau Quixano and Kathleen dance with masks and fake noses. The inappropriateness of the scene had already been mentioned in Baltimore and Chicago, where Amy Leslie, a non-Jew, regarded it as sacrilegious, though she knew nothing about the holiday and its customs. Before returning to England, Zangwill had responded to this critique in a letter that Tyler distributed to the local press. He good-naturedly explained the origins of the holiday and noted that the carnivalesque nature of the feast was "sacred to nothing unless it be the lord of misrule."[144] As previously, when his public presentation of Jewish life had been criticized for its "bad taste," Zangwill denounced the hypersensitivity of assimilated Jews to the public portrayal of Jewish customs. Such people, he said, had a Marrano mentality and were ashamed of their own "ancient poetic ceremonies." No doubt he believed that their unease fed into Christian objections to "disclosures of the customs of Judea."[145]

Apprehensive about Zangwill's reaction to any tampering with his original script, Tyler had kept the scene as written. However, when objections were raised in New York, with its large Jewish population and its ambivalent critical response, along with the less-than-spectacular box office take—$3,800 during the first week—Tyler decided to cut it. He wrote to Zangwill on September

13, 1909, that since the Washington premiere he had received "damnations" about the "nose business." These he ignored until the playwright's personal friends, artist Leo Mielziner and scholar Herbert Friedenwald, attended the New York production and urged him to eliminate the scene. Zangwill wired back, "Insist retain dance even without noses," offering a compromise where pretty masks would be used—a Queen Esther mask for Kathleen, a "bearded rabbinic" mask for Frau Quixano, and a female mask for Mendel—"exchanging the sexes in innocent jollity." He insisted that the dance be retained so that "the pathos of the boy's playing the last dance to the old mother remains" and cited an article in a leading French magazine that compared the dramatic effect of Frau Quixano and Kathleen's dance to Nora's Tarantella in Ibsen's *A Doll's House*.[146] Tyler, however, would not budge. Further correspondence shows that he ignored Zangwill's instructions, arguing that the play would have faced financial ruin had he not excised the offensive scene. The talk against it was so strong, it had become, he said, "almost a disease" with "every Jew who wished to attack" the play using it as an excuse.[147] In this battle of wills, Tyler's chief argument was that the changes he had made were improving business. Yet in early November he admitted that of the nine weeks *The Melting Pot* had been playing New York, not one had been profitable; he also remarked that it was fortunate the play was done in a small theatre, which looked full all the time.[148] By the end of November he informed Zangwill that business had been so bad that the New York run would be closed by New Year's Day, and they would then take the play on tour.[149]

Unlike most plays, which sink into oblivion when their run is terminated, *The Melting Pot* did not disappear from the public sphere. Now published, it inspired additional productions and adaptations. Actor Leo Cooper of San Francisco developed a "Melting Pot" program that he presented throughout the country in which he offered a lecture combined with readings from the script. The play was periodically done in various educational settings—including Mount Holyoke College (December 1913) and the Chicago Hebrew Institute's Young Players Club (October 1914)—and from 1914 on it became a popular offering on the Chautauqua circuit.[150] *The Melting Pot* was also produced in Yiddish in January 1912 by Jacob Adler at the Thalia Theatre in New York, with himself in the lead, and in June 1912 in London, where it marked the opening of London's East End Yiddish People's Theatre.[151] The play went through a radical change in meaning in a 1915 Warsaw production by the Yiddish Kaminsky Theatre. Surprisingly, the local Yiddish paper, *Haynt*, labeled it a drama in three acts, while the original script includes four. This appears not to be a mistake, as the plot summary offered in the review

Front page of a promotional brochure for a 1916 touring production of *The Melting Pot*. The thirty-week tour was organized by the Redpath Chautauqua Bureau. Redpath Chautauqua Bureau, Special Collections Department, University of Iowa Libraries, Iowa City, Iowa.

concludes with the end of act 3, when the despondent David is rejecting Vera after he recognizes her father as the architect of the Kishinev pogrom and declares, "the melting pot is broken."[152] This deletion of act 4 was certainly done without Zangwill's permission. It subverted the original prophesy of fusion, transforming the message into an abject demonstration of the impossibility of assimilation.

A black-and-white film version of *The Melting Pot* starring Walker Whiteside was produced by William Cort in 1915. It was directed by Oliver D. Bailey and James Vincent, the script written by Bailey and Catherine Carr. According to *Variety,* its screening on a Sunday afternoon drew a full house at the Hippodrome, New York's largest theater.[153] A number of mass scenes, praised for their attention to detail, depicted Jewish life in Russia and the crowded steamer voyage of immigrants to America, with extras recruited from New York's Lower East Side. The film's most exciting scene was a graphic representation of the Kishinev pogrom, which *Variety* described as "thrilling, gripping and horrifying in its terrorism."[154] The grisly scene, said the British film periodical *The Bioscope,* transcended verbal description. The reviewer was especially struck by the moment when David finds among the ruins of his destroyed home the dead body of his little sister, her hand still clasping a tattered doll.[155] Both reviews hailed the visual presentation of David's symphony, a symbolic spectacle that showed throngs of America's component races passing downward into "God's Melting Pot." This scene may have been the inspiration for the oft-cited 1916 melting pot pageant organized by the Ford Motor Company, where immigrants in original native dress descended into a large pot topped by a sign inscribed with *E Pluribus Unum,* then reemerged in American business clothes, holding an American flag and naturalization papers. Although the film garnered critical acclaim in America and England, it did not become a success, due to Cort's sudden financial collapse. The correspondence between Zangwill and his New York attorney, Lawrence A. Steinhardt, includes numerous letters referring to Cort's default on royalties due and his refusal to surrender the film's negatives, even when Zangwill was offered a then-handsome ten thousand dollars from another firm interested in buying the rights.[156] The negative was eventually turned over to Steinhardt in 1925, but the film disappeared and must have physically disintegrated, as is the case with the great majority of films from that period.

Six years passed from the Washington premiere of *The Melting Pot* to the opening of its English-language production in London on January 25, 1914, staged in tandem with republication of the play in an expanded edition that included newly compiled appendixes, all of them reproduced in the present

Poster [in color] of the film version of *The Melting Pot* that appeared on the cover of the British periodical *Kinematograph and Lantern Weekly* in anticipation of the April 4, 1919, London trade show screening of *The Melting Pot.* Edna Nahshon's personal collection.

text.[157] Opening at the Court Theatre, this staging was a modest showcase production presented by the Play Actors, a group formed in 1907 and dedicated to quality drama, with the hope of attracting financial backing for a commercial run. It opened on a Sunday evening, when the commercial theaters were dark, with only one other performance scheduled, a Monday matinee. The Play Actors boasted no big names. Harold Chapin, who would be killed in World War I, played David, and Phyllis Relph appeared as Vera. Inez Bensusan, active in the Actresses Suffrage League and the only Jew in the cast, appeared as Frau Quixano, her portrayal hailed as a gem of character acting. The production was covered lightly in the general press but prominently featured in Jewish papers. Like other matinees, it received the obligatory reviews of the two theatrical papers, the *Era* and *The Stage,* and a very brief notice in the London *Times.*[158] They reported a warm audience response but were taken aback by the emotional rhetoric, with *The Stage* suggesting that Zangwill's playwriting would improve if he gave up his "assumed mantle of a prophet." A highly favorable review was given in *The Athanaeum,* which was not at all opposed to Zangwill's use of the stage as a pulpit and welcomed the fact that a "racial" play was finally making itself present on the London stage.[159]

Gaston Mayer, a producer who the previous year had worked with Tyler in organizing the American tour of the Irish Players, decided to invest in a commercial run. Walker Whiteside was rushed to London to take over the role of David, which he had by then played for three years across America and Canada. The production opened on February 7, 1914, at the Queen's Theatre and became an instant success with the public and much of the daily press. Its attributes were again proclaimed in a booklet that basically replicated its American precursor. The triumph was visible to all passers-by. A week after the opening, a queue of seven hundred people formed in front of the theater on Shaftesbury Avenue, and the production broke the house record for both pit and gallery.[160] On February 20 the *Jewish Chronicle* proudly listed the names of celebrities who had seen the play—lords and viscounts, politicians, intellectuals, and artists, as well as dignitaries of the Anglo-Jewish elite. On April 13 the play was moved to the Comedy Theatre, where on May 5 it celebrated its one hundredth performance, an established mark of success. Overall, with the seating capacity of nearly one thousand at Queen's, and the Comedy's nearly eight hundred, the play had been seen by nearly one hundred thousand Londoners, quite a feat for a serious drama, especially one where the cast had no drawing power, the star was an unknown American, and the author, though well entrenched in literary circles, had no great reputation as a playwright.

The Jewish response to the play in London was more complex than that in New York. Zangwill was Anglo-Jewry's most glorified talent, a fiery promoter of Jewish causes, and a celebrity who, unlike many successful Jews, remained umbilically connected to his origins. On the other hand, his play's assimilatory message was regarded with alarm, as it was in America, as a call for the willing disappearance of the diasporic Jew. The *Jewish World* expressed this complexity in a bitter commentary that oscillated between vituperation and reverence.[161] Attacks, however, were not the norm. The usual strategy adopted by Jewish reviewers and commentators consisted of an enthusiastic acknowledgment of the author's stature and of the artistic value of the play, a commendation of its Jewish elements, a refutation of its assimilatory message, and an invocation of its story as a cautionary tale utilized as a springboard for an antiassimilatory message. This tactic was especially noticeable in the *Jewish Chronicle,* by then owned and edited by Leopold Greenberg (1862–1931), a leading Zionist as well as a friend, admirer, and disputant of Zangwill's since the days of "The Wanderers." The paper's extensive review of the Court Theatre opening began with a paean: "A play by Mr. Zangwill necessarily calls for the closest attention, as indeed does the product of any genius such as he."[162] It went on to interpret the message of the play as a warning of the deadly forces of assimilation and concluded with the expressed hope that *The Melting Pot* would find a place on the commercial stage. In his column, "In the Communal Armchair," Greenberg attacked the play's assimilatory message but was careful not to discredit the author.[163] He praised the writing and the astute depiction of the Jewish characters, but resolutely dismissed the play's advocacy of amalgamation of Jews and Christians. His consternation over the future of Jews in a free society is palpable. Jewish assimilation, he wrote, was spreading with appalling rapidity, with thousands of children receiving less than minimal religious education and with intermarriage growing in popularity not only among the Anglo-Jewish upper echelon but also among East End immigrants. Assimilation, he emphatically noted, was the mark of weaklings, of those sapped of strength, its results being both dissolution and anti-Semitism, for the Gentiles would hold the Jews in a contempt that was bound to turn into hatred.

The impact of the production was also reflected in London's more liberal pulpits. In a sermon delivered at the West London Synagogue, Isidore Harris (1853–1925) used the play to promote the ideal of Palestine as a religious and cultural center for world Jewry.[164] He acknowledged that *The Melting Pot* offered an authentic picture of Jewish life in the diaspora, whose fortitude was being undermined by modernity, and contended that in order to resist the forces that stand against it Judaism needed to create a center in Zion. He spoke with enthusiasm about plans for the establishment of a modern university in Palestine where Hebrew would be the language of instruction and supported the reestablishment in Jerusalem of a Sanhedrin—an authoritative central body that would grapple with religious issues pertaining to Jews worldwide. The effect of the play on the Jewish community can also be gauged by the fact that when it was no longer a novelty, it served as the theme of a passionate sermon delivered by Morris Joseph (1848–1930) of the Berkley Street Synagogue on the first day of Passover.[165] Joseph did not mention Zangwill or the play by name. His congregation knew precisely to which "stage play" he was alluding, who "the modern Jewish dramatist" was, and what dramatic character spoke of "our people's paralysis" and advocated the glory of America over that of Rome and Jerusalem. He vigorously attacked Zangwill's thesis, praised Frau Quixano, denounced David, and declared, "the Jew is reserved for something more inspiring than extinction." Referring to the holiday's celebration of the biblical Exodus from the "iron-furnace" of Egypt, he insisted that the Jew's gaze remain fixed not only on the Statue of Liberty but also on the pillar of fire that "led his fathers to freedom under the yoke of God."[166]

The production also resonated in the immigrant community and was chosen as the topic for an address delivered on February 28, 1914, by the aristocratic Lily H. Montagu (1873–1963), a pioneer of Liberal Judaism in England and a social activist and philanthropist.[167] She spoke at the West Central Jewish Working Girls' Club, an institution she had founded in 1893 that offered evening courses, ranging from English literature to artificial flower–making, to nearly three hundred young women who held day jobs in the clothing industry. Imbued with its founder's religious beliefs, the club regularly concluded its activities with services. Montagu explained that she chose to focus on *The Melting Pot* because it was a work of genius that stimulated a deep reverence for the devotion of the past and a recognition of the spiritual striving of the present and, like the others, set out to read into it her own agenda, namely, a warning against drifting toward materialism and away from faith. She concluded her graceful sermon with a stirring summons for a communal commitment to "develop our understanding of Judaism, by seeking to renew the covenant of our fathers."[168]

The Melting Pot's advocacy of racial fusion became the subject of many lectures and discussions in non-Jewish forums as well. Herbert Burrows, with a mixture of sympathy and alienation, rejected Zangwill's theory of amalgamation outright. There could be no fusion in matters religious, he said. The Jew lives in a world of his own, with customs such as fasting on Yom Kippur and a prohibition against mixing meat and dairy that Christians could not understand.[169] He went on to offer a stereotypical list of the qualities of various races and nationalities—the Englishman typified by "virile energy" and "fixity of purpose," the Frenchman by "penetrating culture," the German by a "cool, steady brain," and the negro by "gaiety"—and pronounced that what the world needed was not fusion but cooperation, with the Jew "playing his part" in providing the world with "moral courage" and "tenacity of ideal."[170]

The London press also devoted ample attention to the production and the published version of the play, and leading intellectual figures debated its teachings. The themes of the play's central grand idea, of the use of stage as pulpit, and of the drama's structural weakness were addressed by nearly all reviewers. The *English Review,* though judging the play somewhat ama-teurish in technique, called it "an astonishingly interesting piece of work" imbued with a "rare honesty" of art and purpose.[171] It admired the richness and authenticity of the characters and the playwright's blend of the tragic and ridiculous, citing the Purim "nose scene" as a wonderful mixture of realism and Aristophanic satire. It praised Zangwill's use of the stage as rostrum and went on to expound against the slippage of theater into simplistic entertain-ment, a development it blamed on the rigid system of censorship, which had led to the avoidance of discussions of serious issues on the stage. On the other hand, Wilfred Whitte of *The Bookman* was less enthusiastic. No fan of the "drama of ideas," he did not consider the play itself "great" but praised it for tackling a "great idea," and directing attention to "a great vision" of the modern world.[172]

The play evoked some pro-Jewish sentiment, as many readers and specta-tors were shaken by its graphic description of Russian anti-Semitism. It also provided fodder for racist and anti-Semitic sentiment. This was especially ap-parent in comments that appeared in two periodicals: *The New Age,* a leftist publication that was a hotbed of literary modernism, and the *New Witness,* whose campaign against governmental corruption was imbued with anti-Se-mitic accusations against "alien usurers" and such metaphors as "locusts," "weevils," and "larvae" in its discussion of Jews.[173] Ironically, both papers oc-casionally paid lip service to Zionism, this support primarily motivated by a desire to rid English society and its body politic of Jewish participation. The *New Age* rejected the liberal notion of racial equality and promoted pseudo-scientific race theories that regarded miscegenation as the harbinger of cata-strophic consequences for the nation. The fusion advocated by Zangwill was anathema to its ideology. His melting pot, wrote John Francis Hope, was a "witch's kettle," and the world it would create could become one "run-over by a race of devils."[174] As for Jews, Hope admitted that the massacres of the Jews in Kishinev deserved the condemnation of "civilised men," but noted with cold detachment that "one pogrom is like another."[175] He faulted Zangwill for generating clamorous Jewish propaganda and with stony casualness noted that there was no savagery peculiar to the persecution of the Jews. The horrors of Kishinev, he wrote, could be matched by those of the Boxer rebellion in China, the Indian Mutiny, and the French Revolution.

G. K. Chesterton (1874–1936), reviewing the published play for *The Illustrated London News,* also attacked the notion of racial amalgamation and compared the union of Jews and Christians to that of Caucasians and blacks in America, where, he argued, it increased rather than allayed prejudice. In line with racist theories, he regarded the Jew's traits, like the negro's, as over-powering and predicted that the Quixanos' grandchildren "would always be throwing their Jewish grandfather and their pogrom grandmother at each other's head."[176] With a mixture of sexism and racism and mocking hauteur, he predicted that "little Arthur" would always pull "Polly's Slavonic hair," and Polly would always be pulling "Arthur's Semitic nose." The racist discourse of the immutability of Jewishness, to which was added the charge of Jewish control over Europe outside of Russia, was furthered by playwright J. E. Harold Terry, who reviewed the production for the *British Review*.[177] "I cannot follow Mr. Zangwill's argument," he wrote, for "the Jew will never rid himself of the brand of his race." Jews, he said, had been plunged into a hundred melting pots, yet had not lost "one iota of those strangely persistent characteristics that make their origins."[178] He went so far as to cite the persistence of anti-Semitism as proof for the permanence of Jewish traits and exclaimed, "the Jew in our midst is accorded rare tolerance, a tolerance that I, for one, gladly would see circumscribed." "Poor old England," he eulogized, was "fast degenerating into a dependency on Judaea, with London as a sort of pro-Jerusalem."[179]

An even more offensive voice was that of Cecil Chesterton (1879–1918), G. K.'s younger brother and editor of the *New Witness*. A recent convert to Roman Catholicism, he longed for the order of a mythical medieval past and was convinced that race was destiny, that miscegenation as well as women's suffrage would be disastrous. His anti-Jewish sentiments escalated to shrillness after he was prosecuted for criminal libel in 1913 over his scurrilous allegations regarding the "Marconi Scandal," when he made the accusation that a powerful Jewish ring with government connections had pocketed ill-gotten gains from a contract with the Marconi wireless company. Cecil was the first to attack *The Melting Pot* on Christian religious grounds. Incensed over Kathleen's exclamation that David Quixano's symphony was "like Midnight Mass," he wrote that this heresy made him "understand pogroms." Zangwill responded with a sharp letter, in which he pointed out that *The Melting Pot* had played in heavily Catholic cities in the United States and Canada without any objections to this line. Further, with characteristic panache, he informed Chesterton that although it went against his "conscience as an artist," he had instructed the Queen's Theatre to change the line to "it was like the music at Midnight Mass."[180] He proceeded to blast Chesterton for drawing a skewed equation of Russians and Jews that suggested the possible truth of blood-libel accusations according to which Jews had murdered Christian children whose blood they needed for religious rituals. Chesterton had written as follows: "Why, if we are asked to believe that Russians do abominable things to Jewish children, we should at the same time be asked to regard it as incredible that Jews do abominable things to Russian children—at Kieff, for example?"[181] By "Kieff" he was referring to the notorious trial of Mendel Beilis, a Jew framed for the murder of a boy whose mutilated body was found just before Easter of 1911 in a nearby cave. Beilis spent two years in prison, only to be found not guilty by a Russian jury, which was no mean feat. The trial attracted international attention and was seen as a vicious manipulation by Russian reactionaries to use Jews as scapegoats for political ends. Zangwill, infuriated by Chesterton's insinuation wrote:

> What a syllogism! If hooligans throttle Quakers, why is it incredible that Quakers should throttle hooligans? But you are *not* "asked to believe" that Russians murder and mutilate Jewish children—it is done brazenly, publicly, and on a colossal scale. What you *are* "asked to believe" (by Russia) is in the reality of crimes which, rare even upon the most hostile testimony, have never once in the whole course of history been witnessed or legally proved. Nor are you "asked to believe" that it is "incredible" a Jew should ever murder and mutilate a Christian child. What is "incredible" is that the murder could be "ritual" since there is no such rite.
>
> By the side of these sinister specimens of your logic on momentous questions, your ill opinion of my plays "The War God" or "The Next Religion" sinks into insignificance. But there is no justification for your misrepresenting my teaching or that of "The Melting Pot." It is simply monstrous to say that the play and Mr. Zangwill teach Jews "the abandonment of their nationality for all that America can give of pride and power and wealth" when David Quixano, in the depth of poverty and obscurity, expressly rejects the money of the American millionaire and yearns to build in America "the Kingdom of God," and when I myself have laboured for more than fifteen years at your own ideal of "creating a real jewish nationality with a fatherland."
>
> It is Christendom that is the failure—Christendom that will not give us a square deal, much less a square inch. Canada and Australia, with all their millions of virgin acres, have refused my organisation the tiniest territory. The Turk holds Palestine, and the Arab populates it. There are twelve millions of us. Where are we to go, if not to America?[182]

The Great War erupted in August 1914. Russia was now an ally, and the British government wished to dissuade anti-Russian sentiment. In June 1915 *The Melting Pot* was abruptly pulled from the stage while playing in Edinburgh. A question regarding this came before the House of Commons on June 17, and a verbatim report of the proceedings was published in the London *Times*.[183] It reads like a political satire:

> Mr. ANDERSON (Sheffield, Attercliffe, Lab.) asked the Under-Secretary of State for Foreign Affairs whether Mr. Zangwill's play, *The Melting Pot,* had been withdrawn from performance at Edinburgh owing to the intervention of the Foreign Office, and on what ground this action had been taken.
>
> Mr. KING (Somerset, N.L.), who asked a question on the same subject, stated that the play had frequently been performed in England, and was conciliatory, more particularly towards Russia and the United States.
>
> LORD R. CECIL (Hitchin, U.).—The performance of the play in question was not prohibited, but, at the request of the Foreign Office, it was suggested informally through the Scottish Office to the producers of the play that, in present circumstances, they should replace it by another play. This they were good enough to do.
>
> Mr. KING asked the Under-Secretary whether he was aware that this play had been seen by a member of the Cabinet, who expressed approval of it, and whether he would make inquiries on the point if the name were given him in confidence.
>
> LORD R. CECIL.—I am not responsible for the literary taste of the whole Cabinet. (Laughter.)

The Melting Pot did not have a major commercial revival in England, but neither did it completely disappear from its stage. It was produced in December 1920 by Norman Macdermott at his Everyman Theatre in Hampstead, a nonprofit outfit devoted to quality drama. Nearly simultaneously, Henry Baynton, a popular Shakespearean actor and one of England's last actor-managers, starred in a special performance at the Savoy Theatre on December 23. Baynton kept it in repertory and was still performing it in Yorkshire by 1925. As in America, the play faded from the mainstream but was occasionally revived by amateur groups and dramatic societies.

In 1923, fifteen years after its Washington premiere, Zangwill arrived in New York on his fifth and last visit to America. He had returned to the Zionist camp when the British government published the Balfour Declaration six years earlier and was now invited by Dr. Stephen S. Wise, who pronounced Zangwill "the foremost living Jewish publicist," to address the newly reorganized American Jewish Congress. "We have chosen him," explained Wise, also chairman of the congress, "because we know that no one is qualified as he to make the world listen to the word of the Jew."[184] Titled "Watchman, What of the Night?" the speech was delivered on October 14 at Carnegie Hall and broadcast by radio. It was grand, erudite, and militant, suffused with desperation over conditions in Europe and Palestine. It railed against the apologetics and timidity of the American Jewish leadership, accused them of a merely perfunctory commitment to political Zionism, and ended with the provocative "if die you must, go down like your forefathers, flag in hand."[185] The speech, widely reported in the media, was a landmark event, which flabbergasted his American hosts and alienated some of his closest friends. Once again, and for the last time, Zangwill caused the Jewish pulpits of America to rock with praise, debate, and denunciation. Rabbi Samuel Schulman of Temple Beth-El, who in the distant past had come out against Zangwill's *Children of the Ghetto* and *The Melting Pot,* now attacked Zangwill's attackers. He called the fifty-nine-year-old author a "great Jewish seer," whose "fearless soul has dared to speak the truth" to a strange and wicked world that did not wish to face it. "Watchman, What of the Night?" he said, was an address "inspired by truth, made strong by its comprehensiveness, touched by heroism, by its magnificent courage, and hallowed by the deep abiding love for the Jewish people."[186]

On the day he departed for England, Zangwill spoke about America and the indignation caused by his criticism:

> I do not dislike America; I love her. When I wrote "The Melting Pot" I believed her the hope of humanity. How much more terribly true that is today! One feels that she may be the last hope. With Europe suffering as she is among the ruins of her outworn, inadequate systems of government, one turns to America with a faith that has something frantic in it.[187]

The Melting Pot

Drama in Four Acts

The Cast

[As first produced at the Columbia Theatre, Washington,
on the fifth of October 1908]

David Quixano	Walker Whiteside
Mendel Quixano	Henry Bergman
Baron Revendal	John Blair
Quincy Davenport Jr.	Grant Stewart
Herr Pappelmeister	Henry Vogel
Vera Revendal	Chrystal Herne
Baroness Revendal	Leonora Von Ottinger
Frau Quixano	Louise Muldener
Kathleen O'Reilly	Mollie Revel
Settlement Servant	Annie Harris

Produced [directed] by Hugh Ford

ACT I

The scene is laid in the living-room of the small home of the QUIXANO*s in the Richmond or non-Jewish borough of New York, about five o'clock of a February afternoon. At centre back is a double street-door giving on a columned veranda in the Colonial style. Nailed on the right-hand door-post gleams a* Mezuzah, *a tiny metal case, containing a Biblical passage. On the right of the door is a small hat-stand holding* MENDEL*'s overcoat, umbrella, etc. There are two windows, one on either side of the door, and three exits, one down-stage on the left leading to the stairs and family bedrooms, and two on the right, the upper leading to* KATHLEEN*'s bedroom and the lower to the kitchen. Over the street door is pinned the Stars-and-Stripes. On the left wall, in the upper corner of which is a music-stand, are bookshelves of large mouldering Hebrew books, and over them is hung a* Miz-rach, *or Hebrew picture, to show it is the East Wall. Other pictures round the room include Wagner, Columbus, Lincoln, and "Jews at the Wailing place." Down-stage, about a yard from the left wall, stands* david*'s roll-desk, open and displaying a medley of music, a quill pen, etc. On the wall behind the desk hangs a book-rack with brightly bound English books. A grand piano stands at left centre back, holding a pile of music and one huge Hebrew tome. There is a table in the middle of the room covered with a red cloth and a litter of objects, music, and newspapers. The fireplace, in which a fire is burning, occupies the centre of the right wall, and by it stands an armchair on which lies another heavy mouldy Hebrew tome. The mantel holds a clock, two silver candlesticks, etc. A chiffonier stands against the back wall on the right. There are a few cheap chairs. The whole effect is a curious blend of shabbiness, Americanism, Jewishness, and music, all four being combined in the figure of* MENDEL QUIXANO, *who, in a black skull-cap, a seedy velvet jacket, and red carpet-slippers,* *is discovered, standing at the open street-door. He is an elderly music master with a fine Jewish face, pathetically furrowed by misfortunes, and a short grizzled beard.*

Mendel

Good-bye, Johnny! . . . And don't forget to practise your scales. (*Shutting door, shivers.*) Ugh! It'll snow again, I guess. (*He yawns, heaves a great sigh of relief, walks toward the table, and perceives a music-roll.*) The chump! He's forgotten his music! (*He picks it up and runs toward the window on the left, muttering furiously.*) Brainless, earless, thumb-fingered Gentile! (*Throwing open the window.*) Here, Johnny! You can't practise your scales if you leave 'em here! (*He throws out the music-roll and shivers again at the cold as he shuts the window.*) Ugh! And I must go out to that miserable dancing class to scrape the rent together. (*He goes to the fire and warms his hands.*) Ach Gott! What a life! What a life!

(*He drops dejectedly into the armchair. Finding himself sitting uncomfortably on the big book, he half rises and pushes it to the side of the seat. After an instant an irate Irish voice is heard from behind the kitchen door.*)

Kathleen

(*Without*) Divil take the butther! I wouldn't put up with ye, not for a hundred dollars a week.

Mendel

(*Raising himself to listen, heaves great sigh.*) Ach!, Mother and Kathleen again!

Kathleen

(*Still louder*) Pots and pans and plates and knives! Sure 'tis enough to make a saint chrazy.

Frau Quixano

(*Equally loudly from kitchen*) Wos schreist du? *Gott in Himmel, dieses Amerika.*

Kathleen

(*Opening door of kitchen toward the end of FRAU QUIXANO's speech, but turning back, with her hand visible on the door.*) What's that ye're after jabberin' about America? If ye don't like God's own counthry, sure ye can go back to your own Jerusalem, so ye can.

Mendel

One's very servants are anti-Semites.

Kathleen

(*Bangs her door as she ENTERS excitedly, carrying a folded white table-cloth. She is a young and pretty Irish maid-of-all-work.*) Bad luck to me, if iver I take sarvice again with haythen Jews. (*She perceives* MENDEL *huddled up in the armchair, gives a little scream, and drops the cloth.*) Och, I thought ye was out!

Mendel   (*Rising*) And so you dared to be rude to my mother.

Kathleen   (*Angrily, as she picks up the cloth*) She said I put mate on a butther-plate.

Mendel   Well, you know that's against her religion.

Kathleen   But I didn't do nothing of the soort. I ounly put butther on a mate-plate.

Mendel   That's just as bad. What the Bible forbids—

Kathleen   (*Lays the cloth on a chair and vigorously clears off the litter of things on the table.*) Sure, the Pope himself couldn't remimber it all. Why don't ye have a sinsible religion?

Mendel   You are impertinent. Attend to your work. (*He seats himself at the piano.*)

Kathleen   And isn't it laying the Sabbath cloth I am? (*She bangs down articles from the table into their right places.*)

Mendel   Don't answer me back. (*He begins to play softly.*)

Kathleen   Faith, I must answer *somebody* back—and sorra a word of English *she* understands. I might as well talk to a tree.

Mendel   You are not paid to talk, but to work. (*Playing on softly.*)

Kathleen   And who *can* work wid an ould woman nagglin' and grizzlin' and faultin' me? (*She removes the red table-cloth.*) Mate-plates, butther-plates, *kosher, trepha,* sure I've smashed up folks' crockery and they makin' less fuss ouver it.

Mendel   (*Stops playing.*) Breaking crockery is one thing, and breaking a religion another. Didn't you tell me when I engaged you that you had lived in other Jewish families?

Kathleen   (*Angrily*) And is it a liar ye'd make me out now? I've lived wid clothiers and pawnbrokers, and Vaudeville actors, but I niver shtruck a house where mate and butther couldn't be as pace-able on the same plate as eggs and bacon—the most was that some wouldn't ate the bacon unless 'twas killed *kosher*.

Mendel

(Tickled) Ha! Ha! Ha! Ha! Ha!

Kathleen

(*Furious, pauses with the white table-cloth half on.*) And who's ye laughin' at? I give ye a week's notice. I won't be the joke of Jews, no, begorra, that I won't. (*She pulls the cloth on viciously.*)

Mendel

(*Sobered, rising from the piano*) Don't talk nonsense, Kathleen. Nobody is making a joke of you. Have a little patience—you'll soon learn our ways.

Kathleen

(*More mildly*) Whose ways, yours or the ould lady's or Mr. David's? To-night being yer Sabbath, *you'll* be blowing out yer bedroom candle, though ye won't light it; Mr. David'll light his and blow it out too; and the misthress won't even touch the candleshtick. There's three religions in this house, not wan.

Mendel

(*Coughs uneasily.*) Hem! Well, you learn the mistress's ways—that will be enough.

Kathleen

(*Going to mantelpiece*) But what way can I understand her jabberin' and jibberin'?—I'm not a monkey! (*She takes up a silver candlestick.*) Why doesn't she talk English like a Christian?

Mendel

(*Irritated*) If you are going on like that, perhaps you had better *not* remain here.

Kathleen

(*Blazing up, forgetting to take the second candlestick*) And who's axin' ye to remain here? Faith, I'll quit off this blissid minit!

Mendel

(*Taken aback*) No, you can't do that.

Kathleen

And why can't I? Ye can keep yer dirthy wages. (*She dumps down the candlestick violently on the table, and EXITS hysterically into her bedroom.*)

Mendel

(*Sighing heavily*) She might have put on the other candlestick. (*He goes to mantel and takes it. A rat-tat-tat at street-*

door.) Who can that be? (*Running to* KATHLEEN'*s door, holding candlestick forgetfully low.*) Kathleen! There's a visitor!

Kathleen (*Angrily from within*) I'm not here!

Mendel So long as you're in this house, you must do your work.

(KATHLEEN'*s head emerges sulkily.*)

Kathleen I tould ye I was lavin' at wanst. Let you open the door yerself.

Mendel I'm not dressed to receive visitors—it may be a new pupil.

(*He goes toward staircase, automatically carrying off the candlestick which* KATHLEEN *has not caught sight of. EXIT on the left.*)

Kathleen (*Moving toward the street-door*) The divil fly away wid me if ivir from this 'our I set foot again among haythen furriners—

(*She throws open the door angrily and then the outer door.* VERA REVENDAL, *a beautiful girl in furs and muff, with a touch of the exotic in her appearance, steps into the little vestibule.*)

Vera Is Mr. Quixano at home?

Kathleen (*Sulkily*) Which Mr. Quixano?

Vera (*Surprised*) Are there two Mr. Quixanos?

Kathleen (*Tartly*) Didn't I say there was?

Vera Then I want the one who plays.

Kathleen There isn't a one who plays.

Vera Oh, surely!

Kathleen Ye're wrong entirely. They both plays.

Vera (*Smiling*) Oh, dear! And I suppose they both play the violin.

Kathleen Ye're wrong again. One plays the piano—ounly the young ginthleman plays the fiddle—Mr. David!

Vera	(*Eagerly*) Ah, Mr. David—that's the one I want to see.
Kathleen	He's out. (*She abruptly shuts the door.*)
Vera	(*Stopping its closing*) Don't shut the door!
Kathleen	(*Snappily*) More chanst of seeing him out there than in here!
Vera	But I want to leave a message.
Kathleen	Then why don't ye come inside? It's freezin' me to the bone. (*She sneezes.*) Atchoo!
Vera	I'm sorry. (*She comes in and closes the door.*) Will you please say Miss Revendal called from the Settlement, and we are anxiously awaiting his answer to the letter asking him to play for us on—
Kathleen	What way will I be tellin' him all that? I'm not here.
Vera	Eh?
Kathleen	I'm lavin'—just as soon as I've me thrunk packed.
Vera	Then I must *write* the message—can I write at this desk?
Kathleen	If the ould woman don't come in and shpy you.
Vera	What old woman?
Kathleen	Ould Mr. Quixano's mother—she wears a black wig, she's that houly.
Vera	(*Bewildered.*) What? . . . But why should she mind my writing?
Kathleen	Look at the clock—(*VERA looks at the clock, more puzzled than ever.*) If ye're not quick, it'll be *Shabbos.*
Vera	Be what?
Kathleen	(*Holds up hands of horror*) Ye don't know what *Shabbos* is! A Jewess not know her own Sunday!
Vera	(*Outraged*) I, a Jewess! How dare you?
Kathleen	(*Flustered*) Axin' your pardon, miss, but ye looked a bit furrin and I—

Vera	(*Frozen*) I am a Russian. (*Slowly and dazedly*) Do I understand that Mr. Quixano is a Jew?
Kathleen	Two Jews, miss. Both of 'em.
Vera	Oh, but it is impossible. (*Dazedly to herself*) He had such charming manners. (*Aloud again*) You seem to think everybody Jewish. Are you sure Mr. Quixano is not Spanish?—The name sounds Spanish.
Kathleen	Shpanish! (*She picks up the old Hebrew book on the armchair.*) Look at the ould lady's book. Is that Shpanish? (*She points to the Mizrach.*) And that houly picture the ould lady says her pater-noster to! Is that Shpanish? And that houly table-cloth with the houly silver candle—(*Cry of sudden astonishment*) Why, I've ounly put—(*She looks toward mantel and utters a great cry of alarm as she drops the Hebrew book on the floor.*) Why, where's the other candleshtick! Mother in hivin, they'll say I shtole the candleshtick! (*Perceiving that* VERA *is dazedly moving toward door*) Beggin' your pardon, miss—(*She is about to move a chair toward the desk.*)
Vera	Thank you, I've changed my mind.
Kathleen	That's more than I'll do.
Vera	(*Hand on door*) Don't say I called at all.
Kathleen	Plaze yerself. What name did ye say?
	(*MENDEL ENTERS hastily from his bedroom, completely transmogrified, minus the skull-cap, with a Prince Albert coat, and boots instead of slippers, so that his appearance is gentlemanly. KATHLEEN begins to search quietly and unostentatiously in the table-drawers, the chiffonier, etc., etc., for the candlestick.*)
Mendel	I am sorry if I have kept you waiting—(*He rubs his hands importantly.*) You see I have so many pupils already. Won't you sit down? (*He indicates a chair.*)
Vera	(*Flushing, embarrassed, releasing her hold of the door handle*) Thank you—I—I—I didn't come about pianoforte lessons.
Mendel	(*Sighing in disappointment*) Ach!

Vera   In fact I—er—it wasn't you I wanted at all—I was just going.

Mendel   (*Politely*) Perhaps I can direct you to the house you are looking for.

Vera   Thank you, I won't trouble you. (*She turns toward the door again.*)

Mendel   Allow me! (*He opens the door for her.*)

Vera   (*Hesitating, struck by his manners, struggling with her anti-Jewish prejudice*) It—it—was your son I wanted.

Mendel   (*His face lighting up*) You mean my nephew, David. Yes, *he* gives violin lessons. (*He closes the door.*)

Vera   Oh, is he your nephew?

Mendel   I am sorry he is out—he, too, has so many pupils, though at the moment he is only at the Crippled Children's Home— playing to them.

Vera   How lovely of him! (*Touched and deciding to conquer her prejudice*) But that's just what *I* came about—I mean we'd like him to play again at our Settlement. Please ask him why he hasn't answered Miss Andrews's letter.

Mendel   (*Astonished*) He hasn't answered your letter?

Vera   Oh, I'm not Miss Andrews; I'm only her assistant.

Mendel   I see—Kathleen, whatever are you doing under the table?

    (*KATHLEEN, in her hunting around for the candlestick, is now stooping and lifting up the table-cloth.*)

Kathleen   Sure the fiend's after witching away the candle-shtick.

Mendel   (*Embarrassed*) The candlestick? Oh—I—I think you'll find it in my bedroom.

Kathleen   Wisha, now! (*She goes into his bedroom.*)

Mendel   (*Turning apologetically to* VERA) I beg your pardon. Miss Andrews, I mean Miss—er—

Vera	Revendal.
Mendel	(*Slightly more interested*) Revendal? Then you must be the Miss Revendal David told me about!
Vera	(*Blushing*) Why, he has only seen me once—the time he played at our Roof-Garden Concert.
Mendel	Yes, but he was so impressed by the way you handled those new immigrants—the Spirit of the Settlement, he called you.
Vera	(*Modestly*) Ah, no—Miss Andrews is that. And you will tell him to answer her letter at once, won't you, because there's only a week now to our Concert. (*A gust of wind shakes the windows. She smiles.*) Naturally it will *not* be on the Roof Garden.
Mendel	(*Half to himself*) Fancy David not saying a word about it to me! Are you sure the letter was mailed?
Vera	I mailed it myself a week ago. And even in New York—
	(*She smiles. Re-ENTER* KATHLEEN *with the recovered candlestick.*)
Kathleen	Bedad, ye're as great a shleep-walker as Mr. David! (*She places the candlestick on the table and moves toward her bedroom.*)
Mendel	Kathleen!
Kathleen	(*Pursuing her walk without turning*) I'm not here!
Mendel	Did you take in a letter for Mr. David about a week ago? (*Smiling at* MISS REVENDAL) He doesn't get many, you see.
Kathleen	(*Turning*) A letter? Sure, I took in ounly a postcard from Miss Johnson, an' that ounly sayin'—
Vera	And you don't remember a letter—a large letter—last Saturday—with the seal of our Settlement?
Kathleen	Last Saturday wid a seal, is it? Sure, how could I forget it?
Mendel	Then you *did* take it in?

Kathleen	Ye're wrong entirely. 'Twas the misthress took it in.
Mendel	(*To* VERA) I am sorry the boy has been so rude.
Kathleen	But the misthress didn't give it him at wanst—she hid it away bekaz it was *Shabbos*.
Mendel	Oh, dear—and she has forgotten to give it to him. Excuse me. (*He makes a hurried EXIT to the kitchen.*)
Kathleen	And excuse me—I've me thrunk to pack. (*She goes toward her bedroom, pauses at the door.*) And ye'll witness I don't pack the candleshtick. (*Emphatic EXIT.*)
Vera	(*Still dazed*) A Jew! That wonderful boy a Jew! . . . But then so was David the shepherd youth with his harp and his psalms, the sweet singer in Israel. (*She surveys the room and its content with interest. The windows rattle once or twice in the rising wind. The light gets gradually less. She picks up the huge Hebrew tome on the piano and puts it down with a slight smile as if overwhelmed by the weight of alien antiquity. Then she goes over to the desk and picks up the printed music.*) Mendelssohn's Concerto, Tartini's Sonata in G Minor, Bach's Chaconne . . . (*She looks up at the book-rack.*) "History of the American Commonwealth," "Cyclopaedia of History," "History of the Jews"—he seems very fond of history. Ah, there's Shelley and Tennyson. (*With surprise*) Nietzsche next to the Bible? No Russian books apparently—
	(*Re-ENTER* MENDEL *triumphantly with a large sealed letter.*)
Mendel	Here it is! As it came on Saturday, my mother was afraid David would open it!
Vera	(*Smiling*) But what *can* you do with a letter except open it? Any more than with an oyster?
Mendel	(*Smiling as he puts the letter on* DAVID's *desk*) To a pious Jew letters and oysters are alike forbidden—at least letters may not be opened on our day of rest.
Vera	I'm sure I couldn't rest till I'd opened mine.
	(*ENTER from the kitchen* FRAU QUIXANO, *defending herself*

with excited gesticulation. She is an old lady with a black wig, but her appearance is dignified, venerable even, in no way comic. She speaks Yiddish exclusively, that being largely the language of the Russian Pale.)

Frau Quixano   *Obber ich hob gesogt zu* Kathleen—

Mendel   (*Turning and going to her*) Yes, yes, mother, that's all right now.

Frau Quixano   (*In horror, perceiving her Hebrew book on the floor, where* KATH-LEEN *has dropped it.*) *Mein Buch!* (*She picks it up and, kisses it piously.*)

Mendel   (*Presses her into her fireside chair*) *Ruhig, ruhig. Mutter!* (*To* VERA) She understands barely a word of English—she won't disturb us.

Vera   Oh, but I must be going—I was so long finding the house, and look! it has begun to snow! (*They both turn their heads and look at the falling snow.*)

Mendel   All the more reason to wait for David—it may leave off. He can't be long now. Do sit down. (*He offers a chair.*)

Frau Quixano   (*Looking round suspiciously*) *Wos will die Shikseh?*

Vera   What does your mother say?

Mendel   (*Half-smiling*) Oh, only asking what your heathen ladyship desires.

Vera   Tell her I hope she is well.

Mendel   *Das Fräulein hofft dass es geht gut*—

Frau Quixano   (*Shrugging her shoulders in despairing astonishment*) *Gut? Un' wie soll es gut gehen—in Amerika!* (*She takes out her spectacles, and begins slowly polishing and adjusting them.*)

Vera   (*Smiling*) I understood that last word.

Mendel   She asks how can anything possibly go well in America!

Vera   Ah, she doesn't like America.

Mendel	(*Half-smiling*) Her favourite exclamation is "*A Klog zu Columbessen!*"
Vera	What does that mean?
Mendel	Cursed be Columbus!
Vera	(*Laughingly*) Poor Columbus! I suppose she's just come over.
Mendel	Oh, no, it must be ten years since I sent for her.
Vera	Really! But your nephew was born here?
Mendel	No, he's Russian too. But please sit down, you had better get his answer at once. (*VERA sits.*)
Vera	I suppose *you* taught him music.
Mendel	I? I can't play the violin. He is self-taught. In the Russian Pale he was a wonder-child. Poor David! He always looked forward to coming to America; he imagined I was a famous musician over here. He found me conductor in a cheap theatre—a converted beer-hall.
Vera	Was he very disappointed?
Mendel	Disappointed? He was enchanted! He is crazy about America.
Vera	(*Smiling*) Ah, *he* doesn't curse Columbus.
Mendel	My mother came with her life behind her: David with his life before him. Poor boy!
Vera	Why do you say poor boy?
Mendel	What is there before him here but a terrible struggle for life? If he doesn't curse Columbus, he'll curse fate. Music-lessons and dance-halls, beer-halls and weddings—every hope and ambition will be ground out of him, and he will die obscure and unknown.

(*His head sinks on his breast. FRAU QUIXANO is heard faintly sobbing over her book. The sobbing continues throughout the scene.*)

Vera	(*Half-rising*) You have made your mother cry.
Mendel	Oh, no—she understood nothing. She always cries on the eve of the Sabbath.
Vera	(*Mystified, sinking back into her chair*) Always cries? Why?
Mendel	(*Embarrassed*) Oh, well, a Christian wouldn't understand—
Vera	Yes I could—do tell me!
Mendel	She knows that in this great grinding America, David and I must go out to earn our bread on Sabbath as on weekdays. She never says a word to us, but her heart is full of tears.
Vera	Poor old woman. It was wrong of us to ask your nephew to play at the Settlement for nothing.
Mendel	(*Rising fiercely*) If you offer him a fee, he shall not play. Did you think I was begging of you?
Vera	I beg your pardon—(*She smiles.*) There, *I* am begging of *you.* Sit down, please.
Mendel	(*Walking away to piano*) I ought not to have burdened you with our troubles—you are too young.
Vera	(*Pathetically*) I young? If you only knew how old I am!
Mendel	You?
Vera	I left my youth in Russia—eternities ago.
Mendel	You know our Russia! (*He goes over to her and sits down.*)
Vera	Can't you see I'm a Russian, too?
	(*With a faint tremulous smile*) I might even have been a Siberian had I stayed. But I escaped from my gaolers.
Mendel	You were a Revolutionist!
Vera	Who can live in Russia and not be? So you see trouble and I are not such strangers.
Mendel	Who would have thought it to look at you? Siberia, gaolers,

revolutions! (*Rising*) What terrible things life holds!

Vera   Yes, even in free America.

(*FRAU QUIXANO's sobbing grows slightly louder.*)

Mendel   That Settlement work must be full of tragedies.

Vera   Sometimes one sees nothing but the tragedy of things. (*Looking toward the window*) The snow is getting thicker. How pitilessly it falls—like fate.

Mendel   (*Following her gaze*) Yes, icy and inexorable.

(*The faint sobbing of FRAU QUIXANO over her book, which has been heard throughout the scene as a sort of musical accompaniment, has combined to work it up to a mood of intense sadness, intensified by the growing dusk, so that as the two now gaze at the falling snow, the atmosphere seems overbrooded with melancholy. There is a moment or two without dialogue, given over to the sobbing of FRAU QUIXANO, the roar of the wind shaking the windows, the quick falling of the snow. Suddenly a happy voice singing "My Country 'tis of Thee" is heard from without.*)

Frau Quixano   (*Pricking up her ears, joyously*) Do ist Dovidel!

Mendel   That's David! (*He springs up.*)

Vera   (*Murmurs in relief*) Ah!

(*The whole atmosphere is changed to one of joyous expectation. DAVID is seen and heard passing the left window, still singing the national hymn, but it breaks off abruptly as he throws open the door and appears on the threshold, a buoyant snow-covered figure in a cloak and a broad-brimmed hat, carrying a violin case. He is a sunny, handsome youth of the finest Russo-Jewish type. He speaks with a slight German accent.*)

David   Isn't it a beautiful world, uncle? (*He closes the inner door.*) Snow, the divine white snow—(*Perceiving the visitor with amaze*) Miss Revendal here! (*He removes his hat and looks at her with boyish reverence and wonder.*)

Vera   (*Smiling*) Don't look so surprised—I haven't fallen from heaven like the snow. Take off your wet things.

David Oh, it's nothing; it's dry snow. (*He lays down his violin case and brushes off the snow from his cloak, which* MENDEL *takes from him and bangs on the rack, all without interrupting the dialogue.*) If I had only known you were waiting—

Vera I am glad you didn't—I wouldn't have had those poor little cripples cheated out of a moment of your music.

David Uncle has told you? Ah, it was bully! You should have seen the cripples waltzing with their crutches! (*He has moved toward the old woman, and while he holds one hand to the blaze now pats her cheek with the other in greeting, to which she responds with a loving smile ere she settles contentedly to slumber over her book.*) Es war grossartig, Granny. Even the paralysed danced.

Mendel Don't exaggerate, David.

David Exaggerate, uncle! Why, if they hadn't the use of their legs, their arms danced on the counterpane; if their arms couldn't dance, their hands danced from the wrist; and if their hands couldn't dance, they danced with their fingers; and if their fingers couldn't dance, their heads danced; and if their heads were paralysed, why, their eyes danced—God never curses so utterly but you've *something* left to dance with! (*He moves toward his desk.*)

Vera (*Infected with his gaiety*) You'll tell us next the beds danced.

David So they did—they shook their legs like mad!

Vera Oh, why wasn't I there?

(*His eyes meet hers at the thought of her presence.*)

David Dear little cripples, I felt as if I could play them all straight again with the love and joy jumping out of this old fiddle. (*He lays his hand caressingly on the violin.*)

Mendel (*Gloomily*) But in reality you left them as crooked as ever.

David No, I didn't. (*He caresses the back of his uncle's head in affectionate rebuke.*) I couldn't play their bones straight, but I played their brains straight. And hunch-*brains* are worse than hunch-*backs* . . . (*Suddenly perceiving his letter on the desk*) A letter for *me!* (*He takes it with boyish eagerness, then hesitates to open it.*)

Vera   (*Smiling*) Oh, you may open it!

David   (*Wistfully*) May I?

Vera   (*Smiling*) Yes, and quick-or it'll be *Shabbos!*

         (*DAVID looks up at her in wonder.*)

Mendel (*Smiling*) You read your letter!

David   (*Opens it eagerly, then smiles broadly with pleasure.*) Oh, Miss Revendal! Isn't that great! To play again at your Settlement. I *am* getting famous.

Vera   But we can't offer you a fee.

Mendel (*Quickly sotto voce to VERA*) Thank you!

David   A fee! I'd pay a fee to see all those happy immigrants you gather together—Dutchmen and Greeks, Poles and Norwegians, Welsh and Armenians. If you only had Jews, it would be as good as going to Ellis Island.

Vera   (*Smiling*) What a strange taste! Who on earth wants to go to Ellis Island?

David   Oh, I love going to Ellis Island to watch the ships coming in from Europe, and to think that all those weary, sea-tossed wanderers are feeling what *I* felt when America first stretched out her great mother-hand to *me!*

Vera   (*Softly*) Were you very happy?

David   It was heaven. You must remember that all my life I had heard of America—everybody in our town had friends there or was going there or got money orders from there. The earliest game I played at was selling off my toy furniture and setting up in America. All my life America was waiting, beckoning, shining—the place where God would wipe away tears from off all faces. (*He ends in a half-sob.*)

Mendel	(*Rises, as in terror*) Now, now, David, don't get excited. (*Approaches him.*)
David	To think that the same great torch of liberty which threw its light across all the broad seas and lands into my little garret in Russia, is shining also for all those other weeping millions of Europe, shining wherever men hunger and are oppressed—
Mendel	(*Soothingly*) Yes, yes, David. (*Laying hand on his shoulder*) Now sit down and—
David	(*Unheeding*) Shining over the starving villages of Italy and Ireland, over the swarming stony cities of Poland and Galicia, over the ruined farms of Roumania, over the shambles of Russia—
Mendel	(*Pleadingly*) David!
David	Oh, Miss Revendal, when I look at our Statue of Liberty, I just seem to hear the voice of America crying: "Come unto me all ye that labour and are heavy laden and I will give you rest—rest—" (*He is now almost sobbing.*)
Mendel	Don't talk any more—you know it is bad for you.
David	But Miss Revendal asked—and I want to explain to her what America means to me.
Mendel	You can explain it in your American symphony.
Vera	(*Eagerly—to DAVID*) You compose?
David	(*Embarrassed*) Oh, uncle, why did you talk of—? Uncle always—my music is so thin and tinkling. When I am *writing* my American symphony, it seems like thunder crashing through a forest full of bird songs. But next day—oh, next day! (*He laughs dolefully and turns away.*)
Vera	So your music finds inspiration in America?
David	Yes—in the seething of the Crucible.
Vera	The Crucible? I don't understand!
David	Not understand! You, the Spirit of the Settlement! (*He rises and crosses to her and leans over the table, facing her.*) Not un-

derstand that America is God's Crucible, the great Melting-Pot where all the races of Europe are melting and re-forming! Here you stand, good folk, think I, when I see them at Ellis Island, here you stand (*graphically illustrating it on the table*) in your fifty groups, with your fifty languages and histories, and your fifty blood hatreds and rivalries. But you won't be long like that, brothers, for these are the fires of God you've come to—these are the fires of God. A fig for your feuds and vendettas! Germans and Frenchmen, Irishmen and Englishmen, Jews and Russians—into the Crucible with you all! God is making the American.

Mendel   I should have thought the American was made already—eighty millions of him.

David   Eighty millions! (*He smiles toward* VERA *in good-humoured derision.*) Eighty millions! Over a continent! Why, that cockle-shell of a Britain has forty millions. No, uncle, the real American has not yet arrived. He is only in the Crucible, I tell you—he will be the fusion of all races, perhaps the coming superman. Ah, what a glorious Finale for my symphony—if I can only write it.

Vera   But you have written some of it already! May I not see it?

David   (*Relapsing into boyish shyness*) No, if you please, don't ask. (*He moves over to his desk and nervously shuts it down and turns the keys of drawers as though protecting his MS.*)

Vera   Won't you give a bit of it at our Concert?

David   Oh, it needs an orchestra.

Vera   But you at the violin and I at the piano—

Mendel   You didn't tell me you played, Miss Revendal!

Vera   I told you less commonplace things.

David   Miss Revendal plays quite like a professional.

Vera   (*Smiling*) I don't feel so complimented as you expect. You see I did have a professional training.

Mendel	(*Smiling*) And I thought you came to *me* for lessons!
	(DAVID *laughs.*)
Vera	(*Smiling*) No, I went to Petersburg—
David	(*Dazed*) To Petersburg—?
Vera	(*Smiling*) Naturally. To the Conservatoire. There wasn't much music to be had at Kishineff, a town where—
David	Kishineff! (*He begins to tremble.*)
Vera	(*Still smiling*) My birthplace.
Mendel	(*Coming toward him, protectingly*) Calm yourself, David.
David	Yes, yes—so you are a Russian! (*He shudders violently, staggers.*)
Vera	(*Alarmed*) You are ill!
David	It is nothing, I—not much music at Kishineff! No, only the Death-March! . . . Mother! Father! Ah—cowards, murderers! And you! (*He shakes his fist at the air.*) You, looking on with your cold butcher's face! O God! O God! (*He bursts into hysterical sobs and runs shamefacedly, through the door to his room.*)
Vera	(*Wildly*) What have I said? What have I done?
Mendel	Oh, I was afraid of this, I was afraid of this.
Frau Quixano	(*Who has fallen asleep over her book, wakes as if with a sense of the horror and gazes dazedly around, adding to the thrillingness of the moment*) Dovidel! Wu is' Dovidel! Mir dacht sach—
Mendel	(*Pressing her back to her slumbers*) Du traumst, Mutter! Schlaf!
	(*She sinks back to sleep.*)
Vera	(*In hoarse whisper*) His father and mother were massacred?
Mendel	(*In same tense tone*) Before his eyes—father, mother, sisters, down to the youngest babe, whose skull was battered in by a hooligan's heel.

Vera	How did *he* escape?
Mendel	He was shot in the shoulder, and fell unconscious. As he wasn't a girl, the hooligans left him for dead and hurried to fresh sport.
Vera	Terrible! Terrible! (*Almost in tears.*)
Mendel	(*Shrugging shoulders, hopelessly*) It is only Jewish history! . . . David belongs to the species of *pogrom* orphans—they arrive in the States by almost every ship.
Vera	Poor boy! Poor boy! And he looked so happy! (*She half sobs.*)
Mendel	So he is, most of the time—a sunbeam took human shape when he was born. But naturally that dreadful scene left a scar on his brain, as the bullet left a scar on his shoulder, and he is always liable to see red when Kishineff is mentioned.
Vera	I will never mention my miserable birthplace to him again.
Mendel	But you see every few months the newspapers tell us of another *pogrom* and then he screams out against what he calls that butcher's face, so that I tremble for his reason. I tremble even when I see him writing that crazy music about America, for it only means he is brooding over the difference between America and Russia.
Vera	But perhaps—perhaps—all the terrible memory will pass peacefully away in his music.
Mendel	There will always be the scar on his shoulder to remind, him—whenever the wound twinges, it brings up these terrible faces and visions.
Vera	Is it on his right shoulder?
Mendel	No—on his left. For a violinist that is even worse.
Vera	Ah, of course—the weight and the fingering. (*Subconsciously placing and fingering an imaginary violin.*)
Mendel	That is why I fear so for his future—he will never be strong enough for the feats of bravura that the public demands.
Vera	The wild beasts! I feel more ashamed of my country than ever.

	But there's his symphony.
Mendel	And who will look at that amateurish stuff? He knows so little of harmony and counterpoint—he breaks all the rules. I've tried to give him a few pointers—but he ought to have gone to Germany.
Vera	Perhaps it's not too late.
Mendel	(*Passionately*) Ah, if you and your friends could help him! See—I'm begging after all. But it's not for myself.
Vera	My father loves music. Perhaps *he*—but no! he lives in Kishineff. But I will think—there are people here—I will write to you.
Mendel	(*Fervently*) Thank you! Thank you!
Vera	Now you must go to him. Good-bye. Tell him I count upon him for the Concert.
Mendel	How good you are! (*He follows her to the street-door.*)
Vera	(*At door*) Say good-bye for me to your mother—she seems asleep.
Mendel	(*Opening outer door*) I am sorry it is snowing so.
Vera	We Russians are used to it. (*Smiling, at EXIT*) Good-bye— let us hope your David will turn out a Rubinstein.
Mendel	(*Closing the doors softly*) I never thought a Russian Christian could be so human. (*He looks at the clock.*) *Gott in Himmel*— my dancing class!
	(*He flurries into the overcoat hanging on the hat-rack. Re-ENTER DAVID, having composed himself, but still somewhat dazed.*)
David	She is gone? Oh, but I have driven her away by my craziness—Is she very angry?
Mendel	Quite the contrary—she expects you at the Concert, and what is more—
David	(*Ecstatically*) And she understood! She understood my Cru-

	cible of God! Oh, uncle, you don't know what it means to me to have somebody who understands me. Even you have never understood—
Mendel	(*Wounded*) Nonsense! How can Miss Revendal understand you better than your own uncle?
David	(*Mystically exalted*) I can't explain—I feel it.
Mendel	Of course she's interested in your music, thank Heaven. But what true understanding can there be between a Russian Jew and a Russian Christian?
David	What understanding? Aren't we both Americans?
Mendel	Well, I haven't time to discuss it now. (*He winds his muffler round his throat.*)
David	Why, where are you going?
Mendel	(*Ironically*) Where *should* I be going—in the snow—on the eve of the Sabbath? Suppose—we say to synagogue!
David	Oh, uncle—how you always seem to hanker after those old things!
Mendel	(*Tartly*) Nonsense! (*He takes his umbrella from the stand.*) I don't like to see our people going to pieces, that's all.
David	Then why did you come to America? Why didn't you work for a Jewish land? You're not even a Zionist.
Mendel	I can't argue now. There's a pack of giggling schoolgirls waiting to waltz.
David	The fresh romping young things! Think of their happiness! I should love to play for them.
Mendel	(*Sarcastically*) I can see you are yourself again. (*He opens the street-door—turns back.*) What about your own lesson? Can't we go together?
David	I must first write down what is singing in my soul—oh, uncle, it seems as if I knew suddenly what was wanting in my music!
Mendel	(*Drily*) Well, don't forget what is wanting in the house! The

rent isn't paid yet.

(*EXIT through street-door. As he goes out, he touches and kisses the* Mezuzah *on the door-post, with a subconsciously antagonistic revival of religious impulse.* DAVID *opens his desk, takes out a pile of musical manuscript, sprawls over his chair and, humming to himself, scribbles feverishly with the quill. After a few moments* FRAU QUIXANO *yawns, wakes, and stretches herself. Then she looks at the clock.*)

Frau Quixano   *Shabbos!*

(*She rises and goes to the table and sees there are no candles, walks to the chiffonier and gets them and places them in the candlesticks, then lights the candles, muttering a ceremonial Hebrew benediction.*) *Boruch atto haddoshem ellôheinu melech hoôlam assher kiddishonu bemizvôsov vettzivonu lehadlik neir shel habbos.* (*She pulls down the blinds of the two windows, then she goes to the rapt composer and touches him, remindingly, on the shoulder. He does not move, but continues writing.*) *Dovidel!* (*He looks up dazedly. She points to the candles.*) *Shabbos!* (*A sweet smile comes over his face, he throws the quilt resignedly away and submits his head to her hands and her muttered Hebrew blessing.*) *Yesimcho elôhim ke-efrayim vechimnasseh—yevorechecho haddoshem veyishmerecho, yoer hadoshem ponov eilecho vechunecho, yisso hadoshem ponov eilecho veyosem lecho sholôm.* (*Then she goes toward the kitchen. As she turns at the door, he is again writing. She shakes her finger at him, repeating*) *Gut Shabbos!*

David   *Gut Shabbos!*

(*Puts down the pen and smiles after her till the door closes, then with a deep sigh takes his cape from the peg and his violin-case, pauses, still humming, to take up his pen and write down a fresh phrase, finally puts on his hat and is just about to open the street-door when* KATHLEEN *ENTERS from her bedroom fully dressed to go, and laden with a large brown paper parcel and an umbrella. He turns at the sound of her footsteps and remains at the door, holding his violin-case during the ensuing dialogue.*)

David   You're not going out this bitter weather?

Kathleen   (*Sharply fending him off with her umbrella*) And who's to shtay me?

David	Oh, but you mustn't—*I'll* do your errand—what is it?
Kathleen	(*Indignantly*) Errand, is it, indeed! I'm not here!
David	Not here?
Kathleen	I'm lavin', they'll come for me thrunk—and ye'll witness I don't take the candleshtick.
David	But who's sending you away?
Kathleen	It's sending meself away I am—yer houly grandmother has me disthroyed intirely.
David	Why, what has the poor old la—?
Kathleen	I don't be saltin' the mate and I do be mixin' the crockery and—!
David	(*Gently*) I know, I know—but, Kathleen, remember she was brought up to these things from childhood. And her father was a Rabbi.
Kathleen	What's that? A priest?
David	A sort of priest. In Russia he was a great man. Her husband, too, was a mighty scholar, and to give him time to study the holy books she had to do chores all day for him and the children.
Kathleen	Oh, those priests!
David	(*Smiling*) No, *he* wasn't a priest. But he took sick and died, and the children left her—went to America or heaven or other far-off places—and she was left all penniless and alone.
Kathleen	Poor ould lady.
David	Not so old yet, for she was married at fifteen.
Kathleen	Poor young crathur!
David	But she was still the good angel of the congregation—sat up with the sick and watched over the dead.
Kathleen	Saints alive! And not scared?

David	No, nothing scared her—except me. I got a broken-down fiddle and used to play it even on *Shabbos*—I was very naughty. But she was so lovely to me. I still remember the heavenly taste of a piece of *Motso* she gave me dipped in raisin wine! Passover cake, you know.
Kathleen	(*Proudly*) Oh, *I* know *Motso*.
David	(*Smacks his lips, repeats*) Heavenly!
Kathleen	Sure, I must tashte it.
David	(*Shaking his head, mysteriously*) Only little boys get that tashte.
Kathleen	That's quare.
David	(*Smiling*) Very quare. And then one day my uncle sent the old lady a ticket to come to America. But it is not so happy for her here because you see my uncle has to be near his theatre and can't live in the Jewish quarter, and so nobody understands her, and she sits all the livelong day alone—alone with her book and her religion and her memories—
Kathleen	(*Breaking down*) Oh, Mr. David!
David	And now all this long, cold, snowy evening she'll sit by the fire alone, thinking of her dead, and the fire will sink lower and lower, and she won't be able to touch it, because it's the holy Sabbath, and there'll be no kind Kathleen to brighten up the grey ashes, and then at last, sad and shivering, she'll creep up to her room without a candlestick, and there in the dark and the cold—
Kathleen	(*Hysterically bursting into tears, dropping her parcel and untying her bonnet-strings*) Oh, Mr. David, I won't mix the crockery, I won't—
David	(*Heartily*) Of course you won't. Good night.

(*He slips out hurriedly through the street-door as* KATHLEEN *throws off her bonnet, and the curtain falls quickly. As it rises again, she is seen strenuously poking the fire, illumined by its red glow.*)

ACT II

The same scene on an afternoon a month later. DAVID *is discovered at his desk, scribbling music in a fever of enthusiasm.* MENDEL, *dressed in his best, is playing softly on the piano, watching* DAVID. *After an instant or two of indecision, he puts down the piano-lid with a bang and rises decisively.*

Mendel   David!

David   (*Putting up his left hand*) Please, please—(*He writes feverishly.*)

Mendel   But I want to talk to you seriously—at once.

David   I'm just re-writing the Finale. Oh, such a splendid inspiration! (*He writes on.*)

Mendel   (*Shrugs his shoulders and reseats himself at piano. He plays a bar or two. Looks at watch impatiently. Resolutely*) David, I've got wonderful news for you. Miss Revendal is bringing somebody to see you, and we have hopes of getting you sent to Germany to study composition. (DAVID *does not reply, but writes rapidly on.*) Why, he hasn't heard a word! (*He shouts.*) David!

David   (*Writing on*) I can't, uncle. I *must* put it down while that glorious impression is fresh.

Mendel   What impression? You only went to the People's Alliance.

David   Yes, and there I saw the Jewish children—a thousand of 'em—saluting the Flag. (*He writes on.*)

Mendel   Well, what of that?

David   What of that? (*He throws down his quill and jumps up.*) But just fancy it, uncle. The Stars and Stripes unfurled, and a thousand childish voices, piping and foreign, fresh from the

296

lands of oppression, hailing its fluttering folds. I cried like a baby.

Mendel — I'm afraid you *are* one.

David — Ah, but if you had heard them—"Flag of our Great Republic"—the words have gone singing at my heart ever since—(*He turns to the flag over the door.*) "Flag of our Great Republic, guardian of our homes, whose stars and stripes stand for Bravery, Purity, Truth, and Union, we salute thee. We, the natives of distant lands, who find (*half-sobbing*) rest under thy folds, do pledge our hearts, our lives, our sacred honour to love and protect thee, our Country, and the liberty of the American people for ever." (*He ends almost hysterically.*)

Mendel — (*Soothingly*) Quite right. But you needn't get so excited over it.

David — Not when one hears the roaring of the fires of God? Not when one sees the souls melting in the Crucible? Uncle, all those little Jews will grow up Americans!

Mendel — (*Putting a pacifying hand on his shoulder and forcing him into a chair*) Sit down. I want to talk to you about your affairs.

David — (*Sitting*) My affairs! But I've been talking about them all the time!

Mendel — Nonsense, David.
(*He sits beside him.*) Don't you think it's time you got into a wider world?

David — Eh? This planet's wide enough for me.

Mendel — Do be serious. You don't want to live all your life in this room.

David — (*Looks round*) What's the matter with this room? It's princely.

Mendel — (*Raising his hands in horror*) Princely!

David — Imperial. Remember when I first saw it—after pigging a week in the rocking steerage, swinging in a berth as wide as my

	fiddle-case, hung near the cooking-engines; imagine the hot rancid smell of the food, the oil of the machinery, the odours of all that close-packed, sea-sick—
Mendel	(*Putting his hand over DAVID's mouth*) Don't! You make me ill! How could you ever bear it?
David	(*Smiling*) I was quite happy—I only had to fancy I'd been shipwrecked, and that after clinging to a plank five days without food or water on the great lonely Atlantic, my frozen, sodden form had been picked up by this great safe steamer and given this delightful dry berth, regular meals, and the spectacle of all these friendly faces . . . Do you know who was on board that boat? Quincy Davenport.
Mendel	The lord of corn and oil?
David	(*Smiling*) Yes, even we wretches in the steerage felt safe to think the lord was up above, we believed the company would never dare drown *him*. But could even Quincy Davenport command a cabin like this? (*Waving his arm round the room.*) Why, uncle, we have a cabin worth a thousand dollars—a thousand dollars a *week*—and what's more, it doesn't wobble! (*He plants his feet voluptuously upon the floor.*)
Mendel	Come, come, David, I asked you to be serious. Surely, some day you'd like your music produced?
David	(*Jumps up*) Wouldn't it be glorious? To hear it all actually coming out of violins and 'cellos, drums and trumpets.
Mendel	And you'd like it to go all over the world?
David	All over the world and all down the ages.
Mendel	But don't you see that unless you go and study seriously in Germany—?
	(*ENTER KATHLEEN from kitchen, carrying a furnished tea-tray with ear-shaped cakes, bread and butter, etc., and wearing a grotesque false nose. MENDEL cries out in amaze.*) Kathleen!
David	(*Roaring with boyish laughter*) Ha! Ha! Ha! Ha! Ha!
Kathleen	(*Standing still with her tray*) Sure, what's the matter?

David	Look in the glass!
Kathleen	(*Going to the mantel*) Houly Moses! (*She drops the tray, which* MENDEL *catches, and snatches off the nose.*) Och, I forgot to take it off—'twas the misthress gave it me—I put it on to cheer her up.
David	Is she so miserable, then?
Kathleen	Terrible low, Mr. David, to-day being *Purim.*
Mendel	*Purim!* Is to-day *Purim?*
	(*Gives her the tea-tray back.* KATHLEEN, *to take it, drops her nose and forgets to pick it up.*)
David	But *Purim* is a merry time, Kathleen, like your Carnival. Haven't you read the book of Esther—how the Jews of Persia escaped massacre?
Kathleen	That's what the misthress is so miserable about. Ye don't *keep* the Carnival. There's noses for both of ye in the kitchen—didn't I go with her to Hester Street to buy 'em?—but ye don't be axin' for 'em. And to see your noses layin' around so solemn and neglected, faith, it nearly makes me chry meself.
Mendel	(*Bitterly to himself*) Who can remember about *Purim* in America?
David	(*Half-smiling*) Poor granny, tell her to come in and I'll play her a *Purim* jig.
Mendel	(*Hastily*) No, no, David, not here—the visitors!
David	Visitors? What visitors?
Mendel	(*Impatiently*) That's just what I've been trying to explain.
David	Well, I can play in the kitchen.
	(*He takes his violin. EXIT to kitchen.* MENDEL *sighs and shrugs his shoulders hopelessly at the boy's perversity, then fingers the cups and saucers.*)
Mendel	(*Anxiously*) Is that the *best* tea-set?
Kathleen	Can't you see it's the Passover set! (*Ruefully*) And shpiled

	intirely it'll be now for our Passover . . . And the misthress thought the visitors might like to thry some of her *Purim* cakes. (*Indicates ear-shaped cakes on tray.*)
Mendel	(*Bitterly*) *Purim* cakes! (*He turns his back on her and stares moodily out of the window.*)
Kathleen	(*Mutters contemptuously*) Call yerself a Jew and you forgettin' to keep *Purim*! (*She is going back to the kitchen when a merry Slavic dance breaks out, softened by the door; her feet unconsciously get more and more into dance step, and at last she jigs out. As she opens and passes through the door, the music sounds louder.*)
Frau Quixano	(*Heard from kitchen*) Ha! Ha! Ha! Ha! Ha! Kathleen!!
	(MENDEL's *feet, too, begin to take the swing of the music, and his feet dance as he stares out of the window. Suddenly the hoot of an automobile is heard, followed by the rattling up of the car.*)
Mendel	Ah, she has brought somebody swell! (*He throws open the doors and goes out eagerly to meet the visitors. The dance music goes on softly throughout the scene.*)
Quincy	(*Outside*) Oh, thank you—I leave the coats in the car.
	(ENTER *an instant later* QUINCY DAVENPORT *and* VERA REVENDAL, MENDEL *in the rear.* VERA *is dressed much as before, but with a motor veil, which she takes off during the scene.* DAVENPORT *is a dude, aping the air of a European sporting clubman. Aged about thirty-five and well set-up, he wears an orchid and an intermittent eyeglass, and gives the impression of a coarse-fibred and patronisingly facetious but not bad-hearted man, spoiled by prosperity.*)
Mendel	Won't you be seated?
Vera	First let me introduce my friend, who is good enough to interest himself in your nephew—Mr. Quincy Davenport.
Mendel	(*Struck of a heap*) Mr. Quincy Davenport! How strange!
Vera	What is strange?
Mendel	David just mentioned Mr. Davenport's name—said they

travelled to New York on the same boat.

Quincy   Impossible! Always travel on my own yacht. Slow but select. Must have been another man of the same name—my dad. Ha! Ha! Ha!

Mendel   Ah, of course. I thought you were too young.

Quincy   My dad, Miss Revendal, is one of those antiquated Americans who are always in a hurry!

Vera   He burns coal and you burn time.

Quincy   Precisely! Ha! Ha! Ha!

Mendel   Won't you sit down—I'll go and prepare David.

Vera   You've not prepared him yet?

Mendel   I've tried to more than once—but I never really got to—(*he smiles*) to Germany.

              (*QUINCY sits.*)

Vera   Then prepare him for *three* visitors.

Mendel   Three?

Vera   You see Mr. Davenport himself is no judge of music.

Quincy   (*Jumps up*) I beg your pardon.

Vera   In manuscript.

Quincy   Ah, of course not. Music should be heard, not seen—like that jolly jig. Is that your David?

Mendel   Oh, you mustn't judge him by that. He's just fooling.

Quincy   Oh, he'd better not fool with Poppy. Poppy's awful severe.

Mendel   Poppy?

Quincy   Pappelmeister—my private orchestra conductor.

Mendel   Is it *your* orchestra Pappelmeister conducts?

Quincy   Well, *I* pay the piper—and the drummer too! (*He chuckles.*)

Mendel   (*Sadly*) *I* wanted to play in it, but he turned me down.

Quincy   I told you he was awful severe. (*To* VERA) He only allows me comic opera once a week. My wife calls him the Bismarck of the baton.

Mendel   (*Reverently*) A great conductor!

Quincy   Would he have a twenty-thousand-dollar job with me if he wasn't? Not that he'd get half that in the open market—only I have to stick it on to keep him for my guests exclusively. (*Looks at watch.*) But he ought to be here, confound him. A conductor should keep time, eh, Miss Revendal? (*He sniggers.*)

Mendel   I'll bring David. Won't you help yourselves to tea? (*To* VERA) You see there's lemon for you—as in Russia.

              (*EXIT to kitchen—a moment afterwards the merry music stops in the middle of a bar.*)

Vera   Thank you. (*Taking a cup*) Do you like lemon, Mr. Davenport?

Quincy   (*Flirtatiously*) That depends. The last I had was in Russia itself—from the fair hands of your mother, the Baroness.

Vera   (*Pained*) Please don't say my mother, my mother is dead.

Quincy   (*Fatuously misunderstanding*) Oh, you have no call to be ashamed of your step-mother—she's a stunning creature; all the points or a tip-top Russian aristocrat, or Quincy Davenport's no judge of breed! Doesn't speak English like your father—but then the Baron is a wonder.

Vera   (*Takes up teapot*) Father once hoped to be British Ambassador—that's why I had an English governess. But you never told me you met him in *Russia.*

Quincy   Surely! When I gave you all those love messages—

Vera   (*Pouring tea quickly*) You said you met him at Wiesbaden.

Quincy   Yes, but we grew such pals I motored him and the Baroness back to St. Petersburg. Jolly country, Russia—they know how to live.

Vera	(*Coldly*) I saw more of those who know how to die . . . Milk and sugar?
Quincy	(*Sentimentally*) Oh, Miss Revendal! Have you forgotten?
Vera	(*Politely snubbing*) How should I remember?
Quincy	You don't remember our first meeting? At the Settlement Bazaar? When I paid you a hundred dollars for every piece of sugar you put in?
Vera	Did you? Then I hope you drank syrup.
Quincy	Ugh! I hate sugar—I sacrificed myself.
Vera	To the Settlement? How heroic of you!
Quincy	No, not to the Settlement. To you!
Vera	Then I'll only put milk in.
Quincy	I hate milk. But from you—
Vera	Then we *must* fall back on the lemon.
Quincy	I loathe lemon. But from—
Vera	Then you shall have your tea neat.
Quincy	I detest tea, and here it would be particularly cheap and nasty. But—
Vera	Then you shall have a cake! (*She offers plate.*)
Quincy	(*Taking one*) Would they be eatable? (*Tasting it.*) Humph! Not bad. (*Sentimentally*) A little cake was all you would eat the only time you came to one of my private concerts. Don't you remember? We went down to supper together.
Vera	(*Taking his tea for herself and putting in lemon*) I shall always remember the delicious music Herr Pappelmeister gave us.
Quincy	How unkind of you!
Vera	Unkind?
	(*She sips the tea and puts down the cup.*) To be grateful for the music?

Quincy   You know what I mean—to forget *me!* (*He tries to take her hand.*)

Vera   (*Rising*) Aren't you forgetting yourself?

Quincy   You mean because I'm married to that patched-and-painted creature? She's hankering for the stage again, the old witch.

Vera   Hush! Marriages with comic opera stars are not usually domestic idylls.

Quincy   I fell a victim to my love of music.

Vera   (*Murmurs, smiling*) Music!

Quincy   And I hadn't yet met the right breed—the true blue blood of Europe. I'll get a divorce. (*Approaching her*) Vera!

Vera   (*Retreating*) You will make me sorry I came to you.

Quincy   No, don't say that—promised the Baron I'd always do all I could for—

Vera   You promised? You dared discuss my affairs?

Quincy   It was your father began it. When he found I knew you, he almost wept with emotion. He asked a hundred questions about your life in America.

Vera   His life and mine are for ever separate. He is a Reactionary, I a Radical.

Quincy   But he loves you dreadfully—he can't understand why you should go slaving away summer and winter in a Settlement— you a member of the Russian nobility!

Vera   (*With faint smile*) I might say, *noblesse oblige.* But the truth is, I earn my living that way. It would do *you* good to slave there too!

Quincy   (*Eagerly*) Would they chain us together? I'd come to-morrow. (*He moves nearer her. There is a double knock at the door.*)

Vera   (*Relieved*) Here's Pappelmeister!

Quincy   Bother Poppy—why is he so darned punctual?

(*ENTER* KATHLEEN *from the kitchen.*)

Vera   (*Smiling*) Ah, you're still here.

Kathleen   And why would I not be here?

(*She goes to open the door.*)

Pappelmeister   Mr. Quixano?

Kathleen   Yes, come in.

(*ENTER* HERR PAPPELMEISTER, *a burly German figure with a leonine head, spectacles, and a mane of white hair—a figure that makes his employer look even coarser. He carries an umbrella, which he never lets go. He is at first grave and silent, which makes any burst of emotion the more striking. He and* QUINCY DAVEN-PORT *suggest a picture of "Dignity and Impudence." His English, as roughly indicated in the text, is extremely Teutonic.*)

Quincy   You're late, Poppy!

(*PAPPELMEISTER silently bows to* VERA.)

Vera   (*Smilingly goes and offers her hand.*) Proud to meet you, Herr Pappelmeister!

Quincy   Excuse me—(*Introducing*) Miss Revendal!—I forgot you and Poppy hadn't been introduced—curiously enough it was at Wiesbaden I picked him up too—he was conducting the opera—your folks were in my box. I don't think I ever met anyone so mad on music as the Baron. And the Baroness told me he had retired from active service in the Army because of the torture of listening to the average military band. Ha! Ha! Ha!

Vera   Yes, my father once hoped *my* music would comfort him. (*She smiles sadly.*) Poor father! But a soldier must bear defeat. Herr Pappelmeister, may I not give you some tea? (*She sits again at the table.*)

Quincy   Tea! Lager's more in Poppy's line. (*He chuckles.*)

Pappelmeister   (*Gravely*) *Bitte.* Tea. (*She pours out, he sits.*) Lemon. Four lumps . . . *Nun,* five! . . . Or six! (*She hands him the cup.*) *Danke.*

(*As he receives the cup, he utters an exclamation, for* KATH-LEEN, *after opening the door has lingered on, hunting around everywhere, and having finally crawled under the table has now brushed against his leg.*)

Vera	What are you looking for?
Kathleen	(*Her head emerging*) My nose! (*They are all startled and amused.*)
Vera	Your nose?
Kathleen	I forgot me nose!
Quincy	Well, follow your nose—and you'll find it. Ha! Ha! Ha!
Kathleen	(*Pouncing on it*) Here it is! (*Picks it up near the armchair.*)
Omnes	Oh!
Kathleen	Sure, it's gotten all dirthy. (*She takes out a handkerchief and wipes the nose carefully.*)
Quincy	But why do you want a nose like that?
Kathleen	(*Proudly*) Bekaz we're Hebrews!
Quincy	What!
Vera	What *do* you mean?
Kathleen	It's our Carnival to-day! *Purim.* (*She carries her nose carefully and piously toward the kitchen.*)
Vera	Oh! I see.
	(*EXIT* KATHLEEN.)
Quincy	(*In horror*) Miss Revendal, you don't mean to say you've brought me to a Jew!
Vera	I'm afraid I have—I was thinking only of his genius, not his race. And you see, so many musicians are Jews.
Quincy	Not *my* musicians. No Jew's harp in my orchestra, eh? (*He sniggers.*) I wouldn't have a Jew if he paid *me.*

Vera	I daresay you have some, all the same.
Quincy	Impossible. Poppy! Are there any Jews in my orchestra?
Pappelmeister	(*Removing the cup from his mouth and speaking with sepulchral solemnity*) Do you mean are dere any Christians?
Quincy	(*In horror*) Gee-rusalem! Perhaps *you're* a Jew!
Pappelmeister	(*Gravely*) I haf not de honour. But, if you brefer, I will gut out from my brogrammes all de Chewish composers. *Was?*
Quincy	Why, of course. Fire 'em out, every mother's son of 'em.
Pappelmeister	(*Unsmiling*) Also—no more comic operas!
Quincy	What!!!
Pappelmeister	Dey write all de comic operas!
Quincy	Brute!

(*PAPPELMEISTER's chuckle is heard gurgling in his cup. Re-ENTER MENDEL from kitchen.*)

Mendel	(*To VERA*) I'm so sorry—I can't get him to come in—he's terrible shy.
Quincy	Won't face the music, eh? (*He sniggers.*)
Vera	Did you tell him *I* was here?
Mendel	Of course.
Vera	(*Disappointed*) Oh!
Mendel	But I've persuaded him to let me show his MS.
Vera	(*With forced satisfaction*) Oh, well, that's all we want.

(*MENDEL goes to the desk, opens it, and gets the MS and offers it to QUINCY DAVENPORT.*)

Quincy	Not for me—Poppy!

(*MENDEL offers it to PAPPELMEISTER, who takes it solemnly.*)

Mendel   (*Anxiously to* PAPPELMEISTER) Of course you must remember his youth and his lack of musical education—

Pappelmeister *Bitte, das Pult!* (MENDEL *moves* DAVID's *music-stand from the corner to the centre of the room.* PAPPELMEISTER *puts* "MS" *on it.*) So! (*All eyes centre on him eagerly,* MENDEL *standing uneasily, the others sitting.* PAPPELMEISTER *polishes his glasses with irritating elaborateness and weary "achs," then reads in absolute silence. A pause.*)

Quincy   (*Bored by the silence*) But won't you play it to us?

Pappelmeister Blay it? Am I an orchestra? I blay it in my brain. (*He goes on reading, his brow gets wrinkled. He ruffles his hair unconsciously. All watch him anxiously—he turns the page.*) So!

Vera   (*Anxiously*) You don't seem to like it!

Pappelmeister I do not comprehend it.

Mendel   I knew it was crazy—it is supposed to be about America or a Crucible or something. And of course there are heaps of mistakes.

Vera   That is why I am suggesting to Mr. Davenport to send him to Germany.

Quincy   I'll send as many Jews as you like to Germany. Ha! Ha! Ha!

Pappelmeister (*Absorbed, turning pages*) Ach!—ach!—So!

Quincy   I'd even lend my own yacht to take 'em back. Ha! Ha! Ha!

Vera   Sh! We're disturbing Herr Pappelmeister.

Quincy   Oh, Poppy's all right.

Pappelmeister (*Sublimely unconscious*) Ach so—so—SO! *Das ist etwas neues!* (*His umbrella begins to beat time, moving more and more vigorously, till at last he is conducting elaborately, stretching out his left palm/or pianissimo passages, and raising it vigorously for forte, with every now and then an exclamation.*) Wunderschon! . . . *pianissimo!*—now the flutes! Clarinets! *Ach, ergotzlich* . . . bassoons and drums! . . . *Fortissimo!* . . . *Kolossal! Kolossal!* (*Conducting in a fury of enthusiasm.*)

Vera	(*Clapping her hands*) Bravo! Bravo! I'm so excited!
Quincy	(*Yawning*) Then it isn't bad, Poppy?
Pappelmeister	(*Not listening, never ceasing to conduct*) *Und* de harp solo . . . *ach, reizend!* . . . Second violins—!
Quincy	But Poppy! We can't be here all day.
Pappelmeister	(*Not listening, continuing pantomime action*) Sh! Sh! *Piano.*
Quincy	(*Outraged*) Sh to *me!* (*Rises.*)
Vera	He doesn't know it's you.
Quincy	But look here, Poppy—
	(*He seizes the wildly-moving umbrella. Blank stare of* PAPPEL-MEISTER *gradually returning to consciousness.*)
Pappelmeister	*Was giebt's* . . . ?
Quincy	We've had enough.
Pappelmeister	(*Indignant*) Enough? Enough? Of such a beaudiful symphony?
Quincy	It may be beautiful to you, but to us it's damn dull. See here, Poppy, if you're satisfied that the young fellow has sufficient talent to be sent to study in Germany—
Pappelmeister	In Germany! Germany has nodings to teach him, he has to teach Germany.
Vera	Bravo! (*She springs up.*)
Mendel	I always said he was a genius!
Quincy	Well, at that rate you could put this stuff of his in one of my programmes. *Sinfonia Americana,* eh?
Vera	Oh, that *is* good of you
Pappelmeister	I should be broud to indroduce it to de vorld.
Vera	And will it be played in that wonderful marble music-room overlooking the Hudson?

Quincy	Sure. Before five hundred of the smartest folk in America.
Mendel	Oh, thank you, thank you. That will mean fame!
Quincy	And dollars. Don't forget the dollars.
Mendel	I'll run and tell him. (*He hastens into the kitchen,* PAPPELMEIS-TER *is re-absorbed in the MS, but no longer conducting*)
Quincy	You see, I'll help even a Jew for your sake.
Vera	Hush! (*Indicating* PAPPELMEISTER.)
Quincy	Oh, Poppy's in the moon.
Vera	You must help him for his own sake, for art's sake.
Quincy	And why not for heart's sake—for my sake? (*He comes nearer.*)
Vera	(*Crossing to* PAPPELMEISTER) Herr Pappelmeister! When do you think you can produce it?
Pappelmeister	*Wunderbar!* . . . (*Becoming half-conscious of* VERA) Four lumps . . . (*Waking up*) *Bitte?*
Vera	How soon can you produce it?
Pappelmeister	How soon can he finish it?
Vera	Isn't it finished?
Pappelmeister	I see von Finale scratched out and anoder not quite completed. But anyhow, ve couldn't broduce it before Saturday fortnight.
Quincy	Saturday fortnight! Not time to get my crowd.
Pappelmeister	Den ve say Saturday dree veeks. Yes?
Quincy	Yes. Stop a minute! Did you say Saturday? That's my comic opera night! You thief!
Pappelmeister	Somedings must be sagrificed.
Mendel	(*Outside*) But you must come, David.
	(*The kitchen door opens, and* MENDEL *drags in the boyishly*

shrinking DAVID. PAPPELMEISTER thumps with his umbrella,
VERA claps her hands, QUINCY DAVENPORT produces his eyeglass
and surveys DAVID curiously.)

Vera	Oh, Mr. Quixano, I am so glad! Mr. Davenport is going to produce your symphony in his wonderful music-room.
Quincy	Yes, young man, I'm going to give you the smartest audience in America. And if Poppy is right, you're just going to rake in the dollars. America wants a composer.
Pappelmeister	(*Raises hands emphatically*) *Ach Gott, ja!*
Vera	(*To DAVID*) Why don't you speak? You're not angry with me for interfering—?
David	I can never be grateful enough to you—
Vera	Oh, not to me. It is to Mr. Davenport you—
David	And I can never be grateful enough to Herr Pappelmeister. It is an honour even to meet him. (*Bows.*)
Pappelmeister	(*Choking with emotion, goes and pats him on the back.*) *Mein braver Junge!*
Vera	(*Anxiously*) But it is Mr. Davenport—
David	Before I accept Mr. Davenport's kindness, I must know to whom I am indebted—and if Mr. Davenport is the man who—
Quincy	Who travelled with you to New York? Ha! Ha! Ha! No, *I'm* only the junior.
David	Oh, I know, sir, you don't make the money you spend.
Quincy	Eh?
Vera	(*Anxiously*) He means he knows you're not in business.
David	Yes, sir; but is it true you are in pleasure?
Quincy	(*Puzzled*) I beg your pardon?
David	Are all the stories the papers print about you true?
Quincy	*All* the stories. That's a tall order. Ha! Ha! Ha!

David	Well, anyhow, is it true that—?
Vera	Mr. Quixano! What *are* you driving at?
Quincy	Oh, it's rather fun to hear what the masses read about me. Fire ahead. Is what true?
David	That you were married in a balloon?
Quincy	Ho! Ha! Ha! That's true enough. Marriage in high life, they said, didn't they? Ha! Ha! Ha!
David	And is it true you live in America only two months in the year, and then only to entertain Europeans who wander to these wild parts?
Quincy	Lucky for you, young man. You'll have an Italian prince and a British duke to hear your scribblings.
David	And the palace where they will hear my scribblings—is it true that—?
Vera	(*Who has been on pins and needles*) Mr. Quixano, what possible—?
David	(*Entreatingly holds up a hand.*) Miss Revendal! (*To* QUINCY DAVENPORT) Is this palace the same whose grounds were turned into Venetian canals where the guests ate in gondolas—gondolas that were draped with the most wonderful trailing silks in imitation of the Venetian nobility in the great water fêtes?
Quincy	(*Turns to* VERA) Ah, Miss Revendal—what a pity you refused that invitation! It was a fairy scene of twinkling lights and delicious darkness—each couple had their own gondola to sup in, and their own side-canal to slip down. Eh? Ha! Ha! Ha!
David	And the same night, women and children died of hunger in New York!
Quincy	(*Startled, drops eyeglass.*) Eh?
David	(*Furiously*) And this is the sort of people you would invite to hear my symphony—these gondola-guzzlers!
Vera	Mr. Quixano!

Mendel	David!
David	These magnificent animals who went into the gondolas two by two, to feed and flirt!
Quincy	(*Dazed*) Sir!
David	I should be a new freak for you for a new freak evening—I and my dreams and my music!
Quincy	You low-down, ungrateful—
David	Not for you and such as you have I sat here writing and dreaming; not for you who are killing my America!
Quincy	*Your* America, forsooth, you Jew-immigrant!
Vera	Mr. Davenport!
David	Yes—Jew-immigrant! But a Jew who knows that your Pilgrim Fathers came straight out of his Old Testament, and that our Jew-immigrants are a greater factor in the glory of this great commonwealth than some of you sons of the soil. It is you, freak-fashionables, who are undoing the work of Washington and Lincoln, vulgarising your high heritage, and turning the last and noblest hope of humanity into a caricature.
Quincy	(*Rocking with laughter*) Ha! Ha! Ha! Ho! Ho! Ho! (*To* VERA) You never told me your Jew-scribbler was a socialist!
David	I am nothing but a simple artist, but I come from Europe, one of her victims, and I know that she is a failure; that her palaces and peerages are outworn toys of the human spirit, and that the only hope of mankind lies in a new world. And here—in the land of to-morrow—you are trying to bring back Europe—
Quincy	(*Interjecting*) I wish we could!—
David	Europe with her comic-opera coronets and her worm-eaten stage decorations, and her pomp and chivalry built on a morass of crime and misery—
Quincy	(*With sneering laugh*) Morass!—
David	(*With prophetic passion*) But you shall not kill my dream!

There shall come a fire round the Crucible that will melt you and your breed like wax in a blowpipe—

Quincy (*Furiously, with clenched, fist*) You—

David America *shall* make good . . . !

Pappelmeister (*Who has sat down and remained imperturbably seated throughout all this scene, springs up and waves his umbrella hysterically.*) Hoch Quixano! Hoch! Hoch! Es lebe Quixano! Hoch!

Quincy Poppy! You're dismissed!

Pappelmeister (*Goes to* DAVID *with outstretched hand*) Danke. (*They grip hands.* PAPPELMEISTER *turns to* QUINCY DAVENPORT.) Comic Opera! Ouf!

Quincy (*Goes to street-door, at white heat.*) Are you coming, Miss Revendal? (*He opens the door.*)

Vera (*To* QUINCY, *but not moving*) Pray, pray, accept my apologies—believe me, if I had known—

Quincy (*Furiously*) Then stop with your Jew! (*EXIT.*)

Mendel (*Frantically*) But, Mr. Davenport—don't go! He is only a boy. (*EXIT after* QUINCY DAVENPORT.) You must consider—

David Oh, Herr Pappelmeister, you have lost your place!

Pappelmeister And saved my soul. Dollars are de devil. Now I must to an appointment. *Auf baldiges Wiedersehen.* (*He shakes* DAVID'S *hand.*) Fräulein Revendal! (*He takes her hand and kisses it. EXIT.* DAVID *and* VERA *stand gazing at each other.*)

Vera What have you done? What have you done?

David What else could I do?

Vera I hate the smart set as much as you—but as your ladder and your trumpet—

David I would not stand indebted to them. I know you meant it for my good, but what would these Europe-apers have understood of *my* America—the America of my music? They look back on Europe as a pleasure ground, a palace of art—but I know (*getting hysterical*) it is sodden with blood, red with bestial massacres—

Vera	(*Alarmed, anxious*) Let us talk no more about it. (*She holds out her hand.*) Good-bye.
David	(*Frozen, taking it, holding it*) Ah, you are offended by my ingratitude—I shall never see you again.
Vera	No, I am not offended. But I have failed to help you. We have nothing else to meet for. (*She disengages her hand.*)
David	Why will you punish me so? I have only hurt myself.
Vera	It is not a *punishment*.
David	What else? When you are with me, all the air seems to tremble with fairy music played by some unseen fairy orchestra.
Vera	(*Tremulous*) And yet you wouldn't come in just now when I—
David	I was too frightened of the others . . .
Vera	(*Smiling*) Frightened indeed!
David	Yes, I know I became overbold—but to take all that magic sweetness out of my life for ever—you don't call that a punishment?
Vera	(*Blushing*) How could I wish to punish you? I was proud of you! (*Drops her eyes, murmurs*) Besides it would be punishing *myself*.
David	(*In passionate amaze*) Miss Revendal! . . . But no, it cannot be. It is too impossible.
Vera	(*Frightened*) Yes, too impossible. Good-bye. (*She turns*)
David	But not for always? (*VERA hangs her head. He comes nearer. Passionately.*) Promise me that you—that I—(*He takes her hand again.*)
Vera	(*Melting at his touch, breathes*) Yes, yes, David.
David	Miss Revendal!

(*She falls into his arms.*)

Vera	My dear! my dear!
David	It is a dream. You cannot care for me—you so far above me.
Vera	Above you, you simple boy? Your genius lifts you to the stars.
David	No, no; it is you who lift me there—
Vera	(*Smoothing his hair*) Oh, David. And to think that I was brought up to despise your race.
David	(*Sadly*) Yes, all Russians are.
Vera	But we of the nobility in particular.
David	(*Amazed, half-releasing her*) You are noble?
Vera	My father is Baron Revendal, but I have long since carved out a life of my own.
David	Then he will not separate us?
Vera	No. (*Re-embracing him*) Nothing can separate us. (*A knock at the street-door. They separate. The automobile is heard clattering off.*)
David	It is my uncle coming back.
Vera	(*In low, tense tones*) Then I shall slip out. I could not bear a third. I will write. (*She goes to the door.*)
David	Yes, yes . . . Vera (*He follows her to the door. He opens it and she slips out.*)
Mendel	(*Half-seen at the door, expostulating*) You, too, Miss Revendal? (*Re-ENTERS.*) Oh, David, you have driven away all your friends.
David	(*Going to window and looking after* VERA) Not all, uncle. Not all. (*He throws his arms boyishly round his uncle.*) I am so happy.
Mendel	Happy?

David	She loves me—Vera loves me.
Mendel	Vera?
David	Miss Revendal.
Mendel	Have you lost your wits? (*He throws DAVID off.*)
David	I don't wonder you're amazed. Maybe you think *I* wasn't. It is as if an angel should stoop down—
Mendel	(*Hoarsely*) This is true? This is not some stupid *Purim* joke?
David	True and sacred as the sunrise.
Mendel	But you are a Jew!
David	Yes, and just think! She was bred up to despise Jews—her father was a Russian baron—
Mendel	If she was the daughter of fifty barons, you cannot marry her.
David	(*In pained amaze*) Uncle! (*Slowly*) Then your hankering after the synagogue was serious after all.
Mendel	It is not so much the synagogue—it is the call of our blood through immemorial generations.
David	*You* say that! You who have come to the heart of the Crucible, where the roaring fires of God are fusing our race with all the others.
Mendel	(*Passionately*) Not *our* race, not your race and mine.
David	What immunity has our race? (*Meditatively*) The pride and the prejudice, the dreams and the sacrifices, the traditions and the superstitions, the fasts and the feasts, things noble and things sordid—they must all into the Crucible.
Mendel	(*With prophetic fury*) The Jew has been tried in a thousand fires and only tempered and annealed.
David	Fires of hate, not fires of love. That is what melts.
Mendel	(*Sneeringly*) So I see.
David	Your sneer is false. The love that melted me was not Vera's—it

was the love *America* showed me—the day she gathered me to her breast.

Mendel   (*Speaking passionately and rapidly*) Many countries have gathered us. Holland took us when we were driven from Spain—but we did not become Dutchmen. Turkey took us when Germany oppressed us, but we have not become Turks.

David   These countries were not in the making. They were old civilisations stamped with the seal of creed. In such countries the Jew may be right to stand out. But here in this new secular Republic we must look forward—

Mendel   (*Passionately interrupting*) We must look backwards, too.

David   (*Hysterically*) To what? To Kishineff? (*As if seeing his vision*) To that butcher's face directing the slaughter? To those—?

Mendel   (*Alarmed*) Hush! Calm yourself!

David   (*Struggling with himself*) Yes, I will calm myself—but how else shall I calm myself save by forgetting all that nightmare of religions and races, save by holding out my hands with prayer and music toward the Republic of Man and the Kingdom of God! The Past I cannot mend—its evil outlines are stamped in immortal rigidity. Take away the hope that I can mend the Future, and you make me mad.

Mendel   You are mad already—your dreams are mad—the Jew is hated here as everywhere—you are false to your race.

David   I keep faith with America. I have faith America will keep faith with us. (*He raises his hands in religious rapture toward the flag over the door.*) Flag of our great Republic, guardian of our homes, whose stars and—

Mendel   Spare me that rigmarole. Go out and marry your Gentile and be happy.

David   You turn me out?

Mendel   Would you stay and break my mother's heart? You know she would mourn for you with the rending of garments and the seven days' sitting on the floor. Go! You have cast off the God of our fathers!

David	(*Thunderously*) And the God of our children—does *He* demand no service? (*Quieter, coming toward his uncle and touching him affectionately on the shoulder.*) You are right—I do need a wider world. (*Expands his lungs.*) I must go away.
Mendel	Go, then—I'll hide the truth—she must never suspect—lest she mourn you as dead.
Frau Quixano	(*Outside, in the kitchen*) Ha! Ha! Ha! Ha! Ha! (*Both men turn toward the kitchen and listen.*)
Kathleen	Ha! Ha! Ha! Ha! Ha!
Frau Quixano & Kathleen	Ha! Ha! Ha! Ha! Ha!
Mendel	(*Bitterly*) A merry *Purim!* (*The kitchen door opens and remains ajar.* FRAU QUIXANO *rushes in, carrying* DAVID's *violin and bow.* KATHLEEN *looks in, grinning.*)
Frau Quixano	(*Hilariously*) *Nu spiel noch! spiel!* (*She holds the violin and bow appealingly toward* DAVID.)
Mendel	(*Putting out a protesting hand*) No, no, David—I couldn't bear it.
David	But I must! You said she mustn't suspect. (*He looks lovingly at her as he loudly utters these words, which are unintelligible to her.*) And it may be the last time I shall ever play for her. (*Changing to a mock merry smile as he takes the violin and bow from her*) *Gewiss,* Granny! (He starts the same old Slavic dance.)
Frau Quixano	(*Childishly pleased*) He! He! He! (*She claps on a false grotesque nose from her pocket.*)
David	(*Torn between laughter and tears*) Ha! Ha! Ha! Ha! Ha!
Mendel	(*Shocked*) *Mutter!*
Frau Quixano	*Un' du auch!*
	(*She claps another false nose on* MENDEL, *laughing in childish glee at the effect. Then she starts dancing to the music, and* KATHLEEN *slips in and joyously dances beside her.*)

David   (*Joining tearfully in the laughter*) Ha! Ha! Ha! Ha! Ha!

(*The curtain falls quickly. It rises again upon the picture of
FRAU QUIXANO fallen back into a chair, exhausted with laughter,
fanning herself with her apron, while KATHLEEN has dropped
breathless across the arm of the armchair; DAVID is still playing
on, and MENDEL, his false nose torn off, stands by, glowering. The
curtain falls again and rises upon a final tableau of DAVID in his
cloak and hat, stealing out of the door with his violin, casting a
sad farewell glance at the old woman and at the home which has
sheltered him.*)

ACT III

April, about a month later. The scene changes to MISS REVENDAL'S *sitting-room at the Settlement House on a sunny day. Simple, pretty furniture: a sofa, chairs, small table, etc. An open piano with music. Flowers and books about. Fine art reproductions on walls. The fireplace is on the left. A door on the left leads to the hall, and a door on the right to the interior. A servant enters from the left, ushering in* BARON *and* BARONESS REVENDAL *and* QUINCY DAVENPORT. *The* BARON *is a tall, stern, grizzled man of military bearing, with a narrow, fanatical forehead and martinet manners, but otherwise of honest and distinguished appearance, with a short, well-trimmed white beard and well-cut European clothes. Although his dignity is diminished by the constant nervous suspiciousness of the Russian official, it is never lost; his nervousness, despite its comic side, being visibly the tragic shadow of his position. His English has only a touch of the foreign in accent and vocabulary and is much superior to his wife's, which comes to her through her French. The* BARONESS *is pretty and dressed in red in the height of Paris fashion, but blazes with barbaric jewels at neck and throat and wrist. She gestures freely with her hand, which, when ungloved, glitters with heavy rings. She is much younger than the* BARON *and self-consciously fascinating. Her parasol, which matches her costume, suggests the sunshine without.* QUINCY DAVENPORT *is in a smart spring suit with a motor dust coat and cap, which he lays down on the mantel-piece.*

Servant	Miss Revendal is on the roof-garden. I'll go and tell her. (*EXIT, toward the hall.*)
Baron	A marvellous people, you Americans. Gardens in the sky!
Quincy	Gardens, forsooth! We plant a tub and call it Paradise. No, Baron. New York is the great stone desert.

321

Baroness	But ze big beautiful Park vere ve drove tru?
Quincy	No taste, Baroness, modern sculpture and menageries! Think of the Medici gardens at Rome.
Baroness	Ah, Rome!
	(*With an ecstatic sigh, she drops into an armchair. Then she takes out a dainty cigarette-case, pulls off her right-hand glove, exhibiting her rings, and chooses a cigarette. The* BARON, *seeing this, produces his match-box.*)
Quincy	And now, dear Baron Revendal, having brought you safely to the den of the lioness—if I may venture to call your daughter so—I must leave *you* to do the taming, eh?
Baron	You are always of the most amiable. (*He strikes a match.*)
Baroness	*Tout a fait charmant.*
	(*The* BARON *lights her cigarette.*)
Quincy	(*Bows gallantly*) Don't mention it. I'll just have my auto take me to the Club, and then I'll send it back for you.
Baroness	Ah, zank you—zat street-car looks horreeble. (*She puffs out smoke.*)
Baron	Quite impossible. What is to prevent an anarchist sitting next to you and shooting out your brains?
Quincy	We haven't much of that here—I don't mean brains. Ha! Ha! Ha!
Baron	But I saw desperadoes spying as we came off your yacht.
Quincy	Oh, that was newspaper chaps.
Baron	(*Shakes his head.*) No—they are circulating my appearance to all the gang in the States. They took snapshots.
Quincy	Then you're quite safe from recognition. (*He sniggers.*) Didn't they ask you questions?
Baron	Yes, but I am a diplomat. I do not reply.
Quincy	That's not very diplomatic here. Ha! Ha!

Baron	*Diable!* (*He claps his hand to his hip pocket, half-producing a pistol. The* BARONESS *looks equally anxious.*)
Quincy	What's up?
Baron	(*Points to window, whispers hoarsely*) Regard! A hooligan peeped in!
Quincy	(*Goes to window*) Only some poor devil come to the Settlement.
Baron	(*Hoarsely*) But under his arm—a bomb!
Quincy	(*Shaking his head smilingly*) A soup bowl.
Baroness	Ha! Ha! Ha!
Quincy	What makes you so nervous, Baron?
	(*The* BARON *slips back his pistol, a little ashamed.*)
Baroness	Ze Intellectuals and ze *Bund,* zey all hate my husband because he is faizful to Christ (*crossing herself*) and ze Tsar.
Quincy	But the Intellectuals are in Russia.
Baron	They have their branches here—the refugees are the leaders—it is a diabolical network.
Quincy	Well, anyhow, *we're* not in Russia, eh? No, no. Baron, you're quite safe. Still, you can keep my automobile as long as you like—I've plenty.
Baron	A thousand thanks. (*Wiping his forehead.*) But surely no gentleman would sit in the public car, squeezed between working-men and shop-girls, not to say Jews and Blacks.
Quincy	It *is* done here. But we shall change all that. Already we have a few taxi-cabs. Give us time, my dear Baron, give us time. You mustn't judge us by your European standard.
Baron	By the European standard, Mr. Davenport, you put our hospitality to the shame. From the moment you sent your yacht for us to Odessa—
Quincy	Pray, don't ever speak of that again—you know how anxious I was to get you to New York.

Baron	Provided we have arrived in time!
Quincy	That's all right, I keep telling you. They aren't married yet—
Baron	(*Grinding his teeth and shaking his fist*) Those Jew-vermin—all my life I have suffered from them!
Quincy	We all suffer from them.
Baroness	Zey are ze pests of ze civilisation.
Baron	But this supreme insult Vera shall not put on the blood of the Revendals—not if I have to shoot her down with my own hand—and myself after!
Quincy	No, no, Baron, that's not done here. Besides, if you shoot her down, where do *I* come in, eh?
Baron	(*Puzzled*) Where *you* come in?
Quincy	Oh, Baron! Surely you have guessed that it is not merely Jew-hate, but—er—Christian love. Eh? (*Laughing uneasily.*)
Baron	You!
Baroness	(*Clapping her hands*) Oh, *charmant, charmant!* But it ees a romance!
Baron	But you are married!
Baroness	(*Downcast*) *Ah, oui. Quel dommage,* vat a peety!
Quincy	You forget. Baron, we are in America. The law giveth and the law taketh away. (*He sniggers.*)
Baroness	It ees a vonderful country! But your vife—*hein?*—vould she consent?
Quincy	She's mad to get back on the stage—I'll run a theatre for her. It's your daughter's consent that's the real trouble—she won't see me because I lost my temper and told her to stop with her Jew. So I look to you to straighten things out.
Baroness	*Mais parfaitement.*
Baron	(*Frowning at her*) You go too quick, Katusha. What influence have I on Vera? And *you* she has never even seen! To kick out

the Jew-beast is one thing . . .

Quincy	Well, anyhow, don't *shoot* her—shoot the beast rather. (*Sniggeringly.*)
Baron	Shooting is too good for the enemies of Christ. (*Crossing himself.*) At Kishineff we stick the swine.
Quincy	(*Interested*) Ah! I read about that. Did you see the massacre?
Baron	Which one? Give me a cigarette, Katusha. (*She obeys.*) We've had several Jew-massacres in Kishineff.
Quincy	Have you? The papers only boomed one—four or five years ago—about Easter time, I think—
Baron	Ah, yes—when the Jews insulted the procession of the Host! (*Taking a light from the cigarette in his wife's mouth.*)
Quincy	Did they? I thought—
Baron	(*Sarcastically*) I daresay. That's the lies they spread in the West. They have the Press in their hands, damn 'em. But you see I was on the spot. (*He drops into a chair.*) I had charge of the whole district.
Quincy	(*Startled*) You!
Baron	Yes, and I hurried a regiment up to teach the blaspheming brutes manners—(*He puffs out a leisurely cloud.*)
Quincy	(*Whistling*) Whew! . . . I—I say, old chap, I mean Baron, you'd better not say that here.
Baron	Why not? I am proud of it.
Baroness	My husband vas decorated for it—he has ze order of St. Vladimir.
Baron	(*Proudly*) Second class! Shall we allow these bigots to mock at all we hold sacred? The Jews are the deadliest enemies of our holy autocracy and of the only orthodox Church. Their *Bund* is behind all the Revolution.
Baroness	A plague-spot muz be cut out!
Quincy	Well, I'd keep it dark if I were you. Kishineff is a back num-

ber, and we don't take much stock in the new massacres. Still, we're a bit squeamish—

Baron   Squeamish! Don't you lynch and roast your niggers?

Quincy   Not officially. Whereas your Black Hundreds—

Baron   Black Hundreds! My dear Mr. Davenport, they are the white hosts of Christ (*crossing himself*) and of the Tsar, who is God's vicegerent on earth. Have you not read the works of our sainted Pobie-donostzeff, Procurator of the Most Holy Synod?

Quincy   Well, of course, I always felt there was another side to it, but-still—

Baroness   Perhaps he has right, Alexis. Our Ambassador vonce told me ze Americans are more sentimental zan civilised.

Baron   Ah, let them wait till they have ten million vermin overrunning *their* country—we shall see how long they will be sentimental. Think of it! A burrowing swarm creeping and crawling everywhere, ugh! They ruin our peasantry with their loans and their drink shops, ruin our army with their revolutionary propaganda, ruin our professional classes by snatching all the prizes and professorships, ruin our commercial classes by monopolising our sugar industries, our oilfields, our timber-trade . . . Why, if we gave them equal rights, our Holy Russia would be entirely run by them.

Baroness   *Mon dieu! C'est vrai.* Ve real Russians vould become slaves.

Quincy   Then what are you going to do with them?

Baron   One-third will be baptized, one-third massacred, the other third emigrated here. (*He strikes a match to relight his cigarette.*)

Quincy   (*Shudderingly*) Thank you, my dear Baron,—you've already sent me one Jew too many. We're going to stop all alien immigration.

Baron   To stop *all* alien—? But that is barbarous!

Quincy   Well, don't let us waste our time on the Jew-problem . . . our own little Jew-problem is enough, eh? Get rid of this little fiddler. Then *I* may have a look in. Adieu, Baron.

Baron   Adieu. (*Holding his hand*) But you are not really serious about Vera?

(*The* BARONESS *makes a gesture of annoyance.*)

Quincy   Not serious, Baron? Why, to marry her is the only thing I have ever wanted that I couldn't get. It is torture! Baroness, I rely on your sympathy. (*He kisses her hand with a pretentious foreign air.*)

Baroness   (*In sentimental approval*) Ah! *l'amour! l'amour!* (*EXIT* QUINCY DAVENPORT, *taking his cap in passing.*) You might have given him a little encouragement, Alexis.

Baron   Silence, Katusha. I only tolerated the man in Europe because he was a link with Vera.

Baroness   You accepted his yacht and his—

Baron   If I had known his loose views on divorce—

Baroness   I am sick of your scruples. You are ze only poor official in Bessarabia.

Baron   Be silent! Have I not forbidden—?

Baroness   (*Petulantly*) Forbidden! Forbidden! All your life you have served ze Tsar, and you cannot afford a single automobile. A millionaire son-in-law is just vat you owe me.

Baron   What I owe you?

Baroness   Yes, ven I married you, I vas tinking you had a good position. I did not know you were too honest to use it. You vere not open viz me, Alexis.

Baron   You knew I was a Revendal. The Revendals keep their hands clean . . . (*With a sudden start he tiptoes noiselessly to the door leading to the hall and throws it open. Nobody is visible. He closes it shamefacedly.*)

Baroness   (*Has shared his nervousness till the door was opened, but now bursts into mocking laughter.*) If you thought less about your precious safety, and more about me and Vera—

Baron   Hush! You do not know Vera. You saw I was even afraid to give my name. She might have sent me away as she sent away the Tsar's plate of mutton.

Baroness   The Tsar's plate of—?

Baron   Did I never tell you? When she was only a schoolgirl—at the Imperial High School—the Tsar on his annual visit tasted the food, and Vera, as the show pupil, was given the honour of finishing his Majesty's plate.

Baroness   (*In incredulous horror*) And she sent it avay?

Baron   Gave it to a servant. (*Awed silence.*) And then you think I can impose a husband on her. No, Katusha, I have to win her love for myself, not for millionaires.

Baroness   (*Angry again*) Alvays so affrightfully selfish!

Baron   I have no control over her, I tell you! (*Bitterly*) I never could control my womenkind.

Baroness   Because you zink zey are your soldiers. Silence! Halt! Forbidden! Right Veel! March!

Baron   (*Sullenly*) I wish I did think they were my soldiers—I might try the lash.

Baroness   (*Springing up angrily, shakes parasol at him*) You British barbarian!

Vera   (*Outside the door leading to the interior*) Yes, thank you, Miss Andrews. I know I have visitors.

Baron   (*Ecstatically*) Vera's voice!

(*The* BARONESS *lowers her parasol. He looks yearningly toward the door. It opens. ENTER* VERA *with inquiring gaze.*)

Vera   (*With a great shock of surprise*) Father!!

Baron   *Verotschka!* My dearest darling! . . . (*He makes a movement toward her, but is checked by her irresponsiveness.*) Why, you've grown more beautiful than ever.

Vera	You in New York!
Baron	The Baroness wished to see America. Katusha, this is my daughter.
Baroness	(*In sugared sweetness*) And mine, too, if she vill let me love her.
Vera	(*Bowing coldly, but still addressing her father*) But how? When?
Baron	We have just come and—
Baroness	(*Dashing in*) Zat charming young man lent us his yacht—he is adorahble.
Vera	What charming young man?
Baroness	Ah, she has many, ze little coquette—ha! ha! ha! (*She touches* VERA *playfully with her parasol.*)
Baron	We wished to give you a pleasant surprise.
Vera	It is certainly a surprise.
Baron	(*Chilled*) You are not very . . . daughterly.
Vera	Do you remember when you last saw me? You did not claim me as a daughter then.
Baron	(*Covers his eyes with his hand*) Do not recall it; it hurts too much.
Vera	I was in the dock.
Baron	It was horrible. I hated you for the devil of rebellion that had entered into your soul. But I thanked God when you escaped.
Vera	(*Softened*) I think I was more sorry for you than for myself. I hope, at least, no suspicion fell on you.
Baroness	(*Eagerly*) But it did—an avalanche of suspicion. He is still buried under it. Vy else did they make Skovaloff Ambassador instead of him? Even now he risks everyting to see you again. Ah, *mon enfant,* you owe your fazer a grand reparation!

Vera	What reparation can I possibly make?
Baron	(*Passionately*) You can love me again, Vera.
Baroness	(*Stamping foot*) Alexis, you are interrupting—
Vera	I fear, father, we have grown too estranged—our ideas are so opposite—
Baron	But not now, Vera, surely not now? You are no longer (*he lowers his voice and looks around*) a Revolutionist?
Vera	Not with bombs, perhaps. I thank Heaven I was caught before I had done any *practical* work. But if you think I accept the order of things, you are mistaken. In Russia I fought against the autocracy—
Baron	Hush! Hush! (*He looks round nervously.*)
Vera	Here I fight against the poverty. No, father, a woman who has once heard the call will always be a wild creature.
Baron	But (*lowering his voice*) those revolutionary Russian clubs here—you are not a member?
Vera	I do not believe in Revolutions carried on at a safe distance. I have found my life-work in America.
Baron	I am enchanted, Vera, enchanted.
Baroness	(*Gushingly*) Permit me to kiss you, *belle enfant*.
Vera	I do not know you enough yet; I will kiss my father.
Baron	(*With a great cry of joy*) Vera! (*He embraces her passionately.*) At last! At last! I found my little Vera again!
Vera	No, father, *your* Vera belongs to Russia with her mother and the happy days of childhood. But for their sakes—(*She breaks down in emotion.*)
Baron	Ah, your poor mother!
Baroness	(*Tartly*) Alexis, I perceive I am too many! (*She begins to go toward the door.*)
Baron	No, no, Katusha. Vera will learn to love you, too.

Vera	(*To* BARONESS) What does my loving you matter? I can never return to Russia.
Baroness	(*Pausing*) But ve can come here—often—ven you are married.
Vera	(*Surprised*) When I am married? (*Softly, blushing*) You know?
Baroness	(*Smiling*) Ve know zat charming young man adores ze floor your foot treads on!
Vera	(*Blushing*) You have seen David?
Baron	(*Hoarsely*) David! (*He clenches his fist.*)
Baroness	(*Half aside, as much gestured as spoken*) Sh! Leave it to me. (*Sweetly.*) Oh, no, ve have not seen David.
Vera	(*Looking from one to the other*) Not seen—? Then what—whom are you talking about?
Baroness	About zat handsome, quite adorahble Mr. Davenport.
Vera	Davenport!
Baroness	Who combines ze manners of Europe viz ze millions of America!
Vera	(*Breaks into girlish laughter*) Ha! Ha! Ha! So Mr. Davenport has been talking to you! But you all seem to forget one small point—bigamy is not permitted even to millionaires.
Baroness	Ah, not boz at vonce, but—
Vera	And do you think I would take another woman's leavings? No, not even if she were dead.
Baroness	You are insulting!
Vera	I beg your pardon—I wasn't even thinking of you. Father, to put an end at once to this absurd conversation, let me inform you I am already engaged.
Baron	(*Trembling, hoarse*) By name, David.
Vera	Yes—David Quixano.

Baron	A Jew!
Vera	How did you know? Yes, he is a Jew, a noble Jew.
Baron	A Jew noble! (*He laughs bitterly.*)
Vera	Yes—even as you esteem nobility—by pedigree. In Spain his ancestors were hidalgos, favourites at the Court of Ferdinand and Isabella; but in the great expulsion of 1492 they preferred exile in Poland to baptism.
Baron	And you, a Revendal, would mate with an unbaptized dog?
Vera	Dog! You call my husband a dog!
Baron	Husband! God in heaven—are you married already?
Vera	No! But not being unemployed millionaires like Mr. Davenport, we hold even our troth eternal. (*Calmer*) Our poverty, not your prejudice, stands in the way of our marriage. But David is a musician of genius, and some day—
Baroness	A fiddler in a beer-hall! She prefers a fiddler to a millionaire of ze first families of America!
Vera	(*Contemptuously*) First families! I told you David's family came to Poland in 1492—some months before America was discovered.
Baron	Christ save us! You have become a Jewess!
Vera	No more than David has become a Christian. We were already at one—all honest people are. Surely, father, all religions must serve the same God—since there is only one God to serve.
Baroness	But ze girl is an ateist!
Baron	Silence, Katusha! Leave me to deal with my daughter. (*Changing tone to pathos, taking her face between his hands.*) Oh, Vera, *Verotschka,* my dearest darling, I had sooner you had remained buried in Siberia than that—(*He breaks down.*)
Vera	(*Touched, sitting beside him*) For you, father, I *was* as though buried in Siberia. Why did you come here to stab yourself afresh?
Baron	I wish to God I had come here earlier. I wish I had not been

so nervous of Russian spies. Ah, *Verotschka,* if you only knew how I have pored over the newspaper pictures of you, and the reports of your life in this Settlement!

Vera   You asked me not to send letters.

Baron   I know, I know—and yet sometimes I felt as if I could risk Siberia myself to read your dear, dainty handwriting again.

Vera   (*Still more softened*) Father, if you love me so much, surely you will love David a little too—for my sake.

Baron   (*Dazed*) I—love—a Jew? Impossible. (*He shudders.*)

Vera   (*Moving away, icily*) Then so is any love from me to you. You have chosen to come back into my life, and after our years of pain and separation I would gladly remember only my old childish affection. But not if you hate David. You must make your choice.

Baron   (*Pitifully*) Choice? I have no choice. Can I carry mountains? No more can I love a Jew. (*He rises resolutely.*)

Baroness   (*Who has turned away, fretting and fuming, turns back to her husband, flapping her hands*) Bravo!

Vera   (*Going to him again, coaxingly*) I don't ask you to carry mountains, but to drop the mountains you carry—the mountains of prejudice. Wait till you see him.

Baron   I will not see him.

Vera   Then you will hear him—he is going to make music for all the world. You can't escape him, *papasha,* you with your love of music, any more than you escaped Rubinstein.

Baroness   Rubinstein vas not a Jew.

Vera   Rubinstein was a Jewish boy-genius, just like my David.

Baroness   But his parents vere baptized soon after his birth. I had it from his patroness, ze Grande Duchesse Helena Pavlovna.

Vera   And did the water outside change the blood within? Rubinstein was our Court pianist and was decorated by the Tsar. And you, the Tsar's servant, dare to say you could not meet a

	Rubinstein.
Baron	(*Wavering*) I did not say I could not meet a Rubinstein.
Vera	You practically said so. David will be even greater than Rubinstein. Come, father, I'll telephone for him; he is only round the corner.
Baroness	(*Excitedly*) Ve vill not see him!
Vera	(*Ignoring her*) He shall bring his violin and play to you. There! You see, little father, you are already less frowning—now take that last wrinkle out of your forehead. (*She caresses his forehead.*) Never mind! David will smooth it out with his music as his Biblical ancestor smoothed that surly old Saul.
Baroness	Ve vill not hear him!
Baron	Silence, Katusha! Oh, my little Vera, I little thought when I let you study music at Petersburg—
Vera	(*Smiling wheedlingly*) That I should marry a musician. But you see, little father, it all ends in music after all. Now I will go and perform on the telephone, I'm not angel enough to bear one in here. (*She goes toward the door of the hall, smiling happily.*)
Baron	(*With a last agonized cry of resistance*) Halt!
Vera	(*Turning, makes mock military salute*) Yes, *papasha*.
Baron	(*Overcome by her roguish smile*) You—I—he—do you love this J—this David so much?
Vera	(*Suddenly tragic*) It would kill me to give him up. (*Resuming smile*) But don't let us talk of funerals on this happy day of sunshine and reunion. (*She kisses her hand to him and EXIT toward the hall.*)
Baroness	(*Angrily*) You are in her hands as vax!
Baron	She is the only child I have ever had, Katusha. Her baby arms curled round my neck; in her baby sorrows her wet face nestled against little father's. (*He drops on a chair, and leans his head on the table.*)

Baroness	(*Approaching tauntingly*) So you vill have a Jew son-in-law!
Baron	You don't know what it meant to me to feel her arms round me again.
Baroness	And a hook-nosed brat to call you grandpapa, and nestle his greasy face against yours.
Baron	(*Banging his fist on the table*) Don't drive me mad! (*His head drops again.*)
Baroness	Then drive me home—I vill not meet him . . . Alexis! (*She taps him on the shoulder with her parasol. He does not move.*) Alexis Ivanovitch! Do you not listen! . . . (*She stamps her foot.*) Zen I go to ze hotel alone. (*She walks angrily toward the hall. Just before she reaches the door, it opens, and the servant ushers in* HERR PAPPELMEISTER *with his umbrella. The* BARONESS's *tone changes instantly to a sugared, society accent.*) How do you do, Herr Pappelmeister? (*She extends her hand, which he takes limply.*) You don't remember me? *Non?* (*EXIT servant.*) Ve vere with Mr. Quincy Davenport at Wiesbaden—ze Baroness Revendal.
Pappelmeister	*So!*
	(*He drops her hand.*)
Baroness	Yes, it vas ze Baron's entousiasm for you zat got you your present position.
Pappelmeister	(*Arching his eyebrows*) *So!*
Baroness	Yes—zere he is! (*She turns toward the* BARON.) Alexis, rouse yourself! (*She taps him with her parasol.*) Zis American air makes ze Baron so sleepy.
Baron	(*Rises dazedly and bows*) Charmed to meet you, Herr—
Baroness	Pappelmeister! You remember ze great Pappelmeister.
Baron	(*Waking up, becomes keen*) Ah, yes, yes, charmed—why do you never bring your orchestra to Russia, Herr Pappelmeister?
Pappelmeister	(*Surprised*) Russia? It never occurred to me to go to Rus-

sia—she seems so uncivilised.

Baroness	(*Angry*) Uncivilised! Vy, ve have ze finest restaurants in ze vorld! And ze best telephones!
Pappelmeister	*So?*
Baroness	Yes, and the most beautiful ballets—Russia is affrightfully misunderstood. (*She sweeps away in burning indignation. PAPPELMEISTER murmurs in deprecation. Re-ENTER VERA from the ball. She is gay and happy.*)
Vera	He is coming round at once—(*She utters a cry of pleased surprise.*) Herr Pappelmeister! This is indeed a pleasure! (*She gives PAPPELMEISTER her hand, which he kisses.*)
Baroness	(*Sotto voce to the BARON*) Let us go before he comes. (*The BARON ignores her, his eyes hungrily on VERA.*)
Pappelmeister	(*To VERA*) But I come again—you have visitors.
Vera	(*Smiling*) Only my father and—
Pappelmeister	(*Surprised*) Your fader? *Ach so!* (*He taps his forehead.*) Revendal!
Baroness	(*Sotto voce to the BARON*) I vill not meet a Jew, I tell you.
Pappelmeister	But you vill vant to talk to your fader, and all *I* vant is Mr. Quixano's address. De Irish maiden at de house says de bird is flown.
Vera	(*Gravely*) I don't know if I ought to tell you where the new nest is—
Pappelmeister	(*Disappointed*) *Ach!*
Vera	(*Smiling*) But I will produce the bird.
Pappelmeister	(*Looks round*) You vill broduce Mr. Quixano?
Vera	(*Merrily*) By clapping my hands. (*Mysteriously*) I am a magician.
Baron	(*Whose eyes have been glued on VERA*) You are, indeed! I don't know how you bewitched me.

(*The* BARONESS *glares at him.*)

Vera Dear little father! (*She crosses to him and strokes his hair.*) Herr Pappelmeister, tell father about Mr. Quixano's music.

Pappelmeister (*Shaking his head*) Music cannot be talked about.

Vera (*Smiling*) That's a nasty one for the critics. But tell father what a genius Da—Mr. Quixano is.

Baroness (*Desperately intervening*) Good-bye, Vera. (*She thrusts out her hand, which* VERA *takes.*) I have a headache. You muz excuse me. Herr Pappelmeister, *au plaisir de vous revoir.*

(PAPPELMEISTER *hastens to the door, which he holds open. The* BARONESS *turns and glares at the* BARON.)

Baron (*Agitated*) Let me see you to the auto—

Baroness You could see me to ze hotel almost as quick.

Baron (*To* VERA) I won't say good-bye, *Verotschka*—I shall be back. (*He goes toward the hall, then turns.*) You will keep your Rubinstein waiting? (VERA *smiles lovingly.*)

Baroness You are keeping *me* vaiting.

(*He turns quickly. Exeunt* BARON *and* BARONESS.)

Pappelmeister And now broduce Mr. Quixano!

Vera Not so fast. What are you going to do with him?

Pappelmeister Put him in my orchestra!

Vera (*Ecstatic*) Oh, you dear! (*Then her tone changes to disappointment.*) But he won't go into Mr. Davenport's orchestra.

Pappelmeister It is no more Mr. Davenport's orchestra. He fired me, don't you remember? Now I boss—how say you in American?

Vera (*Smiling*) Your own show.

Pappelmeister *Ja,* my own band. Ven I left dat comic opera millionaire, dey all shtick to me almost to von man.

Vera How nice of them!

Pappelmeister   All egsept de Christian—he vas de von man. He shtick to de millionaire. So I lose my brincipal first violin.

Vera   And Mr. Quixano is to—oh, how delightful! (*She claps her hands girlishly.*)

Pappelmeister   (*Looks round mischievously*) *Ach*, de magic failed.

Vera   (*Puzzled*) Eh!

Pappelmeister   You do not broduce him. You clap de hands—but you do not broduce him. Ha! Ha! Ha! (*He breaks into a great roar of genial laughter.*)

Vera   (*Chiming in merrily*) Ha! Ha! Ha! But I said I have to know everything first. Will he get a good salary?

Pappelmeister   Enough to keep a vife and eight children!

Vera   (*Blushing*) But he hasn't a—

Pappelmeister   No, but de Christian had—he get de same—I mean salary, ha! ha! ha! not children. Den he can be independent—vedder de fool-public like his American symphony or not—*nicht wahr?*

Vera   You *are* good to us—(*hastily correcting herself*) to Mr. Quixano.

Pappelmeister   (*Smiling*) And aldough you cannot broduce him, I broduce his symphony. *Was?*

Vera   Oh, Herr Pappelmeister! You are an angel.

Pappelmeister   *Nein, nein, mein liebes Kind!* I fear I haf not de correct shape for an angel. (*He laughs heartily. A knock at the door from the hall.*)

Vera   (*Merrily*) *Now* I clap my hands. (*She claps.*) Come! (*The door opens.*)Behold him! (*She makes a conjurer's gesture. DA-VID, bareheaded, carrying his fiddle, opens the door, and stands staring in amazement at PAPPELMEISTER.*)

David   I thought you asked me to meet your father.

Pappelmeister   She is a magician. She has changed us. (*He waves his um-*

brella.) Hey presto, *was?* Ha! Ha! Ha! (*He goes to* DAVID, *and shakes hands.*) *Und wie geht's?* I hear you've left home.

David   Yes, but I've such a bully cabin—

Pappelmeister   (*Alarmed*) You are sailing avay?

Vera   (*Laughing*) No, no—that's only his way of describing his two-dollar-a-month garret.

David   Yes—my state-room on the top deck!

Vera   (*Smiling*) Six foot square.

David   But three other passengers aren't squeezed in, and it never pitches and tosses. It's heavenly.

Pappelmeister   (*Smiling*) And from heaven you flew down to blay in dat beer-hall. *Was?* (DAVID *looks surprised.*) I heard you.

David   You! What on earth did you go *there* for?

Pappelmeister   Vat on earth does one go to a beer-hall for? Ha! Ha! Ha! For vawter! Ha! Ha! Ha! Ven I hear you blay, I dink mit myself—if my blans succeed and I get Carnegie Hall for Saturday Symphony Concerts, dat boy shall be one of my first violins. *Was?* (*He slaps* DAVID *on the left shoulder.*)

David   (*Overwhelmed, ecstatic, yet wincing a little at the slap on his wound*) Be one of your first—(*Remembering*) Oh, but it is impossible.

Vera   (*Alarmed*) Mr. Quixano! You must not refuse.

David   But does Herr Pappelmeister know about the wound in my shoulder?

Pappelmeister   (*Agitated*) You haf been vounded?

David   Only a legacy from Russia—but it twinges in some weathers.

Pappelmeister   And de pain ubsets your blaying?

David   Not so much the pain—it's all the dreadful memories—

Vera   (*Alarmed*) Don't talk of them.

David	I *must* explain to Herr Pappelmeister—it wouldn't be fair. Even now (*shuddering*) there comes up before me the bleeding body of my mother, the cold, fiendish face of the Russian officer, supervising the slaughter—
Vera	Hush! Hush!
David	(*Hysterically*) Oh, that butcher's face—there it is—hovering in the air, that narrow, fanatical forehead, that—
Pappelmeister	(*Brings down his umbrella with a bang*) *Schluss.* No man ever dared break down under me. My baton will beat avay all dese faces and fancies. Out with your violin! (*He taps his umbrella imperiously on the table.*) *Keinen Mut verlieren!* (*DAVID takes out his violin from its case and puts it to his shoulder,* PAPPEL-MEISTER *keeping up a hypnotic torrent of encouraging German cries.*) *Also! Fertig! Anfangen!* (*He raises and waves his umbrella like a baton.*) Von, dwo, dree, four—
David	(*With a great sigh of relief*) Thanks, thanks—they are gone already.
Pappelmeister	Ha! Ha! Ha! You see. And ven ve blay your American symphony—
David	(*Dazed*) You will play my American symphony?
Vera	(*Disappointed*) Don't you jump for joy.
David	(*Still dazed but ecstatic*) Herr Pappelmeister! (*Changing back to despondency*) But what certainty is there your Carnegie Hall audience would understand me? It would be the same smart set. (*He drops dejectedly into a chair and lays down his violin.*)
Pappelmeister	*Ach, nein.* Of course, some—ve can't keep peoble out merely because dey pay for deir seats. *Was?* (*He laughs.*)
David	It was always my dream to play it first to the new immigrants—those who have known the pain of the old world and the hope of the new.
Pappelmeister	Try it on the dog. *Was?*
David	Yes—on the dog that here will become a man!
Pappelmeister	(*Shakes his head*) I fear neider dogs nor men are a musical

breed.

David   The immigrants will not understand my music with their brains or their ears, but with their hearts and their souls.

Vera   Well, then, why shouldn't it be done here—on our Roof-Garden?

David   (*Jumping up*) A *Bas-Kôl!* A *Bas-Kôl!*

Vera   What *are* you talking?

David   Hebrew! It means a voice from heaven.

Vera   Ah, but will Herr Pappelmeister consent?

Pappelmeister   (*Bowing*) Who can disobey a voice from heaven? . . . But ven?

Vera   On some holiday evening . . . why not the Fourth of July?

David   (*Still more ecstatic*) Another *Bas-Kôl!* . . . My American Symphony! Played to the People! Under God's sky! On Independence Day! With all the—(*Waving his hand expressively, sighs voluptuously.*) That will be too perfect.

Pappelmeister   (*Smiling*) Dat has to be seen. You must permit me to invite—

David   (*In horror*) Not the musical critics!

Pappelmeister   (*Raising both hands with umbrella in equal horror*) *Gott bewahre!* But I'd like to invite all de persons in New York who really undershtand music.

Vera   Splendid! But should we have room?

Pappelmeister   Room? I vant four blaces.

Vera   (*Smiling*) You are severe! Mr. Davenport was right.

Pappelmeister   (*Smiling*) Perhaps de oders vill be out of town. *Also!* (*Holding out his hand to David*) You come to Carnegie to-morrow at eleven. Yes? *Fraülein.* (*Kisses her hand.*) *Auf Wiedersehen!* (*Going*) On de Roof-Garden—nicht wahr?

Vera   (*Smiling*) Wind and weather permitting.

Pappelmeister   I haf alvays mein umbrella. *Was?* Ha! Ha! Ha!

Vera   (*Murmuring*) Isn't he a darling? Isn't he—?

Pappelmeister   (*Pausing suddenly*) But ve never settled de salary.

David   Salary! (*He looks dazedly from one to the other.*) For the honour of playing in your orchestra!

Pappelmeister   Shylock!! . . . Never mind—ve settle de pound of flesh tomorrow. *Lebe wohl!* (*EXIT, the door closes.*)

Vera   (*Suddenly miserable*) How selfish of you, David!

David   Selfish, Vera?

Vera   Yes—not to think of your salary. It looks as if you didn't really love me.

David   Not love you? I don't understand.

Vera   (*Half in tears*) Just when I was so happy to think that now we shall be able to marry.

David   Shall we? Marry? On my salary as first violin?

Vera   Not if you don't want to.

David   Sweetheart! Can it be true? How do you know?

Vera   (*Smiling*) *I'm* not a Jew. I asked.

David   My guardian angel! (*Embracing her. He sits down, she lovingly at his feet.*)

Vera   (*Looking up at him*) Then you *do* care?

David   What a question!

Vera   And you don't think wholly of your music and forget me?

David   Why, you are behind all I write and play!

Vera   (*With jealous passion*) Behind? But I want to be before! I want you to love me first, before everything.

David   I do put you before everything.

Vera   You are sure? And nothing shall part us?

David	Not all the seven seas could part you and me.
Vera	And you won't grow tired of me—not even when you are world-famous—?
David	(*A shade petulant*) Sweetheart, considering I should owe it all to you—
Vera	(*Drawing his head down to her breast*) Oh, David! David! Don't be angry with poor little Vera if she doubts, if she wants to feel quite sure. You see father has talked so terribly, and after all I was brought up in the Greek Church, and we oughtn't to cause all this suffering unless—
David	Those who love us *must* suffer, and *we* must suffer in their suffering. It is live things, not dead metals, that are being melted in the Crucible.
Vera	Still, we ought to soften the suffering as much as—
David	Yes, but only Time can heal it.
Vera	(*With transition to happiness*) But father seems half-reconciled already! Dear little father, if only he were not so narrow about Holy Russia!
David	If only *my* folks were not so narrow about Holy Judea! But the ideals of the fathers shall not be foisted on the children. Each generation must live and die for its own dream.
Vera	Yes, David, yes. You are the prophet of the living present. I am so happy. (*She looks up wistfully.*) You are happy, too?
David	I am dazed—I cannot realise that all our troubles have melted away—it is so sudden.
Vera	You, David? Who always see everything in such rosy colours? Now that the whole horizon is one great splendid rose, you almost seem as if gazing out toward a blackness—
David	We Jews are cheerful in gloom, mistrustful in joy. It is our tragic history—
Vera	But you have come to end the tragic history; to throw off the coils of the centuries.

David   (*Smiling again*) Yes, yes, Vera. You bring back my sunnier self. I must be a pioneer on the lost road of happiness. To-day shall be all joy, all lyric ecstasy. (*He takes up his violin.*) Yes, I will make my old fiddle-strings *burst* with joy! (*He dashes into a jubilant tarantella. After a few bars there is a knock at the door leading from the hall; their happy faces betray no sign of hearing it; then the door slightly opens, and* BARON REVENDAL's *head looks hesitatingly in. As* DAVID *perceives it, his features work convulsively, his string breaks with a tragic snap, and he totters backward into* VERA's *arms. Hoarsely*) The face! The face!

Vera   David—my dearest!

David   (*His eyes closed, his violin clasped mechanically*) Don't be anxious—I shall be better soon—I oughtn't to have talked about it—the hallucination has never been so complete.

Vera   Don't speak—rest against Vera's heart—till it has passed away. (*The* BARON *comes dazedly forward, half with a shocked sense of* VERA's *impropriety, half to relieve her of her burden. She motions him back.*) This is the work of your Holy Russia.

Baron   (*Harshly*) What is the matter with him?

         (DAVID's *violin and bow drop from his grasp and fall on the table.*)

David   The voice! (*He opens his eyes, stares frenziedly at the* BARON, *then struggles out of* VERA's *arms.*)

Vera   (*Trying to stop him*) Dearest—

David   Let me go. (*He moves like a sleep-walker toward the paralysed* BARON, *puts out his hand, and testingly touches the face.*)

Baron   (*Shuddering back*) Hands off!

David   (*With a great cry*) A-a-a-h! It is flesh and blood. No, it is stone—the man of stone! Monster! (*He raises his hand frenziedly.*)

Baron   (*Whipping out his pistol*) Back, dog! (VERA *darts between them with a shriek.*)

David   (*Frozen again, surveying the pistol stonily*) Ha! You want *my*

	life, too. Is the cry not yet loud enough?
Baron	The cry?
David	(*Mystically*) Can you not hear it? The voice of the blood of my brothers crying out against you from the ground? Oh, how can you bear not to turn that pistol against yourself and execute upon yourself the justice which Russia denies you?
Baron	Tush! (*Pocketing the pistol a little shamefacedly.*)
Vera	Justice on himself? For what?
David	For crimes beyond human penalty, for obscenities beyond human utterance, for—
Vera	You are raving.
David	Would to heaven I were!
Vera	But this is my father.
David	Your father! . . . God! (*He staggers.*)
Baron	(*Drawing her to him*) Come, Vera, I told you—
Vera	(*Frantically, shrinking back*) Don't touch me!
Baron	(*Starting back in amaze*) Vera!
Vera	(*Hoarsely*) Say it's not true.
Baron	What is not true?
Vera	What David said. It was the mob that massacred—*you* had no hand in it.
Baron	(*Sullenly*) I was there with my soldiers.
David	(*Leaning, pale, against a chair, hisses*) And you looked on with that cold face of hate—while my mother—my sister—
Baron	(*Sullenly*) I could not see everything.
David	Now and again you ordered your soldiers to fire—
Vera	(*In joyous relief*) Ah, he *did* check the mob—he *did* tell his soldiers to fire.

David	At any Jew who tried to defend himself.
Vera	Great God! (*She falls on the sofa and buries her head on the cushion, moaning*) Is there no pity in heaven?
David	There was no pity on earth.
Baron	It was the People avenging itself, Vera. The People rose like a flood. It had centuries of spoliation to wipe out. The voice of the People is the voice of God.
Vera	(*Moaning*) But you could have stopped them.
Baron	I had no orders to defend the foes of Christ and (*crossing himself*) the Tsar. The People—
Vera	But you could have stopped them.
Baron	Who can stop a flood? I did my duty. A soldier's duty is not so pretty as a musician's.
Vera	But you could have stopped them.
Baron	(*Losing all patience*) Silence! You talk like an ignorant girl, blinded by passion. The *pogrom* is a holy crusade. Are we Russians the first people to crush down the Jew? No—from the dawn of history the nations have had to stamp upon him— the Egyptians, the Assyrians, the Persians, the Babylonians, the Greeks, the Romans—
David	Yes, it is true. Even Christianity did not invent hatred. But not till Holy Church arose were we burnt at the stake, and not till Holy Russia arose were our babes torn limb from limb. Oh, it is too much! Delivered from Egypt four thousand years ago, to be slaves to the Russian Pharaoh to-day. (*He falls as if kneeling on a chair, and leans his head on the rail.*) O God, shall we always be broken on the wheel of history? How long, O Lord, how long?
Baron	(*Savagely*) Till you are all stamped out, ground into your dirt. (*Tenderly*) Look up, little Vera! You saw how *papasha* loves you—how he was ready to hold out his hand—and how this cur tried to bite it. Be calm—tell him a daughter of Russia cannot mate with dirt.

Vera   Father, I will be calm. I will speak without passion or blindness. I will tell David the truth. I was never absolutely sure of my love for him—perhaps that was why I doubted his love for me—often after our enchanted moments there would come a nameless uneasiness, some vague instinct, relic of the long centuries of Jew-loathing, some strange shrinking from his Christless creed—

Baron   (*With an exultant cry*) Ah! She is a Revendal.

Vera   But now—(*rises and walks firmly toward* DAVID) now, David, I come to you, and I say in the words of Ruth, thy people shall be my people and thy God my God! (*She stretches out her hands to* DAVID.)

Baron   You shameless—! (*He stops as he perceives* DAVID *remains impassive.*)

Vera   (*With agonised cry*) David!

David   (*In low, icy tones*) You cannot come to me. There is a river of blood between us.

Vera   Were it seven seas, our love must cross them.

David   Easy words to you. You never saw that red flood bearing the mangled breasts of women and the spattered brains of babes and sucklings. Oh! (*He covers his eyes with his hands. The* BARON *turns away in gloomy impotence. At last* DAVID *begins to speak quietly, almost dreamily.*) It was your Easter, and the air was full of holy bells and the streets of holy processions—priests in black and girls in white and waving palms and crucifixes, and everybody exchanging Easter eggs and kissing one another three times on the mouth in token of peace and goodwill, and even the Jew-boy felt the spirit of love brooding over the earth, though he did not then know that this Christ, whom holy chants proclaimed re-risen, was born in the form of a brother Jew. And what added to the peace and holy joy was that our own Passover was shining before us. My mother had already made the raisin wine, and my greedy little brother Solomon had sipped it on the sly that very morning. We were all at home—all except my father—he was away in the little Synagogue at which he was cantor. Ah, such a voice he had—a voice of tears and thunder—when he prayed it was like a wounded soul beating at the gates of Heaven—but he sang even more beautifully in the ritual of home, and how we were looking forward to his hymns at the Passover table—(*He breaks down. The* BARON *has gradually turned round under the spell of* DAVID'*s story and now listens hypnotised.*) I was playing my cracked little fiddle. Little Miriam was making her doll dance to it. Ah, that decrepit old china doll—the only one the poor child had ever had—I can see it now—one eye, no nose, half an arm. We were all laughing to see it caper to my music . . . My father flies in through the door, desperately clasping to his breast the Holy Scroll. We cry out to him to explain, and then we see that in that beloved mouth of song there is no longer a tongue—only blood. He tries to bar the door—a mob breaks in—we dash out through the back into the street. There are the soldiers—and the Face—

(VERA'*s eyes involuntarily seek the face of her father, who shrinks away as their eyes meet.*)

Vera   (*In a low sob*) O God!

David   When I came to myself, with a curious aching in my left shoulder, I saw lying beside me a strange shapeless Something . . . (DAVID *points weirdly to the floor, and* VERA, *hunched forwards, gazes stonily at it, as if seeing the horror.*) By the crimson doll in what seemed a hand I knew it must be little Miriam. The doll was a dream of beauty and perfection beside the mutilated mass which was all that remained of my sister, of my mother, of greedy little Solomon—Oh! You Christians can only see that rosy splendour on the horizon of happiness. And the Jew didn't see rosily enough for you, ha! ha! ha! the Jew who gropes in one great crimson mist. (*He breaks down in spasmodic, ironic, long-drawn, terrible laughter.*)

Vera   (*Trying vainly to tranquillise him*) Hush, David! Your laughter hurts more than tears. Let Vera comfort you. (*She kneels by his chair, tries to put her arms round him.*)

David   (*Shuddering*) Take them away! Don't you feel the cold dead pushing between us?

Vera   (*Unfaltering, moving his face toward her lips*) Kiss me!

David	I should feel the blood on my lips.
Vera	My love shall wipe it out.
David	Love! Christian love! (*He unwinds her clinging arms; she sinks prostrate on the floor as he rises.*) For this I gave up my people—darkened the home that sheltered me—there was always a still, small voice at my heart calling me back, but I heeded nothing—only the voice of the butcher's daughter. (*Brokenly*) Let me go home, let me go home. (*He looks lingeringly at VERA's prostrate form, but overcoming the instinct to touch and comfort her, begins tottering with uncertain pauses toward the door leading to the hall.*)
Baron	(*Extending his arms in relief and longing*) And here is *your* home, Vera!
	(*He raises her gradually from the floor; she is dazed, but suddenly she becomes conscious of whose arms she is in, and utters a cry of repulsion.*)
Vera	Those arms reeking from that crimson river! (*She falls back.*)
Baron	(*Sullenly*) Don't echo that babble. You came to these arms often enough when they were fresh from the battlefield.
Vera	But not from the shambles! You heard what he called you. Not soldier—butcher! Oh, I dared to dream of happiness after my nightmare of Siberia, but you—you—(*She breaks down for the first time in hysterical sobs.*)
Baron	(*Brokenly*) Vera! Little Vera! Don't cry! You stab me!
Vera	You thought you were ordering your soldiers to fire at the Jews, but it was my heart they pierced. (*She sobs on.*)
Baron	. . . And my own . . . But we will comfort each other. I will go to the Tsar myself—with my forehead to the earth—to beg for your pardon! . . . Come, put your wet face to little father's . . .
Vera	(*Violently pushing his face away*) I hate you! I curse the day I was born your daughter! (*She staggers toward the door leading to the interior. At the same moment DAVID, who has reached the door leading to the hall, now feeling subconsciously that VERA is*

going and that his last reason for lingering on is removed, turns the door-handle. The click attracts the BARON's attention, he veers round.)

Baron   (*To* DAVID) Halt! (*DAVID turns mechanically.* VERA *drifts out through her door, leaving the two men face to face. The* BARON *beckons to* DAVID, *who as if hypnotised moves nearer. The* BARON *whips out his pistol, slowly crosses to* DAVID, *who stands as if awaiting his fate. The* BARON *hands the pistol to* DAVID.) You were right! (*He steps back swiftly with a touch of stern heroism into the attitude of the culprit at a military execution, awaiting the bullet.*) Shoot me!

David   (*Takes the pistol mechanically, looks long and pensively at it as with a sense of its irrelevance. Gradually his arm droops and lets the pistol fall on the table, and there his hand touches a string of his violin, which yields a little note. Thus reminded of it, he picks up the violin, and as his fingers draw out the broken string he murmurs*) I must get a new string. (*He resumes his dragging march toward the door, repeating maunderingly*) I must get a new string.

(*The curtain falls.*)

ACT IV

Saturday, July 4, evening. The Roof-Garden of the Settlement House, showing a beautiful, far-stretching panorama of New York, with its irregular sky buildings on the left, and the harbour, with its Statue of Liberty on the right. Everything is wet and gleaming after rain. Parapet at the back. Elevator on the right. Entrance from the stairs on the left. In the sky hang heavy clouds through which thin, golden lines of sunset are just beginning to labour. DAVID discovered, on a bench, hugging his violin case to his breast, gazing moodily at the sky. A muffled sound of applause comes up from below and continues with varying intensity through the early part of the scene. Through it comes the noise of the elevator ascending. MENDEL steps out and hurries forward.

Mendel	Come down, David! Don't you hear them shouting for you? (*He passes his hand over the wet bench.*) Good heavens! You will get rheumatic fever!
David	Why have you followed me?
Mendel	Get up—everything is still damp.
David	(*Rising, gloomily*) Yes, there's a damper over everything.
Mendel	Nonsense—the rain hasn't damped your triumph in the least. In fact, the more delicate effects wouldn't have gone so well in the open air. Listen!
David	Let them shout. Who told you I was up here?
Mendel	Miss Revendal, of course.
David	(*Agitated*) Miss Revendal? How should *she* know?
Mendel	(*Sullenly*) She seems to understand your crazy ways.

351

David	(*Passing his hand over his eyes*) Ah, *you* never understood me, uncle . . . How did she look? Was she pale?
Mendel	Never mind about Miss Revendal. Pappelmeister wants you—the people insist on seeing you. Nobody can quiet them.
David	They saw me all through the symphony in my place in the orchestra.
Mendel	They didn't know you were the composer as well as the first violin. Now Miss Revendal has told them. (*Louder applause.*) There! Eleven minutes it has gone on—like for an office-seeker. You *must* come and show yourself.
David	I won't—I'm not an office-seeker. Leave me to my misery.
Mendel	Your misery? With all this glory and greatness opening before you? Wait till you're *my* age—(*Shouts of "QUIXANO!"*) You hear! What is to be done with them?
David	Send somebody on the platform to remind them this is the interval for refreshments!
Mendel	Don't be cynical. You know your dearest wish was to melt these simple souls with your music. And now—
David	Now I have only made my own stony.
Mendel	You are right. You are stone all over—ever since you came back home to us. Turned into a pillar of salt, mother says—like Lot's wife.
David	That was the punishment for looking backward. Ah, uncle, there's more sense in that old Bible than the Rabbis suspect. Perhaps that is the secret of our people's paralysis—we are always looking backward. (*He drops hopelessly into an iron garden-chair behind him.*)
Mendel	(*Stopping him before he touches the seat*) Take care—it's sopping wet. You don't look backward enough. (*He takes out his handkerchief and begins drying the chair.*)
David	(*Faintly smiling*) I thought you wanted the salt to melt.
Mendel	It *is* melting a little if you can smile. Do you know, David, I haven't seen you smile since that *Purim* afternoon?

David	You haven't worn a false nose since, uncle. (*He laughs bitterly.*) Ha! Ha! Ha! Fancy masquerading in America because twenty-five centuries ago the Jews escaped a *pogrom* in Persia. Two thousand five hundred years ago! Aren't we uncanny? (*He drops into the wiped chair.*)
Mendel	(*Angrily*) Better you should leave us altogether than mock at us. I thought it was your Jewish heart that drove you back home to us; but if you are still hankering after Miss Revendal—
David	(*Pained*) Uncle!
Mendel	I'd rather see you marry her than go about like this. You couldn't make the house any gloomier.
David	Go back to the concert, please. They have quieted down.
Mendel	(*Hesitating*) And you?
David	Oh, I'm not playing in the popular after-pieces. Pappelmeister guessed I'd be broken up with the stress of my own symphony—he has violins enough.
Mendel	Then you don't want to carry this about. (*Taking the violin from DAVID's arms.*)
David	(*Clinging to it*) Don't rob me of my music—it's all I have.
Mendel	You'll spoil it in the wet. I'll take it home.
David	No—(*He suddenly catches sight of two figures ENTERING from the left—FRAU QUIXANO and KATHLEEN clad in their best, and wearing tiny American flags in honour of Independence Day. KATHLEEN escorts the old lady, with the air of a guardian angel, on her slow, tottering course toward DAVID. FRAU QUIXANO is puffing and panting after the many stairs. DAVID jumps up in surprise, releases the violin-case to MENDEL.*) They at my symphony!
Mendel	Mother *would* come—even though, being *Shabbos,* she had to walk.
David	But wasn't she shocked at my playing on the Sabbath?
Mendel	No—that's the curious part of it. She said that even as a boy

	you played your fiddle on *Shabbos,* and that if the Lord has stood it all these years, He must consider you an exception.
David	You see! She's more sensible than you thought. I daresay whatever I were to do she'd consider me an exception.
Mendel	(*In sullen acquiescence*) I suppose geniuses *are.*
Kathleen	(*Reaching them; panting with admiration and breathlessness*) Oh, Mr. David! it was like midnight mass! But the misthress was ashleep.
David	Asleep! (*Laughs half-merrily, half-sadly.*) Ha! Ha! Ha!
Frau Quixano	(*Panting and laughing in response*) He! He! He! *Dovidel lacht widder.* He! He! He! (*She touches his arm affectionately, but feeling his wet coat, utters a cry of horror.*) *Du bist nass!*
David	*Es ist gor nicht.* Granny—my clothes are thick. (*She fusses over him, wiping him down with her gloved hand.*)
Mendel	But what brought you up here, Kathleen?
Kathleen	Sure, not the elevator. The misthress said 'twould be breaking the *Shabbos* to ride up in it.
David	(*Uneasily*) But did—did Miss Revendal send you up?
Kathleen	And who else should be axin' the misthress if she wasn't proud of Mr. David? Faith, she's a sweet lady.
Mendel	(*Impatiently*) Don't chatter, Kathleen.
Kathleen	But, Mr. Quixano—!
David	(*Sweetly*) Please take your mistress down again—don't let her walk.
Kathleen	But *Shabbos* isn't out yet!
Mendel	Chattering again!
David	(*Gently*) There's no harm, Kathleen, in going *down* in the elevator.
Kathleen	Troth, I'll egshplain to her that droppin' down isn't ridin'.
David	(*Smiling*) Yes, tell her dropping down is natural—not *work,*

like flying up. (*KATHLEEN begins to move toward the stairs, explaining to FRAU QUIXANO.*) And, Kathleen! You'll get her some refreshments.

Kathleen   (*Turns, glaring*) Refreshments, is it? Give her refreshments where they mix the mate with the butther plates! Oh, Mr. David! (*She moves off toward the stairs in reproachful sorrow.*)

Mendel   (*Smiling*) I'll get her some coffee.

David   (*Smiling*) Yes, that'll keep her awake. Besides, Pappelmeister was so sure the people wouldn't understand me, he's relaxing them on Gounod and Rossini.

Mendel   Pappelmeister's idea of relaxation! *I* should have given them comic opera. (*With sudden call to KATHLEEN, who with her mistress is at the wrong EXIT.*) Kathleen! The elevator's *this* side!

Kathleen   (*Turning*) What way can that be, when I came up *this* side?

Mendel   You chatter too much.

(*FRAU QUIXANO, not understanding, EXIT.*)

Come this way. Can't you see the elevator?

Kathleen   (*Perceives FRAU QUIXANO has gone, calls after her in Irish-sounding Yiddish.*) Wu geht Ihr, bedad? (*Impatiently*) Houly Moses, komm' zurick! (*EXIT anxiously, re-ENTER with FRAU QUIXANO.*) Begorra, we Jews never know our way.

(*MENDEL, carrying the violin, escorts his mother and KATHLEEN to the elevator. When they are near it, it stops with a thud, and PAPPELMEISTER springs out, his umbrella up, meeting them face to face. He looks happy and beaming over DAVID's triumph.*)

Pappelmeister   (*In loud, joyous voice*) Nun, Frau Quixano, was sagen Sie? Vat you tink of your David?

Frau Quixano   Dovid? Er ist meshuggah. (*She taps her forehead.*)

Pappelmeister   (*Puzzled, to MENDEL*) Meshuggah! Vat means *meshuggah*? Crazy?

Mendel   (*Half-smiling*) You've struck it. She says David doesn't know enough to go in out of the rain.

(*General laughter.*)

David   (*Rising*) But it's stopped raining, Herr Pappelmeister. You don't want your umbrella.

(*General laughter.*)

Pappelmeister   *So.* (*Shuts it down.*)

Mendel   *Herein, Mutter.* (*He pushes* FRAU QUIXANO's *somewhat shrinking form into the elevator.* KATHLEEN *follows, then* MENDEL.) Herr Pappelmeister, we are all your grateful servants.

(PAPPELMEISTER *bows; the gates close, the elevator descends.*)

David   And you won't think *me* ungrateful for running away—you know my thanks are too deep to be spoken.

Pappelmeister   And zo are my congratulations!

David   Then, don't speak them, please.

Pappelmeister   But you *must* come and speak to all de people in America who undershtand music.

David   (*Half-smiling*) To your four connoisseurs? (*Seriously*) Oh, please! I really could not meet strangers, especially musical vampires.

Pappelmeister   (*Half-startled, half-angry*) Vampires? Oh, come!

David   Voluptuaries, then—rich, idle aesthetes to whom art and life have no connection, parasites who suck our music—

Pappelmeister   (*Laughs good-naturedly*) Ha! Ha! Ha! Vait till you hear vat dey say.

David   I will wait as long as you like.

Pappelmeister   Den I like to tell you now. (*He roars with mischievous laughter*) Ha! Ha! Ha! De first vampire says it is a great vork, but poorly performed.

David   (*Indignant*) Oh!

Pappelmeister   De second vampire says it is a poor vork, but greatly performed.

David   (*Disappointed*) Oh!

Pappelmeister   De dird vampire says it is a great vork greatly performed.

David   (*Complacently*) Ah!

Pappelmeister   And de fourz vampire says it is a poor vork poorly performed.

David   (*Angry and disappointed*) Oh! (*Then smiling*) You see you *have* to go by the people after all.

Pappelmeister   (*Shakes head, smiling*) Nein. Ven critics disagree—I agree mit mineself. Ha! Ha! Ha! (*He slaps* DAVID *on the back.*) A great vork dat vill be even better performed next time! Ha! Ha! Ha! Ten dousand congratulations. (*He seizes* DAVID'S *hand and grips it heartily.*)

David   Don't! You hurt me.

Pappelmeister   (*Dropping* DAVID'S *hand, misunderstanding*) Pardon! I forgot your vound.

David   No—no—what does my wound matter? That never stung half so much as these clappings and congratulations.

Pappelmeister   (*Puzzled but solicitous*) I knew your nerves vould be all shnapping like fiddle-shtrings. Oh, you cheniuses! (*Smiling.*) You like neider de clappings nor de criticisms,—*was?*

David   They are equally—irrelevant. One day to wrestle with one's own art, one's own soul, *alone!*

Pappelmeister   (*Patting him soothingly*) I am glad I did not let you blay in Part Two.

David   Dear Herr Pappelmeister! Don't think I don't appreciate all your kindnesses—you are almost a father to me.

Pappelmeister   And you disobey me like a son. Ha! Ha! Ha! Vell, I vill make your excuses to de—vampires. Ha! Ha! Also, David. (*He lays his hand again affectionately on* DAVID'S *right shoulder.*) *Lebe wohl!* I must go down to my popular classics. (*Gloomily*) Truly a going down! *Was?*

David   (*Smiling*) Oh, it isn't such a descent as all that. Uncle said you ought to have given them comic opera.

Pappelmeister   (*Shuddering convulsively*) Comic opera . . . Ouf! (*He goes toward the elevator and, rings the bell. Then he turns to* DAVID.) Vat vas dat vord, David?

David   What word?

Pappelmeister   (*Groping for it*) Mega-megassbu . . .

David   (*Puzzled*) *Megasshu?*

(*The elevator comes up; the gates open.*)

Pappelmeister   *Megusshah!* You know. (*He taps his forehead with his umbrella.*)

David   Ah, *meshuggah!*

Pappelmeister   (*Joyously*) Ja, meshuggah! (*He gives a great roar of laughter.*) Ha! Ha! Ha! (*He waves umbrella at* DAVID.) Well, don't be . . . meshuggah. (*He steps into the elevator.*) Ha! Ha! Ha! (*The gates close, and it descends with his laughter.*)

David   (*After a pause*) Perhaps I *am* . . . meshuggah. (*He walks up and down moodily, approaches the parapet at back.*) Dropping down is indeed natural. (*He looks over.*) How it tugs and drags at one! (*He moves back resolutely and shakes his head.*) That would be even a greater descent than Pappelmeister's to comic opera. One *must* fly upward—somehow. (*He drops on the chair that* MENDEL *dried. A faint music steals up and makes an accompaniment to all the rest of the scene.*) Ah! the popular classics! (*His head sinks on a little table. The elevator comes up again, but he does not raise his head.* VERA, *pale and sad, steps out and walks gently over to him; stands looking at him with maternal pity; then decides not to disturb him and is stealing away when suddenly he looks up and perceives her and springs to his feet with a dazed glad cry.*) Vera!

Vera   (*Turns, speaks with grave dignity*) Miss Andrews has charged me to convey to you the heart-felt thanks and congratulations of the Settlement.

David	(*Frozen*) Miss Andrews is very kind . . . I trust you are well.
Vera	Thank you, Mr. Quixano. Very well and very busy. So you'll excuse me. (*She turns to go.*)
David	Certainly . . . How are your folks?
Vera	(*Turns her head*) They are gone back to Russia. And yours?
David	You just saw them all.
Vera	(*Confused*) Yes—yes—of course—I forgot! Good-bye, Mr. Quixano.
David	Good-bye, Miss Revendal.

(*He drops back on the chair.* VERA *walks to the elevator, then just before ringing turns again.*)

Vera	I shouldn't advise you to sit here in the damp.
David	My uncle dried the chair. (*Bitterly*) Curious how every one is concerned about my body and no one about my soul.
Vera	Because your soul is so much stronger than your body. Why, think! It has just lifted a thousand people far higher than this roof-garden.
David	Please don't you congratulate me, too! That would be too ironical.
Vera	(*Agitated, coming nearer*) Irony, Mr. Quixano? Please, please, do not imagine there is any irony in my congratulations.
David	The irony is in all the congratulations. How can I endure them when I know what a terrible failure I have made!
Vera	Failure! Because the critics are all divided? That is the surest proof of success. You have produced something real and new.
David	I am not thinking of Pappelmeister's connoisseurs—*I* am the only connoisseur, the only one who knows. And every bar of my music cried "Failure! Failure!" It shrieked from the violins, blared from the trombones, thundered from the drums. It

was written on all the faces—

Vera   (*Vehemently, coming still nearer*) Oh, no! no! I watched the faces—those faces of toil and sorrow, those faces from many lands. They were fired by your vision of their coming brotherhood, lulled by your dream of their land of rest. And I could see that you were right in speaking to the people. In some strange, beautiful way the inner meaning of your music stole into all those simple souls—

David   (*Springing up*) And *my* soul? What of *my* soul? False to its own music, its own mission, its own dream. That is what I mean by failure, Vera. I preached of God's Crucible, this great new continent that could melt up all race-differences and vendettas, that could purge and re-create, and God tried me with his supremest test. He gave me a heritage from the Old World, hate and vengeance and blood, and said, "Cast it all into my Crucible." And I said, "Even thy Crucible cannot melt this hate, cannot drink up this blood." And so I sat crooning over the dead past, gloating over the old blood-stains—I, the apostle of America, the prophet of the God of our children. Oh—how my music mocked me! And you—so fearless, so high above fate—how you must despise me!

Vera   I? Ah no!

David   You must. You do. Your words still sting. Were it seven seas between us, you said, our love must cross them. And I—I who had prated of seven seas—

Vera   Not seas of blood—I spoke selfishly, thoughtlessly. I had not realised that crimson flood. Now I see it day and night. O God! (*She shudders and covers her eyes.*)

David   There lies my failure—to have brought it to your eyes, instead of blotting it from my own.

Vera   No man could have blotted it out.

David   Yes—by faith in the Crucible. From the blood of battlefields spring daisies and buttercups. In the divine chemistry the very garbage turns to roses. But in the supreme moment my faith was found wanting. You came to me—and I thrust you away.

Vera	I ought not to have come to you . . . I ought not to have come to you to-day. We must not meet again.
David	Ah, you cannot forgive me!
Vera	Forgive? It is I that should go down on my knees for my father's sin. (*She is half-sinking to her knees. He stops her by a gesture and a cry.*)
David	No! The sins of the fathers shall not be visited on the children.
Vera	My brain follows you, but not my heart. It is heavy with the sense of unpaid debts—debts that can only cry for forgiveness.
David	You owe me nothing—
Vera	But my father, my people, my country . . . (*She breaks down. Recovers herself.*) My only consolation is, you need nothing.
David	(*Dazed*) I—need—nothing?
Vera	Nothing but your music . . . your dreams.
David	And your love? Do I not need that?
Vera	(*Shaking her head sadly*) No.
David	You say that because I have forfeited it.
Vera	It is my only consolation, I tell you, that you do not need me. In our happiest moments a suspicion of this truth used to lacerate me. But now it is my one comfort in the doom that divides us. See how you stand up here above the world, alone and self-sufficient. No woman could ever have more than the second place in your life.
David	But you have the *first* place, Vera!
Vera	(*Shakes her head again*) No—I no longer even desire it. I have gotten over that womanly weakness.
David	You torture me. What do you mean?
Vera	What can be simpler? I used to be jealous of your music, your prophetic visions. I wanted to come first—before them all!

	Now, dear David, I only pray that they may fill your life to the brim.
David	But they cannot.
Vera	They will—have faith in yourself, in your mission—good-bye.
David	(*Dazed*) You love me and you leave me?
Vera	What else can I do? Shall the shadow of Kishineff hang over all your years to come? Shall I kiss you and leave blood upon your lips, cling to you and be pushed away by all those cold, dead hands?
David	(*Taking both her hands*) Yes, cling to me, despite them all, cling to me till all these ghosts are exorcised, cling to me till our love triumphs over death. Kiss me, kiss me now.
Vera	(*Resisting, drawing back*) I dare not! It will make you remember.
David	It will make me forget. Kiss me.
	(*There is a pause of hesitation, filled up by the Cathedral music from "Faust" surging up softly from below.*)
Vera	(*Slowly*) I will kiss you as we Russians kiss at Easter—the three kisses of peace. (*She kisses him three times on the mouth as in ritual solemnity.*)
David	(*Very calmly*) Easter was the date of the massacre—see! I am at peace.
Vera	God grant it endure! (*They stand quietly hand in hand.*) Look! How beautiful the sunset is after the storm!
	(*DAVID turns. The sunset, which has begun to grow beautiful just after VERA's entrance, has now reached its most magnificent moment; below there are narrow lines of saffron and pale gold, but above the whole sky is one glory of burning flame.*)
David	(*Prophetically exalted by the spectacle*) It is the fires of God round His Crucible. (*He drops her hand and points downward.*) There she lies, the great Melting Pot—listen! Can't you hear the roaring and the bubbling? There gapes her mouth (*he*

points east)—the harbour where a thousand mammoth feed-
ers come from the ends of the world to pour in their human
freight. Ah, what a stirring and a seething! Celt and Latin,
Slav and Teuton, Greek and Syrian,—black and yellow—

Vera   (*Softly, nestling to him*) Jew and Gentile—

David   Yes, East and West, and North and South, the palm and the
pine, the pole and the equator, the crescent and the cross—
how the great Alchemist melts and fuses them with his purg-
ing flame! Here shall they all unite to build the Republic of
Man and the Kingdom of God. Ah, Vera, what is the glory
of Rome and Jerusalem where all nations and races come to
worship and look back, compared with the glory of America,
where all races and nations come to labour and look forward!
(*He raises his hands in benediction over the shining city.*) Peace,
peace, to all ye unborn millions, fated to fill this giant continent—the God of our *children* give you Peace.

(*An instant's solemn pause. The sunset is swiftly fading, and the
vast panorama is suffused with a more restful twilight, to which
the many-gleaming lights of the town add the tender poetry of
the night. Far back, like a lonely, guiding star, twinkles over the
darkening water the torch of the Statue of Liberty. From below
comes up the softened sound of voices and instruments joining in
"My Country, 'tis of Thee."*)

(*The curtain falls slowly.*)

Appendixes

The following appendixes were prepared by Zangwill for the 1914 republication of *The Melting Pot.*

APPENDIX A

The Melting Pot in Action
Aliens Admitted to the United States
in the Year Ended June 30th, 1913

African (black)	9,734	**Brought forward**	875,975
Armenian	9,554	Japanese	11,672
Bohemian and Moravian	11,852	Korean	74
		Lithuanian	25,529
Bulgarian, Servian, Montenegrin	10,083	Magyar	33,561
Chinese	3,487	Mexican	15,495
Croatian and Slavonian	44,754	Pacific Islander	27
Cuban	6,121	Polish	185,707
Dalmatian, Bosnian, Herzegovinian	4,775	Portuguese	14,631
		Roumanian	14,780
Dutch and Flemish	18,746	Russian	58,380
East Indian	233	Ruthenian (Russniak)	39,405
English	100,062	Scandinavian	51,650
Finnish	14,920	Scotch	31,434
French	26,509	Slovak	29,094
German	101,764	Spanish	15,017
Greek	40,933	Spanish-American	3,409
Hebrew	105,826	Syrian	10,019
Irish	48,103	Turkish	2,132
Italian (north)	54,171	Welsh	3,922
Italian (south)	264,348	West Indian (except Cuban)	2,302
Carried forward	875,975	Other peoples	3,512
		Total	1,427,227

APPENDIX B

The Pogrom
(I) A RUSSIAN ON ITS REASONS
[From *The Nation*, November 15, 1913]

It is now over thirty years since the crew of the sinking ship of Russian abso-
lutism first tried this unworthy weapon to save their failing cause. This was
when Plehve organised an anti-Semitic agitation and Jewish pogroms in 1883
in South Russia, where the Jews formed almost the only merchant class in the
villages, and where the ignorant peasants, together with some crafty Russian
tradesmen, had a natural grudge against them. The result was that the prevailing discontent of the masses was diverted against the Jews. A large public
meeting of protest was organised at that time in the London Mansion House,
the Lord Mayor taking the chair. English public opinion rightly appreciated
the value of this criminal method of using Jews as scapegoats for political
purposes. Now we see merely a further, and let us hope a final, development
of the same tactics. They have been used on many occasions since 1883. One
of the largest Jewish pogroms of the latest series in Kishineff in 1903 has
been clearly traced to the same experienced hand of Plehve, when the passive
attitude of the local administration and the military was explained by the
presence in the town of a mysterious colonel of the Imperial Gendarmerie
who arrived with secret orders and a large supply of pogrom literature from
St. Petersburg, and who organised the scum of the town population for the
purpose of looting and killing Jews.

The repulsive stories of further pogroms all over the country immediately
after the issue of the constitutional manifesto of October 17, 1905, are fresh
in the memory of the civilised world. At that time anti-Semitic doctrine was
openly preached, not only against Jews, but against the whole revolutionary
upheaval. Pogroms against both were organised under the same pretext of
saving the Tsar, the orthodoxy, and the Fatherland. Local police and military
officials had secret orders to abstain from interference with the looting and
murdering of Jews or "their hirelings." Processions of peaceful citizens and
children were trampled down by the Cossack horses, and the Cossacks received formal thanks from high quarters for their excellent exploits.

N. W. Tchaykovsky.

(II) A NURSE ON ITS RESULTS
[From *Public Health*, Nurses' Quarterly, Cleveland, Ohio, October 1913]

I was a Red Cross nurse on the battlefield.

The words of the chief doctor of the Jewish Hospital of Odessa still ring in my ears. When the telephone message came, he said, "Moldvanko is running in blood; send nurses and doctors." This meant that the Pogrom (massacre) was going on.

Dr. P—— came into the wards with these words: "Sisters, there is no time for weeping. Those who have no one dependent upon them, come. Put on your white surgical gowns, and the red cross. Make ready to go on the battlefield at once. God knows how many of our sisters and brothers are already killed." Tears were just running down his cheeks as he spoke. In a minute twelve nurses and eight doctors had volunteered. There was one Red Cross nurse who was in bed waiting to be operated on. She got up and made ready too. Nobody could keep her from going with us. "Where my sisters and brothers fall, there shall I fall," she said, and with these words, jumped into the ambulance and went on to the City Hospital with us. There they had better equipment, and they sent out three times as many nurses as the Jewish Hospital. At the City Hospital they hung silver crosses about our necks. We wore the silver crosses so that we would not be recognised as Jewish by the Holiganes (Hooligans).

Then we went to Molorosiskia Street in the Moldvanko (slums). We could not see, for the feathers were flying like snow. The blood was already up to our ankles on the pavement and in the yards. The uproar was deafening but we could hear the Holiganes' fierce cries of "Hooray, kill the Jews," on all sides. It was enough to hear such words. They could turn your hair grey, but we went on. We had no time to think. All our thoughts were to pick up wounded ones, and to try to rescue some uninjured ones. We succeeded in rescuing some uninjured who were in hiding. We put bandages on them to make it appear that they were wounded. We put them in the ambulance and carried them to the hospital, too. So at the Jewish Hospital we had five thousand injured and seven thousand uninjured to feed and protect for two weeks. Some were left without homes, without clothes, and children were even without parents.

My dear reader, I want to tell you one thing before I describe the scenes of the massacre any further; do not think that you are reading a story which could not happen! No, I want you to know that everything you read is just exactly as it was. My hair is a little grey, but I am surprised it is not quite white after what I witnessed.

The procession of the Pogrom was led by about ten Catholic (Greek) Sisters with about forty or fifty of their school children. They carried ikons or pictures of Jesus and sang "God Save the Tsar." They were followed by a crowd containing hundreds of men and women murderers yelling "Bey Zhida," which means "Kill the Jews." With these words they ran into the yards where there were fifty or a hundred tenants. They rushed in like tigers. Soon they began to throw children out of the windows of the second, third, and fourth stories. They would take a poor, innocent six-months-old baby, who could not possibly have done any harm in this world, and throw it down on to the pavement. You can imagine it could not live after it struck the ground, but this did not satisfy the stony-hearted murderers. They then rushed up to the child, seized it and broke its little arm and leg bones into three or four pieces, then wrung its neck too. They laughed and yelled, so carried away with pleasure at their successful work.

I do wish a few Americans could have been there to see, and they would know what America is, and what it means to live in the United States. It was not enough for them to open up a woman's abdomen and take out the child which she carried, but they took time to stuff the abdomen with straw and fill it up. Can you imagine human beings able to do such things? I do not think anybody could, because I could not imagine it myself when a few years before I read the news of the massacre in Kishineff, but now I have seen it with my own eyes. It was not enough for them to cut out an old man's tongue and cut off his nose, but they drove nails into the eyes also. You wonder how they had enough time to carry away everything of value—money, gold, silver, jewels—and still be able to do so much fancy killing, but oh, my friends, all the time for three days and three nights was theirs.

The last day and night it poured down rain, and you would think that might stop them, but no, they worked just as hard as ever. We could wear shoes no longer. Our feet were swollen, so we wore rubbers over our stockings, and in this way worked until some power was able to stop these horrors. They not only killed, but they had time to abuse young girls of twelve and fourteen years of age, who died immediately after being operated upon.

I remember what happened to my own class-mates. They were two who came from a small town to Odessa to become midwives. These girls ran to the school to hide themselves as it was a government school, and they knew the Holiganes would not dare to come in there. But the dean of the school had ordered they should not be admitted, because they were Jewish, as if they had different blood running in their veins. So when they came, the watchman refused to open the doors, according to his instructions. The crowd of Holiganes found them outside the doors of the hospital. They abused them right there in the middle of the street. One was eighteen years old and the other was twenty. One died after the operation and the other went insane from shame.

Some people ask why the Jews did not leave everything and go away. But how could they go and where could they go? The murderers were scattered throughout the Jewish quarters. All they could do was hide where they were in the cellars and garrets. The Holiganes searched them out and killed them where they were hidden. Others may ask, why did they not resist the murderers with their knives and pistols? The grown men organised by the second day. They were helped by the Vigilantes, too, who brought them arms. The Vigilantes were composed of students at the University and high-school boys, and also the strongest man from each Jewish family. There were a good many Gentiles among the students who belonged to the Vigilantes because they wanted justice. So on the second day the Vigilantes stood before the doors and gave resistance to the murderers. Some will ask where were the soldiers and the police? They were sent to protect, but on arriving, joined in with the murderers. However, the police put disguises on over their uniforms. Later, when they were brought to the hospital with other wounded, we found their uniforms underneath their disguises.

When the Vigilantes took their stations, the scene was like a battlefield. Bullets were flying from both sides of the Red Cross carriages. We expected to be killed any minute, but notwithstanding, we rushed wherever there were shots heard in order to carry away the wounded. Whenever we arrived we shouted "Red Cross, Red Cross," in order to help make them realise we were not Vigilantes. Then they would stop and let us pick up the wounded. They did this on account of their own wounded.

The Vigilantes could not stop the butchery entirely because they were not strong enough in numbers. On the fourth day, the Jewish people of Odessa, through Dr. P—, succeeded in communicating to the Mayor of a different State. Soldiers from outside, strangers to the murderers, came in and took charge of the city. The city was put under martial law until order could be restored.

On the fifth day the doctors and nurses were called to the cemetery, where there were four hundred unidentified dead. Their friends and relatives who came to search for them were crazed and hysterical and needed our attention.

Wives came to look for husbands, parents hunting children, a mother for her only son, and so on. It took eight days to identify the bodies and by that time four hundred of the wounded had died, and so we had eight hundred to bury. If you visit Odessa, you will be shown two long graves, about one hundred feet long, beside the Jewish Cemetery. There lie the victims of the massacre. Among them are Gentile Vigilantes whose parents asked that they be buried with the Jews. . . .

Another case I knew was that of a married man. He left his wife, who was pregnant, and three children, to go on a business trip. When he got back the massacre had occurred. His home was in ruins, his family gone. He went to the hospital, then to the cemetery. There he found his wife with her abdomen stuffed with straw, and his three children dead. It simply broke his heart, and he lost his mind. But he was harmless, and was to be seen wandering about the hospital as though in search of some one, and daily he grew more thin and suffering.

This story is told in the hope that Americans will appreciate the safety and freedom in which they live and that they will help others to gain that freedom.

APPENDIX C

The Story of Daniel Melsa

Another example of Nature aping Art is afforded by the romantic story of Daniel Melsa, a young Russo-Jewish violinist who has carried audiences by storm in Berlin, Paris and London, and who had arranged to go to America last November [probably referring to 1913]. The following extract from an interview in the *Jewish Chronicle* of January 24, 1913, shows the curious co-incidence between his beginnings and David Quixano's:

"Melsa is not yet twenty years of age, but he looks somewhat older. He is of slight build and has a sad expression, which increased to al-most a painful degree when recounting some of his past experiences. He seems singularly devoid of any affectation, while modesty is obvi-ously the keynote of his nature.

"After some persuasion, Melsa put aside his reticence, and, com-plying with the request, outlined briefly his career, the early part of which, he said, was overshadowed by a great tragedy. He was born in Warsaw, and, at the age of three, his parents moved to Lodz, where shortly after a private tutor was engaged for him.

"'Although I exhibited a passion for music quite early, I did not receive any lessons on the subject till my seventh birthday, but before that my father obtained a cheap violin for me upon which I was soon able to play simple melodies by ear.'

"By chance a well-known professor of the town heard him play, and so impressed was he with the talent exhibited by the boy that he advised the father to have him educated. Acting upon this advice, as far as limited means allowed, tutors were engaged, and so much progress did he make that at the age of nine he was admitted to the local Conservatorium of Professor Grudzinski, where he remained two years. It was at the age of eleven that a great calamity overtook the family, his father and sister falling victims to the pogroms.

"Melsa's story runs as follows:

"'It was in June of 1905, at the time of the pogroms, when one afternoon my father, accompanied by my little sister, ventured out into the street, from which they never returned. They were both killed,' he added sadly, 'by Cossacks. A week later I found my sister in a Christian churchyard riddled with bullets, but I have not been able to trace the remains of my father, who must have been buried in some out-of-the-way place. During this awful period my mother and myself lived in imminent danger of our lives, and it was only the recollection of my playing that saved us also falling a prey to the vodka-besodden Cossacks.'"

APPENDIX D

Beilis and America

The close relation in Jewish thought between Russo-Jewish persecution, and America as the land of escape from it is well illustrated by the recent remarks of the *Jewish Chronicle* on the future of the victim of the Blood-Ritual Prosecution in Kieff. "So long as Beilis continues to live in Russia, his life is unsafe. The Black Hundreds, he himself says, have solemnly decided on his death, and we have seen, in the not distant past, that they can carry out diabolical plots of this description with complete immunity. . . . He would gladly go to America, provided he was sure of a living. The condition should not be difficult to fulfil, and if this victim of a barbarous *régime*—we cannot say latest victim, for, as we write, comes the news of an expulsion order against 1200 Jewish students of Kieff—should find a home and place under the sheltering wing of freedom, it would be a fitting ending to a painful chapter in our Jewish history."

That it is the natural ending even the Jew-baiting Russian organ, the *Novoe Vremya,* indirectly testifies, for it has published a sneering cartoon representing a number of Jews crowded on the Statue of Liberty to welcome the arrival of Beilis. One wonders that the Russian censor should have permitted the masses to become aware that Liberty exists on earth, if only in the form of a statue.

APPENDIX E

The Alien in the Melting Pot

Mr. Frederick J. Haskin has recently published in the *Chicago Daily News* the following graphic summary of what immigrants have done and do for the United States:

I am the immigrant.

Since the dawn of creation my restless feet have beaten new paths across the earth.

My uneasy bark has tossed on all seas.

My wanderlust was born of the craving for more liberty and a better wage for the sweat of my face.

I looked towards the United States with eyes kindled by the fire of ambition and heart quickened with new-born hope.

I approached its gates with great expectation.

I entered in with fine hopes.

I have shouldered my burden as the American man of all work.

I contribute eighty-five per cent. of all the labour in the slaughtering and meat-packing industries.

I do seven-tenths of the bituminous coal mining.

I do seventy-eight per cent. of all the work in the woollen mills.

I contribute nine-tenths of all the labour in the cotton mills.

I make nine-twentieths of all the clothing.

I manufacture more than half the shoes.

I build four-fifths of all the furniture.

I make half of the collars, cuffs, and shirts.

I turn out four-fifths of all the leather.

I make half the gloves.

I refine nearly nineteen-twentieths of the sugar.

I make half of the tobacco and cigars.

And yet, I am the great American problem.

When I pour out my blood on your altar of labour, and lay down my life as a sacrifice to your god of toil, men make no more comment than at the fall of a sparrow.

But my brawn is woven into the warp and woof of the fabric of your national being.

My children shall be your children and your land shall be my land because my sweat and my blood will cement the foundations of the America of To-Morrow.

If I can be fused into the body politic, the Melting-Pot will have stood the supreme test.

AFTERWORD

I

The Melting Pot is the third of the writer's plays to be published in book form, though the first of the three in order of composition. But unlike *The War God* and *The Next Religion,* which are dramatisations of the spiritual duels of our time, *The Melting Pot* sprang directly from the author's concrete experience as President of the Emigration Regulation Department of the Jewish Territorial Organisation, which, founded shortly after the great massacres of Jews in Russia, will soon have fostered the settlement of ten thousand Russian Jews in the West of the United States.

"Romantic claptrap," wrote Mr. A. B. Walkley in the *Times* of this "rhapsodising over music and crucibles and statues of Liberty." As if these things were not the homeliest of realities, and rhapsodising the natural response to them of the Russo-Jewish psychology, incurably optimist. The statue of Liberty is a large visible object at the mouth of New York harbour; the crucible, if visible only to the eye of imagination like the inner reality of the sunrise to the eye of Blake, is none the less a roaring and flaming actuality. These things are as substantial, if not as important, as Adeline Genée and Anna Pavlova, the objects of Mr. Walkley's own rhapsodising. Mr. Walkley, never having lacked Liberty, nor cowered for days in a cellar in terror of a howling mob, can see only theatrical exaggeration in the enthusiasm for a land of freedom, just as, never having known or never having had eyes to see the grotesque and tragic creatures existing all around us, he has doubted the reality of some of Balzac's creations. It is to be feared that for such a play as *The Melting Pot* Mr. Walkley is far from being the *Xapiels* of Aristotle. The ideal spectator must have known and felt more of life than Mr. Walkley, who resembles too much the library-fed man of letters whose denunciation by Walter Bagehot he himself quotes without suspecting *de te fabula narratur.* Even the critic, who has to deal with a refracted world, cannot dispense with primary experience of his own. For "the adventures of a Soul among masterpieces" it is not only necessary there should be masterpieces, there must also be a soul. Mr. Walkley, one of the wittiest of contemporary writers and within his urban range one of the wisest, can scarcely be accused of lacking a soul, though Mr. Bernard Shaw's long-enduring misconception of him as a brother in the spirit is one of the comedies of literature. But such spiritual vitality as Oxford failed to sterilise in him has been largely torpified by his profession of play-taster, with its divorcement from reality in the raw. His cry of "romantic claptrap" is merely the reaction of the club armchair to the "drums and tramplings" of the street. It is in fact (he will welcome an allusion to Dickens almost as much as one to Aristotle) the higher Podsnappery. "Thus happily acquainted with his own merit and importance, Mr. Podsnap settled that whatever he put behind him he put out of existence. . . . The world got up at eight, shaved close at a quarter past, breakfasted at nine, went to the City at ten, came home at half-past five, and dined at seven."

Mr. Roosevelt, with his multifarious American experience as soldier and cowboy, hunter and historian, police-captain and President, comes far nearer the ideal spectator, for this play at least, than Mr. Walkley. Yet his enthusiasm for it has been dismissed by our critic as "stupendous *naïveté*." Mr. Roosevelt apparently falls under that class of "people who knowing no rules, are at the mercy of their undisciplined taste," which Mr. Walkley excludes altogether from his classification of critics, in despite of Dr. Johnson's opinion that "natural judges" are only second to "those who know but are above the rules." It is comforting, therefore, to find Mr. Augustus Thomas, the famous American playwright, who is familiar with the rules to the point of contempt, chivalrously associating himself, in defence of a British rival, with Mr. Roosevelt's "stupendous *naïveté*."

"Mr. Zangwill's 'rhapsodising' over music and crucibles and statues of Liberty is," says Mr. Thomas, a very effective use of a most potent symbolism, and I have never seen men and women more sincerely stirred than the audience at *The Melting Pot*. The impulses awakened by the Zangwill play were those of wide human sympathy, charity, and compassion; and, for my own part, I would rather retire from the theatre and retire from all direct or indirect association with journalism than write down the employment of these factors by Mr. Zangwill as mere claptrap."

"As a work of art for art's sake," also wrote Mr. William Archer, "the play simply does not exist." He added: "but Mr. Zangwill would not dream of appealing to such a standard." Mr. Archer had the misfortune to see the play in New York side by side with his more cynical *confrère,* and thus his very praise has an air of apologia to Mr. Walkley and the great doctrine of "art for art's sake." It would almost seem as if he even takes a "work of art" and a "work of art for art's sake" as synonymous. Nothing, in fact, could be more inartistic. "Art for art's sake" is one species of art, whose right to existence the author has amply recognised in other works. (*The King of Schnorrers* was even read aloud by Oscar Wilde to a duchess.) But he roundly denies that art is any the less artistic for being inspired by life, and seeking in its turn to inspire life. Such a contention is tainted by the very Philistinism it would repudiate, since it seeks a negative test of art in something outside art—to wit, purpose, whose presence is surely as irrelevant to art as its absence. The only test of art is artistic quality, and this quality occurs perhaps more frequently than it is achieved as in the words of the Hebrew prophets, or the vision of a slum at night, the former consciously aiming at something quite different, the latter achieving its beauty in utter unconsciousness.

II

It will be seen from the official table of immigration that the Russian Jew is only one and not even the largest of the fifty elements that, to the tune of nearly a million and a half a year are being fused in the greatest "Melting Pot" the world has ever known; but if he has been selected as the typical immigrant, it is because he alone of all the fifty has no homeland. Some few other races, such as the Armenians, are almost equally devoid of political power, and, in consequence, equally obnoxious to massacre; but except the gipsy, whose essence is to be homeless, there is no other race—black, white, red, or yellow—that has not remained at least a majority of the population in some area of its own. There is none, therefore, more in need of a land of liberty, none to whose future it is more vital that America should preserve that spirit of William Penn which President Wilson has so nobly characterised. And there is assuredly none which has more valuable elements to contribute to the ethnic and psychical amalgam of the people of to-morrow.

The process of American amalgamation is not assimilation or simple surrender to the dominant type, as is popularly supposed, but an all-round give-and-take by which the final type may be enriched or impoverished. Thus the intelligent reader will have remarked how the somewhat anti-Semitic Irish servant of the first act talks Yiddish herself in the fourth. Even as to the ultimate language of the United States, it is unreasonable to suppose that American, though fortunately protected by English literature, will not bear traces of the fifty languages now being spoken side by side with it, and of which this play alone presents scraps in German, French, Russian, Yiddish, Irish, Hebrew, and Italian.

That in the crucible of love, or even co-citizenship, the most violent antitheses of the past may be fused into a higher unity is a truth of both ethics and observation, and it was in order to present historic enmities at their extremes that the persecuted Jew of Russia and the persecuting Russian race have been taken for protagonists—"the fell incensèd points of mighty opposites."

The immigrant is, moreover, the toughest of all the white elements that have been poured into the American crucible, the race having, by its unique experience of several thousand years of exposure to alien majorities developed a salamandrine power of survival. And this asbestoid fibre is made even more fireproof by the anti-Semitism of American uncivilisation. Nevertheless, to suppose that America will remain permanently afflicted by all the old European diseases would be to despair of humanity, not to mention superhumanity.

III

Even the negrophobia is not likely to remain eternally at its present barbarous pitch. Mr. William Archer, who has won a new fame as student of that black problem, which is America's nemesis for her ancient slave-raiding, and who favours the creation of a Black State as one of the United States, observes: "It is noteworthy that neither David Quixano nor anyone else in the play makes the slightest reference to that inconvenient element in the crucible of God—the negro." This is an oversight of Mr. Archer's, for Baron Revendal defends the Jew-baiting of Russia by asking of an American: "Don't you lynch and roast your niggers?" And David Quixano expressly throws both "black and yellow" into the crucible. No doubt there is an instinctive antipathy which tends to keep the white man free from black blood, though this antipathy having been overcome by a large minority in all the many periods and all the many countries of their contiguity, it is equally certain that there are at work forces of attraction as well as of repulsion, and that even upon the negro the "Melting Pot" of America will not fail to act in a measure as it has acted on the Red Indian, who has found it almost as facile to mate with his white neighbours as with his black. Indeed, it is as much social prejudice as racial antipathy that to-day divides black and white in the New World; and Sir Sydney Olivier has recorded that in Jamaica the white is far more on his guard and his dignity against the half-white than against the all-black, while in Guiana, according to Sir Harry Johnston in his great work "The Negro in the New World," it is the half-white that, in his turn, despises the black and succeeds in marrying still further white-wards. It might have been thought that the dark-white races on the northern shore of the Mediterranean—the Spaniards, Sicilians, &c.—who have already been crossed with the sons of Ham from its southern shore, would, among the American immigrants, be the natural links towards the fusion of white and black, but a similar instinct of pride and peril seems to hold them back. But whether the antipathy in America be a race instinct or a social prejudice, the accusations against the black are largely panic-born myths, for the alleged repulsive smell of the negro is consistent with being shaved by him, and the immorality of the negress is consistent with her control of the nurseries of the South. The devil is not so black nor the black so devilish as he is painted. This is not to deny that the prognathous face is an ugly and undesirable type of countenance or that it connotes a lower average of intellect and ethics, or that white and black are as yet too far apart for profitable fusion. Melanophobia, or fear of the black, may be pragmatically as valuable a racial defence for the white as the counter-instinct of philoleucosis, or love of the white, is a force of racial uplifting for the black. But neither colour has succeeded in monopolising all the virtues and graces in its specific evolution from the common ancestral ape, and a superficial acquaintance with the work of Dr. Arthur Keith teaches that if the black man is nearer the ape in some ways (having even the remains of throat-pouches), the white man is nearer in other ways (as in his greater hairiness).

And besides being, as Sir Sydney Olivier says, "a matrix of emotional and spiritual energies that have yet to find their human expression," the African negro has obviously already not a few valuable ethnic elements—joy of life, love of colour, keen senses, beautiful voice, and ear for music—contributions that might somewhat compensate for the dragging-down of the white and, in small doses at least, might one day prove a tonic to an anaemic and art-less America. A musician like Coleridge-Taylor is no despicable product of the "Melting Pot," while the negroes of genius whom the writer has been privileged to know—men like Henry O. Tanner, the painter, and Paul Laurence Dunbar, the poet—show the potentialities of the race even without white admixture; and as men of this stamp are capable of attracting cultured white wives, the fusing process, beginning at the top with types like these, should be far less unwelcome than that which starts with the dregs of both races. But the negroid hair and complexion being, in Mendelian language, "dominant," these black traits are not easy to eliminate from the hybrid posterity; and in view of all the unpleasantness, both immediate and contingent, that attends the blending of colours, only heroic souls on either side should dare the adventure of intermarriage. Blacks of this temper, however, would serve their race better by making Liberia a success or building up an American negro State, as Mr. William Archer recommends, or at least asserting their rights as American citizens in that sub-tropical South which without their labour could never have been opened up. Meantime, however scrupulously and justifiably America avoids physical intermarriage with the negro, the comic spirit cannot fail to note the spiritual miscegenation which, while clothing, commercialising, and Christianising the ex-African, has given "rag-time" and the sex-dances that go to it, first to white America and thence to the whole white world.

The action of the crucible is thus not exclusively physical—a consideration particularly important as regards the Jew. The Jew may be Americanised and the American Judaised without any gamic interaction.

IV

Among the Jews *The Melting Pot*, though it has in some instances served to interpret to each other the old generation and the new, has more frequently been misunderstood by both. While a distinguished Christian clergyman wrote that it was "calculated to do for the Jewish race what 'Uncle Tom's Cabin' did for the coloured man," the Jewish pulpits of America have resounded with denunciation of its supposed solution of the Jewish problem by dissolution. As if even a play with a purpose could do more than suggest and interpret! It is true that its leading figure, David Quixano, advocates absorption in America, but even he is speaking solely of the American Jews and asks his uncle why, if he objects to the dissolving process, he did not work for a separate Jewish land. He is not offering a panacea for the Jewish problem, universally applicable. But he urges that the conditions offered to the Jew in America are without parallel throughout the world.

And, in sooth, the Jew is here citizen of a republic without a State religion—a republic resting, moreover, on the same simple principles of justice and equal rights as the Mosaic Commonwealth from which the Puritan Fathers drew their inspiration. In America, therefore, the Jew, by a roundabout journey from Zion, has come into his own again. It is by no mere accident that when an inscription was needed for the colossal statue of Liberty in New York Harbour, that "Mother of Exiles" whose torch lights the entrance to the New Jerusalem, the best expression of the spirit of Americanism was found in the sonnet of the Jewess, Emma Lazarus:

> *Give me your tired, your poor,*
> *Your huddled masses yearning to breathe free,*
> *The wretched refuse of your teeming shore.*
> *Send these, the homeless, tempest-tost to me,*
> *I lift my lamp beside the golden door.*

And if, alas! passing through the golden door, the Jew finds his New Jerusalem as much a caricature by the crumbling of its early ideals as the old became by the fading of the visions of Isaiah and Amos, he may find his mission in fighting for the preservation of the original Hebraic pattern. In this fight he will not be alone, and intermarriage with his fellow-crusaders in the new Land of Promise will naturally follow wherever, as with David Quixano and Vera Revendal, no theological differences divide. There will be neither Jew nor Greek. Intermarriage, wherever there is social intimacy, will follow, even when the parties stand in opposite religious camps; but this is less advisable as leading to a house divided against itself and to dissension in the upbringing of the children. It is only when a common outlook has been reached, transcending the old doctrinal differences, that intermarriage is denuded of those latent discords which the instinct of mankind divines, and which keep even Catholic and Protestant wisely apart.

These discords, together with the prevalent anti-Semitism and his own ingrained persistence, tend to preserve the Jew even in the "Melting Pot," so that his dissolution must be necessarily slower than that of the similar aggregations of Germans, Italians, or Poles. But the process for all is the same, however tempered by specific factors. Beginning as broken-off bits of Germany, Italy, or Poland, with newspapers and theatres in German, Italian, or Polish, these colonies gradually become Americanized, their vernaculars, even when jealously cherished, become a mere medium for American conceptions of life; while in the third generation the child is ashamed both of its parents and their lingo, the newspapers dwindle in circulation, the theatres languish. The reality of this process has been denied by no less distinguished an American than Dr. Charles Eliot, ex-President of Harvard University, whose prophecy of Jewish solidarity in America and of the contribution of Judaism to the world's future is more optimistic than my own. Dr. Eliot points to the still unmelted heaps of racial matter, without suspecting—although he is a chemist—that their semblance of solidity is only kept up by the constant immigration of similar atoms to the base to replace those liquefied at the apex. Once America slams her doors, the crucible will roar like a closed furnace.

Heaven forbid, however, that the doors shall be slammed for centuries yet. The notion that the few millions of people in America have a moral right to exclude others is monstrous. Exclusiveness may have some justification in countries, especially when old and well-populated; but for continents like the United States—or for the matter of that Canada and Australia—to mistake themselves for mere countries is an intolerable injustice to the rest of the human race.

The exclusion of criminals even is as impossible in practice as the exclusion of the sick and ailing is unchristian. Infinitely more important were it to the gates of *birth* free from undesirables. As for the exclusion of the able-bodied, whether illiterate or literate, that is sheer economic madness in so empty a continent, especially with the Panama Canal to divert them to the least developed States. Fortunately, any serious restriction will avenge itself not only by the stagnation of many of the States, but by the paralysis of the great liners which depend on steerage passengers, without whom freights and fares will rise and saloon passengers be docked of their sailing facilities. Meantime the inquisition at Ellis Island has to its account cruelties no less atrocious than the ancient Spanish—cruelties that only flash into momentary prominence when some luxurious music-hall lady of dubious morals has a taste of the barbarities meted out daily to blameless and hard-working refugees from oppression or hunger, who, having staked their all on the great adventure, find themselves hustled back, penniless and heartbroken, to the Old World.

V

Whether any country will ever again be based like those of the Old World upon a unity of race or religion is a matter of doubt. New England, of course, like Pennsylvania and Maryland, owes its inception to religion, but the original impulse has long been submerged by purely economic pressures. And the same motley immigration from the Old World is building up the bulk of the coming countries. At most, the dominant language gives a semblance of unity and serves to attract a considerable stream of immigrants who speak it, as of Portuguese to Brazil, Spaniards to the Argentine. But the chief magnet remains economic, for Brazil draws six times as many Italians as Portuguese, and the Argentine two and a half times as many Italians as Spanish. It may be urged, of course, that the Italian gravitation to these countries is still a matter of race, and that, in the absence of an El Dorado of his own, the Italian is attracted towards States that are at least Latin. But though Brazil and the Argentine be predominantly Latin, the minority of Germans, Austrians, and Swiss is by no means insignificant. The great modern steamship, in fact—supplemented by its wandering and seductive agent—is playing the part in the world formerly played by invasions and crusades, while the economic immigrant is more and more replacing the refugee, just as the purely commercial company working under native law is replacing the Chartered Company which was a law to itself. How small a part in the modern movement is played by patriotism proper may be seen from the avidity with which the farmers of the United States cross the borders to Canada to obtain the large free holdings which enable them to sell off their American properties. How little the proudest tradition counts against the environment is shown in the shame felt by Argentine-born children for the English spoken by their British parents.

The difference in the method of importing the ingredients makes thus no difference to the action of the crucible. Though the peoples now in process of formation in the New World are being recruited by mainly economic forces, it may be predicted they will ultimately harden into homogeneity of race, if not even of belief. For internationalism in religion seems to be again receding in favour of national religions (if, indeed, these were ever more than superficially superseded), at any rate in favour of nationalism raised into religion.

If racial homogeneity has not yet been evolved completely even in England—and, of course, the tendency can never be more than asymptotic—it is because cheap and easy transport and communication, with freedom of economic movement, have been late developments and are still far from perfect. Hence, there has never been a thorough shake-up and admixture of elements, so that certain counties and corners have retained types and breeds peculiar to them. But with the ever-growing interconnection of all parts of the country, and with the multiplication of labour bureaux, these breeds and types will be—alas, for local colour!—increasingly absorbed in the general mass. For fusion and unification are part of the historic life-process. "Normans and Saxons and Danes" are we here in England, yes and Huguenots and Flemings and Gascons and Angevins and Jews and many other things.

In fact, according to Sir Harry Johnston, there is hardly an ethnic element that has not entered into the Englishman, including even the missing link, as the Piltdown skull would seem to testify. The earlier discovery at Galley Hill showed Britannia rising from the apes with an extinct Tasmanian type, not unlike the surviving aboriginal Australian. Then the west of Britain was invaded by a negroid type from France followed by an Eskimo type of which traces are still to be seen in the West of Ireland and parts of Scotland. Next came the true Mediterranean white man, the Iberian, with dark hair and eyes and a white skin and then the round-headed people of the Bronze Age, probably Asiatic. And then the Gael, the long-headed, fair-haired Aryan, who ruled by iron and whose Keltic vocabulary was tinged with Iberian, and who was followed by the Brython or Belgian. And, at some unknown date, we have to allow for the invasion of North Britain by another Germanic type, the Caledonian, which would seem to have been a Norse stock, foreshadowing the later Norman Conquest. And, as if this mish-mash was not confusion enough, came to make it worse confounded the Roman conquerors, trailing like a mantle of many colours the subject-races of their far-flung Empire.

Is it wonderful if the crucible, capable of fusing such a motley of types into "the true-born Briton," should be melting up its Jews like old silver? The comparison belongs to Mr. Walkley, who was more moved by the beauty of the old and the pathos of its passing than by the resplendence of the new, and who seemed to forget that it is for the dramatist to register both impartially—their conflict constituting another of those spiritual duels which are peculiarly his affair. Jews are, unlike negroes, a "recessive" type, whose physical traits tend to disappear in the blended off-spring. There does not exist in England to-day a single representative of the Jewish families whom Cromwell admitted, though their lineage may be traced in not a few noble families. Thus every country has been and is a "Melting Pot." But America, exhibiting the normal fusing process magnified many thousand diameters and diversified beyond all historic experience, and fed not by successive waves of immigration but by a hodge-podge of simultaneous hordes, is, in Bacon's phrase, an "ostensive instance" of a universal phenomenon. America is *the* "Melting Pot."

Her people has already begun to take on such a complexion of its own, it is already so emphatically tending to a new race, crossed with every European type, that the British illusion of a cousinly Anglo-Saxon people with whom war is unthinkable is sheer wilful blindness. Even to-day, while the mixture is still largely mechanical not chemical, the Anglo element is only preponderant; it is very far from being the sum total.

VI

While our sluggish and sensual English stage has resisted and even burked the writer's attempt to express in terms of the theatre our European problems of war and religion, and to interpret through art the years of the modern, years of the unperformed," it remains to be acknowledged with gratitude that this play, designed to bring home to America both its comparative rawness and emptiness and its true significance and potentiality for history and civilisation, has been universally acclaimed by Americans as a revelation of Americanism, despite that it contains only one native-born American character, and that a bad one. Played throughout the length and breadth of the States since its original production in 1908, given, moreover, in Universities and Women's Colleges, passing through edition after edition in book form, cited by preachers and journalists, politicians and Presidential candidates, even calling into existence a "Melting Pot" Club in Boston, it has had the happy fortune to contribute its title to current thought, and, in the testimony of Jane Addams, to "perform a great service to America by reminding us of the high hopes of the founders of the Republic."

I. Z.
January 1914

The King of Schnorrers

Introductory Essay

The 1899 *Jewish Year Book,* published in London, included a comprehensive "Glossary of Jewish Terms" that defined the term "schnorrer" as follows: "The technical name for a Jewish beggar, who is distinguished from all other beggars by his Chutzpa." It went on to explain, "Duties to Jews are their privileges . . . , consequently your Jewish schnorrer regards himself as doing you a favour in giving you the opportunity of performing the duty of helping the poor, and his gratitude is considerably mingled with a feeling of condescension. These characteristic traits have been admirably portrayed in Mr. Zangwill's 'King of Schnorrers.'"[1] Such incorporation of Zangwill's fictional work into a cultural/lexical definition, which also occurs in a more detailed entry for "schnorrer" in *The Jewish Encyclopedia,* demonstrates the extent to which this type was seen through the author's fanciful lens. This resulted in a fusion of fact and hyperbole and helped to establish the schnorrer as a mythologized Jewish figure.[2] Following the popularity of his novella, *The King of Schnorrers,* published in 1893, the word "schnorrer" entered the English language, where it has taken permanent root. Dictionaries usually offer "beggar" as a synonym, which although technically correct is also reductive and devoid of cultural specificity. In his essay on "Language and Jewish Life," Zangwill mused on the intranslatability of the term and humorously relegated it to a gallery of "humble or sordid" occupations that transcended their lowly status, at least in the eyes of their practitioners. He joked that the "larger brotherhood of Israel" made every Jew "the equal of his superiors without robbing him of his natural superiority."[3]

Zangwill had been fascinated with schnorrers since his early days with the *Jewish Standard,* when as a twenty-two-year-old he lamented the disappearance of this "picturesque apparition" from the communal landscape and suggested a scholarly work on schnorrers, to which he contributed two entertaining episodes.[4] Schnorrer anecdotes also appear in his novel *Children of the Ghetto,* which he wrote at nearly the same time as *Schnorrers.* A correspondence between the two works can be found in the intrinsic similarity between the characters of Melchitsedek Pinchas and Manasseh Bueno Barsillai Azevedo Da Costa, both larger-than-life cadgers who combine a measure of erudition or artistic talents with a grandiloquent sense of self-importance and entitlement that justifies the fleecing of lesser mortals. In his entertaining essay "In Defence of Gambling," written in the early 1890s, the young Zangwill expressed an instinctive sympathy for the creative panhandler: "A forlorn, shabby creature, pathetically spruced up, arrives from a ten-mile tramp. He has been a journalist or a poet, but owing to this or that he is on his beamends. He has eaten nothing for two days. His wife is dying, his children are weeping for food. His voice breaks beautifully as he tells me I am his last hope." "What is to be done?" Zangwill asks. His answer: "to give always."[5] For there are two possibilities: either the man is in genuine need, or he is a gifted performer who has composed, edited, and directed his own script, spruced it up with affective details, and highlighted its delivery with carefully devised costumes and props. The vagabond con man, then, is to be entertained as a fellow artist whose performance merits compensation for its careful crafting, just like a stage actor. On the surface, this jolly approbation seems like no more than the flippant wisecrack of a young Victorian bohemian, but it also bespeaks Zangwill's lifelong compassion for the marginalized denizens of society. "Powers and principalities he could tempestuously assail," said Louis Golding, his friend and literary heir, "but if he hurt the newspaper's-boy's feelings, or the plumber's, he was miserable for days."[6]

Zangwill's performative interpretation of the schnorrer was gleefully espoused by Leopold Greenberg, editor of the *Jewish Chronicle,* who in a 1924 column told the story of a man who had recently been sentenced to six weeks' hard labor and recommended for deportation for begging at his own son's wedding.[7] Apprehended with two hundred pounds on him, a small fortune back then, the man explained to the court that he was not motivated by desperate need, but that begging was his avocation. Under his pen name, Mentor, Greenberg wrote:

> What, however, puzzles me, is why this man met the common fate of an ordinary beggar, just as if some physical deformity or the most pressing penury compelled him to seek alms. In such cases, circumstances over which the beggar has little, or perhaps no, control induce his way of gaining a living. But apparently with this man, who could at one moment be the well-dressed, proud father of a son entering

into the bonds of matrimony, and at the next a piteous supplicant for *Tsedakah* [charity], what made him a beggar was a well thought out and clever plan, in which many of the faculties that go to adorn the profession of actor and most of those that make a business man were exhibited in full force. It seems a pity to reward genius of this sort by imprisonment and deportation. Many an actor with less capacity for make-up and characterisation than this remarkable *Schnorrer,* has from popular prosceniums won the applause and *encores* of thronged audiences. And many a man with much less business acumen than this beggar evidently possesses, has become what in these days it is fashionable to term either a bloated Capitalist or a profiteer. There really ought to be a society for the protection of talent from such mere social conventions as this man fell foul of!⁸

Often the subject of jokes that ridiculed their reluctance to engage in real work and their elevated notion of entitlement, schnorrers were in fact products of devastation. The so-called schnorrer period, a phrase coined by Joseph Jacobs, began after the catastrophic Chmielnicki massacres (1648–1649), when more than one hundred thousand Polish Jews were slaughtered, some three hundred communities were destroyed, and thousands of survivors were reduced to total destitution. As they were fleeing westward, many of the refugees headed to Germany and Western Europe, their livelihood depending on the generosity of local Jewish communities. In his study of Jewish beggary in Germany, Ahron Bornstein makes the point that although the word "schnorrer" derives from German, it was a term used exclusively for Jewish beggars. He traces the etymology of the word to "schnurre," meaning a comic tale, a joke, a story, and describes the wandering "schnorrers," or "storytellers," as an established institution in German Jewish communal life.⁹ The interaction between the mercurial wanderers and their local benefactors was unique. Schnorrers relied on native residents to be taken in for temporary room and board and charitable donations. In return, they regaled their hosts with tales of their journeys, news of world affairs, and the latest from the Jewish communities they had visited. Over time they gained a reputation for humor, sauciness, and a measure of erudition. Poet Jakob Lowenberg (1856–1929) wrote about the beggars who used to frequent his hometown: "We were embarrassed in front of our Christian friends that the filthy, dirty, rag-clad beggars were Jews. On the Sabbath my father would invite them to the Sabbath meal and would discuss with them Talmudic issues. It became clear to me that these Polish Jews had great spiritual qualities."¹⁰ Over time the term "schnorrer" expanded to refer to local perennial Talmudic students of unspecified skill who were given a small allowance by Jews engaged in secular pursuits.

When Zangwill was a young man, Jewish charity work had been largely systematized. One-on-one schnorring was frowned upon, and with growing secularization schnorrers were increasingly portrayed as uppity and lazy parasites who made their Friday collection rounds with the persistence of tax collectors. Still, they enjoyed a certain mystique, and stories, anecdotes, and jokes about them abounded and were reproduced in various anthologies of Jewish humor, even finding their way into Freud's *Jokes and Their Relation to the Unconscious.*[11] Zangwill made good use of this folkloristic material, which may explain the enormous popularity of *The King of Schnorrers* with acculturated Jewish readers of his day. In his 1977 autobiography, *From Berlin to Jerusalem,* the renowned scholar Gershom Scholem mentions the book as one of only two works of Jewish fiction found in his parents' library.[12] As with *Children of the Ghetto,* many Jewish readers savored the delectable tale yet were discomfited by the idea that it would be read by Gentiles. A highly favorable review of the book that appeared in 1894 in the *American Hebrew* concluded with the comforting information that Zangwill was about to "abandon this field" of ghetto literature in the future. Many, it said, would "be glad to hear of it," for despite the merit of his work, "they doubt the wisdom of exposing to vulgar gaze, failings that are due to the peculiar environment of these people."[13]

Zangwill anchored his glamorized schnorrer in eighteenth-century London and the intracommunal tensions between the Sephardim, descendants of the Jews who were expelled from Spain and Portugal, who constituted the older and richer stratum of London Jewry, and the Ashkenazim, German-Slavonic Jews who were later arrivals, with considerably lesser means and social prestige. Although there was some cooperation between the two groups, they did not mingle and maintained separate social and religious institutions where they practiced their own rituals. The authorities of the Bevis Marks Synagogue, which served as the center of religious life for the Sephardic community since its establishment in 1698, zealously preserved their separateness by opposing intermarriage with Ashkenazim, whom they called "Tedescos" (Teutons, Germans). A scandal broke in 1745 when Jacob Israel Bernal, a warden at the synagogue, appealed to the Mahamad, the synagogue's Council of Elders, for permission to marry a "Tudesca." Approval was finally granted after long and heated discussion, but the wedding was stigmatized as a second-class affair. Despite the groom's position, which he had to renounce, none of the rabbis or cantors of Bevis Marks were allowed to attend, the bridegroom was not given the traditional honor of being called to the Torah, no offering was given in his honor, and no celebration took place inside the synagogue.[14] Increased liberalization set in at the beginning of the nineteenth century when members of the aristocratic Montefiore and Moccatta families married women with such prominent Ashkenazi last names as Rothschild and Goldsmid.

Zangwill was drawn to the historical background of eighteenth-century London Jewry for personal and artistic reasons. He was motivated by a fascination with communal roots that was enhanced by his association with the scholarly Moses Gaster (1856–1939), the Romanian-born *Chacham* (Chief Rabbi) of London's Spanish and Portuguese community, and by the rich collection of Jewish prints and caricatures of the period assembled by his friend Asher Myers. The picturesque nature and historical distance of the era allowed for much poetic license, especially since it was a relatively little-explored period in Jewish history. Zangwill may have also felt the need to creatively disassociate himself from the historical canvas on which he was then creating *Children of the Ghetto.* And last but not least, historical distancing into a seemingly simpler world of wholesome Jewishness, one into which he could write a scene where magnate and pauper compete on a Sabbath eve for the same fish in the market, offered a feeling of Jewish communion for which he always pined, while at the same time enabling a subversiveness that allowed him to vent the anger of the immigrant peddler's son against the Anglo-Jewish oligarchy that treated the likes of Moses Zangwill with contempt. Beneath the jolly veneer of the story, one can detect not only a deeper cheerless sense of Jewish pauperism, but also the fury of a young author whose only source of power, like Da Costa's, was his nimbleness with words, flashing wit, precise memory, and erudite confidence with text and scripture. Look in the historicized mirror, he seems to be saying to the "somebodies" of Anglo-Jewry—so ill at ease with the poor East European immigrants in their midst—and you will find yourselves. You are as rigid and obnoxious as the members of the Mahamad, who are easily manipulated by a smart schnorrer, and as philistine as Grobstock—a name that points to coarse origins—who fears the impression he makes on his own servant, a favorite Zangwill theme that often characterizes his upwardly mobile Jews. It is the schnorrer, the audacious and enterprising confidence man, who towers over rich twits and has them wrapped around his intellectual pinky. Yet *The King of Schnorrers* concludes not with chaos and revolution, but with orderly power-sharing and acceptance. Manasseh's admission to the ranks of the mighty benefits all: the lovers are married, artificial boundaries are removed, and Israel is united.

The obligation of rich and comfortable Jews to invest themselves in alleviating the misery of their persecuted brothers runs throughout Zangwill's literary and political work. In his presidential address at the Manchester ITO conference in 1907, he admonished:

> Hunting and horse-racing, balls and dinners and operas are legitimate enough in the piping times of peace; but when we are on a war footing, when the agony of our people cries to us from the shambles of Russia to the *Mellahs* of Morocco, and from the *Hara* of Tunis to the ruined villages of Roumania, then I say that if our upper classes do not pause in their pleasurings and make a supreme effort of salvation, the blood of their brothers will cry out against them from the ground. And not only against them, but against every Jew, however lowly, who has done less than his utmost. Judea expects every man to do his duty.[15]

Manasseh Da Costa, with his pride in pedigree and sense of noblesse oblige, and Yankele, his simpleton sidekick, have been compared to Don Quixote and Sancho Panza. Literary critic Holbrook Jackson put Manasseh in the same league with two of the greatest comic characters of English literature, Shakespeare's Sir John Falstaff and Dickens's Wilkins Micawber. Da Costa radiates the sort of presence that naturally appeals to theater people, and the fact that the novella was written largely in dialogic form suggested it as an ideal candidate for dramatization. However, the transfer from page to stage turned out to be more laborious than one may expect.

The King of Schnorrers made its theatrical debut in a 1905 Yiddish adaptation produced in New York by Jacob P. Adler. According to critic Louis Lipsky, Adler "mangled" it and "tore it beyond recognition," eliminating characters and turning it into a lighthearted operetta that mixed Zangwill's lines with "rhymster Shmuelewitz's *coupletten.*"[16] Zangwill strongly objected to Adler's low comedy. In a letter to Bernard Richards, a New York friend, he wrote, "I am particularly annoyed at Mr. Adler's misconduct. We meant him to make a dignified character-creation in comedy. The third act, for example, is almost tragic, and could not possibly resemble 'musical farce.'"[17]

An English-language staging was slow in the making. Although major actors and producers—notably Richard Mansfield, George Tyler, Herbert Beerbohm Tree, and Louis Calvert—considered a production at various times between 1898 and 1918, nothing happened. There is good reason to assume that had *Children of the Ghetto* been the success Tyler had hoped, he would have produced *King of Schnorrers,* though in his correspondence with the author he expressed reservations regarding the overpowering presence of the protagonist and the absence of a strong romantic interest. The hostility with which *Children of the Ghetto* was received in New York certainly dampened his and other producers' interest for a second production about Jewish life. Producers may have also been wary to invest in a text so firmly grounded in tradition and belief specific to Jewish culture for fear it would not attract the general theatergoing public.

It is not clear when the playscript was actually written. In April 1899 *The Bookman* noted that "Mr. Zangwill has dramatised his *King of the Schnorrers* [*sic*], and is now engaged on an adaptation from *The Children of the Ghetto.*"[18] However, although *Schnorrers* is discussed in Zangwill's 1899 correspondence with Tyler, there is no reference to an actual written playscript, suggesting that the project did not go beyond the proposal stage. A script did exist by 1918, as evidenced by Zangwill's August 21 letter to Tyler: "I sent last week the MS. of my play 'The King of Schnorrers' to America at the request of Louis Calvert."[19] It was not until six years later, however, during the summer of 1924, that newspapers in England and America announced that Zangwill was working on a dramatization of the novella and that it would be presented in England during the summer, with prospects for a fall opening in America. These announcements do not mention the existence of an earlier script. Like-wise intriguing is a small item that appeared in the October 23, 1925, "Music and Drama" section of the *Jewish Chronicle,* which reported that Zangwill had prepared a libretto based on *The King of Schnorrers* for a musical version writ-ten and arranged by French composer Octave Crémieux.[20] The musical was to open in Vienna and had been anticipated by a January 5 production in Monte Carlo. Although the source for this information must have been Zangwill, his papers from that period, which are neatly organized, offer no further data.

The King of Schnorrers finally made its English-language stage debut at London's Scala Theatre on November 1, 1925. It was presented by the non-profit Jewish Drama League and was a modest affair, unbefitting the grandil-oquence of its main character. It was a "one-nighter," presented on a Sunday, when the commercial theaters were dark. Though the actors were profession-als, the lead, played by Lewin Mannering, was not in the league of a Richard Mansfield or a Herbert Beerbohm Tree. The reviews in the *Times, The Stage,* and the *Observer* were mixed. The short *Times* piece dismissed the play for its "talkative impossibility" and critiqued the absence of a proper antagonist to Da Costa's loquacious heroics.[21] *The Stage* criticized the play's verbosity but was charmed by the novelty and magnetism of the Da Costa character and by the conflict between Sephardim and Ashkenazim, a bit of historical information completely new to the reviewer.[22] The writer for the *Observer* was the only critic familiar with Zangwill's work, and his words are the most discerning: "Mr. Zangwill continues to astonish us no less by his foibles as a dramatist than by his strength. Many lesser men have written plays whose prevailing quality is good, bad, or indifferent. He alone can box the compass with such aplomb."[23] Parts of the play, he said, were tiresome, others, superb, and, like his colleagues, he expressed the need for the play to be "purged" and compressed and suggested that the first two acts be trimmed and combined. But the third act, where Da Costa duels with the Mahamad, captured his heart. He noted that while the horseplay of the first and second acts could have been the work of a clever schoolboy, the third was a work of genius.

Throughout his career Zangwill had been faulted for a tendency toward verbal avalanches that begged pruning. This "orgy of wit" was the one major criticism voiced by Holbrook Jackson in his overall admiring portrait written in 1914 for *The Bookman*. There were times, he wrote, when "the readiness of his wit overbalances his sense of proportion" and his cleverness "verges on the prodigious and the prodigality of his wit is always astounding and often disturbing."[24] This was undoubtedly the result of the brilliant yet overactive mind and a nervous energy that had been grasped by Abraham Cahan, who in 1898 likened Zangwill to the mythological *Sambatyon*. During the last three years of his life, this trait would contribute to Zangwill's severe insomnia, and finally to the nervous breakdown that preceded his death in the summer of 1926.

The King of Schnorrers was revived in London in December 1930 by the Arts Theatre Workshop. Only six performances were given. Lewis Mannering repeated his role as Da Costa but attracted little critical attention. The one short review that did appear began with, "I cannot for the life of me see why the Arts Theatre Club has introduced Israel Zangwill's 'The King of Schnorrers' to a West-end audience. It is a play which, however much interest it may have for Jews, is largely incomprehensible to Christians."[25] The reviewer was not familiar with Zangwill's work, seen from his comment that the play gave the impression that the book on which it is based was a good one. In November 1931, four Sunday evening performances were put up at the Ambassadors Theatre, again with Mannering in the lead. The limited number of performances suggests that it was geared to Jewish audiences, which most probably explains one rather unpleasant review commenting that the overwhelmingly Jewish social and emotional "colour" of the production was "an embarrass-

The cast of *The King of Schnorrers.* The photographic collage appeared in London's weekly *Jewish World* in conjunction with the 1930 London revival of the play. Library of the Jewish Theological Seminary of America.

ment for a mere Gentile."[26] These responses to the 1930–1931 productions seem to confirm the *Jewish Chronicle's* 1925 prediction that the "average non-Jew" who saw the play would fail to understand the underlying humor of the play.[27]

A postwar West End revival opened at the Saville Theatre on October 2, 1950, and ran for a total of twenty-one performances. Joseph Leftwich, Zangwill's friend, admirer, and biographer, was disappointed with the results. He felt that Ernest Milton as Da Costa missed the "big, impudent, swaggering robust bravado" of the part and that the Yiddish actor Meier Tzelniker, who played Yankele, was but a "low comedian." The spirit of the play was wrong, he said, and the production dragged, with the actors striking attitudes and poses as if in tableaux.[28] The English press was considerably more accepting than Leftwich, its reviews standing in marked contrast to the prewar treatment of the play's Jewish aspects. A second world war and the Holocaust must have altered sensibilities. Gone are the snappy remarks about the play's excessive Jewishness and incomprehensibility, and the term "schnorrer" is now felt to require no explanation. Indeed, it appears as though some of the stiltedness that Leftwich disliked may even be the result of the director's and star's need to treat the postwar Stage Jew with excessive and possibly suffocating respect. No longer a confidence man, Da Costa's schnorring loses its credibility. *The Stage*, in a favorable review, mused that Milton was "too much of the intellectual grandee and not enough of the Jew who draws knowledge not only from books and observation, but from instincts nourished by ancient culture."[29] Indeed, it appears that reviewer and actor were united in a desire for a "noble Jew," as can be seen from *The Stage's* remark that at the end a "Jew of immense dignity emerges," one who thrills the audience with his "controlled, flickering magnificence."[30] Yet it was the review in *The New Statesman and Nation* that would have most pleased Zangwill, whose work, wrote Montagu Slater, came as a welcome surprise to someone "woefully ignorant" of it.[31] "The writing is so good," he exclaimed, "that once again we have to marvel at the English theatre's rule" that "no conscientious writer [be] admitted, at least not while alive." Slater adored the freshness of the theme of Jewish life in eighteenth-century London and concluded with the recommendation that "anyone who wants a genuinely new flavour in the theatre should try this one."

As with *Children of the Ghetto*, the playscript of *The King of Schnorrers* disappeared from the public eye, though the novella inspired sporadic amateur and quasi-professional theatrical adaptations. *Schnorrers* finally reached New York's off-Broadway in November 1979. It was a musical comedy loosely based on Zangwill's novella, with book, lyrics, and music by Judd Woldin. Reflecting the spirit of the time, it told the story of David Ben-Yonkel, a young cabinetmaker who falls in love with the revolutionary-minded Deborah. In order to win his beloved's hand, he needs to prove his schnorring skills to her father, "Da Costa," the King of Schnorrers. He succeeds in his mission and also reveals himself as an underground revolutionary, his intended's ideal. The musical numbers included such titles as "Petticoat Lane," "Chutzpah," "I'm Only a Woman," and "The Fine Art of Schnorring." The production had a cast of ten and ran for sixty-three performances.

The most recent adaptation of *The King of Schnorrers* was a modest two-man show that played at the Edinburgh Festival in 2000. It was a high-energy romp that combined Story Theatre methods with athletic choreography and clowning. It was performed by two young Londoners who had never heard of Zangwill before chancing upon the novella. They became enthusiastic devotees and breathed new life into the old tale.

The King of Schnorrers

A Ghetto Grotesque in Four Acts
Adapted from his popular novel
by
ISRAEL ZANGWILL

[Editor's Note: *The King of Schnorrers* opened on November 1, 1925, at the Scala Theatre, London. It was presented by the Jewish Drama League and produced (directed) by Mr. George Owen. The major roles were played by Lewin Mannering (Manasseh da Costa, the King of Schnorrers), Geoffrey Wilkinson (Yankele, the Death-Rattler), Edward Petley (Joseph Grobstock), Orlando Barnett (Moses Belasco), Denys Blakelock (Beau Belasco), Clifford Cobbe (Wilkinson), John C. Laurence (Chief of the Elders), Chas. R. Stone (the Treasurer), Charles Poulton (Warden of the Congregation), Frank Snell (Warden of the Captives), William Lorrimer (Warden of the Holy Land), Alexander Field (the Chancellor), Constance Robertson (Mrs. Grobstock), Nancy Atkin (Leah Grobstock), and May Grew (Deborah Da Costa).]

CHARACTERS

Manasseh Bueno Barsillai Azevedo
Da Costa . . . . King of Schnorrers
Yankele . . . . The Death-Rattler
Joseph Grobstock. . . . . East India Director
Moses Belasco. . . . . President of the Mahamad
Beau Belasco . . . . His Son
Wilkinson. . . . . A flunkey
Blind Jonathan
Stumpy Sol
Armless Isaac . . . . Beggars
Black Nathan
Red Raphael
Fine Sammy
Titleboam
The Chief of the Elders
The Treasurer
The Warden of the Congregation . . . . . Councillors of the Mahamad
The Warden of the Captives
The Warden of the Holy Land
The Chancellor . . . . Secretary of the Mahamad

Gomez. . . . . Beadle of the Mahamad
Mrs. Grobstock . . . . The Director's Wife
Leah Grobstock . . . . The Director's Daughter
Deborah Da Costa. . . . . The King's Daughter
Jenny. . . . . A Passing Street-Seller
Policemen, Beggars, Vendors,
Street Crowd ad lib

ACT I
Outside Grobstock's House

ACT II
In Mrs. Grobstock's Salon

ACT III
Council Chamber of the Mahamad

ACT IV
Library of Moses Belasco

*The action passes in the London Jewry at the
end of the eighteenth century.*

ACT I

*The scene represents the façade of Grobstock's house in the pictur-
esque old London street near Aldgate. The door is in the centre
of the stage and is led up to by two stone steps, up which stretches
a little crowd of* BEGGARS *with tangled beards and long curls,
one or two in gaberdines with tangled beards and earlocks, coloured handkerchiefs round loins and staves in hand, but most
in shabby knee-breeches and many-buttoned jackets. They include* STUMPY SOL (*one-legged*), ARMLESS ISAAC (*one-armed*),
BLACK NATHAN (*with a big black beard and earlocks*), RED
RAPHAEL (*red-headed*), BLIND JONATHAN (*with a green shade
over his eyes*).

(*There is opportunity for a street-market scene, with the old
London street-cries, e.g.,*
      "I have ripe strawberries!"
      "Fine Salmon! Fine Salmon!"
      "Will ye buy a very fine brush?"
      "Shoe-laces. Flint and Steel!"
      "White radish. White young radish!"
      "Will ye buy my sack o' small coals?"
      "Come, buy my sand, fine silver sand!"
      "I have fresh cheese and cream!")

(*Other passing figures could be seen such as a* CHIMNEY SWEEP
with his cry of "Chimney Sweep!" *A* RAT-CATCHER, *bearing a
placard painted with dead rats, and crying:* "Ha' ye any rats or
mice to kill?" *and a* COLLECTOR *with a basket crying:* "Bread
and meat for the poor debtors in prison.")
(*If this scene is introduced, begin with the entry of* POLICEMAN,
otherwise with STUMPY SOL's *first speech.*)

(*ENTER a "Robin Redbreast," or eighteenth-century* POLICE-

406

MAN, *in a long coat, with big pocket-flaps, red waistcoat, short trousers, shoes, and a broad-brimmed hat, armed with a stick in his left hand and a rattle in his right.*)

Policeman	(*To* CROWD *and* VENDORS) Move on! Pass along!

(*The* CROWD *begins to melt away, all except the* SCHNORRERS *and* FINE SAMMY, *the fishmonger.*)

Fine S.	Why can't we earn an honest living?
Policeman	You're obstructing the street with your stalls and baskets.
Fine S.	But look at *them!* (*Points to* SCHNORRERS.)
Policeman	They're doing nothing.
Fine S.	No, they never do. Dirty beggars! (*Wheels out his barrow left, crying.*) Fine Salmon! Plaice and So-ell! Fine Salmon! (*EXIT on right.*)

(*The* POLICEMAN *follows him sternly to see he really goes.*)

(*The stage is empty of all save the* SCHNORRERS. *As they are now unobserved,* STUMPY SOL *has two legs,* ARMLESS ISAAC *two arms, and* BLIND JONATHAN *two good eyes.*)

Stumpy S.	(*Looking at his gold watch hidden in his bosom.*) Time Grobstock came with our Sabbath allowance, curse him!
Armless I.	Patience, Stumpy Sol!
Stumpy S.	Pox take you! He's kept me on my legs nearly half an hour. I'll bash his knocker in! (*Tries to get at it—*THEY *all push him back with a cry of* "No! No!")
Black N.	But it is yet many hours to Sabbath. He will not fail to feed his flock like a shepherd, as it is writ in Isaiah.
Stumpy S.	May the worm feed sweetly on him, as it is writ in Job. Last Friday he only gave us a groat each.
Black N.	I thank the Lord for small mercies. They come regularly, like my wife's babies—small but sure. What do *you* say, Blind Jonathan?

Blind J.	I say, visit, and see.

(*JENNY, a Christian female peddlar in a Gainsborough hat crosses the stage, laden with miscellaneous objects.*)

Jenny	What d'ye lack? Shoe-laces, flint, and steel, ballads, chap-books, quills, now's your time; pretty ribbons, the true Dream Book, wax and wafers, what d'ye lack? What d'ye lack? (*Pushes among the BEGGARS, trying to do business.*)
Red R.	Ve lack monneys, my good vomans.
Jenny	(*Disgusted*) Then why don't you work for it, you miserable Jews?
Red R.	Vork for it, you minx! Vot you take us for? Ve're *Schnorrers.*
Jenny	Snorers! You look it!
Various Beggars	(*Correctingly*) *Schnorrers! Schnorrers!*
Jenny	Schnorrers? What's that?
Blind J.	Listen to the *shiksah!* Don't you know vot *Schnorrers* are?
Red R.	Vait till you see old Grobstock come out of dis door vid his money-bags.
Jenny	(*Contemptuously*) Oho! Beggars waiting for crumbs!
Red R.	Ve ain't beggars—ve're broders.
Jenny	*You* brothers of Grobstock, the great Jew merchant. Ha! Ha! Ha! Tell that to the horse marines.
Red R.	Vot for I boder myself vid de horse marines? Dey give me noddings! *Meshuggas!*

(*The accent of the BEGGARS after this is not further indicated in the text, but it should be varied ad lib, some more Yiddish, some more Cockney.*)

Black N.	It's true, though. All Israel are brethren.
Jenny	Well, I'm glad I'm not your sister . . . (*ENTER DEBORAH DA*

COSTA. *She wears a head-shawl, but as she and it are pretty it only adds to her Eastern charm.*) Shoe-laces, flint, and steel . . . what d'ye lack?

Deborah	I lack ribbons. I'll take those.
Jenny	(*Handing them to her, then suddenly snatching them back.*) No, you don't! I recognise you! You're the daughter of that diabolical Da Costa!
Deborah	And what if I am?
Jenny	*He* caught me like that. Refused to pay for the goods because I'd asked "What d'ye lack?" (*SCHNORRERS burst into laughter.*) (*JENNY flounces out indignantly and her voice is heard from without.*) The True Dream Book, The Complete Fortune Teller . . .
	(*Seeing the queue,* DEBORAH *tries to get into it. The SCHNOR-RERS push her away.*)
Armless I.	(*Pushing with both hands*) You shameless creature! A woman's place is the home.
Deborah	But I've got no money.
Stumpy S.	And so you come trying to take ours! Go home to your husband and children or—(*Menaces a kick with his hidden leg.*)
Deborah	But I haven't got a husband or children.
Schnorrers	Well go and get them.
Deborah	But I must get my dowry first.
Blind J.	That's for your father to provide. Surely I've seen you with one.
Deborah	You don't know my father. He takes even what *I schnorr.*
Red R.	And now you want him to get what we *schnorr!* Be off with you.
Schnorrers	Off with you!

(*THEY drive her out. From the opposite wing is heard the cry of* FINE SAMMY, *the fishmonger.*)

Fine S.   (*Crying outside.*) Plaice and So-ell! Plaice and So-ell! Fine Salmon! All alive O!

Black N.   Hullo, here's Fine Sammy! (*FINE SAMMY entering, wheeling barrow. Goes up to barrow.*) How much that salmon?

Fine S.   Only two left—goin' cheap—fifty shillings the pair!

Black N.   (*After handling the salmon slowly, like a purchasing connoisseur.*) Give you five for this one.

Schnorrers   Ha! Ha! Ha!

Fine S.   (*Seizing a plaice.*) I'll give you a dab in the eye.

Black N.   (*Seriously*) But look here, Fine Sammy—

Fine S.   Paws off. (*Wheeling his barrow off*) Yah! You couldn't raise fifty shillings among the lot of you.

Schnorrers   (*Fiercely*) What!

Blind J.   (*Waving a bank-note*) Do you see that, sonny? A fiver!

(*The house door opens suddenly, and* GROBSTOCK, *a jovial heavy-jowled old gentleman with a periwig and pigtail, and an imposing presence, habited in a blue body-coat with a row of big yellow buttons, a frilled shirt front, high collar and copious white handkerchief, appears carrying a large canvas money-bag.* BLIND JONATHAN *is the first to become aware of him.*)

Blind J.   (*Hiding his money with an instantaneous transition, cries:*) Pity a poor blind man! (*The* BEGGARS, *catching his cue, in various voices, and not quite simultaneously, shoving one another, and plucking at* GROBSTOCK)
May the Lord bless you!
Bread for the hungry!
The Lord grant you long life!
Remember the poor with no fish for the Sabbath.
The Lord give you peace!
A wife and ten children.
The Lord cause his countenance to shine upon you, the

Lord—

Joseph	(*Jovially*) The Lord knows what you're all saying.
Fine S.	(*In the distance*) All alive O! All alive O!
Joseph	(*Listening*) Oh bother! I wanted a salmon. Never mind, business before pleasure. Now, now, no shoving, one at a time.
Red R.	I was here first.
Joseph	First come, last served.
Beggars	Ha! Ha! Ha!
Joseph	(*Pleased at his own humour*) Who came last?
All	Me! Me!
Joseph	Then you've time to wait. (*Laughter.*) Now, (*Dips into bag, bringing out a small white paper packet.*) Here's a thing and a very pretty thing, and who will be the owner of this pretty thing?
Beggars	(*As before, hustling and plucking at* GROBSTOCK.) May the Lord bless you! Bread for the hungry! The Lord grant you long life! Etc. Etc.
	(*GROBSTOCK [JOSEPH] places the packet in the palm furthest from him,* BLACK NATHAN's. *The* BEGGAR *opens it amid a dead silence, with all eyes upon him.*)
Black N.	(*Ecstatically*) A silver florin! God bless you!
Beggars	(*As before*) May the Lord bless you! The Lord grant you long life, etc. etc.
	(*JOSEPH dips again with deliberate enjoyment and puts the next packet into the palm of the nearest* BEGGAR, *RED RAPHAEL. He opens it amid same excitement.*)
Red R.	(*Lugubrious*) You've given me a copper by mistake.
Joseph	Keep it for your honesty.

Beggars	Ha! Ha! Ha!
Joseph	Ha! Ha! These are *prize*-packets.
	(*Dips again and hands to* BLIND JONATHAN. *Same excitement.*)
Some Beggars	(*Prematurely*) A shilling!
Blind J.	Nay, gold, gold!
Beggars	Gold!
Blind J.	A golden guinea! May you live to see your children's children under the marriage canopy! Gold, gold. (*Capers about.*)
Joseph	Ah, last come, first served. (*Gives him packet.*)
Stumpy S.	(*Opening packet*) What's this? Nothing.
Beggars	Ha! Ha! Ha!
Joseph	Ha! Ha! A blank. You've got no luck.
Stumpy S.	But I've got no legs.
Joseph	Can't help that. Fair is fair. If you're a schlemihl [luckless dog]—However. (*Softening and drawing coins from his trouser's pocket.*) Here's a shilling for each leg.
Stumpy S.	Bless you! Wish I'd no arms either.
Joseph	Then you couldn't take my money.
Beggars	Ha! Ha! Ha!
Red R.	(*Unappeased*) Yes, but if fair's fair, what's this? (*Holds up his penny.*)
Joseph	A penny for your thoughts.
Beggars	Ha! Ha! Ha!
Red R.	But I've got a wife and fifteen children and we've been a week without bread.
Joseph	Passover week, when 'tis forbidden, hey, you rascal? Well,

well, (*softening*) catch if you can. (*Throws some of the packages in the road.* BEGGARS *scramble wildly on hands and knees.*)

Manasseh (*Appearing suddenly LEFT, in a voice of thunder with outstretched stick.*) You dog! (*He is a tall, black-bearded, turbaned, strange-cloaked, shabby, picturesque, prophetic figure—see description in Novel.* ["None but a *Schnorrer* would wear a home-made turban, issue of a black cap crossed with a white kerchief; none but a *Schnorrer* would unbutton the first nine buttons of his waistcoat, or, if this relaxation were due to the warmth of the weather, counteract it by wearing an over-garment, especially one as heavy as a blanket, with buttons the size of compasses and flaps reaching nearly to his shoe-buckles, even though its length were only congruous with that of his undercoat, which already reached the bottoms of his knee-breeches. Finally, who but a *Schnorrer* would wear this overcoat cloak-wise, with dangling sleeves, full of armless suggestion from a side view? Quite apart from the shabbi-ness of the snuff-coloured fabric, it was amply evident that the wearer did not dress by rule or measure. Yet the disproportions of his attire did but enhance the picturesqueness of a personality that would be striking even in a bath, though it was not likely to be seen there. The beard was jet black, sweeping and unkempt, and ran up his cheeks to meet the raven hair, so that the vivid face was framed in black; it was a long, tapering face with sanguine lips gleaming at the heart of a black bush; the eyes were large and lambent, set in deep sockets under black arching eyebrows; the nose was long and Coptic; the brow low but broad, with straggling wisps of hair protruding from beneath the turban. His right hand grasped a plain ashen staff" (p. 7).]) (*BEGGARS, startled, cease scrambling. JOSEPH stares, paralyzed, gripping his bag.*)

Joseph Eh?

Manasseh (*Advancing slowly towards JOSEPH, raising his stick as if to strike. JOSEPH holds bag defensively before his face. Lowers stick contemptuously.*) You murderer!

Joseph	(*Bewildered*) Murderer! (*His bag droops in his hand.*)
Manasseh	Ay, stands it not in the Talmud that he who shams a brother is like to one who spills blood? And are you not putting to shame your brethren in Israel? And you, ye swine, wallowing in street garbage, who degrade the honourable status of the *schnorrer*, up, up, up. (*Whirls his stick among them; they scramble in alarm.*) On your legs like men!
Stumpy S.	I've got no legs.
Red R.	(*Apologetically to* MANASSEH) *I've* got no money, I've been cheated.
Joseph	Do you mean I cheated you, you knave?
Red R.	Did you not give me a packet of mockery?
Joseph	Do you suppose I knew what was in the packet?
Manasseh	Then your steward has robbed him! You let him make up the packets and he has stolen this man's money, the thief, the transgressor, thrice-cursed who robs the poor.
Joseph	Nonsense! I made up the packets myself.
Manasseh	And yet you say you did not know what was in them?
Joseph	Nay, hear me out. In some I placed gold, in the greater number silver, in a few copper. If this man has drawn a blank or thereabouts it is his misfortune—his *Schlimmozel.*
Manasseh	Nay, it is *your* misfortune. The man who hath pity on the poor lends to the Lord, and the good deed you might have had to your account in the heavenly books is lost to you.
Joseph	Maybe. But what of all the others? Have you all not had of my gold and silver? Bear witness—
Beggars	(*As before*) The Lord bless you! The Lord cause His countenance to shine upon you. Etc. Etc.
Manasseh	You have given, but for your own diversion. But what says the Talmud? There is a wheel rolling in the world—not he

who is rich to-day is rich to-morrow but this one He brings up, and this one He brings down, as is said in the seventy-fifth Psalm. Therefore lift not up your horn on high, nor speak with a stiff neck.

Joseph

You are an uncharitable man. I did it not from wantonness but from faith in Heaven. I know well that God sits turning a wheel—therefore I did not presume to turn it myself. Did I not let Providence select who should have the silver and who the gold, who the copper, and who the emptiness? Besides, God alone knows who really needs my assistance. I have made him my almoner; I have cast my burden on the Lord.

Manasseh

Epicurean! Blasphemer! Is it thus you would palter with the sacred texts? Do you forget what the next verse says? "Bloody and deceitful men shall not live out half their days." Shame on you—you a Treasurer of the Great Synagogue! You see I know you, Joseph Grobstock. Has not the beadle of your congregation boasted to me that you have given him a guinea for brushing your spatterdashes? Would you think of offering him a problematic prize-packet? Nay, it is the poor that are trodden on—they whose merits are in excess of those of beadles. But the Lord will find others to take up His loans. You are no true son of Israel.

Joseph

(*With recovered dignity, more quietly*) If you really knew me, you would know that the Lord is considerably in my debt. When next you would discuss me, speak with the poor psalm-sayers, not with the beadle. Never have I neglected those in want.

Manasseh

(*With corresponding quiet*) That is untrue. You have neglected *me*.

Joseph

You? Are *you* in want?

Manasseh

Of everything.

Joseph

Eh?

Manasseh

You are astonished. Those who have everything are amazed that others should want it.

Joseph	But who are you?
Manasseh	(*Proudly*) A beggar.
Beggars	(*With quick contempt*) A *schnorrer!*
Joseph	(*With dazed contempt*) A beggar!
Manasseh	Ay, I should have said—one of these. But (*with withering contempt*) they are unworthy of the poverty with which the Almighty has blessed them. Godless grovellers, was it for this that the Almighty ordained that the poor shall never cease out of the land? Do you not know that without the poor to give charity to, the rich would never get to Paradise, that each poor man is a rung in the Jacob's ladder by which the rich man may mount to Heaven?
Joseph	(*Now complacently superior*) And what may be the name of this particular rung in the Jacob's ladder?
Manasseh	Manasseh Bueno Barzillai Azevedo Da Costa.
Joseph	Oh! A Spaniard!
Manasseh	Is it not written on my face, even as it is written on yours that you are German?
Joseph	(*Still superior*) Humph! And so you are in want of everything. Are you married?
Manasseh	You correct me—wife and children are the only things I do *not* lack.
Joseph	(*Himself again, smiling*) No *Schnorrer* does.
Manasseh	(*Sternly*) No, the poor man has the fear of Heaven. He obeys the Law and the Commandments. He marries while he is young, nor is his spouse with barrenness. It is the rich man who transgresses the Statute, who delays to come under the Canopy.
Joseph	You're wrong there, my fine fellow. I *have* got a wife, and here (*Magnificently*) is a guinea in her name.
Beggars	Oh! (*Murmur of awe and astonishment.*)

Manasseh	(*Taking it quietly*) If I wished to ensure *my* wife's happiness in the World-to-Come, I would give more than a beadle's tip for brushing gaiters.
Joseph	(*Angrily*) You are too—too (*awed by* MANASSEH'S *eye*) too hasty. And as my spouse is *not* barren either, here is another guinea in my daughter's name.
Beggars	Oh. (*More of a growl of protest.*)
Manasseh	It is the first time I have taken gold from a German.
Joseph	(*Taken aback*) Oh, indeed.
Manasseh	Yes, are not we, the old Spanish and Portuguese Jews of London, far richer than your parvenu community? What need have I to take the good deeds away from my own people? They have too few opportunities for beneficence as it is, too few rungs in their celestial ladder, being so many of them wealthy: brokers and West India merchants, and—
Joseph	But, I too, am an East India Director.
Manasseh	Maybe; but your community is yet young and struggling, your rich men are as rare as good men in Sodom. You are the immigrants of yesterday, refugees from the Ghettos of Poland and Germany. But we, as you are aware, have been established here for generations; in the Peninsula our ancestors controlled the purse-strings of princes. In Holland we held the empery of trade. Ours have been the poets and scholars in Israel. You cannot expect that we should recognize your Yiddish-speaking rabble which prejudices us in the eyes of England. We made the name of the Jew honourable: you degraded it. You are as the mixed multitude which came up with our forefathers out of Egypt.
Joseph	Nonsense. All Israel are brethren.
Manasseh	Esau was the brother of Jacob, yet he was only fit for the wilderness. But you will excuse me if I go a-marketing. My wife awaits her Sabbath fish. It is such a pleasure to handle gold. (*EXIT.*)
Beggars	Give us gold, too. Give us gold, too.

Joseph	(*Drawing bag-strings tight*) Off, off, you blood-suckers.
Red R.	Job's boils be on you.
Beggars	He is only a *schnorrer.*
Joseph	Ay, horse-leech. Begone! (*Whirls round his bag.*)
Beggars	(*Muttering as they disperse*) An evil spirit in your bones. A sudden death! May you suffer all the plagues of Egypt! May you be hanged like Haman on a high tree! Etc. (*JOSEPH turns his back to them and inserts his key in his door. ENTER YANKELE, a greasy, shabby Polish beggar, rattling his pyx, a copper money-bag with a handle and a lid closed by a padlock. His speech is Cockney-Yiddish.*)
Black N.	(*Joyfully*) Ah, here's the Death-Rattler.
Red R.	(*Rubbing his hands*) Oh, good! Now we shall know who's in need of our prayers. (*THEY listen eagerly.*)
Yankele	(*Rattling his moneybox in between the phrases like a street-crier's bell*) Simeon Titleboam—of de Orange Market—peace be upon him—Funeral on Sunday mornin' at ten.
Fine S.	(*Without*) All alive O! All alive O!
Yankele	(*Rattling*) Service of Mourners at de house at six.
Beggars	At the Orange Market or in Hackney?
Yankele	De Orange Market. (*BEGGARS hasten off. STUMPY SOL stumping in the rear.*) (*Approaching JOSEPH who has paused to listen and seems much moved.*) Ah, ve are all cut down like grass (*rattling*), but Charity delivers from Death. Give me something for de poor.
Joseph	(*Dropping in coin*) Poor Titleboam! Tut, tut, tut. (*Covers face with hands.*)
Fine S.	(*Without*) All alive O! Plaice and So-ell! Fine Sammin! All alive O!

Yankele	(*Rattling*) Funeral on Sunday mornin' at ten.
Fine S.	(*Wheeling his barrow and talking to MANASSEH off.*) Not a groat less. This is my last sammin and the price is two guineas. Fine Sammin! Fine Sammin!
	(*MANASSEH appears at the wing and stands in dignity.*)
Joseph	(*Opening eyes*) Ah, Fine Sammy! What have you got? (*Comes down.*)
Fine S.	Mornin', Mr. Grobstock. One last sammin.
Joseph	(*Surveying it*) And a truly fine one.
Manasseh	(*Throwing money contemptuously on barrow*) Here's two guineas.
Joseph	(*Becoming aware of MANASSEH*) Eh? What? That salmon's mine, sir. Here, Sammy, three guineas.
Manasseh	(*Moving to barrow*) Pardon me—this is not an auction. (*Seizes the salmon by the tail.*)
Joseph	(*Apoplectic*) You—you—you—rogue! How dare you buy my salmon?
Manasseh	Rogue yourself! Would you have me steal salmon?
Joseph	You have stolen my money, knave, rascal!
Manasseh	Murderer! Shedder of blood! Did you not give me the money as a freewill offering for the good of the souls of your wife and daughter? I call on you to confess, in the presence of the Death-Rattler—that you are a slanderer.
Joseph	Slanderer indeed! I repeat, you are a knave and a jackanapes. You—a pauper—a *schnorrer*—with a wife and children, how can you have the face to go and spend two guineas— two whole guineas—all you have in the world—on a mere luxury like salmon?
Manasseh	If I do not buy salmon when I have two guineas, when *shall* I buy salmon? In the name of my wife and daughter, I ask you to clear my good name, which you have bespattered in

	the presence of my very fishmonger. Come! Do you deny you gave the two guineas in charity?
Joseph	(*Bewildered*) No.
Manasseh	In the name of my wife I thank you. She loves salmon and fries with unction. And now, since you have no further use for that bag of yours, I will relieve you of its burden by taking my salmon home in it. (*Takes the money-bag and drops the salmon in. Its head protrudes.*) A pleasant Sabbath! (*Perceives* YANKELE *as he is sauntering out, and says graciously*) Ah, Yankele, we shall see you this evening, I suppose?
Yankele	Vould I miss dat fish? (*Rattling in front of* JOSEPH) Simeon Titleboam—
Joseph	D——n Simeon Titleboam.
Yankele	(*Rattling*) Peace be upon him.
Joseph	Peace yourself. (*Drives him out.*)
	(FISHMONGER *offers substitute.*)
Fine S.	Fine so-ell, Mr. Grobstock?
Joseph	D——n your sole! (*EXIT* FINE SAMMY.) Come back, Da Costa, come back!
Manasseh	(*Turning*) Can I do anything for you?
Joseph	That bag is not empty. There are a number of prize-packets still left.
Manasseh	So much the better. You will be saved from the temptation to continue humiliating the poor, and I shall be saved from spending *all* your bounty upon salmon—an extravagance you were right to deplore.
Joseph	But—but—
Manasseh	No—no "buts." (*Waving bag*) You admitted you were wrong before. Shall I be less magnanimous now? I ought not to have wasted two guineas on this one fish. It is not worth it—no, indeed!

Fine S.	(*Without*) Plaice and So-ell! Plaice and So-ell!
Manasseh	It is Fine Sammy that is the rogue. This salmon is not worth two guineas—if you had not come up I should have got it for twenty-five shillings at most.
Joseph	And what then?
Manasseh	Well, you won't let me be the loser by your arrival. If I find *less* than seventeen shillings in this bag, you will make it up to me.
Joseph	Eh?
Manasseh	I know you are a gentleman capable of behaving as finely as any Spaniard. And so I should not like you to have it on your soul that you had done a poor man out of a few shillings.
Joseph	You will find more than seventeen shillings in the bag.
Manasseh	Ah, why were you not born a Spaniard? Do you know what I have a mind to do? To come and be your Sabbath-guest this evening.
Joseph	What?
Manasseh	Then we can both enjoy the salmon. It will be a happy compromise.
Joseph	Compromise?
Manasseh	(*With growing enthusiasm*) Yes, this very evening I will take supper with you: we will welcome the bride, the Holy Sabbath, together. Never before have I sat at the table of a German. But you—you are a man after my own heart. Your soul is a son of Spain. Till this evening. *A Dios!*
Joseph	But—come back! But I do not have Sabbath guests.
Manasseh	Then the sooner you revive that pious old custom, the better for your soul. Did you not hear me invite that poor Death-Rattler? Yes, I, Manasseh Barzillai Azevedo Da Costa, have Yankele at my Sabbath table of a Friday evening—Yankele, a German, a Pole even. And why should I draw the line there?

Why should I not permit you, a German, to return the hospitality to me, a Spaniard?

Joseph   But—but I have a wife and daughter.

Manasseh   So have I. Do you mean I bring my Sarah and Deborah too?

Joseph   (*Almost apoplectic*) No—no—I mean—er—my daughter—being of marriageable age—likes only *young* men about the house.

Manasseh   (*Sublimely*) But I do not come as a suitor! Reassure her—it is as a *Schnorrer* that I am coming, purely as a *Schnorrer*. (*Moves off with dignity.*)

Joseph   (*Distracted*) The devil! But wait! Wait a moment!

Manasseh   (*Going*) I am sorry. But I have other clients. If I have accepted your invitation for to-night, it does not mean that I can give you my day too.

Joseph   (*Overwhelmed*) You have accepted my invitation?

Manasseh   (*Benignly*) Did I not make it clear?

Joseph   (*Savagely*) Oh, quite clear. (*With an idea*) Then perhaps you won't mind accepting some of my clothes—

Manasseh   Your cast-off clothes?

Joseph   Not at all. Clothes I'm still wearing—(*Significantly*) Clothes fit for *Sabbath* wearing. My old clothes were already given away at Passover to Mordecai, the Psalm-sayer.

Manasseh   I would beg you to excuse me.

Joseph   (*Anxiously*) Oh, but why not?

Manasseh   I cannot.

Joseph   (*Pleadingly*) But they will just about fit you.

Manasseh   That makes it all the more absurd for you to give them to a shrimp like Mordecai the *Psalm*-sayer. Still, since he *is* your clothes-receiver, I could not think of interfering with his office. It is not etiquette.

Joseph	But he is *not* my clothes-receiver. Last Passover was the first time I gave them to him, because my cousin, Hyam Rosenstein, who *was* my clothes-receiver, has just died.
Manasseh	But surely Mordecai considers himself your cousin's heir. He expects all your old clothes henceforth.
Joseph	No. I gave him no such promise.
Manasseh	(*Graciously*) Well, in that case—
Joseph	(*Anxiously*) In that case?
Manasseh	On condition that I have the appointment permanently, of course—
Joseph	Of course.
Manasseh	Say no more. I will come in with you at once. (*Moves to door.*)
Joseph	(*Alarmed*) No! I will send them to your home.
Manasseh	(*Waving hand and moving forward*) Good deeds should be completed instanter. As it is written, "I made haste and delayed not."
Joseph	But—but—(*Takes out snuff-box in agitation and snuffs himself.*)
Manasseh	Stand still a second.
Joseph	What is it?
Manasseh	You have spilt snuff all down your coat front. Hold the bag a moment while I brush it off.
	(*JOSEPH accepts bag and MANASSEH scrupulously removes every grain.*)
Joseph	(*Impatiently*) Thank you. That will do.
Manasseh	(*Continuing*) No, it will not do. I cannot have my coat spoiled. By the time it comes to me, it will be a mass of stains if I don't look after it.
Joseph	Oh, is that why you took so much trouble.

Manasseh   Why else? Do you take me for a beadle, a brusher of gaiters? There now. That is the cleanest I can get it. You would escape those droppings if you held your snuff-box so—(*Takes snuff-box and snuffs himself.*)

(*The house-door opens and* WILKINSON *appears in the doorway.*)

Joseph   Oh, Wilkinson!

Wilkinson   This salmon to the kitchen?

Joseph   (*Weakly*) Ye-es. (*Hands it over.*)

Manasseh   Eh?

Joseph   (*To* MANASSEH, *as if addressing a carrier*) Wait a minute—I will settle with you.

(WILKINSON *disappears.*)

Manasseh   (*Angrily*) What! You covet the poor man's salmon as Ahab coveted the vineyard of Naboth. Sir, when I placed my fish trustfully in your hands, I thought you were a man of honour.

Joseph   I—I had to give it up to Wilkinson.

Manasseh   You had to give *my* salmon to Wilkinson?

Joseph   Yes—I could not appear to be your fish-carrier.

Manasseh   Oh, we will soon put that right. (*Bawls into hall*) Wilkinson!

Joseph   No! No! I will repay your money.

Manasseh   Sir! I prefer my wife should rejoice in a Sabbath salmon.

Joseph   Here are the two guineas—you will easily get another, and more cheaply. As you pointed out, you could have got this for twenty-five shillings.

Manasseh   Two guineas. Why you offered Fine Sammy three?

Joseph   Well, here are three guineas.

Manasseh	(*Contemptuously*) Three guineas. And what of my profit?
Joseph	Profit!
Manasseh	Since you have made me a middle-man, since you have forced me into the fish-trade, I must have my profits like any other fishmonger.
Joseph	Here is a crown extra!
Manasseh	(*Spurning it still*) And my compensation?
Joseph	Compensation! Compensation for what?
Manasseh	(*With the Talmudic sing-song*) For what? In the first place, compensation for not eating the salmon myself. For it is not as if I offered it you—I merely entrusted it to you and it is ordained in Exodus that if a man shall deliver unto his neighbor an ass, or an ox, or a sheep, or any creature to keep, then for every matter of trespass, whether it be for ox, for ass, for sheep, for raiment, or for any manner of lost thing, the man shall receive double, and therefore you should pay me six guineas. And secondly—
Joseph	Not another farthing.
Manasseh	Very well! (*Bawls*) Wilkinson!
Joseph	Hush! What do you want of Wilkinson?
Manasseh	I will tell him to bring back my property.
Joseph	Wilkinson will not obey you.
Manasseh	Not obey *me*. A servant! At Baron D'Aguilar's mansion in Broad Street Buildings there is a retinue of twenty-four varlets, and they tremble at my nod.
Joseph	And what is your second claim?
Manasseh	Compensation for being degraded to fishmongering. I am not of those who sell things in the streets. I am a son of the Law, a student of the Talmud.
Joseph	If a crown piece will satisfy each of these claims—

Manasseh	I am not a blood-sucker—as it is said in the Talmud, Tractate Passover, "God loves the man who gives not way to wrath nor stickles for his rights";—that makes altogether three guineas and three crowns.
Joseph	(*Grimly*) Yes, here they are.
	(*WILKINSON re-appears.*)
Wilkinson	You called me, sir?
	(*JOSEPH is embarrassed.*)
Manasseh	No, *I* called you. I wished to give you a crown.
Wilkinson	(*Surprised*) Thank you, sir. (*Retires.*)
Manasseh	Did I not get rid of him cleverly? You see how he obeys me!
Joseph	Ye-es!
Manasseh	I shall not ask you for more than a bare crown I gave him to save your honour.
Joseph	To save my honour!
Manasseh	Would you have had me tell him the real reason I called him was that his master was a thief? No sir, I was careful not to shed your blood in public, though you had no such care for mine.
Joseph	(*Savagely*) Here is the crown! Nay, here are three! (*Angrily turns out his breeches-pockets to exhibit there absolute nudity.*)
Manasseh	No, no, I shall take but two. You had best keep the other— you may want a little silver. (*Presses a crown into his hand.*) You should not be so prodigal in the future. It is bad to be left with nothing in one's pocket—I know the feeling. And now to your wardrobe!
Joseph	Ah! (*Looks down the street.*)
Manasseh	What attracts you?
Joseph	My wife.
Manasseh	That is well.

Joseph	No, it is not well—she will make a fuss about my giving away my clothes. Go, I beg you. In ten minutes I shall be at this door with all I can spare.
Manasseh	Far be it from me to mar the peace of households. I know well that women have two pet passions; to keep their husband's clothes old and their own new. My time is money. (*EXIT right.*)
	(*MRS. GROBSTOCK arrives LEFT in a sedan chair.*)
Joseph	(*Hurrying to help her out of her chair*) But where have you lost Leah?
Mrs. G.	She's coming home—walking with Beau Balasco.
	(*The CHAIRMEN go off with the chair.*)
Joseph	What! They are together again! And you, I am sure, told your porters to hurry on, so as to leave the couple to themselves.
Mrs. G.	And why should I not be a grandmother?
Joseph	You know very well why. The Mahamad will never allow a Spanish Jew to marry one of us—(*Bitterly*) even their beggars ride horseback upon us!
Mrs. G.	But Benjamin's father is the President of the Mahamad! He can change the law.
Joseph	On the contrary. He will enforce it the more severely against his own son. Besides, Benjamin is a Godless aper of the Christian gallants, who frequent the playhouses, not the synagogue. And you so pious!
Mrs. G.	(*Sulkily*) Leah will convert him, and I will teach my grandchildren the prayers. Anyhow I have invited him to supper to-night.
Joseph	Great heavens! (*Hurries to steps to the open door.*)
Mrs. G.	Where are you going?
Joseph	To find clothes. (*Disappears*)

Mrs. G.	(*Shouting after him*) He only minds about his own clothes— he won't mind yours.
Beau B.	(*Outside on LEFT*) But Leah!
Mrs. G.	Here they are! (*Rushes within and bangs door.*)
	(*LEAH ENTERs, followed by the protesting BEAU. She is a very pretty but common-sense girl. He is a dandy of exaggerated elegance, aping moreover the chivalry and romance of the heroes of the stage.*)
Beau B.	(*Repeats*) But Leah!
Leah	I will not hear another word. Good-bye.
Beau B.	But I can't quarrel with my father.
Leah	Why not?
Beau B.	You know he would cut me off. I must consider my tradesmen. Consideration is my one foible.
Leah	Then are we to dangle unmarried?
Beau B.	My darling! You spoil all the romance.
Leah	Better than spoiling our lives.
Beau B.	But surely you enjoy feeling ourselves like Romeo and Juliet between the Montagues and the Capulets.
Leah	Romeo and Juliet came to a bad end.
Beau B.	Bad? I positively gloat over the idea of dying together. Don't you?
Leah	No.
Beau B.	Oh fie!
Leah	I gloat over the idea of living together.
Beau B.	My sweetness! Excellency turned.
Leah	Turned! Turned! You'll turn my brain. You're only thinking of phrases from the playhouses. You don't really love me one bit.

Beau B.	Oh Juliet!
Leah	There you go again. I'm not Juliet—I'm plain Leah.
Beau B.	Not plain.
Leah	Plain-spoken, anyhow. If your fine words were anything but theatrical foolery, you'd want to marry me whatever your father did. Haven't I got enough money for both?
Beau B.	I, a fortune hunter! Never! Independence is my one foible.
Leah	You'd be a fortune-loser, too.
Beau B.	(*Puts hands in ears.*) Silence, sweet siren. Never shall it be said that a Belasco owed anything to anybody except his tradesmen.
Leah	Then good-bye! If you really insist on dying, you must do it alone. (*EXIT pathetically. Door bangs in his face.*)
Beau B.	(*Yearning*) My Juliet!
	(*ENTER DEBORAH, who walks up to BEAU BELASCO.*)
Deborah	Give me a shilling, sir.
Beau B.	(*Startled*) Away—don't you see I am suffering? (*The door re-opens. LEAH re-appears.*) Ah, I knew thou couldst not leave me so unsatisfied.
Leah	Wilkinson has just given me this parcel addressed to you here. (*Hands it.*)
Beau B.	Ha! My clothes!
Leah	Your clothes? Why did it come here?
Beau B.	For the same reason that I do. Let it stay, please. (*Pushes it back.*)
Leah	But don't you want to take it with you?
Beau B.	No, no. I must keep a spare suit of clothes here. For, don't you see, a spatter of gravy, a servant's carelessness with the soup, a catastrophe with a coffee-cup, and I am left *hors de combat*. No, your true exquisite should always be able to call

up his reserves.

Leah	You are as pious with your clothes as mother with her pots and pans. Have you ordered a special shroud?
Beau B.	Your mockery is cruel. I didn't mean we were to die together just yet.
Leah	Only to sup together, I see. But at the worst, dear, I can always console myself with your clothes. (*Hugs parcel.*) Till six, then, my Spanish Romeo. (*Door shuts.*)
Beau B.	Oh, my German Juliet! How can I live till six?

(*He leans in a theatrical love-trance against the door. ENTER YANKELE.*)

Yankele	(*Rattling*) Service of mourners at six!

(*ENTER DEBORAH the opposite way. He gives a joyful cry.*)

Deborah!

Deborah	(*Glaring*) How dare you?
Yankele	It popped out from my mouth itself—like de vind. How is your fader?
Deborah	How dare you claim my acquaintance?
Yankele	Vot! Ven I sup vid your fader every—
Deborah	But *I* don't invite you.
Yankele	No, t'ank God! So bold-faced are you not. But you know vy I come?
Deborah	Because you're hungry.
Yankele	(*Advancing*) Yes—for you!
Deborah	(*Retreating*) You German scare-crow!
Yankele	And who cares vot you t'ink? I settle it vid your fader.

(*DEBORAH laughs in loud mockery.*)

Beau B.	(*Turning*) Who is it mocks my ecstasy? Begone, minx! Stay, you seem a capable wench, and I must hasten home to think out my clothes. Do you know the Flower Market at Charing Cross?
Deborah	Of course! My father gets all his flowers from there.
Beau B.	(*Surprised*) Really? Well, run and tell them to make me the finest bouquet, and send it here this evening. I shall owe them five pounds for it. (*Scribbles on card.*) Give them that! Quick! (*Hurrying away.*)
Deborah	(*Calling after him*) But what do *I* get?
Beau B.	(*Impatient*) Oh—bring it yourself and you shall have a gold piece.
Deborah	Not *owing*, I hope.
Beau B.	No, paid on the nail.
Deborah	On Sabbath evening? What would Mrs. Grobstock say?
Beau B.	Zounds! Ask for me and I will slip it into your hand unseen.
Deborah	(*Holds out her hand.*) Nothing on account?
Beau B.	(*Seizing it*) Since you insist! (*Presses it to his lips.*)
Yankele	(*Rattling in jealous fury*) Funeral on Sunday at ten.
Deborah	Ha! Ha! Ha! (*Runs off jeeringly.*)
	(*BEAU BELASCO's eye follows her approvingly. YANKELE rushes menacingly on the BEAU, his pyx raised like a weapon. The BEAU turns and instinctively claps his hand to his sword. YANKELE collapses into his professional whine.*)
Yankele	(*Rattling*) Charity delivers from death!
Beau B.	(*Laughing.*) The delivery I need is from debt.
	(*EXIT one way as MANASSEH comes on from another with packages protruding from every pocket.*)

Manasseh	Ah, Yankele! You will come in handy to carry my clothes.
Yankele	(*Looking at packages*) That ain't clothes?
Manasseh	I refer to those I left too long, with Grobstock! (*Points to house.*)
Yankele	(*Astonished*) You get Grobstock's clothes?
Manasseh	He was so pressing. I could well not refuse.
Yankele	I wish he'd give *me* some to wear.
Manasseh	To wear? What do *you* want with fine clothes?
Yankele	It's—it's de maidens—dey call me a scarecrow.
Manasseh	Well, you're not a cedar of Lebanon.
Yankele	I've seen uglier bridegrooms.
Manasseh	You want to go under the canopy?
Yankele	If I could have a Spanish fader-in-law!
Manasseh	Well, a German can't expect that. But—let me see. There's your grave-digger's daughter—in your own funeral circle!
Yankele	(*Revolted*) Peninah! Vy, she's ugly enough to keep the Messiah from coming.
Manasseh	Beauty is a vain and deceitful good.
Yankele	Not when it comes from a good hondsome fader. Ah, my benefactor, cannot you t'ink of a girl like dat?
Manasseh	Such girls are very rare.
Yankele	Not many like your Deborah.
Manasseh	No, indeed.
Yankele	(*Desperately*) Ah, by van I not hope to call *you* fader-in-law?
Manasseh	(*Paralyzed*) You dream of that!
Yankele	Ah, I know it's a dream. (*Rattling*) Funeral on Sunday at

ten. Ah, vy vas I not born a Spaniard!

Manasseh	It is too late now.
Yankele	I could learn to pronounce Hebrew in your superior vay.
Manasseh	The Mahamad would not consider that anything. It is a question of blood.
Yankele	(*Agonizedly*) Yes, of my 'eart's blood! But vy did you become my friend, vy did you invite me to your Sabbath table and make me believe you cared for me, so that I t'ink of you day and night—and now ven I ask you to be my fader-in-law you say it cannot be. It is like—like—(*sobs*) slaughtering a bullock. T'ink 'ow proud and 'appy I should be to call you my fader-in-law. All my life vould be devoted to you—my von tought to be vordy of such a man.
Manasseh	You are not the first I have been compelled to refuse.
Yankele	Vat helps me that there are other *schlemihls* [luckless dogs]. How can I live midout you for a fader-in-law!
Manasseh	(*Turning to him like a tiger*) How can you live? What! Do you expect me to support you? Why, even if I become your father-in-law, mind, I only say if, and if the Mahamad permitted my Deborah to marry you—mind, I only say if—not only would I not keep you, but you would have to keep my Deborah.
Yankele	Even dat I am prepared for.
Manasseh	But you are not able to keep a wife.
Yankele	Not able? Who told you dat?
Manasseh	You yourself! Why, aren't you always telling me you are blood-poor!
Yankele	Dat I tell you as a *schnorrer*. But now I speak as a suitor.
Manasseh	(*Sternly*) Then it's all untrue about your inability to afford fish even on a Sabbath?
Yankele	(*Enthusiastically*) Lies and falsehood!

Manasseh	And you've wormed your way to my table on false pretenses?
Yankele	It vas your feet, not your table I vised to sit at—Oh vat a rest from death-rattling to drink in your visdom!
Manasseh	(*Drily*) And my wine.
Yankele	De vine vas thrown in. I tell you I can afford to keep *two* vives.
Manasseh	You want *two* fathers-in-law!!
Yankele	No, no—I don't even need *von*. I make a hundred and fifty a year—
Manasseh	A hundred and fifty! (*Suspiciously*) In gold?
Yankele	(*With a gesture of the hands*) Silver and copper are also good.
Manasseh	But it doesn't all come by *schnorring*. You work—not only as Death-Rattler, but as a professional Psalm-sayer and Congregational-Man. You are a Synagogue-Knocker too, waking up people for prayers. And work is always so uncertain. People may become less pious and you lose your Synagogue-Knocking. Or more pious, and they do their own praying. No, *schnorring* is the only occupation that is regular all the year round. Everything else may fail—the greatest commercial houses may totter to the ground; as it is written, "He humbleth the proud." But the *schnorrer* is always secure. Whoever fails, there are always enough left to look after *him*. If you were a father, Yankele, you would understand my feelings. How can a man allow his daughter's future happiness to repose on a basis so uncertain as work? No, no. What do you make by your district visiting? Everything turns on that.
Yankele	Twenty-vive shillings a week.
Manasseh	Really?
Yankele	Law of Moses! In sixpences, shillings and half-crowns. Vy, in Houndsditch alone I have a round of five streets.

Manasseh	But are they safe? Population shifts. Good streets go down. Still, I am glad you visit the rich in their own homes—it does them good. I believe in living personal contact, not in the cold machinery of the charity institution which freezes the heart. Still, twenty five shillings a week is only sixty five pounds a year, and as this is your only secure source of income, it behooves me as a father, before even considering your candidature, to put your *schnorring* powers to the test.
Yankele	To a test? Ven I've *schnorred* from *you*.
Manasseh	We Spaniards are bountiful. You must *schnorr* from a German and a miser—Simeon Titleboam of the Orange Market, let us say.
Yankele	But he's the man I'm rattling for.
Manasseh	Ah, yes. Poor fellow—what a wrench to part with all that money. But look! Providence sends us his son!
Yankele	But his son's worse than *he* vas.
Manasseh	All the better. *Schnorr* his dead father's clothes.
Yankele	(*In despair*) But I beg of you.
Manasseh	Not of me. Of him!
Yankele	(*Rattling hopelessly*) Funeral on Sunday at ten . . . (*Frantically*) Find another test!
Manasseh	Find another father-in-law.
	(*ENTER TITLEBOAM*)
Yankele	(*Pretending at first not to see him*) Simeon Titleboam of the Orange Market—may the memory of the righteous be a blessing. Ah, Mr. Titleboam. I vish you long life. Vat a blow for de community.
Simeon T.	It comforts me to hear you say so.
Yankele	(*Sobbing*) Ah yes. Your fader vas a great and good man. Just my size.
Simeon T.	I've already given them away to Barnet the Glazier.

Yankele	But Barnet has his glaziering, and I have noding but de clothes I stand in, and dey don't fit me half as well as your fader's.
Simeon T.	You are too late. (*EXIT.*)
Yankele	(*Rattling vigorously*) Funeral—for two—(*aside*) next Sunday at ten.
Manasseh	You see you are a bungler.
Yankele	But he had given dem avay already!
Manasseh	If anyone had given away *my* clothes, I should have demanded compensation. No, wisely said the Talmud—"To give your daughter to an uncultured man is like throwing her bound to a lion."
Yankele	Me a lion! (*Weepingly*) *Oi Voi! Oi Voi!*
	(*The door opens.*)
Manasseh	Ah, here come *my* clothes. Behold.
	(*JOSEPH appears burdened as if burglariously with a large variety of garments, hats, and shoes. He slips through the door with quick caution and all but closes it behind him, heaping the clothes on the doorstep.*)
Joseph	There, I think that's all I can spare.
Manasseh	(*Glancing indifferently*) Ah!
Joseph	(*Apologetic*) You see they are not all old.
Manasseh	Well, they're not all new—*Shemah Yisroel* [Hear, O Israel]. (*Pushes open door and runs in.*)
Joseph	Here, come back, what—
Manasseh	To the kitchen, just one minute. (*Disappears within.*)
Joseph	Oh, lord! He'll get the salmon back after all. I only hope my wife won't meet him.
Yankele	(*Rattling*) Funeral on Sunday at ten!

Joseph	Go away, go away.
Yankele	But is is my vork.
Joseph	Ah, that's true. It is a pleasure to find *some one* working for his living.
Yankele	But I *schnorr* also. (*Extending palm*)
Joseph	Off with you! (*Drives him off scene.*) Gracious goodness. (*Surveying clothes*) I've put on my only new pair of pantaloons by mistake. (*Snatches them up—they are of the Regency pattern, fastening at the calves with ribbons*) Ah, he's coming. (*Tries in terror to hide them behind his legs.*)
	(*WILKINSON comes out instead. JOSEPH utters a sigh of relief and absent-mindedly wipes his perspiring brow with the pantaloons.*)
Wilkinson	That fellow's in the kitchen.
Joseph	(*Thrusting the pantaloons into his hand*) Yes yes—slip 'em into the trunk you carried down. Quick! Don't let him see.
Wilkinson	(*Dazedly*) Yes, sir. (*Takes them.*)
Joseph	Ouf! Lucky I saw them in time.
Wilkinson	But he's quarreling with cook.
Joseph	(*Waves him within*) May she be an atonement for all of us. (*WILKINSON re-ENTERs, still dazed. YANKELE is stealing back.*) I told you to be off.
Yankele	But I was ordered to carry Mr. Da Costa's clothes.
Joseph	(*Purpling*) Mr. Da Costa's. I'll kick both your breeches.
Yankele	Mine ain't vorth kicking. You couldn't spare me a better pair?
	(*Re-ENTER MANASSEH*).
Manasseh	(*Waving bag*) I have recovered it. As it is written, "And David recovered all that the Amalekites had taken."

Joseph	The salmon!
Manasseh	Sir! That is yours! You paid for it—not magnificently but honestly. It is my packets of silver that you had stolen *with* the salmon.
Joseph	How came you to think of it so suddenly?
Manasseh	Looking at your clothes reminded me. I was wondering if you had left anything in the pockets.
Joseph	(*Startling*) Ah! Do you—do you—mind my looking?
Manasseh	Am I a dog? Am I a thief that you should never go over my pockets? If I should find anything that is of no value to anybody but to you do you fear I will not return it?
Joseph	No, but—but—
Manasseh	But what? Surely you remember the Law of Moses: "When thou reapest thine harvest in thy field and hast forgot a sheaf in the field, thou shalt not go again to fetch it; it shall be for the stranger, for the fatherless, and the widow."
Joseph	(*Pointing to the heap of clothes*) Well, well—take them away.
Manasseh	(*Turns to them, utters a cry of indignation.*) Oh! (*Turns and looks at JOSEPH.*)
Joseph	What is it now?
Manasseh	I miss a pair of pantaloons?
Joseph	Nonsense! Nonsense!
Manasseh	I—miss—a—pair—of—pantaloons.
Joseph	Oh no—you have all I can spare there.
Manasseh	(*Accentuating angrily by striking heap with stick*) I—miss—a—pair—of—pantaloons. With ribbons.
Joseph	Oh, perhaps you m-mean the new pair I found had got accidentally mixed up with them.
Manasseh	Of course I mean the new pair. And so you took them away.

Just because I wasn't looking. I trusted you as a man of honour but you have broken the Law of Moses again. If you had taken an old pair I shouldn't have minded so much. But to rob a poor man of his brand new breeches—his only perfect pair.

Joseph   (*Shouting angrily*) I *must* have them. I have to go to a reception to-morrow and they are the only pair I shall have to wear. You see I—

Manasseh   Oh, very well. (*He folds the other garments in stern rebuking silence.*) But what am I to take them in?

Joseph   Humph! I'll find you a sack somewhere.

Manasseh   A sack? Would you have me look like an old clo' man. I must have a box.

Joseph   A box?

Manasseh   Yes—I saw one in the hall.

Joseph   But—but—that's not empty; there is—there are a few things in it.

Manasseh   Oh, well, you can throw those few things in with *this* lot; then the box *will* be empty, so far as *you* are concerned. Yankele.

Yankele   Yes, Mr. Da Costa?

Manasseh   Drag me that box from the hall.

Yankele   Yes, Mr. Da Costa.

(*Drags it, perspiring, while* JOSEPH *stands in apoplectic acquiescence.*)

Manasseh   I need not detain you further, Mr. Grobstock. We shall meet this evening.

Joseph   If I've anything to wear. (*Goes in banging door.*)

Yankele   (*Grinning*) Vell, *you'll* have plenty to vear, Mr. Da Costa.

Manasseh   I? I wear another man's clothes? You are to carry them to Samuel the Dealer. Don't stare at me. Bustle. Bustle, or you won't be back here by Sabbath.

Yankele   (*Still more astonished*) Back here?

Manasseh   Yes, you sup with me here this evening.

Yankele   (*Overwhelmed*) Sup with you here?

Manasseh   (*Airily*) Don't you always sup with me on Sabbath evening?

(*YANKELE dazedly throws things from the heap into box. MANASSEH looks on majestically, leaning on stick.*)

CURTAIN

END OF ACT I

ACT II

Elegant Salon in JOSEPH GROBSTOCK's *house. Two doors RIGHT and LEFT. The chandelier is lit but the blinds are not drawn. He is at the window. His wife and daughter are seated with books.*

Mrs. G.	You're very fidgety, Joseph. What's the matter?
Joseph	Fidgety? (*Leaves window*) Nonsense! Nonsense! (*Walks about, returns to window.*)
Leah	Is there anything to be seen in the street, father?
Joseph	The old man of the sea, ouf! (*Draws breath, as if throwing him off.*)
Leah	(*Goes to the window*) Where? I see no old man.
Joseph	You don't, eh? Perhaps you've only got eyes for the young men. And do you expect your precious Benjamin this evening?
Leah	I won't have Mr. Belasco spoken of like that.
Joseph	But don't you call him your precious Benjamin?
Leah	Not in that tone.
Joseph	Oh, it's the tone, is it? Well, do you expect (*mimicking love tone*) your precious Benjamin?
Mrs. G.	How you tease the child. Of course she expects him. Didn't I tell you he has placed a reserve of clothes here?
Joseph	As a sign of a long siege, I know. (*Walks and looks out of window. Sits down at little writing table in a far corner and takes up pen.*)
Mrs. G.	(*Horrified*) Joseph.

Joseph	Wh-a-a-t!
Mrs. G.	It's the Sabbath. You are going to write?
Joseph	Oh, but it isn't quite Sabbath yet. (*Looks at watch.*)
Mrs. G.	Joseph! I've already lit the Sabbath lamp.
Joseph	You were a little fast.
Mrs. G.	My dear, my watch is heaven! Look! (*Points to window.*) The sun has set!
Joseph	It was a little fast. (*Writes.*)

(*MRS. GROBSTOCK looks at LEAH in horror and shakes her head. GROBSTOCK rings the bell*)

(*WILKINSON ENTERS*)

Wilkinson	Yes, sir.
Joseph	Tell Pedro to take this to Mr. Belasco.
Wilkinson	Mr. Belasco, junior?
Joseph	Of course, you nincompoop, Beau Belasco. Who else?

(*EXIT WILKINSON.*)

Leah	What have you been writing to Mr. Belasco?
Joseph	I have asked your precious beau not to come to-night.
Leah	Not to come?
Joseph	Politely, of course.
Leah	But why?
Joseph	Why? Why?
Mrs. G.	Yes, why?
Joseph	I don't want him to come.
Leah	Why not?
Joseph	Why not? Why not?

Mrs. G.	Yes, why not?
Joseph	Why not? Because—because I want to be alone with my family.
Mrs. G.	Alone? Didn't you tell me you expect a stranger?
Joseph	And don't I tell you I won't have Beau Belasco here to-night? Good heavens. Am I not to be master in my own house? Am I not to say who shall and who shall not come? Is not an Englishman's house his castle?
Leah	If this means you are asking Benjamin to cease his attentions you might have the courage to say so.
Joseph	Courage! Ha, ha! Courage! In one's own house. To one's own wife and daughter. I tell you, Miss Impudence, that if I wanted to kick your young gentleman out of the house, I wouldn't ask your permission to put on my boots. And what's the use of his sporting his fancy waistcoats about the place or even laying up reserve forces here?
Leah	You know he'd marry me to-morrow but for that ridiculous law of the Spanish Jews.
Joseph	Confound those Spaniards. Ain't we as good as they? What does Beau Belasco mean by coming here, and thinking himself superior? D——d little fop.
Mrs. G.	Oh, Joseph. You know it's only his father—
Leah	Yes, father knows very well it's because old Moses Belasco is head of the Mahamad.
Mrs. G.	Yes, and because old Moses would cut him off with a shilling—
Joseph	Just enough for starching a waistcoat, eh? Well, you're a pair of foolish women to encourage him—I act in your interest, Leah, in keeping him away—he only keeps off others. It can never come to anything.
Leah	Oh, but his father can't live for ever.
Joseph	Hoity toity. So that's what the young people say of us, eh?

Hang it, miss, we'll live longer than you think—and you shorter. Honour your father and mother, that your days may be long in the land, hey?

Leah	If Benjamin doesn't sup here to-night, I'll not either.
Joseph	(*Gleefully*) Oh, you won't, won't you?
Leah	No, I'll go to bed at once.
Joseph	That's a good little girl.

(*LEAH bangs the door and EXITS.*)

Mrs. G.	Here's a pretty disturbance of the Sabbath, Joseph. And you never told me who—etc.
Joseph	It's not my doing.
Mrs. G.	Yes it is—it all comes from your writing. God's punishment for your sin.
Joseph	Sin! It's one's charity one suffers from.
Mrs. G.	Blasphemer. You talk like Tom Paine.
Joseph	(*Feebly smiling*) I don't feel like Tom Pleasure.
Mrs. G.	Now, you talk like Tom Fool—you know you never told me who *was* coming to supper. What's his name?
Joseph	Manasseh something—too long to tell. I'm tired.
Mrs. G.	But you'll have to introduce him.
Joseph	That's why I wish to spare myself fatigue now.
Mrs. G.	How does he look then?
Joseph	Like—like a King.
Mrs. G.	Like King George?
Joseph	No, no, a king in Israel.
Mrs. G.	Very rich, do you mean?
Joseph	He spends two guineas on a salmon.

Mrs. G.	As extravagant as you. And does he dress as fashionably?
Joseph	Quite—quite—you'd hardly know his clothes from mine.
Mrs. G.	Oh, you darling. (*Throws her arms round him.*)
Joseph	(*Gasping*) What—what's the matter?
Mrs. G.	I begin to understand.
Joseph	(*Alarmed*) You do?
Mrs. G.	Yes, forgive me for having doubted your paternal heart. Of course I know who this visitor is, and why you don't want Beau Belasco to meet him. Oh, my dear Joseph. (*Kisses him soundly.*) You are right. Beau Belasco is a blind alley. But this rich man, that might lead to something.
Joseph	(*Grimly*) It might. Maria, if you dare breathe a word to our visitor—
Mrs. G.	No, not to him, of course. But to Leah. She must be coaxed to come down. I'll go and coax her. Don't look so cross—you know how I long to be a grandmother. (*EXITS hurriedly*)
Joseph	Oh these mothers in Israel. Why, if that horse-leech had a shadow of a hint, he'd be my son-in-law before I could say *Shemah Isroel.* (*Goes to window and looks out.*) *Shemah Yisroel.* (*Runs to bell and rings violently.*)
	(*ENTER WILKINSON.*)
Joseph	I see two beggars coming to the door—I'm not at home.
Wilkinson	No, sir. (*Is going.*)
	(*LOUD KNOCKING heard.*)
Joseph	Wilkinson.
Wilkinson	Yes, sir?
Joseph	I've been taken ill suddenly.
Wilkinson	Gone to a hospital, do you mean, sir.
Joseph	No, no,—in bed here.

Wilkinson	I see. (*Going.*)
	(*Knocking grows more furious.*)
Joseph	Wilkinson.
Wilkinson	Yes, sir.
Joseph	I *am* in hospital.
Wilkinson	Yes, sir.
Joseph	Wilkinson.
Wilkinson	Yes, sir.
Joseph	Hadn't I better die outright?—But no, our Death Rattler would have had word. He's *with* him—Ah, I have it.
Wilkinson	What have you, sir?
Joseph	Smallpox. Quick! Stop!
Wilkinson	Yes, sir.
Joseph	No illness. To visit the sick is a Jewish duty, and he's so plaguily pious. (*The door heard banging—JOSEPH is appalled.*) Some one's let 'em in.
Wilkinson	Must be Pedro come back from delivering your note—I gave him my key.
Joseph	(*Furious*) You gave him your key? Why?
Wilkinson	I can't open the door to a black slave.
Joseph	I'll black and blue you—go and head 'em off at once.
Wilkinson	Yes, sir—but are you sick or dead?
Joseph	Neither, you dolt. Out of town. (*EXITS—rushes to the door to turn the key.*) D———n. Where's the key? (*Opens door finds the key on the wrong side.*) Why the deuce do they keep the key the wrong side? (*Turns and tugs at it to get it out.*)
Manasseh	(*Outside*) Liveried liar. Stand aside!
Wilkinson	But he's out of town, I tell you.

Manasseh	This way, Yankele.
Joseph	God help me. (*Retreats within.*)

(*MANASSEH throws open the door. YANKELE follows, then WILKINSON. Neither of the BEGGARS removes his hat.*)

Manasseh	(*Majestically*) *Sholem Aleichem* [Peace be to you].
Joseph	(*Faltering*) *Aleichem Sholem* [To you be peace].
Manasseh	(*Solemnly*) The Sabbath peace be upon all this house. (*Changing manner as he turns to WILKINSON.*) But not upon pig-tailed pagans. Sir, this gilded varlet would have lost you the good deed your Sabbath guest brings you. 'Tis fortunate for him that I may not carry my stick on the Sabbath.
Wilkinson	Look here, Mr. Grobstock, I . . .
Joseph	Go down, go down.
Wilkinson	But you said—
Joseph	None of your impertinence or I'll sack you.

(*EXIT WILKINSON*)

Manasseh	Nay, remember your job—"despise not the cause of thy manservant when he contends with thee."
Joseph	(*Roaring*) I haven't Job's patience. What is this ragamuffin doing here?
Manasseh	He always sups with me on Friday evening
Joseph	But I didn't invite him.
Manasseh	No, God bless you, you left me my own good deed. You did not grudge Naboth his vineyard.
Joseph	Hum! The grapes are sour, I'm afraid. Where are my clothes?
Manasseh	(*Going to door*) Wilkinson.
Joseph	What has Wilkinson to do with it?
Manasseh	Am *I* your clothes keeper?

Joseph	I wish you were. Where are the clothes I gave you?
Manasseh	O-o-oh. *My* clothes you mean. I have sold them of course.
Joseph	Sold them?
Manasseh	Yes, and very little they fetched too. Sam the Dealer said they were nearly all the worse for wear.
Joseph	And why didn't you wear the better ones then?
Manasseh	What? Have I not clothes of my own? Was that your charity—that I should wear your well-known garments abroad in my comings and in my goings, that my pantaloons should preach your philanthropy in my risings up and sittings down? That I should carry your goodness as a phylactery upon my arm, and bind it as a front-let upon my forehead, so that even as the heavens declare the glory of the Lord, so every square inch of my frame should declare your glory?
Joseph	You are unjust, unjust. I desired only that you should be better clad. Let me lend you something to wear to-night—to-night when there is no public to see—look—there is a rent in your cloak.
Manasseh	It is the rent of mourning for Jerusalem. What? While Zion lies waste and her Temple in ruins, shall Israel be spruce? Shall the exile be clad in white garments and cry Hosanna? Nay, let him be clothed in the sackcloth and ashes of righteousness and repentance. Alas! But for the *Schnorrers* there would be none in Israel with rent garments. See! Yankele, too, is tattered and torn.
Yankele	But Sabbath cancels de mourning for Jerusalem. Ve may wear good clothes to-night.
Joseph	Ah! Just so, just so!
Manasseh	*You* may borrow garments if you please, Yankele. But as for me—I never borrow. It is against my principles.
Joseph	Oh well, I'll give 'em to you.
Manasseh	I do not *schnorr* on the Holy Sabbath, save from the Almighty alone. I may be poor, but do not rob me of my one

treasure, the Law.

Joseph	Then I'll find something for Yankele. Nothing of mine would fit him, but providentially there's a parcel of clothes in the house belonging to a young gentleman about his size. Excuse me a moment. (*EXIT*)
Yankele	You see how I can *schnorr!* You, vill give me your daughter now?
Manasseh	To a jackdaw—in borrowed plumes?
Yankele	You judge too quick. My principle is really de same as yours. You never borrow. I never return.
Manasseh	Pooh! Any fool can keep loans. No, I shall find a better test than that.
Yankele	But if I pass your test, your daughter vill have a dowry vordy of her position?
Manasseh	If the Mahamad permits. First of all there would be all the money she gets from the synagogue. Our synagogue gives considerable dowries to portionless girls. There are large bequests for the purpose.
Yankele	Ah, vat gentlemen you Spaniards be!
Manasseh	Then I daresay I should hand over to my son-in-law all my Jerusalem land.
Yankele	(*Eagerly*) Have you property in de Holy Land?
Manasseh	First class with an unquestionable title. And of course I would give you a street or two in London.
Yankele	Vat?
Manasseh	Could I do less? My own flesh and blood, remember.
Yankele	Ah, you be de King of *Schnorrers*. (*Kisses the hem of his garment.*)
Manasseh	If the Mahamad permits.
	(*ENTER JOSEPH GROBSTOCK with some of the BEAU's clothes.*)

Joseph	Ah, try this. (*YANKELE gingerly puts on a rich laced coat*) There, why, it might have been made for you.
Yankele	It *vas* made for me.
	(*Business ad lib, including fitting him with a wig, silk stockings and knee-breeches. A footstep is heard without.*)
Joseph	Quick! It may be my wife. (*YANKELE clutches desperately at his breeches.*) (*ENTER WILKINSON. YANKELE relaxes his haste. WILKINSON stares open-mouthed at his gilded upper half and his bare legs.*) (*Angrily*) What do you want?
Wilkinson	A young woman's come—
Yankele	A young voman—(*Thrusts a hurried leg into his breeches.*)
Wilkinson	With a bouquet for Mr. Benjamin Belasco.
Joseph	Let her leave it in the hall.
Wilkinson	But she says she must see him personally.
Joseph	But he's not coming.
Wilkinson	But she won't go without a gold piece he promised.
Joseph	Confound her! Send her up to me.
Wilkinson	Yes, sir. (*Going*)
Joseph	(*Pointing to dirty heap of YANKELE's clothes*) But take away those things first.
Wilkinson	(*Glaring at clothes, disgusted*) Me?
Manasseh	(*Reassuringly*) Yes—it's a tip. Though you don't deserve it.
Wilkinson	(*Witheringly*) I will summon a rag-picker. (*EXITS with dignity.*)
Joseph	Oh, those domestics. (*Gets tongs and carries clothes gingerly outside door LEFT.*)
Yankele	(*Strutting in his new-finery*) Ah, dese vill do to be married in, eh?
Manasseh	You are premature. I have not yet set the test.

(*Re-ENTER JOSEPH*)

Joseph	And now won't you sit down?
Manasseh	Won't you sit down, Yankele? I am sorry to keep you so long. I hope you are not hungry.
Joseph	I expect Mrs. Grobstock down every minute and then we will go in to supper.
Manasseh	Ah. That reminds me. I hope you keep your butter and meat plates separate.
Joseph	Of course.
Manasseh	Because unless everything is strictly *kosher,* I cannot eat with you.
Joseph	You can't? (*Eagerly*) Well, I'm not quite sure—
Manasseh	Then I must go down to the kitchen and make sure.
Joseph	(*Stopping him*) Oh, no need. My wife's father was the saintly Aaron Bemberg. And she inherited all his piety.
Manasseh	Ah, the best of all dowries—I congratulate you. But since you have raised my doubts, I must lay them myself. Do not forget it is the first time I have eaten at a German table.
Joseph	(*Frantically*) But I assure you—(*Runs after him.*)
	(*YANKELE, timid at being left alone, makes as if to follow.*)
Wilkinson	(*Outside, throwing open door RIGHT.*) This way, Miss.
	(*ENTER DEBORAH, now clad coquettishly in her Sabbath finery and carrying the BEAU's bouquet. Door closes.*)
Yankele	(*Turning with a cry of joy*) Deborah!
Deborah	(*With her eyes starting out of their sockets*) That's never you!
Yankele	Dat *is* me. Inside, I mean. You didn't like my clothes, so I got a new suit. I didn't think you'd come after me so quick—vid flowers, too.
Deborah	Don't be silly. These flowers are for Beau Belasco—you heard

	him order them. It's you that seem to have come after me.
Yankele	May my next mouthful choke me, if I bodered my 'ead about you.
Deborah	Then what brought you here?
Yankele	My legs. (*Strokes his shimmering hose.*)
Deborah	Don't be silly, I tell you. What are you doing in this grand house?
Yankele	Vaiting for supper vid it's master.
Deborah	You fibber. You know he'd only have you in the kitchen.
Yankele	Clothes like dis can eat anyveres.
Deborah	(*More and more impressed*) Then you aren't eating with father to-night?
Yankele	(*Indignantly*) Do you tink I desert old friends?
Deborah	Then isn't it time you came along?
Yankele	But it is *'ere* ve eat. Ve are both invited.
Deborah	He leaves his family?
Yankele	He takes some of it vid him!
Deborah	What do you mean?
Yankele	Ask my fader-in-law.
Deborah	And who is dat?
Yankele	Dat's *your* fader. See?
Deborah	I don't see.
Yankele	(*Sighs*) Love is blind. Your fader and my fader-in-law—dat's von. So you and me—dat's von, too.
Deborah	(*Half angry yet not at all displeased in view of his fine clothes.*) One, too? Do you mean to say my father has accepted you—?
Yankele	Ve have even settled de dowry.

Deborah	(*Flaring up*) And what about me?
Yankele	*You* go vid de dowry.
Deborah	Impudent face.
Yankele	I told you I'd arrange vid your fader.
Deborah	You conceited puppy. Why didn't you let *me* arrange with him?
Yankele	You?
Deborah	He's sure to diddle *you.*
Yankele	Vat?
Deborah	Who but me knows his ways? I could have got twice as much dowry out of him . . . where *is* he?
Yankele	(*Points kitchenwards.*) Down dere. Inspecting de kitchen.
Deborah	Hold this. (*Dumps the bouquet into his arms and hurries door LEFT.*)
Yankele	(*Bothered with the bouquet*) No, no—don't go to him—'ve haven't quite—and it ain't a voman's business—(*Pursues her.*) Grobstock's there too. Don't leave me alone in this palace.
	(*She runs out—the door bangs in his face. LEAH and her mother are heard approaching outside the other door.*)
Leah	Very well, I'll come to supper. But I warn you—
Yankele	(*Panic-stricken*) *Gott in Himmel.*
	(*ENTER MRS. and MISS GROBSTOCK. YANKELE snatches up a book and turns an alarmed back to them.*)
Mrs. G.	(*Sotto voce to LEAH*) You see. Quite as beautiful as your Beau!
Leah	Let me be, I tell you.
Mrs. G.	(*Advancing*) Delighted to welcome you, sir. (*YANKELE tee-totums round and grins and bows awkwardly.*) This is my

daughter Leah. (*LEAH makes a stiff movement. YANKELE bows to the ground.*) You have brought a bouquet for her. How kind. (*Advances to take it.*)

Yankele	(*In his nervousness rattling the bouquet and uttering his cry.*) Funeral at ten.
Mrs. G.	(*Starting back*) A funeral bouquet?
Yankele	(*Trying to explain*) It's Mr. Benjamin Belasco's.
Leah	(*Hysterically*) Benjamin dead?
Yankele	God forbid—I mean de flowers.
Mrs. G.	(*Taking it*) The flowers are far from dead—it is a beautiful bouquet. (*Tenders it to LEAH who refuses sulkily.*) Won't you sit down, sir.
Yankele	Tank you. (*Goes towards door LEFT.*)
Mrs. G.	Where are you going, sir?
Yankele	To sit in de kitchen. I am not a "sir"! (*Hurries out LEFT.*)
Mrs. G.	Goodness gracious. He's only the servant. What must the master be? Here, Leah, take his marvellous bouquet!
Leah	I won't. I want neither his flowers nor his proposal. So that's the reason father wrote Benjamin not to come. Oh, I'll go back to bed.
Mrs. G.	No, no, you must not be so rude. He is a person of the highest consideration.
Leah	I don't care. I'll marry for love, and love only.
Mrs. G.	Ah me, I always told your father we should suffer from your ungodly bringing-up. Love? In my young days no respectable Jewish girl thought of such a thing; any more than a Jewish youth thought of ruffling it with a sword. Now all heads are stuffed with Christian notions. It's scandalous. If you had listened to me, instead of this moonshine romance with an unmarriageable Spaniard, I should have long since been a grandmother.

Leah	It is two souls that should be united under the wedding canopy, not two money-bags, nor four grandparents.
Mrs. G.	Oh, dear, dear, what will become of the Fifth Commandment?

(*WILKINSON throws open door, announces*)

Wilkinson	Mr. Benjamin Belasco.

(*Door closes—BEAU ENTERS*)

Leah	Benjamin!
Mrs. G.	(*Startled and annoyed*) Did you not get the note Mr. Grobstock sent you?
Beau B.	The note?
Mrs. G.	You must have left before it arrived.
Beau B.	Well, he can tell me its contents by word of mouth. What wonderful flowers, Madam; symbol of your beauty though they will fade before it. But where, by the way, is the bouquet I ordered for your daughter? Wilkinson assures me the young woman brought it up here.
Mrs. G.	I have seen no young woman with flowers—it was a young man brought these for Leah.
Beau B.	(*Hand on sword*) A young man. Where is he?
Mrs. G.	In the kitchen.
Beau B.	The kitchen?
Mrs. G.	Yes, he brought the flowers from his master.
Beau B.	Then where's the master?
Mrs. G.	Not yet arrived.
Beau B.	Zounds, madam, after leading me to believe it was *my* suit you smiled on—I suppose the fellow has gold.
Mrs. G.	A Croesus, I understand. And you know that your father

will never—

Beau B.	'Sdeath. I'll slit his gizzard asunder. My steel against his gold.
Mrs. G.	(*Frightened*) Joseph! Leah! Where is your father? (*Runs out distractedly door RIGHT.*)
	(*LEAH seats herself at the desk and begins a note*)
Beau B.	(*Approaching jealously*) To whom are you writing?
Leah	To your rival, of course.
Beau B.	You shameless creature.
Leah	(*Smiling*) And you are to slip my note into his hand.
Beau B.	I?
Leah	Didn't you see I hadn't taken his flowers? This is only to tell him my heart is not free—an appeal to his chivalry to withdraw his suit.
Beau B.	(*Indignantly*) Appeal? To a commercial Croesus. Give me the pen. (*Seizes it.*) I, too, can write notes—in blood.
Leah	(*Alarmed*) You don't mean—
Beau B.	I do. Chalk Farm. Dawn. Sunday. Swords or pistols.
Leah	Great Heavens.
Beau B.	Silence, Juliet. I hold you against all comers. (*Strikes attitude.*)
Leah	But my note appeals to his honour.
Beau B.	So does mine.
Leah	If he is a man of honour he will withdraw.
Beau B.	If he is a man of honour he will fight.
Leah	But if he killed you.
Beau B.	You said I must die alone.

Leah	But, dearest.
	(*Re-ENTER* MRS. GROBSTOCK, *still distracted.*)
Beau B.	But I can shoot a sparrow at fifty paces.
Mrs. G.	I don't mind your shooting sparrows—but sons-in-law are sacred. Joseph! Joseph. Where are you?
	(*Re-ENTER* MR. GROBSTOCK LEFT. *She gives a cry of relief.*)
	Oh, Joseph.
Joseph	What's the matter? (*Perceives the* BEAU.) You here?
Beau B.	(*Advancing*) Punctuality is my one foible. So glad, sir, to see you looking so well.
Joseph	(*Murmuring*) You're very kind.
	(WILKINSON, ENTERING, *offers the* BEAU *a note on a salver.*)
Wilkinson	It came back from your house, sir. (*EXIT.*)
Beau B.	Excuse me. It is marked urgent. What is this? "Please don't come to-night, as I am ill in bed—Joseph Grobstock." (*Crumples note angrily.*) I congratulate you on your courtesy and your veracity. (*Turns to go.*)
Leah	No. Benjamin, you mustn't go.
Joseph	(*Embarrassed*) It wasn't discourtesy. The truth is there is a person I didn't want you to meet.
Beau B.	(*Grimly*) So I understand.
Joseph	No, you don't. Even my wife doesn't. Maria, you mustn't be surprised at our new guest's clothes.
Mrs. G.	Nothing would surprise me—after the way his very servant dresses.
Joseph	What servant?
Mrs. G.	You didn't see the man who brought these beautiful flowers? A little fellow. (*Exhibits bouquet.*)

Joseph	Oh—ah—yes—I did see him. But what I want to warn you is, it is the—the master you might take for the servant, judging by his dress.
Mrs. G.	But you said he dressed like you.
Joseph	On week-days. On Sabbaths, when other people put on Sabbath finery, he puts on Sabbath shabbiness. And he wears holes in his clothes for Jerusalem's sake. You might take him—ha! ha! ha!—for a beggar.
Beau B.	(*Disgusted*) A beggar?
Joseph	He's too pious even to take off his hat.
Leah	Deplorable.
Mrs. G.	Adorable. The very man for a Jewish girl.
Leah	Pah! I'd rather sit at table with his servant.
Joseph	You will.
Mrs. G.	What?
Joseph	Yes, he insists that on Sabbath master and man are equal and both must take their rest in common.
Mrs. G.	My father told me of such goings on in Poland. But what will Wilkinson say?
Joseph	You, you'd hardly know the man from our young friend, the Beau . . . they might go to the same tailor.
Beau B.	What's that? A servant go to my tailor? A menial ape my creations? What? I shall toil and moil to create and clods shall have the benefit of my taste? The filthy snip! I'll pay his bill at once.
Joseph	No, no violent measures.
Beau B.	(*With a terrible cry*) Gadzooks and odsbodkins.
All	What has happened?
Beau B.	I've spilt ink on my waistcoat. Leah, where's my parcel?
Joseph	(*Alarmed, rushing to inspect it*) That speck! Why, it needs a

	microscope.
Beau B.	It looks to me like a cart-wheel.
Joseph	Positively improves the pattern.
Beau B.	Does it?
Joseph	Puts it beyond imitation. . . . Have a glass of wine before supper? (*Rings.*) I have a magnum of Madeira of a wonderful year. It's a capital appetizer.
Beau B.	I must confess Madeira is my one foible.
Mrs. G.	But why doesn't the Master arrive?
Joseph	(*Embarrassed*) He's already in the kitchen.
Mrs. G.	(*Amazed*) The kitchen?
Joseph	Yes—you see—hush! (*ENTER WILKINSON*) Bring me the last of that old Madeira.
Beau B.	And give these notes to the gentleman in the kitchen.
Wilkinson	(*Coldly*) What gentleman?
Joseph	(*Hastily*) The tall one. Go along. (*Shepherds him out door LEFT.*)
Mrs. G.	But what is he doing in the kitchen?
Joseph	It's that piety you admire. He's testing your pots and pans.
Mrs. G.	(*Affronted*) Testing? Oh, you oughtn't to have permitted that—even to a suitor.
Joseph	(*Grimly*) A suitor? Maria—
	(*VOICES without.*)
Manasseh	(*Outside*) No test, no marriage, I tell you.
Joseph	Good Lord! (*MANASSEH opens the door and ENTERS pompously. YANKELE slinks in behind him.*) My dear, this is Mr. Da Costa.
Manasseh	(*Bowing*) Manasseh Bueno Barzillai Azevedo Da Costa, and

this is Yankele, a poor friend of mine.

(*YANKELE bows awkwardly*)

Mrs. G.	Your *friend* is welcome.
Manasseh	Of that I was assured. The reputation of Aaron Bemberg's beautiful daughter for hospitality is only second to the proverb of her piety.
Mrs. G.	(*Smiling and greatly pleased*) Ah, but you doubted my piety.
Manasseh	Never, madam.
Mrs. G.	You examined my pots and pans.
Manasseh	Only because your husband said he wasn't sure.
Mrs. G.	Joseph!
Joseph	If we reached *his* standard.
Manasseh	And your husband felt I was responsible for my friend.
Joseph	(*Gratefully*) Yes, yes.
Manasseh	(*Clapping YANKELE on the shoulder*) But it reaches even your standard, does it not, Yankele? I'm so glad you were able to come. (*Looking towards LEAH*) And this, I suppose, is the young lady who has written to me?
Joseph & Mrs. G.	Written to you?
Manasseh	She has done me that honour.
Beau B.	(*Aggressively*) We both wrote to him. I hope you got *my* note too.
Manasseh	Yes, sir; but I am afraid its value as an autograph is slight. Ah, Master Benjamin, had you been as attentive to your synagogue as to your toilette or your pistol practice, you would have had a better acquaintance with me.
Beau B.	You are of *our* synagogue?

Manasseh	A humble subject of the Mahamad.
Mrs. G.	(*Disappointed*) You, too?
Leah	How fortunate!
Manasseh	It is indeed our good fortune. Would we were worthy of it. But alas! Only the other day our President was lamenting to me—
Leah	You knew Mr. Belasco's father?
Manasseh	He is one of my chief supporters.
Joseph	(*Involuntarily*) Ha! Ha! Ha! (*Recollecting himself*) You mean in your synagogue schemes.
Manasseh	Whatever I have in hand. But it is useless reckoning on this young gentleman's assistance.
Beau B.	I pay my poll-tax and every bill the rascals send me. Monstrous fine sums, too, egad.
Manasseh	But you never go there.
Mrs. G.	Oh fie, Mr. Belasco!
Beau B.	A man of fashion cannot be everywhere. Routs and rigotti play the deuce with one's time.
Manasseh	What a pity! One misses you there. 'Tis no edifying spectacle—a slovenly rabble with none to set the standard of taste.
Beau B.	Ah, the clods. The fusty shop-keepers. But your man there—by Gad! He knows more than the whole Mahamad. Where did you get those clothes from?
	(*JOSEPH GROBSTOCK looks appealingly to the SCHNORRERS as begging them not to betray him.*)
Yankele	My Maker.
Beau B.	Yes, but who's that?
Manasseh	You are profane, sir. He means the Almighty, blessed be He, who clothes us even as He clothes the dumb creation.

Beau B.	But not with such taste as this. This looks like my own doublet. Nobody else has the design.
Manasseh	Ah, my dear Beau, are not your cast-off clothes sold in Rag Fair, where every tailor in London is on the watch to snap up your inventions?

(*GROBSTOCK gives him grateful look.*)

Beau B.	True, true.
Manasseh	What is the remedy? *Give* your clothes to the poor.
Beau B.	The poor, the poor, always the poor. Charity's all very well for your trading rabble. But I have such extravagant tastes. In fact if your Dan Mendoza fails to lick Dick Humphreys at Doncaster—
Manasseh	You back up a bruiser, a defacer of God's image. He should be excommunicated by the Mahamad.
Joseph	No, by God, no. You should have seen him lick the Badger in thirty-five minutes on a twenty-four-foot stage.
Mrs. G.	Joseph!
Manasseh	I would willingly exchange our Mendoza for your David Levi, the writer.
Joseph	What? Do you know of our mad hatter? He makes nothing at all out of his books.
Manasseh	You should subscribe for more copies.
Joseph	(*Meaningly*) I would, if *you* wrote them.
Manasseh	I took a dozen.
Joseph	You can afford them. I have to earn my money.
Mrs. G.	Well, even if Mr. Da Costa hasn't to earn his, it's none the less to his credit. How many men born to great possessions remain indifferent to learning?
Manasseh	Most true. And yet learning and intellect are the only things in the world essentially valuable. Money? It can always be

had for the asking. It passes from hand to hand. But who can pass on genius or taste?

Beau B.   That is true. (*ENTER WILKINSON with the Madeira and glasses.*) Ah, here is something to pass *round*.

Joseph   (*Perceiving WILKINSON's astonishment at the motley company as he opens the bottle.*) That will do, Wilkinson. (*EXIT WILKINSON. Business, GROBSTOCK begins pouring out the wine.*) Sit, gentlemen, sit.

Manasseh   One moment, Mr. Grobstock. Is this the consecration wine?

Joseph   Oh no! That's on the supper-table. Why do you ask?

Manasseh   Because if this had been wine for the ceremony, I should have asked you to wait for my daughter.

Joseph   Your daughter?

Mrs. G.   You have a daughter, too?

Yankele   (*Proudly*) My Deborah.

Joseph   Your Deborah?

Manasseh   But I introduced her to you in the kitchen.

Joseph   But I never invited her.

Manasseh   Your wife called you away suddenly. I repaired your omission.

Joseph   (*Angrily*) I must do my own repairs, thank you.

Manasseh   Oh, no apology. We all quite understood. She is making her toilette in one of your too numerous spare rooms. I am glad she will be in time for the consecration ceremony.

Beau B.   Meantime, we are letting good Madeira spoil.

Joseph   I beg your pardon. (*Resumes pouring.*) (*Business—LEAH hands the wine.*) Give mother one, even if you're afraid yourself.

Mrs. G.	No, no.
Joseph	Yes, Yes. (*MRS. GROBSTOCK is given a glass—GROBSTOCK raises his.*) *Lechayim,* gentlemen [to your lives, gentlemen].
All	*Lechayim* [to your life].
Yankele	(*After a rapturous sip*) No vonder Noah got drunk.
Manasseh	I am so glad you like our fare, Yankele. You must come again. (*Drains his glass.*) Delicious indeed. My cousin Barzillai's cellar holds no better.
Joseph	(*Amazed*) Barzillai of Fenchurch Street, the big West India merchant?
Manasseh	The same—an excellent man, a bit stockish, perhaps.
Joseph	And he is your cousin?
Manasseh	So he says. (*Sips*) A beautiful bouquet.
Beau B.	Very choice indeed.
Joseph	(*Gratified*) There'll be another glass all round.
Manasseh	(*Aside to YANKELE*) I've got the marriage test. Get me the rest of the bottle.
Yankele	(*Groaning in despair*) *Oi Voi!*
Leah	What's the matter?
Manasseh	A little heart attack—he'll soon get over it. I was glad to see, Mrs. Grobstock, that your cook knows the right sauce for my salmon.
Mrs. G.	Was that *your* salmon?
Manasseh	It was—this morning.
Mrs. G.	How good of you to present it to us. Joseph, why didn't you tell me—?
	(*JOSEPH, agitated, spills wine over his coat.*)
Manasseh	Take care, Mr. Grobstock, take care. You are spilling wine all down my coat. Bestir yourself, Yankele. (*Aside*) Ah, nobody

	makes sauce like Hyman of the London Tavern.
Joseph	Oh, I'll back cook. (*Rising*) Let's finish this and we'll go and test the point. (*He rises and takes up the bottle to re-fill the glasses.*)
Manasseh	(*Aside to* YANKELE) One drop lost, you lose my daughter.
	(*YANKELE trembles all over*)
Beau B.	(*Raising glass towards* GROBSTOCK.) I drink to a connoisseur.
Yankele	(*Screams*) *Oi Voi!*
All	Is it your heart?
Yankele	(*Clasping hand to stomach*) No, my belly.
	I feel a pain here—if de vine should be poisoned.
Others	Poisoned?
	(*BEAU B. sets down his glass*)
Joseph	Poisoned, sir? I'd have you know this wine comes direct from the vaults of the treasurer of our synagogue, Nathan Mordecai.
Yankele	(*Desperately*) *Olov Hasholom* [peace be upon him].
Joseph	(*Pausing, bottle in hand*) What did you say?
Yankele	Yes, he died dis afternoon.
All	Dead?
Yankele	(*Nods*) Poor soul.
Joseph	(*Putting down bottle*) Mordecai, of our synagogue, are you sure?
Yankele	Who should know if not me? (*In professional tones*) Funeral on Sunday at eleven.
Joseph	But I saw him in the street this morning.
Yankele	And den he fell down dead.

Mrs. G.	Heart disease?
Yankele	No, apoplexy.
Joseph	(*Very affected*) Tut, tut, tut.
Leah	Well, after all, he was an old man, father. Drink a little more Madeira. (*Takes up bottle.*)
Yankele	Yes, but his daughter vasn't old—such a bright bonny creature, *olov hasholom* [peace be upon her].
Leah	(*Putting down bottle*) The daughter dead too?
Yankele	Ven dey brought home de body—heart disease.
Leah	Oh! (*Totters into the* BEAU'S *arms.*)
Mrs. G.	(*Starting up*) A drop of wine. (*Takes up bottle.*)
Yankele	So dey vill all dree be buried on Sunday—
Mrs. G.	(*Putting down bottle*) All three?
Yankele	You did not suppose de moder could bear such a double shock—her rest be Eden. You look pale, Mr. Da Costa. Some vine. (*Helps him and stands over him with bottle.*)
Manasseh	Ah, Mr. Grobstock, does it not remind us that we are all God's beggars? (*Sipping*) Naked we came into the world and naked we leave it. Rejoice, O young man, in your strength. (*Sips*) But a day will come when the corpse-watchers will perform your toilette. In plain white they will dress you, and the worms will never know what a dandy you were. (*Drinks.*) (ALL *sit round miserably.* YANKELE *re-fills* MANASSEH'S *glass*) Bear up, Mr. Grobstock, remember the saying of the Talmud; there are ten strong things in the world. The rock is strong, but iron breaks it. (*Sips*) The iron's strong, but fire can melt it. (*Sips*) The fire is strong, but water—(*long sip*) can quench it. (YANKELE *refills glass.*) Water is strong, the clouds—(*long sip*) absorb it. The clouds are strong, the wind disperses them. The wind is strong, a man—(*sips*) withstands it. A man is strong, but fear unmans him. (YANKELE *fills glass.*) Man's fear is strong, but wine—(*sips*) removes it. (*Holds up glass for last drop.*) And wine is

strong—(*drinks to dregs*) but sleep dispels it. (*Rising*) But stronger than all these is—Death; yet CHARITY delivers from Death. (*MANASSEH walks meditatively about. YANKELE follows him. OTHERS sit gloomily.*)

Yankele	Congratulate me.
Manasseh	On what?
Yankele	On my fader-in-law.
Manasseh	I cannot congratulate you on your methods. You slaughtered too many for your wedding-feast.
Yankele	But I get de land in Jerusalem, and de streets in London?

(*WILKINSON throws open the door and DEBORAH ENTERS still more spruced up. Her entry breaks the gloom.*)

Beau B.	(*Springing up*) Ah, at last!
Manasseh	I said she would be in time.
Beau B.	(*To DEBORAH*) But where are my flowers?
Deborah	There they are!

(*Points to MRS. GROBSTOCK, still holding bouquet.*)

Beau B.	(*Dazed*) Then it's my own gizzard I've sworn to slit.
Manasseh	And here, Madam, is *my* flower—my rose of Sharon—my daughter Deborah.
Wilkinson	(*Who has remained at door*) Supper is served, Madam.
Mrs. G.	Your daughter is welcome—will you take in mine? (*MANASSEH does not stir*) Mr. Belasco, your arm. (*He gives it her. She turns.*) Mr. Da Costa, will you take in my daughter?
Manasseh	Certainly not.

(*Sensation.*)

Mrs. G.	Sir!
Manasseh	Madam! (*Dramatic pause*) Do you imagine I allow strange young ladies to hang on my arm? You will next expect me

to dance a minuet with my hand in hers. Ah, where is the ancient piety, when even Aaron Bemberg's daughter—? Nay, my young lady, do not imagine I am rude, but such attentions are reserved for my wife, God bless her.

Mrs. G.   Your wife?

Manasseh   Ay, your husband knows well I have a wife and I am astonished it should have entered into his head that I would give her a bill of divorcement—

Joseph   (*Gasping*) Wh-a-a-t!

Manasseh   (*In tremulous tones*) My old, faithful Sarah, mother of my children.

Joseph   But it never entered my head.

Manasseh   Did you expect me then to commit bigamy? Are these your German morals?

Joseph   But I never suggested you as a son-in-law.

Manasseh   (*Displaying note*) Then why does your daughter appeal to me to withdraw my suit? Did you think I would give up my independent life to be attached tamely to a luxurious household—and that a German's? Or that I would foist myself upon an unwilling heart, upon a heart already pledged?

Leah   (*With shining eyes*) Sir, I am vastly obliged to you.

Manasseh   It is nothing. To a Spanish Jew love is sacred. Who has sung of love in all our Hebrew literature since the exile? Only the Spanish poets? Only Jehuda Halevi, only Moses Ibn Ezra?

Beau B.   Sir, you are a man after my own heart. Here's my hand on it.

Manasseh   (*Spurning it*) Nay, there is blood on that hand.

Mr. & Mrs. G.   Blood!

Manasseh   In intention! This young whipper-snapper has challenged me to a duel.

Mrs. G.   (*Distraught*) I knew he would!

Manasseh	Ay, he is not content to ape the Christian gallants in his clothes, he yearns to flesh his blade for a pretty face. But these customs, young sir, ill befit a race whose greeting to the living is—Peace, whose prayer over the dead is—Peace, whose message to mankind is—Peace. (*Takes out note*) Choose your weapons, he says. But where? I know no Jew who possesses an armoury, or I should choose as many as I could *schnorr*. No, my sweet young lady, be not alarmed for him. I shall not rip up those laces and velvets and waste some poor man's substance. Take him whole and sound. The hand he just now offered me I give to you. The hand your father offered me I give to him. (*Joins their hands, carefully not touching the girl's.*) Be happy.
Joseph	But this is nonsense. They cannot be happy.
Mrs. G.	No, they cannot marry.
Manasseh	(*Imperiously*) Who forbids them?
Joseph	Your synagogue—your *superior* synagogue.
Leah	(*Half weeping*) Your cruel Mahamad. We are of the German community.
Manasseh	It is a misfortune for you. I had forgotten for the moment. (*Broods, with hand to brow.*)
Yankele	(*Murmurs gloomily*) If de Mahamad permits.
Leah	(*Hysterically*) Oh, if this cruel law could only be abolished. Oh, Mr. Da Costa. (*Coming to him with pleading arms*) You who have always synagogue schemes in hand—
Manasseh	(*Thunderously*) Enough! It shall be abolished.
	(*Sensation*)
Leah	Oh, our good angel! (*Breaks into sobs of relief.*)
Joseph	(*Angrily*) *You* will abolish this law?
Manasseh	I will. Times are changed. These laws were framed when your community was a rabble of uncultured pedlars. Now that I have come *among* them I see that there are some who would not disgrace our own community.

Beau B.	A Daniel come to judgment.
Manasseh	Who dares to say that a union between this young exquisite and this . . . exquisite young lady is a descent—for her? No, away with these obsolete traditions! This marriage shall be blessed by the Mahamad.
Leah	(*Through her sobs*) Oh, thank you! Thank you!
Joseph	(*Sternly*) Da Costa, I'll have no fooling with my daughter's happiness. You know you have no power to do this.
Beau B.	But if my father is one of his chief supporters!
Manasseh	With his support or without it, it shall be done. Only one thing, young sir, if I do this for you, what will you do for the synagogue?
Mrs. G.	A Judas Maccabeus come to judgment.
Beau B.	The synagogue shall not find me lacking in good example.
Manasseh	Well spoken! Then I abrogate the Law at once. I set the first precedent. Stand forth, Yankele.
Yankele	(*Wonderingly*) Yes, Mr. Da Costa.
Manasseh	And you, Deborah! (*Very solemnly and slowly*) I, Manasseh Bueno Barzillai Azevedo Da Costa, a Spaniard, give unto you, Yankele ben Yisroile, of the Genrian community, my daughter Deborah, in marriage.
Yankele	My benefactor. (*Falls at feet, embracing them.*)
Joseph	(*Dazed*) Yes, but how does that help us? Belasco and Leah?
Manasseh	Oh, blind, blind! The Mahamad will summon me before it to censure me for my daughter's announced marriage, I shall appear—but it is not I that shall be censured. We shall stand face to face; on the one side the Mahamad in full council, on the other Reason and Justice. We shall see which is the stronger. My daughter shall be the test-case; she shall strike off the bonds from yours. She shall be the martyr of her sex, the scapegoat of her sisters. An end to the infamous Law!
Leah	(*In tears*) Heaven bless you, sir.

Yankele	(*Looking up from the floor*) But you'll make it vorth her vile to be a scapegoat?
Joseph	Stop fooling with my daughter, I tell you. How can a man in your position stand up against the Elders of the Synagogue?
Manasseh	(*Rising to his full height*) You doubt that I can stand up—? (*JOSEPH withers palpably. MANASSEH turns to YANKELE.*) What do *you* think, Yankele?
Yankele	I tink you could stand up to de Devil himself and *schnorr* souls out of hell.
Manasseh	Nay, nay. Not unless they deserved it.
Joseph	Well, all I can say is, if you do succeed, I'll give you a thousand pounds!
Manasseh	(*Overtowering him, immense, prophetic*) Sir!
Joseph	(*Mystified*) I beg your pardon?
Manasseh	You talk business on my Sabbath!
Mrs. G.	For shame, Joseph.
Manasseh	And do you not think that to dry the tears of beauty is not sufficient reward for a son of Spain?
Leah	(*Impulsively*) Oh, sir!
	(*He draws back from the pollution of her touch, waving her back.*)
Beau	Will you take my hand now? (*Extends it.*)
Manasseh	(*Taking it*) Ay, I will take you in to the Sabbath meal. Come now, Yankele, get on your legs and take in our host. And do you, Mrs. Grobstock, bring up the rear with our daughters, as is correct for women. (*Leading procession*) And now let us eat and drink and bless the Lord for all His mercies.

CURTAIN

END OF ACT II.

ACT III

Council-Chamber of the Mahamad with Norman windows and decorated by gold-lettered panes inscribed with the names of pious donors. In an alcove behind the table which stretches horizontally across the stage is the Presidential seat—six chairs around the table. The door is at RIGHT. A revolving bookcase LEFT. Candles in old-fashioned candelabra could be lit.

(The CHANCELLOR, i.e. the Secretary, a little man, an odd medley of meekness and pomp, with a snuff-smeared upper lip and a nose that has dipped in the wine when it is red, is discovered laying out pens and paper and agenda papers for the Council. He places the Minute Book before the Presidential chair, likewise a bowl of sand for blotting. Having completed his work, the CHANCELLOR produces a phial of brandy from an inner Docket and is taking a swig when the door opens and BEAU BELASCO and LEAH appear at the aperture.)

Beau B.	This is the Council Chamber—! (*The CHANCELLOR in comic confusion hides his phial*) Hullo, who are you?
Chancellor	(*Spluttering with indignation and confusion*) Who—who am I? Unprecedented! *I'm* the *Chancellor* of the Mahamad. (*Angrily*) Who are you?
Beau B.	The Secretary of the Mahamad forgets himself—as well as me. (*Pleased with himself*) Well-turned that, eh, Leah?
Leah	The door-handle wasn't. You should have knocked.
Beau B.	A Belasco knock for a menial! I knew my father and the Council were not yet due.
Chancellor	I—I beg your pardon. Are you not Belasco's son?
Beau B.	I, Mr. Belasco's son! No, sir! *He's* my father!

Chancellor	What's the difference?
Beau B.	Precisely that! Mr. Belasco's son—what does that say, outside the Exchange? But Beau Belasco's father—gad! that has a meaning from Bond Street to Bath.
Leah	(*Points to alcove*) And is that where your father sits? I feel all of a tremble.
Beau B.	Compose yourself! (*Offers her a chair, she sits.*)
Chancellor	Unprecedented! Madam, these chairs are for the Council!
Leah	I know. I'm going to sit in the gallery.
Chancellor	The gallery?
Leah	Isn't there a gallery like in Christian courts?
Chancellor	The gentlemen of the Mahamad do not play to a gallery.
Leah	(*To BEAU B*) I thought you said—
Beau B.	I did think there would be a niche somewhere to shelter you.
Leah	Well, I can sit quiet behind that book stand.
Chancellor	Impossible, Madam! Unprecedented!
Leah	(*Half-weeping*) Oh dear. And I did so want to see how Mr. Manasseh manages the Mahamad!
Chancellor	(*Dazed*) How what, madam?
Beau B.	Haven't you got some case coming on to-day? Ah! (*Seizes agenda.*)
Chancellor	(*Trying to take it away*) That is private, sir.
Beau B.	So is this.
	(*Slips banknote into his hand.*)
Chancellor	(*Overwhelmed*) Five pounds!
Beau B.	Unprecedented, eh? But to establish precedents is my one

foible. Ah, here it is! "Proposed Marriage of a Pauper's Daughter with a Member of the Other Nation." That's the case this young lady would have liked to hear.

Chancellor	(*Further dazed*) *She* isn't the pauper's daughter!
Beau B.	No, no—but she's interested in her.
Chancellor	In a hussy who wants to marry one of *us!*
Leah	I only want to hear the case argued.
Chancellor	Argued! There will be no argument. The gentlemen of the Mahamad will simply prohibit the marriage. The case has no interest whatever—it'll all be over in two minutes.
Beau B.	The devil it will!
Leah	But if she insists on marrying—
Chancellor	Then she will be buried—
Leah	(*Startled*) Alive?
Chancellor	No, no. Outside the pale. When she dies, of course.
Leah	And if it is a man who defies the Mahamad?
Chancellor	He, too, will be buried behind the boards.
Beau B.	Have done, both of you. You make my flesh creep. Let me see you to a coach. (*Raising her*) I will come back and report to you.
Chancellor	Oh, sir, *you* cannot stay, either!
Beau B.	What—the President's son!
Chancellor	Not the monarch's son himself, unless duly elected a member of the Mahamad.
Beau B.	Ridiculous!
Chancellor	Would you walk into Mr. Pitt's Cabinet?
Beau B.	If I were Mr. Pitt's son, I should certainly feel quite at home there.

Leah	Let them be, Benjamin. They are a set of cold-blooded autocrats—worse than the Council of Venice! Oh, (*shakes her fist at the Presidential seat*) to think that beings like these have the control of human hearts! (*Shakes chair near her.*)
Chancellor	(*Dismayed*) Madam! That is the Warden's chair!
Leah	(*Hysterically*) I wish I had a bodkin for it. (*Fiercely*) Who sits here?
Chancellor	The *Parnass* of the Holy Land.
Beau B.	Jerusalem!
Leah	And who sits here?
Chancellor	That, madam, is the President of the Congregation.
Beau B.	But I thought my father—
Chancellor	Your father is something much bigger—the President of the Mahamad.
Beau B.	I see. (*Touches another chair.*) And what ill-dressed individual plumps his blatant breeches here?
Chancellor	Oh, sir! That is the Treasurer.
Beau B.	(*Smiling*) Ha! The man with the deficit!
Chancellor	Oh no, sir. We never have deficits here.
Beau B.	(*Glumly*) I don't feel as much at home as I thought.
Leah	Then let us go and await our friend's report. (*Viciously to chair she has risen from*) Well, I sat on *you*, anyhow!
Chancellor	The Chief of the Elders, madam!
Leah	Ha! I'd like to sit on them all. How many more are there?
Chancellor	Only the Warden of the Captives.
Leah	So you keep prisoners too! Brutes! (*Shakes fist.*)
Chancellor	No, madam. It's the Moorish corsairs and the Turks that keep the prisoners. We ransom them from the brutes—that

	is—if they are *Yahadim* . . . (*Voices without*) I hear them coming! (*Agitated*)
Leah	The brutes?
Chancellor	No, no, the gentlemen of the Mahamad. You mustn't be caught here.
Beau B.	We can always appeal to the Warden of the Captives.
	(*BEADLE appears at door in gold-laced uniform.*)
Beadle	Quick, sir, quick!
Beau B.	A Belasco never hurries. It is our one foible.
	(*He gives his arm to LEAH and EXEUNT with dignity.*) (*The anxious CHANCELLOR at last closes the door and wipes his forehead with a large bandanna handkerchief.*)
Chancellor	Ouf! Unprecedented! (*He snuffs himself copiously.*)
	(*GOMEZ, the beadle, re-opens the door and stands respectful. ENTER in conversation the WARDEN OF THE HOLY LAND, the CHIEF OF THE ELDERS, and the WARDEN OF THE CAPTIVES. They are all in elegant eighteenth-century costume, with powdered wigs.*)
Warden Cap	And the next step, I suppose, will be solicitor in Chancery.
Chief Elder	That Joseph Abrahams will go far. (*They take their seats and look at Agenda.*) Not very heavy business.
Warden Cong	No; as for my department, it might as well be abolished. Warden of the Captives indeed!
Chief Elder	What can you expect? The world is getting too civilised for piracies.
Warden Cong	And I doubt if the Turks will ever have war-prisoners again.
Warden HL	Then why not hand over your surplus—for Palestine! (*ALL laugh and BEADLE opens door for the TREASURER, a specially dignified gentleman with a sword.*)
Warden Cong	Here comes the Treasurer—put it to him!

Treasurer	How do you do, gentlemen? (*Looks at his watch*) The President is late. (*Takes his seat.*)
Chief Elder	Ah, you can tell us—is the Joseph Abrahams, who has just been admitted an attorney of the King's Bench, one of us?
Treasurer	Yes—and not very forward to pay me his fines.
	(*A titter.*)
Warden HL	He should make a good lawyer. (*ALL laugh.*)
	(*GOMEZ opens door for PRESIDENT OF THE CONGREGATION.*)
President	(*Looks at watch*) The President is late.
Warden HL	It's Mr. Pitt's new loan. The Exchange is very agitated, they say. But we are talking of Joseph Abrahams.
President	Yes—isn't it wonderful? A Jew actually admitted attorney. At this rate we shall soon be at the bar.
Chief Elder	Not so fast. As well expect a Jew on the bench!
	(*Laughter.*)
Treasurer	(*Sarcastically*) Or Lord Chief Justice!
	(*More laughter.*)
Warden HL	Or the President to be punctual.
	(*More laughter—followed by a sudden awe as the BEADLE throws open the door. ALL rise respectfully. ENTER PRESIDENT [MOSES]. BEADLE closes door.*)
Moses	I fear I am a little late.
Omnes	Oh no, no, Mr. Belasco—not a minute.
	(*PRESIDENT takes his seat solemnly. CHANCELLOR sits at his side. Silence.*)
Chancellor	Shall I read the minutes?
Moses	Sh! (*Waves him away*) Mr. Treasurer!
Treasurer	Sir?

Moses	Have you not forgotten to leave your sword in the ante-room?
Treasurer	A thousand pardons. (*Hurries to door*) Gomez!
Chancellor	(*Murmurs*) Unprecedented!

(*TREASURER hands out sword. Returns, like a chastened school-boy, to seat.*)

Moses	The Chancellor will read the minutes.
Chancellor	(*After nervously clearing his throat*) The usual meeting of the Council was postponed to the 17th inst owing to the incidence of the Feast of Tabernacles. Mr. Moses Belasco, President of the Mahamad, occupied the chair, and was supported by the Council in complete Mahamad. Almost the entire sitting was occupied with the proposition moved by the Chief of the Elders and supported by the Warden of the Holy Land that the Chief Rabbi shall not be allowed to recommend to the Council applicants for its charities. It was urged that the respect which the Council naturally feels for its venerable *Haham,* must unduly prejudice it in favour of his candidates. After an exhaustive discussion it was therefore agreed nem. con. that the respected Rabbi be forbidden in future to nominate applicants for charity of any description. Owing to the length of the discussion the other main item on the Agenda—to wit whether the Council should obey the ruling of the Lord Mayor of London in the matter of tithes—was adjourned. The following fines and penalties were voted unanimously: forty pounds on Isaac Elkan for declining to serve as Bridegroom of the Law; five pounds on Samson Assunta for offending the President and claiming another Yahid's seat in synagogue, with the further penalty that he now sit behind the reading desk; ten pounds on Moses Martine for persuading a Christian clergyman to turn Jew; withdrawal of the franchise from Joseph Portal for making his father's tombstone longer than six and a quarter feet; disqualification of Emmanuel Elzas as Elder by reason of his bankruptcy; and the prohibition of Antonio Mendes from shaving during the period of seven weeks, for having exaggerated the unhappiness of a married couple petitioning for a divorce.

Moses	Is it your pleasure, gentlemen, these minutes be confirmed? (*Murmur of assent.* PRESIDENT *signs them and* CHANCELLOR *puts sand on his signature.*) Gentlemen, the first item on the agenda is the question whose discussion was postponed from our last meeting, the question of whether we were to bow to the ruling of the Lord Mayor of London in the matter of tithes. On the advice of the Chancellor we referred the matter to him that he might look up the precedents.
Councillor	Hear, hear!
Chancellor	Mr. President and gentlemen of the Mahamad, I have to report that it is unprecedented, unprecedented. (*Cheers*) Your community is an ancient, autonomous body, obeying its own *Ascamot* and only subject to the general laws of England; it registers its own births, celebrates its own marriages, divorces its own incompatibles, and performs its own funerals. The Lord Mayor of London has never had such authority as he now claims. (*Cheers*) It is unprecedented, unprecedented.
Moses	Then I certainly do not see why we should be intimidated by a mushroom Lord Mayor.
	(*Loud cheers*)
Chief Elder	(*Springing up*) I beg to move, in the name of the Elders, that the Lord Mayor be respectfully informed that the Mahamad declines.
	(*Cheers and laughter*)
Warden Cong	I beg to second.
Moses	The Chief of the Elders moves, and the Warden of the Congregation seconds that the Lord Mayor's ruling be rejected. Those who are in favour—
Councillor	All!
Moses	Carried unanimously in complete Mahamad. (*Cheers*) Then write the Lord Mayor so, Mr. Chancellor—respectfully. (*Laughter*)
Treasurer	At the same time might we not intimate to him our inability

	to continue our little present to his lordship of fifty guineas a year? (*Cheers*)
Moses	I take it that the sense of the meeting is with this suggestion. (*Cheers*) Add that, Mr. Chancellor.
Chancellor	It is disturbing a time-honoured precedent, gentlemen.
Treasurer	But it increases our surplus. (*Cheers and laughter*)
Moses	The next item, gentlemen; the petition against a clause in the Sedition Act, must I fear stand over, as our Deputados of the Portuguese nation with whom we were to confer have not yet met. This brings us to the last item of our agenda, which is also the least. It merely concerns the marriage of a daughter of Manasseh Da Costa, one of the worst beggars in our community, to a man who is not only German but professionally connected with that alien community in the role of Death-Rattler. The case appears on the customary list of applications for permission to marry forwarded us by the Reverend Haham and at the instigation of our Argus-eyed Chancellor. (*CHANCELLOR coughs modestly*) This fellow, Da Costa, has been cited to appear before us.
Warden HL	Is it suggested that we should forbid the marriage?
Councillor	(*Half springing up*) Sir! Mr. Villareall!
Warden HL	(*Laughingly*) I only mean, would the marriage of a beggar matter?
Moses	Well, if we can't control our beggars, whom shall we control?
Chancellor	But it would be a very bad precedent, sir, if our minister were allowed to perform the ceremony.
Warden Cong	True, that at once cuts the bride off from our community.
Chief Elder	An impertinent rascal, in any case. After fattening and battening on our funds, to arrogate to himself a license which we ourselves dare not permit ourselves.
Moses	Dare not, sir? It is to be hoped we do not desire it.
Chief Elder	I spoke unthinkingly, Mr. President.

| President | There is nothing to think about; the evil must be eliminated instanter. Let Da Costa enter! |
| | |

(*CHANCELLOR throws open the door fussily, beckons* DA COSTA, *his eyes on the* MAHAMAD. *After a while becomes conscious there is no* MANASSEH.)

Beadle	(*Half ENTERING*) You beckoned me, sir.
Chancellor	No, not you, Gomez. Da Costa. Where is Da Costa?
Beadle	(*Calls*) Da Costa! He was in the room a moment ago. Da Costa, Da Costa! Ah, here he comes! Da Costa! Didn't you hear me calling?
Manasseh	(*At door*) I fancied I heard you calling one of your drinking companions. My name is *Mr.* Da Costa.
Chancellor	*Mr.* Da Costa then, the gentlemen of the Mahamad are waiting for you.
Manasseh	Tell the gentlemen of the Mahamad I am engaged in conversation with my future son-in-law and shall presently give myself the pleasure of saluting them. (*EXIT*)
Chancellor	(*Frantically*) Mr. Da Costa! (*Turning to* COUNCILLORS) The fellow has left the ante-room.
Moses	I heard. Let the Beadle drag him back by the scruff of the neck.
Chancellor	Do you hear, Mr. Beadle?
Beadle	He is powerfully built, Mr. Chancellor.
Moses	(*Tattooing angrily*) Go and help him, Mr. Chancellor.
Chancellor	Oh, sir, that is unprecedented.
Moses	(*Thundering*) Go, sir! Tell him the President of the Mahamad desires his President instanter.
Beadle	He is coming back, sir.
Councillor	(*Relieved*) Ah!

(*ENTER* MANASSEH *slowly.*)

Manasseh	*Shalom aleichem,* Mr. Belasco and gentlemen.
President	You have kept us waiting.
Manasseh	Not so long as you have kept *me* waiting. If I had known you expected me to cool my heels in the ante-room, I should not have come.
President	You are impertinent.
Manasseh	I think, Mr. Belasco, it is you who owe me an apology, and, knowing the courtesy and high breeding which has always distinguished the noble family of Belasco, I can only explain your present tone by your being unaware I have a grievance. No doubt it is your Chancellor who cited me to appear at too early an hour.
President	Eh? (*Looks at* CHANCELLOR.)
Chancellor	(*Stammering confusedly*) It is a matter of immemorial precedent to summon persons for the commencement of the meeting. We cannot tell how long the prior business will take.
Manasseh	But, gentlemen, we are not all rich idlers. I am a *schnorrer* with heavy rounds to go and antiquated apparel to collect. (*COUNCILLORS look at one another helplessly.*) However, I will not press the point now, nor will I draw the attention of the Committee to the careless perfunctory manner in which the document summoning me was drawn up, so that, had I been a stickler for accuracy, I need not have answered to the name Manasseh Da Costa.
Chancellor	But that *is* your name.
Manasseh	If you will examine—(*very magnificently*) the Charity List—you will see that my name is Manasseh Bueno Barzillai Azevedo Da Costa. But you are keeping the gentlemen of the Mahamad waiting. (*Seats himself in empty chair at foot of table, leans on elbows, and gazes at* PRESIDENT *opposite.*)
Chancellor	(*Wounded in inmost instincts*) Stand up, sir. These chairs are for the gentlemen of the Mahamad.

Manasseh	And being gentlemen, they know better than to keep an old man on his legs any longer.
Chancellor	If you were a gentleman, you would take that thing off your head.
Manasseh	If you were not a Man-of-the-Earth, you would know that it is not a mark of disrespect for the Mahamad, but of respect for the Law of Moses, which is even higher than the Mahamad. The rich man can afford to neglect our holy religion, but the poor man has only the Law. It is his sole luxury.
President	Let him be, Mr. Chancellor, let him be.
Chancellor	But, sir—
President	Hold your peace.
Manasseh	He means well, Mr. Belasco. He cannot be expected to have the fine instincts of the gentlemen of the Mahamad. (*PRESI-DENT tattoos angrily on the table.*) May I ask you, sir, to proceed with the business for which you have summoned me? I have several appointments to keep with clients.
President	(*Thunderously*) Is it true, sir, is it true?
Manasseh	(*Offers book*) Would you like to see my diary?
President	Confound your diary. What are you talking of? Is it true that you desire to give your daughter in marriage to an alien Jew?
	(*Dread silence*)
Manasseh	No.
	(*Sensation*)
President	(*Gurgling*) No?
Warden Cong	(*On MANASSEH'S right*) Why, your daughter admitted it to my wife.
Manasseh	(*Tilting his chair confidentially to the WARDEN OF THE CAP-TIVES*) An alien Jew desires to marry my daughter, but I do not desire to give her to him.

Warden Cong	(*Holding chair back*) Oh, then, you will refuse your consent.
Manasseh	(*Drawing his chair nearer, in surprised accents*) By no means. I have already consented.
President	None of your quibbles, sirrah! Do you not know that the union you contemplate is disgraceful and degrading to you, to your daughter, and for the community which has done so much for you? What? A Spaniard marry a German! Shameful!
Manasseh	And do you think I have not felt the shame as deeply as you? Do you think, gentlemen, I have not suffered from this passion of an alien for my daughter? I came here expecting your sympathy, and do you offer me reproach? Perhaps you think, sir—(*Wheeling to right-hand neighbour who half turns his back on his argumentative fore-finger.*) Perhaps you think because I have consented, because I have conquered my native sentiments by considerations of reason and justice, that I cannot condole with you; that I cannot sympathise with you, who are yet unconverted, in your lamentations over the blot on our common scutcheon. But if I have consented, sir (*swiftly wheeling his chair round to the next COUNCILLOR, the PRESIDENT OF THE CONGREGATION.*) it is because the Law of Moses ordains that our daughters must wed—
President	Yes, but not anybody—
Manasseh	A fellow-Jew is not anybody.
Warden Cong	Quibbles again.
Manasseh	(*Turning toward him*) No, sir, plain fact, and what my daughter feels.
President	Then you should disown her, cast her off.
Manasseh	That would cost you money, gentlemen. She would become practically an orphan, and as such entitled to receive the larger marriage-dowry for orphans bequeathed by Abraham Rodriques Marques, *olov hashalom*.
President	This is no laughing matter, sir.

Manasseh	No, indeed. (*Half wheels round sympathetically towards* PRES-IDENT.)
President	Ho! So you are aware of the penalties you risk by persisting in your course!
Manasseh	I risk no penalties.
President	Indeed! Then do you think anyone may trample with impunity upon our ancient *Ascamot!*
Manasseh	(*In surprised tones*) Our ancient *Ascamot!* What have they to say against a Spaniard marrying a German? (*Sensation.* COUNCILLORS *survey one another. Pause of astonishment.*) They have nothing to say. There is no such *Ascama.* (*Dread pause*)
President	Do you deny the first principle of our constitution? Do you deny that your daughter is a traitress? Do you—?
Manasseh	Ask your Chancellor. He is a Man-of-the-Earth, but he should know your statutes, and he will tell you that my daughter's conduct is nowhere forbidden.
President	Silence, sir. Mr. Chancellor, read the *Ascama.*
Chancellor	(*Wriggles, flushes, pales, hunts for Statute book, turns over pages.*) Hem, ah—(*Coughs, takes snuff, blows nose elaborately.*) There is n-n-no express *Ascama.* (*Dazed silence.* MANASSEH *sits still in unpretentious triumph.*)
Chief Elder	Of course it was never actually put into writing. It has never been legislated against, because it has never been conceived possible. These things are an instinct with every right-minded Sephardi. Have we ever legislated against marrying Christians?
Manasseh	(*Veering round*) Certainly we have. In Section XX, Paragraph 2. (*Quotes sonorously*) "It is also expressly prohibited to every Yahid or Congregant to contract marriage with a person of another faith, or to consent to any such person passing

by his name, this being at once a high religious offence, and tending to the injury and disquiet of the congregation." If our legislators had intended to prohibit inter-marriage with the German Jews, they would have prohibited it, too.

Chancellor   There is the Traditional Law as well as the Written. It is so in our holy religion, it is so in our constitution. The precedents—

President Con   Yes, what of the precedents?

Chancellor   There is the case of one of our Treasurers in the time of George II. He wanted to marry a beautiful alien Jewess.

Warden HL   And was interdicted, of course?

Chancellor   Hem! He—was only permitted to marry her under humiliating conditions. The Elders forbade the attendance of the members of the house of Judgment or of the Cantors; no celebration was to take place in the synagogue; no offerings were to be made for the bridegroom's health, nor was he even to receive the bridegroom's call to the reading of the Law.

Manasseh   (*Wheeling round* COUNCILLOR's *chair, and now next to the* CHIEF OF THE ELDERS) But the Elders will not impose any such conditions on *my* son-in-law and I address myself to the Chief of the Elders to instruct him in particular. In the first place, my son-in-law is *not*, like your Treasurer in George the Second's time, one of us. His desire to join us is a compliment. If anyone has offended your traditions, it is my daughter. But then she is not a male, like the Treasurer cited. Nor is she an active agent. She has not gone out of her way to choose an alien—she has been chosen. Your masculine precedents cannot touch her.

Treasurer   Ay, but we can touch you.

Manasseh   Is it fines you are thinking of, Mr. Treasurer? Very well, fine me—if you can afford it. You know that I am a student, a son of the Law, who has few resources but what you allow him. If you care to pay this fine, it is your affair. There is always room in your poor-box. I am always glad to hear of fines. You had better make up your mind to the inevitable, gentlemen. Have I not had to do so? There is no *ascama* to prevent my son-in-law having all the usual privileges. In fact it was to ask that he might receive the bridegroom's synagogue honours on the Sabbath before his marriage that I really came here. By Section III, Paragraph 1, you are empowered to admit any person about to marry the daughter of a Yahid.

Chancellor But you are *not* a Yahid. A Yahid means a full voting member of the Congregation. And by Paragraph V of the same Section, anyone whose name appears on the Charity List ceases to be a Yahid.

Manasseh (*Ironically*) And a vastly proper law! Everybody may vote but the *Schnorrer*. (*Confidentially to* CHIEF OF ELDERS) It is curious how few of your Elders perceive that those who take the charity are the pillars of the Synagogue. What keeps your community together? Fines. What ensures respect for your constitution? Fines. What makes every man do his duty? Fines. What rules this very Mahamad? Fines. And it is the poor who provide an outlet for all these monies. Egad, do you think your members would for a moment tolerate your penalties, if they did not know the money was laid out in "good deeds"? Charity is the salt of riches, says the Talmud, and indeed it is the salt that preserves your community.

President Have done, sir! Have done! Do you forget to whom you are talking?

Manasseh I am talking to the Chief of the Elders. But if you would like me to address myself to you—(*Wheels his chair round the* CHIEF OF THE ELDERS, *and arrives on the left of the* PRESIDENT.)

President (*Shrinking back*) Silence, fellow! You have no right to a vote at all; as the Chancellor has reminded us, you are not even a Yahid, a congregant.

Manasseh Then the laws do not apply to me. It is only the Yahid who is privileged to do this, who is prohibited from doing that. No *ascama* mentions the *Schnorrer* or gives you any authority over *him*.

Chancellor On the contrary, he is bound to attend the week-day services. But this man hardly ever does, sir.

Manasseh	(*Glaring at him across the* PRESIDENT) That is untrue.
Chancellor	Untrue? (*Glares back, the* PRESIDENT *being uncomfortably sandwiched between the two quarrelling figures.*)
Manasseh	Yes, I *never* do. That, gentlemen, is another of the privileges I have to forgo in order to take your charity; I cannot risk appearing to my Maker in the light of a mercenary.
Chancellor	Humph! And what prevents you taking your turn in the graveyard watches?
Manasseh	What prevents me? My age. It would be a sin against heaven to spend a night in the cemetery. If the body-snatchers did come, they might find a corpse to their hand—in the watch tower. But I do my duty—I always pay a substitute.
Treasurer	No doubt. I remember your asking me for the money to keep an old man out of the cemetery. Now I see what you meant.
Wardens HL & C	Yes, and I remember.
President	Order, gentlemen, order. You must not argue with the man. Hark you, my fine fellow, we refuse to sanction this marriage. That is all. You may go.
Manasseh	Go? Without your seeing the bridegroom? (*Goes to door and calls.*) Yankele!
President	We don't need to see him. Good-day.
Manasseh	But I have cited him to appear here. He will charge me for his time. Yankele!
President	Beadle! Stop that alien!
Manasseh	(*To without*) Use that sword, Yankele, if he dares touch you. Ha! Your beadle, gentlemen, knows better than to insult a stranger.

(YANKELE *appears at the door, sheepish, in* BEAU BELASCO'S *finery.*)

Yankele	Vat you vant?
	(*The* COUNCILLORS *are taken aback by his get-up.*)
Manasseh	Step forward, Yankele. There, gentlemen, you see what a cavalier I bring you. Fit to grace this council table itself. Head up, Yankele.
Yankele	(*With an awkward effort*) Yes, fader!
Manasseh	Now, Mr. President, look on this picture and on that. (*Points to* CHANCELLOR) If you forbade me to give my daughter to *that,* I could understand.
President	(*Gruffly*) We don't go by the eye.
Yankele	Vell, look at his nose!
President	Be serious, sir. We have no claim to authority over a member of your nation. Only if you presume to marry a daughter of ours, no minister of ours shall perform the ceremony, and do not dream that we shall recognise you as a Yahid and admit you to membership.
Yankele	Den admit me to your charity lists.
President	(*Startled*) You a *schnorrer* too.
Manasseh	Can't you see by his clothes?
President	(*Puzzled*) By his clothes? Oh—I catch your meaning . . . Why, surely they're not my son's?
Manasseh	Yes, Mr. President, your son's first good deed, if unwitting. It is Yankele who is leading your Benjamin heavenwards—and that is the man you would shut out from the congregation.
President	We shall shut you both out.
Manasseh	(*Quietly*) Is it excommunication you threaten?
President	This scandal must be stopped.
Manasseh	The gentlemen of the Mahamad could stop it in a moment. The Chief of the Elders, if he only chose!
Chief Elder	If I only chose!

Manasseh	If you only chose my daughter. Are you not a bachelor?
Yankele	(*Alarmed*) *Oi voi!*
Chief Elder	(*Angrily*) A bachelor? Certainly not. I am a widower.
Manasseh	Still better. You bring experience. And having lost one wife, you will be less careless with the second. (*YANKELE tugs at MANASSEH's robe.*) Don't be alarmed, Yankele. They are not in earnest. They denounce the scandal, but which of them is willing to save the community from it? Not one.
Yankele	Tank Gawd!
Manasseh	And yet, it is a handsome creature, who would not disgrace even a house in Hackney.
Yankele	I can move to Hackney too.
Manasseh	God forbid! You would drive my best clients still further afield.
Yankele	You could get oders.
Manasseh	Not so easy. *Schnorrers* can't be choosers.
President	Kindly continue these wrangles outside. You know our decision, Da Costa. Give your daughter to an alien, and you shall be cut off from us in life and death. Alive, you shall worship without our walls, and dead you shall be buried beyond the cemetery pale, "Behind the boards."
Manasseh	Unsay those words, Mr. President, for he that diggeth a pit for another falls into it himself. The unhallowed grave you dig for me behind the boards—your own son shall occupy it.
President	My son?
Manasseh	Yes, Mr. Belasco, your own Benjamin. As sure as I stand here, he loves a German maiden, and will lead her under the canopy.
President	You lie, fellow.
Manasseh	Where does he pass his Friday evenings? Is he ever at home?

Nay, as little as he is at the synagogue. Where do you suppose he met Yankele and was led heavenwards? At the house of a German, of course.

Yankele	I undressed in de drawing room—ven de ladies vas avay.
Manasseh	That will do, Yankele. You can order your marriage contract at the scribes.
Yankele	(*Effusively*) Tank you, tank you. (*Going—pauses.*) At 'oose expense?
Manasseh	At Mr. Belasco's.
Yankele	(*To* PRESIDENT, *with deep awkward bow*) Tank you, sir. (*EXITS. The* PRESIDENT *gasps.*)
Manasseh	He misunderstood. I referred to your son—they are both to be married under the same canopy.
President	(*Choking*) You repeat your slander.
Manasseh	Ask your Chancellor—he lends them the Council Chamber for their love-makings.
Councillor	Eh? What?
President	Is this true, Mr. Chancellor?
Chancellor	No, sir—yes, sir.
President	(*Ranting*) If this is true he shall join you in your exile.
Manasseh	Nay, there is no exile for either of us. There is no law in your Statute-Book that empowers you, and if there were it would be ridiculous.
Councillor	(*Half rising*) Ridiculous?
Manasseh	Yes—and you too, gentlemen; while you stand for justice and reason, and for the due conservation of our community, I bow my head to you, I am your humble subject, as it is written: "Obey the authorities"; but when you perpetuate a prejudice that has grown cobwebbed and worm-eaten, then I tell you, in complete Mahamad, that your authority is naught. If I, Manasseh Bueno Barzillai Azevedo Da Costa,

deign to waive my pride of blood before honest merit, who shall say me nay, and who shall prevent your Benjamin following in my footsteps?

President   (*Apoplectic*) And who are you?

Manasseh   An Israelite and as the subject of God and His Law the equal of any of you. All Israel are brethren.

Chief Elder   You—you dictate to us, you the least in Israel.

Manasseh   Ay, for what says the Talmud? Blessed is that generation in which the great listen to the small. And I, the small, tell you, Mr. President, the great, that this love of your Benjamin for the fair daughter of the Treasurer of the Great Synagogue, for he has made no mean or unworthy choice, will be the redeeming power of his life. What have you made of him? A pagan swashbuckler, an apish gallant, a mincing swaggerer in fine linen. Leah Grobstock will make a man, ay and a Jew of him again. Only the fear of your wrath prevents him following his best impulses and leading her under the canopy. Let me go back to the young couple, let me tell them you have seen the error of your ways and that the law they feared does not even exist.

President   (*Choking*) Leave the room, fellow. You have heard my ultimatum.

Manasseh   Ay, and you shall hear mine. Do not forget, Mr. President, that you and I owe allegiance to the same brotherhood. Do not forget that the power which made you can unmake you at the next election; do not forget that if I have no vote I have vast influence; that there is not a voter whom I do not visit weekly; that there is not a *schnorrer* who would not follow me in my exile. Do not forget that there is another community to turn to—ay, that very community you condemn; a community that waxes daily in wealth and greatness while you sleep in your sloth, while you dream of the past and fancy it is to-day. Yes, I will join your rivals—and your Benjamin shall be my first follower, as it is written: "Benjamin, the son of my right hand"; and this Death-Rattler's marriage that you would prevent shall be the Death-Rattle of your community.

President   Jackanapes! Blasphemer! Shameless renegade! (*Darts to the bell and tugs at it madly.*)

Manasseh   I shall not leave this Chamber till I choose. (*Drops into* PRESIDENT's *chair and folds arms. A cry of horror from all—*THEY *leap to their feet.*) Nay, keep your seats, gentlemen. (*The* PRESIDENT *glares—then staggers against wall.* GOMEZ *rushes in and stares.*) Don't stare at me, Gomez, can't you see the President wants a glass of water?

President   You—(*Gurgles and falls sideways.*)

Manasseh   (*Springs from the chair and catches him.*) Bestir yourselves, gentlemen, don't you see the President is ill? (THEY *help him to lay the* PRESIDENT *on the table. He sweeps the Minute Book maliciously to the floor.* GOMEZ *ENTERS and drops his glass of water.*) Has anyone any brandy? Come, come, Mr. Chancellor, bring out a phial.

Chancellor   (*Shamefully producing it*) My physician orders it.

Manasseh   (*Forcing brandy down throat*) And, I, too. He has had a slight stroke, but he can bear transporting home. Has any of you his equipage without?

Chief Elder   I have my chariot.

Manasseh   Call it, Gomez. (*EXIT* BEADLE) You see, gentlemen, how insecure is earthly power. It is swallowed up in an instant, as Lisbon was engulfed. Cursed are they who despise the poor. How is the saying of our sages verified—"The house that opens not to the poor opens to the physician." Bear a hand, gentlemen.

      (*Under* MENASSEH's *supervision, the* COUNCILLORS *begin to carry out the* PRESIDENT.)

Chancellor   (*Stands overwhelmed*) Unprecedented! Unprecedented!

Manasseh   Than *make* it a precedent, Mr. Chancellor. Enter it in the minutes. Enter it—that the Council, in complete Mahamad, no longer sanctions the prejudice against inter-marriage with eligible Jews of the other nation.

Chancellor   But—I—gentlemen? (*Looks wildly.*)

Manasseh	Then enter, sir—the Council wished to interfere, in complete Mahamad, with the right of Manasseh Bueno Barzillai Azevedo Da Costa to give his daughter in marriage to a German, but the Almighty intervened. That is so, gentlemen?
Councillor & Members	(*Murmur*) Yes, yes.
Manasseh	Enter it then, sir. Ay, and enter also that the Mahamad sought to interfere with the marriage of its President's son, but the Almighty sent a sign. (*The CHANCELLOR writes. The MEMBERS bear out the PRESIDENT.*) Is it written?
Chancellor	Yes, Mr. Da Costa.
Manasseh	You are dismissed for the day. (*CHANCELLOR creeps out, returns for brandy-bottle, but catching MANASSEH's eye creeps out again. MANASSEH takes key out of door, and with a vindictive thrust puts it on the other side; GOMEZ returns.*) Ah, Gomez, you must have your perquisite, as per *precedent,* I suppose. Here is a crown.
Beadle	(*Overwhelmed*) Oh, but the President gives me only half-a-crown.
Manasseh	Yes, but he may not be able to attend the next meeting. And I may be absent too. Here, take away that brandy!
	(*In Cromwell's tone of dissolving the Rump. Shuts door behind him with a great bang, the key is heard turning in the lock, then is sharply withdrawn.*)

CURTAIN FALLS ON EMPTY STAGE

END OF ACT III

ACT IV

(*SCENE: Oak-panelled Library of Moses Belasco's Mansion in Devonshire Square. The* PRESIDENT OF THE MAHAMAD *discovered at writing-table with papers.*)

Moses	Ten thousand pounds in one morning. Good!
Manasseh	(*Outside*) But I must convince my own eyes that he is better. (*ENTERING*) *Shalom Aleichem!*
Moses	The devil!
Manasseh	No, only I. Your time is not yet. Heaven be praised, my prayers were not unheard.
Moses	You prayed for me?
Manasseh	I have said Psalms *without fee* every morning, in order that you might be preserved for the greater glory of the Mahamad and to see your son under the canopy.
Moses	You begin that again—
Manasseh	Have a care! Have a care! Surely you do not disregard Heaven's warning: surely you have already consented to your son's union.
Moses	On the contrary. By my physician's advice I have refrained from all agitating conversation and I shall therefore be vastly obliged to you if you will leave me in peace.
Manasseh	I need not the assurance of your gratitude to do that. I *will* leave you in peace. I will remove all those agitating thoughts which threaten the stability of our synagogue's corner-stone. (*Makes for bell.*)
Moses	What are you going to do?

Manasseh	To ring for your son; to exorcise his despair.
Moses	His despair? I have just left him in the hands of his hair-dresser.
Manasseh	He does not wear his heart on his wig. It bleeds silently. I'll go and fetch him to you. (*Going*)
Moses	No, no! Leave me, I pray you.
Manasseh	That, Mr. Belasco, would be to flout the maxim of the Talmud: "The bidding of your host obey, Except he bid you go away."
Moses	(*Apoplectic*) I—I—
Manasseh	Tut! Tut! Tut! Pray be calm. I'll fetch Benjamin.
Moses	But I haven't decided what to say to him.
Manasseh	Decide? Why should a man in your state of health be troubled to decide? Leave it all to me, Mr. Belasco. You have helped me many a time, let me now help you. The lion and the mouse, eh?
Moses	I wonder which of us is the lion and which the mouse. I don't want your help to-day, anyhow.
Manasseh	Not to-day? But I have promised the poor young lady all shall be settled to-day. You would not have me break my promise to a lady.
Moses	But I have never seen her.
Manasseh	Ah, now you hit the nail. Hence all these tears. Had you but seen her once—but I have arranged all that! She will wait upon you this very morning to pay her respects to her father-in-law.
Moses	A strange young lady call on *me!* Oh,—but—but—this is quite out of form.
Manasseh	Do you imagine I had not invited her parents, too? Did you suspect *me* of a breach of etiquette? No, sir, Joseph Grobstock, the generous Treasurer of the Great Synagogue, and his charming and pious spouse will assist to arrange the be-

	trothal in due form.
Moses	The devil they will!
Manasseh	It behooves not a man in your state of health to mention the devil so frequently. He is at your elbow now, tempting you to order me off your prosperous premises. But, my friend, the Death-Rattler is below. If you decline to see the Grobstocks, he will bear a countermanding message. He is used to bearing messages—messages that countermand the best-laid human schemes.
Moses	(*Faltering*) Oh—well—there's—there's—there's no harm in seeing them.
Manasseh	No harm! I bring you, sir, a beautiful bride to renew the house of Belasco, and provide leaders of the councils of the community of the third and fourth generation; no bedizened vixen, no penniless adventuress, such as your graceless son might have ogled through his spying-glass at Vauxhall, no Doll Tearsheet, no gallivanting, grimacing actress from Covent Garden, but a true Jewish maiden and a true Jewish purse, as befits the daughter of the Treasurer of the Great Synagogue. And what do I ask in return? Nothing. Nothing—but my usual commission as marriage-broker.
Moses	Oh, if it's the commission you're after—I'll write you out a cheque.
Manasseh	Sir! I withdraw my girl! If I make marriages, it is primarily that the command may be obeyed: "Be fruitful and multiply." The Almighty Himself, the Talmud teaches us, is always making marriages. But let your son go to the devil you invoked, let him dice and duel unchecked, let him play ducks and drakes with the fortune you will soon bequeath him, let him make the immemorial house of Belasco a mockery and a by-word. Farewell! I withdraw my girl! She will find a more eager bidder, and I, a higher commission. And you—you will die out, you and your seed, and who knows if your Benjamin will even say the *Kaddish* for your soul. The Death-Rattler is without—he shall bear the message to the Grobstocks. Farewell! (*Is going out*)
Moses	But—but I've already said I didn't mind seeing them.

Manasseh	(*Quietly*) Then I'll call your son. (*Opens door.*) I know he is at his toilette in yonder room. From your own lips he shall hear the blessed words that will raise him to the seventh heaven.
Moses	But he doesn't know you!
Manasseh	Pardon me—he has even wished to fight a duel with me.
Moses	What! (*Collapses*)
Manasseh	Yes—you see from what I am saving him. (*Calls out*) Enter, Moses son of Benjamin!
	(*ENTER BEAU BELASCO, tying his cravat*)
Beau B.	You wish to see me, sir?
Moses	So Mr. Da Costa says.
Manasseh	Your father wishes to tell you that he has consented to your marriage with Leah Grobstock.
Beau B.	You might have waited till I had tied my cravat.
Moses	You can think of tying your cravat, when it is a question of marriage!
Beau B.	One knot at a time. Everything should be done elegantly and composedly.
Moses	(*To MANASSEH*) Is this the raging love you told me of?
Manasseh	Take away his cravat and you will see.
Moses	His cravat?
Manasseh	Yes, take away his cravat, and the girl will scarcely console him. But take away his girl and he will hang himself on his cravat.
Moses	It doesn't look like it.
Manasseh	The two passions of his life are dress and Leah Grobstock. He puts the girl on an equality with the garments—what greater love? And it is a touchstone of the higher foppishness to be startled by nothing. Have I interpreted you aright,

	Beau Belasco?
Beau B.	Gad, you have the instincts of a gentleman. Ah, I took it for granted *you* would straighten out the tangles. That was why I wasn't surprised. If I saw you on the throne of England, d——n it, Da Costa, if I'd be surprised.
Manasseh	It would surprise *me*. It would mean I had vowed allegiance to the State Church, and that I will never do. No, Mr. Benjamin, *you* may undervalue the glorious traditions of Sinai—
Beau B.	But I don't. Am I not marrying a Jewess?
Moses	But are you perfectly sure, my boy, you desire this particular Jewess?
Beau B.	She has such excellent taste.
Moses	And does she desire you?
Beau B.	She has such excellent taste.
Moses	But are you sure you couldn't live without her?
Manasseh	Not at his present rate, Mr. Belasco. My principal, Mr. Grobstock, empowers me to promise ten thousand pounds for his dowry.
Moses	Only ten thousand pounds! I made as much this morning.
Manasseh	Then you Belascos have made twice as much this morning. I congratulate you the more sincerely since I make no claim to commission on the first ten thousand. This, however, is merely a nest-egg and is not exclusive of the bride's own income of two thousand a year.
Beau B.	My tradesmen are in luck!
Moses	(*Wavering*) I must admit they seem respectable people.
Manasseh	Respectable, Mr. Belasco? There are few people in our own community so charitable. And inferior in blood as they are, yet what says the Talmud? In choosing a friend, ascend a step; in choosing a wife, descend a step. (*Goes to door*) Yankele!
Yankele	(*ENTERING in his clothes*) Yes, Mr. Da Costa.

Manasseh	The President of the Mahamad—and whom you will remember meeting—has consented to your marrying my daughter.
Yankele	Heaven bless you, sir! May you see your own children under de canopy!
Manasseh	I have arranged that, too. Beau Belasco will be married under the same canopy as you.
Beau B.	The deuce he will!
Manasseh	Sir, do you not know that the canopy is for all men, as the blue canopy of Heaven overspreads us all? You promised me to remember the Synagogue if I won you your bride: do not begin by rejecting its teachings.
Moses	He promised to remember the Synagogue!
Manasseh	Ay! (*Witheringly*) *That* was to be my commission—from *him*!
Moses	Forgive me! (*Extends hand*)
	(*The* BEAU *goes on tying his cravat.*)
Manasseh	(*Takes* MOSES BELASCO's *hand.*) The Synagogue demands living services from all of us. Grobstock will be making handsome gifts to it in honour of his daughter's marriage, surely you will not let *my* daughter be less honoured. You will enable *her* father to endow the Synagogue—
Moses	(*Dropping his hand*) Oh, but surely that is Grobstock's concern.
Manasseh	True, but I give *you* the good deed.
Moses	I already give you a commission as marriage-broker, you really ought to go to Grobstock for anything extra.
Manasseh	Sir, you are skillful—nay, a famous financier. You know what stocks to buy, what stocks to sell, when to follow a rise and when a fall. When the Premier advertises the loans, a thousand speculators look to you for guidance. What would you say if *I* presumed to interfere in your financial affairs—if I told you to issue these shares or call in those? You would tell

me to mind my own business; and you would be perfectly right. Now *schnorring* is *my* business. Trust me, I know best whom to come to. You stick to stocks and leave *schnorring* alone.

Moses	What a man! What a man! Will ten pounds satisfy you?
Manasseh	Humph! You could have *schnorred* as much yourself. What do you say, Yankele?
Yankele	I vish my vife to be honoured as befits Da Costa's daughter.
Manasseh	A compromise. Spanish bonds are low. Give me twenty pounds worth of them and I'll accept them as at par.
Moses	You rascal! You've heard something?
Manasseh	I heard at the Coffee House in Change Alley that you had been buying Spanish.
Moses	Well?
Manasseh	And you yourself told me you had made some ten thousand pounds this morning.
Moses	You rogue! Ha! Ha! Ha! You shall have your twenty pounds in good gold!
Manasseh	Only twenty pounds?
Moses	(*Angrily*) What! Not satisfied with even twenty?
Manasseh	Not when you have the power of adding to their number. Invest them—let them increase and multiply.
Moses	Be your broker!
Manasseh	Not mine—but the Synagogue's.
Moses	But suppose I lose the money.
Manasseh	Impossible. Do you think the Almighty will suffer His money to be lost?
Moses	Then why not speculate yourself with it?
Manasseh	The Almighty's honour must be guarded. What? Shall He be less served than an earthly monarch? You see, I know of

	your financial relations with the Court. The service of the Almighty demands the best men. I was the best man to obtain the money—you are the best to invest it.
Moses	(*Taking out his watch*) Then it had better be invested instanter—before the Hamburg packet comes in.
Manasseh	Oh, you have some private information.
Moses	Naturally. I run a schooner of my own to bring the news in advance. The foolish Gentiles never think of that.
Manasseh	Did I not say you were the Almighty's ablest agent? Be off now to do his work. I will do my best to entertain the Grobstocks till you return. (*Hurrying him out.*) (*Then turning to the BEAU, still tying his cravat before a hand-glass he has set up, he slaps him on the back.*) Ha! Ha! A good old man, your father. So now you may order your clothes for the wedding.
Beau B.	Eh? I'd have you know, Da Costa, my wardrobe is astonished at no emergency. Preparedness is my one foible. I have six new suits, any of which would harmonize with the canopy.
Manasseh	But none of which, I hope, resembles the present!
Beau B.	Why? What—
Manasseh	Those buckskin breeches—
Beau B.	(*In consternation*) They were the result of nine separate measurings.
Manasseh	They scarcely do justice to your eminent reputation.
Beau B.	They fit me to bursting.
Manasseh	It were better they burst. No, no, Mr. Belasco, from you one expects originality or nothing. These breeches, why Yankele there might wear them.
Beau B.	He shall! I'll change them on the instant. (*Going*)
Manasseh	And while you are about it, pray set aside your embroidered doublet—it has been on my mind to tell you I saw it worn at Tunbridge Wells when I was taking the waters two years ago.

Beau B.   Is it possible? And I designed it specially to go with frilled shirts.

Manasseh   It was an unconscious plagiarism. No, no, all that does not speak to the man of polish and invention is tawdry frippery on *your* person. Though on Yankele's, who is fortunately about the same size, it would show as elegant embellishment.

Beau B.   I thank you for the suggestion! I will go at once and weed out my wardrobe. I'll shoot the rubbish into the box-room. (*EXIT.*)

Manasseh   (*Slapping* YANKELE *on the back*) And now, Yankele, that I have *schnorred* your wedding garments, you will be able to be married as handsomely as he.

Yankele   (*Bending and kissing the hem of his garment*) Oh, my good angel! You be not a *schnorrer,* you be a miracle. And ven do I get de dowry?

Manasseh   The dowry! You are not satisfied with the tailor's shop I've given you!

Yankele   But you promised me—

Manasseh   Can't you wait till the marriage?

Yankele   Den I get de dowry on de marriage morning?

Manasseh   Humph! On that morning you shall get my daughter without fail. Surely that will be enough for one day.

Yankele   But ven do i get de money your daughter gets from de synagogue?

Manasseh   When she gets it from the synagogue.

Yankele   How much vill it be?

Manasseh   (*Pompously*) It may be a hundred and fifty pounds . . . and it may be less.

Yankele   How much less?

Manasseh   (*With equal pomposity*) A hundred and fifty pounds.

Yankele	Do you mean to say I may get nodings?
Manasseh	Certainly if *she* gets nothing. These dowries are according by lot. By winning my daughter you stand to win a hundred and fifty pounds too. It is a handsome amount. There are not many fathers who do as much for their daughters.
Yankele	But about the Jerusalem estate? I don't vant to live dere. De Messiah is not yet come.
Manasseh	No, you will hardly be able to live on it.
Yankele	You don't object to my selling it, den?
Manasseh	Oh no! If you are so sordid, if you have no true Jewish sentiment.
Yankele	Ven can I come into possession?
Manasseh	On the wedding-day if you like.
Yankele	Von may as vell get it over. As de Talmud says, von peppercorn to-day is better den a basketful of pumpkins to-morrow.
Manasseh	Very well. I will bring it to the synagogue.
Yankele	You mean de deed of transfer.
Manasseh	Eh? Do you think I waste my money on solicitors! No, I will bring the property itself.
Yankele	But how can you bring de property?
Manasseh	Where is the difficulty? Surely a child could carry a casket of Jerusalem earth to the synagogue!
Yankele	A casket of eart'! Is your property in Jerusalem only a casket of eart'?
Manasseh	Did you expect it would be a casket of diamonds? To a true Jew a casket of Jerusalem earth to be thrown upon his grave is worth all the diamonds in the world.
Yankele	(*Angrily*) But your Jerusalem property is a *schwindel*.
Manasseh	On no, you may be easy on that point. It's quite genuine.

I know there is a good deal of spurious Palestine earth in circulation, but this casket I was careful to obtain from a Rabbi of extreme sanctity. It was the only thing he had worth *schnorring*.

Yankele

(*Still angry*) I don't suppose I shall get more dan a crown for it.

Manasseh

That's what annoys me. To think that a son-in-law of mine should mediate selling my holy soil for a paltry five shillings.

Yankele

(*Hopelessly*) And—dose streets—in London I vas to have?

Manasseh

You shall choose your own. We will get a large map and I will mark off in red pencil the domain in which I *schnorr*. You shall choose two main streets with all their dependencies, by-ways, passages, turnings, courts, and alleys, and mark them off in blue pencil, and whatever province of my kingdom you pick, I undertake not to *schnorr* in from your wedding-day onwards. I need not tell you how valuable such a province already is; under careful administration such as you would be able to give it, the revenue from it might be doubled, trebled. I should not expect a tribute of more than ten percent.

Yankele

(*Tearing his hair*) I shall be as poor as ever.

Manasseh

Nay, nay, remember the rabbinic text: "Who is rich, he that hath a beautiful wife." I shall send her to console you while I go and see that the Grobstocks are not sent away because Mr. Belasco is out. (*Calls at door*) Come, my willow of the brook! Come and comfort your bridegroom. (*EXIT, pushing DEBORAH within.*)

Yankele

Oi voi! Oi voi!

Deborah

(*Rushing to him*) What is it? What is it?

Yankele

(*Retreating*) Vy you make such a fuss?

Deborah

Because you are dear to me. Why do you push me away?

Yankele

Because you are *too* dear—I can't afford you!

Deborah	What?
Yankele	Your dowry is a svindle!
Deborah	What did I tell you? I knew he'd only give you soft soap.
Yankele	Yes, vat I get vid you is bubbles.
Deborah	Well, you said it wasn't a woman's business. Next time perhaps you'll let the bride manage.
Yankele	(*Eagerly*) Next time? Den you'll give me up?
Deborah	How can you say such a thing? You must give *me* up!
Yankele	Vat's de difference?
Deborah	Why, then I cry my heart out and pine away.
Yankele	And vat good vill that do *me?*
Deborah	Why, silly, he will have to buy you back to save my life. You can name your own price.
Yankele	And if de trick fails—if he von't buy me back?
Deborah	Then we can marry just the same—you're no worse off.
Yankele	Yes, I am—I've got *you!*
Deborah	You miserable Polish Jew! I thought you loved me.
Yankele	I can love and yet look ahead. Suppose ve get all girls—vere's deir dowry to come from?
Deborah	From our synagogue, of course.
Yankele	But dat's only a lottery, your fader says.
Deborah	Then the more girls one gets, the more chance of winning it.
Yankele	And ain't marriage a lottery enough? You can't have life *all* lotteries.
Manasseh	(*Throws open door*) Enter, enter, good friends. (MR. AND MRS. GROBSTOCK *and* LEAH *come in, bowing.*) So happy to see you all here. Mr. Belasco will be here presently—pray excuse

	him, I have sent him on an errand. Mr. Benjamin is also oc-cupied in preparing friend Yankele's wedding wardrobe. You remember Yankele and my undefiled dove?
Leah	Yes, indeed. Can I ever forget the wretch who gave us such a turn? Why did you say those Mordecais were all dead? Why, we saw them all at the Charity Ball last Sunday.
Yankele	Charity delivers from death.
Joseph	Oho! Come!
Yankele	Yes, dey must have been on de point of death and de report got ahead.
Deborah	Dear Yankele is too conscientious. He rushes to rattle.
Mrs. G.	Nonsense! They outdanced everybody.
Yankele	For joy of deir deliverance.
Deborah	Fiddlesticks!
Yankele	Yes, de fiddlesticks played de music.
Leah	I am afraid you think announcing death is rattling good fun.
Manasseh	Ha! Ha! Ha! Wit, beauty—all the graces. Ah, how I envy your fiancé.
Leah	He is not my fiancé yet.
Manasseh	Why, he is preparing his wedding wardrobe.
Leah	You said Yankele's.
Manasseh	What is left will be for his own. He and Yankele are to be married on the same day, eh, Yankele?
Yankele	If the Mahamad permits.
Manasseh	We permit all. Mrs. Grobstock, may I be the first to con-gratulate you on your daughter's marriage.
Mrs. G.	Then Leah is to be married?
Joseph	Old Belasco has already given in?

Manasseh	Why else did I send for you here?
Joseph	You said Mr. Belasco wished to talk it over.
Manasseh	I have talked *him* over.
Mrs. G.	Heaven bless you, Mr. Da Costa!
Manasseh	It is heaven's blessing merely to oblige a mother in Israel.
Leah	Ah, Mr. Da Costa, father has confessed to us you are only a *Schnorrer*. I think it is we who should confess *we* are only *Schnorrers*. We owe you all.
Joseph	(*Blowing his nose*) I will look after your daughter's dowry.
	(*YANKELE pricks up his ears*)
Deborah	O my benefactor. (*Seizes his hand and kisses it.*) But can you afford it?
Joseph	Afford it?
Deborah	My father promised Yankele such a large dowry.
Manasseh	Yes, I foresaw his patron's generosity. A true prince in Israel.
Yankele	(*To JOSEPH*) But your 'ighness vill pay de dowry direct to *me?*
Manasseh	(*Bridling*) And do you suppose *I* wish to intercept it? True, 'tis the man who has fed and clothed the bride from the cradle to the canopy to whom reimbursement is really owing. Nevertheless, Yankele, I give you my lily of the valley without deducting a single shekel from my promise, and all I ask from your princely subsidiser is my own thousand pounds.
Joseph	Your thousand pounds?
Manasseh	Did you not offer me a thousand pounds if I made the match—when I dined at your house?
Leah	So you did, father.
Joseph	Yes, yes—but you refused them. You wouldn't discuss busi-

ness on a Sabbath.

Manasseh	Exactly, but to-day is a week-day.
Joseph	You mean to say—
Manasseh	I saved you from breaking the Fourth Commandment and in reward you wish to rob me and break the Eighth.
Joseph	But you said it was enough reward to dry the tears of beauty.
Manasseh	But they would gush afresh at her father's meanness.

(*ENTER BEAU BELASCO hastily, waving pantaloons.*)

Beau B.	Look at *these* breeches—Oh, I beg your pardon. (*Hides them behind him.*) Ladies, your humble servant. Mr. Grobstock, I salute you.
Mrs. G.	(*Embracing him passionately*) And I salute you, my dearest Benjamin.
Beau B.	Mind my cravat.
Manasseh	(*Relieving the embarrassed BEAU of his breeches, then leading GROBSTOCK into a corner.*) Let us be kindly blind to all these amatory exuberances, and pursue the pecuniary point you are so clumsily evading.

(*YANKELE goes out with DEBORAH, each feeling in the breeches pockets with one hand. MANASSEH argues with GROBSTOCK in dumb show.*)

Leah	Well, Benjamin, when you are finished making love to mother—
Beau B.	Even that is preferable to embracing *you* in public. Heigho.
Leah	(*Bridling*) You wish to back out?
Beau B.	My precious, what an inelegant expression. But when the Montagues and Capulets make it up, and you change back from Juliet to Leah, don't you find the romance evaporating?
Leah	No, that's when I find it beginning. But if you are dependent

on *other* people for your romance—

Beau B.	Charming! Charming! Other people? No, Juliet. (*Kisses her*) I depend only on you for it.
Mrs. G.	Now you talk sense.
Beau B.	Do I? I plumed myself on talking nonsense.
Leah	In love the two are one.
Beau B.	Exquisite. I see you are capable of infusing romance into marriage. (*Embracing her*)
Joseph	(*Helplessly beaten*) Very well, you shall have the fifteen hundred. (MANASSEH *about to speak.*) Not another word—or you'll get it up to two thousand.
	(*ENTER MOSES BELASCO.*)
Manasseh	(*Advancing to him with warning forefinger pointing to the lovers.*) Hush! Hush! You see?
Moses B.	Yes, I see. (*Turns to the old couple.*) Mr. and Mrs. Grobstock, I presume. (*Bowing*)
Mrs. G.	(*Bowing*) Pleased—
Moses B.	Benjamin!
Beau B.	(*Startled*) Sir!
Moses B.	May I not have a glimpse of the young lady?
Beau B.	Certainly, sir—you have excellent taste.
Moses B.	(*Bowing to Leah*) So have you. And confound it, it's the first time I've thought so. My dear. (*Giving her his hand*) I hope I shall be not only your father-in-law but your friend.
Leah	(*Curtseying*) Sir, I hope I shall be not only your daughter-in-law but in reality. (*Kisses him*)
Beau B.	Charming! Charming!
Manasseh	(*Blowing his nose with emotion*) I am proud of my work. It is its own reward. And—(*mastering himself*) what of the synagogue investment, Mr. Belasco?

Moses B.	I was just in time. The Synagogue will reap no less than five hundred pounds on the transaction.
Manasseh	It shall be counted to you for righteousness. Will you promise me to crown your good deed by instructing the Mahamad to institute a new charity fund with the five hundred, the annual income of which shall go to a poor and deserving member of the community?
Moses B.	I promise with pleasure.
	(*ENTER* YANKELE *and* DEBORAH, *carrying a large sack between them.*)
Beau B.	What have you there?
Yankele	My vedding vardrobe. (*BEAU BELASCO looks at it, pulls out a cocked hat,* YANKELE *murmurs.*) Funeral Service at six.
Beau B.	You never found *this* in the box room.
Yankele	No, but I took it instead of taking a box.
Deborah	You forgot to provide it, sir. He can't be married with a bare head.
Joseph	Barefaced, *I* call it.
Manasseh	(*Turning on his parasite*) You stole it, Yankele? A *schnorrer* sink to theft.
Yankele	But I admired it so much. If I hadn't taken it, I should have been compelled to break the tenth commandment, vich says "Dou shalt not covet."
Beau B.	(*Pleased*) Ah! How true!
Yankele	By taking it, I broke de eighth commandment, vich says "Dou shalt not steal." But as I couldn't escape breaking von commandment or de oder, I thought I might as vell have de hat.
Beau B.	Exquisite! Exquisite! You may keep the hat. Mr. Da Costa, I congratulate you on your son-in-law.
Manasseh	He has indeed the true Talmudic spirit.

Joseph	Humph! I'm not so sure he deserves my dowry.
Mrs. G.	Don't be captious, Joseph, when we're all so happy.
Manasseh	Spoken like a lady Solomon. "Ah, behold how good and pleasant it is for brethren to dwell together in unity." The air is full of unions—union of Spaniard and German after generations of feud. Union of lover and lass, union of rich and poor. In memory whereof, Mr. Belasco, let the five hundred pound synagogue fund for the poor in honour of my daughter's marriage be entitled the Da Costa Peace Offering.
Moses B.	Good.
Leah	Beautiful!
Manasseh	And let it be appointed to me and my heirs for ever.
Moses B.	You take the money for yourself.
Manasseh	(*Putting hands on* YANKELE *and* DEBORAH) And for my children and grandchildren. (YANKELE *and* DEBORAH *squeeze happy hands.*) But I give the Synagogue the honour.
Moses B.	You really are the King of Schnorrers!
Yankele	Gawd save de King!
Omnes	(*Except* MOSES BELASCO) Hear! Hear! Long live the King!
	(THEY *clap their hands.* MANASSEH *bows majestically and the Curtain falls slowly.*)

Epilogue

The November 1925 production of *The King of Schnorrers* was part of a frenetic burst of theatrical activity by Zangwill, who for many years had devoted more of his time and energy to Jewish causes than to literary pursuits and now was eager to reposition himself as a playwright. He had been absent from the London stage for seven seasons, and his last success, *The Melting Pot*, belonged to the prewar era. His most recent commercially produced play, *Too Much Money* (1918), a farce whose theme was the embarrassment of wealth starring Shavian actress Lillah McCarthy, had an unimpressive run of sixty-two performances.[1] Zangwill's comedy *We Moderns,* a satirical look at the postwar young generation, opened at the New Theatre in London on July 7, 1925. The play had debuted in America in 1924 to poor reviews and closed after twenty-two performances. Its London reception was nearly as disappointing, and it closed after thirty-eight performances.

Zangwill would not accept defeat. He decided to invest his money and become his own producer, a move that would prove ruinous. He rented the recently opened Fortune Theatre, a small house owned by Laurence Cowen, brother of his school chum Louis, and declared himself an author-manager, announcing a plan to present a full season of his own plays. His rambling manifesto "Author-Manager!" appeared in the *Daily Express* on September 10, 1925, and was reproduced in Fortune playbills.[2] The disjointed essay revealed his deteriorating condition. He attacked the "Anglo-Saxon public" for failing to appreciate great acting, and the critics, especially A. B. Walkley of the London *Times,* for their class-embedded tyranny: "Why must the critics refrain from studying and learning from me merely because I was born within sound of Bow Bells?" He also railed against the excessive commercialism that had taken over the profession, declaring, "Being a Jew, I am not out for money."[3]

The season began on September 12 with a recast production of Zangwill's *We Moderns,* to which on the sixteenth he added a revival of *Merely*

Mary Ann. He hoped these would be followed by *The War God, The Next Religion, Plaster Saints, The Melting Pot, The Cockpit, The Forcing House, Too Much Money,* and *The King of Schnorrers.* The contract with Cowen may have expired by the end of the year, for while *We Moderns* was completing a 92-performance run at the Fortune, Zangwill had assumed tenancy of the Little Theatre, a 350-seat house where he was producing *Gloriana,* a historical costume drama by Gwen John, which ended up being an expensive project that drew poor press. This was followed by a revival of his *Too Much Money* (42 performances) and a production of *The Forcing House,* Zangwill's new play inspired by the upheaval of the Russian Revolution. The theme of revolution and rapid change from monarchy to Soviet rule was of great interest to the public. Harold Hobson, the influential reviewer at the *Observer,* called it a first-rate play in need of editing and noted that even in its present state it should "reap the success it deserves." "It seemed to me," he wrote, "to have more quality than any contemporary play I have seen for months."[4] The compliment arrived too late, though.

Some years earlier, in an interview with George Sylvester Viereck, Zangwill described the condition of postwar Europe thus: "we are like passengers in a train driven by mad engineers."[5] The metaphor could now be applied to himself. His roller-coaster theatrical adventure ended on March 20, 1926, with the final performance of *The Forcing House,* along with total mental, physical, and financial collapse. Zangwill's friends Louis Golding and Joseph Leftwich remembered the theatrical season with pain. Zangwill's theaters were empty, and he was envious of the success and packed houses he saw around him. In Golding's words, he was "like a boy in the sixth form who sees some terrifyingly clever youngster in the lower school suddenly snatch up all the open prizes" and was unable to get over the fact that only a few years back "two continents had packed them [his plays] nightly."[6] Old and frail before his time, his body and spirit broken, Zangwill retired to his home in East Preston, Sussex, where Edith cared for him until, at the end, his condition worsened sharply and he had to be transferred to a nursing home. It was a horrifying moment that left his physician and friend, Redcliffe Salaman, shaken. He wrote to Leftwich, "It was the most painful scene I have ever witnessed, and it has always left me with the problem—does a man, even if he is out of his mind, really suffer the agonising pains and terrors that from his wild talk he would appear to do? I think he does—which does not make the situation easier."[7]

When Israel Zangwill died on August 1, 1926, the world of letters lamented his passing, some expressing regret that the Nobel Prize committee had missed the opportunity to recognize his literary and humanitarian contributions. Jews mourned him deeply. "Not since the death of Herzl has the passing of any Jew evoked such grief throughout the Diaspora," said Dr. Stephen Wise in the eulogy.[8] He was "something of a folk hero," explained Alexander Baron, who remembered from his East End childhood the old bearded men who spoke with reverential tones of their "great defenders": Zola, Tolstoy, and Zangwill.[9] On August 5, five days after Zangwill's death, the London *Times* reported that the conference of the Tailors and Garment Workers Union, which met in Leeds the day before, passed a resolution in appreciation of Zangwill's efforts for the emancipation of Jews.[10] The Jewish press framed its front pages with black borders, with the major papers issuing special supplements. In Poland, writer Hirsh David Nomberg expressed the sentiment of many in the Yiddish newspaper *Moment:* "I have never met Zangwill, but his death shocked and depressed me as the death of one very close, the very nearest and dearest to me. You must pardon such sentimentality, but I have the feeling of an orphan."[11] *Ha'aretz,* the Tel Aviv Hebrew daily, announced on its front page on August 2, "the last lightning-flash of the triangular fire that burst forth in the West [Herzl, Nordau, and Zangwill] has been extinguished."[12] Zangwill was "our intellectual Rothschild" of the English world, a "Columbus seeking a new territory for the Jew where prejudice, persecution and sorrow do not exist," lamented the *Jewish Forum* in New York.[13] Louis Marshall pronounced him "an exalted son of Israel, an intellectual prince," one who would be remembered in the annals of his people alongside Maimonides, Mendelsohn, Heine, Spinoza, Ibn Ezra, Disraeli, Pinsker, Emanuel Noah, and Herzl.[14]

In a letter to Rabbi Stephen Wise written after the funeral, Edith Zangwill surmised that her husband would have been pleased with the mixed assembly: "the East End Jews, too poor even to have collars, & the West End Jews with their shiny top hats brought together as closely so closely in a brotherhood of Israel, our Israel."[15] Shared sorrow could not eradicate social barriers and the cultural divide as Edith had imagined. In its coverage of the funeral, the *Jewish World* reported an incident worthy of *Children of the Ghetto:*

> They [the arrangements] were marred only by the abominably rude and disorderly conduct of a number of men and women who, in a number of charabancs [open-sided coaches], which started from the Pavilion Theatre in Whitechapel Road, went up to Golders Green, for the purpose of being present. Evidently no provision had been made for their attendance, which was quite unexpected, and of which

they should have advised those responsible in advance, seeing that it is not exactly usual for "mourners" to arrive in brake-loads [masses]. Besides, there is all the difference between congregating in a cemetery and crushing into but a moderately sized crematorium. As it was, these people who I suppose intended to show their respect for Zangwill, manifested it in a very strange way. When they found the doors of the chapel closed—they had to be prevented from occupying the whole of the available space to the exclusion of everyone else—they attempted to "rush" the attendants and force an entry. What ensued can be imagined, but I must say it would have been worse, but for the way in which the situation was handled, and accommodation quickly improvised.[16]

Israel Zangwill left little in the way of material goods, as the sum total of his estate amounted to 3,267 pounds.[17] The contrast between this amount and what is mentioned in his will, where he left 4,000 pounds to each of his children, reveals the great losses incurred during his final theatrical ventures.[18] Concerned about Edith's financial condition, Stephen Wise spoke to her about the possibility that Zangwill's friends could help. On August 25, Edith thanked him in a letter for the generous offer, but made it clear that she had no need for any help of that sort.[19] Instead, she suggested the establishment of a fund in Zangwill's memory, to which she would also contribute. Two things suggested themselves to her. One of his great desires, she said, was the establishment of a national theater. Though he had been thinking of England, and the contributions came chiefly from America, she suggested that the theater should be built in Jerusalem. Her alternative suggestion was the creation of a unit of two permanent Jewish envoys—a man and a woman—who would be ready to go to any part of the world at the first hint of Jewish persecution and report to the world their findings, for "even the most barbaric nation does not want its barbarities to become generally known."[20]

In her suggestions for suitable commemoration of her husband, Edith talked about what was central to his life: meritorious theater, Jewish artistic expression, Zionism, Jewish safety from persecution, and women's equality. Today, Zangwill's legacy is commemorated in different fashion in the three lands that comprised his emotional and ideological compass. The fabric of the American ethos is ingrained with his metaphor of the melting pot; the State of Israel, whose creation was his great passion, is the guardian of his papers, kept in the capital city at the Central Zionist Archives; and England is the repository of his physical remains and his literary work. Zangwill is commemorated on the wall of the Old Reading Room in the British Museum, where the names of some two hundred notable library ticket-holders are inscribed in alphabetical order. "Israel Zangwill, 1864–1926, Writer" is the next-to-last entry, flanked by "William Butler Yeats, 1865–1939, Poet" and "Vera Zasulich, 1849–1919, Revolutionary." Their company could hardly be more fitting: one male, one female; one an Irish nationalist, poet, and playwright, the other an anti-czarist revolutionary.

In 1925, one year before Zangwill's death, journalist and dramatic critic Charles Solomon had this to say in his survey on "The Jew and the Drama":

> First among the creative artists comes Israel Zangwill, that magic personality who has written plays about Jews that even Jews come to see. Mr. Zangwill has shed lustre on the Jewish name, not only because of the extraordinary power and vitality of his work, but also because he has borne his Judaism like a banner, and has done more, perhaps, than any writer that ever lived to show the Jew as he really is to the Gentile, and (even more important) to the Jew.[21]

Notes

Prologue

1. "The Maccabeans," *Jewish Chronicle,* June 26, 1908, 20. The dinner was held on Sunday, June 21, 1908.
2. "Israel Zangwill—the Poet and Statesman," file A120/178, Central Zionist Archives, Jerusalem (hereafter cited as Zionist Archives). File A120 is the exclusive holder of Zangwill's papers.
3. Studies of Zangwill tend to gloss over his lifelong theatrical career, paying at best minimal attention to stage productions of his plays. The following biographies and full-length studies of Israel Zangwill are listed chronologically: Joseph Leftwich, *Israel Zangwill* (New York: Thomas Yoseloff, 1957); Maurice Wohlgelernter, *Israel Zangwill, A Study* (New York: Columbia University Press, 1964); Elsie Bonita Adams, *Israel Zangwill* (New York: Twayne, 1971); Jacques Ben-Guigui, *Israel Zangwill: Penseur et Ecrivain (1864–1926)* (Toulouse: Imprimerie Toulousaine–R. Lion, 1975); Joseph H. Udelson, *Dreamer of the Ghetto: The Life and Works of Israel Zangwill* (Tuscaloosa: University of Alabama Press, 1990).
4. Israel Zangwill, "The Jewish Race," in *Speeches, Articles, and Letters of Israel Zangwill,* sel. and ed. Maurice Simon, with a foreword by Edith Ayrton Zangwill (London: Soncino Press, 1937), 95.

Introduction

1. Louis Zangwill suggested that his father was eight years old when he arrived in London. See Joseph Leftwich, "Israel Zangwill," *Jewish Historical Society of England Transactions Sessions, 1953–1955* 18 (London, 1958): 85.
2. Israel Zangwill, *Children of the Ghetto* (1892; New York: Grosset & Dunlap, 1895), 65. All page references in the novel are from the 1895 edition (hereafter cited as Zangwill, *Children*).
3. Ibid., 66.
4. Leftwich, *Israel Zangwill,* 72.

519

5. *The Service of the Synagogue*, 6 vols., ed. Herbert M. Adler, trans. Herbert Adler, Arthur Davis, Elsie Davis, Nina Salaman, and Israel Zangwill (London: Routledge, 1904–1909).

6. Israel Zangwill, trans., *Selected Religious Poems of Solomon Ibn Gabirol* (Philadelphia: Jewish Publication Society, 1923).

7. Leftwich, *Israel Zangwill*, 51.

8. According to one source, Moses Zangwill sent his first wife divorce papers and married another woman in Jerusalem. Yosef Nedava, *Negohot min He'avar* [Beacons from the Past] (Tel Aviv: Reshafim, 1961), 146.

9. Israel Zangwill, "To Die in Jerusalem," in Zangwill, *"They That Walk in Darkness": Ghetto Tragedies* (New York: Macmillan, 1899).

10. Biographical sketch, file A120/486, Zionist Archives. The two-page document was prepared in 1949 by Mrs. Mielziner. Much of the information on the family was given to her by Eleanor Cowen, an old friend of the Zangwill family. Mrs. Mielziner notes that she herself first met Israel in 1892 or 1893 in Paris. There is good reason to assume the author was Ella Mielziner, widow of artist Leo Mielziner (1869–1935), a friend of Zangwill.

11. Leftwich, *Israel Zangwill*, 73.

12. See, e.g., Udelson, *Dreamer of the Ghetto*, 61.

13. Zangwill, *Children*, 68.

14. File A120/486, 1–2, Zionist Archives.

15. Lloyd P. Gartner, *The Jewish Immigrant in England, 1870–1914* (Detroit: Wayne State University Press, 1960), 16–17. Gartner (p. 49) records that in 1911, three years before the onset of the Great War, the Jewish immigrant population in England, Scotland, and Wales had grown to 120,000.

16. Ibid., 38–40.

17. "London's Jewry," *American Hebrew*, September 7, 1894, 557.

18. Louis Zangwill, "Civilization Before Herzl," *Menorah* 13 (1927): 209–12.

19. For a comprehensive history of the school, see Gerry Black, *The History of the Jews' Free School, London, since 1732* (London: Tymsder, 1998).

20. Quoted in Gartner, *Jewish Immigrant in England*, 223.

21. Ibid.

22. Mary A. Linderman, "No Longer an Alien, the English Jew: The Nineteenth-Century Jewish Reader and Literary Representations of the Jew in the Works of Benjamin Disraeli, Matthew Arnold, and George Eliot" (PhD diss., Loyola University, 1997), 177.

23. Quoted in Black, *History of the Jews' Free School*, 127.

24. Quoted in Udelson, *Dreamer of the Ghetto*, 62.

25. Zangwill's brother Mark won in 1882; Louis, in 1883.

26. Israel Zangwill, "The Premier and the Painter," in *My First Book*, ed. Jerome K. Jerome (London: Chatto & Windus, 1897), 170–72.

27. For a different interpretation on this topic, see Meri-Jane Rochelson, "Language,

Gender, and Ethnic Anxiety in Zangwill's *Children of the Ghetto*," *English Literature in Transition, 1880–1920* 31 (1988): 399–412.

28. Zangwill, "Premier and the Painter," 168.

29. Israel Zangwill, *Children of the Ghetto: A Study of a Peculiar People* (New York: Macmillan, 1895), v.

30. Holbrook Jackson, *The Eighteen Nineties: A Review of Art and Ideas at the Close of the Nineteenth Century* (1913; Atlantic Highlands, NJ: Humanities Press, 1976).

31. Ibid., 224–25.

32. Israel Zangwill, "Language and Jewish Life," in *The Voice of Jerusalem*, ed. Israel Zangwill (London: William Heinemann, 1920), 248. This essay was written for a book honoring Nahum Sokolow's 25th literary anniversary, where it appears in Hebrew translation (*Sefer ha-Yovel huval shai likhvod Nahum Sokolv: be'yom melot hamesh ve'esrim shana l'avodato ha'sifrutit* [Warsaw: Shuldberg, 1904]).

33. Zangwill, "Language and Jewish Life," 248–49.

34. English translation, from "The *Children of the Ghetto*," *American Hebrew*, July 21, 1905, 229.

35. "Morris Rosenfeld's Recital," *Jewish World*, July 13, 1900, 250.

36. E. Jaffe, "Zangwill," *Jewish World*, October 7, 1926, 7.

37. Leftwich, *Israel Zangwill*, 27.

38. Ibid., 28.

39. The book would gain recognition when reissued in 1896, after its author had made a name for himself. When Katherine Cecil Thurston's best-selling book *The Masquerador* came out in 1905, it was suggested by Sinclair Lewis that it had been "lifted" from *The Premier and the Painter*. Leftwich, *Israel Zangwill*, 25.

40. The novel includes Zangwill's translation of the poem. Imber is identified by his real name and described as the National Poet of Israel. Ibid., 189.

41. Naphtali Herz Imber, "Israel Zangwill: In Memoriam of *The Jewish Standard*," *Jewish Exponent* (Philadelphia), February 26, 1982; reprinted in *Master of Hope: Selected Writings of Naphtali Herz Imber*, ed. Jacob Kabakoff (Cranbury, NJ: Associated University Presses, 1985), 96–99.

42. Imber, "Israel Zangwill," 97.

43. Zangwill, *Children*, 440.

44. Israel Zangwill, "English Judaism," *Jewish Quarterly Review* 1, no. 4 (1889): 376–407.

45. *The Bachelors' Club* was produced by Ideal, a U.K. company, as a silent film in 1921.

46. Israel Zangwill, preface, *The Celibates' Club*, 6th ed. (London: Globe, 1925), x.

47. E. F. Bleir, ed. *Three Victorian Detective Novels* (New York: Dover, 1978), xv, quoted in Uri Eizenzweig, "Zionism and Detective Fiction: A Case in

Narratology," *Telos* 60 (1984): 134.

48. "The Maccabeans," *Jewish Chronicle*, November 18, 1892, 17.

49. N. Schoonderwoerd, *J. T. Grein, Ambassador of the Theatre, 1862–1935: A Study in Anglo-Continental Theatrical Relations* (Assen, Netherlands: Van Gorcum, 1963), 84.

50. In a form completed on January 31, 1890, Zangwill gave his reasons for study as "journalistic and literary work," his address as 113 Victoria Park Road, London NE, and his profession as "Journalist." The application was supported by Sir John Abraham Jacob de Villiers (1863–1931) of the British Museum. I wish to thank Marjorie Caygill of the British Library for this information.

51. On November 16, 1888, Potter noted in her diary, "A long morning at the British Museum reading up *Jewish Chronicle* and suchlike." Beatrice Potter Webb, *The Diary of Beatrice Webb*, ed. Norman and Jeanne MacKenzie (London: Virago, 1982–1985).

52. Ibid.

53. For a detailed biography, see Yvonne Karp, *Eleanor Marx*, 2 vols. (London: Lawrence & Wishart, 1972–1976).

54. Karp, *Eleanor Marx*, 2:258.

55. William J. Fishman, *Jewish Radicals from Czarist Russia to London Ghetto* (New York: Pantheon, 1974), 197.

56. Karp, *Eleanor Marx*, 2:521.

57. Sally Ledger, "Eleanor Marx and Henryk Ibsen," in *Eleanor Marx (1855–1898): Life, Work, Contacts*, ed. John Stokes (Burlington, VT: Ashgate, 2000).

58. When reviewing Max Nordau's play *Dr. Kohn*, for example, critic J. T. Grein remarked, "It is Ibsenish in its simplicity, if not so adroitly structured as Ibsen would have done it; and some of the qualities of the great Norwegian are not wanting." J. T. Grein, "Max Nordau's 'Dr. Kohn,'" in Grein, *Dramatic Criticism* (London, 1899), 1:150.

59. Harley Granville-Barker, "The Coming of Ibsen," in *The Eighteen Eighties: Essays by Fellows of the Royal Society of Literature*, ed. Walter de la Mare (Cambridge: Cambridge University Press, 1930), 159.

60. This was not the first alteration of Ibsen's ending. Henry Arthur Jones's earnest version of 1884, demurely retitled *Breaking a Butterfly*, concluded with a stay-at-home Nora, forgiven and forgiving. Two sequels to the play, one earnest by Walter Besant, the other satirical by George Bernard Shaw, appeared in 1890.

61. Israel Zangwill and Eleanor Marx Aveling, "*A Doll's House* Repaired," *Time*, March 1891, 239–53; reprinted in pamphlet form, published by the authors.

62. Sulzberger was the first Jew to hold the position of judge in Philadelphia's common pleas court. In addition to being a noted jurist, he was a Judaica scholar, a Zionist, and the first president of the American Jewish Committee. For a selection of his thirty-year correspondence with Zangwill, see Isaac M. Fein, "Israel Zangwill and American Jewry: A Documentary Study," in

American Jewish Historical Quarterly 60, nos. 1–4 (1970–1971): 12–36.

63. Bernard Winehouse, "Israel Zangwill's *Children of the Ghetto:* A Literary History of the First Anglo-Jewish Best-Seller," *English Literature in Transition, 1880–1920* 16 (1973): 95.

64. The Jewish part of London had already been described as a "sort of ghetto" in *Dickens's Dictionary of London* (1879), but it was Zangwill who had the vision to replace the suggestion of similarity with unambiguous clarity.

65. Zangwill, *Children,* ix.

66. "London's Jewry," *American Hebrew,* September 7, 1894, 557.

67. Louis Wirth, *The Ghetto,* with a new introduction by Hasia Diner (New Brunswick, NJ: Transaction, 1998), 117–21.

68. Jack London, "The Ghetto," chap. 19 in *The People of the Abyss* (New York: Macmillan, 1903).

69. Letter from William Archer to Zangwill, dated December 31, 1892, and signed "William Archer," file A120/236, Zionist Archives.

70. Israel Abrahams, "*Children of the Ghetto,*" *Jewish Chronicle,* October 14, 1899, 7.

71. Winehouse, "Zangwill's *Children of the Ghetto,*" 94.

72. Charles Kensington Salaman, *Jews as They Are* (London: Simkin, Marshall, 1882).

73. "Address of Dr. Stephen Wise, President, American Jewish Congress," in Zangwill Memorial Committee, *In Memory of Israel Zangwill* (New York: Zangwill Memorial Committee, 1926), 19.

74. Lucien Wolf, "Israel Zangwill," *Jewish Chronicle,* October 29, 1926, 17.

75. Lucien Wolf, "The Jews in London," *Graphic,* November 16, 1889, 599–604.

76. Barbara Kirshenblatt-Gimblett, "Exhibiting Jews," in *Destination Culture: Tourism, Museums, and Heritage* (Berkeley: University of California Press, 1998), 85.

77. Zangwill, *Children,* 350.

78. M. C. Birchenough, "Children of the Ghetto," *Jewish Quarterly Review* 5 (1892): 333.

79. Louis Lipsky, "Israel Zangwill as a Story Writer," *American Hebrew,* April 3, 1914, 641.

80. Cyrus Adler, "Israel Zangwill," in *Lectures, Selected Papers, Addresses* (Philadelphia: privately printed, 1933), 103–97.

81. Ibid., 104.

82. [Clement Scott], "The Great Demonstration," *Theatre,* October 1, 1892, 17.

83. See, e.g., "The Royalty," *Era,* September 24, 1892, 9.

84. William Archer, *Theatrical "World" for 1893* (1894; New York: B. Blom, 1969), 290.

85. *Era,* December 30, 1893, 283.

86. *Sketch,* January 10, 1912, 12.

87. Leftwich, *Israel Zangwill*, 46.

88. J. Balfour, quoted in Jim Davis and Victor Emeljanow, *Reflecting the Audience: London Theatregoing, 1840–1880* (Iowa City: University of Iowa Press, 2001), 242.

89. Wolf, "Jews in London," 602. Wolf's list includes Cumberland's *The Jew*, Tobdin's *Jew and the Doctor*, and Lacy's *Jewess*, and the melodramas *The Jew of Lubeck, Ella Rosenberg, Old Death; or, The Hebrew Twins, Azael the Prodigal, Leah the Forsaken,* and *The Maid of Judea.*

90. "Jewish Actors and Actresses," *Jewish Chronicle*, November 17, 1899, 10.

91. "Jews as Playgoers," *Jewish World*, August 29, 1909, 13.

92. Ibid.

93. Michael R. Booth, *Theatre in the Victorian Age* (Cambridge: Cambridge University Press, 1991), 11.

94. Sir Arthur Wing Pinero, "The Theatre in Transition," in *Fifty Years, Memories and Contrasts: A Composite Picture of the Period 1882–1932 by Twenty-seven Contributors to The Times* (London: Thornton Butterworth, 1932), 71.

95. Ibid., 73.

96. Louis Zangwill, "Herzl Invades England," in *Theodor Herzl: A Memorial*, ed. Mayer W. Weisgal (New York: New Palestine, 1929), 41.

97. Ibid., 42.

98. Ibid.

99. Israel Zangwill, "Zionism," *Lippincott's Magazine*, October 1899, 581.

100. Israel Zangwill, Notes for "Presidential Speech at Playgoers Club," n.d., n.p., file A120/486, Zionist Archives.

101. For a discussion of Jewish racial self-definition, see Eric L. Goldstein, "'Different Blood Flows in Our Veins': Race and Jewish Self-Definition in Late Nineteenth Century America," *American Jewish History* 85, no. 1 (1997): 29–55.

102. Theodor Herzl, *The Complete Diaries of Theodor Herzl*, ed. Raphael Patai, trans. Harry Zohn (New York: Herzl Press and Thomas Yoseloff, 1960), 1:276.

103. Shlomo Avineri, "Theodor Herzl's Diaries as a Bildungsroman," *Jewish Social Studies* 5, no. 3 (1999): 24.

104. Quoted in "Topics of the Week," *New York Times*, November 14, 1903.

105. Zangwill, "Jewish Race," 93.

106. Todd M. Endelman, *The Jews of Britain, 1656 to 2000* (Berkeley: University of California Press, 2002), 189.

107. Zangwill, "Zionism," 584.

108. Zangwill, *Dreamers of the Ghetto* (London: Globe, 1925), 392.

109. Ibid., 393, 396.

110. Reuben Brainin, "Israel Zangwill—Twelve Years Later," *Jewish World*, May 28, 1909, 11.

111. Zangwill, "Zionism," *Contemporary Review* (London) 76 (October 1899): 500–512; *Lippincott's Magazine* (Philadelphia) (October 1899).

112. Zangwill, "Zionism," *Lippincott's,* 587.

113. Zangwill, "Zangwill on Zionism," *Jewish Chronicle,* October 6, 1899, 18.

114. Israel Zangwill, "The Return to Palestine," *New Liberal Review,* December 1901, 628.

115. Ibid., 634.

116. Zangwill, quoting an address he delivered in 1903, "The Voice of Jerusalem," in Zangwill, ed., *Voice of Jerusalem,* 85.

117. Ibid.

118. Stuart A. Cohen, *English Zionists and British Jews* (Princeton, NJ: Princeton University Press, 1982), 82.

119. Israel Zangwill, "The Two Opposing Forces at Work on the Jew," *Menorah* 35, no. 4 (1903): 277.

120. For a detailed list of the period's pogroms, see "From Kishineff to Bialystock: A Table of Pogroms from 1903 to 1906," in *The American Jewish Year Book 5667* (September 20, 1906, to September 8, 1907), ed. Henrietta Szold (Philadelphia: Jewish Publication Society of America), 34–89.

121. In England supporters included Lucien Wolf, Meyer A. Spielman, Leopold de Rothschild, Osmond D'Avigdor-Goldmid, and Lionel Abrahams. See Cohen, *English Zionists and British Jews,* 95. In the United States supporters included Oscar S. Straus, Daniel Guggenheim, Judge Mayer Sulzberger, and Cyrus Sulzberger; in Russia, Israel Jasinowski and Max Mandelstamm; in Germany, Karl Jeremias and Alfred Klee; and in France, Nahum Slouscz.

122. Zangwill, "Voice of Jerusalem," 90–91.

123. Bernard Marinbach, *Galveston: Ellis Island of the West* (Albany: SUNY Press, 1983), 171.

124. "Zangwill and the Territorial Organization," *Menorah* 40, no. 239 (1906): 269.

125. Ibid., 17–18.

126. Naomi W. Cohen, *Jacob H. Schiff: A Study in American Jewish Leadership* (Hanover, NH: University Press of New England for Brandeis University Press, 1999), 168.

127. "The Writing of Plays—By the Men Who Do It," *New York Times,* October 18, 1908, 5.

128. Gartner, *Jewish Immigrant in England,* 16–17.

129. Cyrus Sulzberger, a cousin of Zangwill's mentor, was highly critical of the novel's realistic depiction of Jewish life and accused the author of broadcasting Jewish defects. See *American Hebrew,* December 2, 1892, 151; December 30, 1892, 296–97. In the Jewish Women's Congress that took place in Chicago in 1893, Mary Cohen cautioned her Christian readers that Zangwill's book might evoke an unfavorable impression of its poor Jews, urging them to divert their attention to the characters' religious devotion. Quoted in Kirshenblatt-Gimblett, "Exhibiting Jews," 125–26.

130. Willa Cather, *The World and the Parish: Willa Cather's Articles and Reviews, 1893–1902* (Lincoln: University of Nebraska Press, 1970), 1:491.

131. Isidore Harris, "Mr. Israel Zangwill," *Bookman* 7, no. 2 (1898): 104–7.

132. Booth, *Theatre in the Victorian Age*, 20.

133. Major J. B. Pond, *Eccentricities of Genius, Memories of Famous Men and Women of the Platform and the Stage* (1900; London: Chatto & Windus, 1901).

134. Five hundred dollars in 1898 had the equivalent buying power of more than eleven thousand 2003 dollars (see http://www.eh.net/ehresources/howmuch/dollarq.phpA). On objections to the amount of the fee, see a letter titled "Good Things Come High," signed by "Dreamer," in *American Hebrew*, October 14, 1898, 711. Gustav Gottheil, chief rabbi of the wealthy Reform Temple Emanu-El in New York, had a yearly salary of ten thousand dollars, and his assistant received five thousand dollars. Orthodox East European rabbis at the time earned between six and ten dollars a week. See Kimmy Caplan, "In God We Trust: Salaries and Income of American Orthodox Rabbis, 1881–1924," *American Jewish History* 86, no. 1 (1998): 87, 94.

135. I. Zangwill, *Without Prejudice* (New York: Century Co., 1896), 40. (Also published in London by T. Fisher Unwin, 1896.)

136. Pond, *Eccentricities of Genius*, 470.

137. "I. Zangwill's Lecture Tour," *New York Times*, October 10, 1898, 2.

138. "Zangwill on the Ghetto," *New York Times*, November 16, 1898, 6.

139. Located on Fourth Avenue, between 23rd and 24th Streets, the Lyceum was New York's first completely electrically lit theatre. Originally built in 1884 by Steele MacKaye, it was soon taken over by producer Daniel Frohman. It was torn down in 1902.

140. "Mr. Zangwill Again," *New York Dramatic Mirror*, November 26, 1898, 13.

141. "The Drama as a Fine Art," *Werner's Magazine* (New York), November 1898, 159–66; Pond, *Eccentricities of Genius*, 471.

142. "Drama as a Fine Art," 159.

143. Ibid.

144. Ibid.

145. Cather, *World and the Parish*, 491.

146. Ibid.

147. Ibid., 491–92.

148. For a discussion of racialism and Jewish genius, see Sander L. Gilman, *Smart Jews: The Construction of the Image of Jewish Superior Intelligence* (Lincoln: University of Nebraska Press, 1996).

149. Pond, *Eccentricities of Genius*, 471.

150. "As to Mr. Zangwill," *New York Dramatic Mirror*, October 22, 1898, 14.

151. "The Week at the Theatres," *New York Times*, October 23, 1898, 17.

152. "The Matinee Girl," *New York Dramatic Mirror*, October 29, 1898, 14.

153. "Israel Zangwill at the Judaeans," *American Hebrew*, October 28, 1898, 771.

154. Ibid., 772.
155. Kaufman Kohler, letter to the editor, *American Hebrew,* October 28, 1898, 778.
156. "Dinner to Israel Zangwill," *New York Times,* October 25, 1893, 5. Adolphe S. Ochs, the owner of the *Times,* attended the banquet as one of the Judaeans.
157. Ibid.
158. Pond, *Eccentricities of Genius,* 473.
159. The production made a $500,000 profit; see John Perry, *James A. Herne: The American Ibsen* (Chicago: Nelson-Hall, 1978), 263. It was probably through Caine (1853–1931), a close friend of his, that Zangwill connected with Tyler.
160. George C. Tyler, with J. C. Furnas, *Whatever Goes Up: The Hazardous Fortunes of a Natural Born Gambler* (Indianapolis: Bobbs-Merrill, 1934), 163–64.
161. Tyler's correspondence with Zangwill makes it clear that he also considered, though finally rejected, a stage production based on *King of Schnorrers,* which was clearly regarded as a project auxiliary to *Children of the Ghetto.* See miscellaneous correspondence between Tyler and Zangwill, file A120/562, Zionist Archives.
162. Tyler, *Whatever Goes Up,* 162.
163. A. Kingsley Glover, *Jewish Laws and Customs: Some of the Laws and Usages of the Children of the Ghetto* (Wells, MN: W. A. Hammond, 1900).
164. Ibid., 7.
165. See Lawrence G. Charap, "'Accept the Truth from Whomever Gives It': Jewish Protestant Dialogue, Interfaith Alliances and Pluralism, 1880–1910," *American Jewish History* 89, no. 3 (2001): 261–77.
166. William Dean Howells, "An East Side Ramble," in his *Impressions and Experiences* (New York: Harper & Brothers, 1896), 107.
167. Sadakichi Hartmann, "Picturesque Features of the Ghetto," *Mother Earth* 5, no. 6 (1910): 200.
168. Alan Trachtenberg, *The Incorporation of America: Culture and Society in the Gilded Age* (New York: Hill and Wang, 1982).
169. Walter Fuller Taylor, *The Economic Novel in America* (Chapel Hill: University of North Carolina Press, 1942), 79–80, quoted in Keith Gandal, *The Virtues of the Vicious: Jacob Riis, Stephen Crane, and the Spectacle of the Slum* (New York: Oxford University Press, 1997), 144.
170. Jacob A. Riis, *How the Other Half Lives: Studies among the Tenements of New York,* ed. Sam Bass Warner Jr. (1890; Cambridge: Belknap Press of Harvard University Press, 1970).
171. Irving Howe, introduction to Hutchins Hapgood's *The Spirit of the Ghetto: Studies of the Jewish Quarter of New York, with More than 50 Drawings from Life by Jacob Epstein, with a New Introduction by Irving Howe* (New York: Schocken, 1966), i.
172. Lincoln Steffens, *The Autobiography of Lincoln Steffens* (New York: Harcourt,

Brace, 1931), 244.

173. Ibid., 243.

174. Annie Nathan Meyer, "I: Concerning Sensitive Epiderm," in "The Ghetto in Literature," special issue, *Bookman* (February 1900): 533.

175. Martin B. Ellis, "II: The Other Side," in "The Ghetto in Literature," special issue, *Bookman* (February 1900): 534.

176. Ibid.

177. Ibid., 534–35.

178. Glover, *Jewish Laws and Customs*, 10.

179. Steffens, *Autobiography of Lincoln Steffens*, 244.

180. Wilbur M. Bates, "Children of the Ghetto," *Dramatic Magazine*, October 1899, 196.

181. Quoted in Louis Harap, *The Image of the Jew in American Literature: From Early Republic to Mass Immigration* (Philadelphia: Jewish Publication Society, 1974), 221. Available at the University of Georgia's Virtual Vaudeville Web site, http://www.virtualvaudeville.com/hypermediaNotes/frankbush_JewishHeadlinerF.html

182. George Coleman the Younger, *Random Records*, 1830, 1:317, quoted in Gerald Retlinger, "The Changed Face of English Jewry at the End of the Eighteenth Century," *Jewish Historical Society of England Transactions Sessions 1969–1970* 24 (1971): 38.

183. Hall Caine, "The Jew in Literature," *Literary World*, May 20, 1892, 483.

184. Ibid.

185. "The Stage Jew," *Jewish Comment*, May 9, 1913, 66.

186. "Jews and Music Halls," letter to the editor, signed FAIRPLAY, *Jewish Chronicle*, November 11, 1911, 28.

187. "Jews and the Music Halls," letter to the editor, signed JUDEX, *Jewish Chronicle*, December 8, 1911, 42.

188. "War on the 'Hebrew' Comedians in England," *American Hebrew*, June 18, 1913, 175.

189. Lord Halifax, Diary, September 23, 1942, file A7.8.11, Hickleton Papers, University of York, Borthwick Institute.

190. Harley Erdman, *Staging the Jew: The Performance of an American Ethnicity, 1860–1920* (New Brunswick, NJ: Rutgers University Press, 1997).

191. Ibid., 87.

192. Quoted in Shearer West, "The Construction of Racial Type: Caricature, Ethnography, and Jewish Physiognomy in Fin-de-Siècle Melodrama," *Nineteenth Century Theatre* 21, no. 1 (1993): 18.

193. Harap, *Image of the Jew*, 227.

194. Abraham Dreyfus, *Le Juif au théâtre: conference faite à la Société des études juives le ler mars 1886* (Paris: Quantin, 1886), quoted in "The Jew Upon the Stage," *Times-Democrat*, April 18, 1886, reprinted in Lafcadio Hearn, *Occidental*

Gleanings (London: William Heinemann, 1925), 2:188–89.

195. Israel Abrahams, "Jews and the Theatre," *Jewish Chronicle,* November 13, 1891, 21.

196. M. J. Landa, *The Jew in Drama* (London: P. S. King, 1926), 158.

197. Charles Dickens, *Oliver Twist* (New York: W. Morrow, 1994), chap. 19.

198. Israel Zangwill, "The Legend of the Conquering Jew," in Zangwill, ed., *Voice of Jerusalem,* 189.

199. *Trilby and Other Plays,* ed. and intro. by George Taylor (Oxford: Oxford University Press, 1996), 244.

200. For a survey of the "Noble Jew" on the German-language stage, see Charlene A. Lea, "Tolerance Unlimited: 'The Noble Jew' on the German and Austrian Stage (1750–1805)," *German Quarterly* 64, no. 2 (1991): 166–77.

201. Richard Cumberland, *The Jew,* 2nd ed. (London: Printed for C. Dilly, 1794), act 1, scene 1.

202. Salaman, *Jews as They Are,* 217.

203. Malcolm C. Salaman, "The Late Sir Henry Irving," *Jewish World,* reprinted in *American Hebrew,* November 4, 1905, 637.

204. "Music and Drama," *Jewish World* (London), April 10, 1908, 9.

205. Israel Zangwill, "Shylock and Other Stage Jews," in Zangwill, ed., *Voice of Jerusalem,* 239.

206. Ibid., 241.

207. Ibid., 242.

208. "The Future of Jewish Drama, Interview for 'The Jewish Chronicle' with Mr. Israel Zangwill," *Jewish Chronicle,* April 10, 1925, 16.

Children of the Ghetto: Introductory Essay

1. Zangwill to George Platt Brett at Macmillan, October 13, 1900, Macmillan Company Records, 1889–1960, Humanities Manuscripts, New York Public Library.

2. Zangwill to Brett, February 6, 1901.

3. Ibsen had cut the number of acts from five to four. Most playwrights of the early twentieth century preferred the three-act form, which was reduced later in the century to two. The one-act play is increasingly common nowadays.

4. See David Mayer, "Toga Plays," in *British Theatre in the 1890s: Essays on Drama and the Stage,* ed. Richard Foulkes (Cambridge: Cambridge University Press, 1992).

5. *Sketch,* November 29, 1899, 233.

6. Linda Rozomovits, *Shakespeare and the Politics of Culture in Late Victorian England* (Baltimore: Johns Hopkins University Press, 1998), 3.

7. Zangwill, "Shylock and Other Stage Jews," 228.

8. For Heine on Shylock, see "Shylock (Jessica)," trans. Frederic Ewen, in Heinrich

Heine, *Jewish Stories and Hebrew Melodies* (New York: Markus Wiener, 1987), 83–94.

9. Zangwill, "Shylock and Other Stage Jews," 233–34.

10. *Children of the Ghetto,* The British Library, Lord Chamberlain's Plays, MS no. 28, approved for production November 9, 1899.

11. Tyler to Zangwill, April 11, 1899, file A120/562, Zionist Archives.

12. There are two monographs on Herne: Herbert J. Edwards and Julie A. Herne, *James A. Herne: The Rise of Realism in the American Drama* (Orono: University of Maine Press, 1964), and John Perry, *James A. Herne: The American Ibsen* (Chicago: Nelson-Hall, 1978).

13. Cather, *World and the Parish,* 469; Donald Pizer, ed., *Hamlin Garland's Diaries* (San Marino, CA: Huntington Library, 1968), 146.

14. Pizer, ed., *Hamlin Garland's Diaries,* 146.

15. William Winter, "Ibsenites and Ibsenism," in *The Wallet of Time* (New York: Moffat, Yard, 1913), reprinted in *The American Theatre as Seen by Its Critics,* ed. Montrose J. Moses and John Mason Brown (New York: Norton, 1934), 100–101.

16. James A. Herne, "Art for Truth's Sake in the Drama," *Arena* 17 (1896–1897): 369–70, quoted in Perry, *James A. Herne,* 131.

17. Perry, *James A. Herne,* 154.

18. Edward A. Dithmar, "James A. Herne's *Margaret Fleming,*" *New York Times,* December 10, 1891, reprinted in Moses and Brown, *American Theatre,* 143.

19. Pizer, ed., *Hamlin Garland's Diaries,* 200.

20. Edwards and Herne, *James A. Herne,* 137. Julie Herne's account is valuable but must be viewed with caution. The discrepancy in dates between Tyler's letter to Zangwill cited above and the date she offers may be explained by the fact that she spoke from personal memory and could offer no documentation, since her father's papers were lost in a 1907 fire. Her loyalty to him might also have influenced her interpretation of events. For example, she believed her father's work on Zangwill's play to be detrimental to his health and partially responsible for his premature death in 1901 (ibid., 136), yet neglected to mention any ill effects from his hard drinking (see Pizer, *Hamlin Garland's Diaries,* 145). She also de-emphasized any connection between Herne's acceptance of the directing job and Tyler's agreeing to produce *Sag Harbor* (1900), which proved to be Herne's last production.

21. T-Mss 1937–001, Liebler and Company Records, 1890–1931, series 4, Theatre Manuscripts, New York Public Library for the Performing Arts. The contract is dated November 18, 1898.

22. Tyler to Zangwill, May 2, 1899, file A120/562, Zionist Archives.

23. Tyler to Zangwill, April 4, 1899, file A120/562, Zionist Archives.

24. In the May 2 letter, Tyler asks Zangwill to "tell Mr. Cowen a regular orchestra consists of fifteen men. I am willing to supply at least twenty-four men if

necessary. I understand Mr. Irving & Mr. Tree use thirty-four to forty men in their orchestra. In America they don't expect it and would not appreciate it if it were supplied." Tyler to Zangwill, May 2, 1899, file A120/562, Zionist Archives.

25. The Programme of Music in the playbill for the New York production lists the following: Prelude—"Children of the Ghetto"—[William] Furst; Waltz—"Charming Swing"—Louis Maurice; Selection—"Cavaleria Rusticana"—[Pietro] Mascagni; "Dance of the Hours"—[Amilcare] Ponchielli. The London musical program of the play is different: Prelude—"Children of the Ghetto"—[William Furst]; "Grand Fantasia: Songs of Shakespeare's Time" [J. Hamilton Clarke]; Selection: "Lohengrin" [Richard Wagner]; Waltz—"Fidelity" [Andrew J. Levey]; March—"Tommy's Own" [John Crook]; Selection from "Yeoman of the Guard" [Arthur S. Sullivan].

26. Israel Zangwill, "An Open Letter to Mr. Clement Scott," *Jewish Exponent*, October 27, 1899, 8.

27. X. Y., "An Interview with Mr. Zangwill," *Jewish Chronicle*, November 13, 1899, 13.

28. For a detailed discussion of Warfield, see Erdman, *Staging the Jew*, 107.

29. Norris had no experience playing Jewish parts, though he would later star in the dramatic role of the immigrant Jewish clothing merchant Pincus Mayer in *The Business Man* at McVicker's Theatre in Chicago (1903).

30. Tyler to Zangwill, June 24, 1899, file A120/562, Zionist Archives.

31. Edwards and Herne, *James A. Herne*, 138.

32. Ibid., 140.

33. *Washington Post*, June 23, 1901, 27, quoted in Perry, *James A. Herne*, 265.

34. "The Actor in the Street," *Theatre* (February 1909): 49–50.

35. Adler, "Israel Zangwill," 105.

36. "The Latest Dramatic Attractions," *Leslie's Weekly*, August 26, 1899, 171.

37. I assume it was a press release, given the near-absolute resemblance between the text of the *New York Times*, the Philadelphia *Jewish Exponent*, and the *Jewish Chronicle*. "In the Theatrical World, Zangwill Talks on 'The Children of the Ghetto,'" *New York Times*, September 2, 1899, 6–7; "Zangwill's Play," *Jewish Exponent*, September 15, 1899, 11; "Fear of Production," *Jewish Chronicle*, September 15, 1899, 20.

38. Richard Gottheil, "Children of the Ghetto," *Jewish Chronicle*, November 3, 1899, 12.

39. Ibid.

40. Cyrus Adler, "Zangwill's 'Children of the Ghetto,'" *Jewish Chronicle*, October 6, 1899, 15.

41. Anonymous notice, reprinted as "Zangwill's Play a Success," *Jewish Exponent* (Philadelphia), September 22, 1899, 7.

42. Adler, "Zangwill's 'Children of the Ghetto,'" 15.

43. "Children of the Ghetto," *New York Times,* September 18, 1899, clipping, Billy Rose Theatre Collection, New York Public Library.

44. "Children of the Ghetto," *New York World,* September 18, 1899, clipping, Billy Rose Theatre Collection, New York Public Library.

45. "Children of the Ghetto Dramatised," *Jewish World,* September 22, 1899, 404.

46. Bates, "Children of the Ghetto," 2.

47. John Corbin, "The Jew in Drama," *Harper's Weekly,* October 7, 1899, 10.

48. Substantial excerpts from the local newspapers were reprinted in "Philadelphia City News," *Jewish Exponent* (Philadelphia), October 6, 1899, 8.

49. Ibid.

50. Ibid.

51. "Miss Szold on Zangwill," *Jewish Exponent* (Philadelphia), October 20, 1899, 8.

52. Hoffman was a member of the first graduating class at the Jewish Theological Seminary. I wish to thank Harry D. Boonin for the information regarding the identity of Publius.

53. Publius, "About Men and Things," *Jewish Exponent* (Philadelphia), October 6, 1899, 4.

54. Ibid.

55. Other changes occurred in act 3. David's rant against the injustice of Jewish law was trimmed and toned down, and the comic performance of the Irish maid was subdued. See "Local Play-Bills, *Philadelphia Record,* n.d., clipping, Billy Rose Theatre Collection, New York Public Library.

56. Harrison Fiske, "Herald Square—Children of the Ghetto," *New York Dramatic Mirror,* October 21, 1899, 16.

57. Herman Heijermans Jr., *The Ghetto: A Drama in Four Acts, Freely Adapted from the Dutch of Herman Heijermans, Jr. by Chester Bailey Fernald* (London: William Heinemann, 1899).

58. See Seymour L. Flaxman, *Herman Heijermans and His Dramas* (The Hague: Martinus Nijhoff, 1954).

59. Zangwill, "Open Letter to Mr. Clement Scott," 8.

60. "Zangwill's Play of Little Value, *Sun,* n.d., Billy Rose Theatre Collection, New York Public Library.

61. "Mr. Zangwill Loses Suit against the *Sun,*" *New York Times,* February 27, 1900, 7.

62. Tyler to Zangwill, June 24, 1899, file A120/562, Zionist Archives.

63. Quoted in Peter Hay, *Broadway Anecdotes* (New York: Oxford University Press, 1989), 184.

64. Mrs. Clement Scott, *Old Days in Bohemian London* (London: Hutchinson, 1919).

65. The Theatrical Syndicate was formed in 1896. It included Charles Frohman,

Marc Klaw, Abraham Erlanger, Alfred Hayman, Fred Nixon, and Fred Zimmerman. Its monopoly was eventually broken by the Shubert Brothers. The last of the Syndicate agreements ended in 1916. The Shuberts then retained their national monopoly until 1930. For information on the Syndicate, see Norman Hapgood, *The Stage in America* (London: Macmillan, 1901), 29, and John Frick, "The Changing Theatre: New York and Beyond," in *The Cambridge History of American Theatre*, ed. Don B. Wilmeth and Christopher Bigsby, 2 vols. (Cambridge: Cambridge University Press, 1999), 2:213.

66. "Children of the Ghetto in New York," *Jewish Chronicle*, October 23, 1899, 13.

67. Zangwill, "Open Letter to Mr. Clement Scott," 8.

68. Hapgood, *Stage in America*, 334.

69. Tyler to Zangwill, n.d., 1900, file A120/562, Zionist Archives. The production, starring Sarah Cowell LeMoyne, did not do well, mainly due to the weakness of *The Greatest Thing in the World*.

70. Tyler, *Whatever Goes Up*, 162–63.

71. "Children of the Ghetto," *New York Times*, October 17, 1899, 7.

72. Ab[raham] Cahan, "Zangwill's 'Children of the Ghetto' in People's Theatre" [in Yiddish], *Forward*, January 7, 1905, n.p.

73. Ibid.

74. "Zangwill's Play of Little Value," *Sun*, n.d., Billy Rose Theatre Collection, New York Public Library.

75. Nearly five years later Zangwill drew criticism from literary pundits for compromising artistic integrity by adding a happy ending to his dramatization of *Merely Mary Ann* (1903), his most successful stage play.

76. Hapgood, *Stage in America*, 335.

77. Abraham Cahan, "Zangwill's Play, 'The Children of the Ghetto,'" *Forum* 27 (December 1899): 503–12.

78. Ibid., 503.

79. Tyler, *Whatever Goes Up*, 163.

80. Scott's *Herald* review was reprinted in "Children of the Ghetto in New York," *Jewish Chronicle*, October 23, 1899, 13.

81. Clement Scott, "Clement Scott on Zangwill's Play," *Sketch*, December 13, 1899, 292.

82. C. Lewis Hind, "Clement Scott," *More Authors and I* (London, 1922), 257.

83. Ibid., 259.

84. From Scott's review, reprinted in "Children of the Ghetto in New York," *Jewish Chronicle*, October 23, 1899, 13.

85. Scott, "Clement Scott on Zangwill's Play," 292.

86. Ibid.

87. Ibid.

88. Corbin, "Jew in Drama," 10.

89. Edwin S. Bettelheim, "The Zangwill Play," unidentified clipping, Billy Rose Theatre Collection, New York Public Library.

90. Gottheil, "Children of the Ghetto," 12.

91. Ibid.

92. Scott, "Clement Scott on Zangwill's Play," 292.

93. Ibid.

94. Gottheil, "Children of the Ghetto," 12.

95. Scott, "Clement Scott on Zangwill's Play," 292.

96. John Russell Stephens, *The Censorship of English Drama, 1824–1901* (New York: Cambridge University Press, 1980), 114.

97. This incident is discussed in full by Frank Fowell and Frank Palmer in *Censorship in England* (1913; New York: Burt Franklin, 1970), 214–15.

98. Scott, "Clement Scott on Zangwill's Play," 292.

99. Cahan, "Zangwill's Play, 'The Children of the Ghetto,'" 511.

100. According to Hutchins Hapgood, Zangwill received assistance from the rabbi when he was preparing *Children of the Ghetto* for the stage. Zangwill had him photographed in his study, dressed in his rabbinic garments and surrounded by books. See Hapgood, *Spirit of the Ghetto*, 68–69.

101. Cahan, "Zangwill's Play, 'The Children of the Ghetto,'" 511.

102. Zangwill, "Open Letter to Mr. Clement Scott," 8.

103. Ibid.

104. Gottheil, "Children of the Ghetto," 12.

105. David Halberstam, *The Powers That Be* (New York: Knopf, 1979), 208.

106. Editorial, *New York Times*, October 18, 1899, 6.

107. "Mr. Zangwill's Play," *American Hebrew*, September 8, 1899, 528; "Two Jewish Plays," *American Hebrew*, September 22, 1899, 611.

108. Lewis N. Dembitz, "A Divorced Woman to a Private Priest," *American Hebrew*, November 10, 1899, 12–13.

109. Morris Mandel and Dr. Frederick de Sola Mendes, "Communications," *American Hebrew*, November 10, 1899, 13.

110. Ibid.

111. Gotthard Deutsch, "Zangwill and the Rabbinical Law," *American Hebrew*, November 24, 1899, 82–83.

112. Samuel Schulman, "Zangwill's 'Children of the Ghetto'—An Incomplete Picture of Jews and Judaism," *Menorah* (December 1899): 345–56.

113. Mandel and De Sola Mendes, "Communications," 13.

114. "The Zangwill Play," *American Hebrew*, October 27, 1899, 774.

115. Thomas L. James, "A Non Jewish Point of View," *American Hebrew*, October 27, 1899, 774.

116. Ibid.

117. Letter by Jacob H. Hollander, *American Hebrew*, October 27, 1899, 774.

118. Max Ellinger, "Zangwillism and Sunday Lectures," *American Hebrew*, November

24, 1899, 74.

119. Malka Pinchas and Gertrude Veld, "One Point of View," *American Hebrew,* November 10, 1900, 12.

120. Veld, ibid.

121. Hapgood, *Spirit of the Ghetto,* 63.

122. Curiously, the *Times* published a second review of *Children of the Ghetto* right after the first. Both were mixed though sympathetic in tone.

123. X. Y., "Interview with Mr. Zangwill," 13.

124. Tyler, *Whatever Goes Up,* 164.

125. Tyler to Zangwill, November 13, 1899, file A120/562, Zionist Archives.

126. Tyler to Zangwill, November 6, 1899, file A120/562, Zionist Archives.

127. "Adelphi Theatre," *Times* (London), December 12, 1899, 7.

128. Tyler to Zangwill, November 6, 1899, file A120/562, Zionist Archives.

129. Tyler, *Whatever Goes Up,* 164–65.

130. "The Week at the Play 'Children of the Ghetto,'" *Outlook,* December 16, 1899, 648–49.

131. "The Drama," *Queen,* December 16, 1899, 1020.

132. "Drama," *Athenaeum,* December 16, 1899, 844.

133. "The Week at the Play 'Children of the Ghetto,'" *Outlook,* 648.

134. "The Drama," *Athenaeum,* 844.

135. "Children of the Ghetto," *Era,* December 16, 1899, 15.

136. Ibid.

137. "Adelphi Theatre," *Times* (London), 7.

138. J[acob] T[homas] Grein, "Adelphi: "Children of the Ghetto," in *Premières of the Year* (London: John Macqueen, 1900), 119–23.

139. Ibid., 121.

140. J. T. Grein, "Our Drama in 1899," in *Premières of the Year* (London: John Macqueen, 1900), 135.

141. "Children of the Ghetto Dramatised," *Jewish World,* September 22, 1899, 404.

142. "Jews and the Drama," *Jewish Chronicle,* October 13, 1899, 17; "Jewish Actors and Actresses," *Jewish Chronicle,* November 17, 1899, 10; and Isaac Saphir, "Jewish Playwrights," *Jewish Chronicle,* December 22, 1899, 13.

143. "Children of the Ghetto, Mr. Zangwill's Play at the Adelphi," *Jewish World,* December 15, 1899, 184–85.

144. Grein, "Adelphi," 119.

145. "Children of the Ghetto, Mr. Zangwill's Play at the Adelphi," 184–85.

146. I[srael] A[brahams] "'Children of the Ghetto' at the Adelphi," *Jewish Chronicle,* December 15, 1899, 13.

147. Landa, *Jew in Drama,* 222–23.

148. I. Abrahams, "Children of the Ghetto," 13.

149. Ibid.

150. Tyler to Zangwill, telegram, December 31, 1899, file A120/562, Zionist Archives.

151. Tyler, *Whatever Goes Up,* 167.

152. Cahan, "Zangwill's 'Children of the Ghetto,'" [in Yiddish], *Forward,* n.p.

153. For information on the representation of Jews in silent films, see Lester D. Friedman, "Celluloid Assimilation, Jews in American Silent Movies," *Journal of Popular Film and Television* 15, no. 3 (1987): 129–36.

154. "Children of the Ghetto," *Variety,* February 12, 1915, n.p.

155. Umberto Fortis, *Il ghetto in scena: Teatro giudeo-italiano del Novecento Storia e testi* (Rome: Carucci, 1989), 64.

156. X. Y., "Interview with Mr. Zangwill," 13.

157. Ben Hecht, *A Flag Is Born* (New York: American League for a Free Palestine, 1946), 21.

The Melting Pot: **Introductory Essay**

1. Ben Wattenberg, "The New American," *New York Post,* March 16, 2001, 27.

2. Nancy L. Green, "*Le Melting-Pot:* Made in America, Produced in France," *Journal of American History* 86, no. 3 (1999): 1188–1208.

3. For a discussion of melting pot symbolism, see Philip Gleason's "The Melting Pot: Symbol of Fusion or Confusion," *American Quarterly* 17 (Spring 1964): 20–46. Gleason lists alternative metaphors, which he subdivides into five categories: culinary (pressure-cooker, stew, soup, salad or salad bowl, and mixing bowl); color (flower garden, mosaic, kaleidoscope, and rainbow); musical (orchestra and choir); mechanical (weaving machine and pipeline); and derogatory (dumping ground, village hound, catch basin, and cul-de-sac) (32–34).

4. John Francis Hope, "Drama," *New Age,* February 12, 1914, 473.

5. Ibid.

6. Zangwill, *Dreamers of the Ghetto,* vi.

7. See herein, "Afterword" to *The Melting Pot,* p. 379.

8. Israel Zangwill, *Watchman, What of the Night?* (New York: American Jewish Congress, 1923), 42.

9. The reference to this title appears in a letter from Zangwill to George Tyler dated May 23, 1908, as well as in the cover letter dated June 2, 1908, that accompanied the contract sent from Liebler's New York office. File A120/486, Zionist Archives.

10. Zangwill to Tyler, May 23, 1908, file A120/486, Zionist Archives.

11. Zangwill to Theodore Roosevelt, August 25, 1908, file A120/486, Zionist Archives.

12. Zangwill to Tyler, July 21, 1908, file A120/486, Zionist Archives.

13. Ibid.

14. Ibid.

15. *The Melting Pot,* The British Library, Lord Chamberlain's Plays, MS no. 480 (hereafter LC no. 480).

16. Gleason, "Melting Pot," 22.

17. Ibid., 24.

18. J. Hector St. John de Crèvecoeur, *Letters from an American Farmer* (New York: E. P. Dutton, 1957,) 39, quoted in Richard Conant Harper, *The Course of the Melting Pot Idea to 1910* (New York: Arno, 1980), 101.

19. Edward Waldo Emerson and Waldo Emerson Forbes, eds., *Journals of Ralph Waldo Emerson* (Boston: Houghton Mifflin, 1913), 7:115–16.

20. Rev. Dr. S. Schulman, "Judaism and Intermarriage with Christians," *American Hebrew,* November 20, 1908, 60.

21. Philip Gleason, "Confusion Compounded: The Melting Pot in the 1960s and 1970s," *Ethnicity* 6, nos. 10–20 (1979): 11.

22. Ford Madox Hueffner [Ford], *The Spirit of the People: An Analysis of the English Mind* (London: Alston Rivers, 1907). Later known as Ford Madox Ford (1873–1939), he went on to be founder and editor of the prestigious *English Review* and author of the modernist novel *The Good Soldier* (1915).

23. Hueffner [Ford], *Spirit of the People,* 83.

24. Ibid., 84.

25. Paul Peppis, "Thinking Race in *Avant Guerre:* Typological Negotiations in Ford and Stein," *Yale Journal of Criticism* 10, no. 2 (1997): 376.

26. See herein, "Afterword" to *The Melting Pot,* p. 385.

27. Edward Price Bell, *Is the Ku Klux Klan Constructive or Destructive?: A Debate between Imperial Wizard Evans, Israel Zangwill, and Others, Reported by Edward Price Bell, Staff Writer, The Chicago Daily News* (Girard, KS: Haldeman-Julius, 1924), 28.

28. Hueffner [Ford], *Spirit of the People,* 84.

29. Two years later, Zangwill did publish a piece in the *English Review,* and soon after the outbreak of World War I both he and Ford were among twenty-five leading British authors invited to Wellington House by the War Propaganda Bureau to discuss how to promote British interests and shape public opinion. Other invitees included Arnold Bennett, Arthur Conan Doyle, John Masefield, William Archer, G. K. Chesterton, Sir Henry Newbolt, John Galsworthy, Thomas Hardy, Rudyard Kipling, Gilbert Parker, G. M. Trevelyan, and H. G. Wells.

30. Israel Zangwill, *The Principle of Nationalities* (London: Watts, 1917).

31. Zangwill, "Jewish Race," 93.

32. Ibid.

33. David Biale, "The Melting Pot and Beyond: Jews and the Politics of American Identity," in *Insider/Outsider: American Jews and Multiculturalism,* ed. David Biale, Michael Galchinsky, and Susan Heschel (Berkeley: University of

California Press, 1998), 17–33.

34. Fein, "Israel Zangwill and American Jewry," 23.

35. Bell, *Ku Klux Klan,* 34.

36. "How a Washington Editor Views Zangwill's Play," *American Hebrew,* October 9, 1908, 558. Also quoted in London's *Jewish World,* October 23, 1908, 16.

37. Zangwill, "Jewish Race," 93.

38. Ibid., 95.

39. Reported in "The Melting Pot," *Jewish World,* June 17, 1914, 29.

40. Bell, *Ku Klux Klan,* 27.

41. Biale, "Melting Pot and Beyond," 24.

42. Leftwich, *Israel Zangwill,* 88.

43. *Times* (London), November 27, 1903, 9.

44. Edith Zangwill to Annie Russell, n.d. [1905?], Annie Russell papers, Humanities Manuscripts, New York Public Library.

45. Fein, "Israel Zangwill and American Jewry," 19.

46. "About the World: Israel Zangwill," *Jewish World,* August 5, 1926, 2–3.

47. Leftwich, *Israel Zangwill,* 88; Udelson, *Dreamer of the Ghetto,* 151.

48. Leftwich, *Israel Zangwill,* 88.

49. Ibid.

50. See herein, *The Melting Pot,* act 3, p. 347.

51. LC no. 480, act 1, 10.

52. Leftwich, *Israel Zangwill,* 102.

53. Edith Zangwill to Annie Russell, January 21, 1909, and undated, Annie Russell papers, Humanities Manuscripts, New York Public Library.

54. Brainin, "Israel Zangwill—Twelve Years Later," 11.

55. Zangwill, *Watchman,* 19.

56. Leftwich, *Israel Zangwill,* 103.

57. Amos Elon, *Herzl* (New York: Holt, Rinehart and Winston, 1975), 255.

58. M. W. Weisgal, *The Letters and Papers of Chaim Weizmann* (London: Oxford University Press, 1972), cited in Udelson, *Dreamer of the Ghetto,* 152.

59. Herman Bernstein, "A Week-End with Zangwill," *Jewish Tribune,* n.d. 1926, 22.

60. Israel Zangwill, "My Religion," file A120/486, Zionist Archives. A carefully edited version of the piece appeared in London's *Daily Express* and was later incorporated into the book *My Religion, by Arnold Bennett, Hugh Walpole, Rebecca West, Sir Arthur Conan Doyle, E. Phillips Oppenheim, Compton Mackenzie, J. D. Beresford, Israel Zangwill, H. de Vere Stacpoole, Henry Arthur Jones, and "the unknown man," together with replies from many eminent divines and others* (London: Hutchinson, 1925).

61. Israel Zangwill, "Singer vs. Schechter," *Jewish Chronicle,* October 26, 1900, 7.

62. Floyd S. Fierman, "Israel Zangwill's Family," *Jewish Spectator,* September 1965, 24.

63. Leftwich, *Israel Zangwill*, 98.

64. Biographical note, file A120/486, Zionist Archives.

65. Louis Golding, "Israel Zangwill," *Menorah Journal* 12, no. 6 (1926): 567.

66. LC no. 480, n.p.

67. Jay Bergman, *Vera Zasulich: A Biography* (Stanford, CA: Stanford University Press, 1983), 188.

68. "Judaism in Music" (1850) (pp. 79–100) and "Appendix to 'Judaism in Music'" (1869) (pp. 101–12), in Richard Wagner, *Judaism in Music and Other Essays*, trans. William Ashton Ellis (Lincoln: University of Nebraska Press, 1995).

69. Carl Sandburg, *Chicago Poems* (New York: Henry Holt, 1916), n.p.

70. Walker Whiteside, "The History of a Zangwill Drama," unidentified clipping, stamped (possibly by Tyler's office) January 16, 1910, Billy Rose Theatre Collection, New York Public Library.

71. Zangwill to Tyler, August 26, 1908, file A120/486, Zionist Archives. Whiteside read the speech for the first time at the copyright presentation of the play, a legal procedure required to ensure authorial rights. The other performers included Zangwill reading the roles of Mendel Quixano and the baron; his wife, Edith, as Kathleen; Hertha Ayrton reading Frau Quixano; Louis Zangwill as Pappelmeister; Mrs. Whiteside reading Vera; and Arthur Ponsynby as Quincy Davenport. An audience of two paid a shilling each in order to make the copyright legal.

72. LC no. 840, act 3, 91–92.

73. Ibid., 94.

74. Ibid., 96.

75. Ibid., act 2, 51.

76. Ibid., 52.

77. Ibid., act 4, 110.

78. Ibid., 107.

79. Israel Zangwill, "The Goyim," in Zangwill, ed., *Voice of Jerusalem*, 311–13.

80. Zangwill to Tyler, July 2, 1908, p. 2, file A120/560, Zionist Archives.

81. Jewish Territorial Organization, *Report on the work of the commission sent out by the Jewish Territorial Organization under the auspices of the Governor-General of Tripoli to examine the territory proposed for the purpose of a Jewish settlement in Cyrenaica* (London: ITO Offices, London, January 1909).

82. S. J. F., "Interview with Mr. Zangwill," by Lucien Wolf, *Jewish World*, September 18, 1908, 9.

83. Editorial, *American Hebrew*, October 16, 1908, n.p.

84. Jesse Conway, "Capitol Comment," *Times-Star*, October 13, 1908, n.p.

85. "Itoland and Other Places: Special Interview with Israel Zangwill," *American Hebrew*, October 2, 1908, n.p.

86. Israel Zangwill, "Zion, Whence Cometh My Help," in Simon, ed., *Speeches, Articles, and Letters*, 81.

87. Zangwill to Tyler, July 23, 1909, file A120/560, Zionist Archives.

88. Dr. J. L. Magnes, "The Melting Pot" *American Hebrew,* October 22, 1909, 620.

89. "Zangwill's New Play," *Jewish Comment,* October 2, 1908, 381.

90. "How a Washington Editor Views Zangwill's Play," 558. Also quoted in London's *Jewish World,* October 23, 1908, 16.

91. Between 1913 and 1921 Ford directed thirty-one films. His first was *The Prisoner of Zenda.* In 1916 he wrote the screenplay for *The Moment Before,* based on Zangwill's short play. Directed by Robert G. Vignola, it was produced by the Famous Film Company and distributed by Paramount Pictures.

92. Zangwill to Tyler, May 9, 1908, file A120/560, Zionist Archives.

93. Zangwill to Tyler, November 6, 1908, file A120/560, Zionist Archives.

94. Israel Zangwill, "Mr. Zangwill Explains Some Points," *Jewish Chronicle,* March 6, 1914, 30.

95. Ibid.

96. Israel Zangwill, "The Hebrew's Friday Night," in *Blind Children* (New York: Funk & Wagnalls, 1903), 118.

97. Israel Zangwill, *The Forcing House* (London: Globe, 1925), 29–30.

98. Zangwill to Theodore Roosevelt, August 25, 1908, file A120/559, Zionist Archives.

99. Letter on White House stationery to Zangwill, signed by the secretary to the president, September 7, 1908, file A120/559, Zionist Archives.

100. "Zangwill Play Produced," *Jewish Exponent,* October 9, 1908, 2.

101. Conway, "Capitol Comment," n.p.

102. Prompt-book for the "The Melting Pot" (1909?), Billy Rose Theatre Collection, New York Public Library. This line, minus the reference to "the 400," made it into the published text of the play.

103. "Divorce in America," *Times* (London), October 12, 1908, 6.

104. Roosevelt to Zangwill, n.d. 1911, file A120/559, Zionist Archives.

105. Cited in *Language Loyalties,* ed. James Crawford (Chicago: University of Chicago Press, 1992), 84. The complete version appears in *Annals of America,* vol. 114, 1916–1928 (Chicago: Encyclopedia Britannica, 1968), 129–31.

106. Theodore Roosevelt, *Letters,* sel. and ed. Elting E. Morison (Cambridge: Harvard University Press, 1951–1954), vol. 3, letter #2044, p. 78.

107. "Roosevelt Friend of the Jews," *New York Times,* April 15, 1905, 2.

108. Zangwill, *Watchman,* 21.

109. Guy Szuberla, "Zangwill's *The Melting Pot* Plays Chicago," *Melus* 20, no. 3 (1995): 5.

110. Tyler to Jacob Schiff, October 27, 1908, p. 1, file A120/560, Zionist Archives.

111. Tyler to Zangwill, November 27, 1908, file A120/560, Zionist Archives.

112. Tyler to Zangwill, September 2, 1909, file A120/560 Zionist Archives.

113. Burns Mantle, "The Melting Pot," *Chicago Daily Tribune,* October 20, 1908, n.p.

114. *Unity,* October 29, 1908, 133; Constance Skinner, "'Melting Pot,' at Grand, Play to Remember," *Chicago Evening American,* October 21, 1908, n.p.

115. Skinner, "'Melting Pot,' at Grand," n.p.

116. Percy Hammond, "The Melting Pot," *Chicago Evening Post,* October 20, 1908, n.p.

117. Unidentified clipping, n.d., file A120/165, 45/3 Zionist Archives.

118. "America," lyric sheet, file A120/165, 45/3 Zionist Archives.

119. Amy Leslie, "Grave Play at Grand," *Daily News,* October 21, 1908, n.p.

120. Charles W. Collins, "The Melting Pot," *Inter Ocean,* October 21, 1908, n.p.

121. The special matinee occurred in mid-December 1908. The undated list of invitees who confirmed their attendance is located in file A120/165, 45/3, Zionist Archives.

122. Tyler to Zangwill, November 21, 1908, file A120/560, Zionist Archives.

123. Emil G. Hirsch to *Reform Advocate* (1904), quoted in "Shall the Jew Intermarry?" *Jewish Tribune,* November 20, 1908, n.p.

124. "Intermarriage: Summary of a Discourse Preached by Emil G. Hirsch," *Jewish Exponent,* November 27, 1908, 1.

125. Leon Zolotkoff, "Zangwill's groyser erfolg," *Der Idisher Kuryer* [Daily Jewish Courier], November 13, 1908, n.p.

126. For Fyne, see "At the Montefiore Synagogue," *Jewish Exponent,* November 27, 1908, n.p.; for Rubenstein, see "Dr. Rubenstein Criticises Zangwill and E. G. Hirsch," *Jewish Exponent,* November 27, 1908, n.p.; "Shall the Jew Intermarry?" n.p.

127. "The Melting Pot," *Jewish Exponent,* October 23, 1908, n.p.

128. "Should Jews Marry Christians?" *New York Herald,* November 8, 1908, magazine, 1–2.

129. George Washington, "Letter to the Newport Congregation," *Pennsylvania Packet and Daily Advertiser,* September 16, 1790 [Philadelphia], 4 pp. Correspondence between Moses Seixas and George Washington appears in column 4 of page 2 and column 1 of page 3. Washington's letter reads: "All possess alike liberty of conscience and immunities of citizenship. It is now no more that toleration is spoken of, as if it was by the indulgence of one class of people, that another enjoyed the exercise of their inherent natural rights. For, happily, the government of the United States which gives to bigotry no sanction, to persecution no assistance, requires only that they who live under its protection, should demean themselves as good citizens."

130. "Shall the Jew Intermarry?" *Jewish Tribune,* December 4, 1908, n.p.

131. Intermarriage began to raise concern in Europe, especially in Germany, where the *Frankfurter Zeitung* reported in 1908 that nearly 20 percent of Jews were marrying out of the faith. Cited by Veritas, "Mixed Marriages," *Jewish Chronicle,* May 8, 1908, 27.

132. "The Comedy Theatre," *Morning Sun,* September 7, 1909, n.p.

133. "Out of the Melting Pot Comes Lecture on Zionism," *New York Press,* September

7, 1909, n.p.

134. Tyler to Zangwill, telegram, September 7, 1909, file A120/560, Zionist Archives.

135. "Zangwill Play Opens New Comedy Theatre," *New York Herald,* September 7, 1909, n.p; Charles Darnton, "The New Play," *Evening World,* September 10, 1909, n.p.

136. "New Zangwill Play Cheap and Tawdry," *New York Times,* September 7, 1909, n.p.

137. Alan Dale, "'The Melting Pot' Is Serious, Says Dale," *New York American,* September 7, 1909, n.p.

138. Adolph Klauber, "A Spread-Eagle Play by Israel Zangwill," *New York Times,* September 12, 1909, section 6, p. 10.

139. Louis V. De Foe, "Purpose and Power in 'The Melting Pot,' Yet Its Faults Are Many," *New York World,* September 12, 1909, n.p.

140. Darnton, "New Play," n.p.

141. Acton Davies, "'The Melting Pot' Contains an Awful Zangwill Stew," *Evening Sun,* September 10, 1909, n.p.

142. A. B. Walkley, "The Melting Pot," clipping, *Times* (London), November 10, 1909, file A120/165, 45/3, Zionist Archives.

143. Ibid.

144. Amy Leslie, "He Accounts for 'Purim,'" *Chicago Daily News,* October 31, 1908, n.p.

145. Ibid.

146. Zangwill to Tyler, September 21, 1909, file A120/560, Zionist Archives.

147. Tyler to Zangwill, October 4, 1909, file A120/560, Zionist Archives.

148. Tyler to Zangwill, November 3, 1909, file A120/560, Zionist Archives.

149. Tyler to Zangwill, November 26, 1909, file A120/560, Zionist Archives.

150. Charlotte Canning, "'The Most American Thing in America': Producing National Identities in Chautauqua, 1904–1932," in *Performing America: Cultural Nationalism in American Theater,* ed. Jeffrey D. Mason and J. Ellen Gainor (Ann Arbor: University of Michigan Press, 1999), 101.

151. "Mr. Zangwill's 'Melting Pot,'" *Jewish Chronicle,* June 14, 1912, 36.

152. "Der Shmelts Top," *Haynt,* November 10, 1915, 2.

153. "Fred," "The Melting Pot," *Variety,* June 4, 1915, n.p.

154. Ibid.

155. "The Melting Pot," *Bioscope,* April 10, 1919, 69–70.

156. Letters between Zangwill and Lawrence A. Steinhardt, n.d., file A120/499, Zionist Archives.

157. Zangwill's correspondence with Tyler suggests that some initial thought was given to a parallel London production. In a July 1908 letter to Tyler, Zangwill briefly mentions the prominent English actors John Martin-Harvey (1863–1944), Henry H. Ainley (1879–1945), and Johnston Forbes-Robertson (1853–

1937) as possible candidates for the lead. Zangwill to Tyler, July 17, 1908, file A120/560, Zionist Archives. However, these plans never went further.

158. "Play Actors' Production," *Era,* January 28, 1914, 13; "The Play Actors," *Stage,* January 29, 1914, 25; "The Melting Pot," *Times* (London), January 27, 1914, 9.

159. "Drama," *Athanaeum,* January 31, 1914, 171.

160. Frank Desprez, "Mr. Zangwill and the Masses," *Era,* February 18, 1914, 17.

161. GYP, "Communal Silhouettes, No. XLI—The Child of the Ghetto," *Jewish World,* February 18, 1914, 11.

162. Ibid.

163. Mentor [Greenberg's pen name], "The 'Melting Pot' and the Jew: Some Stray Thoughts," *Jewish Chronicle,* January 30, 1914, 9.

164. Isidore Harris, "Palestine and 'The Melting Pot,'" *Jewish Chronicle,* February 20, 1914, 34.

165. Morris Joseph, "Looking Back," *Jewish Chronicle,* April 17, 1914, 19.

166. Ibid.

167. Lily H. Montagu, address given at the West Central Jewish Working Girls' Club, February 28, 1914, file A120/165, Zionist Archives.

168. Ibid., 12.

169. Herbert Burrows, "The Melting Pot," *Jewish World,* June 10, 1914, 29.

170. Ibid., 30.

171. S. O., "The Melting Pot," *English Review,* April 1914, 130.

172. Wilfred Whitte, "The Melting Pot," *Bookman* (March 1914): 315.

173. F. H. O'Donnell, "A Reply to Mr. Zangwill," *New Witness,* April 9, 1914, 721; F. H. O'Donnell, "The Need For Clean Government," *New Witness,* October 9, 1913, 717, cited in Tom Villis, "Early Modernism and Exclusion: The Cultural Politics of Two Edwardian Periodicals, *The New Age* and *The New Witness,*" *University of Sussex Journal of Contemporary History* 5 (December 2002): 17. The *New Witness* had previously been called *The Eye-Witness* and was edited by Hilaire Belloc in 1911–1912.

174. John Francis Hope, "Drama," *New Age,* February 12, 1914, 474.

175. Ibid., 473.

176. G. K. Chesterton, "Our Note Book," *Illustrated London News,* February 28, 1914, 312.

177. J. E. Harold Terry, "The Melting Pot," *British Review* 6, no. 2 (1914): 306–11.

178. Ibid., 307.

179. Ibid., 307–8.

180. "Mr. Israel Zangwill and Mr. C. Chesterton," *Jewish Chronicle,* March 20, 1914, 27.

181. Ibid.

182. Ibid.

183. "Parliament," *Times* (London), June 17, 1915, 10.

184. Zangwill, "Introductory," *Watchman,* 1.

185. Ibid., 43.

186. Samuel Schulman, *Israel Zangwill's Message and American Judaism* (New York: Temple Beth-El, 1923), 4.

187. "Zangwill, Mirror of the Jewish Soul," *American Hebrew,* August 6, 1926, 356.

The King of Schnorrers: Introductory Essay

1. "Schnorrer" in "Glossary of Jewish Terms," *The Jewish Year Book,* ed. Joseph Jacobs (London, 1899), 316.

2. "Schnorrer," *The Jewish Encyclopedia* (New York: Funk and Wagnalls, 1909–1912), 11:106. The entry was written by Joseph Jacobs and Judah David Eisenstein.

3. Zangwill, "Language and Jewish Life," 249.

4. Israel Zangwill, "Morour and Chorouseth," *Hebrew Standard,* July 13, 1888, 10.

5. Israel Zangwill, "In Defence of Gambling," in *Without Prejudice,* 88.

6. Golding, "Israel Zangwill," 566.

7. Mentor [Greenberg's pen name], "Some Current Topics," *Jewish Chronicle,* January 25, 1924, n.p.

8. Ibid.

9. Ahron Bornstein, *Ha'kabtsanim, perek be'toldot yehudey germanya* [The Beggars: A Chapter in the History of German Jewry] (Jerusalem: Reuven Mass, 1992), 17.

10. Quoted in ibid., 18.

11. Sigmund Freud, *Jokes and Their Relation to the Unconscious* (New York: Norton, 1960).

12. Cited in Sander L. Gilman, *Jewish Self-Hatred: Anti-Semitism and the Hidden Language of the Jews* (Baltimore: Johns Hopkins University Press, 1986), 252.

13. "Zangwill's *King of Schnorrers,*" *American Hebrew,* February 23, 1894, 492.

14. Albert Hyamson, *The Sephardim of England: A History of the Spanish and Portuguese Jewish Community, 1492–1951* (London: Methuen, 1951), 170.

15. Quoted in Holbrook Jackson, "Israel Zangwill," *Bookman* (May 1914): 71–72.

16. L[ouis] L[ipsky], "The Yiddish Theatre," *American Hebrew,* August 7, 1908, 500.

17. Quoted in Leftwich, *Israel Zangwill,* 246.

18. "Chronicle and Comment," *Bookman* 9 (April 1899): 101.

19. Zangwill to Tyler, August 21, 1918, file A120/564, Zionist Archives.

20. "Music and Drama," *Jewish Chronicle,* October 23, 1925, 35.

21. Jewish Drama League, "The King of Schnorrers," *Times* (London), November 3, 1925, 3.

22. "Jewish Drama League," *Stage*, November 5, 1925, 15.

23. "The King of Schnorrers," *Observer*, November 8, 1925, 11.

24. Jackson, "Israel Zangwill," 67.

25. W. A. D., "Dramatising a Novel," unidentified clipping, n.d., n.p.

26. H. M. W., "King of Schnorrers," *Telegraph*, November 2, 1931, n.p.

27. "The King of Schnorrers," *Jewish Chronicle*, November 6, 1925, 35.

28. Leftwich, *Israel Zangwill*, 250–51.

29. "The Saville, 'The King of Schnorrers,'" *Stage*, October 5, 1950, 9.

30. Ibid., 10.

31. Montagu Slater, "The Arts and Entertainment," *New Statesman and Nation*, October 7, 1950, 363.

Epilogue

1. The play opened at the Ambassadors Theatre on April 9, 1918, and closed on May 25. In December 1926 an American film based on the play was released by First National Pictures.

2. Israel Zangwill, "Author-Manager!" file A120/177, Zionist Archives.

3. Fortune Theatre program, n.d. 1925, British Library, item 11795 C70, n.p.

4. H[arold] H[obson], "The Forcing House," *Observer*, February 14, 1926, 11.

5. "The Ascerbities of Israel Zangwill," in George Sylvester Viereck, *Glimpses of the Great* (London: Duckworth, 1930), 280.

6. Golding, "Israel Zangwill," n.p.

7. Leftwich, *Israel Zangwill*, 95.

8. "Israel Zangwill, Address Delivered by Rabbi Dr. Stephen S. Wise," *Jewish Graphic*, August 13, 1916, 3.

9. Alexander Baron, "The Case of Israel Zangwill," in *Caravan: A Jewish Quarterly Omnibus* (New York, 1962), 90.

10. "Tailors' Union and Russia," *Times* (London), August 5, 1926, 6.

11. Cited in *Jewish World*, August 19, 1926, 7.

12. "Israel Zangwill," *Ha'aretz*, August 2, 1926, 1.

13. A[lter] A[belson], "Zangwill an Eternal Dreamer," *Jewish Forum* 9, no. 6 (1926): 342.

14. Louis Marshall, eulogy, in *In Memory of Israel Zangwill* (New York: Zangwill Memorial Committee, 1926), 14.

15. Edith Zangwill to Stephen Wise, August 6, 1926, file A120 243/91, Zionist Archives.

16. "Zangwill's Funeral," *Jewish World*, August 12, 1916, 2.

17. "Wills and Bequests," *Times* (London), December 20, 1926, 18.

18. "Wills and Bequests," *Jewish World*, December 23, 1926, 16.

19. Edith Zangwill to Stephen Wise, August 25, 1926, file A120 243/91, Zionist Archives.

20. Ibid.

21. Charles Solomon, "The Jew and the Drama," in *The Real Jew, Some Aspects of the Jewish Contribution to Civilization*, ed. H. Newman (London: A. & C. Black, 1925), 235.

Index

Abrahams, Israel, 15, 16, 104, 106
Abrahams, Louis, 9
Abrahams, Morris, 27
Acosta, Uriel, 17
Actresses Suffrage League, 255
Addams, Jane, 246, 247
Addison, Thomas, 249
Adler, Cyrus, 11, 23–24, 36, 76, 77–78
Adler, Hermann, 89
Adler, Jacob P., 27, 47, 252, 394
After Dark (Boucicault), 52
Aiton, George Briggs, 242
Al Raschid, Haroun, 26
Alward, Rector, 243
America: Christian interest in the ghetto,
    44–49; as cultural market, 37;
    Jewish immigration to, 34–36; and
    melting pot concept, 219; merging
    with Judaism, 220–21; social anti-
    Semitism, 43
The American Farmer (Crèvecoeur), 215
American Jewish Congress, 243, 263
American Jews, 42; antagonism toward
    ghetto literature, 47–49; clash over
    representation, 47–48
Angel, Moses, 9
Anglicization of Jews, 9
Anglo-Jewish Historical Exhibition, 22
Anti-Semitism, 9, 32, 51, 87, 227,
    259–61; in music, 228–30
Archer, William, 19, 21
"Art for Truth's Sake in the Drama"
    (Herne), 68

Ashkenazim, 392, 396
As You Like It (Shakespeare), 42
Auld Licht Idylls (Barrie), 11
"Author-Manager!" (Zangwill), 513
The Autocrat of the Breakfast Table
    (Holmes), 25
Aveling, Edward, 18, 227
Aveling, Eleanor Marx. *See* Marx [Aveling],
    Eleanor
Avineri, Shlomo, 30
Axelrod, Pavel, 227
Ayrton, Edith. *See* Zangwill [Ayrton],
    Edith (wife)
Ayrton, William E., 221

The Bachelors' Club (Zangwill), 16, 24
Bailey, Oliver D., 254
Balfour, J., 26
Balfour Declaration, 34
Barlow, Jane, 11
Baron, Alexander, 515
The Baron of Offenbach (Zangwill), 24
Barrie, James M., 11, 16, 101
Bates, Blanche, as Hannah Jacobs in
    Children of the Ghetto, 72, 73, 83, 101
"Bath" (Sandburg), 230
Baynton, Henry, 262
Beecher, Henry Ward, 37, 63
Beerbohm, Max, 1
Beilis, Mendel, blood libel trial, 260–61
Belasco, David, 68, 211
belle Juive, 54
The Bells (Lewis), 55

Ben-Hur (Young, based on Wallace), 62
Bensusan, Inez, as Frau Quixano in *The Melting Pot*, 255
Bentwich, Herbert, 15
Berkley Street Synagogue, 257
Bernal, Jacob Israel, 392
Bernhardt, Sarah, 54
Bernstein, Herman, 224
Bettelheim, Edwin S., 88
Bevis Marks Synagogue, 392–93
Biale, David, 218
The Big Bow Mystery (Zangwill), 16
Birchenough, M. C., 23
Blaustein, David, 38
Boer War, 101; Black Week, 105
Bog-land Studies (Barlow), 11
Booth, Charles, 17
Booth, Edwin, 56, 240
Booth, Michael, 27
Bornstein, Ahron, 391
Boston intellectual elite, 68
Boucicault, Dion, 51–52
Bow Bells, 5, 513
Brainin, Reuben, 31
Breslar, Meyer, 10
Bribery in theater, 82
British Museum, 17, 227, 517
Brudno, Ezra S., 228
Bryan, William Jennings, 68
Burrows, Herbert, 258
Bush, Frank, 49–50

Cahan, Abraham, 21, 41, 42, 46, 48, 84–85, 90, 107, 396
Caine, Hall, 16, 41, 44, 50, 62, 221
Calvert, Louis, 394
Cambridge University, 15, 224
Capeman (Simon), 110
Carr, Catherine, 254
Cather, Willa, 36, 40
The Celibates' Club (Zangwill), 16
Censorship, 11, 63, 89
Central Zionist Archives, 225, 516
Chamberlain, Houston Stewart, 229
Chapin, Harold, as David Quixano in *The Melting Pot*, 255

Chaplin, Matilda, 221
Charlie's Aunt (Thomas), 1, 28
Chatrian, Pierre Alexandre, 55
Chautauqua circuit, 252–53
Chesterton, Cecil, 260–61
Chesterton, G. K., 259–60
Chicago Hebrew Institute's Young Players Club, 252
"The Children of the Crucible" (Roosevelt), 242
Children of the Ghetto (film) (Zangwill), 107, 109
Children of the Ghetto (novel) (Zangwill), 5, 7, 11, 14, 15, 17–18, 21–22, 23, 24, 27, 36, 389–90, 392, 393, 515; father-daughter relationship, 63–64; as Jewish drama, 56–57; Yiddish translation, 13
Children of the Ghetto (stage play) (Zangwill), 25, 43, 47, 49, 54, 395, 398; Chicago opening, 106; dramatization of, 44; as ethnic Jewish drama, 56–57; legal validity of marriage in, 93–94; London production, 100–106; music in, 70, 90; New York premiere, 83; New York reception, 83–100; Philadelphia production, 79; Philadelphia reception, 79–80; possible sacrilege in, 89–91; producing and casting, 68–72; reaction, by American Jews, 91–93, 95–96; by English Jews, 104; by Jewish community, 22–23; recasting of the story, 61–63; religious topics in, 62–63; return to Jewish ghetto theme, 65–67; title change, 80–81; Washington premiere, 77; Washington reception, 77–79; Yiddish production of, 107, 108
Chmielnicki massacres, 391
Chovevei Zion Association, 30
The Christian (Caine), 44, 62, 78, 91, 96
Cividalli, Jolanda, 109
Clinton, De Witt, 215
Clover, Lyman B., 106
Cockney, 5, 12
The Cockpit (Zangwill), 514

Cohan, George M., 245
Cohen, Alfred J. *See* Dale, Alan [Alfred J. Cohen]
Cohen, Dayan Susman, 6
Cohen, Isaac, 27
Cohen, Naomi, 35
Cohen, Stuart A., 32–33
Collins, Charles W., 245–46
Continental realism, 103
Cooper, Leo, 252
Copyright(s), 28, 61
Corbin, John, 78–79, 88
Cort, William, 254
Cowen, Eleanor, 7
Cowen, Frederic Hyman, 70
Cowen, Laurence, 513, 514
Cowen, Louis, 13, 24, 513
Cowen, Philip, 38
Crèvecoeur, J. Hector St. John de, 215
The Crucible (Luther), 214
Cumberland, Richard, 54
Curtis, M. B., 51
Cyrano de Bergerac (Rostand), 36, 79
Cyrenaica, 236
Czernowitch Conference, 228

Dale, Alan [Alfred J. Cohen], 250, 251
Daniel Deronda (Eliot), 22, 222
Darrow, Clarence, 246
Darwin, Charles, 68
Davis, Arthur, 15
Deborah (von Mosenthal), 54
DeFoe, Louis V., 250
Degeneration (Nordau), 29
Dembitz, Lewis N., 93
de Mille, Beatrice, 83
d'Ennery, Adolph, 52–53
De Sola Mendes, Frederick, 94
Deutsch, Gotthard, 94
The Devil's Disciple (Shaw), 104
Dialect in literature, 11–13
"Diary of a Meshumad" (Zangwill), 15, 24
Dickens, Charles, 21, 38, 53, 394
Di East-Side Ghetto (Kobrin), 107
d'Indy, Vincent, 229–30
Disraeli, Benjamin, 15, 40, 218

A Doll's House (Ibsen), 18, 19, 84, 252
A Doll's House Repaired (Zangwill and Aveling), 18, 19
Doyle, Arthur Conan, 16
"The Drama as a Fine Art" (Zangwill), 38, 39, 43
Drama, in the 1890s, 28
"Dreamers in Congress" (Zangwill), 31
Dreamers of the Ghetto (Zangwill), 17, 24, 31, 81, 213
Dreyfus, Abraham, 52
Dreyfus Affair, 41, 44–45, 79
Du Maurier, George, 39, 53, 230
Dwyer, Ada, as Malka in *Children of the Ghetto*, 84

East Africa, colonization plan, 32–33
East End, London. *See* London, East End
East Side, New York City. *See* New York City, Lower East Side
Eccentricities of Genius (Pond), 37
Edeson, Robert, as David Brandon in *Children of the Ghetto*, 101
Edinburgh Festival, 398
The Eighteen Nineties (Jackson), 11
Eiseman, Aaron, 249
Eliot, George, 22, 49
Elizabethan Stage Society, 1
Ellinger, Max, 95
Ellis, Havelock, 18
Ellis, Martin B., 48
Elman, Mischa, 230
Emerson, Ralph Waldo, 37, 215
Endelman, Todd M., 30
An Enemy of Society (Ibsen), 18
English Jews: attitude toward East European immigrants, 8–9; concern over image, 22; fear of anti-Semitism, 9; reaction to *Children of the Ghetto* (stage play), 104; reaction to *The Melting Pot* (stage play), 256–58; and Zionism, 29
"English Judaism; a Criticism and Classification" (Zangwill), 16
English Zionist Federation, 15
Epstein, Jacob, 47

Erckman, Emile, 55
Erdman, Harley, 51

Fagin, 17, 53
Falstaff, Sir John, 394
Father-daughter relationship in Victorian
    drama, 63–64
Faust (Gounod), 235
Feinman, Sigmund, as Reb Samuel in
    Children of the Ghetto (Yiddish pro-
    duction), 84, 107
"Fiction, the Highest Form of Truth"
    (Zangwill), 43
Fierman, Floyd S., 224
Fiske, Harrison Grey, 80
A Flag Is Born (Hecht), 110
Flying Scud (Boucicault), 52
Food in Zangwill's Jewish works, 7
The Forcing House (Zangwill), 241, 514
Ford, Harriet, 83
Ford, Hugh, 238, 240
Ford Motor Company pageant, 254
Forrest, Edwin, 56
Fowler, Benjamin Orange, 69
French, Samuel, 25
Freud, Sigmund, 392
Freundschaft Club (New York), 37
Friedenwald, Herbert, 252
Frohman, Charles, 82
From Berlin to Jerusalem (Scholem), 392
The Fugitive (Brudno), 228
Furst, William, 70

Galveston Plan, 34–35, 236
Garland, Hamlin, 68, 69
Gartner, Lloyd, 8
Gaster, Moses, 393
George, Henry, 68
Ghetto: medieval, 20; new use of term,
    20–21
The Ghetto (Heijermans), 81, 89, 101
"The Ghetto" (Steffens), 47
The Ghetto (Wirth), 21
"The Ghetto" (Zangwill), 38, 43
Ghetto Comedies (Zangwill), 24
"The Ghetto in Literature" (Meyer, Ellis),

48
Ghetto literature, 21; causes Jewish anxiety,
    36
Ghetto Silhouettes (Warfield), 21
Ghetto Tragedies (Zangwill), 24
Ghosts (Ibsen), 17
Gladstone, William E., 37
Gleason, Philip, 214, 215, 217
Gloriana (John), 514
"Glossary of Jewish Terms," 389
Glover, A. Kingsley, 45, 49
Goldfaden, Abraham, 27
Golding, Louis, 226, 390, 514
Goldsmid, Julian, 9
Goldsmid family, 393
Gottheil, Richard, 77, 88–89, 91
"The Goyim" (Zangwill), 235–36
Graetz, Heinrich, 16
Granville-Barker, Harley, 19
The Great Demonstration (Zangwill), 24
The Greatest Thing in the World (Ford and
    de Mille), 83
Greenberg, Leopold, 257, 390–91
Grein, J. T. (Jacob Thomas), 17, 103
The Grey Wig (Zangwill), 24
Griffith Davenport (Herne), 69
Grundy, Sidney, 55
Guggenheim, Daniel, 38, 69, 248, 249
Guzkow, Karl, 54

Haggard, Rider, 16
Halberstam, David, 92
Halifax, Lord, 51
Hammond, Percy, 245
Hannah (Cividalli), 109
Hannah Jacobs/David Brandon romance in
    Children of the Ghetto, 20, 61, 64–65
Hannele (Hauptmann), 86
Hapgood, Hutchins, 21, 46–47, 49, 96
Hapgood, Norman, 82, 84
Harap, Louis, 52
Hardy, Thomas, 16
Hare, John, 55
Harmonie Club (New York), 37
Harris, Isidore, 257
Harris, Maurice H., 42–43, 93

Hartmann, Sadakichi, 46, 49
"Hatikvah" (The Hope) (Imber), 14
Hauptmann, Gerhart, 86, 103
Hearts of Oak (Herne with Belasco), 68
Hebrew comics: Jewish resentment of, 51;
      U.K., 50–51; U.S., 49
"The Hebrew's Friday Night" (Zangwill),
      38, 241
Hebrew Union College of Cincinnati, 94
Hebrew University, 15
Hecht, Ben, 110
Heijermans, Herman, 21, 81, 89
Heine, Heinrich, 15–16, 40
Heinemann, William (publisher), 11, 29
Herne, Chrystal: as Vera Revendal in *The
      Melting Pot,* 246; and Zangwill, 72
Herne, James A., 67, 81, 238; compared
      with Ibsen, 69; directing *Children
      of the Ghetto,* 72–74; and stage real-
      ism, 68
Herzl, Theodor, 2, 28–30, 31–33,
      223, 515
Hilfsverein der Deutschen Juden, 34
Hillel, Rabbi, 42
Hind, C. Lewis, 86–87
Hirsch, Emil G., 247–48
Hobson, Harold, 514
Hoffman, Charles I. [Publius], 80
Hollander, Jacob H., 95
Holmes, Oliver Wendell, 25
Hope, Anthony, 1, 41
Hope, John Francis, 259
The House Next Door (Manners), 249
House of Commons, 262
Housman, Laurence, 1
Howe, Irving, 46–47
Howells, William Dean, 45, 68
*How the Other Half Lives: Studies among the
      Tenements of New York* (Riis), 46
Hueffner [Ford], Ford Madox, 217–18
Humor in literature, 16
Hypatia (Kingsley), 17

Ibn Gabirol, Solomon, 6, 24
Ibsen, Henrik, 17–19, 28, 40, 62, 68, 84,
      86, 252

Ibsenism, 18
The Image of the Jew in American Literature
      (Harap), 52
Imber, Naphtali Herz, 14–15, 93
The Incorporation of America
      (Trachtenberg), 46
"In Defence of Gambling" (Zangwill), 390
Independent Theatre, 17
Intermarriage, 221–24, 247–49; and
      Zionist camp, 223
Intermarriage plays, 249
International Socialist Congress (Paris), 17
Irish Idylls (Barlow), 11
Irving, Henry, 19, 37, 55, 56, 68, 86–87
Isaacs, Solomon, 52
Italian Fantasies (Zangwill), 24
ITO (Jewish Territorial Organization),
      33–34, 223, 236, 394
Itoland, 33
Ivanhoe (Scott), 54, 64

Jackson, Harry, 87
Jackson, Holbrook, 11, 394, 396
Jacobs, Joseph, 15, 22, 391
Jacobs, W. W., 16
Jaffe, E., 13
Jail Bird (Townsend), 52
James, Thomas L., 94–95
Janauscheck, Fanny, 54
Jerome, Jerome K., 16, 221
Jerusalem, 6, 7, 30, 38, 221; suggested na-
      tional theater in, 516
Jessica (*The Merchant of Venice*), 63–64
"The Jew and the Drama" (Solomon), 517
The Jew (Cumberland), 54–55
The Jew in Drama (Landa), 53
"The Jew in Literature" (Caine), 50
The Jewish Drama League, 17, 56, 395
The Jewish Encyclopedia, 389
Jewish Historical Society, 11
Jewish law, 61–62, 64
*Jewish Laws and Customs: Some of the Laws
      and Usages of Children of the Ghetto*
      (Glover), 45, 49
Jewish Museum (New York), 110
Jewish nationalism, 222

Jewish nose, 230
Jewish Publication Society, 19, 23, 36, 79
"The Jewish Race" (Zangwill), 30
Jewish Territorial Organization. *See* ITO
      (Jewish Territorial Organization)
Jewish Theological Seminary, 15
Jewish Working Men's Club, 30
Jewish Year Book (1899), 389
Jewish Year Book (1946), 223
The Jew of Malta (Marlowe), 64
Jews: as nation, 30; as race, 29
Jews as They Are (Salaman), 22, 56
Jews' Free School, 8–9
"The Jews in London" (Wolf), 26
Jinny the Carrier (Zangwill), 24, 238
John, Gwen, 514
Johns Hopkins University, 95
Johnson, Samuel, 42
Jokes and Their Relation to the Unconscious
      (Freud), 392
Jones, Henry Arthur, 1, 28, 40, 62
José, Edward, 107
Joseph, Morris, 257–58
Judaean Society, 41
Judah (Jones), 62
"Judaism in Music" (Wagner), 229
Judestaat (Herzl), 29

Kean, Edmund, 56
The King of Schnorrers (novella)
      (Zangwill), 7, 16, 24, 44, 389, 392,
      393
The King of Schnorrers (stage play)
      (Zangwill), 17, 24, 36, 225, 513,
      514; Judd Woldin adaptation, 398;
      London opening, 395–96; London
      revival, 396–98; schnorrer as my-
      thologized Jewish figure, 389; Yiddish
      adaptation of, 394
Kipling, Rudyard, 16, 43
Kishinev pogrom, 32, 221, 227, 243,
      259; reflected in *The Melting Pot*,
      231–34, 254
Kitl, 64, 89
Klauber, Alfred J., 250
Klein, Charles, 211

Kobrin, Leon, 107
Kohler, Kaufman, 43
Kohut, George Alexander, 225
Kosher, 7, 41

Lackaye, Wilton: as Reb Shemuel in
      Children of the Ghetto, 53–54, 72,
      74–76, 79, 84, 104, 107; as Svengali,
      72, 76
The Lady of the Sea (Ibsen), 18
Landa, M. J. (Myer Jack), 53, 105
"Language and Jewish Life" (Zangwill),
      12, 389
Lazarus, Emma, 45, 221, 239
Leah, the Forsaken (von Mosenthal), 54
Lecture tours, 37
Leftwich, Joseph, 6, 25, 222, 224, 397,
      398, 514
Le Gallienne, Richard, 41
Leipziger, Henry M., 41
"Le Juif au theatre" (Dreyfus), 52
Le Juif Polonais (Erckman and Chatrian),
      55
"Le Melting-Pot: Made in America,
      Produced in France," 211
Leslie, Amy, 245, 251
Lessing, Gotthold Ephraim, 54
Lestina, Adolph, as Moses Ansell in
      Children of the Ghetto, 84
Levendall (Kishinev), 227
Levy, Amy, 18, 22
Lewis, Leopold, 55
Liebler and Company, 44, 70, 72, 81, 82,
      100, 243
Life and Labour of the People of London
      (Booth), 17
Linguistic hybridity, 11–12
Lipsky, Louis, 23, 394
Lipton, Thomas, 83
The Little Minister (Barrie), 101
Loeb, Louis, 38, 41, 214
Loeb, William, 241
London: East End, 9, 17–18, 20, 22, 23;
      Jewish community in, 7–8; Jewish
      immigrant quarter, 5–8; Jewish im-
      migration to, 7–8; theatrical activity

in, 27–28

London, Jack, 21

London Jews: fascination by Israel Zangwill, 393; and love of theater, 26–27

London Labour and London Poor (Mayhew), 26

London theater scene in the 1890s, 27

"Long run," 27–28

Lovelace, Richard, 42

Lowenberg, Jakob, 391

Luther, Mark Lee, 214

Lyceum movement, 37

Maccabeans (club), 1, 15; and Zionism, 29, 30

Macdermott, Norman, 262

Mack, Julian W., 42

Macklin, Charles, 55

Macmillan (publishers), 38, 61, 214

Macready, William Charles, 56

Magnes, Judah, 238, 249

Mahamad, 392, 393, 396

Mandel, Morris, 94

Mannering, Lewin, as Manasseh Da Costa in *The King of Schnorrers*, 395, 396

Manners, J. Hartley, 249

Mansfield, Richard, 36, 71, 394, 395

Mantle, Burns, 244

Mantle of Elijah (Zangwill), 24

Marconi Scandal, 260

Margaret Fleming (Herne), 69

Marks, Sarah (Hertha), 221, 222

Marlowe, Christopher, 64

Marshall, Louis, 515

Marx [Aveling], Eleanor, 17–19, 227

Marx, Groucho, 51

Marx, Karl, 17

The Master (Zangwill), 24, 36

Mayer, Gaston, 256

Mayhew, Henry, 26

M. Butterfly (Hwang), 110

McCarthy, Lillah, 513

Melting pot concept, 211–13, 250–51; origin of, 214–17

The Melting Pot (film) (Zangwill), 254

The Melting Pot (stage play) (Zangwill), 513, 514; anti-Jewish response, 259–62; arising sympathy for plight of Russian Jews, 231; at Chautauqua circuit, 252–53; Chicago reception, 244–47; differences between published and unpublished texts, 234–35; dispelling stereotypical image of the Stage Jew, 228–30; at educational settings, 252; English origins of, 238; as expression of Zangwill's experience with settlement issues, 35; general response to, 255–56; intermarriage theme in, 247–49; Jewish response, 256–58; London production, 254–56; melting pot theme, 211, 250–51; nativist response to, 245; New York opening, 249; New York reception, 249–51; pogrom soliloquy, 231; premiere of, 1, 6; previous titles of play, 213–14; publicity campaign, 246, 249; soliloquy suggested by Walker Whiteside, 231–32; timeliness of, 214; use of Yiddish, 226, 228, 251; vision of America in, 30; Washington premiere, 236; Yiddish productions, 252; Yiddish translation, 13; Zangwill's involvement in preparations for and casting of production, 238, 240

Mendes, Pereira, 41, 249

Men's League for Women's Suffrage, 1

The Merchant of Venice (Shakespeare), 55, 56, 63

Merely Mary Ann (Zangwill), 24, 37, 211, 238, 513–14

Meyer and Son (Addison), 249

Meyer, Annie Nathan, 48

Micawber, Wilkins, 394

Michael and His Lost Angel (Jones), 62

Mielziner, Leo, 252

Mielziner, Mrs., 6

Milton, Ernest, as Manasseh Da Costa in *The King of Schnorrers*, 397, 398

Mixed marriage controversy, 247–49

Moccatta family, 393

Mock marriage *(Children of the Ghetto),* 93–94

The Moment of Death (Zangwill), 83, 238

Montagu, Lily H., 258

Montagu, Samuel, 9, 104

Montefiore, Claude, 16

Montefiore, Moses, 45

Montefiore family, 393

"Morour and Chorouseth" (Zangwill), 14

Morrison, Rosabel, as Hannah Jacobs in *Children of the Ghetto,* 101

Morris, William, 17

Morton, Edward, 1

Moses, 2

"Moses and Jesus" (Zangwill), 213

"Motso Kleis" (Zangwill and Breslar), 10

Mount Holyoke College, 252

Mrs. Sidgwick, 22

Mrs. Warren's Profession (Shaw), 87

The Music Master (Klein), 211

"My Country 'Tis of Thee," 235, 245

Myers, Asher, 15, 393

"My Religion" (Zangwill), 224

Nathan the Wise (Lessing), 54

Nationalism, theorizing of, 218

The New American (Wattenberg), 211

New Drama, 18–19, 28, 86, 103

Newspapers and Periodicals (Israel and Poland): *Ha'aretz* (Hebrew, Tel Aviv), 515; *Haynt* (Yiddish, Warsaw), 252; *Moment* (Yiddish, Warsaw), 515

Newspapers and Periodicals (U.K.): *Ariel, or the London Puck,* 16; *The Athenaeum,* 102, 256; *The Bioscope,* 254; *British Review,* 260; *Daily Express,* 513; *Daily Mail,* 30; *Daily Telegraph,* 19, 86; *English Review,* 259; *Era,* 25, 103, 256; *The Graphic,* 22; *The Idler,* 16; *The Illustrated London News,* 259; *Jewish Chronicle,* 14–15, 21, 26, 31, 51, 70, 77, 82, 96, 104–5, 106, 224, 240, 256, 257, 390, 395, 397; *Jewish Quarterly Review,* 16, 23; *Jewish Standard,* 14–15, 18, 389; *Jewish World,* 13, 26, 91, 104–5,

256, 515–16; *Life,* 17; *The New Age,* 213, 259; *The New Statesman and Nation,* 398; *New Witness,* 259, 260; *Observer,* 395, 396, 514; *Outlook,* 102; *Pall Mall Gazette,* 32; *Punch,* 16; *Queen,* 102; *The Sketch,* 63, 86; *The Stage,* 256, 395, 398; *Star,* 16; *Sunday Special,* 103; *Theatre,* 24; *Time,* 19; *Times,* 100, 103, 105, 221, 250, 256, 262, 395, 513, 515

Newspapers and Periodicals (U.S.): *American* (NY), 250–51; *American Hebrew* (NY), 8, 20, 38, 41, 42, 93, 94, 95, 96, 214, 237, 249, 392; *The Arena* (Boston), 68; *The Bookman* (NY), 36, 48, 259, 395, 396; *The Chautauquan* (NY), 215; *Chicago Herald,* 106; *Commercial Advertiser* (NY), 41, 46, 82, 84; *Cosmopolitan* (NY), 214; *Daily News* (Chicago), 245; *Daily Tribune* (Chicago), 244; *Dramatic Magazine* (Chicago), 49; *Evening American* (Chicago), 244; *Evening Item* (Philadelphia), 79; *Evening News* (Philadelphia), 79; *Evening Post* (Chicago), 245; *Evening Sun* (NY), 250; *Evening Telegraph* (Philadelphia), 79; *Evening World* (NY), 250; *The Forum* (NY), 85; *Forward* (NY, Yiddish), 107; *Harper's Weekly* (NY), 36, 78; *Inter Ocean* (Chicago), 245; *Jewish Comment* (Baltimore), 238; *Jewish Exponent* (Philadelphia), 80, 91, 241; *Jewish Forum* (NY), 515; *Jewish Spectator* (NY), 224; *Jewish Tribune* (Portland), 248, 249; *Leslie's Weekly* (NY), 76; *Morning Sun* (NY), 249; *Morning Telegraph* (NY), 81; *New York Dramatic Mirror,* 39, 41, 80; *New York Herald,* 86, 248, 250; *New York Press,* 238, 249; *New York Times,* 35, 41, 69, 78, 83, 84, 92, 96, 109, 250, 251; *New York World,* 78; *North American* (Philadelphia), 79; *Philadelphia Press,* 79; *Public Ledger* (Philadelphia),

79; *Puck* (NY), 215, 216; *Scribner's Magazine* (NY), 46; *Sun* (NY), 81–82, 84; *Unity* (Chicago), 244; *Variety* (NY), 109, 254; *Washington Post,* 218; *Werner's Magazine* (Chicago), 39
New York City: Jewish immigration, 35–36; Lower East Side, 45–47, 49, 88; slums of, 46
New York uptown Jews, 20, 41; and the ghetto, 42
The Next Religion (Zangwill), 63, 89, 514
Nomberg, Hirsh David, 515
Nordau, Max, 29, 223, 515
Norris, William, as Meltchitsedek Pinchas in *Children of the Ghetto,* 71, 84
Nose scene in *The Melting Pot,* 230–31, 252, 259
Nurse Marjorie (Zangwill), 238, 240

Ochs, Adolphe S., 92
Old Days in Bohemian London (Mrs. Scott), 82
An Old Jew (Grundy), 55
The Old Maids' Club (Zangwill), 16, 24
Oliver Twist (Dickens), 53
O'Neill, James, 44, 72
The Only Way (Wills), 104

Pain, Barry, 16
Palestine, under Ottoman rule, 31
Panza, Sancho, 394
Passover, 6, 14, 62, 66, 70, 88–89, 101, 104, 257
Peppis, Paul, 217
Phillpotts, Eden, 16
Philo-Semitic sentiments, 44–45
Pinero, Arthur Wing, 26, 28, 40
Plaster Saints (Zangwill), 63, 514
Play Actors, 255
Playgoers Club, 17, 29
Plays published in book form, 28
Poel, William, 1
Pogrom(s), 6, 32, 33
Pond, J. B. (James Burton) Major, 37, 38, 40–41, 82

Potter, Beatrice, 17
Powell, Frank, 107
The Premier and the Painter; a Fantastic Romance (Zangwill and Cowen), 13, 14, 24
The Principle of Nationalities (Zangwill), 218
The Prisoner of Zenda (Hope), 1
"Professor Grimmer" (Zangwill), 10
Pseudonyms (Zangwill): "Baroness von S.," 15; "J. Freeman Bell," 13, 15; "Shloumi Yoshki ben Shlemeal," 10
Publius. *See* Hoffman, Charles I. [Publius]
Puffing practice, 82
Purim, 230, 251, 259

Quixote, Don, 394

Race Congress (1911), 3, 30
Race riots in Atlanta, 218
Racial comics, 50–51
Racism, 218; British, 217–18, 259–60
Redpath Lyceum Bureau, 37
Reform Judaism, 42, 65–66, 94, 247, 248
Religion and drama, 62–63, 89–90; on Yiddish stage, 90–91
Relph, Phyllis, as Vera Revendal in *The Melting Pot,* 255
"The Return to Palestine" (Zangwill), 31
Reuben Sachs (Levy), 18
The Reverend Griffith Davenport (Herne), 78
The Revolted Daughter (Zangwill), 17, 238
Richards, Bernard, 394
Riis, Jacob A., 46
Roosevelt, Theodore, 43, 214, 218; and Jews, 242–43; and *The Melting Pot,* 241–42, 246
Root, Elihu, 241
Ropes, Arthur R., 1
Rosenfeld, Morris, 13, 21
Ross, Adrian. *See* Ropes, Arthur R.
Rostand, Edmund, 36
Rothschild, Lord, 3, 10, 14
Rothschild family, 9, 44, 393
Royal Society of British Artists, 15

Russell, Annie, 221–22, 223
Russian Jewish Operatic Company, 27
Russian Jews: immigration to U.S., 22–23, 34–35; pogrom at Kishinev, 33
Ruth the Moabite, 222, 228

Sabbath (Jewish), 5, 7, 66, 104, 109, 221, 227, 228, 240, 241, 251, 391, 393; and Fourth of July, 228
Sag Harbor (Herne), 69
Salaman, Charles Kensington, 22, 56
Salaman, Malcolm C., 56
Salaman, Redcliffe, 514
Sambatyon, 42, 396
Sam'l of Posen; or, The Commercial Drummer, 51
Sandburg, Carl, 230
San Toy (Morton), 1
"Satan Mekatrig" (Zangwill), 15
Schecter, Solomon, 15, 16
Schiff, Jacob H., 34–35, 243, 246
Schnorrer: definition of term, 389, 391–92; in Zangwill's works, 14, 389–92
Scholem, Gershom, 392
The School for Scandal (Sheridan), 40
Schreiner, Olive, 18
Schulman, Samuel, 94, 215, 249, 263
Schwartz, Maurice, 13
Scott, Clement, 19, 82, 86–91
Scott, Walter, 54, 64
The Second Mrs. Tanqueray (Pinero), 28, 87
Seligman, Edwin R., 42
Sephardic pedigree, 225
Sephardim, 392, 396
The Serio-Comic Governess (Zangwill), 238
Shakespeare, William, 16, 42, 55, 63, 235, 394
Shame of the Cities (Steffens), 47
Shaw, George Bernard, 17–18, 28, 104
She Stoops to Conquer (Golsmith), 40
Shore Acres (Herne), 68, 78
Shylock (*The Merchant of Venice*), 3, 17, 47, 55–56, 63
The Sign of the Cross (Barrett), 62, 87, 96
Silverman, Joseph, 249

Six Persons (Zangwill), 25
Skinner, Constance, 244–45
Slater, Montagu, 398
Small, Maynard, and Company, 61
Socialist League, 17
Solomon, Charles, 517
Solomon, Isaac, 241
Solomon, Solomon J., 15
Songs of the Ghetto (Rosenfeld), 21
Spencer, Herbert, 68
The Spirit of the Ghetto (Hapgood), 46
The Spirit of the People: An Analysis of the English Mind (Hueffner), 217
The Stage in America (Hapgood), 82
Stage Jew, 49–56, 76, 228, 398
Stanley, Henry M., 37
Statue of Liberty, 221, 239, 258
Steffens, Lincoln, 47, 49
Steinhardt, Lawrence A., 254
Strauss, Oscar, 236, 241, 246
Sulzberger, Judge Mayer, 19–20, 36, 38, 41, 42, 79
Sunday services, 94
Sutro, Alfred, 1
Svengali (*Trilby*), 17, 39, 53–54, 230
Szold, Henrietta, 80
Szuberla, Guy, 243

Tailors and Garment Workers Union, 515
Taliaferro, Mabel, as Esther Ansell in *Children of the Ghetto*, 84
Talmud/Talmudic, 6, 14, 21, 42, 48, 56, 84, 90, 93, 391, 392
Taylor, Walter Fuller, 46
Temple Beth-El (New York), 94, 215, 263
Temple Emanu-El (New York), 92, 238
Temple Israel (New York), 93
Territorialism. *See* ITO (Jewish Territorial Organization)
Terry, J. E. Harold, 260
Theater, Yiddish. *See* Yiddish theater
Theater critics, 82
Theaters (London): Adelphi Theatre, 101, 102; Ambassadors, 396; Arts Theatre Club, 396; Britannia, 25, 27; Comedy, 256; Convent Garden,

26; Court, 255; Drury Lane, 54, 87; Everyman Theatre, 262; Foote's Little Theatre, 50; Fortune Theatre, 513, 514; Garrick (East End), 25, 27, 55; Haymarket, 25; Little Theatre, 514; New Theatre, 513; Pavilion, 25, 27; People's, 252; Queen's, 256; Royal Court, 25; Royalty, 24; Saville, 397; Savoy, 262; Scala, 395

Theaters (New York): Comedy, 249; Fifth Avenue, 86; Herald Square, 83, 95, 101; Hippodrome, 254; Lyceum, 38; People's Theatre, 107; Thalia, 252; Yiddish Art Theatre, 13

Theaters (Poland): Kaminsky Theatre (Yiddish, Warsaw), 252

Theaters (U.S.): Chickering Hall (Boston), 69; Columbia Theatre (Washington, D.C.), 241; Grand Opera House (Chicago), 106, 243, 246, 247; National Theater (Washington, D.C.), 77; Walnut Street Theatre (Philadelphia), 79

Theatre Guild, 109

Theatrical Syndicate, 82, 249

They That Walk in Darkness (Zangwill), 24

Thomas, Brandon, 1

Threepenny Bits (Zangwill), 25

"To Die in Jerusalem" (Zangwill), 6

Toga plays, 62

Tolstoy, Leo, 515

Tomashefsky, Bessie, as Hannah Jacobs in *Children of the Ghetto* (Yiddish production), 107–8

Tomashefsky, Boris, as David Brandon in *Children of the Ghetto* (Yiddish production), 107

Too Jewish?: Challenging Traditional Identities, 110

Too Much Money (Zangwill), 513, 514

Townsend, Charles, 52

Trachtenberg, Alan, 46

Tree, Herbert Beerbohm, 1, 17, 25, 54, 56, 394–95

Trilby (Du Maurier), 29, 39, 230

Trilby (stage play) (Potter), 53–54

Twain, Mark, 15, 37

Tyler, George C., 44, 83, 213, 394; *Children of the Ghetto:* American tour of, 106–7; British production of, 101, 105, 106; producing, 67–72, 81, 82, 96–97; and Jewish public, 231–32; *The King of Schnorrers,* 395; *The Melting Pot* (producing), 240, 243–44

Tzelniker, Meier, as Yankele in *The King of Schnorrers,* 397

Udelson, Joseph H., 7, 222

Uganda Scheme, 32–33

Uncle Tom's Cabin (Beecher Stowe), 23

"Under Sentence of Marriage" (Zangwill), 15

United Hebrew Charities, 14

Uriel Acosta (Guzkow), 54

Usishkin, Menachem, 223

Veld, Gertrude, 95–96

Vera (Wilde), 227

Viereck, George Sylvester, 514

Vincent, James, 254

Violinists, Jewish, 230

Von Mosenthal, Salomon Herman, 54

Wagner, Richard, 228–29

Walkley, Arthur B., 250–51, 513

"The Wanderers," 15, 257

Warfield, David, 21, 70–71, 246

The War God (Zangwill), 17, 514

Washington, George, 248

"Watchman, What of the Night?" (Zangwill), 6, 243, 263

The Watch on the Jordan (Imber), 14

Wattenberg, Ben, 211

The Weavers (Hauptmann), 86, 103

Weizmann, Chaim, 223

Wells, H. G., 16

We Moderns (Zangwill), 109, 513–14

West End Synagogue (New York), 94

West London Synagogue, 257

Wewitzer, 50

Whiteside, Walker, as David Quixano in *The Melting Pot,* 231, 240, 246, 250,

Whiteside, Walker (*continued*)
254, 256
Whitte, Wilfred, 259
Widerwitz, Chaim Yaakov, 90
Wilde, Oscar, 227
William Fox Film Corporation, 107
Wills, Freeman, 104
Winchevsky, Morris, 8
Wine, Samuel, 90–91
Winter, William, dislike for realistic drama,
68, 82
Wirth, Louis, 21
Wise, Isaac Mayer, 92
Wise, Stephen S., 22, 51, 249, 263,
515, 516
Without Prejudice (Zangwill), 24
Woldin, Judd, 398
Wolf, Lucien, 9, 15, 22, 26
Wolf, Simon, 241
Women's suffrage, 2, 224, 516
Women's Trade Union League, 18
Worthing, Frank, as David Brandon in
Children of the Ghetto, 83, 101

Yeats, William Butler, 517
Yekl: A Tale of the New York Ghetto
(Cahan), 21
Yiddish, 11–13, 18; in *Children of the
Ghetto,* 12, 102; in *The Melting Pot,*
13; in theaters, 27; use in literature,
11–13
Yiddish theater, 47; in London, 27; in New
York City, 47

Zangwill [Ayrton], Edith (wife), 19,
221–22, 515, 516; active in Jewish
affairs, 222–23
Zangwill, Ayrton Israel (son), 224
Zangwill, Ellen Hannah (mother), 5, 6–7
Zangwill, Israel: affected by East European
immigration, 8; on America and
Judaism, 220; on Arab population,
34; assimilation into Gentile culture,
235–37; association with Moses,
5–6, 225; attachment to mother,
226; commodification of writ-

ing, 37–38; criticism of American
Judaism, 42–43; death of, 514–16;
defamation as a plagiarist, 81–82;
depiction of Russian immigrant Jews,
21–23; as detective novelist, 16;
education of, 9–10; family life and
children, 224–25; fascination with
communal roots of London Jewry,
393; fascination with schnorrers,
389–90; fascination with Shylock
character, 56; ghetto writings, 24,
28; on human history as process of
fusion, 219; as humorist writer, 16;
immigration views, 220–21; as interpreter of Jewish life, 2–3; involvement
in women's suffrage movement, 19;
Jewish identity of, 23–24, 39–40; on
Jewish languages (Hebrew, Yiddish
and Ladino), 12; Jewish nationalism,
222; as journalist, 14–15; lectures in
U.S., 38–43; literary career beginnings, 10–14; as literary dramatist,
36–37; literary friends of, 17–19; love
of theater, 17–19; marriage to Edith
Ayrton, 221–23; and music, 235; on
Palestine, 30, 31; parents of, 5–7; as
playwright, 24–28, 36–37; political activity of, 28–35; as producer,
513; reception in America, 40–41;
and Reform Judaism, 65–66; as site
of Jewishness, 39–40; of Spanish
blood, 225; teaching career, 13–14;
as Territorialist, 33–35; verbosity
tendencies, 396; view of Jewish history, 237–38; views on intermarriage,
221–24; views on racism, 218; and
Zionism, 29–32, 236–37
Zangwill, Leah (sister), 7
Zangwill, Louis (brother), 8, 29
Zangwill, Margaret Ayrton (daughter), 224
Zangwill, Mark (brother), 70
Zangwill, Moses (father), 5–6
Zangwill, Oliver Louis (son), 224
Zasulich, Vera, 18, 227–28, 234–35, 517;
opposition to anti-Semitism, 227
Zaza (Belasco), 91

"Zion, Whence Cometh My Help"
    (Zangwill), 237
Zionism, 2, 29–34, 225, 237–38, 259; in
    London, 29–30
"Zionism" (Zangwill), 31
Zionist Congress: Fifth, 31; First, 21, 31;
    Seventh, 33; Sixth, 32

Zionist Federation, 31
Zionist movement, 14, 29–34; Basle plat-
    form, 31, 33
Zionists, 29–34; Russian, 33
Zola, Emil, 40, 515
Zolotkoff, Leon, 248
Zoot Suit (Valdez), 110

9 780814 329559